MW01164864

Rethinking Race in Modern Argentina

This book reconsiders the relationship between race and nation in Argentina during the twentieth and twenty-first centuries and places Argentina firmly in dialogue with the literature on race and nation in Latin America, from where it has long been excluded or marginalized as a purportedly white, European exception in a mixed-race region. The contributors, based both in North America and Argentina, hail from the fields of history, anthropology, and literary and cultural studies. Their chapters collectively destabilize widespread certainties about Argentina, showing that whiteness in that country has more in common with practices and ideologies of *mestizaje* and "racial democracy" elsewhere in the region than has typically been acknowledged. The chapters also situate Argentina within the well-established literature on race, nation, and whiteness in world regions beyond Latin America (particularly, other European "settler societies"). The collection thus contributes to rethinking race for other global contexts as well.

PAULINA L. ALBERTO is Associate Professor of History and Romance Languages and Literatures at the University of Michigan.

EDUARDO ELENA is Associate Professor of History at the University of Miami.

Rethinking Race in Modern Argentina

PAULINA L. ALBERTO AND EDUARDO ELENA

CAMBRIDGE
UNIVERSITY PRESS

CAMBRIDGE
UNIVERSITY PRESS

32 Avenue of the Americas, New York, NY 10013–2473, USA

Cambridge University Press is part of the University of Cambridge.

It furthers the University's mission by disseminating knowledge in the pursuit of education, learning, and research at the highest international levels of excellence.

www.cambridge.org
Information on this title: www.cambridge.org/9781107107632

© Paulina Alberto and Eduardo Elena 2016

First published 2016

Printed in the United States of America

A catalog record for this publication is available from the British Library

Library of Congress Cataloging in Publication Data
Rethinking race in modern Argentina / Paulina L. Alberto and Eduardo Elena, eds.
    pages   cm
Includes bibliographical references and index.
ISBN 978-1-107-10763-2 (Hardcopy : alk. paper)
1. Argentina–Race relations.   I. Alberto, Paulina L., 1975– editor, author.   II. Elena, Eduardo, 1972– editor, author.
F3021.A1R48 2015
305.800982–dc23   2015028908

ISBN 978-1-107-10763-2 Hardback

Contents

Figures

Table

Notes on the contributors

Paulina L. Alberto (Ph.D. University of Pennsylvania, 2005) is Associate Professor in the Departments of History and of Romance Languages and Literatures (Programs in Spanish and Portuguese) at the University of Michigan. She is the author of multiple articles on racial activism and racial ideologies in modern Brazil and Argentina, and of *Terms of Inclusion: Black Intellectuals in Twentieth-Century Brazil* (UNC Press, 2011), awarded the Warren Dean Memorial Prize by the Conference on Latin American History (2013) and the Roberto Reis Award by the Brazilian Studies Association (2012). Her current research on the (in)famous *porteño* street character Raúl Grigera ("El Negro Raúl") explores the power of racial stories to construct "whiteness" and "blackness" in twentieth-century Argentina and to shape individual fates.

Eduardo Elena is Associate Professor of History and Research Director for Latin American Policy at the Miami Institute for the Americas at the University of Miami. He is the author of *Dignifying Argentina: Peronism, Citizenship, and Mass Consumption* (University of Pittsburgh Press, 2011), which was awarded the 2013 Book Prize in the Social Sciences by the Southern Cone Studies Section of the Latin American Studies Association. His work on the political, economic, and cultural history of Peronism and midcentury Latin America has appeared in numerous journals and edited volumes. Building from his research on consumption and the study of race and nation, he is currently investigating steam-age globalization in late nineteenth- and early twentieth-century Argentina.

Sandra McGee Deutsch is Professor of History at the University of Texas at El Paso. She is the author of *Counterrevolution in Argentina, 1900–1932: The Argentine Patriotic League* (University of Nebraska Press, 1986); *Las derechas: The Extreme Right in Argentina, Brazil, and Chile, 1890–1939* (Stanford University Press, 1999); and *Crossing Borders, Claiming* *a Nation: A History of Argentine Jewish Women, 1880–1955* (Duke University Press, 2010). She has also written numerous articles on rightist movements, anti-Semitism, gender, and women in Latin America. Currently, she is researching the Junta de la Victoria, a women's antifascist group in Argentina that sent aid to the Allies during World War II, at the regional, national, and transnational levels.

Oscar Chamosa is Associate Professor of History at the University of Georgia. He obtained his Ph.D. in History in 2003 from the University of North Carolina at Chapel Hill. He is the author of *The Argentine Folklore Movement: Sugar Elites, Criollo Workers and the Politics of Cultural Nationalism, 1900–1955* (University of Arizona Press, 2010) and *Breve historia del folklore argentino* (Edhasa, 2012). He is coeditor, with Matthew Karush, of *The New Cultural History of Peronism: Power and Identity in Mid-Twentieth-Century Argentina* (Duke University Press, 2010). Chamosa has published several book chapters in English and Spanish, and his articles have appeared in the *Hispanic American Historical Review* and *The Americas*, among other journals. He is currently working on a project about neoliberalism and folklore in late-twentieth-century Argentina.

Matthew Karush is Professor of History at George Mason University. He is the author of *Culture of Class: Radio and Cinema in the Making of a Divided Argentina, 1930–1946* (Duke University Press, 2012) and *Workers or Citizens: Democracy and Identity in Rosario, Argentina (1912–1930)* (University of New Mexico Press, 2002) and the coeditor, with Oscar Chamosa, of *The New Cultural History of Peronism: Power and Identity in Mid-Twentieth Century Argentina* (Duke University Press, 2010). With a fellowship from the National Endowment for the Humanities, he is currently working on a transnational history of Argentine popular music in the twentieth century.

Rebekah E. Pite is Associate Professor of History and Program Chair for Latin American and Caribbean Studies at Lafayette College. Her research focuses on histories of gender, food, consumption, and labor in Argentina in particular and in southern South America more broadly. Pite's book, *Creating a Common Table in Twentieth-Century Argentina: Doña Petrona, Women, and Food* (University of North Carolina Press, 2013) won the Gourmand Prize for "Best Latin America Cuisine Book" published in the United States and the LASA Southern Cone Studies section prize for "Best Social Sciences Book." She has also published articles in the *Hispanic American Historical Review*, *Revista de Estudios Sociales*, *Apuntes*, *Estudios Interdisciplinarios de América Latina y el Caribe*, *Massachusetts Historical Review*, and a number of edited volumes.

Mariela Eva Rodríguez received an MA in Romance Languages and Literature at the University of Notre Dame and a Ph.D. in Latin American Literature and

Cultural Studies at Georgetown University. She is Researcher at the National Council for Scientific and Technological Research (CONICET) of Argentina, and teaches Anthropology at the University of Buenos Aires (UBA) and at the Latin American Faculty of Social Sciences (FLACSO). Rodríguez is the recipient of several scholarships from Argentine and US institutions and is a member of various Argentine research teams. In her current research on Southern Patagonia, she employs an engaged ethnographic approach with Mapuche and Tehuelche people, analyzing relationships between past and present through orally transmitted memories and archival research. Rodríguez's work is concerned with indigenous re-emergence, processes of patrimonialization, the recovery of indigenous land, human remains repatriations, interculturality, and Tehuelche language revitalization, among other topics. She has published numerous articles in national and international journals and edited volumes.

Ezequiel Adamovsky obtained his Ph.D. in History from University College, London and is Professor in the Department of History at the University of Buenos Aires and Researcher at the National Council for Scientific and Technological Research (CONICET), Argentina's highest public institution for research. He was also Guest Researcher at the CNRS in Paris. Adamovsky's academic work has been mainly in the field of social and intellectual history, with studies on Europe as well as on middle- and lower-class identities in Argentina. He is the author of *Euro-Orientalism* (Oxford University Press, 2006), *Historia de la clase media argentina* (Sudamericana, 2009), and *Historia de las clases populares en Argentina, de 1880 a 2003* (Sudamericana, 2012), among other books. He was awarded the James Alexander Robertson Memorial Prize in 2009 and the *Premio Nacional* (First prize in history) in 2013, the highest distinction of the Argentine state for arts and humanities.

Lea Geler is Researcher at Argentina's National Council for Scientific and Technological Research (CONICET) and at the Interdisciplinary Gender Studies Institute (IIEGE) of the University of Buenos Aires. Using a historical-anthropological approach, her work focuses on Afro-descendants in Buenos Aires from the nineteenth century to the present, exploring questions of Afro-Argentine memory, of (self-)representation, and of race, nation, class, and gender in Argentina. Geler is the author of *Andares negros, caminos blancos. Afroporteños, Estado y Nación Argentina a fines del siglo XIX* (Prohistoria, 2010) and is coeditor (with Florencia Guzmán) of *Cartografías Afrolatinoamericanas. Perspectivas situadas para análisis transfronterizos* (Biblos, 2013). She has also published numerous articles in journals including *African and Black Diaspora, Horizontes Antropológicos, Tabula Rasa, Memoria Americana,* and *Boletín Americanista,* and in several edited volumes.

Gastón Gordillo is Professor in the Department of Anthropology at the University of British Columbia. He has conducted ethnographic research on space, ruination, history, violence, memory, subjectivity, and indigeneity in several areas of northern Argentina since 1987. Born and raised in Buenos Aires, he obtained his Ph.D. from the University of Toronto (1999). He is a Guggenheim Scholar, was a visiting scholar at Harvard and Yale, and taught at Cornell. His most recent book is *Rubble: The Afterlife of Destruction* (Duke University Press, 2014). Based on ethnographic research in the region where the Argentine Andes give way to the Gran Chaco lowlands, the book proposes a theory of ruins as rubble by analyzing the everyday experience of people living in the vicinity of palimpsests of debris from multiple eras. His book *Landscapes of Devils: Tensions of Place and Memory in the Argentinean Chaco* (Duke University Press, 2004) won the American Ethnological Society Sharon Stephens Book Prize. He is also the author of *En el Gran Chaco: Antropologías e historias* (Prometeo, 2006) and *Nosotros vamos a estar acá para siempre: Historias Tobas* (Biblos, 2005). He blogs at *Space and Politics*.

Chisu Teresa Ko (Ph.D. in Spanish, Columbia University) is Assistant Professor of Spanish and Coordinator of Latin American Studies at Ursinus College. Her field of research includes Latin American cultural and literary studies, Asian-Latin American studies, and theories of race with a special focus on race, ethnicity, and multiculturalism in Argentina. She has written about Argentine multiculturalism in "From Whiteness to Diversity: Crossing the Racial Threshold in Bicentennial Argentina," *Ethnic and Racial Studies* 37.14. Her work on the representation of Asians in contemporary Argentine novels, "'Argentina te incluye': Asians in Argentina's Multicultural Novels" appeared in *Symposium: A Quarterly Journal in Modern Literatures* 69.1. Her current research considers from a theoretical and comparative perspective the position of Asian-Argentine Studies within the broader fields of Asian-Latin American or Asian-American Studies. Her book in progress, *Making Identities Visible and Invisible: The Uses of Race in Argentine National Identity*, examines Argentina's changing racial discourses in a variety of cultural products from the founding of the nation to contemporary times.

George Reid Andrews is Distinguished Professor of History at the University of Pittsburgh, where he has taught since 1981. His publications include *The Afro-Argentines of Buenos Aires, 1800–1900* (University of Wisconsin Press, 1980), *Blacks and Whites in São Paulo, Brazil, 1888–1988* (University of Wisconsin Press, 1991), *Afro-Latin America, 1800–2000* (Oxford University Press, 2004), and *Blackness in the White Nation: A History of Afro-Uruguay* (University of North Carolina Press, 2010). His forthcoming book is *Afro-Latin America: Black Lives, 1600-2000* (Harvard University Press, 2016).

Preface

This book is the outcome of many years of conversation among the editors, contributors, and various audiences and readers. Most of the chapters first took shape in a series of panel presentations delivered at the Latin American Studies Association conferences in Toronto (2010), San Francisco (2012), and Washington, D.C. (2013). The volume's authors have also shared their research with colleagues in venues across Argentina as well as with students, activists, and wider publics there and elsewhere. Along the way, we encountered a spectrum of reactions to our project: from enthusiasm and encouragement, to thoughtful critiques, to skepticism and even hostility. Indeed, the range and intensity of these responses not only helped us sharpen our arguments and reframe our assumptions, but they also strengthened our conviction that questions of race and nation in twentieth- and twenty-first-century Argentina merit rethinking.

If the subjects treated in this volume touch a nerve for some readers, it is surely because the chapters reconsider the conventional wisdom about Argentine politics, culture, and society held by many commentators in Argentina and abroad. Raising questions about the racial dimensions of inequality, identity, and power in Argentina is itself controversial. And even among those who agree that those are crucial questions, disagreements persist over how best to pose and answer them. To pick one telling example, the very title of this book, *Rethinking Race in Modern Argentina*, may provoke some unease. In the United States, references to *race* as a social dilemma or as an academic area of inquiry are commonplace. Yet in contemporary Argentina, the term *raza* carries a strongly negative connotation and is thus far less frequently invoked: indeed, it is common for *raza* to be placed within quotation marks even in the writings of researchers who use the concept to expose problems of discrimination. This circumspect treatment of *raza* is intended to emphasize its socially constructed, rather than essential or biological, character (despite the fact that other social constructs like *género* [gender] and *clase* do not require this kind of treatment), or to signal the concept's status as archaic and somehow foreign to Argentina. The pages that follow devote considerable attention to unraveling the many languages of race in Argentina employed since the early twentieth century and assessing their political implications. But even as our title embraces the unquoted use of *race* common in the US academy, the volume takes as its premise the idea that Argentine conceptions of race should not be approached as exotic or benighted deviations from a norm (based, as so many other things, on US and Western European models).

Instead, our goal is to facilitate discussion across geographic borders and disciplinary or conceptual boundaries, generating a sharper understanding of how race-related ideas and practices – especially those surrounding the production of "whiteness" – have molded modern Argentina and other nations across the world. In keeping with this impulse, the volume not only reaches out to experts in the study of Argentina and Latin America but also to scholars of other world regions and to curious readers of all backgrounds and levels of expertise. This approach may occasionally lead us to explain things that seem obvious to Argentines or to experts on the region, but it has the virtue of bringing new participants into the discussion. As the lively community and the exchanges that defined this project come to a close (at least for now), we hope that the finished book will spark further debate, comparison, and questioning in the classroom and beyond.

The making of this edited volume was a collective endeavor in more ways than one. We are grateful for the support received from everyone at Cambridge University Press, first and foremost our editor Deborah Gershenowitz and her assistant Dana Bricken, whose encouragement and vision helped shape the book in important ways. The three anonymous readers selected by Cambridge University Press deserve special recognition for their close readings and their excellent recommendations for how the book might reach its fullest potential. Early in the production process, Kristin McGuire employed her copyediting prowess to ensure that the authors were all on the same page. And, of course, we thank all the contributors to this volume for their cooperation and for their good-tempered responses to our seemingly endless revisions and e-mail queries.

One of the pleasures of undertaking this project was the many opportunities it offered to expand our intellectual community, whether by meeting new people or having new conversations with colleagues and friends. Audience members at talks in Argentina and elsewhere provided invaluable feedback that guided this book to completion. The project also gave us the chance to exchange ideas with a number of researchers who took part in the original LASA panels or who were involved in early versions of the manuscript. Alejandro Frigerio, Valeria Manzano, John Charles Chasteen, Ana Vivaldi, and James Shrader deserve heartfelt recognition for their contributions to the realization of this book. We look forward to upcoming studies by these and other colleagues who will no doubt continue to expand the field in exciting ways. Given the number of people who generously gave their time to discuss and read our work, we have incurred debts too numerous to be properly accounted, but we grate-fully acknowledge the comments offered by Sueann Caulfield, Matthew Coun-tryman, Mark Healey, Jesse Hoffnung-Garskof, and Ashli White.

Paulina Alberto wishes to thank Eduardo Elena for agreeing to embark on this exciting but laborious journey, and for cheerfully keeping us on course through some of its rough patches. We began this project just as I was finishing my monograph on Brazil, and though I had been looking over my shoulder to Argentina for quite some time, the idea of retraining myself as a historian of Argentina seemed daunting. I can imagine no better guide through the peculiar landscape of Argentine historiography than Eduardo. Working closely with Eduardo and the volume's contributors over the past five years and exchanging ideas and arguments has been an incredible education. I cannot thank these colleagues enough for their generosity of spirit. I am also grateful to the friends and colleagues who wished me well in my (only partial) change of course and helped me think through the connections between projects old and new: George Reid Andrews, Rebecca Scott, Sueann Caulfield, Barbara Weinstein, Jeff Lesser, Jerry Dávila, Marc Hertzman, Keila Grinberg, and James Green. Warm thanks go to Mariela Rodríguez and Lea Geler for their invitation to team teach the seminar "Nación, 'Raza', y Mestizaje en América Latina" at the University of Buenos Aires in 2014, and to the undergraduate and graduate students who made it such a lively place to work through many of the ideas that animate this volume. The departments of History and of Romance Languages and Litera-tures as well as the College of Literature, Science, and Arts at the University of Michigan provided important funding for this project and made my extended stay in Argentina possible. My friends and family, for their part, made that time a delight: Julieta Pereira, Zulma Alberto, Fernando Skiarski, the whole Rafaela crew, my parents Néstor and Ana Berta de Alberto, my sisters Cristina and Mariana, as well as Matías Salmoiraghi and the inimitable Luca. My deepest love and gratitude go to my husband Jesse Hoffnung-Garskof for his seemingly unending stores of wisdom and patience, and to little Lalo and Pía, for making any place we go together feel like home.

Eduardo Elena wishes to thank the volume's contributors for making this project so intellectually stimulating. I have learned a great deal from you all. Paulina Alberto in particular has helped steer me through unfamiliar waters, and without her expertise and bighearted guidance I would have surely lost my way. I began this process with a mixture of curiosity and ignorance about the study of race in twentieth- and twenty-first-century Argentina – and, truth be told, a healthy skepticism, born from frustration with how some in the US academy use race to constrict and "orientalize" the study of Latin America and the Caribbean. Thanks to my fellow contributors I now see more clearly how to transcend these limitations, while also gaining in the process a richer under-standing of Argentina's past and present. I am grateful to have received the backing, financial and otherwise, from the University of Miami, above all from my wonderful colleagues in the History Department and Center for Latin

American Studies (now the Miami Institute for the Americas). I wish to recognize Hugo Ratier, Lila Caimari, and Nicolás Quiroga for their insights as specialists and for the opportunities to share my work. *Mil gracias* to the family and friends who have always been at my side, including those in Argentina and Uruguay who hosted me and challenged my thinking: Jorge Elena, Elena Milla de Elena, Victoria Basulado, Vania Markarian, Juan Santarcangelo, Leandro Delgado, and Fanny Cassinoni. Final thanks are reserved, as always, for Ashli White and my daughter Paulina for being constant sources of ideas and inspiration.

Introduction

The shades of the nation

Paulina L. Alberto and Eduardo Elena

Argentina suffers from what marketing experts would call an "image problem." The country rarely fares well in the global media spotlight, where it is
frequently trotted out as an example of spectacular political or economic
failure. But seldom are the results of this scrutiny so unflattering as when issues
of race and national identity come to the fore.[1] As we write this Introduction,
the 2014 World Cup provides the latest occasion for commentary. In a piece
titled "Why So Many World Cup Fans Dislike Argentina," The *New York
Times* informed readers that "across Latin America, Argentina has the most
people rooting against it" – not just because of the country's past successes on
the field against its regional rivals but, more pointedly, because of "how some
Argentines projected their perceptions of economic and cultural superiority in
the region." For the article's authors, the ugliest aspect of this ethnocentrism
lies in "the ways in which some Argentines have traditionally viewed their
nation, which received millions of European immigrants in the nineteenth and
twentieth centuries: as a dominion of racial pre-eminence in the region."[2]
A piece in the *Huffington Post* took a similar angle, asking "Why Are There
No Black Men on Argentina's Roster?" Unlike other Latin American "rainbow
nations [...] conceived by the blend of American-Indians, Spaniards, and
enslaved Africans," Argentina's seemingly all-white roster confirmed, for the
author of this piece, the country's exceptionally violent history of "purg[ing]
their African roots from their socio-historical landscape and conscience," and
even of "ethnic cleansing" and "genocide," in its eagerness to become "South
America's whitest country."[3]

These journalistic assessments are all too familiar. The image of Argentina as
a racial outlier in Latin America has become deeply engrained in popular and
even academic discourses over the last century, and it shows few signs of fading.
Whether celebrating the country's white and European character or condemning the discrimination and violence that sustained this image, commentators in

Argentina and abroad have largely agreed in placing Argentina well outside of the narratives of racially mixed nationhood that characterize much of modern Latin America. The image of Argentina as a racial outlier makes for a good story, whether in the world of sports, in journalism, or in the classroom: it rings true and, as the World Cup coverage demonstrates, it often carries an important moral critique of racism and ethnocentrism. But that image is too often rooted in half-truths, stereotypes, and assumptions rather than in historically and culturally grounded analyses of Argentine society.

This edited volume offers an alternative interpretation. It marks a collective attempt to rethink the meanings and workings of race in twentieth- and twenty-first-century Argentina by interrogating prevailing stories and asking new questions. To this end, we have recruited contributors from multiple disciplines – history, anthropology, and literary and cultural studies – based in academic institutions in both North America and Argentina. The volume's chapters span a wide variety of subjects, but they share an impulse to illuminate the significance of race in Argentina's past and present in ways that open avenues for international comparison and dialogue foreclosed by assertions of Argentina's "exceptional" status as a white and European nation. By placing Argentina more firmly within the vibrant scholarly conversations on race and nation in the Americas and beyond, the chapters in this volume generate insights that, we hope, will be valuable for other national contexts. This volume is thus meant as a contribution to rethinking race *in* modern Argentina, but also *from* Argentina outward to the broader world.

THE PROBLEM OF ARGENTINE RACIAL EXCEPTIONALISM

The idea of Argentine racial exceptionalism stems from early conceptions of national progress rooted in racism and violent exclusion, and it persists as part of more recent attempts to address those legacies and to combat racial discrimination in the contemporary world. It is not by chance that critics often choose Argentina as a cautionary case – indeed, the nation's politicians and thinkers went to great lengths, starting in the nineteenth century, to make racial whiteness and cultural Europeanness central to definitions of Argentine identity and to produce social transformation through overseas immigration and frontier conquest. Argentina's apparent success in this regard – which once earned the country comparisons to Europe or to European "settler societies" like the United States, Canada, and Australia – was in fact a source of pride for many Argentines at a time when dominant social theories questioned Latin Americans' capacity for civilization.[4] Yet as the twentieth century progressed, regional and global changes in ideas of race and national belonging increasingly cast Argentina's proud embrace of whiteness and Europeanness in a negative light. In the first half of the century, many leaders and intellectuals across Latin America began to modify or reject the European standards of civilization and racial whiteness once aspired to by their predecessors, finding new pride instead in what we might call a *mestizo* nationalism: a defense of their nations' racial and cultural hybridity (resulting from centuries of racial mixing or *mestizaje*) and a celebration of supposedly "Latin" traditions of racial coexistence or fusion in contrast to North Atlantic racism and segregation. Although Argentine intellectual, political, and artistic movements participated in this wave of cultural nationalism, Argentina's leaders never embraced mestizaje or racial multiplicity as official national ideologies in the twentieth century.[5] Nor, later in the century, did Argentine leaders follow in the paths of the European nations or multiracial settler societies Argentina had once aspired to emulate. While processes like decolonization, immigration, and civil rights or anti-Apartheid movements forced many of these countries to grapple with histories of racial exclusion, discrimination, and violence, similar discussions have been markedly slower to emerge in Argentine public life. Within Argentina, in fact, many continue to uphold the ideas of homogeneous national whiteness and of the absence of distinct racial groups as proof of the absence of racism. The idea that race is irrelevant or even foreign to Argentina has made it difficult for members of groups who feel targeted by racism or who claim ethnic or racial difference to have their concerns heard, respected, and addressed.

As the World Cup coverage makes clear, then, the "exceptional" whiteness and Europeanness that was once a source of pride (and still is) for many Argentines appears outdated and even shameful at a time when multiculturalism, diversity, and anti-racism have become, at least nominally, dominant values deeply linked to ideas of justice and human rights.[6] Yet in taking up an anti-racist position, commentators within and outside of Argentina too frequently take for granted the success of the whitening project in that country, leaving intact the image of Argentine racial exceptionalism. Critics of social inequality likewise often accept the idea of Argentine exceptionalism, leading them to overlook the issue of race or, at best, to repeat the simplified version of a much more complicated story: that Argentines either exterminated all nonwhite people or erased them from national history and consciousness, or both. Taken to its extreme (as in the *Huffington Post* piece), the attempt to make Argentina into an object lesson of "ethnic cleansing" and "genocide" unintentionally confirms the supposed "disappearance" of indigenous or Afro-descendant people from the nation – the very discourses to which contemporary activists vocally object in their struggles against invisibility. As a result, Argentina is often marginal to or omitted from comparative studies of race in Latin America. In a field overwhelmingly focused on African, indigenous, or mestizo majorities or minorities, this omission indirectly endorses the image of Argentina as white and of "white" as a neutral, un-marked, or transparently intelligible category rather than as the opaque product of local racial ideologies and negotiations.

This volume aspires to move beyond the limiting framework of exceptionalism toward a more robust understanding of race in Argentina's past and present. In approaching this task, the contributors to this volume are conscious of the need to act as translators of sorts between Argentine and foreign conceptions of race (and thus between the distinct scholarly vocabularies and conceptual toolkits that have developed around each). We are aware that by attempting to mediate, we risk dissatisfying both of the constituencies we seek to engage. Yet recent work on Argentina by scholars based both inside and outside the country has broken new ground by beginning to place these different systems of meaning-making around race in conversation with one another. The chapters that follow seek to deepen and amplify those emerging conversations, mapping the points of convergence and divergence among local and foreign traditions of analyzing race, and using each to point out the other's blind spots, hidden assumptions, or contradictions.

Given the longstanding prevalence in Argentina of ideas about the nation as homogeneously white and about the irrelevance of race as a social (and even analytical) category, we believe that providing satisfactory alternatives to the narrative of exceptionalism requires engaging with terms and concepts that have not traditionally been central to Argentine discussions of national identity or to Argentine scholarship. Though terms like "mestizaje," "minorities," "whiteness," and even "race" may seem imported or illegitimate, they have proven adaptable and very useful in helping to explain the workings of social inequality in other parts of the Americas. Their use helps render visible the ways that ideas about race and processes of racialization, even if not always explicitly recognized as such by locals, inflected or shaped other (perhaps more readily recognized) forms of difference and inequality in Argentina.

Yet this operation is useful only if we are simultaneously attuned to local social attitudes, behaviors, and vocabularies of difference. The World Cup coverage cited earlier illustrates the pitfalls of transporting fixed or preconceived ideas about race to a foreign context, and of treating race as somehow more "real" than other forms of difference. Specifically, it demonstrates the limited usefulness of categories like "blackness" and "whiteness" when deployed from a strictly external perspective and helps explain why many Argentine scholars have found them lacking. Yet this journalistic coverage (in spite of itself) also hints at the unexpected meanings that these false cognates might yield up when examined within the context of Argentina. From this perspective, we might ask of the aforementioned *New York Times* article: What do Argentines mean when they say their nation is "white"? How do the meanings of the term vary in different times and places within Argentina, and how do they diverge from understandings of what it means to be white in other parts of the region and the world? How exceptional or extreme are Argentine racial ideologies in the Latin American context, and how do the ways we conceptualize the comparative elements influence our conclusions? Similarly, when the *Huffington Post* piece asks why there are no black men on Argentina's roster, we might reply: How do we know there aren't? By whose definition of "black"? What does it mean that Argentines refer to at least one player on the team colloquially as *el negro*, even though his "blackness" is not obvious to the North American journalist?[7] By posing these kinds of questions, the contributors to this volume seek to *explain* the obliqueness of race in Argentine society rather than celebrate it as an accomplishment or dismiss it as a comparative "lack" or "failure."

RACE IN ARGENTINA: A HISTORICAL PERSPECTIVE

How does one write the history of race in a country that largely denies its relevance? Until recently, because most Argentine scholars were skeptical of the concept, no one had attempted to write an integrated history of race that explained patterns of racial formation and followed multiple racial groups over the long term, analyzing their relationships to racial ideologies and to processes of nation- and state-formation. Though much work remains to be done, the outlines of this history are slowly emerging.[8] The brief overview that follows is meant as a guide for readers, providing useful background for the individual chapters. It also reveals how and why the twentieth century appears to be missing in the literature on race and nation in Argentina, and why interest in race seems to be reemerging in the twenty-first.

During the late colonial period, the territory that would become Argentina was a socially heterogeneous landscape. Like many other peripheral parts of Spanish America, the Viceroyalty of the Río de la Plata lacked the large, settled indigenous populations characteristic of Mexico or Peru, the centers of Spain's New World Empire. Its relatively sparse population included people labeled as Spaniards, Indians, blacks (*negros* or *morenos*, comprising free and enslaved Africans), as well as a range of people in-between. *Mestizo* referred primarily to individuals of mixed indigenous and European ancestry. *Pardo* and *mulato* described people of mixed African and European ancestry, and *zambo* referred to people of mixed indigenous and African heritage.[9] Over time, *criollo*, a term originally applied to American-born Spaniards (and in some areas, to American-born African slaves), was increasingly used to designate anyone born on American soil.

Although it may seem surprising to readers familiar with Argentina's reputation for racial exclusion, in the wake of independence and for much of the nineteenth century, relatively inclusive definitions of national belonging prevailed as elites attempted to create an Argentine "people" out of this heterogeneous, stratified, and formerly colonized population.[10] Dominant conceptions of citizenship as political or voluntarist were, in theory if not always in practice, race-blind or raceless, and the nation's guiding metaphors of inclusion endowed the national soil with the power to generate a shared sense of familial belonging among people of different ancestries.[11] In the first half of the nineteenth century, the exact shape that the Argentine nation would take remained an open question as various factions struggled for power in protracted civil wars. Rival conceptions of republicanism embraced, to greater or lesser degrees, liberal and individualist principles as well as more conservative corporatist ideals. Proponents of these different political tendencies also reached out, to varying degrees and in different ways, to people of indigenous, African, or mixed ancestry in their attempts to recruit or mobilize "the people"; the 1853 Constitution that abolished slavery and granted the right to vote to all adult men embodies the overall expansion of political participation and citizenship in this period.[12] This project is evident in the case of Afro-Argentines, who made up about 30 percent of the population of Buenos Aires in the early nineteenth century (the figures were even higher in parts of the Northwest). Afro-Argentines fought in the country's many wars and were active participants in the nation's politics, including as an important contingent of voters. Together with the politicians who sought their support, Afro-Argentines stressed the power of the land or of soldiering to make them nationals and promoted the idea that nonwhites could be improved through education, military service, labor, and general assimilation to Catholic, European ideals. This was far from an easy or automatic process. Afro-Argentines had to struggle, often against difficult odds, for their rights of citizenship to be respected. They also had to renounce ethnic, cultural, linguistic, or religious differences in the process of becoming unmarked Argentines.[13]

The relationship of Argentine nation-building to indigenous peoples differed in important respects. Regardless of which political faction held power, Argentina's nineteenth-century leaders sought to wrest control over portions of the national territory and areas outside its formal borders from a number of Amerindian polities (although even at their most violent, the nation's shifting frontiers were also places of extensive cultural and economic exchange).[14] Argentine statesmen and intellectuals considered members of unassimilated indigenous groups as "savage" threats to civilization and indeed as foils to the "proper" Argentine citizen, a view that underlay and supported their policy of war and expansion.[15] At the same time, the state's strongly territorial conceptions of citizenship meant that indigenous people who lived inside the national territory and adopted a "civilized" way of life were envisioned as Argentines – if not fully equal to Argentines of European descent, at least no longer "Indian."[16] Yet in this period the boundaries for integration into the nation (conceived by elites as a process of "civilization") appear to have been somewhat more porous for Afro-Argentines than for indigenous people, who continued to bear stronger stigmas of racial and cultural otherness.[17]

In the last quarter of the nineteenth century, ideologies of race and national belonging hardened and narrowed further, reflecting in part the rise of currents of so-called scientific racism in Europe and the United States. In this context, Argentine liberals recast ideals of nationality and of fitness for citizenship more forcefully in terms of racial whiteness and European culture, while enacting disciplinary legislation (regarding labor, vagrancy, education, immigration, military service, and so on) designed to create and enforce homogeneity among the citizenry.[18] It was in this period, as the Argentine state pushed to consolidate a booming agro-export economy, that the national governments launched military campaigns to definitively occupy the remaining expanses of Amerindian lands to the south and northeast. These campaigns killed thousands of indigenous people and violently assimilated survivors through practices like the separation of families, forced relocation, and coerced or low-wage labor.[19] In the wake of the subjugation of independent indigenous groups and the consolidation of the national territory, Argentine observers complacently declared the almost complete disappearance of "Indians" in the nation. "Blacks" too, official histories and statistics of the period asserted, had disappeared or were well on their way toward group extinction, due to their supposedly disproportional rates of death in nineteenth-century wars or epidemics and their high degree of intermixture with the broader population.[20] These disappearances, of course, were a matter of perception. Indigenous people and descendants of Africans continued physically to exist in the nation, but no longer as members of communities recognized as racially or ethnically distinct. Instead, people of indigenous or African ancestry increasingly became part of a many-hued "popular world" composed of the nation's poorer sectors – a group considered white in racial terms but subject to longstanding social prejudices that linked darker skin tones to low socioeconomic status and lack of cultural refinement. Though elites often questioned the popular sectors' fitness for full political participation, many also saw them as capable of improvement through education and disciplinary policies.[21] The victory of a white racial order in Argentina (which earned the country its reputation as exceptional) therefore depended not principally on "extermination," but on the renegotiation of the boundaries of ethno-racial difference in socioeconomic and cultural terms. This process was a result of elites' attempts to produce a homogeneous citizenry, but it also reflected many nonelites' attempts to seize the spaces that assimilationist ideologies provided for their fuller inclusion as citizens.[22]

At the same time that Argentine statesmen waged their campaign of conquest and assimilation in the Interior, they sought to take advantage of the growing stream of migrants leaving Europe and the Mediterranean basin. Other Latin American countries created similar projects to sponsor European immigration in an effort to whiten their populations, but due to a variety of economic factors and other reasons, Argentina stands out in its dramatic success. Census figures suggest that approximately 2.9 million immigrants settled permanently between 1880 and 1916, while millions more came and went among Argentina, their homelands, and other destinations. By the end of this period nearly one-third of Argentina's population was foreign-born (the reader may contrast these levels, among the highest in the world, with the United States today, in which immigrants represent roughly 12.9 percent of the total population).[23] Immigrants to Argentina often came in search of rural work, but many remained in the capital Buenos Aires – which rapidly became the largest metropolis in Latin America – and in other cities, where they too became part of the emergent "popular world." The demographic transformations that immigration wrought allowed Argentine public figures – together with many private citizens – to congratulate themselves on the achievement of a homogeneously white citizenry and to construct personal and national genealogies that stressed European descent. Yet just as the ideas of indigenous extermination and Afro-Argentine disappearance need rethinking, so too does the idea of immigrant whitening. For one thing, although Italian and Spanish immigrants represented the largest groups of resident foreigners, the immigrant population comprised a kaleidoscope of nationalities, ethnicities, religions, languages, and cultural traditions.[24] Second, as anthropologist Claudia Briones has pointed out, imagining Argentine whiteness as the result of a purely European melting pot [*crisol de razas*] obscures the presence of a "hidden" melting pot that included Argentina's significant pre-immigration popular sectors.[25] In short, turn-of-the-century immigration had a profound influence in shaping Argentine society and ideas about national and racial identity as European and white, but these ideas need to be examined, not taken literally.

Indeed, Argentine authorities in this period were hardly satisfied with the whiteness or homogeneity of the national population that they had fashioned through ostensible extermination, disappearance, and immigration. Heavily influenced by the new science of eugenics, in the early twentieth century some leaders worried obsessively about the disorder caused by the intermingling of diverse native- and foreign-born populations and created new policies designed to protect the national "race" from degeneration. The state and allied intellectuals used policies and institutions of social control to police diversity of all kinds – not just along lines of race and ethnicity but also of religion, culture, language, political affiliation, sexuality, psychology, age, and legal condition – and to induct newcomers and locals as nationals by disciplining them in acceptable behavioral norms modeled on Western European standards. In this context, in which behaviors considered "deviant" could be understood as dangers to the health of the nation and its people, "race" came to mean many things: it could denote perceived differences and hierarchies among human groups (like "whites" or "blacks"); it could refer to national populations imagined as distinct (the "Argentine race"), or it could refer more broadly to humankind (the human "race") in discourses about public health and social improvement.[26] As several chapters in this volume demonstrate, race was, in a sense, atomized and absorbed into other forms of marking difference in the early twentieth century, thereby becoming difficult to see or to name. Similarly, as whiteness became ever more firmly established as a natural part of the nation's identity and of what it meant to be Argentine, it too became invisible as a racial construction.[27] Yet even when the main projects to reform the Argentine population no longer identified clearly defined communities of racial others as primary targets, and indeed exported (construing as foreign) the problem of race from the national debate, the differentiating, essentializing, and disciplining logic of racial thought permeated interactions between the state and its citizens and, through micro-mechanisms of self- and mutual "cultural patrolling," among citizens themselves.[28]

The best example of this process is the transformation of the word *negro,* in the early twentieth century, from an explicitly racial referent to a term used primarily to mark social class within the broad field of Argentine whiteness. As Argentina became more urban and industrial and the poor more proletarian, class became central to the vocabulary of mass politics and mass culture alike, thanks in part to the activism of the country's small but vocal labor and leftist movements. The growth of a proletarian sector and the importance of left-wing politics predicated on a belief in the essential historical reality of class and the secondary, ideological, status of other kinds of exclusion, meant that race further receded in visibility as a way of marking or explaining social difference. Yet even as class subsumed racial or ethnic identifications in these decades, race strongly inflected the meanings of class.[29] In the parlance of members of the middle and upper classes, to return to our example, "negro" was unmoored from biological references to African descent and extended more broadly onto working-class sectors and certain provincial populations. In this usage, "negro" – issued as an insult – projected the pejorative connotations once attached exclusively to people of African descent to popular sectors as a whole. This broad application of "negro," though intended as a class-based slur, drew on the term's delegitimizing power (originally based on race and culture) to mark these populations off as less deserving of full citizenship due to their perceived poverty, uncouth behavior, lack of education, or place of residence.[30]

While this rhetorical move did not make members of the lower classes "black" in a way that would be legible to most outside observers (the journalists who produced the coverage of the 2014 World Cup a case in point), it did draw upon the longstanding association in Argentina between dark skin and low socioeconomic status, thus providing a necessary corrective to the idea that race simply ceased to be an important part of Argentine social hierarchies in this period. The transformation of "negro" into a primarily class-based slur diluted the word's racial meanings so thoroughly that they remain difficult to pinpoint today – whether for exposing the racism that the term often carries, or for affirmatively claiming a black racial identity, as chapters in this volume demonstrate. But far from having no racial salience, the term's redefinition at precisely the moment when "white" became the default national race points to the stratifications within Argentine whiteness, a status conditioned by a range of factors: geographic origin, appearance, education, and class affiliation and its attendant cultural forms and behaviors, among others.[31] Nor is "negro" an isolated case. As several chapters in this collection reveal, the use of euphemistic terms like criollo, *paisano,* or *descendiente* to refer to individuals of mixed racial ancestry or to culturally assimilated indigenous people (especially in rural areas) similarly served to facilitate the conceptual transformation of the population to white, while acting as continual reminders of widespread processes of mestizaje and of the persistence of ethnic or racial differences. These various terms, with their oblique racial connotations, bolstered the image of the white nation while creating subtle differentiations within it.[32]

This volume begins, then, with the turn of the twentieth century: the moment when race began to recede from view in official discourses, eclipsed or subsumed by other categories of difference (class, nation, region) that became more visible, even as race continued to shape them. The twentieth century is the period most marked by the turn away from race as a category of historical analysis, and most in need of careful reinterpretation. This volume also tries to make sense of the first decade of the twenty-first century, a period in which questions of racial and ethnic identity, discrimination, and diversity have reemerged as issues of public debate in Argentina (as in many other parts of Latin America). While these conversations have been simmering at least since the country's return to democracy in 1983, the traumatic 2001–2002 economic crisis brought them to the surface with new urgency by dealing a blow to longstanding formulations of Argentine exceptionalism that had linked national progress to whiteness and middle-class status. Building on this conjuncture, on the rise of a multicultural agenda within international organizations and funding institutions, and on the political openings provided by a left-leaning nationalist government from 2003 to 2015, state and non-state actors have increasingly put forth an image of a nation premised on antiracism and on the affirmative inclusion of various ethnic or racial groups. This new image of the nation was clearly on display in the state-organized 2010 Bicentennial celebrations and in the 2010 Bicentennial census, which, for the first time in over a century, included categories for both Afro-descendants and indigenous people.[33] Yet Argentina's multicultural turn, as this volume demonstrates, is far from complete or assured, and in any case, multiculturalism brings with it new problems. Recent xenophobic attacks on mestizo or indigenous migrants from neighboring countries, or denunciations of reemergent "Afro-descendant" or indigenous identities as inauthentic or imported, demonstrate that exclusionary paradigms of nationhood have hardly vanished. And even the newly inclusive census of 2010 has faced criticism for undercounting the presence of Afro-Argentines and indigenous people and omitting other groups entirely. Still, these controversies have fueled lasting discussion among politicians, media commentators, NGOs, intellectuals, artists, and other actors about the contours of national identity, fracturing longstanding ideas of Argentine whiteness or, at the very least, revealing its internal shades and nuances. It is thus an ideal time to revisit the issue of race in modern Argentina, analyzing contemporary transformations as part of our revision.

ARGENTINA IN LATIN AMERICAN CONTEXT

Because the narrative of Argentina's exceptional whiteness depends essentially on a comparison between that country and its regional neighbors, rethinking "exceptionalism" requires that we reassess the terms of that comparison. On the one hand, Argentine thinkers' emphasis on whiteness and cultural Europeanness is noticeably distinct from the efforts of other Latin American national elites – in

Mexico, Peru, Cuba, Bolivia, or Brazil, for example – to emphasize some amount of indigeneity or Africanness as part of mestizo or multiracial national identities. On the other hand, multiracial/mestizaje ideologies elsewhere in Latin America often prized the gradual whitening of the population through mixture, or at least aimed to produce its move away from Africanness and/or Indianness, as in Argentina. Even in situations where national elites stressed multiracialism, coexistence, or colorlessness instead of fusion, the achievement of full belonging for people of color required adherence to cultural norms and forms of behavior based largely on "modern" European ideals.[34] Meanwhile, as several works in this volume argue, whiteness prevailed in Argentina because of a system of racial classification and perception that broadened North Atlantic definitions of the category "white" to include an array of racial origins, phenotypical variations, and shades of color, while suppressing intermediate categories and narrowing the categories "black" or "Indian" almost to the vanishing point.[35] This broad definition of whiteness and its conferral, at least in theory, on most of the nation's inhabitants is thus markedly similar to the tropes of racial and cultural inclusion that came to characterize other Latin American nations in the twentieth century, where elites often incorporated an array of racial origins, phenotypical variations, and shades of color into broadened "mestizo" (or comparable intermediate) categories. If we understand "whiteness" and "mestizaje" in these more nuanced ways, the terms and outcomes of the regional comparison shift: Argentine ideas of whiteness become part of, rather than stark deviations from, a spectrum of regional ideologies of racial and ethnic fusion. As in more iconically "mixed-race" nations, Argentina's racial narratives have also encompassed both an erasure of nonwhite roots at the service of whitening ideas and – less visibly but no less durably – celebrations of some degree of non-whiteness or mixture as the basis of a unique national identity. In this vein, several of the chapters in this volume pay attention to attempts to make mestizaje or nonwhiteness a visible and even central part of the nation, whether in the twentieth century (Adamovsky, Elena, Pite, Karush, Gordillo) or in the early twenty-first (Ko, Geler, Alberto). Argentina also shares with Latin America the relative absence of explicitly and exclusively race-based movements and politics in the twentieth century. Across Latin America, demands for fair treatment by people of color, as well as state-sanctioned celebrations of racial inclusiveness, rarely took a purely "racial" form, but were instead deeply intertwined with tropes of nationalism, regionalism, class, politics, history, culture, or gender.[36]

All of this opens the possibility of comparison, rather than the more traditional contrast, between Argentina's ideology of whiteness and so-called ideologies of racial democracy in the rest of Latin America, whose inclusionary and exclusionary effects scholars and activists have debated for the past half-century or more. One of the strongest criticisms leveled at official ideologies of racial fusion or coexistence, especially in the last decades of the twentieth century, portrays them as smoke-screens or "myths" that proclaimed the inclusion of nonwhite people even as discrimination persisted, making racism difficult to identify and fight, and delegitimizing any demands based on racial or ethnic difference. This powerful critique, thoroughly developed for other parts of Latin America, has not yet reached its full potential for the Argentine case, where assertions or denunciations of the exceptionally successful whitening project have largely preempted (with some notable exceptions) a deeper scholarly examination of the unevenness of whiteness.[37] Some of the chapters in this volume make this kind of critique for Argentina, revealing whiteness to be, in a sense, a "myth."

Yet the authors in this volume are aware that the goal of debunking racial "myths" should not, in the process, hold up another purportedly truer or more foundational "reality" of race (a social construction, after all). They therefore attempt to move beyond treating whiteness simply as a misapprehension or a lie. Rather, they show whiteness to be a complex and deep-rooted racial formation with profound contradictions – an ideology that grants broad inclusion by muting explicit discussions of racial and ethnic difference, but which nonetheless reinscribes those differences through internal hierarchies, frontiers, or margins of belonging within the white nation. The ideology of whiteness, in other words, might be seen as "inclusive" for being conferred broadly and officially upon a majority of Argentines over the course of the twentieth century (thus buttressing the image of the white nation), but it also contains within it vocabularies and visual codes for identifying shades of ethnic or racial difference embedded in performances of class, region, culture, gender, or propriety. These meanings, legible to most of the population, often remain tacit until moments of tension or conflict, when they become readily available for open deployment. The chapters by Deutsch, Rodríguez, Chamosa, Gordillo, Pite, and Geler examine these shifting internal frontiers of whiteness as they affect rural people of indigenous descent, poor or working-class urban Argentines, Sephardic and Ashkenazi Jews, and even white people of African descent. Their chapters show how the making of Argentine whiteness, even when it depended on processes of mestizaje and the strategic or partial inclusion of nonwhite populations, nonetheless produced lasting associations between certain kinds of mestizo-ness or nonwhiteness and foreignness that relegated (and still relegate) many Argentines to a kind of second-class citizenship that has proven almost impossible to articulate openly.

In addition to examining the limitations of dominant ideologies of whiteness, several of the chapters in this volume reprise another important theme in much of the recent scholarship on race and nation in Latin America: an attempt to take seriously – without relapsing into the self-satisfaction of an earlier era – the potential spaces for belonging made possible by discourses of mestizaje or racial inclusion. In this sense, chapters by Adamovsky, Elena, Ko, and Alberto examine the limitations as well as the affordances of shifting definitions of whiteness for making racial, ethnic, or cultural differences visible and politically meaningful over the course of the twentieth and twenty-first centuries. Other chapters move beyond state ideologies and discourses by focusing on the agency and experiences of people of color, or people not obviously or always recognized as white, and their attempts to contest whiteness or negotiate positions within it. In this sense, the chapters by Geler, Karush, Deutsch, and Rodríguez all ask what spaces were available, within the "white" nation, to nonwhite people or to people whose whiteness and Argentineness were and are, as Deutsch and Geler aptly put it, in some sense "insecure" or "marginal" – such as Jews, indigenous people, and Afro-descendants. What is to be gained or lost, these chapters ask, by asserting whiteness or nonwhiteness in different times and places? What factors, other than physical appearance, affected how subjects could claim these identities at different times? What has changed, in this sense, from a twentieth century mostly marked by ideologies of homogeneous whiteness to a Bicentennial era that finds many Argentines newly proud of their nation's official inclusiveness and multiculturality?

Finally, it is useful to measure this rethinking of Argentine exceptionalism in relation to other societies that have, at different times, imagined themselves as essentially or primarily white. Whereas in places like the United States, the United Kingdom, South Africa, or Australia, whiteness was largely constructed in opposition to one or more internal racial others (generally seen as clear and present threats) and in relation to colonies, in Argentina whiteness was constructed in reference to disappearing, distant, or altogether vanished racial others, and in contrast to neighboring nations. The chapters in this volume suggest that, as a result, whiteness in Argentina became highly naturalized, almost coterminous with the nation and blanketing all within its bounds. To readers familiar with the scholarship on race in other "settler societies," the claim of universal whiteness, or whiteness not clearly bounded by a color line, may seem suspicious or even comical. Yet by taking Argentine concepts like "blanco," "negro," "criollo," and "descendiente" seriously, without taking the claim to racelessness literally, these chapters productively challenge the limits of our tolerance for the theoretical insight that whiteness, and race more broadly, are socially constructed and locally situated. Among other questions, these chapters underscore the power of not-strictly biological traits to shape perceptions of whiteness and non-whiteness. In this sense, perhaps, Argentina (with its unique, regionally-situated imaginary of whiteness) can act as a useful link between Latin America and other global regions imagined as primarily white. What might at first glance seem like the country's historically dulled or oblique sense of race or its peculiar form of whiteness can become useful tools for rethinking the apparent obviousness of race or whiteness in other contexts. Moreover, Argentina's present-day experience as a society attempting to become multicultural, multiethnic, and multiracial after a century of official "racelessness" speaks directly to pressing problems of racial visibility and equality in other purportedly "post-racial" or legally "colorblind" societies such as the United States. In sum, the chapters in this volume draw upon, and contribute to, a growing body of scholarship that reminds us that "whiteness" is a product of specific racial ideologies and historical processes.

STRUCTURE AND THEMES

This book is organized into two sections. Part I, "Histories of Race in the Twentieth Century," considers the problem of the "missing twentieth century" in the study of race in Argentina. Through a series of case studies, this section investigates the forging of dominant paradigms of national identity and the parallel emergence of alternative conceptions that recognized, to varying degrees, the "nonwhite" or "non-European" contributions to the nation. Part I begins with Sandra Deutsch's chapter on turn-of-the-century Jewish immigrants of various national origins and their efforts, in cities and rural areas, to position themselves in relation to Argentine debates regarding whiteness, national assimilation, racial degeneracy, and social improvement. Oscar Chamosa's chapter shifts our perspective on the formation of a national race from the consequences of trans-Atlantic migration to domestic explorations of the national territory – in particular, the encounters between Argentine travelers from major cities and residents of Amerindian descent in the Northwestern provinces, which became sites of tourism in the early twentieth century. Chapters by Matthew Karush and Rebekah Pite employ a biographical approach to cultural history topics. Karush's work surveys the life and times of guitarist Oscar Alemán and the permutations of his racial self-presentation as "black" across a long career marked by foreign travel and changing trends and expectations in the music industry. Pite's chapter moves from the Northwest to Buenos Aires to examine debates over what counted as Argentina's authentic national cuisine over the past century (focusing in part on famed cookbook author Doña Petrona C. de Gandulfo), and in so doing elucidates the racial and regional undertones of efforts to define criollo food traditions. Mariela Eva Rodríguez takes us from Argentina's capital city to the Patagonian province of Santa Cruz to reveal the ways in which anthropological and historical inquiry into "vanishing" indigenous populations and trans-Andean migration shaped debates over racial identity, mixture, and family history as well as local contests over land. The closing pair of chapters in this section focuses on articulations of race and nationalism by one of Latin America's most controversial and longest-lived mass political movements: Peronism. In his close analysis of Peronist visual culture, Ezequiel Adamovsky unpacks the interrelated representations of racial harmony, class solidarity, and social justice disseminated during the first and second Juan D. Perón presidencies (1946–55), while situating these initiatives within the context of earlier experiments in cultural nationalism. Eduardo Elena's chapter begins with Peronism's foundational moment in the mid-1940s and advances through the turmoil of Argentina's 1960s and 1970s to the present day, revealing how Peronist authorities, intellectuals, and supporters have employed racial concepts to strikingly flexible political ends and how these evolving treatments compare to other famed Latin American nationalisms.

The volume's Part II, "Race and Nation in the New Century," asks how and why race has become a renewed object of fascination and public discussion in contemporary Argentina, without fully displacing engrained ideas of white exceptionalism. Each of the chapters in this section takes the contemporary moment – with its emerging denunciations of Argentine ideas of homogeneous whiteness, its officially backed ideals of inclusiveness and multiculturalism, and its processes of ethnic and racial "revisibilization" – as its main site of inquiry and point of departure. Yet in order to trace transformations over time, each of these chapters necessarily also doubles back over the long twentieth century. In particular, the first two chapters of Part II, together with the closing chapter of Part I, act as bridges between the twentieth and twenty-first centuries. The contributors to Part II adopt a variety of scholarly approaches, including ethnographic investigation, literary and cultural interpretation, and historical analysis, to study recent challenges to the received wisdom about white nationhood in Argentina. Lea Geler's chapter delves into the obstacles and contradictions faced by Buenos Aires residents who seek to acknowledge African ancestry in their own family past, experiences that demonstrate how powerfully the borders of whiteness are socially enforced. Adopting a similar ethnographic approach, but bridging Buenos Aires with its rural hinterlands, Gastón Gordillo's chapter on the spatial and affective underpinnings of whiteness considers how the figure of the nineteenth-century indigenous raiding party [*el malón*] remains alive in fears of social invasion and of the erosion of white exceptionalism experienced by *porteños* [Buenos Aires city residents] in the past few decades. The final two chapters use recent film and literary works to investigate shifts in contemporary racial ideologies in wider cultural and historical perspective. Chisu Teresa Ko breaks new ground by studying film representations of Asian-Argentines for insights into the impact of globalization on Argentine ideas of national identity and the ultimate limits of multiculturalist, as well as more traditionally nationalist, formulations of racial and ethnic inclusion. Employing a corpus of recently published works of popular historical fiction, Paulina Alberto's chapter asks what it means that mixture and interracial romance among European, Amerindian, and African populations figure so prominently in new imaginings – both fictional and non-fictional – of Argentina's past and present. The volume concludes with a reflection by George Reid Andrews, whose influential book *The Afro-Argentines of Buenos Aires*, published more than three decades ago, first posed many of the questions we address here. Andrews' epilogue brings together insights from the broad-ranging social scientific literature on race and racial ideologies in Latin America, from historical and recent demographic data, and from his reading of the chapters themselves to situate Argentina's trajectory within contemporary regional transformations in matters of racial identities and racial politics.

As this outline suggests, the volume is characterized by its diverse disciplinary and methodological scope as well as by the broad range of topics, locations, populations, and time periods addressed by the contributors. The contributors do not entirely see eye to eye in their interpretations or agree fully on how best to translate across the "internal" and "external" scholarly literatures on race and nation in Argentina – differences that will, with any luck, spark discussion among readers. Nevertheless, there are a number of questions and themes that surface repeatedly in the book and lend the chapters a collective coherence and dynamism. We hope our readers will discover their own interconnections, but it is useful at the outset to identify four major threads that run throughout the volume.

The first originates in the contributors' shared interest in examining how constructions of race intersect with those of class and gender. This approach reflects, of course, a broader scholarly tendency in Latin American studies and other fields. Drawing on these models, the chapters provide a deeper under- standing of the particular ways class and gender have constituted conceptions of race in Argentina, and vice-versa. As we have seen, commonly used Argen- tine epithets like "negro" defy easy categorization as either terms of class or racial prejudice, nor do these local terminologies map neatly onto white-black (or white-indigenous) color lines and spectrums. Accordingly, the volume considers questions such as: Why is it often easier to articulate and acknow- ledge class inequalities in Argentina than practices of discrimination based on skin color and other physical attributes? How have the vocabularies of class provided both the tools to fight against racialized forms of exploitation and to silence discussions about the existence of race and race-based discrimination? What have been the advantages of emphasizing class and what have been the limitations and unforeseen consequences? In regards to gender, the volume's contributors are attuned not only to the different ways that men and women experience racial identification, inclusion, and exclusion, but also to the ways that conceptions of race and nation bear the marks of patriarchal norms. Gender and sexuality feature centrally in how Argentines envisioned the poten- tials and dangers of racial mixture in their nation, as well as in racialized conceptions of the nation itself. Intellectuals and other actors took interracial couplings, both real and imagined, as emblematic of crossing other orders of difference (such as region, political parties, and cultural practices). The chapters probe the workings of gender and sexuality in individual, group, and national racial identities through sources that range from social scientific reports and state documents to family histories and artistic works. The questions posed include: In what ways have men and women been envisioned as the agents of whitening, degeneration, disappearance, or reappearance among populations identified frequently by commentators as racial others? How do performances of certain kinds of gender identities reinforce or undercut subjects' claims to specific racial (or class) identities? More broadly, whereas countries like Cuba, Brazil, or Mexico have projected mixed-race women (the *mestiza* or *mulata)* as emblems of a hybrid and unique national identity, Argentina has mostly upheld white or off-white male figures as symbols of national authenticity, some of whom appear in these chapters: the *gaucho* or mounted cowherd of Argentina's grasslands, of course, but also the *compadrito* or urban tough immortalized by tangos, the *descamisado* or shirtless worker, or the *asador*, preparer of the national grilled meat dish. What, then, are the gendered politics of national authenticity in Argentina, and how do they shape or reflect the tendency to read mestizaje as whitening? Finally, how do contemporary revisions of national historical narratives seek to leverage the relationship between race and gender to reshape ideas of the authentic nation, and to what effects?

In seeking answers to these questions, the volume pays careful attention to the ways that race has (and has not) acquired mainstream political significance in twentieth- and twenty-first-century Argentina. The absence in Argentina of the elaborate legal systems of racial classification and exclusion that characterized other European settler societies in the nineteenth and twentieth centuries did not mean that political institutions – that is, national and provincial governments as well as parties and civil associations – simply ignored matters of race and ethnicity. State actors played a crucial role in the creation and dissemination of paradigms of white nationhood, but they were also involved in periodic efforts to advance rival ideas of national inclusion and, more recently, to inculcate the values of multiracial nationalism among the citizenry. Questions about the politics of race and the race of politics thread their way through the volume: Why have state policies shifted over time, and what are the underlying continuities in political efforts to define the racial or ethnic terms of national belonging in Argentina? How do the politics of race in Argentina compare with those of neighboring Latin American societies and those of societies reliant on formal legal regimes of segregation? How have shifting economic fortunes and demographic trends inspired new forms of political action around race? Accordingly, the chapters consider the multiplicity of motivations, strategies, and consequences of supranational, state, and political organizations in shaping racial ideologies and dynamics, including from the perspective of individuals and populations located throughout the national territory who reacted to these overtures.

Discussions about race in Argentina, however, were hardly confined to the country's political arenas. A third thread that runs through the volume is an attention to how conversations about race took place in various spheres of cultural production and consumption. Contributors analyze influential modes of cultural expression such as literature, social treatises, travelogues, and the visual arts. Yet the existence of elaborate networks of mass media and mass commerce in Argentina from the early twentieth century onward provided additional channels for the production, distribution, and consumption of more popular forms of print and visual culture. The bustling variety of music, film, journalism, and fiction and non-fiction publishing aimed at popular audiences contained powerful representations of national identity and racial thinking. How did audiences in different times and places in Argentina react to discourses of race and nation that circulated through the networks of a modern consumer society? How did older media (such as print and photography) help shape ideas of Argentine nationhood, and how has the appearance of new modes of communications – radio, film, television, and now social media – enabled different representations of race in Argentina's past, present, and future?

Finally, the volume's chapters all pose variations on the question of how race "mapped" onto understandings of space and geography in Argentina. This fourth thread is perhaps the thickest one, as it occupies a prominent place in every chapter; here, too, the contributors seek to engage with scholars who have explored similar topics in other national contexts. Argentina encompasses a vast national territory that spans varied landscapes. It is currently the world's eighth-largest country by area, second only to Brazil in Latin America. Many chapters are grounded in specific places and regions (including the Northwest, Patagonia, Mesopotamia, the Northeast, the Littoral, and Buenos Aires city), while others consider the movement and interaction of populations within the national territory and from overseas. Migration features prominently in these investigations – not surprisingly, given the importance of European immigration to ideas of national whitening, the recent controversies generated by migration from neighboring and other countries, and the status of sustained rural-urban migration as arguably the most significant demographic trend of the past century. How, then, have Argentines envisioned different racial and social "types" as occupying (or originating from) specific regions, provinces, and cities? How has this geography of race shifted over time due to migration and other forces? In what different ways have political and cultural actors grappled with the issues of geographic and racial diversity in Argentina, while also seeking to emphasize themes of national unity and shared identity? How and why do the vocabularies for speaking about and visualizing race and ethnicity vary across the Argentine national territory?

This final question should alert the reader to one general characteristic of the volume: namely, the range of terminologies employed by the contributors in their investigations, both as a reflection of diverse local vocabularies of race and in their own attempts to find appropriate analytical categories. That the terms of racial identity vary across time and place, even within a single nation, has become a point of departure of most recent scholarly works on race and nation in Latin America. Accordingly, each chapter in this volume relies primarily upon the categories used by actors in Argentina's past and present, including terms like "criollo" and "negro" that have been deployed in a dizzying number of ways. Many of the contributors devote considerable attention to analyzing the obliqueness associated with efforts to name race in Argentina, even among people decrying racialized forms of discrimination and injustice. These treatments will no doubt provoke some consternation among readers, including those, in Argentina and abroad, who remain committed to the image of a white Argentina or have certain expectations of how race does or should function. Extricating oneself fully from the racial categories that predominate in places like the United States – and from resultant assumptions about what it "really" means to be white or black, European or Latin American, "pure" or "mixed" – is not an easy task, either for the contributors to this volume or its readers. Nor is it entirely desirable, as one of this volume's goals is to move back and forth between these frames to consider the multiple ways that race has been experienced and understood, throwing into relief the constructed nature of all ideas about race. Yet we ask that readers guard against the temptation of leaping to conclusions based on their own country's norms and instead pay close attention to the possibilities, problems, and contradictions of formulations of race and nation in twentieth- and twenty-first-century Argentina.

In keeping with this spirit of experimentation, the volume is designed to offer an introduction to a field of inquiry that is still very much in formation, rather than providing a concluding summary of an established body of scholarship. Indeed, there are far more Argentina specialists working in this field than could be included in this brief volume, including a younger generation of researchers in the process of completing dissertations as well as established scholars who have participated in the conferences at which early versions of these chapters were discussed. Given recent trends in public debate about race-related questions within Argentina, it is likely that many of the subjects addressed in the volume will attract further academic attention and social commentary – in this sense, and despite the deep history of race in Argentina, the conversation about the "shades of the nation" is just beginning. The editors and contributors hope that the investigations collected in this book will, in ways large and small, help to set the agenda for future research. At the very least, we hope that readers will view tidy assertions of Argentine exceptionalism evoked at the next international sporting event or moment of national crisis with greater skepticism – or even better, with a more historically and culturally grounded understanding of how race in modern Argentina has evolved over time and connects this society to others across the globe.

Notes

1. Even when race and culture do not come explicitly to the fore, these ideas nonetheless inform the standards of economic progress, political stability, financial responsibility, and overall "seriousness" with which commentators (including many Argentines) measure the country. See Joseph, "Taking."
2. Simon Romero and Jonathan Gilbert, "Why So Many World Cup Fans Dislike Argentina," *New York Times*, 10 Jun. 2014.
3. Rachel Décoste, "Why Are There No Black Men on Argentina's Roster?," *The Huffington Post*, 9 Jul. 2014.
4. For examples of this sort of self-congratulation, see Zimmermann, "Racial Ideas," 29–30; Helg, "Race," 43. On earlier formulations of Argentine exceptionalism, see Garguin, "Los Argentinos," 165–66; Shumway, *The Invention*; Halperín Donghi, *Proyecto*.
5. On Argentine cultural nationalism, see Prieto, *El discurso*; Delaney, "Imagining"; Chamosa, *Argentine Folklore*.
6. Gilroy, *Against Race*, 244–45.
7. Ezequiel Garay is known as "El negro Garay." See, for example, http://canchallena .lanacion.com.ar/1709257-el-negro-garay-todavia-le-debe-un-gol-a-la-seleccion.
8. Lea Geler and Mariela Rodríguez's synthetic history of race in Argentina is thus an extremely welcome contribution and an insightful framework for future studies.

Their interpretation informs our account in the next few paragraphs. Geler and Rodríguez, "Argentina." For similarly synthetic approaches to the discursive dimensions of contemporary racism and to contemporary antiracist politics, see Courtis et al., "Racism and Discourse," and Sutton, "Contesting Racism."

9. On "mixed" social and racial categories in the colonial period, see Guzmán, *Los claroscuros*; Farberman and Ratto, *Historias mestizas*.

10. Recent scholarship provides a more nuanced view of the spaces for inclusion that liberalism and republican political culture afforded nonwhite or mixed-race people during much of the nineteenth century, while assessing the costs associated with these formulations of national belonging and highlighting the efforts of nonelite actors in widening those spaces. See especially Di Meglio, *¡Viva...!*; Quijada, Bernand, and Schneider, *Homogeneidad*; Geler, *Andares*; Geler and Rodríguez, "Argentina."

11. On these processes, see Quijada, "Imaginando." Quijada calls this metaphor of territorially generated belonging in the post-independence period "the alchemy of the land," evoking a chemical recombination of diverse elements that explicitly avoided biological connotations of consanguinity or mestizaje. Geler and Rodríguez frame this metaphor slightly differently but also emphasize the mixing of "bloodlines" without mestizaje: "a botanical metaphor [that] stated that the soldiers' blood that was shed over the national territory fed one, and only one, family tree, thus originating the new Argentinean[s]." Geler and Rodríguez, "Argentina"; Geler, "Afro-Porteños," 4–5. On a later incarnation of this chemical/telluric metaphor, see Garguin's discussion of Scalabrini Ortiz in "Los Argentinos," 171.

12. The province of Buenos Aires did not accept this constitution (and therefore did not abolish slavery) until 1861–62. By then most slaves had already obtained their freedom through other means, like manumissions (purchased or granted) or military service.

13. Andrews, *Afro-Argentines*; Geler, *Andares*. For estimates of the African and Afro-descendant population (across the territory and over time), see Picotti, *La presencia*, 41–44.

14. On the state of the nation's frontiers over the course of the nineteenth century, see Mases, *Estado*, chapter 1. On the fluidity of the frontier, see also Mandrini, *Vivir*; Boccara, "Fronteras."

15. Lenton, "De centauros," chapter 1.

16. Quijada, "Indígenas."

17. Briones, "Mestizaje"; Geler, "¡Pobres negros!" Briones points out that processes of "de-indianization," by which indigenous people theoretically became unmarked (white) Argentine citizens, were slowed or conditioned by intermediate stages, like "mestizo," which (through theories of hypodescent) remained closer to "Indian" than to "non-Indian." See Geler, this volume, on the hardening of blackness into a category of radical alterity by the twentieth century.

18. On shifting conceptions of citizenship, see Quijada, "Imaginando." Gabriela Nouzeilles, following E.K. Francis and E. Gellner, frames this as a shift from political or voluntarist models of citizenship to ethnic or genealogical ones. Nouzeilles, *Ficciones*, 18–19. On the homogenizing effects of state disciplinary legislation, see Geler, *Andares* and this volume.

19. Mases, *Estado*; Lenton, "De centauros"; Martínez Sarasola, *Nuestros paisanos*, see 294–96, 508 for figures. Most contemporary scholars who use the term "genocide" to describe these events do so not to suggest complete elimination of indigenous

people, but rather (following the broader UN definition of the term) to condemn the panoply of turn-of-the-century assaults on indigenous people, their societies and cultures, and their ways of life. See e.g. Delrio et al., "Discussing"; Lenton et al., "Argentina's."

20. See Quijada, "Imaginando"; Andrews, *Afro-Argentines*; Geler, "¡Pobres negros!"; Otero, "Estadística."

21. Quijada, "Imaginando"; Margulis and Urresti, *La segregación*; Romero, "Los sectores populares"; Adamovsky, *Clases populares*. On this "mundo popular" in an earlier period, see Di Meglio, *¡Viva...!*.

22. Geler, for instance, demonstrates how Afro-porteño intellectuals negotiated their own "disappearance" by attempting to use this conjuncture to become unmarked citizens in the "modern" nation. See Geler, *Andares*.

23. Brown, *Brief History*, 152–55. For excellent overviews of Argentina's place within these wider migratory flows, see Moya, "A Continent"; Goebel, *Overlapping Geographies*.

24. These migratory trends have long attracted scholarly interest, generating a vast and rich literature on different immigrant collectivities. Major works that have influenced this volume include: Baily, *Immigrants*; Devoto, *Inmigración*; Devoto, *Italianos*; Deutsch, *Crossing Borders*; Freidenberg, *The Invention*; Moya, *Cousins and Strangers*; Sofer, *Pale*; Civantos, *Between*; Goebel, *Overlapping Geographies*.

25. Briones, "Mestizaje."

26. Zimmermann, "Racial Ideas." Cf. Stepan, *Hour*; Vallejo and Miranda, "Los saberes."

27. On whiteness as Argentina's "invisible raciality," see Geler, this volume.

28. Segato, *La nación*, 51.

29. This process is often referred to as a "racialization of class relations" (see Margulis and Belvedere, "La racialización"). However, this formulation implies that class is the "true" or bedrock identification and that race is a mere patina upon it. Recent works, including those in this volume, suggest instead that race and class mutually constituted each other at the turn of the twentieth century; race was inextricable from the language of class that became so central to Argentines' ways of expressing and understanding social difference.

30. On the origins of this metonymic displacement of "negro," see especially Geler, *Andares*; Geler, "Afrodescendencia." See also Ratier, *El cabecita negra*; Frigerio, "Negros," as well as Geler, Gordillo, Adamovsky, and Elena, this volume.

31. Adamovsky, *Clase media*; Garguin, "Los argentinos"; Margulis and Urresti, *La segregación*; Guano, "Color."

32. Escolar, *Los dones*; Chamosa, *Argentine Folklore*. See also Rodríguez, Pite, Chamosa, this volume.

33. The census of 2001 included a question about indigenous, but not Afro-Argentine, ancestry. While the 2010 census included both, these questions appeared only in a special form distributed partially across the national territory for sampling purposes. The census reported 149,493 people who self-recognized as Afro-descendants (0.37% of the total population) and 955,032 self-recognized indigenous people (2.38% of the total population), out of a national population of 40,117,096. For the vast majority of Argentines who did not self-identify as either Afro-descendant or indigenous, no race or ethnicity was given. As Ko argues in her chapter (this volume), the lack of a need to specify "white" as the predominant race

illustrates its deep normativity in Argentina. For census figures, see www.censo 2010.indec.gov.ar/resultadosdefinitivos_totalpais.asp. For recent alternative estimates of racial identity in Argentina, see Andrews, this volume.

34. See, among others, Skidmore, *Black Into White*; Andrews, *Blacks and Whites*; Alberto, *Terms*; Weinstein, *Color*; Bronfman, *Measures*; de la Fuente, *A Nation*; de la Cadena, *Indigenous Mestizos*; Wade, *Blackness*; Wright, *Café con Leche*; Loveman, *National Colors*; Sanjinés, *Mestizaje*; Gould, *To Die*; Andrews, *Blackness*; Knight, "Racism, Revolution."

35. Quijada calls this process "disolución de la percepción fenotípica." Quijada, "Imaginando," 209. Recent comparative studies of whiteness, status, and nation in contemporary Latin America confirm the persistence of these dynamics: see Telles and Flores, "Not Just Color"; Telles and PERLA, *Pigmentocracies*.

36. See, for instance, Fischer, *Poverty*; Lasso, *Myths*; Scott, *Degrees*; Appelbaum, *Muddied Waters*; de la Fuente, *A Nation*; Weinstein, *Color*.

37. Andrews' *Afro-Argentines*, which explores both the mestizaje implicit in Argentine whiteness (and, conversely, the whitening tendencies of mestizaje in Argentina) is a pioneer in this regard. See also Briones, "Mestizaje"; Quijada, Bernand, and Schneider, *Homogeneidad*; Escolar, *Los dones*; Chamosa, "Indigenous"; Otero, "Estadística"; Segato, *La nación*.

PART I

HISTORIES OF RACE IN THE TWENTIETH CENTURY

I

Insecure whiteness

Jews between civilization and barbarism, 1880s–1940s

Sandra McGee Deutsch

With its large percentage of inhabitants descended from European immigrants, Argentina has not had as obvious a racial Other as such Latin American countries as Brazil or Mexico. Scholars have begun to examine in detail Argentine notions of blackness – sometimes identified with persons of African ancestry, more often with *mestizos* from the Interior, and frequently with poor people of varied backgrounds – and how they have changed over time.[1] Yet the construction of whiteness is equally deserving of attention. The prevailing historical narrative contends that before the advent of Peronism, "the nation had been constructed as homogeneously white."[2] It also suggests that Argentines viewed immigrants from Europe and the circum-Mediterranean region as uniformly white.[3] My research indicates that this was not necessarily the case for Jews, whose whiteness was suspect despite their European and Mediterranean origins. How can one conceptualize the racial constructions of Jews, whom Argentines rarely described in explicitly phenotypical terms, yet sometimes seemed to regard as a race apart? How did Jews assert their whiteness? The reflections of two famous literary figures, Manuel Gálvez and Leopoldo Lugones, provide initial clues.

In the early 1900s, an unruly gathering of Eastern European Jews shocked Manuel Gálvez. Aware of his research on the white slave trade, a Jewish antiprostitution organization had invited him to serve on its board, and he and other leaders sat on the stage at the inaugural meeting. According to the young writer, the many poverty-stricken people in the audience moved about "as if possessed by a sickly nervousness," joking, murmuring, scolding each other, their babies shrieking at their mothers' breasts. Apparently incited by one of the speakers, the ill-smelling crowd turned into a "jungle of arms that waved in a threatening manner, the faces congested with fury," as many screamed insults, shook their fists, and emitted ever more sour odors. The board members fled the auditorium when the throng began to throw chairs and other objects at them. "In my life I have never attended such a monstrous scandal," Gálvez claimed many years later. He believed that traffickers had hired the mob to break up the gathering.[4] Whether these people received payment or not, the author regarded them as uncontrollable animals, as observers often have depicted people of color.

Leopoldo Lugones perceived Jews very differently. He defended the Jews of his acquaintance after the Tragic Week of 1919, a bloody labor conflict that pitted authorities and civilian vigilantes against workers, including Russian Jews. Disagreeing with those who conflated Jews with Bolsheviks, Lugones argued that "their laboriousness, their honor, and their orderliness" qualified them to receive the benefits of Argentine hospitality. Having spread the values of charity, freedom, and reason in their diaspora, Jews were "excellent elements of culture," the poet declared. Furthermore, they were incorporating themselves fully into Argentine life and took pride in their children born on Argentine soil.[5] Lugones praised Jews in terms usually reserved for white Europeans.

The two authors proved to be more ambivalent about Jews than these words suggest. In another passage in his memoirs, Gálvez admitted that poverty and oppression had helped shape their demeanor. As Lugones shifted to the right after 1919, he sometimes expressed radical anti-Semitic views. Both would be associated with extreme right-wing *Nacionalismo* in the 1930s.[6] Nevertheless, these contrasting images provide a basis for understanding the racial constructions of Jews in Argentina.

I approach these issues by utilizing the famous binary of civilization versus barbarism, in particular, the way in which President Domingo Faustino Sarmiento (1868–74) distinguished between the "barbaric" *gauchos* [cowboys], usually people of color, and the "civilized" inhabitants of European descent. Other scholars have drawn upon this dichotomy to explain racial discourses during the administrations of Juan D. Perón (1946–55) and Carlos Menem (1989–99).[7] Even earlier, many Argentines were coding "civilized" behavior as white and "barbaric" behavior as nonwhite,[8] and some applied these notions to Jews. Gálvez portrayed them as animal-like, rootless creatures: unwashed, brutish, and frenetic. Their lack of self-control contradicted the calm, restrained manner of civilized persons. Furthermore, their ragged poverty "darkened" them.[9] Concerns about Jewish leftism and religious difference influenced Gálvez's thoughts. Citing these and other traits, real or imagined, some Argentine spokespersons agreed that Jews seemed barbaric and thus nonwhite. On the other hand, Lugones regarded Jews as cultured and hard-working elements of civilization who were assimilating into Argentine life. Jews and non-Jews would borrow these arguments.

The disagreement between Gálvez and Lugones indicated that Jewish whiteness was insecure. In many instances, such as daily interactions, non-Jewish Argentines treated Jews as white, yet at other moments they questioned Jewish whiteness. During debates on immigration, education, and leftist radicalism, some public figures characterized Jews as nonwhite, distinct from other European immigrants, and difficult to absorb. Identifying Jews with the modernity they feared, radical right-wing *Nacionalistas* expressed such notions in strident terms. More moderate spokespersons saw Jews as potential members of civilized society – as long as they proved their value and relinquished aspects of their identities. Thus Jews could reinforce their claim to whiteness by changing their culture. Perceiving Jews in this manner enabled these intellectuals and statesmen to retain the positive view of immigrants that formed part of liberal ideology. It also meant that they could cloak more inhabitants with the mantle of whiteness and bolster the image of a white Argentina.[10]

This chapter surveys not only how prominent non-Jews regarded Jews, but how Jews reacted to their uneasy racial status. I group Jewish statements and actions within three themes.[11] One is the intersection of manliness and racial categorization. Marilyn Lake and Henry Reynolds found that in areas ranging from the Southern United States to European empires in Asia and Africa during the late nineteenth and early twentieth centuries, "white men considered that their manhood rested on the exercise of racial domination."[12] Gender hierarchies overlapped these racial hierarchies. Writing on the evolving patterns of racialization along the US–Mexico border in the early twentieth century, Katherine Benton-Cohen explained how protecting and providing for white women helped define men as white.[13] Furthermore, Latin Americanists Nancy Appelbaum, Anne Macpherson, and Karin Rosemblatt noted that men have asserted their racial superiority over potential rivals by controlling the sexuality of women within their group. Failing to safeguard women's reputations undermined images of respectability and whiteness.[14] Jewish men's resentment of gaucho interest in Jewish women, as well as Jewish concerns about perceptions of sexual and familial disorder in Jewish communities, revealed these tensions. The equation between manliness and self-control also affected impressions of Jews' racial status.

Another theme is spatial in nature. The Interior was the region characterized as barbaric, given its association with *caudillos* [strongmen rulers], economic underdevelopment, and, especially, with indigenous and mestizo inhabitants; here there was a more distinguishable racial Other than in Buenos Aires and other large littoral cities. Many Ashkenazi Jews found opportunities in this setting to contest Gálvez's type of assertions and deploy Lugones', seeking to prove their whiteness through hard work, upward mobility, and educational and cultural achievements. Some asserted their whiteness by distinguishing themselves from *criollos* [native-born, usually mestizo, inhabitants of the Interior], whom they, like Sarmiento, saw as uncouth and barbaric. Not all Ashkenazim, however, accepted this racial binary.[15]

The third theme revolves around Sephardi and Syrian Jews who claimed whiteness largely by distancing themselves from their largely Muslim countries of origin and embracing a Spanish heritage, real or imagined. For these Judeo-Spanish and Arabic speakers, the Interior also was a critical space, albeit for reasons other than those of the Ashkenazim. Here there was less differentiation between groups of varied Mediterranean origins,[16] which facilitated Arab amalgamation with Sephardim and their associations with Spain.

The scholarship on whiteness in the United States has informed my thinking in this chapter. Analyses of the shifting racial placement of Southern and Eastern European immigrants, including Ashkenazi Jews, from nonwhite – or a different shade of white – to white have been especially useful. Such works demonstrate that cultural, economic, and environmental factors, as well as biological ones, define race. Indeed, Karen Brodkin focused her discussion of racialization on class and culture rather than physical appearance. Interestingly, she also used the terms "civilization" and "barbarism" to denote whiteness and nonwhiteness, respectively, in the United States.[17]

In addition, I draw upon an old and rich tradition of writings on race in Latin American countries outside Argentina. These works show that as Latin Americans have recognized race mixture, in contrast to many white US Americans, racial categories arguably have been more complex in the former area than in the latter. They also demonstrate that perhaps even more clearly than in the United States, racial designations in Latin America often have rested on criteria other than genetics or skin color. Many Latin Americans have considered cultural characteristics innate; in Lamarckian style, such "racial" traits could be handed down to one's offspring. Yet they also have thought it possible to change one's race. The well-known adage "money whitens" illustrates this acceptance of racial fluidity.[18] Furthermore, various authors have applied the civilization/barbarism binary to their studies. Barbara Weinstein, for example, explained how Brazilians have coded São Paulo as civilized and European, and the rest of their country, especially the Northeast, as barbaric and racially mixed.[19]

Argentines in the late nineteenth and early twentieth centuries occasionally used the word "race" in an explicitly phenotypical sense. More typically, however, as in the cases of Gálvez and Lugones, they defined race in cultural terms, often blurring the distinctions between culture and biology by essentializing the characteristics of a particular group and regarding them as passing from one generation to the next. Indeed, some students of race have argued that biological and cultural criteria are intertwined. As Peter Wade has observed, little separates the notion that certain cultural traits are "innate and heritable, and considered as fundamental as a soul or spirit" from biology.[20] When persons marginalize a group on the basis of cultural features they consider to be bred in the bone, they are racializing that particular minority. This is what Jews sometimes experienced in Argentina.

A CONTEXT OF SUSPICION AND AMBIGUITY

Argentine racial constructions of Jews were rooted in notions about immigration that surfaced in the Constitution of 1853 and surrounding debates.

Heeding liberal wishes to civilize and modernize the country by altering its population, this document affirmed that the federal government would promote European immigration. Falling short of declaring Catholicism the official religion, the Constitution declared that the federal government would support this faith, yet it also guaranteed freedom of religion for all inhabitants. In doing so, its framers were mindful of Juan Bautista Alberdi's warning: "To summon the Anglo-Saxon race and the populations of Germany, Sweden, Switzerland, and to refuse them the practice of their religion, is the same as not summoning them."[21] Only Northern European settlers could eradicate the barbarism of the Indians and mestizos, according to Alberdi and Sarmiento, and they would never come without a guarantee of their religious rights.

These passages had several implications for Jews. That European immigration meant white immigration seemed implicit. Whether the liberal elite regarded Jews as white, however, was unclear, since they did not belong to the preferred "Anglo-Saxon race." What is clear is that Alberdi and leading thinkers did not favor the entry of Jews and other groups from Southern and Eastern Europe and the Mediterranean.[22] The question of whether Argentina was a Catholic country also led a few authors of the Constitution to ponder whether Jews were good material for the white society they were constructing. Their ruminations may have drawn upon a long history of obsession with blood "purity" in colonial Spanish America, which, according to María Elena Martínez, had promoted the "gradual crystallization of a Christian, Spanish, and white identity."[23] Since these three elements seemed inseparable, these statesmen may not have seen non-Christians as white. Sporadically during the constitutional debates, conservatives expressed discomfort with the Jews' religious difference and doubted they could integrate into Argentina. Regarding the Constitution's uneasy compromise on the nation's religious status, historian Haim Avni concluded that "as a religious group, they [non-Catholics] were to be treated as *almost* equal."[24] Would Catholic Argentines treat Jews as *almost* white, given what Jerry Dávila called the "perceived and parallel significance of whiteness and Christianity for many Latin American elites?"[25]

In their deliberations over the Immigration and Colonization Law, passed in 1876, most legislators again favored the arrival of Northern Europeans. One congressman wanted Argentina to imitate the example of the United States, which this "manly, intelligent race" had made a wealthy country.[26] Since few Jewish immigrants would hail from Northern Europe, Argentine lawmakers may not have considered them manly. Gálvez's description of Jews as nervous, sickly, and lacking in gentlemanly self-restraint indicated that he would not. And while Lugones would praise the intelligence of Jews, other Argentines would denigrate it.

Even before Jews arrived on a mass scale, some members of the elite expressed ambivalence about their racial fitness. In the late 1880s, Sarmiento mocked "the Jewish people dispersed throughout the earth, exercising usury and accumulating millions, rejecting the fatherland in which they are born, . . .

[dying] for an ideal ... to which they do not plan to ever return."[27] The "Semitic race," according to the former president, considered Argentina "an article of negotiable old clothing and material for industry."[28] Peddlers by nature, for Jews anything except their impractical dream of Israel was for sale. By nature itinerant and disloyal to their countries, their whiteness was dubious, and they would never assimilate.

As Baron Maurice de Hirsch, who founded the Jewish Colonization Association in 1891, prepared to purchase land for Jewish settlement, *La Nación* questioned the "quality" of these proposed immigrants. It called for studying their "physical and moral aptitudes" before encouraging their entry, as they could "improve or worsen the conditions of the race." This daily argued that Jews compared poorly even to Spanish and Southern Italian immigrants, as they were "dirty, indolent, incapable of agricultural labor." Statesman Estanislao Zeballos considered them too weak for rural tasks.[29] Evidently their lack of manliness, cleanliness, and discipline called their whiteness into question. So, too, did their sickly nature, according to José María Ramos Mejía, psychiatrist and president of the Consejo Nacional de Higiene, who identified Jews with typhus and insanity.[30]

Jewish avarice was a theme of the well-known book *La bolsa* (1891), in which Julián Martel attributed the financial collapse of 1890 to the machinations of European Jews and their Argentine dupes. In his view, the Jews' greed and their surreptitious and dishonest means of seeking domination contrasted with the manly openness, honor, and trustworthiness of the "Aryan race." Since Aryans were white, the implication was that Jews were not. Unlike Aryans, Jews did not cultivate the land or exercise any useful occupation; instead they took advantage of other people's labor through their pecuniary manipulations. The Jews' monopolization of prostitution further underlined their criminal nature. Lacking true nobility of heart and mind, the Jews' intellectual and artistic endeavors were below par.[31] For Martel, these were racial traits.

Martel constructed Jews using a combination of "innate" cultural and corporeal traits. His villain, the financier Filiberto Mackser, "was a pallid man, blonde, lymphatic, of medium height, and in whose repugnant and effeminate face one observed that expression of hypocritical humility that the custom of a long servility had made the typical stamp of the Jewish race. He had the small eyes ... and the curved nose characteristic of the tribe of Ephraim."[32] Despite his light-colored skin and hair, Mackser's repulsive and unmanly appearance set him off from the white race. Aside from highlighting these racial characteristics, Martel described how Jewish immigrants corrupted Argentines physically and morally. He likened this process to the spread of disease, in which Jews and other foreigners carried the germs of materialism and of imported cosmetics, hair dyes, and fashions that infected Argentine women and disguised the "heritage of Spanish blood."[33] Responsible for corrupting local women and weakening their racial identity, Jews were agents of barbarism.

These notions of Jewish physical difference, greed, and harmful influence leaked into popular theater at the turn of the century. *Sainetes* (the leading genre of popular theater in these years) often portrayed Jewish men as unscrupulous peddlers and usurers whose bearded and filthy looks further set them apart. Even a number of Jewish dramatists accepted some of these stereotypes and considered Jews a separate race. Unlike Martel, however, playwrights conveyed the view that Jews could integrate into Argentine society, albeit by giving up their customs and intermarrying. Several, however, disapproved of relationships between criollas and Jewish men, who might defile them.[34] By declaring native-born Argentine women out of bounds, Martel and these dramatists sought to "protect" them from Jewish men and claimed racial superiority over the latter.

Martel saw the stock market as Semitic; he identified the institution with Jews and the surrounding district with "greasy Turks" (in reality Syrian-Lebanese) who sold cheap goods in the streets.[35] Such associations of Jews and non-Jewish Arabs were common;[36] indeed, the term often used to refer to Jews, *israelitas*, underlined their Middle Eastern origins. These linkages provide clues about racial constructions of Jews. Journalists often lumped Jews, Syrians, and East Asians together as "inherently disease ridden, immoral, and lazy," in historian Carl Solberg's words, and thus as "'inferior' races."[37] That many Jews and non-Jewish Middle Easterners were urban peddlers and merchants, engaged in economic activities that the elite regarded as "unproductive and parasitic," made them undesirable. So, too, did their non-Catholicism, although in fact a majority of the Arab immigrants were Maronite Christians, who were affiliated with the Catholic Church.[38] Jeffrey Lesser argued that in Brazil by 1930 whiteness signified not only being European and Christian, but willing to settle in rural areas. For the Brazilian elite, this definition disqualified Jews and Arabs.[39]

Some distinguished Argentines added to these definitions of whiteness. Around the time of the Tragic Week, the Museo Social Argentino asked progressive and conservative figures to participate in a survey on immigration. Most of the forty-five respondents preferred Northern and Latin Europeans, and many openly favored the "white race." A minority explicitly deemed other "races" unfit and unwanted. "Turks, – Arabs, Jews, and so forth – and especially those without a profession" were unacceptable to engineer Jorge Butza. Conservative Catholic Horacio Beccar Varela rejected Russians, except for farmers and the illiterate. Tomás Amadeo, an agronomist and educator, opposed the entry of proletarians, "yellow races," Russians, beggars, and invalids. Argentina should prohibit the "undesirables of inferior race ... individuals without a profession, sectarians religious and civilian, cripples, etc. and particularly Russian Bolsheviks," wrote Eduardo Gschwind. A member of the anti-leftist strikebreaking Liga Patriótica Argentina, General Proto Ordóñez repudiated "individuals of bad antecedents, disobedient to order and contrary to all principle of authority; the contagious ill, beggars, cripples, Jewish Russians, gypsies, Egyptians, those of the yellow and black race."[40]

These individuals made their remarks during a period of labor militancy and the presidency of Hipólito Yrigoyen (1916–22, 1928–30), the first national government elected under universal male suffrage and secret ballot. Yrigoyen's conservative rivals often disparaged his followers, workers, and leftists as black or indigenous, despite their predominantly European origins.[41] Juxtaposing Jews with Arabs, blacks, East Asians, gypsies, the infirm, vagrants, and urban laborers suggested they were unfit and nonwhite. Some respondents further associated Jews with barbarism by highlighting their rebelliousness. As most Russians in Argentina were Jews, and most Jews were from Russia, many Argentines used the two terms interchangeably. After the Russian revolutions of 1905 and 1917–18, this also meant that they identified Jews with the working class and leftism.[42] Beccar Varela sought to exclude literate urban Russians – signifying Jews – who he believed would not abide by the status quo.[43] Believing that the Jews' level of education promoted their unruliness, he held their intelligence against them.[44]

Only a minority among the respondents, however, expressed such views. Nor did all Argentine thinkers agree that Jews composed a separate racial category. Despite the fact that he had clustered Russians, East Asians, and racial degenerates in 1919, twenty years later Tomás Amadeo claimed that Jews were not a race. Nor were they even a type, for Jews differed by appearance and personality. Nevertheless, he argued that "it is ridiculous to colonize our lands with Jews, if it is true that they are not good agricultural-ists; but for this reason and not because they are Jews." His insinuation that Jews in general performed poorly as cultivators suggested an innate quality that excluded them from the ranks of civilizers.[45] A specialist in psychiatry and criminology, the leftist José Ingenieros was hardly free of racism, as he frowned upon blacks and Indians. Yet in the early 1900s, he claimed that all of the components of the white race, including "Semites," were equal in quality.[46] Sometimes seen as white, sometimes not, Jewish racial status was unstable and insecure.

Shortly after the Tragic Week, the Jewish periodical *Vida Nuestra* queried statesmen and intellectuals on the situation of Jews in Argentina. Their respondents included Leopoldo Lugones, whose words I cited in this chapter's introduction. These contributors tended to see Jews as civilizers, although sometimes with qualifiers. The Socialist professor of abnormal psychology Enrique Mouchet asserted that the "Jewish race" was less criminal than other nationalities. The Jewish community was "intelligent, disciplined, and perse-verant," according to poet Alfonsina Storni. If Jews left Argentina, opined Justo Pallares Acebal, it would damage Argentine "intellectual and economic devel-opment," given that Jews had contributed agricultural settlements and "bril-liant mentalities" to the nation. This journalist, however, added that Jews "usually have more money ... than anyone else." Lawyer Juan P. Ramos, a future Nacionalista, lauded the morality, tenacity, and cultural achievements of this "race" yet doubted its willingness to integrate.[47]

In *Vida Nuestra* José Ingenieros defended Jewish claims to whiteness. He affirmed that Jewish immigrants had contributed their hard work and children to the betterment of Argentina. Native-born Jews would be more engaged with local issues. They would join other Argentines in seeking freedom and social justice for all; indeed, this was their manly duty.[48] Evidently, Jews were capable of changing themselves and assuming this virile role. For Ingenieros as for militant workers in Buenos Aires, Jewish leftist tendencies were praiseworthy and civilized rather than barbaric.[49] Their radicalism did not exclude Jews from the category of whiteness.

Despite some ambivalence and hostility, the government and society generally consented to the Jewish presence. Like other newcomers, many Jews stayed at the Hotel de Inmigrantes upon arrival. They faced no legal impediments such as segregation laws or housing covenants; universities did not impose quotas, nor did hotels forbid them entry. Of the censuses produced during the years under study, only the national one of 1895 and those of the city of Buenos Aires in 1909 and 1936 separated Jews as a category. Officials did not always distinguish them from other Argentines, perhaps because they thought Jews were assimilating, did not see them as different, or did not want to call attention to their difference. Beginning in 1881, the government recruited Russian Jews in Europe to move to Argentina. Eight years later, some immigration officials briefly attempted to deny them entry and subsidized passages. The belief that Jews were responsible for bringing typhus to Argentina, as fostered by Ramos Mejía, led authorities to single them out among other immigrant groups for required disinfection and quarantine in 1895. Nevertheless, successive administrations usually welcomed Jewish newcomers until the 1930s, when they restricted Jewish entry, and treated them as equal under the law, with the important exception of the Tragic Week of 1919. Thus the government implicitly accepted Jews as white.[50] The disagreements among opinion makers and the contradictions in government policies, however, helped make Jewish whiteness insecure.

CLAIMING WHITENESS IN THE COLONIES

Jews absorbed the importance of identifying with whiteness and civilization in classrooms in rural settlements and cities alike.[51] The public school system bore the mark of the educator president, Sarmiento. Here Jews learned about Sarmiento's belief in immigration, the melting pot, and civilizing the country through education, ideas which resonated with their experiences and desire for acceptance and upward mobility.

Acquiring these lessons and realizing their insecure racial status, many Jews felt a need to perform their whiteness, and there was no better place to do so than in the countryside. By taming the wilderness and sinking roots into the soil, Ashkenazi farmers could defy the stereotypes and prove that they were agents of civilization. While not always consciously so, their remarks seemed designed to convince themselves and the elite of their racial identity.

Writer Emilio Berisso noted in the *Vida Nuestra* survey how Jews exerted themselves to cultivate untilled lands in Entre Ríos and keep them productive, "irrigating them with the sweat of their brows."[52] Describing his boyhood experiences, the Socialist legislator Enrique Dickmann claimed that "two or three ordinary peons would have been needed to equal my work" on the farm.[53] "They were hard years, very strenuous" for the men and the women who removed the thick brush and tall grass that covered Entre Ríos and harvested the fields, recalled one resident.[54] More than praising Jewish labor, such remarks portrayed Jews as the most industrious and therefore most Argentine of ethnic groups.[55]

These and other Jewish colonists had proven their whiteness with their heroism and hard work. Not only had they begun to civilize the uncultivated "desert," but they had civilized themselves. Through agricultural pursuits they had divested themselves of their images as undignified and greedy merchants and sickly urbanites. One sees this transformation in Alberto Gerchunoff's well-known book *Los gauchos judíos* (1910). In his prologue, Martiniano Leguizamón contrasted its "handsome and manly new figure" of the Jewish gauchos with that of the decrepit elderly rabbis, the "classic sharp-nosed bearded old Jews," who were destined to fade away. This redemption was tied to the land; Jews who remained in the colonies tended to see those who migrated to the cities as weaklings and cowards[56] – ones who found it difficult to claim whiteness.

Jews also sought to redeem themselves by establishing educational and cultural institutions in the hinterland. In numerous works Jewish authors lauded their schools, libraries, theaters, concerts, debates, and lectures. These accounts stressed how criollos sometimes attended classes in Yiddish culture and listened outside synagogues and community centers.[57] Jewish teachers became Sarmiento's civilizing agents in country schools, where they taught Jews and non-Jews alike.[58] Educator Máximo Yagupsky, who grew up in La Capilla, Entre Ríos, observed that the colonists' efforts to "civilize the environment" included uplifting criollos.[59]

Their complex relations with rural criollos affected the Jews' assertions of whiteness. Even though most of these horsemen had become peons, Jews and others called them gauchos and admired their supposed freedom.[60] Jewish farmers praised their skills, cordiality, and generosity and appropriated gaucho foods and dress. They learned farming, equestrian arts, and the local tongue and customs from these rural denizens. Indeed, gauchos were symbols of the Argentine nationality that Jews sought to acquire. Thus, rooting themselves meant becoming "Jewish gauchos," as in the title of Gerchunoff's book. Yet Argentine leaders and intellectuals viewed these rural criollos ambivalently. Disturbed by the immigrants' political, social, and cultural impact, some had turned against foreigners by the early 1900s and now exalted the gauchos.

At the same time, many still disparaged the dark-skinned criollos as barbaric racial Others.[61] Claiming whiteness seemed to require distinguishing themselves from these locals.[62] Thus Jews both identified with and set themselves apart from them.

Some distanced themselves from criollos through struggles over women's bodies, as described in a memoir published by a settler in 1922. The Russian-born colonist Marcos Alpersohn wondered how "savage gauchos" from near and far had realized that there were beautiful women in Colonia Mauricio, Buenos Aires. Who had informed the "Indian of Patagonia" and the "criollo in the caves and on the slopes of the Andes" that the Jewish colonies contained beautiful "white" women? As if drawn by sirens to the farming community, gauchos arrived on horseback and asked for work, which the colonists readily granted. In their sad songs "we recognized our own souls, their nostalgia for a home spread through our hearts like oil." Yet soon thereafter, Jews found dead butchered cattle and even live heifers missing pieces of flesh, which apparently the gauchos had hacked off and eaten. Lacking the concept of private property, they perceived no difference between what was "mine or yours"; they grabbed what they needed or wanted. As long as they restricted themselves to cattle, which belonged to the Jewish Colonization Association, the settlers looked the other way. But this restraint only emboldened the "semi-savage criollo" to pursue women. In this regard as well, the gaucho was "as free as the bird in the forest," knowing nothing of marriage, morality, or religion. When Jewish women resisted their overtures, criollos assaulted and raped several of them. Only by arming themselves and firing upon intruders, fencing the colony with barbed wire, and calling for police reinforcements did settlers finally solve the problem.[63] By protecting "their" women, Jewish men asserted their whiteness against the dark-skinned interlopers.

As a diasporic Jew, Alpersohn empathized with the gauchos' wanderings and longing for refuge, and envy tinged his sarcastic description of their unfettered habits. Yet their independence was barbaric, as was their lack of sexual control, which also was unmanly.[64] The author underlined what he saw as their brutal, uncivilized, Indian, and, ironically, un-Christian nature. By describing their Jewish prey as white, he implied that the locals were not, thus distinguishing between the two. He set up a hierarchical relationship with Jews as racially predominant over the gauchos.

Colonia Mauricio was not the only place where Jews thought that criollos lusted after "white" Jewish women. In some settlements locals peeped through the windows at Jewish women; to shield themselves, girls in one colony closed the shutters when they undressed. Sons of local Christian landowners and businessmen attended social gatherings hosted by Jewish organizations and danced with Jewish women. While Jewish women may have found their dance partners attractive, the latter's habit of firing celebratory shots in the air seemed menacing.[65] Although these men had higher status and lighter skin than gauchos, Jews conflated them and coded their behavior as uncouth. Jews had additional reasons to see criollos as violent and nonwhite after a labor conflict in Villaguay, Entre Ríos in 1921 (as we shall see), in which authorities and vigilantes of the Liga Patriótica Argentina assaulted and imprisoned workers and Socialists, including Jews, and threatened further attacks. One woman recalled that the presence of men from Villaguay at dances scared her and her friends.[66] Yet there also were Jewish women who had non-Jewish lovers and husbands.[67] Seeking to maintain their communities and reinforce their whiteness, most Ashkenazim frowned on these practices.

Jews distanced themselves from what they regarded as evidence of criollo ignorance and superstition. A Russian-born woman in rural Entre Ríos debated whether to send her son to a *curandera* [healer] to be treated for tapeworm. She decided against it, for if someone spotted her carriage outside the healer's house, it would lower her "cultural image."[68]

Jewish scorn for gauchos was a theme of Samuel Eichelbaum's play, "El judío Aarón" (1926). Born in a colony in Entre Ríos, Eichelbaum described the collision between his protagonist Aarón, a colonist who supported striking Indian laborers and a more equitable social order, and wealthy Jews who despised the native peons. Further adding to his disreputable image, Aarón was having an affair with a criolla and looked unkempt. His leading opponent sneered at Aarón's friendships with dark-skinned country folk: "He gets together with all the scum, and afterwards he's capable of getting angry if someone tells him that he's just like them." Even though Aarón was close to these nonwhites, he did not want to be identified with them.[69] And, like other Argentines, some Jews referred to criollos as *negros*, a more blatantly racialized term than "scum."[70]

Some Jewish teachers, however, opposed racial stereotyping of and discrimination against criollos. The teenaged instructor Sara Dachevsky informed her pupils in La Capilla, Entre Ríos in the early 1900s that the fatherland included even "the little shack that one saw through the schoolhouse window."[71] These remarks suggested that the criollos who lived in such shacks formed part of the nation and could be educated to fit into white society. Other teachers expressed similar ideals. Juanita de Salischiker taught for thirty-two years in schools in and around Carlos Casares, Buenos Aires, beginning in the 1930s. Her concerns about hungry students led her to create a free food program in her school.[72] Teaching in Villa Domínguez, Entre Ríos in the same years, Luisa Furman urged criollos to keep their progeny in school rather than send them to work. She tutored poor children without charge and founded a used clothing service for needy pupils.[73]

Teachers commonly engaged in such charitable practices, yet they had special meanings for Jews. Assigned to enlighten rural inhabitants, Jewish educators identified themselves with civilization. Many of them were genuinely preoccupied with the criollos' lowly position in society. Yet by trying to alleviate their poverty, these Jewish women unintentionally highlighted the racial and class gulf between them and the recipients of their largesse.

Another educator tried to bridge the gap between the two groups. A renowned teacher born in Moisés Ville, Santa Fe, Rosa de Ziperovich connected prejudice against Jews to that against criollos. Some instructors and classmates at the normal school of Rafaela, Santa Fe, where she had studied in the 1930s, had discriminated against her and other Jewish pupils. She recalled that one professor would intervene and discuss racism and the need for mutual understanding with the entire class. Years later, Ziperovich imitated this practice when she witnessed her students taunting underprivileged or dark-skinned classmates.[74]

Some Jews did not fear being linked with people of color. Going far beyond Eichelbaum's fictional character Aarón, who sympathized with the peons, Jewish militants joined criollos to resist employers and the Liga Patriótica Argentina in Entre Ríos. When a primarily criollo union in Villa Domínguez, the heart of the Jewish agricultural zone, called a strike in early 1921, authorities jailed its Jewish secretary, José Axentzoff, and several other militants. Liguistas and police attacked workers and Socialists when they demonstrated in Villaguay against the imprisonments, resulting in many casualties. Police detained seventy-six activists, about eighteen of whom were Jews. Although the violence continued, the prisoners eventually were freed.[75]

By mobilizing alongside criollos, Jewish activists defied their coreligionists' efforts to distinguish themselves from nonwhites. They also stirred up racialized sentiments among some reporters and politicians. Radical party congressman Eduardo Mouesca blamed the incident on anarchist Jews who "for the ill of Entre Ríos had encysted themselves in the bosom of the province," as if they formed a cancerous tumor. He saw their activism as a despicable "custom." *La Provincia* of Concordia depicted the demonstrators as "abnormal Jews and criollos," "barbarians" all.[76]

Jews belonged to at least twelve of the thirty Liga brigades in the Jewish settlement zone of Entre Ríos.[77] Two sons of colonists who were Liga members had attacked Axentzoff, and a Jewish physician who served as the vice-president of the local Liga brigade had refused to treat his wounds. A colonist who applied to join the Liga claimed that most Jews in the province were law-abiding and hardworking Argentines who ignored extremist "Russian sects."[78] Resembling Eichelbaum's characters, some bourgeois Jews set themselves apart from unruly leftist elements who threatened their claim to whiteness.

These self-styled orderly Jews included some of Moroccan descent in Buenos Aires. While it condemned the Liga's attacks on Jews, *Israel*, the voice of this community, insisted that "violence and advanced theories have no place in Judaism" and their perpetrators and advocates were not true israelitas.[79] The editors denied that the Jewish community in Entre Ríos was revolutionary, pointing out that only a few Jews had been arrested in Villaguay. The Jews there were "tranquil citizens who live devoted to their work, love their property, have Argentine homes, have Argentine sons in the army," and in fact were more patriotic than those who opposed the Jews.[80] *Israel* decried assaults on

Jewish militants yet at the same time insisted that Jews possessed civilized qualities that accorded with notions of whiteness. In fact, both sides claimed that Jews were genuinely Argentine, either because of their inherent conservatism or because they defended the criollos' rights in a land of freedom.[81]

According to some non-Jewish critics, however, the Jewish Colonization Association (JCA) impeded Jewish efforts to root themselves. In 1908, describing the difficulties Jewish farmers faced in acquiring titles from this organization, the national daily *La Prensa* portrayed colonists as a breed of "white slaves" who could never become landowners. Observers also questioned whether the JCA schools, staffed with Mediterranean Sephardi teachers who spoke other forms of Spanish, educated their pupils adequately and nurtured true Argentines "in complete communion with the people and the soil where they were born," in writer Ricardo Rojas' words.[82] *La Prensa* acknowledged the settlers' hard work and interest in learning but blamed the JCA for impeding their upward mobility and assimilation. By calling them white slaves, it both recognized and undermined their whiteness, as it linked them to the disreputable practice of prostitution and denied Jewish independence and manliness.[83]

Shortly after this controversy, in *Los gauchos judíos*, Alberto Gerchunoff asserted the whiteness of Ashkenazi colonists – without using this term – by dubiously tying them to Spain. Doing so might once have been problematic, since hegemonic intellectuals had regarded Spain as backward for much of the nineteenth century, but by the time Gerchunoff published his book in 1910, some had revised their opinions. In the context of the centennial of independence, Spaniards represented European civilizers. The text abounded with telling references to this country, its literature, and Jewish life through the time of the Inquisition, allusions that seemed designed to convince the elite that Jews belonged in Argentina. Claiming the great Spanish writer, Gerchunoff referred to "Our Lord Don Miguel de Cervantes." The learned and pious colonist Guedali's "proud bearing – far from suggesting a humble farmer – recalled the noble eras when Hebrew poets and sages formed learned guilds in the towns of medieval Spain," despite his Russian origins. Guedali and other Jewish rural dwellers dreamed of when "our brethren lived peacefully under the protection of the kings of Castile," and they cursed the persecution and expulsion that had set a second diaspora into motion. Yet the ties with Spain were not completely broken, for the language remained. Even Russian Jewish immigrants could appropriate the Spanish tongue. To reinforce the link, Gerchunoff imitated old forms of Castilian in this book.[84]

SEPHARDI AND SYRIAN JEWS

More fittingly, Gerchunoff and other Ashkenazim also identified Sephardi Jews with Spanish culture and aristocratic features. *Los gauchos judíos* referred to the Moroccan Moisés Urquijo de Albinoim, father of a JCA teacher. An erudite heir of the "Talmudists of the Spanish Golden Age," he represented the

"Jews who continued the tradition of the great sages of Jerusalem under the kings of Castile."[85] Ruth, the purported Ashkenazi columnist for *Israel*, praised a Sephardi acquaintance for having the "sparkling loquacity of an Andaluz" and another Sephardi gentleman's "noble pride."[86]

Lugones commended the Spanish Jews' cultural prestige. He observed that when the Russians defeated the Kingdom of the Khazars in Crimea in the tenth century, its poorer Jewish inhabitants migrated to Russia and the "wealthiest and most cultured" moved to Spain. There the Jewish community flourished, and such luminaries as Yehuda Halevi and Maimonides contributed significantly to philosophy and letters.[87]

Sephardi Jews commonly pointed to the ties of language, music, food, and memory that bound them to Spain. Some also prided themselves on an aristocratic lineage that further Europeanized them. Much admired by Argentine intellectuals, claimed *Israel*, was Hortensia Benmuyal de Ambram, a Moroccan-born poet who lived in Rosario. Ambram dedicated a poem to Dr. Angel Pulido that highlighted the Jews' long and distinguished roots in Spain. A liberal Spanish senator and academic, Pulido had rediscovered the Sephardim in the early 1900s. Fascinated by their continuing links to Spain and the Spanish tongue, he believed that the Sephardim were ideally suited to revive Spain's cultural primacy at a time when it had lost its empire.[88] Ambram's poem celebrated his studies of Sephardi culture in Spain and Morocco and his search for these "Spaniards without fatherland," who longed for their homeland with "nostalgia and pain." How could Spain bear to "lose these remnants of genuine aristocracy," she asked, and she imagined Pulido's response: "They are brothers . . . / Exiles innocent of sin, Spain's own sons!" Ambram wondered how to reunite the Sephardim with their ancestral land that had unjustly banished them. "Return to the maternal breast was your [Pulido's] redemptive cry."[89]

Ironically, while Pulido worked for Spanish reconciliation with the Sephardim, he wanted them to promote Spain while residing outside it. Still, Ambram appreciated Pulido's sympathy for her people. She and others agreed with him that they were genuinely Spanish and deserved to be seen as such.

For historical and geographical reasons, Moroccan Jews had an especially strong claim to Spanish and European identity. Spain had controlled the coastal cities of Ceuta and Melilla since 1640 and 1497, respectively; Ceuta formed part of the province of Cádiz, and Melilla part of the province of Málaga until 1995, when they became autonomous. Alegría Levi was a Sephardi Jew who lived in Melilla in the early 1900s and emigrated to Argentina. As she exclaimed, "I was born and brought up in Melilla. I am Spanish! With Spanish papers!"[90] Seats of import-export trade, consulates, and Christian residences, Tetuan and Tangier had long been connected commercially and diplomatically to Europe, and Jews participated in this nexus. Jewish business and cultural ties with that continent expanded during the Spanish occupation of Tetuan between 1860 and 1862. Contact with these Iberians "re-Hispanized" the Moroccan

Jewish tongue Haketia, a mixture of old Spanish with Hebrew, Arabic, Berber, and other influences. Jews not only began to speak a more peninsular form of Spanish, but they adopted elements of French culture. Founded in 1860, the Alliance Israélite Universelle was a French charitable organization that opened schools in the Balkans, West Asia, and North Africa to teach and Europeanize Jewish children. It inaugurated its first school in Tetuan in 1862. As of 1935, the Alliance had forty-one schools in Morocco, far more than in any other territory. Spain created a protectorate in 1912, with its capital in Tetuan, and the French dominated the rest of Morocco.[91] Their presence expedited the Europeanization of Jews.

Tentatively and partially, some Spaniards started to redefine their national identity around the time of expansion into North Africa. Although Catholic, Muslim, and Jewish communities had inhabited medieval Spain, when it expelled the Moors and Jews it reinvented itself as a place that had always been Christian.[92] The 1869 Constitution transcended the past somewhat by declaring limited religious tolerance. In 1924, a decree mainly directed toward residents of ex-Ottoman lands granted citizenship to "former Spaniards or their descendants and, in general, members of families of Spanish origin" who applied for it by the end of 1930. Relatively few Sephardim, however, took advantage of this law. A decree of 1931 allowed citizens of Spanish Morocco, among other countries, to obtain Spanish citizenship after only two years of residency, instead of the ten years required of most applicants. While this law was not specifically aimed at Jews, they benefited from it.[93] These measures, Pulido's campaign, and ongoing liberal and republican attempts to legislate religious freedom in Spain legitimized Sephardi beliefs that they had a right to call themselves Spanish – whether the Spanish government fully agreed or not.[94]

Yet not all Sephardim in the world embraced this right or welcomed Spanish recognition. While treasuring distant memories of Spain, many felt bitter about its treatment of their ancestors. They revered Judeo-Spanish because it was their language but did not feel allegiance to the Spanish nation. Furthermore, the Alliance Israélite Universelle's promotion of French, the integration of Jews into the Balkan nations freed from Ottoman rule, and the rise of Zionism resulted in the decline of Judeo-Spanish.[95]

Nor did Sephardi Argentines base their identities solely on bonds, real or imagined, with Spain. They associated themselves with the places where they and their families had lived, such as Izmir and Rhodes. Moreover, in their new homeland the Sephardim refurbished their Jewish identities in the process of becoming Argentine.[96]

Still, many Sephardim in Argentina profited from this nuanced connection. Jews of Moroccan origin utilized their advantageous link through the names of their institutions and locations of their gatherings. This group founded the Congregación Israelita Latina, their main communal and religious entity, in 1891, the word "Latina" underlining their claim to French and Spanish culture.

Four years later, Moroccans established the Congregación Israelita Latina Sefaradim of Santa Fe. A Moroccan Jewish mutual aid society known as the Asociación Castellana de Beneficencia y Misericordia secured government recognition as a legal society in 1920. In the 1930s, several Moroccan Jewish social clubs held events at the Casal de Cataluña and the Club Catalán; members of this community often met informally at La Cosechera, a Spanish café on the Avenida de Mayo, the hub of Spanish Republican sociability.[97] These markers of identity and the wealth of several early Moroccan Jewish immigrants led some Argentines to regard them as "Spaniards of a superior level"[98] and hence civilized and white.

Many Jewish newcomers from West Asia and North Africa, however, were impoverished and uneducated, a far cry from the intellectuals of medieval Spain or modern-day youths imbued with French culture. Sephardi journalists admitted this cultural lag and feared being seen as retrograde, uncivilized, and non-European. One reason why these immigrants, as well as the less affluent Moroccans, exalted the Spanish past was to draw attention away from their current poverty. In this manner they also demonstrated their worth and potential to their wealthier brethren and to Ashkenazim.[99]

As the Sephardi periodical *La Luz* pointed out in 1931, the Sephardim came from countries that were poorer than the Ashkenazi homelands. Only now were they becoming interested in their children's education. Yet it wondered why Jews from Syria continued to teach their children Arabic, which it saw as an inferior language that lacked a great literature.[100] These comments hinted at the double hazard faced by Mediterranean Jews: not only their Judaism but their identification with Arabs and Islam threatened to cast them as nonwhite.

Fellow Jews regarded some of their habits as uncivilized. Many Mediterranean Jewish men arrived as bachelors and, after saving their earnings, sent for their families or returned to their homelands to marry. In the meantime they often sought community in cafés. *La Luz*'s correspondent in Córdoba in 1933 lambasted its Turkish Jewish residents for loudly playing cards and games in such establishments instead of attending to their businesses or creating institutions. Beneath these remarks lay the fear that this "scandalous" behavior[101] could convince Catholic Argentines that they were barbaric, exotic, and hence nonwhite.

Ashkenazim tended to see Sephardi women as backward. Ruth wrote in her column in 1921 that few young women of these origins attended Jewish social functions, so they were unknown. "Their separation and seclusion create a grave problem," she claimed. Although Ruth admitted this was an issue for other women as well, her observations resembled Orientalist constructions of Middle Eastern women as sequestered and eroticized symbols of barbarism.[102]

Sephardi efforts to identify with European culture were not always successful. The Alliance sent a number of its graduates to the agricultural settlements to educate the colonists' children. As seen earlier, however, some non-Jewish Argentines did not consider these teachers truly fluent in modern Spanish, which weakened Sephardi claims to civilization and whiteness. Nevertheless, some Mediterranean Jews cemented their Iberian roots in the Interior. By the early 1900s, Abram Abisror had left Portugal for Buenos Aires, where he associated with the Jewish Moroccan community and was active in its synagogue. He married a woman of Moroccan descent and they settled in Peyrano, Santa Fe, where he opened a general store and prospered. Spanish settlers in Peyrano, who regarded him as one of them, chose Abisror to preside over the local Sociedad Española.[103]

More than other Jews of Mediterranean origin, Syrians confronted the dilemma of being associated with Arab and Muslim culture. Their ancestors generally had not come from Spain, and they spoke Arabic rather than Judeo-Spanish. Yet they, too, found means of identifying with Spain and Latinity, particularly in the provinces, where the small size of the various Mediterranean Jewish communities prompted interaction among them. While their first institutions in the Interior had the word Syrian in the titles, they increasingly joined with Judeo-Spanish speakers to create groups that styled themselves as Latin or Sephardi. For example, Jews from Aleppo, Izmir, Istanbul, Odessa, and Morocco established what became known as the Asociación Israelita Latina de Corrientes by 1928.[104] Similarly, Syrians participated in the founding of the Comunidad Israelita Sefardí of Córdoba in 1943. Latinizing or "Sephardizing" themselves, as Leonardo Senkman called it, helped Syrians exchange an Arab identity for a European one.[105]

Jews did not belong to the Anglo-Saxon "race" preferred by statesmen in the mid-1800s. Yet now the Sephardim and Syrians among them could claim they formed part of the "Latin race" that policymakers favored by the 1930s.[106] Such performances, however, did not convince the government to admit more Jews into the country.[107]

SENSUALITY AND PROSTITUTION

With European fascism in the background, it became more common for Argentine eugenicists and intellectuals to use the term "white" and advocate the exclusion and marginalization of Jews on explicitly racial grounds in the 1930s–40s.[108] In this context Nacionalistas judged it impossible for any Jews to claim whiteness, as did their counterparts in Europe. These radical rightists conflated leftism, liberalism, international capitalism, and other manifestations of modernity with Jews. One of their targets was sensuality. Like German National Socialists, Nacionalistas associated Jews with libertine behavior, pornography, and prostitution. Drawing upon age-old notions, both movements saw Jewish men as effeminate or feminized, yet at the same time hypersexual. Being circumcised made Jewish men sexually distinct and "Other"; one could expect any depravity from them. Jewish lust and greed, as manifested in the white slave trade, demonstrated this group's focus on the material and the flesh, rather than on higher spiritual values. Carnal and diseased beings who could degrade the social fabric, Jews epitomized barbarism.[109]

Nacionalista writers and cartoonists saw Jewish men as nonwhite. Drawings published in *Clarinada*, a self-styled "anti-Communist and anti-Jewish magazine," delineated their racialized features: large hooked noses; distorted faces; frizzy, African-like hair and beards. Their bloated stomachs and the bags of money they held indicated their appetite for food and other bodily and material pleasures. The cover of one issue showed a Jew with claws for hands, denoting his acquisitive and animal-like nature. Another picture contrasted the Nacionalistas' conception of the archetypical Jewish man with a lean, virile Argentine soldier, suggesting the former's lack of manliness and whiteness.[110] Nacionalista author Walter Degreff further accentuated the Jews' nonwhiteness by distinguishing between them and the inhabitants of the "white" countries that Jews plotted to control.[111]

Judaism was "a factor of corruption," announced an article in *Clarinada*. Its author, Ana Cecilia Fuentes, related how a Jewish man transformed his innocent, devout Catholic girlfriend into a "vulgar woman" ruled by "low passions." "The Jew corrupted her soul, extirpating faith from her spirit, and today, she is a stupid vain toy, whom he manipulates as he pleases." Nor was this an isolated case. This young woman resembled the many who flocked to nightclubs, mostly Jewish owned, she insisted, where cigarettes, adulterated liquor, and sensual music made them susceptible to immorality.[112] These remarks harked back to Martel's theme of Jewish men who contaminated Christian women. According to *Clarinada*, Jewish Communists planned to "destroy the Christian home, prostitute the woman, and relax all virtues, bestializing the human being."[113] Not only did their religion set them apart from Christianity, which Nacionalistas and other Argentines identified with whiteness; Jews aimed to replace spirituality with carnality and thus obliterate Christianity.[114] These agents of "moral perversion"[115] were the opposites of civilization; they were, indeed, a "cursed race."[116]

Nacionalistas claimed that Jews had initiated and organized the local sex trade, which remained in their hands, and internationalized the traffic in women. Other Argentines agreed with some of these inaccurate ideas, although they did not necessarily tie them to an all-encompassing Jewish conspiracy.[117] In contrast, Nacionalistas conflated their demons by insisting that leaders of the Zwi Migdal, the Jewish prostitution ring, were Communists.[118]

Ashkenazi women numbered among the procurers, brothel managers, and prostitutes. Nevertheless, the Nacionalistas only occasionally paid notice to Jewish women, representing them as lewd and bestial.[119] Perhaps they rarely questioned Jewish women's whiteness and sexual innocence because the images of them as white slaves – desirably light-skinned and victimized – were too widespread and powerful. Instead, they blamed sexual commerce on Eastern European Jewish men. The notion of Jewish pimps who monopolized prostitution aptly fit Nacionalista depictions of Jewish men as corrupt, sexually dissolute, and unmanly.

The tension between these competing images of men and women distinguished Jewish attempts to end sexual commerce from those of other communities. So, too, did the need to reaffirm whiteness, which heightened Jewish zealousness. According to Victor Mirelman, there was a higher incidence of prostitution among the French, Spanish, and Italians in Buenos Aires, yet they did not seem as concerned about it as the Jews did. These immigrants "had much less to lose," in Mirelman's words,[120] perhaps because they were Latin, Catholic, and hence more secure in their whiteness.

Prominent Jewish Argentines struggled to terminate Jewish prostitution, police Jewish women's bodies, and wipe out the stigma. They hoped to rescue women from an immoral and degrading life, as they saw it, and remove them from compromising situations. Another aim was to promote respectability and protect Jewish spaces in the nation, and ideals of manliness affected this goal. The failure of impoverished Jewish men to provide for their families weakened their image as upstanding white men and pushed women into sex work.[121] Prostitution, promiscuity, and relations with Catholic men demonstrated the inability of Jewish fathers and husbands to control Jewish women's sexuality and further undermined the community's whiteness. Since not all Jewish men could fulfill the roles of breadwinner and guardian, it was necessary to create a paternal substitute. To this end, the Sociedad Israelita de Protección a Niñas y Mujeres "Ezras Noschim" formed in the 1890s and affiliated with the London-based Jewish Association for the Protection of Girls and Women in 1901. It stepped into the gap by protecting women from Jewish procurers and Jewish and Christian clients and predators, and by disciplining women's sexual habits. In addition, it sought financial support for deserted wives and other needy women who might sell their bodies. The Sociedad hoped to strengthen the reputation of Jewish men and communities as honorable, civilized, and white. That a woman became president of this group in 1930 did not change its character, in part because a male administrator continued to handle much of its work.[122]

Many Jewish Argentines protested organized prostitution and denounced it in Spanish and Yiddish periodicals. They petitioned the government for legal restrictions on this practice, tried to keep the "unclean" out of Jewish institutions, and boycotted Jewish businesses that dealt with sex merchants.[123] The Sociedad addressed Jewish communities in other countries and international antiprostitution activists by sending reports of its cases to the Jewish Association in London, which published a number of these accounts. Sometimes they featured women coerced or deceived into prostitution by Jewish pimps or threatened by male relatives seeking to confine them in brothels. The endangered women turned for help to kindly Jewish men, who alerted the Sociedad or brought them to its doors. As historian Donna Guy observed, in these narratives Jewish men served as guardian angels (and villains), for women never rescued the victims.[124] Since evil men were mocking their rightful roles, other men had to step in to fulfill them. A woman could not take their place, except as a titular head of a group actually run by a man.

In its descriptions of several cases in the 1930s, the Sociedad indicated that fathers and husbands had handed over their duties to this group. Sabina, whose mother had died and whose father had emigrated to Argentina, had lived in Poland with relatives. When she was eighteen, the Sociedad had helped her father pay for her trip to Buenos Aires. After her arrival, he asked the Sociedad to intervene because of her friendships with people he considered bad influences. Its agent discovered that she was having affairs with several men and warned her that since she was a minor she could be imprisoned. It placed her with a family that supervised her more closely than had her father.[125] Unable to fulfill his duties, the father had abdicated his role to the Sociedad, which, as a responsible patriarch, had provided money and counsel and removed his errant daughter.

In 1937, Moisés, a tailor, asked the Sociedad to find his daughter Catalina, who had left home for the fourth time. His brother Ezequiel wrote that the parents' continual abuse had forced the girl to escape. They had removed her from school, refused to dress her properly (or at all), and ordered her to bring money home, suggesting they were pushing her into prostitution. The Sociedad took heed and moved her to another family's care, admonishing Moisés that it was best for Catalina.[126] Again, the agency assumed paternal functions and even reprimanded the father for his treatment of his daughter.

In other cases, the Sociedad not only took on a paternal role but fought barbaric Christian men over Jewish women's bodies. Twenty-year-old Rebecca left her home in 1928 in the company of a young Catholic named Dorenzo. According to the Sociedad, Dorenzo received money from her earnings as a servant for a respectable English family. Apparently he collected money from other women as well, suggesting he was a pimp. This perception of Dorenzo contested Nacionalista notions of Jewish men as the sole procurers and seducers. The police, working with the Sociedad, located Rebecca and the unsavory young man and took her to a reform school. She promised to change her ways and obey her parents, and she returned to her job.[127] In this instance the Sociedad established Jewish moral and racial supremacy over a Christian competitor and won back a girl for the community.

By guarding the sexuality and security of working-class women and fending off Christian rivals for their bodies, the Sociedad took the place of men who failed to comply with their familial duties. Thus it tried to reclaim Jewish manliness, civilized behavior, and whiteness. Since the opprobrium of prostitution persisted long after the decline of this practice among Jews, however, it appears that the Sociedad was unsuccessful.

CONCLUSION

For Gálvez and like-minded Argentines, Jews exemplified barbarism; for Lugones and others, they represented civilization. The focus on cultural features did not make these racial discourses any less biological, as the Jews' supposed traits often were considered innate and inheritable, albeit alterable. Jews participated in this debate, performing whiteness through orderliness, strenuous labor, cultural achievements, manly virtue, and allegiance to Argentina. Those of Mediterranean origins also pointed to their bonds with Spain and Latin Europe.

From the mid-nineteenth century on, opinion makers discussed Jews and race in various forums. Since Jews were by definition not Christian, and few were of the favored Northern European origin, thinkers and leaders did not necessarily see them as white. Perceptions of Jews as rootless, urban, mercantile, leftist, dirty, lazy, and poor reinforced this image. Purported Jewish carnality and criminality further prevented Nacionalistas from ever accepting this group as white. Sephardi and Syrian Jews possessed the additional handicap of their long residence in countries perceived as retrograde. Nevertheless, the federal government generally recognized Jews as white by opening the door to Jewish immigrants before 1930 and treating them as equals.

The countryside became a crucial site for Ashkenazi Jews to claim whiteness. Here they could redeem themselves by tilling the soil and casting off their identities as sickly city dwellers, greedy usurers, and effete rabbis. The rural setting was an equally important place for demonstrating that criollos, not Jews, were the true racial Others. Some Jews distanced themselves from these people of color by alternately uplifting, scorning, and fearing them, even as others, including teachers and leftists, befriended them. To reaffirm their racial and economic status, Jewish landowners, political moderates, and rightists also distanced themselves from Jewish progressives.

Alberto Gerchunoff tried to polish the whiteness of Russian Jewish farmers by connecting them to Spain, yet this strategy was more applicable to the Sephardim. Many Sephardi, Ashkenazi, and non-Jewish observers exalted the Sephardi Spanish heritage. While Moroccans had a particularly compelling claim to Spain, Latinity, and French culture, other Sephardim and even Syrians appropriated these identities. Orientalist views of Sephardi women as recluses and men as idle gamesters, however, made them seem exotic and barbaric.

Asserting manliness was a means of reinforcing Jewish whiteness. Ashkenazi men contested perceptions of sexual dissipation, nervousness, and feebleness. They sought to demonstrate their ability to work hard, provide for their families, and protect their "white" women. They also asserted their racial superiority by attempting to control Jewish women's bodies against gaucho and other Catholic competitors. When men could not play the patriarchal role, the Sociedad Israelita de Protección a Niñas y Mujeres took their place and supervised women's sexuality, although not always effectively.

Studying the racial constructions of Jews teaches us about Jews and whiteness in Argentina. It reveals an unexplored dimension of Jewish struggles for belonging and acceptance in that nation. The contentious discussion among Christian spokespersons and Jewish responses to it tell us that Jewish whiteness was insecure. Not all people of European or Mediterranean backgrounds, or of light skin color, were necessarily seen as white. Studies of Armenians and non-Jewish Arabs are needed to prove whether their whiteness also was insecure.

As historian Daniel Sharfstein observed for the United States, race is "a set of stories that people have told themselves and one another over and over again. Some are rooted in day-to-day living and hard-won experience, while others derive from fear and fantasy, hope and despair."[128] Similar elements abounded in the diverse and contradictory tales Christian Argentines told about Jews, and Jewish Argentines told about themselves, that situated Jews within the ranks of civilization or barbarism.

Notes

I thank Ezequiel Adamovsky, Paulina Alberto, Charles Ambler, Adriana Brodsky, Julia Schiavone-Camacho, Oscar Chamosa, Paul Edison, Eduardo Elena, Federico Finchelstein, Patricia Flier, Marta Goldberg, Donna Guy, Matthew Karush, Jeffrey Lesser, Daniel Lvovich, Margaret Power, Raanan Rein, Mariela Rubinzal, David Sheinin, Heather Sinclair, Mónica Szurmuk, Alejandra Vitale, and Barbara Weinstein for their help.

1. Andrews, *Afro-Argentines*, pioneered such work. For recent historical studies see, among other studies, Adamovsky, *Clase media*, 93–97, passim; Chamosa, "Indigenous," and *Argentine Folklore*; Frigerio, "Negros"; Garguin, "Los Argentinos"; Karush, "Blackness"; Karush and Chamosa, eds., *New Cultural*; Solomianski, *Identidades*. Frigerio, "Negros," 88, notes the black ancestry of many mestizos in the Interior, owing to its relatively high black population in the late colonial period. See also Geler, this volume. David Sheinin, private communication, provided insight into this work.

2. Garguin, "Los Argentinos," 162. Quijada, "Introduction," 9–10, and Frigerio, "Negros," 81, agree.

3. Lesser raises this question for Jews in other Latin American settings in "How," 41 and passim.

4. Gálvez, *Recuerdos*, 185–191, quotes on 187–188, 190. On Jewish "nervousness" see Gilman, *Smart Jews*, 46 and passim.

5. *Vida Nuestra* (Buenos Aires) 7 (Jan. 1919), 147. On the Tragic Week, among numerous works, see Rock, "Lucha civil."

6. Deutsch, *Las derechas*.

7. For the Peronist era see Adamovsky, *Clase media*, esp. 265–86; Garguin, "Los Argentinos," 173–77; and Milanesio, "Peronists," esp. 55–57. On later years see, among other works, Bialogorski and Bargman, "Gaze"; Joseph, "Taking"; Guano, "Color" and "Denial."

8. Svampa, *El dilema*, explores the long-term deployment of Sarmiento's maxim, although race is not her focus. According to Svampa, Sarmiento's treatment of the two terms was more nuanced than that of many later writers. She notes ironically that Gálvez and Lugones revindicated barbarism – but that of the gauchos, not the Jews (104–13).

9. On the racialization of poverty see Garguin, "Los Argentinos," 177.

10. As did census takers and some folklorists. See Andrews, *Afro-Argentines*; Chamosa, "Indigenous" and *Argentine Folklore*. Goldstein makes a similar observation of the United States in *Price*, 5.

11. In doing so I seek to avoid the pitfalls described by Dávila, "Ethnicity," 96, and Weinstein, *Color*, 29. They point out that some historians of race have not explained their criteria for choosing statements and actions to analyze. As a result, their examples have been scattered over time and place and are not necessarily representative.

12. Lake and Reynolds, *Drawing*, 36.

13. Benton-Cohen, *Borderline Americans*. I differentiate between manliness, or the Victorian notion of what made a man genteel and praiseworthy, and masculinity, which came to mean virility and aggressiveness by the early 1900s in the United States. See Bederman, *Manliness*, 17–19.

14. Appelbaum et al., "Racial," 15–17.

15. Argentines commonly distinguish among Ashkenazim, of Eastern European Yiddish-speaking descent; German-, Czech-, and Hungarian-speaking Jews of Central Europe; Sephardim, descendants of Jews expelled from Spain; and Arabic speakers.

16. See Brodsky, "Re-configurando."

17. Brodkin, *How*, and Goldstein, *Price*, have strongly influenced my thoughts. I have also benefited from such foundational works for the United States as Roediger, *Working*; and Jacobson, *Whiteness*.

18. The literature on race in Latin America is vast. Among more recent works, Stepan, *Hour* and Appelbaum et al., *Race and Nation*, have been particularly useful for this chapter.

19. Weinstein, "Racializing."

20. Wade, "Race," esp. 271, 274 (quote). Also see Appelbaum et al., "Racial," 12; Stern, "Mestizophilia," 205 n. 4; Weinstein, *Color*, esp. 13, 24–26.

21. Alberdi, *Bases*, 71. Also see República Argentina, *Constitución*, 5, 7–8, 10–11.

22. Klich, "Arab-Jewish," 13; Quijada, "De Perón," 871–72.

23. Martínez, *Genealogical*, 268.

24. Avni, *Argentina*, (quote) 10, 16–17. Italics in original.

25. Dávila, "Ethnicity," 111.

26. Avni, *Argentina*, 14.

27. Sarmiento, "Somos," 58.

28. "Prevenciones," 59–60. Sarmiento expressed complex shifting views on immigration and Jews; see, for example, Rollansky, *Sarmiento*; Baily, "Sarmiento."

29. Cited in Lewin, *Como fue*, 123–24. Much has been written on Hirsch and Jewish farming in Argentina. For overviews see Elkin, *Jews*, 105–20; Flier, "Historia."

30. Cited in Lvovich, *Nacionalismo*, 55.

31. Martel, *La bolsa*, 61–71. Also see Onega, *La inmigración*, 119–22; Lvovich, *Nacionalismo*, 57–60. European anti-Semites held such views. Regarding Jewish non-creativity, see Gilman, *Smart Jews*, 45–46, 49–50, 55, 75.

32. Martel, *La bolsa*, 61.

33. Cited in Onega, *La inmigración*, 111–12.

34. Castro, "Sainete."

35. See, among other works, Onega, *La inmigración*, 114.

36. See, for example, Klich and Lesser, eds., *Arab and Jewish*; Rein, ed., *Árabes y judíos*; Lesser and Rein, "Together."

37. Solberg, *Immigration*, 20.
38. See, among other works, Solberg, *Immigration*, 87–89; Rein, "Introduction," 14; Klich, "Arab-Jewish," 14 (quote).
39. Lesser, "Jews," 39–49.
40. "La inmigración," 36 (Beccar Varela), 54 (Amadeo), 84 (Ordóñez), 141 (Butza); for Gschwind see Lvovich, *Nacionalismo*, 212–13. Also see Lvovich, *Nacionalismo*, 209–16, and Senkman, "Nacionalismo." On the Liga Patriótica Argentina see Deutsch, *Counterrevolution*, and Caterina, *La Liga*.
41. Svampa, *El dilema*, 151–57; James, *Resistance*, 31; Adamovsky, *Clase media*, 96–97; Garguin, "Los Argentinos," 176. Brodkin, *How*, 55–56, notes that US Americans conflated industrial workers at the turn of the century with nonwhiteness.
42. Milanesio, "Peronists," 55–57, attributes the anti-Peronist prejudice against internal migrants largely to classism. Yet both the respondents in this 1919 survey and anti-Peronists in the 1940s and 1950s melded class, biology, and culture in their racial frameworks. Internal migrants were depicted as barbaric threats to the modern European social order, like Jews in 1919.
43. "La inmigración," 37.
44. Gilman, *Smart Jews*, does not address the correlation between Jewish intelligence and leftism.
45. Amadeo, *El falso*, 121–22, 135.
46. Helg, "Race," 42.
47. *Vida Nuestra* 7 (Jan. 1919), 159 (Mouchet), 173 (Ibarguren), 178 (Storni), 177–78 (Ramos), 185 (Pallares Acebal).
48. *Vida Nuestra* 7 (Jan. 1919), 172–73.
49. Moya makes a similar point in "Stereotype," 78–79. For the elite, however, militant immigrants became the "new barbarians"; see Svampa, *El dilema*, 80–81.
50. Avni, *Argentina*, 22–23 and passim; Lvovich, "Argentina," 26–27, 36, 37, and passim; Senkman, *Argentina*; Diner, personal communication. On the censuses see Deutsch, *Crossing*, 249. Castro, "Sainete," 34, mentions contemporary plays depicting Jews in the Hotel de Inmigrantes.
51. Goldstein, *Price*, 139, observes that Jews learned about whiteness in US schools.
52. *Vida Nuestra* 7 (Jan. 1919), 177.
53. Cited in Solberg, *Immigration*, 47.
54. *Tierra*, 49 (quote), 202–3. Also see Schoijet, *Páginas*, 9–10.
55. Dávila, *Ethnicity*, 109.
56. Leguizamón, "Prólogo." I use Aizenberg's translation in *Parricide*, 34 (quotes)-35. Regarding Jews who left the colonies, see Flier, "Historia."
57. Deutsch, *Crossing*, 34.
58. Ibid., 40, 74–81, passim; Svampa, *El dilema*, 94.
59. Máximo Yagupsky, interview, 1984, no. 68, transcript (Archivo de la Palabra, Centro de Documentación e Información sobre Judaísmo Argentino Marc Turkow, Asociación Mutual Israelita Argentina, Buenos Aires) [hereafter AP].
60. Garfunkel, *Narro*, 325.
61. Chamosa, this volume, discusses how criollos were seen as national symbols yet marginalized. Freidenberg, *Invention*, explores Jewish ambivalence toward gauchos. Karush, "Blackness," shows how Argentines admired but also denigrated black culture.
62. Spitzer, *Hotel*, 130, suggests that Jewish farmers in Bolivia maintained whiteness by distancing themselves from the subtropical environment and the Indians.

According to Wells, *Tropical Zion*, Jewish farmers in the Dominican Republic acted similarly by keeping apart from locals.

63. Alpersohn, *Colonia*, 236–43, quotes on 236–37. Yagupsky, interview, claimed that gauchos in Entre Ríos rarely approached Jewish women unless they thought these women had encouraged them. Gerchunoff, *Los gauchos*, and Leguizamón, "Pró- logo," depicted Jewish girls as attractive and white.
64. Bederman, *Manliness*, 49, 52.
65. Celia Koval Magrán, interview, 1989, no. 84, transcript (AP); Dora Schvartz de Pitasni, interview, 1997 (by Sandra McGee Deutsch, Basavilbaso); Zimerman de Faingold, *Memorias*, 3.
66. María Camín de Efron, interview, 1989, no. 96, transcript (AP). On criollo violence, rape, and robbery see Garfunkel, *Narro*, 286–87, 293, 295–96; Adela Speckman de Klein, interview, n.d., no. 110, transcript (AP); Lote and Heinz Sichel, interview, no. 326, 1996, transcript (AP).
67. I develop this point further in *Crossing*.
68. Olga Kipen, interview, 1997 (by Sandra McGee Deutsch, Basavilbaso). Also see Dora Caplan, interview, 1989, no. 81, transcript (AP).
69. Eichelbaum, "Aaron," 19–54 (quote on 37).
70. See, for example, Sofia Eidman de Tkach, interview, n.d., no. 145, transcript (AP).
71. Yagupsky, interview.
72. *Raíces*, 206.
73. Luisa Furman de Bendersky, interview, 1997 (by Sandra McGee Deutsch, Villa Domínguez); *El Heraldo* (Concordia), 29 Apr. 1994, n.p.
74. Ziperovich, "Memoria," 244.
75. On this incident, see Deutsch, *Counterrevolution*, 129–34; and *Vida Nuestra*, 9 (Mar. 1921). Some Jews identified with blacks. Paloma "Blackie" Efron, a jazz singer born in a colony in Entre Ríos, openly embraced African-American culture. See Deutsch, *Crossing*, 101–102; Karush, "Blackness," 232–33.
76. *La Vanguardia* (Buenos Aires), 19 Feb. 1921, 1, 5, 24 Feb. 1921, 1. In 1944, military authorities fired all the Jewish teachers in Entre Ríos, claiming they were subversives. See Deutsch, *Crossing*, 190.
77. Deutsch, *Counterrevolution*, 133.
78. *La Fronda* (Buenos Aires), 3 Mar. 1921, n.p.
79. *Israel* (Buenos Aires), 15 Jan. 1919, Supplement, n.p.; also see 16 Feb. 1919, 790. See Deutsch, *Counterrevolution*, 78–79, on other Jews who separated themselves from leftist co-religionists.
80. *Israel*, 25 Feb. 1921, 8.
81. Brodkin, *How*, 158, argues that Jews in the US civil rights struggle demonstrated that they were truly American because they supported equality.
82. Rojas, *La restauración*, 127–28; *La Prensa* (Buenos Aires), 28 Dec. 1908, 9. Also see 25 Nov. 1908, 10.
83. On Jewish prostitution see, among other works, Guy, *Sex*; Deutsch, *Crossing*, 105–22.
84. Aizenberg, *Parricide*, (quotes) 107, 159, 161; also see 26, 43, 44, 51, 129, 156. Also see Senkman, *La identidad*, 39–57. Szurmuk, private communication, described the importance of Spain and Spanish for Gerchunoff and how, indeed, Cervantes was his master.
85. Aizenberg, *Parricide*, 123, (quotes) 126.

86. *Israel*, 9 Jun. 1922, 16; 2 Feb. 1923, 15.
87. Lugones in *Vida Nuestra* 7 (Jan. 1919), 148. Gerchunoff mentioned Halevi in *Los gauchos*; see Aizenberg, *Parricide*, 51.
88. Ginio, "Sephardic," 287–96. Also see Díaz-Mas, *Sephardim*, 153–55; Gerber, *Jews*, 260.
89. *Israel*, 20 Jan. 1933, 11. See Pulido, *Españoles*.
90. Gutkowski, *Erase*, (quote) 430. Julia Edéry, a Moroccan in Canada, asserted, "We are Spanish," in Cohen, "Role," 212.
91. Gutkowski, *Erase*, 429–30, 435–36; Vilar, "La emigración," 14–22; *American Jewish Yearbook* 56: 450, 453–54; statistic in *Israel*, 13 Sep. 1935, 3; Díaz-Mas, *Sephardim*, 87–88. Also see Laskier, *Alliance*.
92. Martínez, *Genealogical*, 266.
93. Díaz-Mas, *Sephardim*, 158, 161; Gerber, *Jews*, 259–61. Sephardi Cubans in the 1930s asked Spain for citizenship; see Bejarano, "From," 145.
94. Yet they were not necessarily Spanish citizens, nor did the Franco government (1939–1975) want them in Spain. Still, as Rein, "Diplomacy," notes, some Spanish officials felt a certain commitment to help Sephardim.
95. Ginio, "Sephardic," 293–96; Díaz-Mas, *Sephardim*, 170–74.
96. Adriana Brodsky, private communication.
97. Senkman, "Identidad y asociacionismo," 188–90; Brodsky, "Contours," 103. On the Avenida de Mayo see Schwarzstein, "Entre," 128–30. Regarding the term "Latin" and French attempts to "Latinize" the region, see, for example, Edison, "Conquest."
98. Vilar, "La emigración," 39.
99. Gerber, "Sephardic," 56, made this point for Mediterranean newcomers in the United States.
100. *La Luz* (Buenos Aires), 13 Mar. 1931, 3; 5 Jun. 1931, 161.
101. Ibid., 13 Jan. 1933, 8. Also see Gerber, "Sephardic," 53.
102. *Israel*, 9 Sep. 1921, 13. Whether Sephardi women in Argentina were cloistered, or so distinct from Ashkenazi women, is debatable. See Deutsch, *Crossing*. On Orientalist views of non-Jewish Arabs and their gender relations, see Taub, "La conformación," and Goldberg, "La telenovela."
103. Julia Levi, interview, 2000 (by Sandra McGee Deutsch, Buenos Aires).
104. Sara Salón de Esperanza, interview, 2000 (by Sandra McGee Deutsch, Buenos Aires); Hazan, "Historia."
105. Senkman, "La identidad," 207; Brodsky, "Re-configurando," 119. Yet Mediterranean Jews did not completely ignore their long residence in Muslim countries. See, for example, *Israel*, 13 Apr. and 20 Apr., 1934, 45.
106. On the policymakers' preference, see Museo Social Argentino, *Primer*, 88, 245, 431; Senkman, "Nacionalismo"; Stepan, *Hour*, 141–42.
107. On immigration policy see Avni, *Argentina*, 128–74; Lvovich, "Argentina," 38–47.
108. See, for example, Bunge, *Una nueva*, esp. 27–60; Stepan, *Hour*, 141–43; Garguin, "Los Argentinos," 173–75.
109. Deutsch, "Contra"; Finchelstein, "Anti-Freudian"; Gilman, *Jew's Body*, esp. 119–24.
110. *Clarinada* (Buenos Aires), esp. Jul. 1943, 12, and Jun. 1943, cover. Also see Nov. 1942, 18; Jun. 1943, 6, 12.

111. Degreff, _Judiadas_, 30. On Nacionalista categorizations of Jews as a separate race, see Finchelstein, "Anti-Freudian," 84, 86.
112. _Clarinada_, Nov. 1942, 14.
113. Ibid., 11 (quote) and last page (n.p.).
114. Finchelstein, "Anti-Freudian," 103, 106 n. 112.
115. _Crisol_ (Buenos Aires), 1 Apr. 1934, 1.
116. Rubinzal, "El nacionalismo," 239.
117. Itzigsohn, et al., _Integración_, 206; Guy, _Sex_, 20, 22, and passim. Until the early 1930s "'Rufians,' 'Polacos' and Jews were synonymous terms," according to the _Vigilance Record_ (London), Jun. 1931, n.p.
118. _La Nueva República_ (Buenos Aires), 30 Aug. 1930, 2; Napal, _El imperio_, 256–57. Moya, "Stereotype," 59–61, notes that police linked anarchism with Jewish prostitution. Guy, _Sex_, 141–42, 151, 161–63, 168, discusses the perception that prostitution in general was tied to anarchism. According to Corbin, _Women_, 155, pimps represented the physical proletarian threat to the bourgeoisie. On the Zwi Migdal, see Guy, _Sex_, 120–29; Alsogaray, _Trilogía_; Bra, _La organización_.
119. Rubinzal, "Women's," 229.
120. Mirelman, "La comunidad," 29.
121. On white men as family heads and providers, see Benton-Cohen, _Borderline_.
122. On the Sociedad and Jewish opposition to prostitution, see Deutsch, _Crossing_, 105–22; Guy, _Sex_, 17–21.
123. Mirelman, "La comunidad," 18–27.
124. Guy, _Sex_, 20–21. For such accounts see _Report for 1906_, 26; _Report for 1911_, 52–55; _Report for 1915_, 28.
125. "Memoria de la 'Ezras Noschim' de Buenos Aires, 1936," 35–38 (IWO archive, Buenos Aires).
126. Folder 362–37, V. 91 (IWO archive, Buenos Aires).
127. Copiador (1924–1928), 6 Feb. 1928 (Ezras Noschim papers, CAHJP-INV 4349, Central Archive for the History of the Jewish People, Jerusalem). The archive has since recataloged this collection.
128. Sharfstein, _Invisible_, 10.

2

People as landscape

The representation of the criollo Interior in early tourist literature in Argentina, 1920–30

Oscar Chamosa

In the 1930s, a series of mountain districts in Argentina began receiving thousands of tourists from Buenos Aires and other Argentine cities, attracted to the spellbinding vistas and the brisk mountain air. The most popular destinations, such as Lake Nahuel Huapi in Patagonia, the Andean foothills in Mendoza, the Sierra in Córdoba, and the Calchaquí and Humahuaca valleys in the Northwest, offered a diversity of climates and landscapes for the fledgling Argentine leisure class. The tourism industry brought roads, hotels, and vacation houses where only small rural communities existed before.[1] It also placed the extreme opposites of the Argentine social, ethnic, and regional spectrum in contact with each other: while the privileged vacationers were urban Argentines of primarily European descent – some of them members of the old patrician elite and others middle-class children of the recent wave of European migration – the hosts tended to be poor, rural, dark-skinned peasants. Some of these peasants were indigenous people, such as the Kollas of Humahuaca or the Mapuche in Nahuel Huapi, while others were *mestizo* (*criollo* in Argentine parlance) with strong indigenous roots, such as the inhabitants of the Uco, Punilla, and Calchaquí valleys.[2] The physical development of tourism displaced the existing populations but did not eliminate them. Instead, they became indispensable in sustaining the tourist economy as a source of cheap labor. Furthermore, the dark-skinned, "traditional" peasants became part of the tourist attraction itself, precisely because they represented a visual and cultural contrast with the wealthy, "modern," and light-skinned Argentine tourists.

Arguably, the tourist encounter in these Argentine mountain destinations of the 1930s both revealed and shaped the complexities of national constructions of race and ethnicity. In particular, it hastened the process of racialization of the rural poor, analyzed by anthropologist Claudia Briones, in which the pre-immigration mixed-race population became integrated into the nation in a permanently subordinate position.[3] The peculiarity of the Argentine case, however, rests precisely upon the myth of the white nation that prevailed among Argentine elites since the second half of the nineteenth century.[4] The "darkening" of the subaltern classes not only failed to challenge the notion of a homogeneously white Argentina, but in fact strengthened it by associating dark skin with low socioeconomic status (and, in the case of the rural poor, with rurality), instead of reading dark skin as a sign of belonging to formally recognized, distinct "races." The term "criollo" itself, for instance, indirectly alludes to racial mixture and to the nonwhiteness (or incomplete whiteness) of this dark-skinned population, but on its surface it preserves a racial neutrality that does not necessarily exclude criollos from whiteness. This was one of the many ways in which race operated in Latin America during the first half of the twentieth century.

In the same period, many leading Latin American ideologues defined their nations as primarily mestizo – the result of biological and cultural intermixing among people of indigenous, European and African descent. These intellectuals saw mestizos, especially if they were urban and middle class, as the modern and dynamic segment of the population, the future of the nation.[5] Mestizos, in this view, possessed the superior qualities of spirituality and creativity that nationalist thinkers assigned to Latin European civilizations (in explicit contrast to North European and US materialism). They expected indigenous, black, and poor mestizo peasants to assimilate to this new paradigm of mestizo modernity, or else became ostracized as isolated ethnic minorities. Argentina, as many of the chapters in this volume make clear, belongs instead to the group of Latin American nations and regions that made their claim to exceptionality by stressing the prominence of Iberian and other European settlers in their racial makeup.[6]

The Argentine emphasis on the demographic prevalence of Europeans – both biologically and culturally – left little room for *mesticismo* to function as an assimilationist ideology, yet the myth of the white Argentina (like many other Latin American myths of whiteness) did not entail a claim of racial exclusivity. Instead, it sought both to racialize and subordinate the dark-skinned pre-immigration population and to accommodate it to some specific aspects of the nation-building project, especially as folk types and historical figures celebrated in popular literature.[7] The best example of this phenomenon was the cult of the *gaucho* and the rise of criollo folklore as the aesthetic paradigm of the nation in the early twentieth century. The exploration of pre-Hispanic archeological sites was another way of accommodating an indigenous past into the national history.[8] A lesser-known aspect was the role of criollo and indigenous Argentines as host populations in the tourism destinations of the Interior.[9]

The development of tourism was intimately related to the construction of a visual discourse about Argentina in which the mestizo and indigenous populations played a (limited) role. The images generated through the tourist complex served to make visible the ethnic divide created by the dynamics of Argentina's construction of whiteness. While the white Argentine tourist acts as the active agent who relaxes while producing and consuming images, the dark-skinned local populations in the mountain destinations become subordinated as passive elements, virtually part of the landscape scenery. By the early 1920s, images of dark-skinned people, preferably rural and dressed in traditional clothing, became a trope in pictorial and photographic representations throughout the Western Hemisphere. Group scenes of indigenous people, for instance, were one of the trademarks of the Mexican muralist movement.[10] This visual discourse, in the case of Mexico, was closely related to the state-led project of assimilation of indigenous people in the modern postrevolutionary nation, something that certainly could be said of the representation of racial others in both Latin- and Anglo-American nations more broadly. In Argentina, as elsewhere, internal tourism was one important avenue for the visualization of non-European rural populations as exotic enclaves of tradition amidst the modern nation. In these visualizations, landscape and people formed a continuum of images made attractive by its distinctiveness and contrast with the urban milieu, the places where tourists conducted their everyday lives.

While tourist destinations were not *terra nullius* or empty spaces, the tourism industry modified the sense of place that local societies assigned to these sites by adapting them to the perceived needs of the tourist market.[11] This process involved altering the physical landscape, such as by building artificial lakes or framing the existing landscape with hotels, public buildings, and monuments purposely designed to create a certain sense of place, even if that sense was a borrowed one. In Argentina, tourism promoters tended to project European leisure landscapes onto developing destinations. In this way, the Patagonian lake region became Argentina's Switzerland, both in terms of its landscape and ski resorts and of the architectural style used in private and public buildings. Similarly, Mendoza's Villavicencio thermal springs aspired to be Argentina's answer to the Alpine spas, while Mar del Plata's central beach received the name of Bristol, in honor of the famous British seaside resort town.[12] In Northwestern Argentina, however, the emphasis of the destination-making process was on what we might (in today's terms) call "heritage tourism." Promoters highlighted the role of the region in the colonial and independence periods, organizing tours to visit historical sites. To make the experience of the past more accessible to modern tourists, the national government conducted extensive historical restoration throughout the region. In this context, the Quebrada de Humahuaca (or Humahuaca Valley) and other locations in Northern Jujuy Province saw most of their colonial churches restored and their small towns adapted to appear more colonial than they actually were.[13]

Together with this physical transformation of the landscape, tourism promoters also pre-defined what visitors must see and how they should interpret it. Travel writing in newspapers and magazines, with their accompanying photographs, framed the visual field for visitors, orienting their gaze toward particular aspects of the landscape, monuments, and local culture. Tourism developers, photographers, journalists, and writers collectively determined the visibility and invisibility of the local population. In some cases, such as the Patagonian Lakes, promoters rendered the local indigenous population completely invisible.[14] In Córdoba's sierras, the *serranos,* as local peasants were known, remained visible in a limited way, as they sold crafts and local delicacies to the tourists or served as decorative elements on postcards and promotional posters. Part of the tourist experience in the sierras involved being photographed in traditional ponchos and hats while holding the reins of a burro or llama. In the Calchaquí Valley and the Quebrada de Humahuaca, the local indigenous population and its culture were more evident than those of other resort areas. Images of Kolla peasants, commonly referred to as "Coya," dominated the tourist iconography of the region. Furthermore, developers encouraged local festivals, religious rituals, and carnival celebrations, promoting them as part of the tourist experience.[15] As these folkloric attractions were impossible to reproduce in other settings, the added value of authenticity compensated for the comparably high expenses of traveling to the Northwestern Calchaquí and Quebrada de Humahuaca valleys.

Traveling to these distant regions was indeed a pecuniary and physical sacrifice, but it was justified by the Romantic-nationalist principle of "know your country" that tourist promoters exploited in much of the Western world in the interwar era.[16] Reflecting international trends, the Argentine tourist literature of this period characterized the countryside as embodying the natural and spiritual reserves of the nation and thus promoted tourism to the Interior as a return both to nature and to the historical roots of Argentine nationality. The emphasis on nature, history, and tradition reveals the influence of German Romantic nationalism in shaping Argentine tourism discourse.[17] As in its European version, the Argentine Romantic-nationalist movement emerged in the early twentieth century as a reaction to socialism and anarchism, encouraging a return to "tradition" that also aimed to steer national elites away from positivism and cosmopolitan liberalism.[18] Knowing one's country, or in this case touring the Interior, played a central role in this program. The picturesque and traditional Interior, where nature remained untouched and people moved in a characteristically pre-modern tempo, contrasted, in this view, with the squalor, alienation, and moral decay that nationalists associated with Buenos Aires.[19] By establishing contact with "untouched" nature and communities, the *porteño* travelers could immerse themselves in a process of spiritual and bodily purification that would renew their energies and renovate their ties with their country.

Despite (or indeed because of) these Romantic overtones, rarely was the tourist experience isolated from asymmetrical relations of power. The distant mountains of the Argentine Interior offered the unique combination of landscape, natural settings, and local culture that made possible the wholesome and patriotic experience expected from the intelligent tourist. Yet, on the ground, Romantic-nationalist rhetoric met the reality of the enormous social distance between tourists and locals. Numerous travel articles published in the 1930s treated the rural population of the Interior in tones that ranged from the condescendingly sympathetic to the openly cynical. At best, the mountain dwellers became highlights of the landscape, as much of the promotional material announced. Thus, the same tourist literature that encouraged readers to embrace the nation's diverse local cultures, including its nonwhite population, also determined the boundaries of what the tourists could see and how they should interpret the ethnic differences they encountered in their forays into the distant valleys of Argentina. These textual and visual discourses and experiences of tourism, in turn, contributed to broader understandings of which types of people belonged to the Argentine nation, and which were simply a part of the landscape.

CREATING IMAGES OF THE INTERIOR

"Why are you going there? You won't find anything but *ranchos* [shacks] and *vinchuca* bugs."[20] This is what Argentine naturalist Eduardo Holmberg heard from his porteño friends after they learned of his upcoming trip to the Northwest in 1902. Holmberg used the anecdote to illustrate typical porteño prejudices about the Interior and to highlight the necessity of traveling to change that state of misinformation. Forty years later, those prejudices may have persisted among a minority, but the construction of tourist infrastructure and the promotion of travel to the Interior had by then made inroads in placing the Northwest among the desired destinations for porteño travelers. Over the course of the intervening decades, intellectuals, writers, tourism developers, and government officials championed Romantic-nationalist principles that transformed different localities in the Interior into prestigious tourist destinations, where the tourist would be expected to relax and to learn about the country's landscapes, folk cultures, history, and economic potential. These notions, in turn, informed decisions about the construction of infrastructure and the reconstruction of historical buildings. It is impossible to gauge the extent to which the literature on tourism and government projects shaped the perceptions and actions of actual tourists in these years, but it could still be argued that these discourses shaped the conditions in which the encounter between Argentine tourists and Argentine locals took place. Certainly, this travel literature played a foundational role in bringing the Interior to Buenos Aires, creating discursive and visual panoramas through which the national elites in the capital city saw and in some cases experienced the far Interior.[21]

At the turn of the nineteenth century, the voyage to the far Interior was limited to gentlemen explorers like Holmberg who, upon their return, gave speeches at the Jockey Club, the Argentine Scientific Society, or the Argentine Geographical Institute for the benefit of other curious but less adventurous fellow citizens. During the period between 1880 and 1910, a slew of expert explorers, including Francisco Moreno, Estanislao Zeballos, Juan B. Ambrosetti, Carlos Ameghino, and Holmberg himself, became intermediaries between a select audience of educated Argentines and the people, landscapes, and resources of the remote regions of the country where railroad and tourist amenities were absent. The entire enterprise of exploration and research, as geographer Hortensia Castro argues, consisted of a symbolic process of claiming ownership of the distant regions for the nation.[22] Holmberg, for instance, traveled through the Northwest commissioned by the Ministry of Agriculture on a fact-finding mission in the recently created National Territory of the Andes and the neighboring province of Jujuy.

While these explorers appropriated the patrimony of the Interior in the name of progress, a different group of travelers, this time literary ones, let themselves be appropriated by the Interior and purified from the undesired effects of modernity. The group of authors known as "The Generation of the Centennial" (thus named for the 1910 commemoration of Argentina's break from Spanish rule a century earlier) departed from the positivist ideology of their predecessors and turned their views to the Interior, where they traveled to reconnect with what they saw as the true spirit of the nation. The foundational text of this kind of Romantic-nationalist travel is Ricardo Rojas' *El país de la selva* (1907). Rojas composed his masterpiece as the fictional travelogue of a young resident of Buenos Aires visiting Santiago del Estero, the land of his ancestors. In the scrublands of Santiago, this perceptive youth discovers the wisdom of the rustic criollos and stumbles on customs and traditions believed extinct. At the end of this journey, as in a shamanic quest, our hero meets the squat figure of Zupay, the "numen" or protector-spirit of the forest and its creatures. In a magical vision, Zupay shows the traveler how unchecked logging had laid waste to the land and expelled its dwellers, beasts and humans alike. The narrator returns to Buenos Aires concerned but enlightened, more adult and more identified as Argentine than before his departure. Rojas thus created a new paradigm that conceived of travel to the Argentine Interior as a return to the sources of nature and nation, a rite of passage for urban travelers who, once divested of their urban clothes, could immerse themselves in the poetry of the landscape and in the culture of rural Argentina.

As historians Anahí Ballent and Adrián Gorelik note, the Generation's ideology exerted a decisive influence over the project of physical integration of the country promoted by the conservative governments that ruled the country through the 1930s.[23] Ballent and Gorelik explain that highway construction and other public works projects initiated during this period were inspired by the idea of bringing the countryside to the city and vice-versa. Similarly, Rojas and his colleagues instilled the notion that travel to the Interior was a necessary component of the process of "national restoration" they championed. The far Interior also offered a personal escape from the city and its corrupting forces that would trigger a process of spiritual renovation.

As internal tourism developed in the 1930s as a common activity among the propertied classes, the Romantic notions of spiritual and cultural renovation took root among the various agents involved in tourism development. This was especially true among the specialized journalists who contributed to the travel sections in wide-circulation newspapers and magazines. In 1937, art critic Juan Zocchi elaborated on this pastoralist view as it applied to tourism in an article in the influential Buenos Aires daily *La Nación*: "Whichever the motive for the ... vacation, travel to the seaside, the mountain or the pampas. ... there is always a return to the origins, a going back to nature, for this prodigal child who returns from the city morally, physically, and economically van-quished."[24] Here, Zocchi follows the Romantic paradigm popularized by the nationalist writers, in which the city appears as a giant grinder pulping the human essence into an artificial, shapeless mass. In the Sierras de Córdoba, the shapes, lights, and scents of nature had the property of freeing the soul from the walls of the city and thus restoring its vital force.

But the refurbishing of inner energies went hand in hand with active learn-ing, something that citizens were expected to take seriously. "To know the homeland is a duty [*Conocer la patria es un deber*]," was the slogan adopted by the Directorate of National Parks in 1934.[25] Similarly, Minister of Public Works Salvador Oria expressed during the opening ceremony of the "Hotel de Turismo" in Catamarca: "Helping Argentines to know their country and to know each other is a contribution to the consolidation of national unity."[26] These mottos were consistent with the goals established by different offices of the national government and by articles published in the press, and they follow an international trend at the time in the promotion of domestic tourism.[27] "To travel to the Interior [*internarse*] at least once a year should be mandatory for porteños as a complement to formal education," wrote Mario S. Ayala in the magazine *El Hogar*.[28] Like many contemporary nationalist authors, Ayala deplored the tendency among porteños to imagine the Interior of Argentina as an extension of modern and wealthy Buenos Aires. He therefore asked urban Argentines to travel, not just to revise such assumptions but also to form a bond of empathy with the land and its people. Tourism reached a higher purpose when the visitor ventured beyond the more accessible destinations and entered the territory of ancient Argentina, where the nation's deep history waited to be discovered.

To know Argentina was to visit, to sightsee, to discover and apprehend the spirit of the place. In his article, Ayala expressed his desire for porteños to return from the Interior with a piece of native soil affixed to their souls. In that regard, the first step was to try to achieve a deep perception of the environment using all the physical senses. Zocchi, in his article for *La Nación*, recommended observing and memorizing the color and shape of the mountains. A further step: listening to the whistle of the wind, the rustle of leaves, the murmur of water, and letting the aroma of the air stir one's emotions. At this point, the tourist should feel that she has returned to the "warm womb of nature, like a lost child found after so much crying."[29] Zocchi further poses the question: "What do you see in the sierras, man from the city?"[30] The question is rhetorical but not trivial. The implication is that the tourist reaches the heartland numbed by the noises and smog of the city, unable to tune his senses to this new environment. Celestina P. de Saint Antonin, staff writer of *Automovilismo*, the Argentine Automobile Club magazine, confessed that in view of the Andean range "the eyes grow weary from seeing, from wanting to see everything, from chasing all possible details and imprinting them in the retina."[31] Similar articles recommended traveling by car, allowing tourists to stop to appreciate the view or take detours to explore beyond the beaten track. Car travel was also touted for producing a more lively impression of the changing landscape and luminosity than horseback riding. Delfina Bunge de Gálvez compared the experience of admiring the landscape from the seat of a moving car to that of a sharp reader who has the ability to capture the organization and argument of a novel without losing sights of the details.[32] But travel writers also recommended stopping the car and allowing the landscape to penetrate the senses.

In addition to appreciating the landscape, according to these writers, a complete travel experience required paying homage to different cultural and historical aspects of the tourist destination. Antecedents of that form of travel to the Interior were the so-called patriotic pilgrimages. Since the late nineteenth century, different institutions around the country organized these collective trips to Tucumán on the occasion of Independence Day.[33] Groups of twenty to sixty people, usually members of patriotic associations or student organizations, would travel to Tucumán to visit the ruins of the site where the Congress of the United Provinces of the Río de la Plata declared independence on July 9, 1816 (the original house was mindlessly demolished in the mid-nineteenth century). The action-packed program typically included a Te Deum in the cathedral, speeches at the historical site, a reception hosted by the provincial governor, and an evening gala at the governor's palace. These patriotic pilgrimages continued into the twentieth century and expanded to other provinces. In 1914, for example, the inauguration of the monument to the "Army of the Andes" (led by independence hero General José de San Martín) in Cerro de la Gloria, Mendoza, established this province as a new patriotic destination.

The number of destinations for patriotic tourism increased dramatically in the 1930s and 1940s. With funding from the national government and input from provincial elites, numerous ambitious construction projects honoring patriotic dates and figures broke ground within a span of fifteen years. In 1931, Salta unveiled a monument to Martín Miguel de Güemes, an independence-era hero, posing serious competition to Mendoza's Cerro de la Gloria.[34] Immediately thereafter, a similar monument was under construction in Humahuaca. Beginning in 1938, the Dirección Nacional de Museos, Monumentos y Lugares Históricos [National Directorate of Museums, Monuments, and Historical Sites] commissioned major reconstruction work on the Independence House in Tucumán, the Cabildo of Buenos Aires, the Jesuit estates in Córdoba and Misiones, the colonial chapels in Quebrada de Humahuaca and Puna, and the birthplace of General San Martín in Yapeyú, Corrientes, as well as his headquarters in El Plumerillo, Mendoza.[35] These places became prestigious landmarks which, reproduced in posters, magazines, and school readers, came to constitute a recognizable historical-patriotic topography. The act of visiting them and experiencing them in person was supposed to inspire respect for the civilizing mission of the Church in the colonial period (and certainly not for the pre-existing indigenous population) and admiration for the founding fathers of the nation, all necessary steps in the process of initiation into the restored sense of nationality. Visiting these monuments and historical sites also encouraged the establishment of a link with the rural criollo culture, as nationalist intellectuals recommended, since most of those historical landmarks were located amidst criollo communities of old settlement.

In order for any of this to happen, however, the country needed decent roads. In the mid-1930s, the national government began to finance critical infrastructure that made travel possible for urban tourists. The public works program initiated by President Agustín P. Justo (1932–38) and continued under his successors, from Roberto Ortiz (1938–42) to Juan D. Perón (1946–55), included the construction of roads, hotels, and the organization of national parks. Although tourists from Buenos Aires could and did ride the train to popular vacation destinations like the seaside resort town of Mar del Plata or the province of Córdoba, highway construction allowed more tourists to reach outlying historical sites and natural landscapes.[36] In the summer season of 1937, for example, the railroad companies sold over 100,000 tickets to Mar del Plata and 50,000 to Córdoba, but only 3,500 to Mendoza's Andean foothills, and 2,267 to Lake Nahuel Huapi.[37] The same publication that compiled this data estimated that over 11,000 cars made the thousand-mile trip on gravel roads toward the Patagonian lake district. (Unfortunately, neither this publication, nor any other source, provides an estimate of car travel to the Northwest). With the expansion of the nation's travel infrastructure, more Argentines from Buenos Aires, Rosario, and other locations in the area of European settlement could fulfill the romantic vision of heading to the Interior to restore their bodies and reconnect with the sources of authentic nationality.

Even as the national government was busily building the main highway networks, the lack of backcountry roads made excursions to the most scenic and traditional districts of the Interior an ordeal worthy of a classic hero. Consider a trip from Buenos Aires to the stunning and pleasantly breezy Tafí del Valle in the mid-1930s. The trip by train from Retiro station in downtown Buenos Aires to the rail terminal in San Miguel de Tucumán took an average of 36 hours, not counting the usual long maintenance stops. For most of that time a cloud of dust hovered in the passenger cars, regardless of the class. Reaching Tucumán, the verdant surroundings and tree-lined streets offered some relief, but only if the traveler could tolerate humid subtropical weather, or, if traveling in winter, the thick smog spouting from the sugar mill smokestacks. From the provincial capital of San Miguel another shorter train trip took the traveler to Acheral in the foothills of the Aconquija range. Most travelers would almost certainly have had to be guests of one of the four Tucumán elite families that owned most of the private property in the Tafí valley, and thus they could count on their hosts having already made the arrangements for the final leg of the trip between Acheral and Tafí.[38] A train of mules with their drivers would be waiting for the visitors in the vicinity of the Acheral station. The mules would then negotiate an uphill, pebble-strewn riverbed that served as a road, surrounded by the thick tropical vegetation that covers the eastern slopes of the Aconquija range and the damp mist that penetrates both clothes and hair. Sudden torrential rains were common year round, causing dangerous rockslides and flash floods. Fortunately for these weary travelers, their landowning hosts in Tafí enjoyed legendary fame for their hospitality and would likely have waited for them with refreshments of empanadas, olives, fresh cheese, and wine, all locally produced, which alone would have justified the risky adventure.

Travelers who lacked friends with vacation homes in the sub-Andean valleys had to content themselves with touring the less dramatic landscapes of the lower Sierras. In 1937, the agency Exprinter offered off-season a sixteen-day, all-expenses-included package to Tucumán, Salta, and Jujuy for 310 pesos per person.[39] The package included visits to tourist spots located in the vicinity of the provincial capitals (Villa Nougués in Tucumán, San Bernardo in Salta, and Termas de Reyes in Jujuy). For a similar amount, Exprinter offered sixteen-day cruise deals to Rio de Janeiro, including admission to the casino; resisting such foreign temptations was probably the first trial in our tourist-hero's quest for national knowledge. But the biggest ordeal was without a doubt the price. Even the well-priced 310 pesos per person package was beyond the reach of any wage earner in pre-Peronist Argentina.[40]

Promoters of tourism discouraged train travel in favor of cars, downplaying the difficulties of driving more than a thousand miles from Buenos Aires to Humahuaca and other destinations. In 1938, an article in *Automovilismo* made reference to the "erroneous belief that the lack of roads make [the scenic landscapes of the Northwest] inaccessible."[41] The year before, the same magazine sent an investigative reporter to assess the state of the roads in the Northwest. The reporter covered over 300 miles of gravel roads, commenting that while the authorities were busy building new bridges, they lacked resources to maintain the road surfaces. But nevertheless, the author recommended that porteños choose car travel over the train. The article explains that the excursions organized by agencies (such as that advertised by Exprinter) were limited in reach and curtailed the individuals' freedom to experience the places on their own terms.[42] In a letter to *Automovilismo* a reader reported that a recent car trip to the Northwest had made him revise his previous opinion on that region, which had been based solely on train travel: "Having traveled around in Switzerland, Austria, France and Germany, I can attest that, if our panoramas are somehow different, they are equally attractive and, often, even more grandiose."[43] This car enthusiast, who clearly enjoyed plenty of time and money, is probably fairly representative of the profile of tourists who could afford the Northwestern trip. Considering the social provenance and education of those sophisticated tourists makes one wonder whether they would in fact immerse themselves in criollo culture as Romantic nationalists expected.

TOURISTS, LOCALS, AND THE LIMITS OF ROMANTIC-NATIONALIST DISCOURSE

Tourism promoters made great use of photographs in magazines and newspapers to teach readers what to see and do in each destination. Photomontages emphasized the range of choices when visiting the Interior: alpine landscapes in Nahuel Huapi, tropical lushness at Iguazú Falls, glamour and fun in Mar del Plata, brisk mountain air and pristine waters in Mendoza, health and relaxation in the Sierras de Córdoba. For the Northwest, and to a lesser extent also for the Sierras de Córdoba, they emphasized history and traditions. Images of pre-Hispanic ruins, whitewashed chapels, and historical buildings from the independence period invited the tourist to travel to the mythical time when the motherland was in its infancy. Snapshots of the Interior often included images of dark-skinned peasants wearing homespun clothes. In the case of photographs from the Northwest, most urban Argentines would recognize in these images the Coyas, indigenous inhabitants of the Puna, but only the few viewers who were acquainted with the works of turn-of-the-century explorers would have more than a vague idea about those fellow Argentines.

By the 1930s, the inclusion in tourist materials of images of individuals representing pre-modern populations was a well-established practice worldwide. Remarkably, Mexican postcards and promotional posters tended to depict indigenous and mestizo peasants as often they showed landscapes or landmarks. Historians Alex Saragoza and Eric Zolov interpret the portrayal of peasants in tourist material as a form of self-exoticization for foreign consumption.[44] The goal was to counteract pervasive images of a grim and violent Mexico among potential US tourists with images that conveyed primeval innocence as well as welcoming comfort. Arguably, the pictures of Coyas or of mestizo criollos in Argentine tourist materials represented a similar form of exoticization. However, since these images were aimed at a domestic market, travel writers and tourism promoters faced the problem of how to define the rural population in terms of ethnicity and their relation to the nation as a whole.

Using images of non-European Argentines as exotic others made for effective promotional material, but by doing this, the tourist literature was caught in an apparent contradiction. First, the presence of Argentines of indigenous ancestry (including mestizo criollos) contradicted the view of Argentina as a white country populated by European immigrants. Second, the practice of portraying these populations as "exotic" clashed with the Romantic-nationalist discourse for which rural Argentines were not merely part of the national population but *the* authentic Argentines. The imperative of "know your country" required that tourists, actual Argentines, meet their rural counterparts, the "authentic" Argentines, and acquire from them the wisdom of the nation that poor farmers and herders had preserved from time immemorial. In sum, the exotic Other was at the same time the authentic national Self.

One way to untangle this riddle was to emphasize the local boundaries of these exotic Argentines by referring to the rural population as "types." Images portraying people in peasant dress or performing traditional practices often included captions such as *tipos serranos* [types from the sierra] or *tipos del altiplano* [highland types]. In typifying local populations for tourist consumption, the Argentine tourism boosters were, again, following well-established international trends. From the European point of view, people who fell into the category of "types" were those who belonged to racial, ethnic, and regional minorities – as well as unassimilated immigrants, colonial subjects, and the urban poor – in short, everyone excluded, by chance or design, from the benefits of modern capitalism.[45] By the turn of the nineteenth century, the mechanical reproduction of images helped generalize the use of human "types" in illustrated magazines, trademark logos, and postcards, usually showing men and women donning "traditional" garments and performing tasks that modernity had rendered obsolete. It would not take long before the tourism industry adopted those types as cultural markers aimed at increasing the destinations' exotic appeal.[46] Rather than representing individuals, the persons in the pictures represented group categories whose physical features, dress, and demeanor not only had characteristic local flavor but also differed noticeably from the social class and ethnicity of the tourists.

Tourist promotional graphics drew heavily from the tradition of *pintura costumbrista* [paintings of country scenes], a genre that dominated Argentine visual arts in the 1920s and 30s.[47] Influential artists such as Cesareo Bernaldo de Quirós and Alfredo Gramajo Gutiérrez portrayed gauchos and peasants from the rural Interior in a way that cultivated the cult of gaucho masculinity while fusing landscape and humans in a continuum. This was particularly true in the case of Gramajo Gutiérrez, who was originally from Tucumán but who became a regular member of mid-century Buenos Aires' beaux-arts scene.[48] This painter specialized in portraying groups of Northwestern criollo and indigenous peasants engaged in both mundane and ritual activities. In form, if not in content, these paintings evince the strong influence of the Mexican muralist movement, including a tendency to reflect racialized group typology rather than individuality.[49] Late-impressionist techniques used by most *costumbrista* scene painters allowed for the erasure of signs of individuality while still conveying bodies codified as "ethnic" through the accentuation of skin color, hair, and eyelid shape. Not unlike Paul Gauguin's Breton peasants, the characteristic ponchos, dresses, and hats of the Northwestern peasants in Gramajo Gutiérrez's paintings highlighted regional difference and helped make visible

the survival of primitive traditions within a modern nation.[50] Gramajo Gutiérrez's human groups, whether attending the wake of an *angelito* [a dead infant]
or dancing a *zamba*, seemed to belong in their colors and shapes to the negative
space of the mountains, trees, or thatched roofs that emerged behind them.[51]
When the iconographic subject was an individual and not a group, racial
typology seemed to guide the artists' inspiration. Many oeuvres by Northwestern artists such as *tucumano* sculptor Juan Carlos Iramain and the Humahuaca painter of Spanish origin Francisco Ramoneda are specifically devoted to
exemplifying regional types, as can be readily observed in the private museums
kept by these artists' descendants in San Miguel de Tucumán and Humahuaca,
respectively.[52]

Highlighting human racial typologies became a trope of early–twentieth-
century visual culture in Europe and the Americas, and tourism offered the
lucky few who could travel an opportunity to appreciate these types in the
exclusive theater of their own local spaces. In Argentina, according to many
articles on tourism, observing these *tipos populares* was one of the main
attractions of the Northwest. The Andean valleys with their small villages
offered a living version of an ethnographic museum exhibit. A back cover
feature in a 1941 issue of *Automovilismo*, titled "Tipos del Norte," made
this point unambiguous: "A factor of indubitable attraction for the tourist
traveling through the northern region is the diversity of types. . . In that sense,
Salta, Jujuy, Catamarca, and Tucumán frequently offer popular types and
costumes that strongly grab the attention of the visitor."[53] The accompanying
pictures show a young man looking at the camera while holding a *bombo*
[a type of drum], market women wearing Andean peasant dress in San Salvador de Jujuy, and a group of women marching on foot, according to the
caption, for their day of work to the sugar mills. The visitor, the article
concludes, could appreciate this diversity of types in a setting of extraordinary
beauty.

Other articles recommended observing the locals in their daily activities as
well as in rituals and fiestas. One magazine article argued that religious festivals, such as that of the Virgen del Valle in Catamarca, were a good opportunity to observe the heterogeneous crowd of "characteristic types" from the
northern provinces.[54] Another occasion to observe the congregation of types
from the various northern provinces was the annual sugar harvest in Tucumán.
Automovilismo, in its yearly promotion of winter tourism in the Northwest,
featured the *zafra*, or sugar cane harvest, as one of the region's tourist attractions.[55] The fact that such activity was not a traditional craft did not matter
here, since the tourist's curiosity would be aroused by "the movement of
thousands of men who, according to a custom that is rooted in them, travel
long distances to the sugar mills across sierras and mountains carrying along all
their possessions: children, women, and animals."[56] Perhaps not surprisingly,
the same writer who presupposed that the harvesters' seasonal migration was a
voluntary practice had the indelicacy of listing women and children as male

FIGURE 1 In this photo essay on Northwestern Argentina, *Automovilismo* magazine recommends that tourists observe the local "types," including seasonal workers marching to the sugar cane harvest in Tucumán and market women bringing their wares to the city of Jujuy. Source: *Automovilismo* 12:257, May 1941, n.p.

possessions. The same article included a number of clichés about the good nature, humbleness, and endurance of "the race [*la raza*]" – an undefined term often used in relation to dark-skinned rural Argentines. It also recommended paying attention to the beautiful colors and "Incaic motifs" of the migrants' garments and ponchos. All these "vistas," it argued, were worthy of observation and photographic record, so as to ensure future memories of such delightful times.[57]

Being constructed as a human "vista" effectively makes the rural Argentines of the Northwest part of the landscape. Jujuy's representative to the First National Congress on Tourism, Teodoro Sánchez de Bustamante, summarized in his presentation what all tourist iconography and discourse attempted to say with respect to the rural population of the Northwest: "In the Puna and Quebrada de

FIGURE 2 An artist's rendering of the Argentine tourist visiting her country.
Source: *Automovilismo* 19:236, Aug. 1939, n.p.

Humahuaca, the Indian, descendant of the primitive inhabitants, is an *integral part of the landscape*, and as such he seizes the interest of the tourist for his garments, customs, music, and beliefs."[58] The meaning of "integral part of the landscape" is unequivocal: landscape and people cannot be separated. A visit to the Quebrada would not be complete without seeing the local population and their culture. The sounds and colors produced by traditional people enrich the landscape and increase its touristic value. The local people, on the other hand, can only be appreciated in their natural habitat. Only there do their customs, rituals, and garments become a source of attraction. As long as indigenous or

FIGURE 3 Under the title "Argentina: Country of Tourism," the cover of *Automovilismo* shows a stylish Argentine woman packing golf clubs in preparation for a trip to the Interior. On the superimposed picture, a peasant drives burros over one of the recently built mountain roads. Source: *Automovilismo* 18:228, Dec. 1938, n.p.

mestizo rural workers remained both traditional and attached to their land they would retain their picturesque condition.

The same tourist literature that constructed the local population as types and as part of the landscape also constructed the tourist as the curious, smart observer. These tourists were also imagined as white, modern, and middle- or upper-class. The cover of a 1939 issue of *Automovilismo* devoted to the Northwest features an illustration of a slender, well-groomed, ivory white, light-blonde young woman dressed in elegant winter clothes taking a suitcase out of a parked car. A whitewashed chapel stands in the background against the gentle contours of nearby mountains. The woman's Hollywoodesque air is consistent with images of women on other contemporary magazine covers as well as with advertising portraying Argentine travelers in the Interior. As a matter of fact, almost the exact same female image appears in advertising for a wide range of products, appealing perhaps to the perceived (or idealized) self-image of potential consumers. But in contrast to other advertisements that idealized their subjects, this particular cover image is both improbable (no dust, no appropriate clothes) and preposterously out of touch with the humility of the surroundings. But let us remember that, in the visual imagery of tourism literature, the tourist is there to relax and enjoy her vacation as well as to learn about the mysteries of deep Argentina. If we were to believe the travel literature accompanying those images, these urban creatures would return to the city entirely transformed and purified by the experience of contemplating the complex scenery of nature and people.

Although articles on travel in the Northwest and the Interior in general urged tourists to establish an empathic connection with the landscape and the local culture, they stopped short of establishing a principle of equality and reciprocity between locals and tourists. This discourse, in its visual and textual forms, constructed two kinds of subjects: one active and one passive. The active subject, the *turista argentino*, is urban, wealthy, worldly, curious, and educated, the one who observes and knows how to read the landscape. The passive subject, the "local type," is rural, traditional, simple, and noble if a bit diffident, the one who is being observed: a mere tourist attraction. To say that the former represents the modern and the latter the past is to state the obvious. What complicates this pairing of subjects is that while members of one group represented (in the language of Romantic nationalism) the "authentic Argentines," it was the members of the other group who were considered the "actual" Argentines.

Prevalent conceptions of race and ethnicity shaped the language of Argentine domestic tourism. In turn, the development of that industry helped modify (and reinforce) the myth of the white Argentina by including indigenous and mestizo peasants from the Interior into the narrative of the nation. Through the first half of the twentieth century the notion that Argentina was a white country, both culturally and biologically, proved resilient but evolved to accommodate the realization that a sizable part of the Argentine population was of non-European origin. This discursive adjustment, mostly promoted by Romantic-nationalist intellectuals but widely shared among different segments of the public sphere, continued to celebrate the markedly modern European outlook of the country, but created a niche for the descendants of the pre-immigration population. Rather than excluding this population, the modified myth of the white Argentina recognized in the criollos (notably, a term that avoids explicitly naming the group's nonwhiteness) the purveyors of the ancient spirit of the Argentine nation and linked them both to the epics of early national history and to the romanticized landscape of the vast Interior. Thus, while in symbolic terms indigenous and criollo Argentines moved to the center as archetypes of the nation, they remained in the geographical and temporal periphery. In the meantime, the dynamic center of modern Argentina continued to be occupied by the business and political elite: mainly, the European immigrants that arrived after 1870 and their Argentine-born children. As the promoters of internal tourism invited urban white Argentines to visit the criollo ancestral homelands, the country's racial/ethnic hierarchies were simultaneously revealed and reified. In Humahuaca, the Calchaquí Valley, or Córdoba, tourists looked at the dark-skinned peasants as frozen–in-time folk types that, together with whitewashed chapels and historical monuments, complemented the rugged landscape. This particular discourse reached maturity by the mid-1930s, in consonance with the construction of infrastructure that made the tourist experience possible. In an ironic reversal, however, the same infrastructure that brought tourists to the distant valleys also allowed dark-skinned rural criollos to migrate to the cities in search of better living conditions. Once there, out of their habitat and deprived of accessories such as ponchos or llamas, the criollos lost their picturesque appeal and became outsiders. Instead of being subjected to the curious gaze of the tourists, they have since had to withstand the disapproving stare of urban Argentines.

Notes

1. Pastoriza, *La conquista*; Fernández Balzano, *El turismo*; Schlüter, *El turismo*; Schlüter, *Áreas protegidas*; Ospital, "Turismo"; Getino, *Turismo*.
2. On the process of incorporation of the indigenous population into the Argentine nation, see Escolar, *Los dones*; Farberman and Ratto, *Historias mestizas*; Farberman and Gil Montero, *Los pueblos*; Lorandi, "Ni tradición," 108; Paz, "Campesinos"; Gordillo and Hirsch, "Indigenous Struggles," 4–30.
3. Briones, "Formaciones," 32–33.
4. Quijada, "Hijos," 469–510; Guano, "Color," 148–71.
5. Lomnitz-Adler, *Exits*, 39; Pérez Montfort, "Indigenismo," 343–83; Lehmann, "Gilberto Freyre," 208–17; Miller, *Rise and Fall*; Appelbaum et al., *Race and Nation*, 7–8; Stern, "Mestizophilia," 187–210.
6. Other "white nations" or regions included Uruguay, Chile, Southern Brazil, Costa Rica, the Cauca Valley in Colombia, and Arequipa in Perú. See Rama, "Hispanismo," 136–73; Appelbaum, *Muddied Waters*; Weinstein, "Racializing," 237–60; Andrews, *Blacks and Whites*; Andrews, *Blackness*.
7. Adamovsky, "La cuarta función," 50–92; Ludmer, *Gaucho Genre*; Prieto, *El discurso*.
8. Endere, *Management*.
9. For a discussion of this topic in current tourism see Logan, "Constructing," 405–31; Verdesio, "Invisible," 339–56.
10. Anreus, Linden, and Weinberg, *The Social*, xiii–xxii; Coffey, *Revolutionary Art*, 1–24.
11. Kirshenblatt-Gimblett, *Destination Culture*; Babb, *Tourism Encounter*; for the concept of place in Latin American studies, see Escobar, "Culture," 139–74.
12. References to the Patagonian lake district as the Argentine Switzerland appear in tourism articles from the 1920s and continue into Peronist school textbooks from the 1940s. "La región de los grandes lagos del Sur," *Automovilismo* (Buenos Aires) 123 (Feb. 1929), 61–62; García and Miralles, "Tierra," 203–25; Tabanera, "Organización," 480–82.
13. Reboratti, "Una visión," 37–39.
14. Kropff, "Debates," 83–99.
15. De Castro Esteves, "En pro," 585.
16. Löfgren, "Know your Country," 137–54.
17. Semmens, *Seeing*, 11.

18. Devoto, *Nacionalismo, fascismo*, 40–53; Rock, "Antecedents," 1–33; Zanatta, *Dallo stato*; Spektorowski, "Ideological Origins," 166–69.
19. For further discussion, see Chamosa, *Argentine Folklore*, 40–46.
20. Holmberg, "Investigación," 6–7.
21. The results of these voyages were often published in newspapers or popular magazines such as *Caras y Caretas* (Buenos Aires) as well as in scientific journals; eventually they were republished as books: Moreno, *Viaje*; Holmberg, *Viaje*; Payró, *Por tierras*; Ambrosetti, *Viaje*; Quiroga, *Calchaquí*; Zeballos, *Viaje*.
22. Castro, "Otras miradas."
23. Ballent and Gorelik, "País urbano," 143–200.
24. Juan Zocchi "Estética de las sierras de Córdoba," *La Nación* (Buenos Aires), 14 Feb. 1937.
25. Ospital, "Turismo."
26. Cited in *Automovilismo* 22:257 (May 1941), n.p.
27. Löfgren "Know your Country," 6–153.
28. Mario S. Ayala, "La Argentina empieza por dentro," *El Hogar* (Buenos Aires) 35:1537 (31 Mar. 1939), n.p.
29. Zocchi, "Estética," 3.
30. Ibid.
31. Celestina P. de Saint Antonin, "A orillas del Nahuel Huapi," *Automovilismo* 10:132 (Nov.–Dec. 1929), 99.
32. Delfina Bunge de Gálvez "La sierra cordobesa," *Automovilismo* 10:124 (Mar. 1929), 15–16.
33. Vignoli, "Formación," 45–68.
34. Villagrán, *Un héroe*, 74–76.
35. "Libros de Actas de la Comisión Nacional de Museos, Monumentos y Lugares Históricos," Buenos Aires, 23 May 1938 to 25 Sep. 1939. Archivo de la Comisión Nacional de Museos, Monumentos y Lugares Históricos.
36. Pastoriza, *La conquista*, 141–56.
37. "Es extraordinaria la afluencia de turistas a la tierra del sol," *Turismo* (Buenos Aires) 333 (Feb. 1937), 3; "El turismo del último verano representa más que una soberbia promesa, el principio de una hermosa realidad," *Turismo* 28:335 (Apr. 1937), 17.
38. "Vida Social de Tafí del Valle," *El Orden* (San Miguel de Tucumán), 27 Jan. 1927, 4.
39. *La Nación*, 18 Jul. 1937, 11.
40. For reference, monthly salaries in the public administration in the mid-1930s ranged from 200 pesos to 500 pesos. See Argentina, Leyes Nacionales, nos. 12295 a 12356, período parlamentario de 1936 y sesiones extraordinarias de 1937 (Buenos Aires, Imp. Bernabé y Cía, 1937), passim.
41. "Hacia el norte de la República," *Automovilismo* 18:221 (May 1938), n.p.
42. "El turismo a las provincias del Norte Argentino," *Automovilismo* 17:208 (Mar. 1937), n.p.
43. "A través del norte Argentino en viaje de turismo," *Automovilismo* 19:399 (Sep. 1939), n.p.
44. Saragoza, "The Selling," 93–95; Zolov, "Discovering," 234–52.
45. Löfgren, *On Holiday*, 103–5; Edwards, "Postcards," 197–21; Dann, "The People," 61–81.
46. Hale, *Races on Display*.

47. Payró, "La Pintura," 131–98; Forn, "La construcción," 9–17.
48. Forn, "La construcción," 7.
49. On the influence of Mexican muralism in Argentina see Anreus, "Siqueiros' Travels," 177–95.
50. Cariou, *L'Aventure*; Wigmore, *American*, 3.
51. See as an example Gramajo Gutiérrez's "Un velorio de angelito."
52. "Artistas Tucumanos que triunfan en el mundo: Juan Carlos Iramain," *El Orden*, 16 Mar. 1929, 1.
53. "Tipos y costumbres del Norte," *Automovilismo* 22:254 (May 1941), n.p.
54. The same article mentions in a different section that travel across the mountain roads is an opportunity to observe the skillfulness of the "tipos regionales" in riding their mules on the mountain paths. "La Provincia de Catamarca brinda múltiples atractivos al turista," *Automovilismo* 19:234 (Jun. 1939), n.p.
55. "Tucumán Jardín de la Republica," *Automovilismo* 18:223 (Jul. 1938), n.p.
56. "El turismo a las provincias del Norte Argentino," *Automovilismo* 17:208 (Mar. 1937), n.p.
57. In 1939 another article emphasized the spectacle of the workers arriving to the zafra with their diverse costumes and dresses. "Tucumán: Una de las regiones más bellas del Norte Argentino," *Automovilismo* 19:235 (Jul. 1939), n.p. Finally, a 1940 article highlights the preoccupation of the mill owners with the well-being of their workers. "La industria azucarera en la provincia de Tucumán," *Automovilismo* 21:247 (Jul. 1940), 13–15.
58. Sánchez de Bustamante, "Ponencia," 649; italics mine.

3

Black in Buenos Aires

The transnational career of Oscar Alemán

Matthew B. Karush

In 1973, the African American magazine *Ebony* sent its international editor, Era Bell Thompson, to Buenos Aires to do a feature on Argentina's tiny black community. Although Afro-Argentines represented nearly one third of the population of colonial Buenos Aires, they had since virtually disappeared from official records. Miscegenation, war, and disease contributed to this demographic decline, but as historian George Reid Andrews showed many years ago, the invisibility of Afro-Argentines was at least as much the product of racism and of the hegemonic idea of Argentina as a white nation.[1] For the *Ebony* article, "Argentina: Land of the Vanishing Blacks," Thompson interviewed every self-identifying Afro-Argentine she could find. Among them was Oscar Marcelo Alemán, a jazz guitarist who had enjoyed substantial fame and commercial success in Paris in the 1930s and in Buenos Aires during the 1940s and 1950s. By the time Thompson met him, Alemán had recently been rediscovered by Argentine jazz aficionados after a decade in obscurity, during which he had supported himself by giving guitar lessons in his home. Although he told Thompson that he was the son of a Spanish father and an Indian mother, Alemán insisted on his blackness: "'Some of my six brothers are even darker than I,' he smiled, 'we think there was a black man somewhere.'"[2]

Throughout his long career, audiences both at home and abroad perceived Alemán as a black man, a perception that was made possible by his dark complexion and his own avowal of a black identity, but also by his association with jazz music. Nevertheless, the precise meanings that attached to his blackness changed over the years. This chapter will trace the vicissitudes of his career while reconstructing the shifting discursive landscape within which that career developed. Alemán was a talented musician who played the music he loved, but as with any artist, both his musical creations and the popular reception of those creations were shaped by the world in which he lived. Alemán responded creatively to his audiences' varied racial expectations, performing multiple black identities over the years. In the Parisian nightclubs of the 1930s, being black gave him a certain cachet. Similarly, once he returned to Buenos Aires in 1940, his racial identity strengthened his claim to being Argentina's most authentic jazz musician. Yet as a black jazz musician, he challenged ideas about Argentine national identity in ways that ultimately limited his career horizons.

Alemán's artistic production as well as his commercial successes and failures illuminate the transnational construction of blackness in the middle decades of the twentieth century and complicate our understanding of race in Argentina. Scholars have generally interpreted Argentine racism as a byproduct of the desire to join the modern, civilized world.[3] Yet Alemán's career demonstrates that other transnational forces were also at work. Under the influence of North American jazz and French "negrophilia," Argentines were powerfully drawn to blackness as an emblem of modernity. Alemán's reception in his own country was shaped by local appropriations and re-workings of these transnational discourses as well as by Argentine attitudes toward Brazil, where the guitarist had spent many of his formative years. Anthropologist Alejandro Frigerio has argued convincingly that Argentina's self-image as a white nation is premised on the active denial of phenotypic evidence of African ancestry and the firm association of blackness with foreignness. In this way, Afro-Argentines are located in the nation's past and rendered invisible in the present.[4] Yet at the same time, the ambiguous status of blackness in Argentina created space for Alemán to re-invent himself as an attractive exotic in his own country. By developing an exciting and entertaining musical style and by navigating these complex racial discourses, Alemán became a star for two decades in a country thought to be averse to any reminders of its own blackness.

BEGINNINGS: *CRIOLLISMO* AND EXOTICISM

Oscar Alemán was born in 1909 in the remote province of Chaco in North-eastern Argentina. As a child, he performed alongside his father and siblings in the so-called Moreira Sextet, a music and dance troupe that specialized in the traditions known collectively as *criollismo*.[5] The dominant trend in Argentine popular culture during the first two decades of the twentieth century, criollismo involved the celebration of the nation's rural traditions. During this period of massive immigration and rapid modernization, native Argentines looked back nostalgically to the culture of the legendary *gauchos*, brave and violent cowboy figures who roamed the vast *pampas*, or plains, outside Buenos Aires. At the same time, many foreign-born newcomers also embraced these cultural practices as a means to assimilate. Both groups were likely to read the pulp fiction that narrated the heroics of gaucho rebels, to join criollista clubs, and to attend the criollo circus, where gauchos performed equestrian feats. Although Alemán never explained why his father, the Uruguayan-born Jorge Alemán Moreira, used his maternal surname for the family group, it was likely a strategic choice. While "Alemán" sounded foreign, "Moreira" would have reminded audiences

FIGURE 4 Photograph of the Moreira Sextet, 1917. Source: *Crisis*, Jan. 1975, 30.

of the most popular literary gaucho of the period, Juan Moreira, whose exploits were first described by Eduardo Gutiérrez in a pulp serial published between 1878 and 1880 before becoming a staple of criollista literature and theater.[6] Alemán's father chose the group's name, its costumes, and its repertoire with an eye toward cashing in on the popular craze for gaucho traditionalism.

At the age of five or six, Oscar accompanied his family to Buenos Aires, where they performed at two well-known venues, the Teatro Nuevo in Luna Park and the Parque Japonés. Oscar specialized in dancing the *malambo*, the stiff-backed, stamping dance performed by gauchos in head-to-head competitions. A 1917 photograph shows him dressed in an elaborate gaucho costume, dancing with his sister while his father sits behind them strumming a guitar. The photograph leaves little doubt that audiences would have seen the two children as Argentines of African descent. With his dark complexion and traditional costume, Oscar embodied a well-known criollo type: the black gaucho. Blacks were quite visible in the culture of criollismo, particularly as competitors in *payadas*, the improvisatory rhyming duels waged by gaucho guitarists. Criollista literature, such as José Hernández's celebrated epic, *Martín Fierro*, had prominently featured black gauchos, and many of the most famous real-life payadores were Afro-Argentine. Despite the endemic racism of the period, blacks were recognized as authentic participants in the native, rural culture of Argentina.[7] Within the racial codes of criollismo, then, Alemán's blackness served the Moreira Sextet's effort to depict itself as an authentic gaucho troupe. For very pragmatic reasons, Oscar Alemán began his performing career with an unequivocally racialized persona.

From Buenos Aires, the Alemáns took their act to Brazil, where Jorge also hoped to make money in the cotton trade. Business did not go well, and when word came of the death of Oscar's mother, who had stayed behind in Buenos Aires, the family fell apart. After his father's suicide, the ten-year-old Oscar found himself alone in the port city of Santos in Southern Brazil. While making a living opening car doors for tips, he taught himself how to play the *cavaquinho*, the small, four-string guitar used in Brazilian *samba* and *choro*. By 1924, Alemán was performing on cavaquinho at a Santos hotel when he was discovered by a Brazilian guitarist named Gastão Bueno Lobo. Lobo and Alemán formed a duo called Les Loups, a name created by translating Lobo's last name into French. Although the duo's repertoire was varied, Les Loups specialized in what was known as Hawaiian guitar. In other words, they offered popular songs from a range of different genres, in instrumental versions that featured a guitar played flat on the performer's lap and fretted with a metal slide. Although Alemán later claimed that he and his partner traded roles, Lobo, who had apparently visited Hawaii years earlier, was the Hawaiian guitar specialist, while Alemán typically accompanied him on *guitarra criolla* – "native" or Spanish-style guitar. The duo performed on the radio and on stage in Rio de Janeiro and elsewhere in Brazil before traveling to Buenos Aires in 1927 as part of a variety troupe led by the Argentine comedian Pablo Palitos.[8]

Over the course of a decade in Brazil, Oscar Alemán had become a professional guitarist, specializing in music that was quite different from the criollismo of his childhood. In the process, he shed one racial persona in favor of another. In Argentina, Les Loups were marketed as an exotic import. The duo was a big enough hit to receive a contract from Victor, the North American multinational record company whose Argentine branch specialized in recording local tango bands.[9] In Les Loups' official photograph for Victor, Alemán and Lobo appear seated, dressed in white suits with neckties and fancy shoes. Alemán fingers a chord on his guitar, while Lobo holds his flat on his lap, Hawaiian-style. To signal the duo's musical identity, each of the two musicians has a *lei* around his neck. The popular music magazine *La Canción Moderna* printed the photo under the headline "Bewitching Guitars [*Guitarras brujas*]" along with a notice describing Les Loups as a "notable duo of Hawaiian guitar soloists, marvelous interpreters of popular regional music."[10] The magazine did not mention the musicians' racial or national origins, and there was no hint that Alemán was a native son. On the contrary, the leis, combined with the group's French name and Alemán's dark skin (in the photo, he appears much darker than Lobo) suggested a vague exoticism. In 1917, Alemán's blackness had reinforced the Moreira Sextet's claims to Argentine authenticity within the criollista idiom. A decade later, he might still be read as black, but instead of dressing as a gaucho and dancing the malambo, he wore a lei and performed in a Hawaiian guitar duo. In this context, his phenotype now accentuated his exoticism.

FIGURE 5 Photograph of Les Loups. Source: *La Canción Moderna* 1:6, 30 Apr. 1928, n.p.

The music of Les Loups was part of an international fad. Sparked by the hit Broadway musical *Bird of Paradise* (1911), as well as by the appearance of Hawaiian musicians at the Panama-Pacific International Exposition in San Francisco in 1915, a Hawaiian music craze swept the United States. Tin Pan Alley publishers produced hundreds of songs with Hawaiian themes, while companies like Edison, Columbia, and Victor rushed to record Hawaiian musicians playing ukuleles and lap steel guitar for the mainland market.[11] Although the Hawaiian music fad waned in the 1920s, the sound of the lap steel guitar proved easy to assimilate into other genres. While some Hawaiian artists continued to record and perform throughout Europe and the United States, the slide guitar was widely adopted by North American musicians specializing in blues, country, and jazz.[12] In order to situate Les Loups within the Argentine record market, it is also important to remember that genre boundaries were less tightly policed in the 1920s than they would be later.

Argentine tango bands played fox-trots and "shimmies" in order to please audiences who wanted to dance to the latest North American rhythms, and visiting jazz bands often repaid the favor by playing tangos. In this context, Les Loups' Hawaiian records represented the application of a recognizably exotic sound (slide guitar) and look (white suits, leis) to familiar musical genres.

Between December 1927 and December 1928, Les Loups recorded nine two-sided records for Victor. The following year, the record company added the tango violinist Elvino Vardaro, named the group the Trio Victor, and cut six more sides. Taken together, these records feature ten tangos, ten waltzes, and four fox-trots.[13] All of the records are built around Lobo's Hawaiian-style slide guitar or Vardaro's violin, relegating Alemán to the role of accompanist. In the absence of any other instruments, the job of maintaining rhythmic propulsion falls to Alemán, and he responds with regular, somewhat stiffly strummed chords. At the end of each phrase, however, Alemán typically plays a single note run that intertwines with Lobo's melody.

Alemán's own accounts of his musical development during this period are vague, but close listening reveals several possible sources of influence. On the waltz "La criollita," Alemán plays improvised bass lines that are reminiscent of the approach of the Brazilian string ensembles that specialized in choro music.[14] Another possible indication of Brazilian influence is the fact that unlike most North American jazz guitarists, Alemán played without a plectrum. As a result, he could maintain a simple bass line with his right thumb while using his other fingers to pick out single notes. But even if Alemán's playing on these early records shows signs of Brazilian influence, his approach is also comparable to that of tango guitarists like the Afro-Argentine José Ricardo, Carlos Gardel's long-time accompanist, or even that of the jazz guitar pioneer Eddie Lang, whom Alemán would later cite as an influence. These stylistic similarities reveal the broad overlap among choro, tango, and jazz, musical genres that are too often seen as discrete, unrelated traditions. Thanks to the development of the radio and to the worldwide reach of multinational recording companies like Victor, the globalization of popular music was well underway in the 1920s. This transnational cross-pollination is evident in Les Loups' varied repertoire. In 1927, the Paul Whiteman jazz orchestra's recording of "In a Little Spanish Town" (Wayne) spent 15 weeks at number one on the North American Billboard chart and was number 21 in Brazil.[15] The following May, Les Loups recorded it as the b-side to a tango composed by Lobo. Thus, a North American pop tune meant to evoke a quaint Spanish village gained a South American audience and was re-recorded by an Argentine/Brazilian duo featuring Hawaiian slide guitar. While jazz, tango, and choro cannot be considered exclusively black genres – Paul Whiteman, Eddie Lang, and most tango musicians were white – they were all associated with blackness in the popular imagination.[16] Alemán's racial appearance, so useful as an indicator of his exoticism, made sense in musical terms as well.

BLACK GUITARIST: JAZZ STARDOM IN PARIS

In late 1928, Harry Flemming, a black tap dancer from the Danish Virgin Islands then on a South American tour, heard Les Loups in a Buenos Aires nightclub and asked the duo to join his show. Lobo and Alemán accepted the invitation, performing their Hawaiian guitar repertoire as part of Flemming's "Hello Jazz" revue at Montevideo's Teatro 18 de Julio in January 1929. The next month, Flemming and his troupe left for an extensive tour of Europe, and with them were Les Loups. Although Lobo and Alemán split up after two years, Alemán remained in Europe for more than a decade after the tour. Based primarily in Paris, he worked regularly in the touring and recording band of the legendary African American performer Josephine Baker, played alongside dozens of other well-known North American and European jazz musicians, and honed his guitar technique. By the end of the 1930s, he was an accomplished player with a recognizable, hard-swinging style of improvisation. When the Nazi invasion of France made life increasingly difficult for him, Alemán returned to Buenos Aires, where he was celebrated as Argentina's most famous and most authentic jazz musician.

During his years in Europe, Alemán's blackness was reconfigured once more. Arriving several years after the *tumulte noir* that overtook the continent in the 1920s, Alemán's racial appearance conferred a certain legitimacy that his Argentine origins could not. No longer an indication of a rural Argentine "criollismo" nor of a vague, tropical exoticism, his blackness now resonated with cosmopolitan images of jazz modernity.

By the time Alemán arrived in Europe, black musicians were not the novelty they had once been. African American performers had danced the cakewalk in Paris as early as 1902, but it was World War I that incited a new French fascination for blackness by bringing thousands of black soldiers to the continent. James Reese Europe's Harlem Hellfighters regimental band achieved enormous popularity performing a mixture of classical music, minstrel tunes, and early jazz throughout France in 1918. Other African American groups soon followed, including Will Marion Cook's Southern Syncopated Orchestra, eliciting an enthusiastic response on tours of Britain and France. The fascination of Picasso and other modernists with African sculpture and masks had prepared the Parisian avant-garde to embrace jazz as an expression of an essential blackness. Between 1918 and 1925, "negrophilia" was, in Bernard Gendron's words, "the most widespread fashion movement in Parisian cultural life."[17]

Unlike belly dancing and tango, two of the most popular Parisian fads of the 1910s, jazz eventually lost its association with exotic spectacle and thereby achieved a more enduring place in French popular culture. At first, jazz had been criticized as an alien import threatening French tradition. Particularly problematic was the widespread notion that only black (and therefore foreign) musicians could play the music well. But beginning in the late 1920s, several

French musicians gained acceptance as jazz musicians. This trend culminated with the founding in 1932 of the musical appreciation society called the Hot Club de France and its sponsorship two years later of a new quintet led by gypsy guitarist Django Reinhardt and featuring only French musicians. While jazz retained its associations with blackness, the idea of French jazz was no longer oxymoronic.[18]

At the same time, French audiences developed a more nuanced understanding of blackness itself. In particular, Josephine Baker, France's most iconic black performer, engineered a rather dramatic transformation of her public image. Although Baker's initial appeal lay in her performance of primitive, black sexuality, she was also figured as an emblem of modernity. This duality reflected the attitudes of French avant-gardists, for whom jazz represented both African primitivism and cutting-edge modernism. The famous images of Baker created by poster artist Paul Colin explicitly linked her erotic blackness to modern skyscrapers and Art Deco design. By 1930, Baker had abandoned the banana skirt and crafted a much more sophisticated, high-fashion image. Starring in advertisements for skin lotion, hair pomade, and cigarettes, Baker was figured as the epitome of the modern woman. In her movement from savagery to refinement, Baker seemed to enact the civilizing mission of France's colonial project.[19] In any case, by 1931, when Oscar Alemán arrived in Paris to join her band, French audiences were accustomed to thinking of jazz music and of black musicians as both sophisticated and ultra-modern.

While discussions of jazz in Europe often depict it as an instance of bilateral cultural exchange, the jazz milieu of the 1920s and 1930s is more accurately seen as a broader Atlantic World phenomenon.[20] Jazz traveled along circuits forged by the Argentine tango and the Brazilian *maxixe*, which had aroused North American and European enthusiasm during the 1910s. It was not a coincidence that one of the first magazines dedicated to promoting jazz in France was called *Jazz-Tango*.[21] Since the first Paul Whiteman records had become available in Buenos Aires in 1918, jazz had attracted South American fans and musicians. During the 1920s, Brazilian bands that specialized in choro and maxixe also played jazz, as did the leading Argentine tango bands. Moreover, Parisians in the grip of negrophilia did not limit their consumption of blackness to its North American variants. The legendary Brazilian band Oito Batutas, led by the samba pioneer Pixinguinha, enjoyed a six-month stay in Paris in 1922, earning enough acclaim to significantly improve its reputation back home.[22] Likewise, many of the African American jazz musicians who performed in Europe also toured Brazil and Argentina. Violinist and clarinetist Paul Wyer, a pool shark known as "the Pensacola Kid," played in W.C. Handy's Memphis Blues Band in the 1910s before touring England and France as a member of the Southern Syncopated Orchestra and several other jazz bands. In 1923, he traveled to Buenos Aires, performing in both the Argentine capital and in Rio de Janeiro. He would remain in Argentina for the rest of his life, leading several outfits including the Dixie Pals, whose long residency at the swank Alvear Palace Hotel made it one of the most prominent Argentine jazz bands of the 1930s.[23] And Wyer was not alone. The Philadelphia-born pianist Sam Wooding first toured Europe in 1925 as the leader of the pit band for a revue called *The Chocolate Kiddies*. Wooding's band played throughout Argentina for six months in 1927, igniting the enthusiasm of Argentine jazz fans anxious to get their first look at an authentic band composed entirely of African Americans. Two years later, Josephine Baker herself brought her scandalous version of jazz performance to Buenos Aires and Rio de Janeiro.[24]

As a member of a Hawaiian guitar duo, Oscar Alemán was already a part of this transnational jazz scene. The duo's recordings of fox-trots, as well as its inclusion in a revue called *Hello Jazz*, suggest that jazz's various associations – as modern, cosmopolitan, and black – also attached to Les Loups. After Alemán moved to Europe, these associations only deepened. Unlike in South America, European advertisements for Harry Flemming's *Hello Jazz* foregrounded race, announcing that the troupe was composed of "whites and blacks."[25] In the revue's European sojourn, which included stops in France, Belgium, and Italy, as well as an extensive tour of Spain, jazz took on greater prominence. Flemming hired European and North American jazz musicians, including trumpeter Robert De Kers and trombonist Jules Testaert, both from Belgium, as well as saxophonist Ray Butler, and formed a jazz band called Flemming's Bluebirds specializing in "real North American music." In Spain, they shared a bill with Sam Wooding's band, now back in Europe.[26] Alemán was still not playing jazz music – at least not in public – but he was closely connected to the world of jazz.

Alemán became a jazz musician in 1931 when he left Les Loups and joined Josephine Baker's newly formed band, the 16 Baker Boys. Robert De Kers and Jules Testaert were members of the new band, and it was likely they who recommended the Argentine guitarist to Baker. But Alemán's South American roots, and particularly his Brazilian background, were also helpful. Baker had established enduring ties with Brazilian musicians during her 1929 visit. In particular, she was a fan of Romeu Silva's Jazz-Band Sul-Americano. Silva's group emulated the classy and refined sound of Paul Whiteman's orchestra, recording sambas, maxixes, tangos, and foxtrots for Odeon in the 1920s. Silva spent much of the late 1920s and early 1930s touring Europe, performing alongside Baker at the Casino in 1931. When Baker returned to the studio for Columbia Records in 1931 and 1932, she enlarged her backing group with several Brazilian members of the Jazz-Band Sul-Americano: Romeu Silva on tenor sax, Luis Lopes da Silva on bass sax, and the drummer Bibi Miranda. The guitarist on these recording sessions was Oscar Alemán.[27] Led by an African American singer and composed of a mixture of Europeans and South Americans, Baker's recording band was a microcosm of the transatlantic jazz world; as a capable player who had lived for years in Brazil and therefore spoke Portuguese, Alemán fit right in.

Alemán's ascent within the Parisian music scene was rapid. He immediately became an integral part of Baker's touring band. In addition to his jazz guitar work, he sang in Portuguese, French, and Spanish, played the *pandeiro* (a Brazilian tambourine) and the cavaquinho, danced rumba, and occasionally played Hawaiian guitar. Despite his inability to read music, Alemán even served for a while as the band's musical director. On stage, he was often a comic presence; one photograph shows him imitating Baker herself, wearing skimpy briefs, spangled gloves, an elaborate headdress and women's dancing shoes. When he was not touring with Baker, Alemán gained steady work as a studio musician, sideman, and bandleader, and by 1935 he was, along with Django Reinhardt, one of the two most prominent guitarists on the Parisian jazz scene.[28]

European audiences saw Alemán as a person of African descent. Charles Delaunay, the long-time leader of the Hot Club de France, described the Argentine guitarist in overtly racialized terms: "Oscar was a small *bonhomme* with copper-colored skin – a *métisse* [sic], as we said – sharp and quick as a monkey, always ready for a joke."[29] On a tour of Rome, some audience members refused to let Alemán go on because they took him for an Ethiopian.[30] For his part, Alemán loudly objected to any hint of racism. Once the Italian fans had been convinced of Alemán's national origins, the guitarist honored the terms of his contract, but he refused to play any encores. An anecdote told by North American trumpeter Bill Coleman is even more revealing. Alemán had a regular gig for a while playing in Coleman's band at a Parisian nightclub called the Villa d'Este. According to Coleman, the French heavyweight boxer Georges Carpentier, a regular visitor to the club, used to call Alemán "little monkey" in English. The guitarist did not speak English, but he eventually asked his bandmates what the word meant. The next time Carpentier came by the club, Alemán shouted out from the bandstand, "Hello Georges Carpentier, you big white monkey!"[31] That Alemán felt free to respond so confrontationally illuminates both his personality and the racial context that shaped his life in France. Like the many African American jazz musicians who chose to live and work in Paris during the interwar years, Alemán was able to take advantage of the relative freedom afforded by French negrophilia.[32]

Within European jazz circles, Alemán's blackness could be an asset. According to one anecdote, Duke Ellington visited Josephine Baker in Paris and asked to meet Alemán, about whom he had heard great things. Impressed with the guitarist's chops, he invited Alemán to tour the United States as a soloist with the Ellington band. Baker, however, refused to part with Alemán, explaining that it would be impossible to replace a guitarist who could also sing and dance and for whom she had had seven suits and pairs of shoes custom made. But her final argument was the most telling: any replacement for Alemán would have to be black.[33] Alemán was often the only black member of Baker's band, and she valued him in part for helping her satisfy her audience's desire for jazz authenticity, which it associated with blackness. Similarly, a poster for a

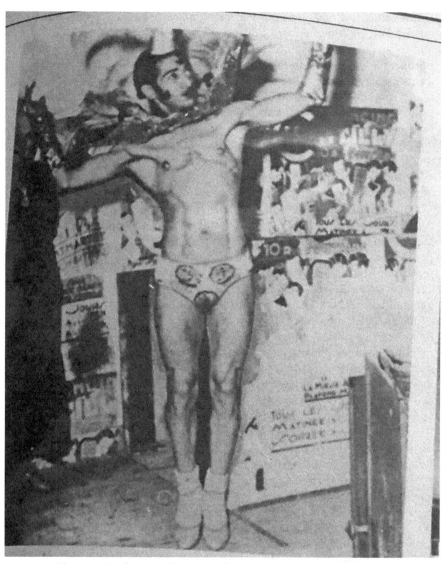

FIGURE 6 Photograph of Oscar Alemán performing in Josephine Baker's stage show. Source: *Crisis*, Jan. 1975, 31.

1939 Dutch jazz festival featuring Alemán billed him as "the extraordinary black guitarist," while an announcement in a local magazine explained the relevance of race: "he will bring the authentic element, being the only black man at the Jazzwereldfeest."[34] Interestingly, North American and British observers, for whom an Argentine jazz guitarist was much more of an anomaly than a black one, did not often remark on Alemán's blackness. For example, the famous British critic Leonard Feather, a great admirer of Alemán, referred to him as an "Argentinian Indian."[35] But in France and in much of the rest of Europe, the modernity and excitement of jazz was still deeply connected to its status as black music. In that context, Alemán's dark skin conferred prestige. Of course, in France Alemán's blackness also underscored his foreignness. Despite being seen as an authentic black guitarist, he did not enjoy the sponsorship that the Hot Club de France conferred on Django Reinhardt, who despite his gypsy origins could be depicted as the hero of French jazz. According to Reinhardt's biographer, this sponsorship enabled him to record hundreds of sides and helps explain why the legendary gypsy guitarist has eclipsed his now obscure Argentine rival in jazz history.[36]

Like Reinhardt, Alemán developed a guitar style that was not steeped in African American blues, typically considered the wellspring of jazz. Neither guitarist played with the behind-the-beat, relaxed feel and blues tonalities of Eddie Lang, the Italian American who performed on countless jazz and blues records in the 1920s and early 1930s.[37] Yet Alemán was no Django copy. Unlike Reinhardt, who famously played a Selmer Maccaferri, Alemán preferred a metal-bodied, National tricone resonator guitar (visible in Fig. 7), which had a much heavier, almost electric tone. More interesting are the stylistic contrasts. As an accompanist, Alemán often combined chords with single-note ostinatos reminiscent of his playing in Les Loups, while Reinhardt preferred the percussive, up-and-down strum known as *la pompe*. Alemán's solos tended to be more restrained and perhaps more thought out than those of Reinhardt, who was given to displays of reckless virtuosity and seemingly spontaneous improvisation. It is tempting to attribute these differences to genealogy: whereas Reinhardt applied gypsy melodies and styles to jazz, Alemán must have drawn on Brazilian and Argentine traditions.[38] Without ruling out those influences, I would argue that other factors were more decisive. Alemán was an entertainer before he was a jazz guitarist, and he developed his style over the course of a career dedicated to showmanship. The Josephine Baker show was long on crowd appeal and short on jazz virtuosity. Bill Coleman's account of his Villa d'Este stand with Alemán makes it clear that customers came to the club not to sit and listen, but to dance.[39] Meanwhile, as a sideman on jazz recordings, Alemán had developed the ability to express a complete musical idea over the course of a short solo.

These influences are apparent in the handful of sides Alemán recorded in 1938 and 1939, his only sessions as a front man during his European phase. Inspired by the success Reinhardt had enjoyed with the jazz standard "Limehouse Blues," Alemán recorded the tune with a sextet including the Brazilian drummer Bibi Miranda and the Danish violinist Svend Asmussen. Unlike the Reinhardt version, in which the guitarist solos with his usual joyful virtuosity, Alemán's take on the song seems built for dancing. The track opens with a brief, heavily syncopated drum break from Miranda, signaling the group's

FIGURE 7 Photograph of Oscar Alemán with Josephine Baker. Source: *Sintonía*, 25 Nov. 1942, n.p.

emphasis on rhythm. Alemán's solo never ventures far from the melody; instead, he focuses on clever ornamentation and rhythmic play, offering short repeated phrases, quick runs, and sustained notes struck with heavy vibrato. The result is a deeply swinging feel and a fun, extremely danceable record. Given his appearance and given the racial expectations of his European audiences, Alemán probably *sounded* black, but this was a blackness that did not express itself via the serious melodrama of the blues. Instead, Alemán's guitar style was forged in the light popular entertainment of the music revues.

LOSING THE JAZZ WARS: RACE AND THE RISE OF BEBOP IN BUENOS AIRES

Alemán returned to Buenos Aires shortly after the Nazis occupied France in May 1940. In his hurried departure he left most of his possessions behind, and his two metal-bodied National guitars were confiscated at the border to be melted down and used for the German war effort. Still, he brought something far more valuable from his decade in Europe: a reputation as a jazz guitarist who had earned commercial success and critical acclaim in Paris. Welcoming him home as a national hero, one local jazz magazine declared him "the most famous Argentine musician in the world of jazz" and marveled that "an Argentine is, on his instrument, one of the greatest practitioners in the world."[40] The jazz columnist for the music magazine *Sintonía* could not contain his astonishment: "It is difficult to believe that a phenomenon like that represented by Oscar Alemán could occur among us."[41] Alemán quickly translated his reputation into paying work. By May 1941, he had formed a new quintet with Argentine jazz musicians and was performing at Gong, a Buenos Aires [or *porteño*] nightclub.[42] In October, his quintet played a major concert at the Teatro Casino and began appearing twice weekly on Radio Belgrano, the city's most popular radio station.[43] The following month, Alemán signed a contract with Odeon Records and recorded the first of dozens of sides that he would record for the company over the next two decades. Alemán remained a significant presence in the porteño entertainment world until the late 1950s: throughout this period, his groups enjoyed regular nightclub and radio gigs and toured Chile, Brazil, and Uruguay. But if Alemán was celebrated as an Argentine jazz musician, he was also seen as a black man, and for local critics, his blackness was closely articulated with a particular version of jazz, one that gradually fell out of favor as time passed. In this way, race imposed clear constraints on Alemán's Argentine career.

Despite some significant overlap, the meanings that attached to jazz in Argentina were different from those that accompanied the music in France. Argentines were not immune to negrophilia: local critics had responded to Josephine Baker's visit in 1929 with the same mixture of condescension and awe as their French counterparts.[44] But black musicians remained far less numerous and therefore far more exotic in Buenos Aires than in Paris. With a handful of exceptions, such as Paul Wyer and the saxophonist and clarinetist Booker Pittman, who was a major presence on the local scene in the late 1930s and early 1940s, most jazz musicians in Buenos Aires were white Argentines. Jazz was extremely popular both on the radio and on the dance floors, but it was always a distant second to tango, which reigned supreme throughout the 1940s. In 1941, jazz accounted for 18% of the music programs heard on porteño radio stations, a substantial portion but a far cry from the 52% dedicated to tango.[45] Given the well-known popularity of jazz in the United States and Europe, Argentines perceived the genre as the sonic expression of modernity itself. Yet no Argentine jazz band could ever express Argentine national identity in the way that Django Reinhardt's Quintette du Hot Club de France could express Frenchness.

As a black Argentine jazz musician, Alemán challenged the categories through which Argentines understood jazz. Nevertheless, he could not single-handedly nationalize the music. In fact, his association with the genre occasionally put him at odds with Argentine nationalism. At one concert in 1943, Alemán was about to take the stage after a succession of tango bands, only to find that the master of ceremonies, the self-proclaimed "defender of tango" Julio Jorge Nelson, refused to announce him.[46] More seriously, Alemán sometimes had difficulty navigating the intense nationalism of the Juan D. Perón regime (1946–55). Asked at the last minute to perform at an official event at which the president and first lady were to speak, Alemán, no fan of the government, recognized that he had little choice but to accept the invitation. But when he showed up with his quintet, he was told that President Perón did not want to hear any North American music. Alemán managed to avoid sanction by playing "Caminos Cruzados," a song by the Cuban composer Ernesto Lecuona. It may not have been Argentine music, but at least it avoided the taint of imperialism.[47] For the most part, Alemán did not face official harassment, but as a jazz musician in Argentina he played a foreign music.

Although Alemán's association with jazz sometimes called his Argentine identity into question, his blackness was initially a boon to his jazz career, just as it had been in Paris. In fact, Alemán's reception in Argentina was decisively shaped by the fact that local jazz fans and critics saw the music through the lens of race.[48] During the 1920s, the Argentine media used stereotypical images of blackness to mark jazz as exotic. Local jazz bands often painted caricatures of smiling black people on their bass drums, while fan magazines illustrated their jazz coverage with cartoons of thick-lipped, dark-skinned, and carefree musicians.[49] In the 1930s, the growing international prominence of African American musicians and bandleaders reshaped the way jazz was understood in Argentina. The immense talents and professional self-presentation of musicians like Louis Armstrong, Duke Ellington, Coleman Hawkins, and Fletcher Henderson demanded a more complex response than simple exoticism. Yet even when they raved about the musical innovations of African American jazz musicians, Argentine critics and commentators rarely failed to mention their race. In one typical issue of *Sintonía*, the magazine's jazz writers referred to "the black trumpeter and singer Luis [sic] Armstrong," hailed Ellington as "the first figure of black jazz," and noted that the latest recording by the Fletcher Henderson Orchestra had "all the characteristics of black 'swings' [sic]."[50] These writers considered black musicians as a category apart, treating "black jazz" and "white jazz" as two distinct genres.

From the moment he returned to Argentina, Alemán was inserted into this racialized discourse; his blackness was both obvious and obviously relevant. In 1941, Argentine jazz guitarist Jorge Curutchet published an overview of the major practitioners of the instrument for a local jazz magazine. As was typical in such articles, Curutchet divided the world's jazz guitarists into black ones and white ones, insisting that the latter "cultivate a very different style." Alemán, "an Argentine guitarist with phenomenal technique and good jazz ideas," was the last guitarist Curutchet listed in the black category.[51] Five years later, Alemán provided the musical accompaniment for a recital of poetry by black authors from throughout the Americas. The racial essentialism that characterized press descriptions of the event make it clear that Alemán was chosen at least in part for his blackness:

How the throats of black people heat up with their songs of pain and hope! What a feeling of palm trees and cotton, sensuality and mysticism strangely married . . .What anxious happiness, what rhythmic sadness . . . That atmosphere erupted in the Empire Theater during the recital of black music and poetry offered by the actress Lisa Marchev – immense eyes, voice of the jungle – and the world famous artist of color Oscar Alemán.

Asked by the reporter about his rapport with Marchev, Alemán commented that blacks and Jews have historically faced similar mistreatment. "Meanwhile," he went on, "black people sing . . . I am not a politician. I am black. And all of the black people of the world can be in my beat [*pueden estar en mi tam-tam*] and in the . . . mouth of Lisa Marchev."[52] Reports like these highlighted Alemán's blackness as well as the spirituality, intensity of emotion, and rhythmic expertise that were stereotypically associated with it.

Alongside his commercial and critical success in Europe, Alemán's blackness gave him instant jazz credibility. At the same time, the inverse was also true: it was his association with jazz that made his blackness so visible. This becomes apparent if we compare Alemán's reception in Argentina with that of another prominent musician of ostensibly African descent, the tango pianist and bandleader Horacio Salgán.[53] Beginning in the mid-1940s, Salgán's tango band was a fixture on porteño dance floors and on the radio. In 1952, when his band replaced Alemán's as the main attraction on Radio Belgrano's "Brilliant Rhythms" program, the two musicians appeared together in a photograph published in *Antena* magazine. The accompanying note referred to Salgán as "an authentic value of our popular music," but did not mention his race.[54] This silence was typical of coverage of Salgán in the popular press of the 1940s and

FIGURE 8 Photograph of Oscar Alemán (on the left) shaking hands with Horacio Salgán. Source: *Antena*, 2 Dec. 1952, n.p.

1950s: unlike Alemán, the pianist was never described as black. The two musicians were friends, and it does appear that Alemán saw Salgán as black. In an interview conducted in 1975, Alemán's praise for the pianist included a subtle allusion to race: "he has that rhythm that is born inside one."[55] But for most Argentines, Salgán's blackness was rendered invisible by his association with tango.

In the early decades of the twentieth century, Afro-Argentines had figured prominently among tango musicians and composers. Yet by the 1920s, when the birth of the recording and radio industries transformed tango from dance music to a genre of songs, lyrics rarely mentioned black characters, and the term "negro" was applied as a nickname to many tango performers who lacked any identifiable African ancestry. In this context, blackness alluded not to race but to class, signifying a populist affiliation with the poor Argentine communities from which the tango was said to have emerged.[56] During the 1940s, a popular revival of the older genres *milonga* and *candombe* reminded audiences of tango's origins in the music and dance of Afro-Argentines, while firmly locating tango's racial blackness in the distant past.[57]

The modern tango was the quintessential musical representation of Argentine national identity and as such it was white music. Within Argentine popular music, therefore, the visibility of blackness varied with the nationality ascribed to the genre. African ancestry was visible in an Argentine musician who played jazz, a foreign music, but not in one who played tango. Notwithstanding their phenotypic similarity, jazz blackened Alemán, while tango whitened Salgán.

During Alemán's period of commercial success in Argentina, the pages of local jazz magazines were filled with debates over the alleged racial essence of the music. In an essay published in an Argentine jazz magazine, the Chilean musician and critic Pablo Garrido insisted that jazz arose from "the anguish and tribulation of an oppressed race. Jazz is, then, exclusively black-American [*negro-americano*], and for that reason its authentic interpreters are black-American musicians."[58] Similarly, Uruguayan critic Francisco Mañosa argued that jazz was "an essentially black music" and that white jazz musicians could only be imitators; to the extent that they improved on the work of their black colleagues, they were no longer playing jazz.[59] On the other hand, just three years later, the same magazine published a column that ridiculed a radio commentator for insisting on the blackness of jazz, noting that whoever hired the Argentine jazz band that played on the same show must not have seen the musicians' faces.[60]

By the 1950s, this debate over race intersected with another series of arguments provoked by the rise of new subgenres of jazz. In a development that replayed events in Europe and the United States, the Argentine jazz community split between traditionalists and modernizers. Inspired by its French namesake, the Hot Club de Buenos Aires was founded in 1948 to promote local bands who specialized in the old "hot" jazz style associated with New Orleans and, especially, with Louis Armstrong. Just two years later, fans, critics, and musicians who embraced bebop and other styles of so-called modern jazz founded the Bop Club Argentino.[61] Rejecting traditionalism and nostalgia, this group celebrated the vanguardism implicit in new forms of jazz that were as sophisticated and challenging as any modern art. Since modern jazz required an educated audience, the Bop Club organized a series of lectures aimed at "elevating the listener's degree of comprehension."[62] As one of the group's members put it, "jazz is not the result of a strong dose of enthusiasm, but rather it requires preparation and extremely intense study, as well as a very profound knowledge of music."[63]

The dispute between traditionalists and modernizers was not fundamentally about race, yet it was fought on discursive terrain that was marked by race. The leaders of the bebop revolution – musicians like Charlie Parker and Dizzy Gillespie – were African American, as were many of their most important successors, including Miles Davis and John Coltrane. But while the Bop Club's members praised these artists, they also celebrated the innovations of white musicians like Stan Kenton, Stan Getz, and Lennie Tristano. The embrace of jazz modernism weakened the hold of racial essentialism; it opened a path to jazz authenticity that did not require blackness. In an essay called "Jazz and Modern Art," the young pianist Lalo Schifrin, perhaps the leading Argentine musician in the modern camp, compared the best modern jazz to the works of avant-garde composers like Paul Hindemith and Igor Stravinsky. This argument had racial implications: "It is said that only blacks can play jazz . . . These are no more than absurd and snobbish arguments and cannot be considered serious artistic theories. Jazz is no longer a mythological legend."[64] Similarly, Luis Borraro of the Bop Club Argentino argued that like all great art forms, jazz needed to evolve with the times. "You may speak to me about the feeling of the oppressed race. [But] while jazz began as exclusively black, it has universalized. Jazz can be played not just by a black person, but also by a Pole or a Lapp, and authentically."[65] In these formulations, the argument against traditionalism coincided with the argument against racial essentialism. As a black guitarist who specialized in swing, Oscar Alemán was on the losing side of both debates.

Between 1941 and 1957, Alemán recorded more than 100 sides for Odeon, first as the leader of a sextet and after 1951, at the helm of a nine-piece "orchestra."[66] These recordings reveal a guitar style rooted in swing and marked by an easy virtuosity. Having lost his National guitars, Alemán now played a Selmer Maccaferri, the same guitar as Django Reinhardt, but his playing still sounded quite different. His tone was thicker, and his improvisations still hewed closer to the melody. He now developed a theatrical tendency to punctuate his riffs with a ringing harmonic, a high-pitched double stop, or a sustained note struck with heavy vibrato. Above all, Alemán's records betray a musical personality characterized by humor and showmanship. His rendition of the standard "Sweet Georgia Brown," recorded in 1941 in his very first session for Odeon, is less inventive and adventurous than the version Reinhardt recorded for Decca three years earlier, but it is a crowd pleaser. Alemán first offers a largely straightforward reading of the melody and then develops playful, heavily syncopated variations, before finishing with a couple of rapid-fire riffs and an explicit allusion to Gershwin's "Rhapsody in Blue." His English-inspired vocalizations throughout the piece – "yeah!" – add to the mood of levity. Alemán's showmanship was even more evident on stage. In a scene from the 1949 film *El ídolo del tango* (Canziani), Alemán performs his song "Improvisaciones sobre boogie woogie" at a fancy porteño nightclub. He does a comic, rubbery-legged dance while playing the guitar, puts the instrument down to do some enthusiastic scat singing, and then jumps off the stage to dance with one of the female patrons.

In his initial recording sessions for Odeon, Alemán's repertoire was comprised exclusively of instrumental jazz tunes – either North American standards or his own originals. But this changed in 1943 when his band cut a light-hearted, up-tempo, swing version of "Bésame Mucho" (Velázquez), a bolero first recorded two years earlier by the Mexican singer Emilio Tuero. On the flip side, the band recorded "Nega do cabelo duro, [nappy-haired black woman]" a *batucada* that had been a hit in Brazil during the carnival season of 1942. These two sides marked Alemán's debut as a singer: he sings the bolero in Spanish and the batucada in Portuguese. They also established a pattern. Over the next fifteen years, Latin American pop songs, especially from Brazilian genres like samba, choro, and *baião*, featured prominently in Alemán's discography, often paired with jazz numbers. In contrast to his take on "Bésame Mucho," which he played as if it were a swing tune, Alemán did not generally "jazz up" his Brazilian material. The rhythm section plays the appropriate Brazilian beat, and while Alemán's jazz phrasings are still evident in his guitar playing, he generally avoids taking improvised solos, focusing instead on playing the melody with minor embellishments. In 1951, Alemán recorded a version of Waldir Azevedo's current choro hit "Delicado," labeled the biggest record of the year by one Argentine magazine.[67] Already covered by some seven Argentine acts by the time Alemán recorded it, the original was a catchy, instrumental baião that Azevedo played on a cavaquinho. Alemán played it on the guitar against a more prominent bass drum pulse and ornamented the melody with flashy riffs, including a series of lightning-fast triplets. The result was not recognizable as a jazz record. Alemán's recordings of Brazilian pop music were the work of a jazz musician open to another musical tradition, but they were also commercial products, with which Odeon clearly hoped to tap into a bigger market than the one composed of jazz aficionados.

Alemán's commercialism raised the hackles of Argentine music journalists. For *Sintonía's* jazz critic, he was "a black guy [*un morocho*] who can do whatever he wants with the strings, who feels the rhythm and what it transmits, but . . . [h]e has two personalities: one legitimate and one commercial."[68] Such critics were particularly offended by Alemán's comic scat singing – his "*grititos* [little shouts]" – which seemed to militate against musical seriousness.[69] And as the proponents of modern jazz gained prominence within Argentine jazz circles, negative reviews became more common. For these writers, Alemán's records were hackneyed, commercial fare, good for dancing to and appealing to his uninformed fans, but lacking substance. The tone of these reviews was dismissive: "a series of riffs in Oscar's more-or-less habitual arrangement . . . it certainly won't add much to his harvest but it will no doubt please his followers and those who love to dance."[70] "Why won't he try to rise to the challenge of renovation and of doing something really serious that will elevate him among those who 'know' what jazz is?"[71] Critics particularly lambasted Alemán for his Brazilian and other non-jazz material. *Jazz Magazine's* reviewer ostentatiously declined to comment on records like "Delicado" and often gave Alemán's foxtrots the backhanded compliment, "at least it's in 4/4 time."[72] One typical review dismissed the latest Alemán release as "strictly dance music" and pleaded with him to return to jazz: "now that Django has hopped the fence to bebop, [Alemán] is one of the few who remain to defend a school that seems destined to disappear."[73] Even if modern jazz aficionados could accept Alemán's old-fashioned style, they could not forgive his betrayal of jazz itself.

The antipathy of the hardcore jazz audience was not racially motivated. These writers rejected Alemán's commercialism, his fondness for comic singing and dancing, and his enthusiasm for non-jazz material, not his blackness. Nevertheless, the rise of bebop and other modern genres had disrupted the racial essentialism implicit in the idea of jazz as the expression of African American experience. In so doing, it altered the landscape in which Alemán's blackness had functioned as a badge of authenticity. For the jazz avant-garde, sophistication, technical mastery, and artistic seriousness were the hallmarks of the authentic musician; being black was no longer sufficient to guarantee Alemán's jazz credibility. Had Alemán been North American and had his musical style been clearly derived from the blues tradition, it might not have mattered. But Alemán's blackness was associated not with oppressive cotton plantations or seedy New York bars, but with fancy Paris nightclubs and, secondarily, with Brazil. By the early 1950s, Alemán had been marginalized by the jazz critics of Buenos Aires.

This critical disdain had little effect on Alemán's ability to earn a living. Until 1957, he continued to record prolifically for Odeon, to appear on the radio, and to perform in Buenos Aires and abroad. Only at the end of the decade did these gigs begin to dry up. Alemán's career could withstand bad reviews in specialized jazz magazines but not the dramatic change in the musical tastes of the mass audience. By the late 1950s, both big-band jazz and tango had lost their position of dominance on porteño radio waves and dance floors, replaced by new imports from the United States, including singers like Frank Sinatra and, most importantly, rock 'n' roll. This transformation represented a major blow to all Argentine musicians associated with styles that now seemed antiquated.[74] Yet some survived better than others. In particular, some tango stars who could no longer afford to maintain their large orchestras re-emerged in small-group contexts. Horacio Salgán, for example, dissolved his tango band in 1957. Later that year, he formed a duo with guitarist Ubaldo de Lío. By 1960, he was performing and recording alongside other tango legends in the Quinteto Real.[75] In this way, Salgán was able to negotiate the end of the dance-band era. Like jazz in the United States, which had evolved from big-band dance music to the more cerebral, small-group style of bebop, tango was now music for listening rather than dancing. The musician who would best embody this new, more sophisticated version of tango was, of course, Astor Piazzolla. But even if Salgán never achieved the stature of Piazzolla nor even recovered his own earlier prominence, he was able to thrive on a more modest scale. Alemán, by contrast, disappeared into obscurity.

The contrasting career trajectories of Salgán and Alemán reflected primarily the very different status of tango and jazz in Argentina. Whereas tango was the music *par excellence* of Buenos Aires, jazz was a foreign import. No matter how old-fashioned it seemed, tango would always appeal to nationalist nostalgia. By contrast, once swing jazz came to seem outdated, it was simply jettisoned in favor of the next new import. But race mattered here as well. As we have seen, Salgán's blackness was invisible in the 1940s and 1950s. As a result, he avoided any association with the primitive, African roots of tango and could be seen as a member of the avant-garde. As early as 1956, the mainstream press linked Salgán to Piazzolla, describing both as key players in a "New Guard" of innovative musicians who were modernizing tango by ignoring the dancers and injecting the music with quality and sophistication.[76] Alemán's blackness, saturated as it was with associations of frivolity, comedy, corporality, and the Parisian nightlife, closed this path to him. Other Argentine jazz musicians were able to join the jazz vanguard; some – Lalo Schifrin, Gato Barbieri – even became international stars. Alemán's roots in an older style as well as his particular way of being black prevented him from doing so.

After more than a decade away from the limelight, Alemán was rediscovered in the early 1970s. In 1971, EMI/Odeon re-issued some of his 1940s and 1950s material on LP, and over the next three years, Redondel, a small Argentine label, released three albums of new recordings. Now in his sixties, Alemán returned to public performance and drew the attention of a new generation of music journalists. Press reports from this era focus even more attention on Alemán's race than those of earlier decades. At the beginning of his rediscovery, one article introduced him as follows: "Oscar Marcelo Alemán, 61, one of the greatest guitarists in the world, a black thing [*cosa negra*] possessed by all the spirits of rhythm and of music."[77] The following year, a concert review highlighted his "black fingers" and his "black rhythm."[78] In an extended interview published in 1975 in the left-wing magazine *Crisis*, Gerardo Sopeña asked Alemán if he thought a musician's race influenced the music he played, "or in your case, does African descent determine a natural sense of rhythm?"[79] For Alemán, whose answer was a qualified "yes," blackness once again seemed to open doors rather than close them. Alongside his instrumental virtuosity and his Parisian past, his blackness itself was now a factor that attracted the attention of journalists. By this time, debates over the racial essence of jazz had long since lost relevance, but the black roots of contemporary popular music, including North American jazz and rock as well as Brazilian and Caribbean genres, were well-established. In this context, Alemán's blackness was *musically* interesting. Blackness no longer anchored a claim of jazz authenticity – the idea of a white jazz musician was entirely unproblematic by the 1970s – but it still carried with it essentialist associations of rhythmic aptitude.

Alemán's career played out within a set of overlapping circuits that structured transnational, mass cultural exchange in the mid-twentieth century. Jazz music was not simply disseminated outward from the United States; rather, it flowed in various directions among a number of key sites throughout the Atlantic World. Alemán's connection to the music came by way of Brazil and the cosmopolitan jazz scene in Paris. His position within these circuits shaped his choice of repertoire and his musical style, but it also informed his racial identity: Alemán embodied a blackness that alluded to Parisian nightclubs and frivolous Brazilian tropicalism, rather than to the tropes of African American suffering and oppression. His commercial success in Buenos Aires, as well as the limits of that success, demonstrates that popular music represented a privileged space within which Argentines experimented with evolving, transnational racial discourses. The existence of a black Argentine jazz musician of Alemán's caliber enabled local fans to engage with images of black modernism and authenticity. Yet his blackness, made visible by his association with jazz, prevented him from embodying Argentine national identity. As a result, his commercial fortunes were directly tied to the international status of blackness. When jazz lost its position as the quintessential musical expression of modernity, Alemán became yet another invisible Afro-Argentine. In the late 1960s and early 1970s, decolonization, black power, and soul music revived Argentine interest in blackness and, not coincidentally, Alemán's career. Unfortunately, the positive associations that attached to blackness in the musical sphere did not reshape Argentine racial attitudes more generally. In a country that remained committed to a vision of itself as white, it was Alemán's status as a well-known musician that protected him from discrimination. As he explained in the *Ebony* article, he was "accepted everywhere" in Argentina, but "with another black man . . . it might be different."[80]

Notes

The author would like to thank Paulina Alberto, Eduardo Elena, Alison Landsberg, Bryan McCann, Mike O'Malley, Sergio Pujol, and Greg Robinson for reading and commenting on earlier drafts of this chapter.

1. Andrews, *Afro-Argentines*.
2. Thompson, "Argentina," 80.
3. See Quijada, Bernard, and Schneider, *Homogeneidad*.
4. Frigerio, "Negros," 88–93.
5. Information on Alemán's early years comes from several interviews that he granted after he was rediscovered by the Argentine media in the early 1970s. See "Oscar Alemán," in Ardiles Gray, *Historias*, 287–92; Sopeña, "Oscar Alemán." Other useful sources are Pujol, *Jazz*, 91–101, and the documentary film by Hernán Gaffet, *Oscar Alemán: Vida con swing* (2002).

6. Prieto, *El discurso*.
7. On the role of Afro-Argentines in criollismo, see Solomianski, *Identidades*; Castro, *Afro-Argentine*; Chasteen, *National Rhythms*, 51–70.
8. On Lobo, see Mello, "Gastão Bueno Lobo."
9. The Les Loups records appeared in Victor's local advertisements. See *Caras y Caretas* (Buenos Aires), 3 Mar. 1928; 7 Apr. 1928; 10 Nov. 1928; 19 Jan. 1929; 6 Apr. 1929.
10. *La Canción Moderna* (Buenos Aires) I:6, 30 Apr. 1928.
11. Garrett, *Struggling*, 165–202.
12. For a good selection of Hawaiian steel guitar across a range of musical genres in the late 1920s and early 1930s, see the CD *Slidin' on the Frets*.
13. For this and all recording information, I am entirely dependent on the online Oscar Alemán discography meticulously assembled by Hans Koert: www.oscar-aleman .opweb.nl/.
14. www.oscar-aleman.blogspot.com/2011/09/les-loups-criollita.html. "La criollita" is the only Les Loups song on which Lobo plays the cavaquinho instead of the Hawaiian guitar.
15. www.tsort.info/music/yr1927.htm.
16. On tango's associations with blackness, see Karush, "Blackness."
17. Gendron, *Between*, 103–16; quotation on 107. On the impact of James Reese Europe, the Southern Syncopated Orchestra, and Louis Mitchell in England, see Parsonage, *Evolution*.
18. Jackson, *Making*, 123–35.
19. Jules-Rosette, *Josephine Baker*, 144–79; Archer-Straw, *Negrophilia*, 113–33; Wood, *Josephine Baker*. On Colin and Baker, see Dalton and Gates, Jr., "Josephine Baker."
20. Micol Seigel has revealed and examined the Brazilian dimension of this multipolar exchange. See Seigel, *Uneven Encounters*, 95–135.
21. Jackson, *Making*, 132–33.
22. Seigel, *Uneven Encounters*, 97–107; Davis, *White Face*, 20–28; Hertzman, *Making Samba*, 103–13.
23. Rye, "Southern," 66.
24. Pujol, *Jazz*, 24–27, 36–39; Seigel, *Uneven Encounters*, 127.
25. See, for example, *La Voz* (Madrid), 9 Nov. 1929, 6.
26. Koert, "Oscar Alemán, 1930–1931."
27. Thompson, "Globetrotting." See also Seigel, *Uneven Encounters*, 125–26.
28. Ardiles Gray, *Historias*, 292–94; Pujol, *Jazz*, 91–96; Bergmeier and Lotz, "James Arthur Briggs," 141.
29. Quoted in Dregni, *Django*, 101.
30. *Sintonía* (Buenos Aires), 25 Nov. 1942.
31. Coleman, *Trumpet Story*, 99.
32. Stovall, *Paris Noir*.
33. Ardiles Gray, *Historias*, 297. For other versions of the story, see *Crisis*, Jan. 1975, 30; *La Nación Revista* (Buenos Aires), 27 May 1979.
34. Koert, "Oscar Alemán: Star."
35. Quoted in Dexter Johnson, liner notes to *Oscar Alemán*.
36. Dregni, *Django*, 102–03.
37. On the complex racial politics of Lang's work, see O'Malley, "Blind Imitation."

38. The historian Sergio Pujol discusses Brazilian influence on Alemán's guitar style in Gaffet, *Oscar Alemán.*
39. Coleman, *Trumpet Story,* 99–100.
40. *Síncopa y Ritmo* (Buenos Aires), Apr. 1941, 4.
41. *Sintonía,* 25 Jun. 1941, 33.
42. *Síncopa y Ritmo,* May–Jun. 1941, 2.
43. *Síncopa y Ritmo,* Oct.–Nov. 1941, 16.
44. See Seibel, "La presencia," 202.
45. Matallana, "*Locos,*" 95.
46. *Sintonía,* 1 May 1943, 13.
47. This anecdote is related in Gaffet, *Oscar Alemán.*
48. On the treatment of race in Argentine jazz criticism of this period, see Borge, "Dark Pursuits."
49. See, for example, *Sintonía,* 2 Sep. 1933, 7; *Canción Moderna* (Buenos Aires), 16 Jul. 1928.
50. *Sintonía,* 9 Mar. 1935.
51. *Síncopa y Ritmo,* Apr. 1941, 26. For another example of this sort of racial determinism in Argentine jazz criticism, see *Síncopa y Ritmo,* Dec. 1941–Feb. 1942, 4–5.
52. *Sintonía,* Mar. 1946, 40.
53. For a biography of Salgán, see Ursini, *Supervivencia.* Although Ursini does not mention his race, more recent accounts describe him as Afro-Argentine. See Frigerio, "Negros," 88–93; Thompson, *Tango,* 194–99.
54. *Antena* (Buenos Aires), 2 Dec. 1952.
55. *Crisis,* Jan. 1975, 32.
56. On the processes by which the meanings of the term "negro" shifted from race to class in the early twentieth century, see Geler, this volume; on its uses throughout the century, see Gordillo, Elena, Adamovsky, this volume.
57. Karush, "Blackness."
58. *Síncopa y Ritmo,* Feb.–May 1944, 10–11.
59. *Jazz Magazine* (Buenos Aires), Aug.–Sep. 1953, 6.
60. *Jazz Magazine,* Apr.–May 1956, 16–17.
61. Pujol, *Jazz,* 120–32. On this controversy as it played out in France and the United States, see Jackson, *Making,* 196–97; Stowe, *Swing Changes,* 180–245.
62. *Jazz Magazine,* Mar. 1954, 29.
63. *Jazz Magazine,* Jun.–Aug. 1956, 22.
64. *Jazz Magazine,* Dec. 1951, 7.
65. *Jazz Magazine,* May 1951, 5–6.
66. Mysteriously, Alemán's sextet was always known as his "Quinteto de swing."
67. *El Disco* (Buenos Aires), Oct. 1951, 5.
68. *Sintonía,* Nov. 1947.
69. *Sintonía,* 1 Apr. 1945, 22B; see also *Sintonía,* Apr. 1948, 23.
70. *Jazz Magazine,* Jul.–Aug. 1952, 19.
71. *Jazz Magazine,* Mar.–Apr. 1953, 20.
72. *Jazz Magazine,* Jan.–Feb. 1952, 10; Oct. 1952, 18–19; Dec. 1953, 24.
73. *Jazz Magazine,* Nov. 1951, 20.
74. See Karush, *Culture,* 200–01.
75. Ursini, *Supervivencia,* 67–89.

76. *Mundo Argentino* (Buenos Aires), 29 Feb. 1956, 7–9.
77. *Primera Plana* (Buenos Aires), 15 Dec. 1970, 8.
78. *Primera Plana*, 21 Sep. 1971, 45.
79. *Crisis*, Jan. 1975, 30.
80. Thompson, "Argentina," 80.

4

La cocina criolla

A history of food and race in twentieth-century Argentina

Rebekah E. Pite

In 1889, an Italian visitor to Santiago del Estero praised the liberal "progress" sweeping this Northwestern provincial capital. He celebrated the new market, buzzing commercial center, and renovated homes filled with products from Europe and Buenos Aires. He emphasized his appreciation for the renovated kitchens that, in his view, "reveal[ed] a step forward in the manner of eating." Citing writer Brillat-Savarin's famous aphorism 'tell me what you eat and I will tell you what you are,' he argued that this new manner of cooking and eating among the *santiagueño* elite embodied "true progress."[1] Even in this relatively sleepy city far from the national capital, cosmopolitan culinary practices had recently begun to have a marked impact. While our visitor did not specify the exact nature of the foods consumed, in Santiago, as in Buenos Aires and Córdoba, it was likely French fare or at least local dishes dressed up with French names and served at elegant, well-set tables.[2]

The question of who Argentines were as well as what and how they should eat received a considerable amount of attention during the late nineteenth century and throughout the twentieth. Around the turn of the century, many Argentine scientists and politicians embraced a version of Lamarckian eugenics that held that changing a combination of biological and environmental factors, including people's diets, would improve the population.[3] Given the association of French cuisine with high civilization across the Americas, Argentine elites (like their counterparts in Mexico or Brazil) publicly embraced French dishes to cement their own respectability and that of their nation. At the same time, in more private, quotidian settings, they also enjoyed specialties with local ingredients and techniques.[4]

As massive numbers of immigrants – most from Italy and Spain – made their way to Argentina around the turn of the century, they shaped new ideas about what defined Argentine food. Even today, most urbanites describe Spanish and Italian influences as particularly prominent in the development of a national cuisine. As one elderly gentleman of Italian descent explained to me in Buenos Aires in 2003, "Here the main influence [on food] is Spanish and Italian [...] After that there are evidently *other influences*."[5] Such notions about the roots of Argentine cuisine parallel racial ideologies that held that the massive wave of immigrants had displaced earlier Indo-Afro-Hispanic society and its legacies. And yet, while this discourse celebrated European contributions to Argentina's foodways, these Southern European currents (like the immigrants who brought them) were not quite the "French" and Northern European influences to which some elites had aspired.

While the few works written on Argentine food explore the (mainly European) ethnic backgrounds of particular foods or the people who made them, race has not been a topic of analysis.[6] Yet as historian Rebecca Earle has demonstrated, since the early colonial era, people in Latin America have imagined that the foods they eat (or avoid) shape not only their bodies but also their racial status.[7] Mainstream discourses around food in twentieth-century Argentina expressed varying levels of anxiety about eating from the table of the "other," but they have consistently downplayed the culinary contributions of nonwhites. This is despite the fact that cooks with indigenous and African roots played a significant role in creating what would come to be considered quintessentially "Argentine" dishes. Northwestern cooks with indigenous or mixed ancestry and *gauchos* [iconic Argentine cattle-hands who were frequently mixed-race but increasingly portrayed as white] were the early creators of what would become national dishes like *locro* [a traditional Andean stew made with hominy, squash, beans, potatoes, hot peppers, and sometimes, beef] and *asado* [beef barbecue]. Afro-Argentines, among the least recognized contributors, also played a key role in forging what would be considered classic local preparations like *mondongo* [stew made with tripe], *puré de zapallo* [pumpkin puree],[8] and even *parrillada mixta* [mixed grill of beef].

By tracing shifting definitions of what counted as Argentina's local cuisine or *cocina criolla* over the course of the twentieth century, this chapter seeks to contribute to our understanding of the racial and ethnic undertones of the idea of *criollo* culture in Argentina. It does so by analyzing a range of cookbooks as well as a sampling of advertisements, culinary festivals, and oral histories. Argentina's wildly popular twentieth-century culinary expert, Doña Petrona C. de Gandulfo, merits special attention. Following her personal trajectory and that of other culinary figures who helped make certain foods emblematic of local cuisine, this chapter considers a variety of regional vantage points, especially Buenos Aires and the Central and Northwestern provinces, which became the principal regional inspirations for cocina criolla. Attention to region-specific ideas about food and identity helps reveal competing visions of the nation and varying racial or ethnic formations in different parts of the country.[9] While Argentina's unique version of cocina criolla in fact relied upon a diverse array of culinary contributions and cooks,[10] the discourse surrounding this cuisine tended to homogenize those influences.

"LO CRIOLLO" IN ARGENTINA

Unlike many other Latin Americans, Argentines never widely adopted the term *mestizo* to describe people with mixed indigenous, European and/or African heritage or to celebrate these groups as emblems of a hybrid national "essence." But the term "criollo," with its wide range of meanings, sometimes played a similar role. As historian Florencia Guzmán explains, this was especially the case in the Northwestern provinces where, during the late colonial period and into the nineteenth century, the term "criollo" was deployed to convey the sense of mixture more directly referenced in the term "mestizo."[11] Over the course of the national period, "criollo" became another way of saying that someone or something was local, though not necessarily native.[12] Using the term this way alluded to meanings that dated back to the colonial period, when subjects used "criollo" to refer to the white, American-born descendants of European parents, to people of African descent born in the New World, or even to animals and plants of European origin that thrived on American soil.

While "criollo" was generally not applied to those who preserved an indigenous identity, the categories were sometimes flexible. As historian Oscar Chamosa has shown, when early-twentieth-century state actors sought to construct a "white Argentina," they did so in part by attempting to turn people indigenous to the Northwestern Calchaquí Valley from "Indians" into "criollos."[13] Although this process of re-labeling suggests that elites considered indigenous people capable of transformation, it also resulted in their being relegated to a kind of a second-class status within the nation, as anthropologist Claudia Briones notes. People of indigenous and mixed descent became nominally white, thus solidifying Argentina's claims to whiteness, but they remained marked within this category through cultural, linguistic, and/or phenotypical differences.[14]

Who (and what) was considered criollo was profoundly shaped by region, class, politics, and the passage of time. During the early twentieth century, as nationalism began to manifest itself in new ways, urbanites disenchanted with the city used the term "criollo" as a flexible descriptor to refer primarily to rural people and traditions, including the gaucho and his idealized rough-and-tumble lifestyle on the countryside. They also used it to describe symbolically important urban cultural forms including the tango and popular literature. In claiming the gaucho, the tango, and criollo literature as their own, urban Argentines sought to distinguish themselves and their national culture from that of the recent wave of immigrants.[15] In contrast, very few rural actors used the term "criollo" to self-identify, preferring other terms like *paisano* [from the country].[16] Nevertheless, during the twentieth century "criollo" gained strength in urban areas to signal the presence of nonwhite and mestizo populations within Argentina.[17] The porous category "criollo" thus provides important insights into the processes by which, as some scholars have recently argued, a sense of

Argentine homogeneity was laboriously and unevenly constructed from the nation's significant racial, ethnic, and regional heterogeneity.[18]

What can "cocina criolla" – with its simultaneous connotations of localism, ethno-regional difference, and melting-pot-style fusion – tell us about this process of racial construction? As we shall see, over the course of the twentieth century, there was a significant shift in urban Argentines' appreciation of provincial cooking and mixed-race culture as key elements of an authentic criollo Argentine identity, with the most explicit embrace occurring in the 1960s and 1970s. Nevertheless, if we shift our gaze to Northwestern Argentina, we can see a divergent and less explicit strand of criollismo that preceded Buenos Aires' belated admiration of "deep Argentina," and which had long taken for granted the Indo-Hispanic roots of local cuisine. In categorizing different ways of cooking and eating, urban and rural actors made ethno-racial claims about who and what was valued, local, and ultimately, Argentine.

PROVINCIAL FOODWAYS AND EARLY COOKBOOKS

There is perhaps no better embodiment of these trends than Argentina's unparalleled culinary celebrity and best-selling cookbook author, Doña Petrona Carrizo de Gandulfo (ca. 1896–1992). A woman from the provinces, Doña Petrona touted her European training and cuisine in the nation's capital beginning in the late 1920s, but by the 1960s she was emphasizing regional dishes like *empanadas* [hand-held savory pies] along with her Northwestern provincial roots.

Petrona Carrizo was born on the outskirts of the city of Santiago del Estero. Named Petrona after San Pedro, the saint who shared her birthday, she was the sixth of seven children (five girls and two boys). Her father Manuel was apparently of Spanish descent and her mother Clementina of Italian and indigenous heritage.[19] During the early twentieth century, those with some indigenous ancestry (including Petrona's mother Clementina) who wished to present themselves as acculturated Argentines could do so by speaking Spanish, practicing Catholicism, living in urban environments, and eating European-influenced foods.[20] Still, even as the Carrizo family spoke both Spanish and Quechua (like many in Santiago del Estero),[21] lived near the provincial capital, and were Catholic, they appear not to have been among the elite (described by our Italian visitor to that city) who ate fancy French foods prepared in renovated kitchens. Petrona's father died when she was just six years old, and some five years later her mother moved the family to the provincial capital and established a *pensión*, or boarding house. There, Petrona learned how to make *pastelitos de dulce* [quince-filled pastries], and delivered empanadas and other foods to the boarding house's male clientele with her younger brother.[22]

Foods like empanadas and pastelitos, which drew from both indigenous and colonial-era Spanish foods and cooking methods, would eventually be considered classic staples of cocina criolla in Argentina. Still, during the early twentieth century most provincial families like the Carrizos did not characterize the dishes they ate as "criollo." In fact, historian Fernando Remedi explains that in the province of Córdoba it was the newer Italian and French foods that carried an explicit ethnic marker during the early twentieth century, and not the foods forged by natives and Spaniards during the colonial era (considered simply the local cuisine).[23] The same was true in Santiago del Estero and other Northern provinces. Indeed, while some South Americans began to label their dishes "criollo" around the turn of the century,[24] fewer seemed to do so regularly within Argentina. In 1890, the accomplished Argentine writer Juana Manuela Gorriti published *Cocina ecléctica* [Eclectic Cuisine], a cosmopolitan set of recipes compiled from the submissions of her Argentine, Peruvian, and Bolivian friends.[25] (Gorriti had been born into an elite political family in the Northwestern Argentine province of Salta and spent much of her life exiled in Bolivia and Peru). The few dishes that carried the name "criollo" in this compilation were from Peru and not Argentina.[26]

That same year (1890), Susana Torres de Castex, a less-famous elite woman from Buenos Aires, also published the first edition of a cookbook. She titled it *La perfecta cocinera argentina* [The Perfect Argentine Cook], and authored it under the pseudonym Teófila Benavento. Like Gorriti, Torres de Castex suggested the Argentine cook learn a wide range of cosmopolitan recipes drawn from both Argentina and Europe, where she traveled regularly.[27] Both Gorriti and Torres de Castex's approaches reflected the importance of local and international foodways in shaping cooking in Argentina, especially in urban areas like Buenos Aires. Unlike Gorriti, Torres de Castex suggested that the "the perfect Argentine cook" might wish to cook a few "criollo" dishes as well. She included seven recipes dubbed "*a la criolla*." Tellingly, all but one (a dessert called "*ambrosia a la criolla*") required beef or beef lard. By this point, most Argentines considered cattle, which had originally been imported from Europe during the sixteenth century, to be local rather than foreign. But this association between beef and criollo food remained tacit in Torres de Castex's work, for even as she associated beef with local cuisine, only a minute fraction of her 628 original recipes earned the label "criollo." Among the few other recipes for which she specified origins, most involved a particular region in Europe or Argentina, such as *salsa catalana* [Catalan sauce], *croquetas de bacalao francesas* [French cod croquettes], *empanadas mendocinas* [empanadas from Mendoza], and *chafaina cordobesa* [chafaina from Córdoba]. By contrast, a recipe for *humita en chala* – a preparation of creamed corn cooked in a husk, derived from pre-colonial indigenous Andean culinary traditions – was not labeled as criollo, indigenous, or Andean. This cookbook was more cosmopolitan and provincial than it was nationalist or criollo.

The first cookbook explicitly focused on cocina criolla was published in Argentina a couple of decades later. In 1914, Mercedes Cullen de Aldao, an elite woman from the province of Santa Fe, published *La cocinera criolla* under the pseudonym Marta.[28] Like Susana Torres de Castex before her, Mercedes Cullen de Aldao, who "laid claim to two of the most exalted last names" in Santa Fe, hid her upper-class identity and instead conjured up an image of an everyday "*cocinera criolla* [criolla cook]."[29] This was a way not only of protecting herself from the social biases that relegated cooks and other servants to the bottom of the social hierarchy, but also of recognizing that non-elite women did most of the cooking (for their own and for other families) in early-twentieth-century Argentina.

Like *Cocina ecléctica* before it, *La cocinera criolla* was a cooperative and cosmopolitan effort – in this case the aim was to raise money for a chapel for a local hospital. Even though its author hailed from the province of Santa Fe, it was published in Barcelona, Spain, with a glossary that translated Argentine culinary terms for other Spanish-speaking audiences. Perhaps due to this desired external audience, it was the most local and self-consciously criollo cookbook published by an Argentine author to date. This approach reverberated with the growing nationalism of the times, which frequently manifested itself in Argentines' attempts to embrace local cultural forms derived from an old Spanish heritage to distinguish national culture from that of newer immigrants. Cullen de Aldao explained that she sought to "create a publication that would conserve and perpetuate our healthy *cocina criolla* and reproduce the foreign ways [of cooking] that we have assimilated, incorporating them into *nuestra mesa* [literally, 'our table,' or figuratively, 'our repertoire']." In this spirit, she organized her cookbook by dividing it in two parts; the first focused on cocina criolla and the second on *cocina cosmopolita* [cosmopolitan cooking].

While dishes in both sections used ingredients native to the Americas and to Europe, Cullen de Aldao made more explicit than her predecessors the relationship between cocina criolla and *grasa vacuna* [beef lard]. Many Argentines used beef lard as their principal cooking fat, and it had become a key ingredient that distinguished local preparations from foreign ones. This was especially the case in a province like Santa Fe, where cattle predominated. For example, Cullen de Aldao's recipes for *facturas* included in the cocina criolla section described pastries inspired by European techniques but made with beef lard instead of butter or pig's lard. Other recipes for beef dominated the section on local foods. In contrast, the section on "cocina cosmopolita" presented recipes from Spain or Italy featuring fish or fowl but little beef. Echoing the dynamics in Córdoba and Santiago del Estero, this author from the province of Santa Fe reserved mention of specific ethnic and regional identities for Spanish and Italian recipes (referring to them as "*caldo gallego* [Galician soup]" or "*arroz a la milanesa* [Milan-style rice]"), thereby reinforcing the notion that "cocina criolla" was the regular – unmarked – Argentine fare.

One year later, in 1920, a congregation of nuns in the province of Tucumán published a second cookbook from the Argentine provinces. They adopted the generic title *El arte de cocinar* [The Art of Cooking], and combined recipes of foods popular in Argentina with those inspired by diverse South American and European foodways. In contrast to *La cocinera criolla*'s broader audience, this cookbook seems to have been originally directed to people in Tucumán, and it was not a deliberate presentation of cocina criolla. *El arte de cocinar* featured Spanish techniques and ingredients in special sections dedicated to how to prepare *bacalao* [cod] and *croquetas* [croquettes], and reflected the influence of the local sugar industry with a large number of dessert recipes and advertisements. Tellingly, it was not until subsequent editions, including one published in 1974, that dishes were labeled "criollo," and the introduction to this latter edition belatedly recognized that the recipes in its collection were, in fact, "*cocina regional* [regional cooking]."[30] In other words, these recipes were "cocina criolla" that in the 1920s had not yet considered itself as such – it was simply "everyday cooking" in these regions.

As provincial cookbooks made their way to Buenos Aires (where they were usually printed and easiest to find), and as the number of provincial migrants to that city grew during the early twentieth century, Northern regional cooking began to gain an identity as cocina criolla in the capital city. A series of nine photos from 1936 in Argentina's National Archive showcase "*Cocina Gaucha* [Gaucho cooking]" and "*Comidas típicas criollas* [Typical creole cuisine]" for a presumably urban audience. The photographs seem eager to "class up" primarily rural fare by placing dishes including tamales, empanadas, carbonada, humitas, and asado, which were generally served in a more rustic manner, on a table with a white linen tablecloth, fancy plates, and a bottle of wine. Some three years later, the popular women's magazine *Para Ti* published recipes for a similar range of dishes. The article's author lamented, however, that "*la cocina criolla* does not occupy the place it should on daily menus." Instead, the magazine explained, in a likely reference to the tastes of *porteños* [residents of Buenos Aires], "there is a preference for French and Italian cooking."[31]

Despite the growing attention that cooks and magazine editors began to pay to cocina criolla in these years, it was not this kind of home cooking but rather the asado or beef barbecue associated with the rural gaucho that would become the most sought-after provincial preparation in early-twentieth-century Buenos Aires. An Afro-Argentine chef, Antonio Gonzaga, played a particularly important role in urbanizing the asado by bringing it to homes and white-linen restaurants of the capital. Known at the time as "*el negro Gonzaga* [black Gonzaga]," his nickname spoke to how his contemporaries understood his racial identity.[32] Gonzaga had gained experience as a military cook before serving as chef for the Argentine Senate and moonlighting at other fine restaurants in Buenos Aires, including the Jockey Club's. He had achieved such esteem for his culinary talents that in 1929, when he was around eighty years old, he presented a sold-out live cooking show in the Palace Theater and received a standing ovation.[33]

FIGURE 9 Photograph of tamales from series of culinary photographs titled "*Cocina Gaucha*" [Gaucho Cuisine] from July 1936. Source: *Archivo General de la Nación*, neg. B.119.116. Courtesy of Archivo General de la Nación.

Just one year earlier, Antonio Gonzaga had published his first cookbook, *La cocina argentina y francesa* [Argentine and French Cooking] in Buenos Aires. In this text, he included a brief biography in which he characterized himself as a proud patriot who had gone to great lengths to provide the military men he had served with the flavors of Buenos Aires (especially fresh bread) aboard Atlantic naval ships and on the Bolivian border. Such patriotic claims resonated with those of previous Afro-Porteño intellectuals of the late nineteenth century, who, as historian Lea Geler has shown, emphasized that their community's military service helped build the Republic and therefore made them (and other patriot soldiers) into full-blooded Argentines.[34] In this vein, in his biographical note Gonzaga also relayed an incident from 1900 in which the foreman of one of the first ships on which he served as a cook had referred to him as "el criollo" and "el negro." He explained that the latter description "did not affect me at all, as I would have experienced great pain if they had distorted or wanted me to give up my nationality." (If that had happened, he noted playfully, no one aboard would have eaten bread for the rest of the trip).[35] In other words, to Gonzaga, racial labels mattered less than his shipmates' ultimate respect for his Argentineness.

La cocina argentina y francesa was one of the most self-consciously nationalist cookbooks published in Argentina to date. Unlike Cullen de Aldao, Gonzaga did not divide sections into local and foreign cooking. Instead, the French influences manifested themselves primarily in recipes for sauces and sweets, while the Argentine influences and the meat-centric approach for which Gonzaga had become famous were more persistent throughout, flanked by local versions of Italian and Spanish preparations. Rather uniquely, Gonzaga affirmatively named several of his recipes "Argentine," including *Sopa argentina* [Argentine soup], *Asado con cuero tipo tradicional argentino* [traditional Argentine asado cooked in its own hide or "leather"], and *Macitas argentinas* [Argentine fine biscuits]. Drawing on what appears to have been his birthplace in the province of Corrientes, he also included a soup and stew from that region. But with this exception, Gonzaga, like other authors who included provincial preparations, did not identify the regional or (indigenous) ethnic origins of dishes like humita and *mazamorra*.

In contrast to previous cookbook authors who emphasized urban provenance primarily when the cities in question were European, Gonzaga associated recipes with specific Argentine cities. For example, the cities of Buenos Aires and Mar del Plata claimed recipes like *Salsa porteña a la jamón* and *Potage Mar del Plata*. Indeed, even though this cookbook included classic French recipes, its author ultimately seemed more interested in celebrating the culinary contributions of his own country. To this end, Gonzaga closed his biographical note with a plea to his fellow Argentines not to favor things from abroad as they had tended to do in the past but instead to embrace a "*nacionalismo sincero* [sincere nationalism]" that placed more value on local knowledge and accomplishments.[36]

In 1931, Antonio Gonzaga published his second cookbook, *El cocinero práctico argentino: Nuevo tratado de economía doméstica, pastelería, repostería y helados* [The Practical Argentine Cook: A New Treatise on Home Economics, Pastries, Confectioneries, and Ice Creams]. Here Gonzaga presented himself in an opening photograph as a serious and respectable figure, with a crisp suit and a confident expression. In addition to providing a variety of tips and treats, this cookbook celebrated numerous ways to cook beef, including a recipe for "*asado con cuero moderno.*" This preparation referred to the large beef barbecues famously cooked by gauchos outside over an open fire with the cow's skin still attached. In Gonzaga's "modern" version, this delicacy could be cooked over a small *parrilla* [outdoor grill]. His recipe for an urban asado found an enthusiastic audience and continues to serve as a referent for the "proper" way to make an Argentine asado.[37] Likewise, his *parrillada* of the innards, ribs, sausage, and other cuts of beef, which he served in restaurants and included in this cookbook, drew from the popular classes' tendencies to eat all parts of the cow.

While Gonzaga became best known for his recipes with beef, this cookbook, even more than his first one, also reflected the growing popularity of immigrant and regional foodways in the capital city. He recognized Italian immigrants' major culinary contributions in chapters for pastas and pestos. Toward the end of his cookbook, he included a chapter titled "various dishes" that included several dubbed "criollo." Preparations in this section tended to be inspired by the provinces, including, for example, a recipe for "*locro de provincia con porotos* [provincial stew with beans]." In contrast to earlier cookbook authors, Gonzaga did not label beef dishes as criollo, making beef "disappear" seamlessly into Argentine everyday cooking, which for him was primarily porteño. This culinary move echoes broader trends. As recent historiography has shown, because Afro-Argentines were deeply assimilated into porteño popular culture, their central roles in helping to forge quintessential Argentine cultural forms have tended to be taken for granted by their peers and overlooked by subsequent generations.[38]

Cookbooks, like other books, were easier to find in Buenos Aires than in the countryside. But that did not mean that there were no cookbooks in the provinces. Elite provincial families, many of whom regularly traveled to Buenos Aires and Europe for business and leisure, also owned and expected their cooks to use cookbooks published abroad or in the capital.[39] But most non-elites continued to cook meals based on local and regional customs that they learned from family, neighbors, and friends. This started to change in the 1930s, when the growing mass media began to provide new, more accessible venues for a culinary education, and when, as a result, Doña Petrona C. de Gandulfo seized this potential to emerge as a star. Over the next several decades, the expansion of the media and of cookbook ownership would encourage more cosmopolitan cooking, and would eventually help foster a greater recognition of, and appreciation for, cocina criolla.

Con 40 años de práctica. — Actual Jefe de cocina de la H. C.
de Diputados de la Nación. Ex-jefe de cocina en uno de los
primeros viajes de la Fragata Sarmiento a las órdenes del
entonces Comandante don Onofre Bedbeder. Ex-jefe de cocina
en el Crucero Patria a las órdenes del Comandante Quiroga
Furque. Del mismo modo en el Buenos Aires en viaje al Brasil.
Fiestas Patrias, a las órdenes del Comandante O'Connor.
Comisión de Límites con Bolivia en viaje de seis meses a las
órdenes del señor Perito Coronel don Manuel Olascoaga y al
servicio de infinidad de distinguidas familias,

FIGURE 10 Photograph of Chef Antonio Gonzaga. Source: *El cocinero práctico argentino* (Buenos Aires: 1931).

ENTER THE ECÓNOMA

Petrona Carrizo arrived in Buenos Aires from Santiago del Estero with her future husband Oscar Gandulfo and his family around 1916. In the national capital, her identity shifted: Petrona was now perceived as a *santiagueña* [woman from the province of Santiago del Estero] and a criolla. Both labels conjured up rural settings, oral cultures, and lower social status in the capital during the early twentieth century.[40] Indeed, as Petrona began to carve out her culinary career, neither she nor her sponsors played up her provincial roots; rather, they downplayed the provincial origins of the woman who would become the public face of Argentine cuisine.

In 1928, Petrona C. de Gandulfo applied for and received a position as an *ecónoma* [corporate home economist] for the British gas company Compañía Primitiva de Gas. Primitiva sent her (along with the other ecónomas it had hired) to study at the French culinary academy Le Cordon Bleu, which was under the leadership of an Italian immigrant named Angel Baldi. The company encouraged its ecónomas to highlight French-inspired food in their cooking demonstrations for potential customers of their gas stoves. Acknowledging the large populations of first- and second-generation immigrants in the capital, they also provided instruction for many Italian- and Spanish-inspired dishes as well as a few British and provincial foods – all of which were tailored to the new gas stoves and the local palate.

This emphasis on creolized (but not explicitly criollo) European cuisine and technology was not only about class and the desire to sell products to status-conscious consumers; it also echoed latent racial and ethnic dynamics. Like the people themselves, the food typically consumed by European (or white) people tended to be associated with modernity and civilization, whereas indigenous and African people's food was associated with backwardness and barbarism. Previous generations of elites had enjoyed criollo fare like *puchero* [stew] at simply set tables, regularly sharing bowls, glasses, and spoons; but by the 1890s porteño elites sat at formally set tables – precisely the development applauded by our Italian visitor to Santiago del Estero around this time.[41] Like elites across the Americas, well-off porteños embraced the status embodied in French-inspired *haute cuisine*. They sought out cooks from France or the local branch of Le Cordon Bleu who could serve their families and their guests. For special occasions, they dined on French dishes that called for ingredients like prawns and cognac, even as they continued to eat more standard criollo dishes for everyday meals.[42]

Thousands of women from the newly wealthy and emerging middle class flocked to watch Primitiva's ecónomas prepare cosmopolitan dishes in the capital starting in the late 1920s. Ofelia F., the teenage daughter of a British homemaker and railroad manager, attended some of these early classes. She recalled that at seventeen years old she clipped an ad in the magazine *El Hogar* and went to watch Petrona and her fellow ecónomas prepare "elaborate

French-style dishes" including desserts and appetizers. She explained that the recipes presented at these sessions represented "all of the most useful foods." To my question about whether they also learned how to make popular provincial dishes like empanadas and locro, she responded, "No, with Petrona we didn't have any of that. How strange, if I think about it, because she was *provinciana* [from the provinces]."[43]

From the outset Petrona and her sponsors seemed to realize that empanadas and locro were a lot less effective than French canapés and British-style cakes in establishing them and their products as useful in the capital city. Therefore, when Petrona C. de Gandulfo published the first edition of her cookbook *El libro de Doña Petrona* in 1934, she also emphasized French techniques and preparations for pastries like *vol-au-vents* and a variety of mousses and patés. Still, like Primitiva's classes, her cookbook was not solely a treatise on French cooking. Although it featured more European-inspired recipes popular in the capital, she also included dishes inspired by provincial cooking. Echoing earlier cookbooks and migratory patterns to Buenos Aires from *both* Europe and Argentina's "Interior," Italian pastas and Spanish seafood dishes were joined by recipes for hominy-based locros and empanadas associated with specific Argentine provinces.[44] The few recipes that included the term "criollo/a" in this cookbook generally called for beef or a mixture of oil, vinegar, tomato, garlic, onion, and parsley, sometimes spiked with indigenous *ají* [chile pepper].[45]

Doña Petrona's cookbook recipes thus implicitly constructed Argentina as racially more white than "brown" by recognizing the Europeanness of its cuisine and downplaying (in part by not naming) the importance of Indigenous and African contributions.[46] Its imagery was even more forthright in conveying this message. For example, an illustration from the mid-1930s showed a pair of fair-skinned hands (meant to represent those of her readers) and included tips, presumably written by Petrona herself, for preserving their beauty by rubbing them with a mixture of sugar and lemon followed by a combination of sugar and olive oil. After applying both rubs, readers were told, "rinse, and you will see how your hands *quedan blancas* [are left white] and the skin velvety."[47] A second color insert, an advertisement for a dairy company, also reveals this explicit preference for white skin by depicting a fair Petrona C. de Gandulfo educating a pale blond woman about the brand's virtues.

Corporations did not use exclusively white women in an effort to sell their products in early-twentieth-century Argentina; a number also depicted black women. In contrast to white professionals or consumers, dark-skinned women were often cast as domestic servants. For example, an advertisement for the Argentine frozen meat company Sansinena, which branded its products under the name "*La Negra* [The Black Woman]" during the early twentieth century, showcased an elegant black woman holding sausages in what might have been a nostalgic reference to domestic slave servants (like Aunt Jemima in the US context), and to the historical association, in Argentina, between black women and the job of butchering and eviscerating beef. This depiction may have been intended to remind homemakers of the emerging middle classes that they did not have help for these bloody and unpleasant tasks and that they should buy new frozen, pre-packaged products to compensate.[48] Likewise, a 1935 advertisement for Tulipán brand butter featured Doña Clarida, a smiling black woman wearing a servant's uniform and pronouncing, in a form of broken Spanish usually associated with the popular world, *"pa' mi no hay otra* [for me there's no other]."[49] This choice was likely meant to remind consumers of the predominant role that African-descended women had played as enslaved and free (but low-paid) cooks serving wealthier, lighter-skinned families; this longstanding association gave the black cook authority in recommending the product.

Neither Petrona C. de Gandulfo nor Primitiva, however, seemed interested in playing on the historical trope of black women's cooking. Instead, both continued to highlight European-style recipes and their urban modernity. Despite the nationalist turn in Argentina during the early-to-mid twentieth century, Doña Petrona and her contemporaries did not emphasize foods that would promote a regional or mestizo national identity, nor, like earlier cookbooks (or like cookbook authors in other Latin American countries), did they associate national authenticity with those kinds of foods.[50] Even as the Peronist government (1946–55) touted its ability to increase poor people's access to food and other consumer goods as evidence of its new nationalist political economy, government officials did not celebrate provincial, indigenous, African, or mestizo-inspired dishes as part of an authentic national cuisine. The Peronist government was more interested in emphasizing the class-based oppression of its followers and the possibility of including them in the privileges of a nation largely imagined as white than in highlighting their racial differences or race-based oppression.[51]

Indeed, instead of celebrating the criollo foods associated with poorer and darker-skinned people from the provinces, the Peronist government would highlight the beef and other prestigious foods that it enabled Buenos Aires' urban poor to enjoy. For example, in the opening celebration for a state-run home for single female workers, *El Hogar de la Empleada*, the menu included melon and prosciutto, crêpes filled with creamed corn and cheese, grilled entrecôte with French fries, and chocolate cake.[52] This multi-course cosmopolitan feast echoed the culinary preferences of the porteño middle and upper classes. In fact, it was a menu that could easily have been inspired by a cookbook like *El libro de Doña Petrona*.

By the mid-twentieth century, porteños could sample provincial fare at the *peñas* or folkloric clubs popping up across Buenos Aires, and the nationalist government occasionally encouraged home cooking of traditional provincial dishes, but the state did not forcefully promote a nationalist cuisine. And even as beef consumption increased significantly for working-class families in Buenos Aires during the late 1940s, it remained relatively low in the Northern and Southern provinces.[53] With the harvest failures of the early 1950s, the Peronist government changed its tune about what and how people in central

Argentina should eat. But even then it did not push provincial fare very aggressively. Instead, it encouraged people to replace beef with other meats and "healthier" foods like dairy, fruits, and vegetables.[54]

Ever-responsive to changing social dynamics, during the Peronist era Doña Petrona sought to make her recipes more accessible to upwardly mobile members of the working class. For example, in 1947 she added to *El libro de Doña Petrona* a less expensive version of the beloved Christmas sweet bread, *Pan dulce de navidad*, which called for replacing eggs with grated squash, and pine nuts or almonds with less expensive nuts like walnuts.[55] Still, she did not explicitly root these new dishes in a particular ethnic or racial identity that would speak to the often mixed-race background of Argentina's poor. (Pan Dulce was, after all, much closer to an Italian panettone than to an indigenous-inspired mazamorra). During the 1940s and 1950s, Doña Petrona continued to emphasize European and increasingly US-style dishes, making them more affordable and, during the 1960s when more middle-class women entered the workforce, quicker to make.[56]

Despite her emphasis on dishes that would speak to people in the capital, Doña Petrona's status as a *provinciana* was unquestionable for those who saw her live performances. And more and more people had the opportunity to do so. In the 1950s, viewers from Buenos Aires watched her cook live on television with her assistant Juanita Bordoy, and by the 1960s she was on air in other urban areas.[57] On television Doña Petrona spoke with a santiagueñan accent and rhythm; she enunciated each word in a marked staccato. She became infamous for a linguistic tic, the "¿no?" she often included at the end of her statements. In 1969, when a journalist asked her if this stemmed from her santiagueñan heritage (along with her empanadas santiagueñas), she retorted, "Hold on a second; I don't say it anymore." She went on to explain, "They gave me such a hard time about it everywhere that I had to stop doing it."[58] In a similar vein, journalists, along with many of the middle- and upper-class Argentines with whom I spoke, laughingly recalled how she would label an outstanding dish "un p*ue*ma," instead of "un poema," as the word "poem" is spelled and generally pronounced in and around Buenos Aires. As with the "¿no?," many in Buenos Aires associated this "mispronunciation" with Petrona's provincial upbringing in Northern Argentina and lack of a higher education. This demonstrates one of the ways – in this case, modifiable – in which the combination of language, culture, and region could mark people within a supposedly uniformly "white" Argentina as ethnically different.[59] At some level, Doña Petrona seemed to recognize this phenomenon, seeking to retrain some of her "ways of being."[60]

But if Doña Petrona's provincial status was immediately apparent to her contemporaries in her manner of speaking, it seems that her ethnic or racial identity remained either tacitly embedded in her provincial roots or insignificant. Many Argentines I spoke with were clearly attuned to Petrona's provincial background, but they seemed genuinely confused by my questions about their understanding of her (or her assistant Juanita's) racial or ethnic identity. When I asked about this, several of the people I interviewed simply stated that Doña Petrona was "provinciana" or "criolla," or did not answer at all. These responses suggest that race and ethnicity are not everyday categories that Argentines have consciously used to label others. This does not mean, however, that racial categories have not been at work. Indeed, such forms of difference might have been folded into terms like "provinciana" or "criolla." Like other Latin Americans, it seems plausible that some of the people I spoke with were regionalizing mestizo-ness in Argentina by locating it in the Northern provinces.[61]

The one person who answered most directly, an archeologist in her fifties named Marta, remarked that Doña Petrona's ethnic identity "was not anything, *estábamos muy mezclados* [we were very mixed]."[62] This comment echoes the widespread acceptance of the ideology of Argentina as a *crisol de razas* [crucible of races], in which people of different ancestries, and particularly Europeans of different national origins, were believed to have combined to form racially unmarked Argentines. As historian Mónica Quijada has demonstrated, this vision of Argentina has emphasized distinct European contributions to this "crucible" but also allowed for the (less-specifically noted) integration of nonwhites.[63]

Because political and social leaders generally succeeded in creating the idea that Argentina was a raceless nation by the early twentieth century, the racism experienced by poor people, who have often had darker skin and/or indigenous or African features, has been regularly overlooked, making it difficult to analyze and confront.[64] On a personal level, Marta made this point, recalling, "My mother always gets very mad when I say it, and she won't admit that she and her generation *eran racistas* [were racist]." Being identified as white, Marta explained, was best according to her mother's view. In contrast, if someone was from the Interior, a "*morochito* [dark person]," they "had to be clean."[65] Such a statement suggests, some three decades later, the continued resonance of the hand-washing advice from early editions of *El libro de Doña Petrona*, intended not only to clean – a modern, "civilized" practice – but also to whiten.

Discrimination extended beyond the perceived "dirtiness" of darker people from the provinces to a suspicion about the foods associated with them. As Marta explained, "Indigenous foods could be very tasty but they were not eaten [...] An empanada with a lot of spice wasn't good."[66] Eating in a properly "Argentine" manner mattered to the second- and third-generation immigrants living in her "middle-class" neighborhood in La Plata. Marta continued, "We lived in an Italian neighborhood and no one could say that they were Jewish or Spanish. Everyone wanted to be Argentine. People had to civilize themselves, to know how to eat." As this quote suggests, by the 1960s eating and being Italian had been thoroughly incorporated into eating and being Argentine in the urban centers of Argentina. But eating spicy foods associated with indigenous people was not part of the assimilation (or "civilization") plan for relatively recent immigrants from Spain or Eastern Europe in this region.

Still, some criollo foods were acceptable and even embraced by urbanites. Marta explained that "locro, as Doña Petrona would say, could pass." This was not to say that this dish was "whitened," but rather that it was "passable" provincial fare, or, in other words, locro occupied a respectable place within the diets of urban middle-class residents. Indeed, dishes like locro and (not too spicy) empanadas were not only acceptable, but also played important symbolic roles by distinguishing local fare from that of Europe.

CELEBRATING COCINA CRIOLLA

During the 1960s, culinary experts and media outlets would begin to celebrate a wider variety of provincial foods. In an early testament to this shift, the magazine *Mucho Gusto* published a cookbook in 1958 entitled *Especialidades de la cocina criolla* [Specialties of Criollo Cooking]. The editors explained that they had collected authentic recipes for cocina criolla, which they explicitly defined as having both indigenous and Spanish roots and hailing from Argentina and other parts of Latin America. While recognizing that their cookbook was not exhaustive, they claimed that the selection of recipes they offered represented "the most complete" treatment of cocina criolla available to "homemakers in the *países hermanos* [brother countries] of Central and South America."[67] The editors of this relatively conservative magazine based in Buenos Aires positioned Argentina and its cuisine as part of the same family tree as other Latin American – as opposed to European – nations. As this move attests, Argentine nationalism drew not just from the Interior but also from broader Latin American referents.

In contrast to previous cookbooks published in Argentina, the recipes in *Especialidades de la cocina criolla* did not focus on dishes of Italian or French origin. Instead, the editors drew inspiration from across Latin America, presenting dishes like Mexican *enchiladas* and Brazilian *feijoada* alongside a number of local Argentine dishes, some featuring beef (like asado) and others not (such as mazamorra). The editors even included a small but notable number of Argentine recipes with indigenous terminology, including *mbaipi de choclos*, which they explained (with an Italian metaphor they assumed to be more familiar to their readers) was "a type of polenta [...] typical of Corrientes."[68]

A couple of years later, Doña Petrona publicly stated for the first time her preference for cuisine from the Americas over the European cuisine with which she had begun her career. In so doing, Doña Petrona both reflected and tapped into new waves of Latin American regional pride and internationalism. When asked by food journalist and cook Marta Beines in 1960 about her favorite foods to prepare, she responded by saying that although she appreciated European cooking, she preferred "what is ours." This was a sentiment that Beines and others clearly appreciated. Beines wrote:

As a professional [Petrona] has access to any secret of the diverse cuisines of the world, [still] what is more than true is that she is not, nor does she want to be, a European-style specialist. What is important is not what can be imitated. Doña Petrona is faithful to what is hers.[69]

As this quote suggests, during this period a number of urban, middle-class Argentines began to appreciate provincial cultures, as opposed to Europeanized urban cultures, as sites of Argentine authenticity.[70]

As a woman from Santiago del Estero, Doña Petrona was particularly well-situated to promote the latest, more provincial version of "faithfulness" to all things Argentine. In journalists' hands, both Petrona and her empanadas came to embody the growing association of Argentine identity with its own rural roots rather than with Europe or Buenos Aires. For example, Beines included Petrona's empanada recipe, along with a description of the sensory experience of eating one: "They have a native flavor: they are juicy, spicy enough to excite the palate without destroying it and they are seasoned with spices that perfume the filling without changing the taste of the meat and of the dough, [which is] light and golden."[71] As this description suggests, Doña Petrona had succeeded in marrying slightly spicy indigenous flavors with beef inside the empanada, a sensually "exciting" union whose outcome would not be "destroyed" by the native element, and which in any case was contained by the European-inspired "light and golden" crust. Through her characterization, Beines suggested such empanadas to be an apt metaphor for the latest, more indigenous-inflected (or "perfumed") iteration of criollo identity in urban Argentina.

While Doña Petrona more actively celebrated provincial foods during the early 1960s, she also continued to present a broad range of cosmopolitan recipes as worthy of women's attention. In contrast, during this same period, the well-known Argentine folk singer Margarita Palacios, a native of the North-western province of Catamarca, began to use her fame and her provincial culinary roots to promote cocina criolla exclusively. In January 1962, she opened a peña in Buenos Aires featuring "Northern foods."[72] Later that year she published a recipe pamphlet called "*Las comidas de mi pueblo* [The Foods of My People]" for the Argentine magazine *Folklore*. In 1963, she began her own television program, showing her viewers how to make dishes popular in Northern Argentina.[73]

In future years, Doña Petrona paid greater attention to economizing (which was a more pressing concern for many of her urban middle-class fans) than to Northwestern recipes, yet she continued to address her provincial identity in a way she had not done previously. In 1969, the magazine *Gente* ran an article with a three-page spread featuring photographs in which Doña Petrona and her family (including her son, daughter-in-law, grandchildren, and assistant Juanita Bordoy) enjoyed empanadas around the traditional outdoor bread oven she had installed in her patio. In this article, Petrona commented, "empanadas should be eaten spicy and warm. 'In the mouth of the oven,' as they say in Santiago. [This is] a very old, and very wise Indian recipe." It seems that by the

DOÑA PETRONA: EMPANADAS SANTIAGUEÑAS

No es necesario presentarla: es Petrona, Doña Petrona, la figura más conocida de nuestra gastronomía. Ella lo sabe y es justo que tenga conciencia de ello; a su público se ha dado con verdadero fervor de oficio. No se limitó a llegar a él a través de las páginas de su libro, uno de los "bestseller" de vida más prolongada, sino que hace años que sus admiradoras y discípulas pueden seguirla en sus clases por radiotelefonía y televisión. En sus conferencias sobre arte culinario se congrega un público adicto que alcanza a llenar salas de espectáculo con miles de butacas; un público atento para no perder sus consejos técnicos y dispuesto a imitar su artesanía en el difícil arte de decorar. Doña Petrona confecciona tortas como juguetes encantados; golosinas que hacen soñar a los niños con soldaditos de caramelo y casas de mazapán, pero no es éste el aspecto más interesante de su capacidad. Como profesional no le es ajeno ningún secreto de las diversas cocinas del mundo, mas lo cierto es que ella no es ni quiere ser una especialista al estilo europeo. Lo importante no es lo que pueda imitarse. Santiagueña de origen, Doña Petrona tiene fidelidad por lo suyo.

Ante la pregunta sobre cuáles son sus preferencias dentro de su especialidad, manifiesta sin dudas que, aunque la entusiasma mucho la cocina europea, prefiere lo nuestro. Es decir lo suyo. Quien ha probado alguna de las famosas empanadas sabe que ella posee el secreto de una manera de hacerlas que las hace diferentes. Tienen el sabor de lo autóctono; son jugosas, picantes para avivar el paladar sin destruirlo y están sazonadas con las especias que perfuman el relleno sin modificar el gusto de la carne y de la masa, ligera y dorada.

De todas las empanadas típicas de nuestras provincias, encuentra que las de la suya son las que más aceptación tienen... "Eso sí —dice sonriéndose con picardía—: para tomarles el gusto hay que comerlas al lado del horno y a mano, envueltas en una servilleta para no quemarse". Y agrega: "La empanada santiagueña no admite ser recalentada; su sabor cambia y la grasa que contiene el relleno impregna la masa..."

Con su cordialidad y llaneza habituales se dispone a redactar una receta dedicada a los lectores de LA NACIÓN. Su secretaria se apresura a complacerla. Doña Petrona trabaja con un equipo organizado de colaboradoras: secretarias y ayudantas de cocina esperan sus órdenes para recorrer su nutrido fichero de recetas o poner en marcha su cocina experimental. Lo que es evidente es que Da. Petrona C. de Gandulfo ama la profesión

Doña Petrona C. de Gandulfo en su famoso laboratorio, donde se armonizan la tradición y la sorpresa

que ha elegido. Habla con entusiasmo sobre sus actividades; trata a sus colaboradoras y amigas que la acompañan con afecto y se advierte en el ambiente donde ella trabaja que la labor se realiza con alegría y buena voluntad.

Marta Beines

EMPANADAS SANTIAGUEÑAS

Elementos para preparar 24 empanadas:

MASA: 600 gramos de harina, 1 cucharadita de sal fina, 125 gramos de grasa de vaca. Agua fría.

SALSA: 500 gramos de grasa de vaca, 600 gramos de cebolla, 1 cucharada de pimentón de buena calidad, 1 cucharada de ají molido, picante; 1 cucharada de agua y 1 cucharadita de sal fina.

RELLENO: ½ kilogramo de carnaza de ternera, 1 cucharada al ras de comino molido, 1 cucharada de ají picante molido y sal fina a gusto.

PREPARACION: Para hacer la salsa hay que cocinar en la grasa la cebolla finamente picada y antes de que se dore agregarle el pimentón, el ají, el agua y la sal; dejar hervir un minuto, retirar en seguida y dejar enfriar.

Para hacer el relleno hay que cortar en pequeños daditos la carnaza, y, una vez cortada, pasarla rápidamente por agua hirviendo, colocarla en un colador y después acomodarla en una fuente grande, bien desparramada, para que se enfríe. Una vez casi fría se condimenta con sal, comino molido y ají picante molido.

Para hacer la masa, colocar sobre una mesa la harina en forma de corona, poner en el medio la grasa y el agua con sal. Formar una masa algo dura, dejarla descansar un cuarto de hora, tapada con una servilleta; después sobarla bien, cortarla en pedacitos, amasar como bollitos, estirarlos, dándoles forma redonda y dejarlos algo finos.

Tener listos tres huevos duros y pasas, a las que se habrá quitado las semillas.

Poner encima de cada masa una cucharada bien llena de carne, sobre ésta una cucharada de salsa y después un poco de huevo duro picado y algunas pasas. Humedecer los bordes de la masa y formar las empanadas con un buen repulgue.

Hornearlas en horno muy caliente; lo máximo que deben estar en el horno es doce minutos.

La Nación

5-6-60

FIGURE 11 Images from a newspaper article titled "What Gastronomy Experts Prefer to Eat: Doña Petrona: Empanadas from Santiago del Estero." Source: *La Nación*, 5 Jun. 1960. Courtesy of *La Nación*.

late 1960s, Petrona was proud of her regional (and perhaps even her indigenous) heritage, and rather than distancing herself from it as she did at the start of her career, she now seemed to embrace the notion of herself as a provincial woman even to the extent of calling the empanada – of primarily Spanish origin – indigenous. She remarked, "Things from the place you were born stay with you."[74]

Over the course of the 1970s, many of the provincial things people had been "born with" became increasingly important to a group of young, politicized middle-class people in urban areas. As historian Valeria Manzano has demonstrated, a burgeoning sense of pan-Latin Americanism and Third-Worldism manifested itself in new youthful patterns of cultural consumption that celebrated Argentina's native and local culture over those of the United States and Europe.[75] This manifested itself in the growing consumption of "folkloric" goods at local fairs, as well as travel to and social work in the provinces. For one young man who traveled to Petrona's native province of Santiago del Estero from the city of Mendoza, the differences were stark. "I could not believe that was also Argentina," he wrote, "but *that* is the true Argentina."[76]

The "true Argentina" was a place one could not only see, but taste. In 1970 in the Northeastern province of Chaco, the provincial capital of Resistencia hosted the "first national festival of *cocina criolla.*" At this festival, men competed to make the best asado con cuero.[77] This festival clearly drew from the cooking practices and mythology surrounding the gaucho, who was the heralded originator of this preparation (and stood in stark contrast to more urbanized styles of cooking in which select cuts of trimmed meat were prepared on domestic grills).[78] This mythic connection between cowboys and beef was something recognized not only at local festivals; it also became a deliberate export. Some seven years prior to this festival, in 1963, E. Rodríguez Long and Jewel B. Groves published a bilingual cookbook (in Spanish and English) in Buenos Aires titled *El asado criollo*, which they translated both as "Roast Spit Barbecue" and, more nationalistically, "Argentine Spit Roast." The authors explained to their desired English-language audience that asado was *the* national dish accepted across the country. They continued, "There is a deep tradition in this country that goes back for many years, from the time of the classic *asado* of the *gauchos* to the very sumptuous roast-on-the-spit *parrilla* of these days."[79] While the practice itself had changed, the asado made on an outdoor grill had become a celebrated, national tradition.

Doña Petrona continued to refrain from making asado outdoors, explaining in 1973 that her husband Atilio was the *"asador de la casa* [griller of the house]."[80] This reflected her (and many of her contemporaries') gender ideology as opposed to her lack of interest in cocina criolla. (The authors of *El asado criollo* also expected men to attend the grill).[81] As she had started to do during the previous decade, during the 1970s Doña Petrona made available to her magazine readership several Northwestern specialties.[82] Likewise, *Mucho Gusto* more emphatically began to celebrate Argentina's provincial culinary heritage in this period. It titled the May 1972 issue of its magazine "*Cocina Criolla con Sabor a Independencia* [Creole Cooking with the Flavor of Independence]." In the introductory note, the editors explained, "This collection of recipes contains culinary secrets from various Argentine provinces offered especially to porteños, who are already tired of eating *fideos con salsa* [noodles and sauce]." Whether or not such boredom existed, the editors emphasized the predominance and monotony of Italian-style preparations in Buenos Aires. Striking a provincial patriotic note, they signed off "With all the flavor from *tierra adentro* ['inland,' but also a historical term for indigenous lands beyond the nation's borders] and the pride of possessing a native cuisine." As in earlier recipe books, beef lard was a key ingredient in many dishes *Mucho Gusto* characterized as "criollas," including empanadas and pastries. Locro was also present, but no other beef-dominant dishes were. Instead, corn, which was both indigenous to and a staple in Northwestern Argentina, played the starring role in recipes for humita, *tamales salteños* [Salta-style tamales], *torta de choclo criolla* [criollo corn tart] and *empanadas de choclo* [corn-filled empanadas]. While most of these recipes were drawn from the Northwestern and Central provinces, there was also a reference to the typical celebratory fare from the Southern part of Argentina (a recipe for *Chivito a la criolla* [criollo-style goat]) and another from the West (a recipe for *Empanadas mendocinas*).[83]

As the provincial and criollo came to play a larger role in defining Argentine national identity, Doña Petrona pointed to her own provincial and mixed-race past more directly than before. In a 1976 interview, she proudly explained that she prided herself on being able to "speak *quechua* perfectly, read four news-papers a day [...and be] interested in politics, soccer, and other things in the world around us."[84] While she refused to publicly talk politics despite (or perhaps because of) the recent military coup, her claim that she was fluent in Quechua emphasized her mastery of an indigenous language widely spoken in her native province of Santiago del Estero.

For its part, the military dictatorship was eager to promote criollo national-ism, and it tapped into the tremendous symbolic nature of food. During the winter of 1976, the government joined forces with commercial interests and a children's charity to carry out what it deemed the first annual *Nacional Jorna-das de Cocina Criolla* [National Conference of Criollo Cuisine]. (They made no reference to the event six years prior in Chaco). Doña Petrona was in attend-ance (with her husband and with fellow ecónoma Choly Berreteaga) and was even named "honorary president."[85] Other participants in the four-day-long conference included cooks, doctors, dietitians, and government officials from across Argentina. Dramatizing the links between the military government and commercial interests, Doña Petrona and Choly Berreteaga sat on a panel that judged the empanada competition along with Roberto Mitchell, Administrative Director of the Ministry of the Economy, and Héctor Adell, the marketing

director for a well-known liquor business.[86] The military government's organization of this conference suggests their interest in showing their government to
be authentically Argentine, even criollo. This notion was replicated in the diet
of military conscripts, who regularly ate what was by then considered quintessentially criollo fare like empanadas and locro.[87] Like previous political leaders,
the military government's interest in female cooking (this was an empanada and
not an asado competition after all) emphasized their broader idea that women's
domestic duties played an important role in the national community and
economy, as well as in sustaining their families.

During the late 1970s, urban men and women alike had come to embrace a
new form of criollismo that incorporated indigenous and mestizo influences
from Northern provinces. Indeed, the gauchos of the plains and criollos of the
Northwest had become "quintessentially Argentine" to a much greater extent
than their counterparts in Patagonia or Northeastern Argentina. This was
reflected in both folklore and food.[88] For example, the authors of a 1978 cookbook titled *La cocina del gaucho* [The Gaucho Cookbook], explained,

... in love with *lo criollo*, aware of how national cosmopolitanism at times harms our
traditions, respectful of the wise culinary base of the Inca period, admiring tasters of our
original variety of ingredients, we believe it important to undertake this work of
organization and of exegesis of the range of food inherited from our remote American
ancestors.[89]

As they suggested in this quote, some of the recipes did indeed draw from pre-
colonial foodways and featured native Andean ingredients including corn and
potato. However, dishes made with local ingredients from other regions, such
as manioc from Northeastern Argentina, were notably absent. In addition, this
cookbook, like other celebrations of cocina criolla, also reflected the profound
impact of the Spanish introduction of cattle on what, by the twentieth century,
had come to be considered uniquely Argentine culinary traditions. The authors
of this text devoted entire chapters to celebrating and explaining how to
prepare asado or *charqui* [jerky].

Doña Petrona became even more interested in promoting recipes for Northwestern provincial cooking during the 1980s. She shared with a journalist in
1985 that she had prepared a new cookbook focused on cocina criolla, or, as
she also put it, "our traditional food," but that it was too expensive and
difficult to find an editor.[90] The santiagueña who established herself as *the*
premiere culinary expert in twentieth-century Argentina would publish over
one hundred editions of her main cookbook *El libro de Doña Petrona*, along
with more specialized cookbooks focused on decoration, economizing, and diet
foods, but she would never publish a cookbook that featured the cooking of her
native province and Northwestern Argentina. Indeed, it was not until the 1990s
and beyond that the next generation of explicitly criollo and provincial cookbooks would be published. And since Doña Petrona died in 1992, such initiatives were left to be undertaken by others.

CONCLUSION

In early-twentieth-century Buenos Aires, "lo criollo" had been tightly linked with a local culture associated with the whitened gaucho and his celebrated open-air asados on the Pampas, idealized by nationalist segments of Argentine society in the face of waves of European immigration. Still, it was not asado criollo or cocina criolla that dominated the culinary ideal in Buenos Aires and other urban settings like Santiago del Estero during this era. Instead, for the Italian visitor to Santiago del Estero, the Compañía Primitiva de Gas, and its star "ecónoma" Doña Petrona, French and other European cuisine reigned supreme during the 1920s through the 1950s. During the 1960s and 1970s, as more urban youth looked to rural spaces for the "real" Argentina, Doña Petrona (like other urbanites) sought to publicly embrace her provincial roots and celebrate the spicy empanadas of Santiago del Estero. Until this point, local foods like these had remained ethnically unmarked in their regions of origin in contrast to "French" or "Italian" fare.

Echoing an earlier trend, ideas about national cuisine in Argentina have continued to be tightly associated with beef. In 2003, the Argentine Secretary of Culture formally inducted *asado de carne vacuna* [beef barbecue] as a "food and specific dish belonging to the Argentine cultural patrimony."[91] This was not just political grandstanding. Many Argentines had come to believe "that a meal without beef should not be called a meal," and that a proper celebration called for an asado.[92] In contrast to much of the world, where starchy grains (corn, rice, wheat) serve as the basis for most people's diets, in central Argentina beef had become an expected staple of the diet and a defining element of local cuisine and identity.

By the late twentieth and early twenty-first centuries, more and less beef-centric versions of cocina criolla had acquired a place at the national table and in the national imaginary. In urban centers, this trend can be seen most dramatically on national holidays when dishes like locro and empanadas enjoy a high-profile status. The growing appreciation for cocina criolla has also manifested itself in a slew of new cookbooks. In 2005, Choly Berreteaga (who had helped judge the 1976 empanada competition with Doña Petrona) published *La cocina de nuestra tierra* [The Cooking of Our Land]. In the prologue, she celebrated Argentina's cocina criolla, which, she explained, had been forged by the "fusion between the Hispanic and indigenous worlds and the later migratory flows from Europe."[93] In distinguishing a previous bedrock Argentine criollo identity from "later" migratory flows, Berreteaga echoed a new (post-2001 economic crisis) discourse about national formation.[94] Further, in contrast to previous generations who celebrated cocina criolla as essentially stemming from culinary traditions from the Northwest and the Central plains, Berreteaga presented a more inclusive version by including not just token recipes but entire chapters focused on dishes from the Northeast, Patagonia, and the mountainous Western region of Cuyo.

This more inclusive vision of Argentina's culinary map came in conjunction with other recent efforts to speak about and even celebrate Argentina's indigenous and mestizo past – efforts that have accelerated in the twenty-first century with Argentina's 2001 economic crisis and 2010 Bicentennial.[95] Still, in looking back at the twentieth century, it bears remembering that the emphasis on criollo culture has often erased or subsumed Argentina's histories of racial difference and mixture, keeping those processes deliberately opaque. Anthropologist Víctor Ramos suggests that even at the start of the twenty-first century, many people with indigenous backgrounds who migrate to urban areas "tend to negate their background and instead affirm their identity as *'provincianos'*," leading to a loss of "particular cultural traits and ethnic traditions."[96] While not directly mentioned in this scholarship, indigenous and Afro-Argentine culinary contributions are among the traditions that have been subsumed and are only recently starting to be recognized. Whereas eating foods inspired by Europe and the United States was considered modern throughout the twentieth century, eating cocina criolla, even when it was celebrated, was primarily associated with tradition and, at times, a hazy indigenous and mestizo heritage, decidedly located in the past.

Notes

I thank Paulina Alberto and Eduardo Elena for the thoughtful work they have put into this chapter, this volume, and the conference panels that preceded this book. I express my appreciation to my co-panelists and to members of the Grupo de Estudios Afrolatinoamericanos for useful feedback. I also thank Carina Perticone for sharing a rare edition of Antonio Gonzaga's first cookbook and the Argentines I interviewed for sharing their food-related memories.

  1. Fazio, *Memoria*; Tasso, *Historia*, 60.
  2. Losada, *La alta sociedad*, 204–08; Remedi, *Entre*, 141–52.
  3. Stepan, *Hour*; Rodríguez, *Civilizing Argentina*.
  4. Losada, *La alta sociedad*, 204–08; Remedi, *Entre*, 141–52.
  5. Emilia S. and Livio S., interview by author, Buenos Aires, 6 Nov. 2003.
  6. Arcondo, *Historia*; Caldo, *Mujeres cocineras*; Remedi, *Entre*.
  7. Earle, *Conquistador*.
  8. Schávelzon, *Historias*, 71–72.
  9. This approach is inspired by Briones, *Cartografías*.
 10. For a comparative study of cocina criolla in Argentina, Cuba, and Mexico, see Pilcher, "Eating."
 11. Guzmán, "Performatividad."
 12. Castro, *Afro-Argentine*, viii; Arrom, "Criollo," 172–76.
 13. Chamosa, "Indigenous."
 14. Briones, "Mestizaje."
 15. Prieto, *El discurso*; Bockelman, "Between."
 16. Chamosa, *Argentine Folklore*, especially 2 and 196 n. 36. See also Rodríguez, this volume.

17. Adamovksy, "La cuarta función."
18. Quijada et al., *Homogeneidad*; Briones, *Cartografías*; Adamovsky, "La cuarta función."
19. Olga C. G. and Olga A. G., interview by author, Santiago del Estero, 4 May 2004.
20. For colonial Latin American trends, see Bauer, *Goods*, especially 46–84.
21. Tasso, *Ferrocarril*, 219.
22. "Goyo" C., interview by author, Santiago del Estero, 6 May 2004.
23. Remedi, *Entre*.
24. For example, Tulio Febres Cordero, *Cocina criolla o guía del ama de casa* (Mérida, Venezuela: Tipografía El Lápiz, 1899).
25. Tobin, "Manly Acts," 53.
26. Pilcher, "Eating."
27. Arcondo, *Historia*, 227.
28. *La cocinera criolla por Marta* [pseudonym] (Barcelona: Luis Gili, 1914); Caldo, *Mujeres cocineras*, 136.
29. Caldo, *Mujeres cocineras*, 136.
30. Congregación de Hijas de María y de Santa Filomena de Tucumán, *El arte de cocinar* (Tucumán, Argentina: Imp. La Comercial de Aníbal L. Medina, 1920 [1st ed.]; 1974 [4th ed.]).
31. *Para Ti* (Buenos Aires), 23 May 1939, 66.
32. While the term "negro" in Argentina can also be used as a class descriptor, it seems that in this case it referred to Gonzaga's color, as he was also called "moreno" and "de color."
33. Antonio Gonzaga, *El cocinero práctico argentino* (Buenos Aires: 1931); www.lanacion.com.ar/1186416-la-cocina-del-negro-que-cautivo-buenos-aires (accessed 18 Apr. 2012).
34. Geler, "Afro-Porteños."
35. Antonio Gonzaga, *La cocina argentina y francesa* (Buenos Aires, 1928).
36. Gonzaga, *La cocina*, 270.
37. See, for example, www.carnesdelolo.wordpress.com/2012/05/01/asado-un-ritual/ (accessed 11 Feb. 2012).
38. Geler, *Andares* and "Afro-Porteños"; Karush, "Blackness."
39. Caldo, *Mujeres cocineras*, especially chapter 4.
40. Cara, "Poetics," 39.
41. Schávelzon, *Historias*, 54–69.
42. Losada, *La alta sociedad*, 204–08.
43. Ofelia F., interview by author, Buenos Aires, 31 Dec. 2003.
44. Petrona C. de Gandulfo, *El libro de Doña Petrona* (Buenos Aires, 1934 [editions through 1992]).
45. Gandulfo, *El libro*; Pilcher, "Eating," 10.
46. On ideas of brownness for the Argentine context, see Alberto, this volume.
47. Gandulfo, *El libro*, eds. 1–2(1934–35), inset before p. 9.
48. Luis Barrantes Molina, *Para mi hogar. Síntesis de economía y sociabilidad domésticas: Escrita expresamente para la Compañía Sansinena de carnes congeladas* (Buenos Aires: 1923), 16.
49. Advertisement for Tulipán, *El Hogar* (Buenos Aires) 5 Apr. 1935.
50. On Mexico, see Pilcher, *Tamales*.

51. See Elena, Adamovsky, this volume.
52. "Fueron habilitadas ayer las instalaciones del Hogar de la Empleada," *Democracia* (Buenos Aires) 20 Jan. 1950, as cited in Acha, "Dos estrategias," 167.
53. Milanesio, "Food Politics," 86–88, 91.
54. For more analysis of Peronist food- and consumption-related initiatives see Billarou, "El ama"; Elena, *Dignifying* and "What the People Want"; Milanesio, "Guardian"; and Pite, *Creating*.
55. Gandulfo, *El libro*, 23rd ed. (1947), 516.
56. For my analysis of these trends, see Pite, *Creating*.
57. For more analysis, see, Pite, "Entertaining Inequalities."
58. Mario Mactas, "Para comerte mejor," *Gente* (Buenos Aires), 25 Sep. 1969, 55.
59. For analysis of this trend, see Briones, "Mestizaje."
60. See Geler, this volume.
61. On the racialization of region in Latin America, see Weinstein, "Racializing"; Appelbaum, *Muddied Waters*; and Wade, *Blackness*.
62. Marta F., interview by author, La Plata, 4 Apr. 2004.
63. Quijada et al., *Homogeneidad*, 9–12.
64. Margulis and Urresti, *La segregación*. See also Geler, Gordillo, Rodríguez, this volume.
65. See Geler, this volume; Marta F., interview by author.
66. Marta F., interview by author.
67. *Especialidades de la cocina criolla: seleccionadas por el personal técnico de la revista Mucho Gusto* (Buenos Aires: Fabril Financiera, 1958), 8.
68. *Especialidades*, 63.
69. Marta Beines, "Qué prefieren comer los grandes gastrónomos, Doña Petrona: Empanadas Santiagueñas," *La Nación* (Buenos Aires), 5 Jun. 1960.
70. On an earlier period, see Chamosa, *Argentine Folklore*.
71. Chamosa, *Argentine Folklore*.
72. "Guía de Peñas," *Folklore* (Buenos Aires), Jan. 1962, 63.
73. "Guía nativa: Radio y TV," *Radiolandia* (Buenos Aires), Sep. 1963, 72.
74. Mactas, "Para comerte mejor."
75. Manzano, "Making."
76. "Cartas," *Nuevo Hombre* (Buenos Aires) Mar. 1972, 12; Manzano, "Making." My emphasis.
77. Emmy de Molina, "Sabor y saber sobre la mesa: Exotismo en nuestro folklore gastronómico," *La Prensa* (Buenos Aires), 25 Nov. 1972, 2a.
78. On gauchos and "lo criollo," see, for example, Prieto, *El discurso*; Bockelman, "Between."
79. E. Rodríguez Long and Jewel B. Groves, *El asado criollo; Roast Spit Barbecue* (Buenos Aires: Artes Gráficas M.A.C.S., 1963), 10.
80. Elsa San Martín, "Petrona C. de Gandulfo: Una mujer positiva," *Mucho Gusto* (Buenos Aires), 12–25 Sep. 1973, 9.
81. Rodríguez Long and Groves, *El asado criollo*, 26–27.
82. Elsa San Martín, "Petrona C. de Gandulfo: Una mujer positiva," *Mucho Gusto*, 12–25 Sep. 1973, 9.
83. "Cocina criolla con sabor a independencia," *Mucho Gusto* 41, May 1972, 35–51.
84. "Cómo viven los argentinos: Petrona C. de Gandulfo: ¿el Gardel de las amas de casa?" *Clarín*, 11 Jun. 1976, n.p.

85. Choly Berreteaga, interview by author, 18 Jun. 2004, Buenos Aires.
86. "Sabor y saber sobre la mesa: La cocina criolla en jornadas," n.p., n.d., courtesy of the Association of Ecónomas.
87. Conversation with a former military conscript who served in 1983, Oct. 2011.
88. Chamosa, "Indigenous," 75.
89. *La cocina del gaucho* (Buenos Aires: Ediciones Gastronómicas el Gato que Pesca, 1978).
90. "Doña Petrona a 50 años de su primer libro, habla con Emmy de Molina, su amiga y colega." *La Prensa*, 9 Apr. 1984, 4.
91. Osés, *Léxico de la carne*, 18.
92. Lovera, *Food Culture*, 37.
93. Choly Berreteaga, *La cocina de nuestra tierra* (Buenos Aires: Editorial Atlántida, 2005), 4.
94. Briones, "La Nación."
95. See also Alberto, Elena, Ko, this volume; Briones, "La Nación;" and Adamovsky, "El color."
96. Margulis and Urresti, *Racismo*.

5

"Invisible Indians," "degenerate descendants"

Idiosyncrasies of mestizaje *in Southern Patagonia*

Mariela Eva Rodríguez

In Argentina's Southern Patagonian region one often hears that the *Tehuelche* people were the "only" and the "true Argentine Indians," that they "became extinct [*se extinguieron*]," and that only a handful of "descendants" remain. Paradoxically, this utterance ("*se extinguieron*") – in the passive voice, with no subject, in which there seems to be no agent responsible for the alleged extinction – takes place in a context of the re-emergence of the Tehuelche people and of an indigenous communitarian reorganization that involves the Tehuelche, as well as the *Mapuche* and *Mapuche-Tehuelche*.[1] The supposed "disappearance" of the Tehuelche is the result of interrelated discourses and practices that a range of agents constructed and deployed over the course of more than a century, in which the ideology of "degenerative *mestizaje*" played a central role. In this chapter I argue that in the mid-twentieth century, the Argentine state, in its eagerness to "whiten" and homogenize its citizenry, suppressed the category *mestizo* (a term traditionally referring to people of mixed European and indigenous origins) from its bureaucratic terminology and replaced it with euphemisms – notably, the term *descendiente* [descendant] – that encompassed a range of interrelated racial, ethnic, class, and national classifications. Using a varied documentary corpus, this chapter analyzes the changing uses of classificatory terms like "mestizo" and "descendiente" over the course of the long twentieth century in what is today the province of Santa Cruz, in Southern Patagonia. In so doing, it sheds light on the tensions between those who had the power to classify and those who were classified, on the strategies used by the latter to enter or to exit taxonomic categories, and on the consequences of those categories in the daily lives of generations of local people who at different times acknowledged varying degrees of indigenous ancestry. Finally, this chapter contributes, from the perspective of Patagonia, to the emerging picture of the regional variations within Argentine ideologies of whiteness, and situates these regional and national ideologies within a broader Latin American context.

Latin American ideologies of mestizaje and whitening, as well as ideologies of racism, have varied widely across time and space, reflecting different patterns in the ways colonial and then national elites constructed hegemony and subalternity. As anthropologist Rita Segato argues, racial ideologies vary according to the particular "matrix of diversity" within every "national formation."[2] Over the course of the past century, some of the region's intellectual elites – such as José Vasconcelos in Mexico and the thinkers associated with the 1952 Bolivian Revolution – chose to celebrate mestizaje and to make it central to an official discourse of nation-building.[3] In other cases, it was subalternized groups (such as *Chicanos* in the United States or *Cholos* in Peru) who appealed to a "resistant mestizaje" as a liberating force capable of challenging hegemonic colonial and neocolonial categories of "ethnicity" and "race."[4]

Further south, however, national elites from Argentina or Uruguay – even as they consolidated "white" nations through the amalgamation of groups of varied backgrounds – did not celebrate mestizaje as a national ideology; indeed, they condemned it as a threat to the desired homogeneity of a "white race." In so doing, they presented their respective nations as "exceptional" in comparison to the rest of Latin America, the products of a more distinctly European melting pot forged through a dual process: campaigns of extermination against indigenous people in the nineteenth century and the simultaneous arrival of massive numbers of European immigrants, which continued into the twentieth century.

As a result, until recently, the dominant view in Argentina's national historiography has held that the nineteenth-century civic-military campaigns resolved the so-called Indian problem. These campaigns – officially titled the "Conquest of the Desert" and carried out by General Julio Argentino Roca – began in 1879 in the central-south region of present-day Buenos Aires Province, pushing far southward to Patagonia and, shortly thereafter, turning north to the Gran Chaco region along the border with Paraguay (a phase known as the "Conquest of the Green Desert," ending in 1917). The indigenous people who were not killed during these campaigns were forcibly incorporated into the nation as nominal citizens and into the national economy as a cheap labor force. Their territories became "public lands" under the control of the state bureaucracy or were sold off as private property. The state also distributed lands among those who had taken part in or sponsored the military conquest as well as among European immigrants, who were invited by the 1853 Constitution to enter the country as settlers and contribute to advancing what elites understood as "order," "civilization," and "progress."

In conjunction with these trends of territorial conquest, Argentina's national leaders and intellectuals crafted narratives that stressed the successful construction of a "white nation" – a political, cultural, and ideological project that sought to render indigenous peoples and Afro-descendants invisible. Even though the process of creating a homogeneously white nation out of a diverse population relied on processes that elsewhere in Latin America would be recognized as mestizaje, in Argentina, the production of whiteness required that processes of mestizaje *not* result in the creation of mestizos, but of "whites." This ideology was reflected in the suppression or erasure of processes and categories of hybridity from official documents, histories, and popular discourse beginning in the late nineteenth century.[5] The result of these transformations, by the early twentieth century, was a nation without "blacks" or "Indians," and also without "mestizos."[6]

The stability of these national narratives, however, was threatened throughout the twentieth- and twenty-first centuries by at least three factors. First, the indigenous survivors of these nation-building processes continued making themselves visible to the state through bureaucratic channels, including by soliciting permissions to settle in their former territories; these demands were part of broader strategies employed by indigenous people to recreate their own social, economic, and political organizations. Second, although trans-Atlantic European immigration dominated national attention at the turn of the twentieth century, immigration from neighboring countries (which reflected long-term movements of people even before national borders were established) continued at a significant pace throughout the century. In Southern Patagonia, a considerable number of immigrants were indigenous people and mestizos who lost their marks of aboriginality[7] after crossing the Chile-Argentina border, fleeing Chile's own wars of frontier expansion. In the official census and in police records these immigrants were commonly registered as "foreigners." Yet far from being a neutral term referring strictly to nationality, the term "foreigner" contained racial meanings, deeply engrained in the common sense of everyday Argentines, which marked these immigrants as Others in the "European" nation. Third, the presidency of Juan D. Perón (1946–55) was characterized by the appearance and heightened visibility in the national capital of supporters from the Interior, whose combination of low socioeconomic status and indigenous and/or African phenotypes (as well as their vocal and unsettling demands for economic and social rights) led members of the anti-Peronist upper and middle classes to pejoratively call them "*cabecitas negras* [little black heads]." Although white urban Argentines (especially in the capital Buenos Aires) portrayed this demographic transformation as sudden or as an "invasion," in fact the "cabecitas negras" drew from populations, hailing mostly from the Interior, that had long combined Afro-descendants, displaced indigenous people, and indigenous or mestizo migrants from neighboring countries.[8]

One way of understanding the tensions in Argentine narratives of whiteness – in their simultaneous inclusion and exclusion of people of non-European descent – is to follow anthropologist Claudia Briones' proposal to imagine Argentine national formation in terms of two simultaneous *crisoles de raza* [racial crucibles or melting pots] that contributed to the creation of a "white nation." Running parallel and subordinate to the celebrated European melting pot, she argues, we might imagine a "hidden" melting pot made up of the nation's "popular sectors" – precisely the kinds of people who in the 1940s came to be known as "cabecitas negras." According to Briones, the nation's popular sectors have historically inhabited a kind of second-class citizenship because of a combination of class position, regional background, educational levels, and phenotype – a combination in which ideas about race were always powerful but whose prominence or visibility varied by context. Briones proposes analyzing this hidden stratification within the "white" nation in terms of practices of "ethnicization" and "racialization," ways of marking difference that produce distinct effects but which operate in concert. "Racializations" – classifications that revolve around differences supposedly rooted in "nature" – deny the possibility of movement across social boundaries and the possibility that marks of difference will be completely diluted by biological miscegenation or cultural homogenization. While in extreme cases processes of racialization justify racial enclaves or apartheid policies, in less dramatic contexts they tend to result either in the reading of mixture as "mestizaje," or in the creation of "categorical anomalies," for which it is difficult to account using the categories provided by the taxonomic system. By contrast, "ethnicization" refers to forms of marking difference based on distinctions rooted in culture, which allow for movement between different social categories. Thus, processes of ethnicization rest on the idea that it is possible to manipulate and to transform marks of belonging and, therefore, that these marks can be made visible (acquirable) or – as is frequently supposed – that they can be made invisible (hidden or eliminated). By using these meta-terms instead of "race" or "ethnicity," Briones seeks to avoid the trap of treating these analytical categories as if they alluded to the supposedly fixed or inherent typological qualities of specific groups. By focusing on *processes* of racialization and ethnicization, she is able to show how these different forms of marking difference tend to operate simultaneously in most cases, though their effects and outcomes vary according to specific contexts of interaction, as we will see in the case of Santa Cruz.[9]

Working from the premise that racial and ethnic classifications vary not only country to country but within nations themselves (by province, state, region, and so forth), the first section of this chapter sheds light on the processes of racialization and ethnicization affecting indigenous and mestizo populations in the province of Santa Cruz, in dialogue with broader national-level processes.[10] It begins by tracing the emergence of a particular discursive formation – produced by state, scientific, and ecclesiastic agents – that declared the Tehuelche people "extinct" and treated the Mapuche people as "foreigners." In contrast to the idealized national subject embodied in the figure of the European "pioneer," state officials, scientists, and priests from the late nineteenth century through the twentieth classified the progeny of those considered "pure Indians" as an inferior copy, distorted by a process of biological, cultural, and morally "degenerative mestizaje." In turn, they affixed racialized and ethnicized labels such as "descendants" and "chilotes" to these populations of indigenous ancestry to highlight their presumed inferiority or their foreignness.

The second part of the chapter examines the records of the federal and provincial public land management agencies (the National Directorate of Land and Colonies and the Provincial Agrarian Council) to uncover how state authorities deployed these categories over the course of the twentieth century and to what effects. In particular, it focuses on how the use of such categories has affected the members of the former indigenous "reservation" of Camusu Aike (renamed by them as a "community" in 2007). I pay particular attention to the year 1943, when land inspectors replaced the term "mestizo" with "descendant." These documents and their shifting language for referring to indigenous people reveal the ways in which processes of "ethnicization" permitted the entrance of these groups into the white nation, where, renamed as "descendants," they became invisible *as indigenous.* Yet simultaneously, processes of racialization based on the idea of degenerative mestizaje continually stigmatized them and prevented them from entering fully into the supposedly white nation. The section ends by demonstrating that what might seem like a mere terminological substitution had practical consequences, ones that have shaped contests over land and processes of self-recognition for members of Camusu Aike even to this day.

THE DISCURSIVE FORMATION OF "EXTINCTION" AND THE IDEA OF "DEGENERATIVE MESTIZAJE"

Although the idea of Tehuelche "disappearance" first emerged in the late nineteenth century, it consolidated over the course of the twentieth through what I have analyzed elsewhere (following Michel Foucault) as the "discursive formation of extinction."[11] By "discursive formation," Foucault means a corpus of utterances that – despite their heterogeneity and their emergence in different times and places – are nonetheless interlinked as part of a system and governed by a set of rules or principles that shape the objects, perspectives, concepts, and themes of discourse.[12] In the case of Southern Patagonia since the late nineteenth century, a group of anonymous (but historically and spatially specific) rules created the conditions of enunciation of a discourse of "extinction" that was acritically reproduced for over a century by a series of actors with the power to write (and which, it should be noted, excluded the voices and perspectives of indigenous people themselves). This corpus includes a set of reports produced by state agents, priests, and missionaries (Anglicans and Salesians), and scientists (naturalists, linguists, anthropologists) who traveled from Buenos Aires to Southern Patagonia between the late nineteenth and the late twentieth centuries. The somewhat later works of local journalists and historians (both amateur and professional), as well as teachers, artists, and folklorists, among others, also make up this corpus and its distinctive discursive profile. Discourses and practices are intimately related, and the consequences of this "discursive formation of extinction" continue to affect indigenous peoples to this day.

Within this discursive formation, several *dispositifs* or knowledge-power apparatuses – including institutions, regulations, laws, administrative measures, and scientific or philosophical precepts – operated in concert, though in slightly different ways, to reinforce the idea of the supposedly imminent and unavoidable extinction of the Tehuelches. Though scientific dispositifs generally constructed and justified racial or cultural taxonomies, while state dispositifs prioritized civilizational and nationalist ones, both converged around two major assumptions. The first assumption, grounded in appeals to the "inevitability" of the laws of progress, held that the Tehuelche were "destined" to disappear – that a few scattered and unproductive "savages" "wandering" in open fields were condemned to "extinction." Followers of Darwin and Spencer, for example, believed that hunter-gatherer groups would perish when they encountered the more advanced and civilized (European) settlers, because such was the inexorable fate of the "inferior races." This was the conviction of many naturalists who traveled to Southern Patagonia financed by the Argentine state in the 1870s and 1880s[13] as well as of several British explorers and travelers.[14]

The second assumption regarding the extinction of the Tehuelche, by contrast, points to a very specific agent: the Mapuche people were responsible for the "disappearance" of the Tehuelche, either because the Mapuche murdered them or because they merged with them, imposing their own biological and cultural features. This idea has a long history: just prior to the so-called Conquest of the Desert, General Roca's advisor, the military explorer and naturalist Estanislao Zeballos, promoted the idea that the Mapuche were "Chilean Indians" invading Argentine territories. In his book *The Conquest of the Fifteen Thousand Leagues* (1878), Zeballos elaborated a set of arguments that would become all too familiar: that such lands constituted valuable territory for the Argentine state and that it should move to occupy them before Chile did; that Indians harmed the national economy (through their frequent raids and through the cost of treaty tribute given to them by the federal government); and that, in any case, the most problematic and "warlike Indians" in Argentina actually originated in Chile. Through this logic, certain indigenous groups from the greater Pampa region previously considered "friendly Indians" became "foreign invaders." This "epic-political scheme," to borrow anthropologist Diana Lenton's phrase, was used by the federal government to legitimize the war.[15]

As the so-called Conquest of the Desert progressed, Zeballos's work helped cast the Río Negro [Black River] as a new symbolic boundary, whereby peoples imagined as located primarily to the river's south (including the Tehuelche) were represented as the "country's original people," "naturally prepared for civilization." As a result, the Tehuelche were included in a plan of forced assimilation as "Argentine Indians," which permitted their entrance into the nation as cheap manual labor: as *peones* or rural hands, as low-level soldiers in the army, or as *baqueanos* [experts in topographic and geographical knowledge] to guide army troops and explorers.[16] The Tehuelche and other indigenous peoples who survived the Army's murderous campaigns and its forced recruitment practices, as well as the subsequent ordeals of state-ordered confinement in concentration camps, torture, displacement, or deportation,[17] were forcibly inducted into a "civilized" and undifferentiated form of citizenship, and further incorporated as low-wage workers into the capitalist order. The Conquest of the Desert thus not only represented a military defeat for indigenous peoples and a permanent seizure of their lands but was also a turning point in the political and cultural process of "invisibilization" of indigenous peoples in Argentina. This process continued to be perfected in subsequent years by travelers' chronicles and (as we will see in the next section) bureaucratic reports that stressed extinction.

In the twentieth century, the works of state-sponsored anthropologists in particular would engage with, and perpetuate, both sets of assumptions about Tehuelche disappearance. In Argentina, as in other countries, the early twentieth century witnessed the spread of eugenicist ideologies and related forms of bio-power, which asserted that human offspring could be improved through the manipulation of natural laws of inheritance.[18] From this vantage, some observers considered certain types of immigration (whether from Europe or neighboring Latin American countries) as a threat to the nation. In light of domestic outbreaks of social and labor conflict in which leftist European immigrants played visible roles, this ideological inclination became more extreme and racist by the 1920s and especially the 1930s (during a military regime), and its xenophobic principles became more closely linked to ideas about the health, purification, order, and progress of the nation. It was in this context that the Spanish anthropologist Salvador Canals Frau coined the term "Araucanization" (1935) to describe the supposed processes by which groups he construed as foreign (like the Mapuche, seen as originating in Chile's Araucanía region) imposed their culture upon local indigenous people, thereby permanently transforming them. This concept directly referenced the ideas about "invasive" Mapuches elaborated by Zeballos in the previous century, granting them scientific legitimacy and further justifying the Conquest of the Desert. In his contribution to the *Handbook of South American Indians* (1946) edited by US anthropologist Julian Steward, Canals Frau argued that General Roca brought "civilization" to the Pampa-Patagonia region by ending the territorial rule of the indigenous. These populations, he asserted, though culturally similar to sixteenth-century Indians who had lived in those parts, were "racially and linguistically different" from their earlier counterparts.[19] In a later book, Canals Frau refined these ideas further, arguing that the "racial types" he called "Patagónidos" and "Pámpidos" (which he conceded were "Argentine") had disappeared as the consequence of a gradual process of "ethnic substitution," which was the outcome of the "infiltration" of foreign groups of "Araucanians" who entered from Chile in the eighteenth century, displacing the former indigenous populations without violence.[20] In general, the ethnological research conducted in the wake of Canals Frau's influential studies did not challenge the notion that "Araucanization" had actually happened; instead, its authors merely debated the timing of this process.[21]

In the wake of World War II and the defeat of Nazism, the concept of "race" (as the description of a biological reality) was increasingly abandoned by anthropologists and other scholars abroad.[22] In Argentine scientific and academic circles, however, explicitly racialist discourses became fused with discourses about ethnicity, informing nationalist ideologies in periods of democracy and dictatorship alike. The term "culture" came to absorb concepts that had previously fallen under the domain of "race" – like, for instance, the notion of "blood" – and, in turn, "race" was re-conceptualized as "culture," in which guise it continued its longstanding functions as a supposed indicator of morality and intelligence.[23]

These theories would in turn shape state policies toward indigenous peoples. During his presidency in the 1940s, Perón used the state apparatus and propaganda to build his image as the champion of the Argentine *pueblo*, especially the humbler classes. This political project, driven in part by a desire to homogenize the nation, interpellated indigenous people as citizens and constructed them as part of a "working class" or as "rural workers." During Perón's presidency, indigenous peoples accessed specific rights, including the right to vote, to obtain personal identification documents, to access credit, to organize themselves into cooperatives, and to obtain property deeds, rental agreements, and property titles. Since many indigenous people in Southern Patagonia worked on extensive sheep farms or "*estancias*," the Statute of the Rural Peon promulgated under Perón allowed them to improve their living conditions and reverse older practices of semi-servile exploitation. These transformations explain why the majority of the indigenous population in this region still identifies with the Peronist party.[24]

However, the tutelary interventions that the Peronist state directed toward these citizens and workers simultaneously made visible the internal hierarchies within the national community. Although the indigenous were encompassed within the collective that Peronists called "the Argentine *pueblo*," public officials consistently presented them as human beings lacking in civilization and plagued by racial deficiencies or ancestral defects. Indeed, it was in this period that Santiago Peralta, an anthropologist and the founder of a new state agency, the National Ethnic Institute [Instituto Étnico Nacional, IEN], created the label "National Ethnic Type [Tipo Étnico Nacional]" in 1946 to designate the national "ideal citizen" against which the indigenous were measured and found wanting.[25] From his post within Perón's government, Peralta positioned himself as an expert, promoting his racial knowledge and introducing the techniques of "applied anthropology" to the state bureaucracy. He often relied on state-generated census data to provide evidence to support and advance his theories, thereby reinforcing ideas about the impartiality of the state and the neutrality of science.[26]

Canals Frau, the architect of the concept of "Araucanization," succeeded Peralta as director of the National Ethnic Institute between 1948 and 1951. During his administration, Canals Frau replaced the category "National Ethnic Type" with "Mediterranean Racial Type of the White Race [Tipo Racial

Mediterráneo de la Raza Blanca]," establishing a list of four features that were fundamental for the construction of this ideal national ideal citizen: (1) a "patriotic education," in which the "true" but disappeared Argentine indigenous groups of the past (like the Tehuelche) would operate as the bedrock for the spiritual unity of the subsequent "modern" nation; (2) "indigenism," an ideology according to which, given that Indians were "different" from the Argentine mainstream, they should be confined in "colonies" and "reserves," where they could be protected, civilized, and fully nationalized; (3) "mental health," revealing the extent to which "difference" between indigenous and non-indigenous in Argentina was premised not only "culture" but also "reason" and mental capacity; and (4) "physical selection," an element whose identification and enforcement required anthropometric measurements of conscripts, immigrants, students, indigenous, and foreigners. This last feature would accomplish a twofold objective: helping to document and diagnose the progress of Argentina's ethnic formation and promoting racial whitening through hybridization and changes to the lived environment.[27] In conjunction with the era's nationalist, anti-communist, and anti-Semitic immigration policies, the National Ethnic Institute combined eugenic surveillance – including the formation of a database based on anthropometric charts (also known as "Identity Kits") – with pedagogical functions executed through educational institutions and museums, including prestigious university institutions such as the Museum of Natural Sciences of La Plata and the Ethnographic Museum in Buenos Aires.

During the Perón administration, the latter museum was directed by José Imbelloni, an Italian-born anthropologist and racial ideologue with a specialization in craniometry whose work would deeply shape state policies and social knowledge regarding indigenous peoples in Southern Patagonia.[28] In his first few years as director, Imbelloni staged an "expedition" to this region to gather information about local indigenous populations and the "cultural traits" that allegedly survived among them from the distant past. Imbelloni was particularly interested in taking anthropometric measurements to determine how many "pure" Tehuelche remained and how much they had mixed with other populations, and to prove if they were really "giants" – as Antonio de Pigafetta, the chronicler of Magellan's expedition, had suggested centuries earlier.[29] Like Pigafetta, Imbelloni focused above all on the two traits he considered distinctive to the group: height and "corpulence." However, since he believed his research should be holistic, he did not limit himself to investigating "racial morphology" (that is, taking anthropometric measurements, making plaster masks, and gathering blood samples). He also aimed, in his own words, to "offer the most rigorous racial and cultural classification possible"[30] of those indigenous people who, as he claimed in his report, were the "prototype" of the nation's human patrimony:

It was necessary to find some effective means of knowing with precision if there still were living remnants [*residuos vivientes*] of the ancient Tehuelche race in Patagonia and if so, how many individuals remained; if they were elderly and sick people unsuitable for the purposes of racial morphology, or if any mature and young specimens still survived; if there were hopes of recovering the key elements of the language spoken when their civilization flourished or any cultural remnants of the ancient heritage.[31]

Imbelloni aspired to find "mature and young specimens" that would fit into his typology, which he called the "Architectural Model of the Patagonian [*Patagón*]" or "Athletic Model," and which he defined as "a fundamental magnificent sculptural form, consisting of a luxuriant skeleton of osseous mass and a stunning muscular system" – in short, "the most harmonious model of the human organism."[32] He asserted that the Tehuelche race was one of three autochthonous Patagonian "races," along with the Andeans [*ándidos*] and the Fuegians [*fuéguidos*] – comprising what Federico Escalada, a contemporary physician and collaborator of Imbelloni's, would call the "Tehuelche Complex."[33] These perspectives on the Tehuelche illustrate the persistence of the idea, even in the mid-twentieth century, that the Tehuelche (narrowly or broadly defined) constituted the proud cornerstone of Argentina's "true" native populations. But this idea, as we will see, would also make the equally persistent notion of the "disappearance" (through "degeneration") of the Tehuelche all the more far-reaching in its implications, effectively canceling out the possibility of the existence of "true" Argentine indigenous in the twentieth century.

During his expedition to Southern Patagonia, Imbelloni, who wished to find "the desert's most authentic specimens," concentrated on rural areas (particularly the indigenous "reservations") where he supposed that his subjects would exhibit a "sharply different physiognomy from those people seen in cities."[34] At the end of his study, however, Imbelloni regretted not having found "young individuals besides the mestizos":[35]

It seems that the integration of the unions among the three Southern races, especially between the Tehuelche and the Mapuche, produced in Patagonia a comprehensive hybridization, whose product is equidistant from its three original models, such that currently it is impossible to discern to which of the three components each individual belongs.[36]

As a consequence of this "comprehensive hybridization," which made it impossible to distinguish one "race" from another, Imbelloni claimed to find only "living remnants [*residuos vivientes*] belonging to the ancient Tehuelche race." Based on his investigations, he concluded that the Tehuelche, as a "racial and social unit, can be considered practically extinct."[37] Imbelloni believed that this "hybridization" was the consequence of the "artificial life lived in the reservations," which generated a "monstrous effect." The indigenous "reservations," he went on to note, "have been centers of racial and moral deterioration" and have led indigenous people to acquire "an indefinable morphology (and physiology)" as a result of the "overlapping of the most diverse genes."[38] In Imbelloni's view, the agents of this degeneration – and those most clearly to blame – were interloping males, for, he asserted, "the few [Tehuelche] women who survive do not pair off with Tehuelche men but with *Araucanos* [a reference to Chile's Araucanía] and *Chilotes* [natives of Chiloé Island, Chile]"[39] who, echoing the longstanding discourse of "Araucanization," Imbelloni construed as foreign "invaders" and agents of "promiscuity."

These pessimistic conclusions did not stop Imbelloni's penchant for measuring, however. Intent on confirming that hybridity really occurred, he used another scientific dispositif: the "Skelic Index [*índice skélico*]" (seated height multiplied by 100/standing height). Building on his earlier convictions about the "corpulence" and size of the Tehuelche as distinctive traits, Imbelloni argued that this index would allow him to identify the prevalence of either the Tehuelche or the Mapuche "races" in a given individual. He concluded that while "males of higher purity" have a lower Skelic index, the number increases when the individual is a "mestizo." This "scientific" equation allowed Imbelloni to validate numerically what he already assumed before conducting his fieldwork – namely, that the Tehuelche were taller than mestizos – and to conclude that the remaining "pure" Tehuelche were few in number and were in decline. Indeed, Imbelloni claimed that there were just twelve cases of "purity" out of a total of forty-five individuals included in his supposedly exhaustive survey.

Upon returning to Buenos Aires from his Southern "expedition," Imbelloni gave a presentation recommending that the federal government take measures to preserve a group of "representatives of the Tehuelche race" – not in formaldehyde nor in the basement of La Plata's Museum (as the nineteenth-century explorer and naturalist Francisco Moreno had done), but in a space to be provided by the General Administration of National Parks and Tourism.[40] In describing this sort of living museum, he suggested that "the artificial preservation of some *stocks*" should include four or five families, which should be kept isolated from each other for three main reasons: (1) to serve as a historical and scientific "example [*semblanza*]" for future study; (2) to shield these indigenous people from further predations (in particular, to "watch and to protect [. . .] the specimens" from traders and thus to "preserve them from others' greed"); and (3) to prevent "physiological hybridization" – that is, to protect them from themselves in the face of the perils of miscegenation.

Imbelloni and his fellow scientific authorities were not alone in reaching such judgments or in warning about the perceived dangers of mixture, both to Indians and to the rest of the Argentine nation. During Perón's presidency, Catholic authorities reached similar conclusions as their counterparts in state agencies and research institutions. They too blamed "hybridization" for producing indigenous extinction and shared similar assumptions about "degeneration" and about the inevitability of evolutionary laws that would ultimately benefit the "superior races." Four years before Imbelloni's expedition, for example, Alberto María de Agostini, a Salesian priest from Italy, argued that the process of fusion between the Tehuelche and the foreign

Chilotes "degenerated" the former's indigenous lineage, making them weak and sickly, whereas contact with the stronger "white race" simply led to an inevitable annihilation:

Frequent marriages with white people, especially with *chilotes* from Chiloé Island, have degenerated the stock, procreating a huge number of weak and sickly *mestizos*. Among the few Indians I was able to photograph, only Uake, Yepelenol, Bampn and a handful of women were able to modestly represent the figure of their ancestors. It is saddening to see how this strong and good race shaped by excellent and athletic forms has come to its end so quickly. It is the fatal fortune that touches all indigenous races, too primitive, when they enter into contact with the stronger and more vigorous white race.[41]

Although de Agostini explicitly includes the "Chilotes" in the collective "white race" that is destined to wipe out indigenous peoples, in noting that Chiloé Island's population is "especially" degenerative to Tehuelches, his language implicitly suggests that the "Chilotes" themselves are mestizos or not fully white. In keeping with the only partial loss of trans-Andean migrants' markers of aboriginality, de Agostini's appreciations suggest that there were "white whites" (members of the "stronger and more vigorous" "white race" of European origin, only indirectly involved here) and others (the Chilotes) who were inferior or only partial members of the "white race."

Along with the works of scientists and priests, census statistics also played a crucial role in the discursive formation of extinction. Census data, in their ability to construct social realities from apparently objective numbers while silencing the ambiguities and subjectivities involved in the processes of creating such data, constitute one of the most effective instruments of bio-power. In 1943, the National Agrarian Council sent a request to the governor of the Territory of Santa Cruz for information regarding the size of the local indigenous population. Four years later, in 1947, the Directorate for the Protection of Aborigines ordered a similar report on "the situation of the indigenous tribes." In both cases, the data gathered in the field – by the local police, it should be noted – underwent several stages of processing and transcribing by the Territory's statistics office before being sent to Buenos Aires, resulting in important modifications. In the final versions of both documents, the detailed descriptions of everyday life included in the local police's first-hand reports were replaced with much more generic terms that occluded the populations' marks of aboriginality. For example, the original description of the female task of "making *quillangos* [a type of cape made from the leather of the *guanaco*, a local camelid]" was replaced in the final report by the more generic phrase "domestic tasks [*quehaceres domésticos*]." Most notably, the "mestizo" category used in the first-hand surveys disappeared from the final versions sent to the national capital.

The *coup d'état* that overthrew Perón in 1955, the self-styled "Liberating Revolution," eliminated the National Ethnic Institute and removed Imbelloni from his posts. Imbelloni's dismissal undercut the political legitimacy that anthropology – with its racializing discourses and typologies – had acquired in previous years. Yet such typologies did not disappear overnight. The expulsion of Peronist Party members from the universities did not expel the followers of the so-called Cultural-Historical School (to which Imbelloni had subscribed) from the anthropological field.[42] Nor did changes in partisan orientation lead the state to stop conducting census surveys informed by these earlier anthropological models. In the following decade, the First National Indigenous Census was conducted under an anti-Peronist government. Resorting to the essentialist equation "race = culture = language," Edelmi Griva and Griselda Dalla Marta, the authors of the report for Santa Cruz Province (published in 1967–68), recorded a total of two hundred and ten "*Aónikenk*" (Tehuelche). According to the authors, this number included "mixed marriages," but, they noted, "if we become more rigorous [. . .] we see that the number diminishes considerably due to the fact that, according to our calculations, right now there would be just 70 speakers of the *aonikó-aish* language."[43] The ten families enumerated in the Camusu Aike "reservation" were registered as belonging to the "Aónikenk-*criollo*-Chileno ethnic group," with the following explanation offered by way of elucidation: "the man is the non-indigenous [member of the family] and the women are Aónikenk." Once again, we see the gendered idea of "foreign" Chilean male interlopers as the agents of the degeneration of a dwindling "pure" Tehuelche community, embodied in a very few women.

This survey also demonstrates the ways in which ideas about language played a role in the discursive formation of Tehuelche "disappearance." Its authors arrived at the conclusion that, since the children of these families at Camusu Aike did not speak the native language, they were "semi-disconnected from their pre-Hispanic ethnic belonging." The authors went on to assert that, "with the exception of the household mothers, none of the offspring self-identify as indigenous. They look upon the Indians of their own *reducción* [a term, similar to reservation, originally used by the Church] as different people."[44] As these statements reveal, during the 1960s the ability to speak an indigenous language acquired pre-eminence as a "distinctive feature" of aboriginality, thus making language into a racial feature and continuing the process by which culture itself took on racial meanings at mid-century. By the 1980s, with a surge of linguistic studies, this tendency would become still more significant. Paradoxically, it was just as the Tehuelche language acquired this scientific value as a marker of aboriginality that older generations of Tehuelche speakers made the decision to interrupt the transmission of their language to their offspring, preventing them from being marked as indigenous and thereby protecting them from discrimination.

Local historians in Santa Cruz province added a final piece to the consolidation of the discourse of extinction during the 1980s. Foremost among these local intellectuals was the journalist Juan Hilarion Lenzi. In his book *Historia de Santa Cruz* (1980) – which has served as a major reference work in countless local family and school libraries – Lenzi argues that the Tehuelche "race" degenerated by an "excessive mixing" with "social waste [*desechos sociales*]."[45] The book underscores the idea that the moral and racial degeneration that befell the Tehuelche came from foreigners (that is, from the Mapuche and from Chilotes). Like Imbelloni, though without citing him, Lenzi blames these nominally "white" foreign males for engendering a defective progeny, but like Imbelloni he qualifies their whiteness as already partially degraded:

The white man penetrated the intimacy of the Tehuelche tent, [where he] was received as a friend, and in his relations with Indian women, [he] procreated, in general, a defective specimen, because the guest was the carrier of human scourges, which are inevitably degenerative factors. Tuberculosis and syphilis on the one hand, alcoholism on the other, and the mental defects [*taras*] typical of individuals who tended to be social waste, mixed in excessive proportions in the blood of the sons of the desert. It was not possible to expect superb products from this amalgam.

According to the author there were, by contrast, a few "happy" examples of "crossbreeding, thanks to contributions of better quality."[46] From such positive hybridization with people of primarily European descent (rather than negative crossings with carriers of "human scourges") there emerged a "miraculous human melting pot" that "has permitted the population's evolution," fusing, absorbing, and incorporating difference, while expelling "what is the effect of error" (meaning "degenerative mestizaje") through the community's "active moral capacity."[47] Lenzi regrets that these positive mixings were not more widely encouraged, that no one "came bravely to the aid" of the Tehuelche, thereby permitting the "ethnic disaster" by which they instead mixed primarily with Chileans of "unsavory lifestyle." Through this *mea culpa*, he argues that "the destiny of this race, nowadays almost extinct, could have been different if society had acted uprightly."[48] Lenzi implies, in other words, that mechanisms should have been put in place to avoid "crossbreeding" with people already degenerated by mixture (meaning "Chilotes") and to foster, instead, "crossbreeding" with "pure" elements (meaning European "pioneers"). Because of society's failure to avoid this tragedy, Lenzi implies, the "authentic last specimens stopped walking their lands many years ago."[49] The collective he imagines as "we the Santacruzian people" thus lost "a well-rooted, agile, strong, physically uncontaminated and morally perfectible subject"[50] by leaving these people "to perish rather than doing something to help them adapt to the new moral climate, to our traditions and customs, to labor and intellectual life," "to progress," and "to our civilization."[51] What Santacruzians were left with, instead, were their "descendants," illegitimate and corrupted copies of the original and true Tehuelche.

In short, we can observe that the utterances and forms of knowledge produced by the state bureaucracy, scientific researchers, members of the Church, and historians combine intertextually into a powerful discursive formation. The disappearance of the Tehuelche People is the result of classificatory dispositifs that envisioned and exalted a racially and culturally "pure" group of people – declared disappeared – in opposition to their children, who survived but were lodged in an anomalous position within the supposedly homoge-neously white nation. In Santa Cruz, individuals with indigenous surnames or phenotypes are pejoratively referred to as "Chilotes" on a routine basis – particularly those individuals suspected of having Mapuche ancestors – while the common term used in the bureaucratic reports since 1943 has been "des-cendant." These terms are similar to "cabecita negra" or "negro," commonly used in other parts of Argentina. Although both of the terms used in Santa Cruz evoke miscegenation, "descendant" allows the possibility of "passing,"[52] some-thing denied to those stigmatized as "Chilotes," who are always marked as foreigners regardless of whether they were born in Argentina or acquired Argentine citizenship. That is, while "Chilote" is a highly racialized xenophobic category that permanently marks its bearers as "external Others," the term "descendant" refers to markings that, depending on the context, may involve ethnicizations or racializations, allowing or not for the people thus marked to hide their aboriginality. If we translate this situation to the national level, we can observe that the paradigm of Argentina as "Europe's replica" discursively enables the "passing" between categories (from "indigenous" or "mestizo" to "white") that would contribute to an overall formal whitening of the citizenry. However, in the actual interactions of everyday life, racialized markings such as "negro" or "cabecita negra" interrupt this fluidity, ensuring the social margin-alization of those who fall into those categories and effectively, though tacitly, creating forms of second-class citizenship.

LAND INSPECTORS, "MESTIZOS," AND "DESCENDANTS"

The taxonomies discussed in the previous section oriented state policies in ways that affected indigenous people's lives and limited the political spaces available to them. Through a "movement toward facticity," some versions of these taxonomies were imposed upon other less-widely circulating ones, thereby creating "reality-effects" as well as effects upon reality.[53] Among such effects was the territorialization of indigenous people in enclaves ("indigenous reser-vations," "missions," and "colonies") following the Conquest of the Desert, and, over the course of the twentieth century, further dispossession and privat-ization as indigenous territories became government-owned plots (*tierras fis-cales*) that could be leased and sold. These processes were supervised by the National Directorate of Lands and Colonies (under the Ministry of the Inter-ior's General Directorate of National Territories) and were carried out through land inspections that included map-making, census-taking, and information-gathering on livestock and agricultural activity, soil quality, and improvements. Inspections in Santa Cruz, however, were not carried out on a regular basis; rather, owing to the centralization of state authority in the national capital and to the institutional instability that characterized national and provincial gov-ernments during the twentieth century (frequent coups that led to a high turnover of public officials), these inspections took place at intervals of two to seventeen years. In this section, I analyze the corpus of documents produced by state inspections conducted on the former indigenous "reservation" (now "community") of Camusu Aike, located in the southern part of Santa Cruz province. The goal is to gain a better understanding of how and why the "mestizo" category was replaced by "descendant" during contests over land management in the 1940s and how this move contributed to a twofold process of ethnicization (which further rendered indigenous people invisible at the provincial and national levels) and racialization (which stigmatized and excluded them), transformations whose consequences persist today.

In 1878, just before the Conquest of the Desert, the federal state created an administrative entity known as the Governorate of Patagonia, which was subdivided into six National Territories six years later. Compared to other Argentine provinces and territories, the new Territory of Santa Cruz was from its inception distinguished by its large expanse, low population density, and remoteness. Although military campaigns did not have the same intensity in Santa Cruz as they did north of the Black River, political authority was exerted by a comparable set of actors: uniformed representatives of the Army and Navy, followed by members of Anglican and Salesian religious orders, who disputed between them the power to influence state policy in these areas. The spaces that official maps had labeled as Indian-controlled until 1879 were first annexed through maps themselves, reflecting a "territorial desire" more than any effective state control, formal occupation, or practical knowledge.[54] The maps made by the Argentine Geographic Institute – founded by explorer Estanislao Zeballos in 1879 – incorporated, conquered, and "civilized" territories through cartographic representational strategies that included plotting nonexistent railway lines, roads, and telegraph lines, along with the "routes of explorers" and abandoned "Indian whereabouts." In so doing, they contributed to the process of imagining a "modern" and "rational" country, a project that lay just on the horizon and that would erase the land's earlier indigenous history and place names, and even the existence of indigenous people themselves.[55] Indigenous territories thus became "government plots" to be quickly distributed as property among a few landowners, giving rise to a new landscape of large-scale landholding.[56]

The state's military onslaught during the Conquest of the Desert voided earlier "peace" treaties between the state and indigenous groups, but it did not completely dismantle indigenous social and political structures and inter-group alliances.[57] Those who survived organized themselves around leaders (typically, renowned elders or *caciques*), who negotiated formal permissions to occupy marginal "grids" of land (i.e., plots formed by imaginary lines and marked off by milestones). Through presidential decrees signed between 1898 and 1927, the national government granted six permits for collective occupation in the Territory of Santa Cruz to families identified as Tehuelche, Mapuche, and Mapuche-Tehuelche. The first decree in Santa Cruz, signed by

President José Evaristo Uriburu, was given to Camusu Aike in 1898, authorizing the "Tehuelche Indian tribe" to settle into five land plots (50,000 hectares) under the "surveillance of the Governor."[58] In cases such as this one, collective status as part of a "reservation" exempted people from paying pasture taxes. Similar concessions applied to indigenous people considered "civilized" by state officials as well as to those who served during the wars as guides or provided other services to the state; members of these groups often obtained individual permits to lease or buy land plots.

The creation of Indian "reservations" was originally proposed by Ramón Lista, a naturalist who served as governor of the Territory of Santa Cruz between 1887 and 1892. Lista supported the ideologies of violent conquest and occupation articulated by General Roca and Zeballos (indeed, Lista was accused by Joseph Fagnano, a Salesian priest, of murdering a group of *Selk'nam* people in the Territory of Tierra del Fuego).[59] Nevertheless, Lista modified his positions later in life. In his book *The Tehuelche People: A Disappearing Race* (1894), he denounces both the Argentine and Chilean governments, accusing them of not having taken measures to prevent the extinction of this indigenous people. Inspired by the case of the Sioux in the United States as well as by that country's discourse of the "vanishing Indian," he demanded that both Argentina and Chile enact a "Law of Indian Land Reserves."[60]

In *The Tehuelche People*, Lista attributed indigenous "extinction" to factors such as murder, the introduction of alcoholic beverages by itinerant merchants [*mercachifles*], and what he termed "generational replacement." He argued that "the Tehuelche dwindle in size and the reason is simple: The elderly are disappearing and the young who replace them are mostly mestizos, that is, children of a white man and an Indian woman."[61] Lista's book did not adopt a xenophobic position against the Chileans, like other observers before and after him, but it appraised the "crossbred" offspring hierarchically, according to the origins of their progenitors:

The recognized intellectual superiority of the pure European element guarantees the results of the crossbreeding. And, indeed, the children of a *criolla* woman and a European man are usually much more beautiful, manly, and intelligent than those who come only from the native element [the indigenous] or the country's traditional element [criollos].[62]

The "extinction" as a result of mestizaje posited by Lista contradicts, however, the situation of his own daughter, who was the product of his close relationship with a Tehuelche woman called Koila (also known as Clorinda Coyle).[63] This relationship – which may explain his change of attitude toward indigenous people – cost him his position as governor, as he was forced to resign. His daughter Ramona, to whom he gave his surname, was subsequently registered on censuses both as an "Aboriginal" and as an "Indigenous" person (as well as "Argentine" and "Chilean" according to different inspection reports). Nevertheless, neither she nor the other members of Camusu Aike doubted her indigenous affiliation. In this case, state racial classifications do not account for socialization processes at the grassroots level, according to which the children of non-indigenous parents raised by indigenous mothers are considered fellow indigenous community members. In most of the cases I have studied, which include six indigenous "reservations" and twelve contemporary "communities," it is clear that, as Lista's own writings suggest, the "principle of hypodescent" prevailed over the principle of "hyperdescent." This means that the mixed category ("descendants" or "mestizos") was absorbed into the marked or subordinate category ("indigenous"), rather than being absorbed into the hegemonic category ("European pioneer," "White," "Argentine type").[64] Thus, in opposition to the hypergamic unions ("marrying up"), the hypogamic marriages ("marrying down") classified the "descendants" closer to the marked parent than to the unmarked one. Such marriages were read by observers from the late nineteenth century through the twentieth as a form of "degenerative mestizaje," which pointed to a supposed biological "degeneration" (racialization) as well as to a cultural-moral "degeneration" (ethnicization), as examined in the previous section.[65]

In 1908, ten years after President Uriburu's initial decree creating Camusu Aike, a group of landowners led by Anglican church official Victor Fenton created the Honorary Commission of Indian Reduction of the Territory of Santa Cruz. Among the Commission's declared aims was to "seek to standardize and legalize marriages, preventing white men from marrying Indian women according to the Indian style, because these informal unions disrupt the descendants' civil status."[66] Exposing his horror toward hybridization, Fenton argued that such unions "alter their children's status" and instead of teaching them civilized habits through their own good example, these "Christians" adopt indigenous practices. This very same idea would be invoked by state officials in subsequent land inspections. The Commission had other objectives as well, including putting an end to indigenous people's hunting practices, resettling them on individualized, fenced plots (one per family), instructing them about sheep farming, and "making them develop a love for farming."[67] In other words, Fenton and his colleagues insisted that local indigenous abandon "a nomadic life," which his Commission considered incompatible with and detrimental to capitalist rural production as well as an impediment to indigenous peoples' becoming fully "civilized." Fenton framed these interventions as "assistance," "providing them [the indigenous] the means to become extinct in peace." Such means involved the transformation of the Tehuelche "reservation" into a "Pastoral Indigenous Colony" by establishing a sheep ranch and founding a "small village with a school, a chapel, some houses for the authorities, a square, a hospital, and a civil registry." He imagined this place – which he bucolically dubbed "*La Estancia*" – as being administered by the Indians themselves. This was, however, only partially true. Although the plan allowed for an indigenous person to hold the post of police sub-commissioner, the colony's general administration would be entrusted by the provincial governor or a local judge to the chief of the Mission Church of the Territory of Santa Cruz who, together with a committee of landowners constituted as "organizers and directors," would be responsible for the "surveillance" of the colony's indigenous population.

The objective of the first inspection of Camusu Aike carried out by the National Directorate of Land and Colonies in 1914 was to evaluate the success of the "*La Estancia*" project.[68] The results of this inspection were negative, as were those of the next inspection in 1918. In both cases, as we will see, inspectors blamed degenerative mestizaje for what they saw as a sad state of affairs. The inspector estimated that the community consisted of 16 tents occupied by a total of 114 people, half of them "purebred Indians" while "the rest are mestizos," especially the young people. The latter, the 1914 inspection concluded, show "signs of physical degeneration" caused by their mixing with "foreign elements" and by alcoholism. Notably, the "mestizos" differed from the "specimens" who "show the characteristic development of the Tehuelche race; that is, they are about two meters tall, have a broad back and a strong musculature." The inspectors believed that "the Tehuelche Indians should be removed from the reserve as a means of promoting the progress of important and numerous sheep farms in that area" (i.e., they should be employed as labor) and should be relocated north of the Santa Cruz River. The report justified the proposal by arguing that "they are extremely poor, and produce almost nothing. They just vegetate in idleness, trying to steal other people's sheep, they do not want to work, and are a true hindrance to the region's progress." Shortly after issuing this report, the Commission concluded that the "*La Estancia*" project, only in its third year of existence, had failed due to obstruction by the indigenous residents and, therefore, that the "reserved" lands should be offered "to the private sector, to be leased or sold."[69] State investments had not yielded the expected results: the indigenous not only had not become civilized, but continued to resist the Commission's surveillance. The 1918 inspection reached similar conclusions. It estimated a similar number of inhabitants and, in the same vein, the inspector in charge declared that "the new generations show signs of physical degeneration caused by the mixing with foreign elements and especially by the pernicious influence of alcohol, to which both men and women are devoted."[70] This inspection restated the idea of relocating the Tehuelche, but in this case the inspector framed the argument in terms of the indigenous persons' own wishes, asserting that "they are not happy in this place and have expressed their desire to be transferred elsewhere, to a place where there still are guanacos so they can hunt them freely."[71]

Seventeen years later, in the midst of a military regime, the National Directorate of Land and Colonies conducted a third inspection of Camusu Aike to check if the indigenous had been relocated.[72] The official in charge of this 1935 inspection collected information through a census and reported that some families had indeed left, carrying their tents with them. He counted the occupants of each of the thirteen adobe and tin-roof houses led by a male head of household (a format that would continue to be used in such censuses until 1984). Under the entry for "nationality," the official wrote "indigenous," without further specification; among the residents were also three individuals identified as Chilean citizens. Given that, by the end of the 1920s, the state had distributed most of the "public land" in this region of Santa Cruz province to private owners,[73] the state inspections of Camusu Aike from the 1930s onward vehemently argued that it was best to leave these families where they were and, in fact, to relocate indigenous people living in other reservations to this site. The subsequent inspection in 1940 observed that among the estimated 25 families, "some of the heads of household [. . .] are not Argentines." In the eight inspection reports that followed between 1943 and 1984, the qualifier "some" appeared less and less frequently, reinforcing the prejudicial view that Camusu Aike occupants were mostly foreigners of Chilean origin. The number of household units, however, remained relatively constant, belying the engrained idea of indigenous "disappearance."

The inspection conducted in 1943 constitutes a turning point in this documentary corpus, since it represents the first time that people from Camusu Aike were referred to as "descendants" (instead of "mestizos") – and, more specifically, as "descendants of the Tehuelche tribe."[74] (Under the section subtitled "Observations," this report also introduces for the first time the term "community" – paradoxically, given the report's ideological position, the term that the residents of Camusu Aike would officially use after 2007 instead of "reservation"). The 1943 report, channeling nationalist ideas, a defense of Christian morality, and well-worn notions of indigenous vagrancy and promiscuity, explicitly associates these "descendants" with the process of "degenerative mestizaje":

Among all aboriginal people, only a few can be properly called authentic indigenous people, because they are mostly mestizo, a degeneration that becomes more marked every day. Notwithstanding the influx of other bloods, they all retain their ancestors' habits and customs, because their way of life is still characterized by indolence, poor labor habits, and promiscuity. This should not come as a surprise, for despite their crossbreeding with individuals of other races, these [latter] were individuals who, having rejected their own condition as Christians, adopted that of the Indians. Hence, any beneficial influence exerted by members of these other races was limited, since most of the time, if not always, they were the elements considered the dregs of humanity. It was thus easier for them to adapt themselves to the indigenous way of life than to modify or improve it.

The 1943 report accepts the premise that "crossing with individuals of other races" has not made indigenous people modify "their lifestyle," since they continue "preferring the breeding of mares, whose meat is one of their favorite foods, nor have they abandoned hunting ostrich and guanaco." The reason for this purported failure to progress is that the "individuals of other races" who have joined with indigenous women are doubly negative people: because they are foreigners to the Argentine nation (the report suggests that these are Chilean men), and because they readily abandoned "civilized" Christian morals to adopt the "immoral" and "savage" lifestyles of indigenous people. Once again, Chilean husbands are presented as agents of moral degeneration among the "purebred Indians" through their bad habits, and as agents of racial degeneration through the creation of inferior offspring. Despite these problems, the state inspector concludes that "the reservation should be preserved," restating previous recommendations that the indigenous living on other reservations be relocated to Camusu Aike to free up more lands for colonization (by idealized white "pioneers").

The pejorative description "dregs of humanity [*hez de la humanidad*]" used by the 1943 inspector to refer to the non-indigenous husbands of Camusu Aike specifically excluded José Macías, who was Ramona Lista's husband. During the inspection, Macías expressed his intention to obtain a formal lease on the land he was already using in order to build a fence – something not allowed inside the "reservation" – to prevent the loss of livestock. Employing the language of capitalist efficiency and civilized governance, the inspector judges that Macías is "in condition to contract with the State" (a clause that, after this first appearance, would recur in subsequent reports) and distinguishes him from the other husbands, arguing that "although he is a Chilean man married to an Indian woman, his entrepreneurial spirit and work habits [...] make him deserving of a better situation." In contrast to traditional hunting practices, the keeping of horses, and high spatial mobility (considered evidence of "savagery"), individual ownership of land and property (contracting with the state to set up a sheep ranch) could earn indigenous people the status of rational beings and adults, allowing them either full and ethnically unmarked citizenship (as "farm owners," "workers," or "peones") or partial citizenship as "descendants."

The ensuing 1947 inspection built further upon these assumptions and categories, for instance by repeating the proposition that "the core of settlers is shaped by descendants of the indigenous [people] of this tribe and by a steady percentage of foreigners."[75] The report specified that among the twelve heads of household, six are "descendants of the Tehuelche," but only three of them "can be called authentic aborigines, the others being mestizos and foreigners who, [...] upon settling in this reserve, found the best way to approximate the lifestyle of the rest of the occupants, distinguishing themselves only by their indolence and their lack of work habits." The number of Chileans, however, remained the same as in the 1935 report. We should recall that this inspection took place during Perón's presidency and at the height of state efforts to create a homogeneous citizenry. In an effort to assimilate indigenous people into this collective state officials produced records that increasingly dissolved the marks of aboriginality within the capacious category of nationality. The classifications produced show inconsistencies over time and even in the same report (as in the 1953 inspection, when Ramona Lista was registered as both "Argentine" and "Chilean"; in other cases, people listed in the "observations" section as "descendants" might appear just a few pages later as "Argentine Indian" or just as "Argentine.") But the effort to dilute the marks of aboriginality in populations classified in primarily national terms would remain for decades.

The last inspection of Camusu Aike carried out by the National Government was in 1957, the year that the Territory of Santa Cruz became a province. In a context favorable to the consolidation of local power networks through personal favors and nepotism, three of the six "reservations" were abolished by 1966, and those that remained lost land in subsequent decades to the usurpations of local landowners or security forces. These land seizures, though carried out by provincial actors, were based in part on information gleaned from the national inspectors' reports. They rested upon two main kinds of arguments: economic (according to which indigenous people supposedly failed to exploit the land in a rational way) and demographic (drawing on censuses indicating that there were "only a few" Indians left, or buying into the alleged "disappearance" of the "Tehuelche race" altogether). Some collectively held reservation lands were sold to indigenous individuals who managed to prove that they "were able to contract with the State,"[76] but in subsequent years, many of these individuals lost their lands either through the mechanics of intergenerational inheritance or as a consequence of underhanded dealings.[77] While the term "descendant" would continue to be used in local land inspection reports (subsequently conducted by the Province), the term "mestizo" ceases to appear in that genre of documents after 1947. It does, however, make a notable appearance in related documents surrounding a legal dispute. One of the parties, a rancher who had illegally settled in Camusu Aike and who for almost fifteen years tried to acquire indigenous lands, staked his claim on the idea that the "Tehuelche Tribe" had ceased to exist and that it was an "ideological reserve that exists exclusively on paper [...] occupied in practice by 'Chilean' and 'mestizo' people."[78] This dispute resulted in the passage of two assimilationist laws during the 1960s, which stand among the first political measures taken by a "young province" that shared the national desire to homogenize its citizenship through a "melting pot" increasingly imagined as white. In this context, however, indigenous peoples did not enter the national community as members of the "Argentine type" and even less as (European) "pioneers." Instead, they were incorporated as second-class citizens – as "descendants" or as "Chilotes," depending on the context.

The same nationalist, racialist, and "civilizing" criteria that had for so long informed the national land inspection reports shaped those carried out in subsequent years by provincial authorities. An inspector from the Provincial Agrarian Council, for instance, stated in 1969 that the "reservations" remained a "problem" in need of "a comprehensive solution." While previous reports had enumerated and assigned the indigenous population to categories such as "purebred Indians," "descendants," and "foreigners," this inspection (executed, it should be noted, during the right-wing military dictatorship led by General Juan Carlos Onganía) quite radically declared all of them to be

Chileans: "of the current population, we can say that they are neither indigenous nor their descendants, but Chilean citizens who have settled in the reserve, thereby distorting the purposes for which the land was destined." The report then clarified that "the indigenous, their descendants, or any who occupy the reserve in that capacity, do not exploit the land in any way."[79] With this familiar trope of indigenous lack of rational productivity, this document paved the way for further dispossession.

The reports produced by national and provincial land bureaus were connected intertextually with information produced by other agencies under civilian and military rule. In 1978, during the dictatorship that styled itself as the "Process for National Reorganization" and in a critical moment of escalating military tensions between Chile and Argentina, the Director of the Ministry of Education and Culture performed an inspection of the Camusu Aike school, which had been shut down the previous year. This report reiterates the long-standing view of the reservation as a desolate place with only a few scattered "*ranchos* [shacks]," on which only "two or three families vegetate in the most profound indigence." This report was attached to a note signed by the Secretary of Agriculture proposing the annulment of all occupation permits for a place that, it noted in the past tense, "had once been an Indian reservation"; the lands, it further proposed, should be offered for sale.[80]

In the corpus of land inspection documents spanning the late nineteenth to the late twentieth centuries, we can see how ideas about disappearance through degenerative mestizaje created the conditions for the impossibility of "authentic" Argentine indigenous people. Within this gradient of purity-impurity, observers argued that there were no "purebred Indians" but only "descendants" ("mestizos"), or not even "descendants" but simply "Chilean lowlifes." In turn, suspicions about indigenous authenticity made it possible to conclude that indigenous "disappearance" was not only individual (a product of mestizaje) but collective. State authorities and their allies stressed that the residents of Camusu Aike lacked "traditional" social and political organization, such as being organized into hunting bands or obeying a cacique, and that they were thus not a "Tribe." Once this dual conclusion of individual and collective disappearance was established, the provincial government legitimated actions that contributed further to the fragmentation and alienation of collective lands.[81] Just as inspections carried out during military regimes tended to be particularly damaging to the interests of indigenous people, those conducted in the period of Argentina's transition to democracy (that is, inspections from 1984 and 1993) produced some positive changes – for instance, officials did not ask whether locals were indigenous or descendants. Yet these trends were not uniform; in 1987, four years after the democratic opening, the Army dispossessed the Tehuelche people of yet another portion of their lands.[82] By 2002, the bureaucratic climate improved once again: the inspector informed residents that they could present complaints to an ombudsman and that they were protected by the National Constitution of 1994 (which newly recognized the ethnic and cultural pre-existence of the nation's indigenous peoples and their rights to communally held land). Problems with access to land persisted, however; of Camusu Aike's remaining 7,000 hectares of land, two heads of household requested 2,000 hectares each, leaving only 3,000 hectares of communal lands (less than 10 percent of the original 50,000 hectares "reserved" in 1898). Not surprisingly, given the incentive structure we can glean from successive reports, it appears that individual property-holding became the only option for Camusu Aike members seeking to avoid the threats of dispossession and eviction that shadowed them from the mid-twentieth century onward.

This documentary collection also reveals that in individual cases in which processes of ethnicization prevailed over racialization – where the indigenous were able to demonstrate that they had become "civilized" and "white," thus reversing the negative valence of "mestizaje"[83] – they were able to get access to private property. In a mutually reinforcing dynamic, landowning status itself operated as a path toward (or evidence of) whitening. Whitening could also occur through filiation (typically, the offspring of "white" fathers and indigenous mothers), through affinity (indigenous women married to non-indigenous men), and through changes of residence (moving from rural areas to urban centers). Whitening was conceived as a unidirectional and irreversible process, one that touched both the people who struggled unsuccessfully to become invisible or unmarked as well as those few who became unmarked against their will, considered "white" despite self-identifying as indigenous. Such was the case of one of Ramona Lista's sons, who was described dismissively in the 1980s by a group of psychiatrists as "a rancher with dubious Tehuelche ancestors."[84]

While we know that in 1943 the term "descendants" appears in the corpus of inspections for the first time, it is more difficult to determine when this term began to operate as a self-ascribed category. The archives provide some evidence, as in the case of Jacinto López, the son of a Chilean man and a woman from Camusu Aike. Jacinto's father, Abdón López, had originally been the opposing party in the legal battle cited earlier; Jacinto took over after his death. In a declaration made in 1977, Jacinto López refers to himself using the term "descendant," but without associating the term with the official logic of degenerative mestizaje or foreign degradation. Instead, he reverses the term's negative moral charge, using it as part of his argument that he is a "civilized" person qualified for land ownership, a "descendant [...] capable of carrying out an efficient and independent sheep ranch." The fact that, some years earlier, his father Abdón (or his lawyer) had taken the opposite tack reflects changes in the political landscape as well as indigenous peoples' shifting political strategies. Seeking to demonstrate that he was in condition to "establish a contract with the State," Abdón had presented himself in court as a "civilized Indian." Examples such as these demonstrate that, in addition to redefining classificatory categories for their own purposes, the indigenous peoples of Southern

Patagonia were able to use institutions of control to their own ends, sometimes exploiting antagonisms between diverse social and political actors in their favor, and creating spaces for political negotiation.[85]

In the political context of contemporary Argentina, in which people who recognize indigenous ancestors are newly able both to occupy new social and physical spaces and to redefine identifications and taxonomies, some individuals linked to Camusu Aike choose to self-identify as members of the Tehuelche people. At the same time, the youngest among them tend to self-recognize as "descendants," reflecting deeper questions they themselves pose about their own "legitimacy." The incipient process of self-ascription does not mechanically lead these individuals to seek to recover dispossessed lands, but the emerging sense of belonging does challenge the "discursive formation" that the Tehuelche people were "extinguished." These processes transmute humiliated subjectivities into ones that can express new pride in indigenous "roots." This, in turn, provides guidance in ongoing struggles to obtain the title of "Indigenous Communal Property" for Camusu Aike in a region where the right to such titles is still very much in dispute.[86]

FINAL WORDS

Argentina's standing as a "white nation" was more than simply a myth or a desire: from the late nineteenth century and through the twentieth, the state tried to make this ideal a reality through policies of removal and displacement of populations and individuals deemed undesirable. The Conquest of the Desert not only successfully erased a long history of negotiations between the state and indigenous peoples; it also erased the continuous existence of its survivors. Cartographic and historiographical dispositifs created by military and civilian officials set the groundwork for subsequent narratives of "disappearance," whether they stressed "annihilation" (often by celebrating the white "heroes" who defended the homeland from Mapuche "savage invaders") or "extinction" (the Tehuelche as "noble savages" destined to become "civilized" or to perish when faced with the inevitable forces of "progress").

As this chapter has demonstrated, the Tehuelche "disappeared" discursively in the ink used to write bureaucratic reports, scientific research papers, and opinion pieces published in national and local newspapers since the late nineteenth century. They "disappeared" because they ceased to conform to racial and ethnic taxonomies that combined phenotypic features considered "distinctive" traits from the sixteenth century onward (height and "corpulence") and a set of cultural practices ascribed to aboriginality (speaking an ancestral language, living in tents, hunting guanacos, and organizing as "tribes"). Through a process of racialization, the Tehuelche came to be considered hybrids, the illegitimate product of a "degenerated purebred race," and through a simultaneous process of ethnicization, they were viewed as products of a once pristine culture that had been lost or diluted.

As the indigenous began moving in greater numbers to Santa Cruz's urban centers in the 1960s, their aboriginality became invisible, although they continued to be placed in positions of subalternity through the workings of class and nationalism, as well as through practices of racialization and ethnicization organized around classist and xenophobic categories. In terms of class, those who had once been labeled "peones" or "rural workers" became the undifferentiated "poor" or "marginals." Nationalist ideologies, for their part, transformed the once-standard category of "descendant" into an anomaly. For according to the ideas of degenerative mestizaje and "disappearance" that shaped discourses on indigenous people throughout the twentieth century, the people in question do not exclusively "descend" from an "internal Other" – the "true Indians," or the "Argentine Indians," who had supposedly become extinct. Rather, they descend from a doubly harmful mixture with foreign "Chilotes," considered threats to state sovereignty and the undesirable product of previous hypogamic mestizaje.

Words became things; discourses became practice.[87] Through a "movement toward facticity," hegemonic discourses on indigenous people in Southern Patagonia created "reality-effects," and the invisibilization of the Tehuelche and other indigenous peoples materialized through policies of territorial dispossession, of the indigenous dead housed in museums, and of indigenous children sent to orphanages and boarding schools.[88] The weight of the discursive formation analyzed in this chapter explains why, in the present day, the processes of Tehuelche re-emergence are, like those of other groups, looked upon with suspicion or deemed inauthentic by many observers. As this chapter has argued, this "re-emergence" does not mean that these indigenous peoples actually ceased to exist, but that their newfound visibility stands in contrast to the dispositifs that rendered them invisible. In recent years, a combination of factors such as the maturing of indigenous struggles across the continent, new research on indigenous peoples in Argentina by engaged scholars, and the internalization of the tenets of interculturality by state officials have produced fissures in the discursive formation analyzed here. New interpretive frameworks generate a shared terrain from which people who self-identify as "indigenous," "Indian," "Tehuelche," "Mapuche," "Mapuche-Tehuelche," "paisano," and even "descendants" can begin to question old taxonomies, to re-accentuate existing categories,[89] and to further their emancipatory actions.

Notes

1. Following the International Labor Organization's Convention 169 (1989) on Indigenous and Tribal Peoples' Rights, I use "people/s" as a juridical category that recognizes preexisting collectives (indigenous peoples and indigenous communities) and their right (among others) to self-identification and self-determination, to exercise control over their own institutions, territories, way of life and economic development, and to maintain and develop their identities, languages, and religions.

2. Segato, "Color-Blind," 129.
3. Sanjinés, *Mestizaje*; Vasconcelos, *Raza cósmica*.
4. Mallon, "Constructing Mestizaje."
5. Andrews, *Los afroargentinos*; Geler, *Andares*; Frigerio and Lamborghini, "Los afroargentinos."
6. On a nation without "mestizos," see Escolar, *Los dones*.
7. On "aboriginality" and its origins in the Australian context, see Beckett, *Past*.
8. Briones, *Cartografías*.
9. Briones, "Mestizaje."
10. For the concept of "provincial formations of alterity," I am indebted to the work of the "Aboriginality, Provinces, and Nation Study Group" (GEAPRONA). See also Briones, *Cartografías*.
11. Rodríguez, "De la 'extinción.'"
12. Foucault, *La arqueología*.
13. Lista, *Mis exploraciones*; Lista, *Viaje*; Moreno, *Viaje*; Moyano, *A través*.
14. Musters, *At Home*; Beerbohm, *Wanderings*; Dixie, *Across*.
15. Lenton, "Los araucanos" and *De centauros*.
16. Lenton, "Los araucanos."
17. Mases, *Estado*; Bayer, *Historia*.
18. See Stepan, *Hour*.
19. Canals Frau, "Expansions."
20. Canals Frau, "La araucanización."
21. Mandrini and Ortelli, "Los araucanos."
22. Lewontin, *La diversidad*.
23. See de la Cadena, *Indigenous*.
24. Delrio, *Memorias*.
25. Lazzari, "Antropología."
26. Ibid.
27. Ibid.
28. On Imbelloni's career and training, see www.dante.edu.ar/web/dic/i.pdf.
29. De Pigafetta, *Primer*.
30. Imbelloni, *Informe preliminar*, 6.
31. Ibid., 3.
32. Imbelloni, "Los Patagones," 55.
33. Escalada, *El complejo*.
34. Imbelloni, "Los Patagones," 27.
35. Ibid., 55.
36. Ibid., 23.
37. Imbelloni, *Informe preliminar*, 8.
38. Imbelloni, "Los Patagones," 23.
39. Ibid., 55.
40. Imbelloni, *Informe preliminar*, 10.
41. De Agostini, *Andes*, 398.
42. Ratier, "La antropología."
43. Censo Indígena Nacional, vol. 3, 108.
44. Ibid., 101.
45. Lenzi, *Historia*, 55.
46. Ibid., 54.

47. Ibid., 562.
48. Ibid., 54.
49. Ibid., 43.
50. Ibid., 54.
51. Ibid., 55.
52. Rappaport, "Mischievous"; Briones, "Mestizaje."
53. Silverstein, "Shifters."
54. Lois, "La Patagonia."
55. Ibid.
56. San Martín, "Memorias."
57. Briones and Carrasco, *Pacta.*
58. Records of the Provincial Agrarian Council (*Consejo Agrario Provincial,* hereafter CAP), file 1074-S-1897 in file 1779/S/914.
59. Nicoletti, "Los Salesianos."
60. Lista, *Los indios tehuelches,* 29.
61. Ibid., 66.
62. Ibid., 132.
63. CAP, file 59,408/48 (joined with file 40,335/52), 235–247.
64. Briones, "La nación."
65. Ibid.
66. CAP, file 7584F/910, 60–66.
67. CAP, file 4349/P/908 and S/4,373, 1–3.
68. CAP, file 9728/S/914, 80–91.
69. CAP, file 6897/915, 68–72.
70. CAP, file 4394 S/908, 40–49.
71. CAP, file 4394/S/908, 43–48.
72. CAP, file 7637/923, 135.
73. Barbería, *Los dueños.*
74. CAP, file 102,599/928, 138–144.
75. CAP, file 40,355/52, 303–308.
76. CAP, file 102,599/28, 138–144.
77. Elsewhere, I discuss the legal figure of "*estelionato,*" a tool of fraud, as it affected several indigenous families; see Rodríguez, "Empezaron."
78. CAP, file 18,804/61, 14.
79. CAP, file 18,804/61, 88–89.
80. CAP, file 486,710/74, 10–21, 35.
81. In 1982, the province donated 8,000 hectares from Camusu Aike to the Air Force and offered approximately 11,000 hectares for sale to the couple constituted by one of Ramona Lista's sons and one of Abdón López's daughters, who sold the land almost immediately (CAP, file 483,409/82).
82. In 1987, the province authorized the Army to occupy 6,000 hectares. That same year, the province reduced the 8,000 hectares it had originally donated to the Air Force in 1982 (see previous note) to 6,000 (still in Camusu Aike), leaving a total of approximately 7,000 hectares for Camusu Aike (CAP, Agreement 79, file 486,799/87).
83. See Geler, this volume.
84. Pagés Larraya et al., *Tehuelches.*
85. Following historian Serge Gruzinski, anthropologist Guillaume Boccara refers to these forms of exerting power and control as "mestizo logics," redefining the term

"mestizo" to suggest cultural flexibility and creativity. Boccara, "Antropología diacrónica."

86. During the National Land Survey of Indigenous Communities (*Relevamiento Territorial de Comunidades Indígenas*, ReTeCI, National Law 26,160/06) conducted in Santa Cruz between 2009 and 2011, the community itself demarcated 37,668.47 hectares, but at that time the Provincial Executive Power only recognized 18,000 hectares.

87. Foucault, *La arqueología.*

88. Rodríguez, "Empezaron."

89. See Voloshinov, *Marxism.*

6

Race and class through the visual culture of Peronism

Ezequiel Adamovsky

The elites who built Argentina claimed that their nation was embodied in a white-European people. At the end of the nineteenth century, members of distinct African or indigenous groups were declared extinct or were acknowledged only as the last few historical remnants of their communities, rapidly dissolving in the massive torrent of European immigrants. Although a few dissident voices made themselves heard, the master narrative of the nation revolved around the idea of a "melting pot [*crisol de razas*]" out of which one unified and homogeneous new *ethnos*[1] emerged. This new Argentine ethnos was almost exclusively connected (both culturally and biologically) to its European cradle, and the "Argentine race" was proclaimed to be "white." This, of course, was a kind of fantasy, as the ethnic backgrounds and phenotypes of large portions of the population did not (and still do not) easily fit into standard definitions of whiteness. For one thing, Afro-Argentines and indigenous groups managed to preserve some ethnic particularities despite the state's homogenizing pressures. The continuity of their physical presence also posed challenges to assertions of whiteness. In addition, a large portion of the Argentine population with no sense of belonging to any particular ethnic minority bore phenotypes that did not fully align with contemporary images and stereotypes of whiteness. All Argentines were formally considered "white," but in terms of physical appearance there was a substantial grey area between those who clearly displayed the right ("European") skin tones and facial features, and those who obviously did not. In theory, Argentina's whiteness was one; but in practice it had its visual and social nuances.

Indeed, although Argentines of non-exclusively European ancestry have been rendered invisible through discourses of whiteness, racist aggressions against the lower classes have been present throughout modern Argentine history, particularly when plebeian sectors have acquired political representation. Both President Hipólito Yrigoyen's and Juan Perón's followers were discredited for being *negros.* Their capacity for citizenship was thus questioned, as the racial allusion evoked shortcomings traditionally associated with irrationality and barbarity. Moreover, as I have shown elsewhere, middle-class identity in Argentina developed around a particular historical narrative that imagined the middle class as a force for civilization and progress supposedly brought to the country by European immigration. It distinguished itself from the plebeian sectors of society, understood to be the descendants of the mixed-race, native-born *criollos* of the pre-immigration nineteenth-century and colonial past, seen as obstacles to national prosperity and order.[2] Although prejudice against the so-called negros has an obviously racist component, it is a racism that, as historian Natalia Milanesio has noted, is subordinate to a discrimination based primarily on class. The use of labels such as negro, *cabecita negra*, and *groncho* during the twentieth century was aimed at the lower classes and at plebeian behavior generically, conveying a "racial" mark that did not translate into a particular physical trait. A lower-class individual could be considered a "negro" even if his skin color and facial features were fully in tune with the stereotype of the white-European Argentine.[3] And yet, possessing a phenotype perceived as nonwhite (or non-stereotypically white) had consequences in twentieth-century Argentina. Although prejudice and racism in Argentina require greater research, individuals of dark complexion and mestizo phenotypes have certainly experienced widespread discrimination in the labor market and have enjoyed fewer educational opportunities.[4]

What was the influence of this racial dimension on lower-class and plebeian political identities? As soon as this question is raised, we are confronted with a seeming paradox: despite skin-color discrimination and the pervasive presence of racist aggression, during most of the twentieth century there seems to have been no collective or sustained public reaction by members of the lower classes to these problems. To be sure, there were efforts by a few intellectuals to embrace ideals of mestizo nationhood. But among the lower classes there is only scattered evidence of efforts to confront the myth of the white-European Argentina, to turn nonwhiteness into an emblem of pride and a weapon to combat stigmas and discrimination. This situation changed after the 1980s and even more markedly in the 1990s. As the country's economic and political crisis spiraled, the state's (and therefore the nation's) capacity to incorporate the lower classes weakened. As anthropologist Rita Segato has argued, under these circumstances, the effectiveness of the "cultural patrolling" that had long enforced the myth of the white-European country diminished, which in turn made room for nonwhite presences to become newly visible.[5] The derogatory meanings ascribed to nonwhiteness certainly remain strong today. But for the first time, lower-class cultural and political forms of expression have directly challenged prevailing national myths by declaring dark skin a source of pride, thus responding to racism and also (albeit vaguely) antagonizing the upper classes. This "negro" identity is not imagined – at least not explicitly – as part of a broader Afro-diasporic community (except, of course, by members of the small groups who claim an Afro-descendant identity). Nor does the term refer to a specific Amerindian ethnos (except among those who recognize themselves as members of indigenous nations), even if it may connote a vague sense of mestizaje. Instead, being an Argentine negro today appears as a *racial marker* in what is fundamentally a *class identity*, rather than an ethnic or racial identity strictly speaking.[6]

The emergence of this non-diasporic "negro" marker in lower-class identities in the past two decades inevitably raises the question of its relationship to the history of race, class, and politics in earlier periods. I will argue that, although perhaps not manifested directly, allusions to the presence of nonwhiteness as a fundamental part of the nation can be found much earlier than the 1980s. Through a range of practices (such as carnival and other public celebrations) and through forms of cultural consumption (from *criollista* productions celebrating Argentina's rural and pre-immigration traditions to diverse popular music genres), the lower classes and some of the political forces that channeled their voices made the nonwhite visible in ways that undermined the implicit homogenization produced by the discourse of a white-European nation. One of the main arenas for these tacit disputes was visual culture. This chapter explores visual representations of the people, the worker, and Peronist supporters during the era of the "First Peronism" (1945–55), contrasting them with images from earlier periods. Although during the first half of the twentieth century the myth of a white-European Argentina was rarely challenged in an openly *verbal and argumentative way* – something that would dramatically change following the 1955 military coup that toppled Perón – one can nonetheless locate underlying disputes over the ethnic profile of the nation in the variety of visual documents produced and disseminated in these years. Indeed, these visual documents and their recuperation of nonwhiteness were of utmost importance to Peronist discourse.

ON VISUAL CULTURE

Although the Peronist state adopted policies in favor of indigenous minorities, the Peronist leadership did not make it central to their agenda to challenge the idea that the Argentine people were basically European. Questions of skin color were not publicly discussed by political authorities. While a few marginal figures in the Peronist movement called attention to nuances of skin tone (like labor leader Cipriano Reyes) or even proudly identified darker-skinned people as the authentic Argentines and the backbone of Peronism (like folk author Buenaventura Luna),[7] there is no evidence that Perón or his wife Evita ever uttered the expression "cabecita negra," let alone gave it a positive connotation.[8] The Peronist leadership acknowledged only one difference among Argentines and it was, in their view, temporary and fixable: the inequity of social class. Any other distinction was a threat to the Peronist vision of the unified people, a vision just as homogenizing as that of the elites who built the nation.

In Argentina, as Peronist authorities and followers proudly declared on many occasions, there was no "racial problem" at all.

However, the fact that issues of race and color were not *verbally* addressed should not blind us to a discussion of these issues in the era's visual culture. Images have a logic of their own, a signifying and also emotional power, which is irreducible to that of verbal communication (even if images and words supplement each other in countless ways).[9] In the public sphere, a number of shared discursive categories – like "workers" or "the people" – define particular ways of alluding to a larger social reality, and in turn enable debates on certain issues while obscuring others. By comparison, images can be more detailed and specific, while at the same time more fluid, than verbal categories. In a visual representation, the racially neutral category of "worker" may become a *white* or a *dark-skinned* worker; the figure in question can be dressed as a *modern* citizen or as a *traditional* inhabitant, and so forth. More importantly, visual language often works in a metonymical way. As a rhetorical figure, the metonym is about naming one thing in place of another, taking advantage of the association or contiguity between the two (for instance, the part standing in for the whole). But in visual language, the metonym is harder to avoid: illustrations are often precisely about choosing a concrete image – one character, one landscape, one situation – to represent something more general or conceptual. In the interaction between visual and verbal languages, the same image may correspond to different categories. Thus, the illustration of a "worker" might also be valid for the categories of "poor," "criollo," or even "indigenous," depending on the context of enunciation and reception. In some cases, this fluidity can open up a space of indeterminacy that is less common in verbal discourse.[10] Visual sources and the act of gazing have often been studied as devices of domination; however, the relationship between images and power is far more contradictory.[11]

Needless to say, visual culture is one of the fundamental resources for hegemony-building, but it is also fertile ground for counter hegemonic exercises. Specifically, visual language – polysemic, vague, and imprecise as it inherently is – can be particularly useful when it comes to grappling with issues that are impossible or too risky to debate openly and explicitly in a given cultural context.[12] It should come as no surprise, then, that the racial dimension we are exploring in this chapter found its way into the visual culture of Peronism a few years before it appeared in public speeches and debates. Peronist sympathizers made good use of visual sources to transmit ideas about ethnic or racial differences without having to engage in discussions that the state would not have welcomed. By using visual representations of plebeian bodies as metonyms of the nation or of their own rank and file (the two were sometimes indistinguishable in Peronist ideologies), the people who produced and circulated these images implicitly undermined the narrative of the white-European Argentina.

The visual culture of Peronism has attracted the attention of scholars who have focused especially on its propagandist and educational purposes and on the ways it helped construct "the People" as a political entity. These images have thus been almost exclusively analyzed in their hegemony-making functions.[13] The racial dimension implicit in the representation of the workers or the people and, more generally, the counter hegemonic power of images in this period, have been largely overlooked.[14] This chapter engages with the visual culture of Peronism with these goals in mind, drawing on a corpus of visual products made or designed by Peronists, published in the Peronist media, or used by state and partisan organizations in public festivities or demonstrations. Given the volume of visual sources in this period, this chapter focuses on static images such as paintings, photos, drawings, illustrations, and symbols printed in books, newspapers and magazines, brochures, placards, and leaflets.

VISUAL CULTURE AND "RACE" BEFORE PERONISM

Scholars have noted that rather than proposing a new culture of its own, Peronism engaged in a rich dialogue with previous cultural forms, discourses, and symbols. Visual culture was no exception. In the turbulent decades that followed the early-nineteenth-century wars of independence, elite projects of nation-building in Argentina faced at least two major obstacles. One of them was the active political participation of the lower classes. Mobilized by state officials and rival *caudillos* or strongmen, urban plebeians and rural *gauchos* became a permanent source of fear and instability for the new nation's elites. The other obstacle was geography. The few and mostly small cities in which the elites resided were simply incapable of controlling vast rural hinterlands with almost no state presence, not to mention the large expanses dominated by indigenous groups. In the mid-nineteenth century, *porteño* [Buenos-Aires based] elites construed the dramatic process of nation-building as a struggle of "civilization" against "barbarism," of urban space against the backward countryside of the Pampas, of a modern Buenos Aires against a more traditional Interior. Of course, these binary oppositions also had social and ethnic corollaries. The fight was also conceived as one of the literate classes against the uncultured lower classes, a struggle of Europeanness against creole and mestizo habits and mentalities, and, in keeping with the racialist thinking of the times, a contest of white versus nonwhite populations.

These oppositions nurtured Argentina's nascent iconography. The landscape of the Pampas and its inhabitants became the favorite topic of early painters of Argentine life, who filled their canvases with scenes of gaucho customs, voyages across the vast solitude of the land, and the much-feared *malones* or raiding parties, during which the Pampean tribes stormed rural populations to steal cattle and take captives. Depictions of *cautivas* [female captives] taken by force were among the most powerful visual (and literary) artifacts of the times, from Johann Rugendas' "El rapto de la cautiva" (1845) to Juan Manuel Blanes' "Rapto de una blanca" (1870s) and Ángel Della Valle's acclaimed "La vuelta del malón" (1892). These paintings communicated the imperative of eradicating barbarism by illustrating the danger of an inter-racial sexual possession of white women by darker-skinned indigenous men. Naturally, these images of wild savages and an exoticized landscape contrasted with those of the "civilized" world, the symbols of progress in Buenos Aires, and the social life of the elites, all of which were also frequent topics for painters.[15]

With the consolidation of the national state in 1880, the civil wars came to an end. The "Conquest of the Desert" launched in 1879 inflicted a definitive defeat on the bellicose indigenous groups of the Pampas, and those of the Northeast would soon suffer the same fate. Meanwhile, welcomed by authorities as the indispensable engine of progress, immigrants flooded the country, the vast majority of them from Europe. By the time of the Centennial celebrations (1910), there seemed to be little doubt that "civilization" definitively prevailed over barbarism, a belief reinforced by the myth of the emergence of a new "Argentine race" that was essentially white-European, as the influential intellectual José Ingenieros put it. Around the same time, technological changes were helping to expand the reach and everyday presence of images. Thanks to turn-of-the-century advances in photolithography and photography, images gained increasing space in postcards, books, popular magazines, and newspapers printed on a massive scale; moreover, printed matter gained an expanded readership in conjunction with the rise of literacy rates.[16] Visual representations of "ordinary" Argentines in advertisements, school books, and newspaper and magazine illustrations – including in socialist and anarchist publications – reinforced the myth of the white-European Argentina. Non-whites did appear occasionally, typically as part of stories situated in the remote past or in representations of supposedly vanishing populations (for example, in postcards featuring indigenous people) or of distant Northern provinces, often accompanied by captions expressing curiosity or satire.[17] But the images of present-day and "mainstream" Argentines overwhelmingly depicted subjects with white phenotypes (something often reinforced with the inclusion of fair-haired characters).[18] These dominant characteristics of Argentine visual culture continued for decades and have endured, in many respects, until the present.

It is also the case, however, that in these years, in reaction to deep anxieties about the flood of overseas immigration, the ethnic diversity of the nation – identified with a deeper colonial heritage – gained a place in visual culture, albeit a less prominent one. Partly in response to the growth of revolutionary working-class movements, elites' attitudes toward immigrants, which had been initially marked by optimism, became increasingly darkened by fears of cosmopolitanism and national dissolution. Nationalist movements began to emerge, first in groups of intellectuals and, by the 1920s, in periodicals and political organizations. For all of their ideological diversity, many within these nationalist groups defended the contributions of native-born criollos to national tradition in a time of cosmopolitanism and mass immigration. This position did not automatically challenge the myth of a white-European Argentina, since a large portion of the nationalists adopted a

Hispanist stance; if the criollo traditions embodied in the figure of the gaucho – now held up as the quintessential symbol of Argentineness – were considered to be of pure Spanish heritage, then these expressions of cultural nationalism posed little threat to the idea that the true Argentine people were white and European. Nevertheless, a few nationalist intellectuals – most notably, Ricardo Rojas – did put forward new notions of nationality in which the mestizo and indigenous legacies (though not the African) were acknowledged and celebrated, albeit as a more abstract cultural heritage than as a concrete and contemporary human presence.

These intellectual currents in turn shaped mass culture during the early twentieth century. The gaucho and related traditions of the rural Pampas – which had been present for decades in popular criollista literature, circus shows, theater plays, and postcards – acquired new legitimacy as emblems of nationality and became favorite topics for the nascent film, recording, and broadcasting industries.[19] With the emergence of a folk music movement in the 1920s, other criollo social types and traditions from beyond the Pampas, especially those from the Northwest, also gained visibility and legitimacy. As historian Oscar Chamosa has argued, though folklore specialists tended to hide or to minimize indigenous contributions to folk music and the mestizo characteristics of criollo populations, by the 1930s, musicians like Atahualpa Yupanqui recorded popular songs that alluded to the "old races" and their contemporary suffering.[20] Finally, due to both local and international influences, in the same decades other popular rhythms such as tango and jazz lent a new sense of legitimacy to African roots and blackness.[21]

Within this context of cultural nationalism, nonwhite (or non-stereotypically white) phenotypes acquired some presence in Argentine visual culture. Ricardo Rojas' syncretic vision of local traditions as a blend of indigenous and European elements, presented in his work *Eurindia* (1924), captured the attention of painters; contemporary artists also drew inspiration from the trip to Buenos Aires, the same year, of a delegation of Peruvian artists of *indigenista* orientation. Thus, the Salón Nacional de Bellas Artes – the most prestigious event in local fine arts – featured portraits in which the ethnic heterogeneity of the nation became more visible. Representations of indigenous or mestizo characters situated in provincial locations – particularly in the Northwest – became more frequent and were more likely to win honors (although it should be noted that these figures were almost always portrayed as ahistoric "types" that suggested no evident connection to the contemporary population).[22] In turn, the gauchos or criollos of the Pampas, as portrayed by artists such as Emilio Centurión, Jorge Bermúdez, Fernando Fader, or Cesáreo Bernaldo de Quirós, sometimes featured darker skins or other phenotypic marks denoting miscegenation. Left-leaning forms of anti-imperialism also played a role in illuminating racial difference. In depicting the suffering of urban workers and rural inhabitants, the painter Antonio Berni captured a diversity of skin colors and phenotypes, notably in his acclaimed works "Manifestación" (1934) and "Jujuy"

(1937). These sorts of depictions, most notably those of Bernaldo de Quirós, found their way to wider audiences through newspapers and magazine reproductions.[23] The most emblematic case in this sense is that of Florencio Molina Campos: several of his famous illustrations for the printed wall calendars issued by the manufacturers of *alpargatas* [a cheap type of shoe used by the lower classes] circulated widely in the 1930s and for a long time thereafter, and featured gauchos of mestizo or even African appearance.[24]

Beyond the world of fine arts, lesser-known artists sometimes included images of non-stereotypically white Argentines (and also of Argentines with indigenous or African features) in their work for periodicals. Traditionalist magazines were particularly generous in this regard: *Nativa* – launched in 1923, one of the most established publications in this genre and the longest lived – continuously published illustrations and photos (usually under the title "From Our Land") featuring lower-class people of mestizo, African, or indigenous appearance.[25] Even in *Caras y Caretas* (1898–1939), the most widely read general interest magazine of its time – where Argentines were overwhelmingly represented by people of white phenotype – there is a gaucho-looking character, "Juan Pueblo" (meant to represent the quintessential Argentine) who in at least three examples was depicted with darker skin in the midst of whiter characters.[26] The entertainment press was also a channel through which pictures of non-stereotypically white Argentines were occasionally disseminated. The photographs devoted to the folklore movement, for example, often featured musicians from the Interior of mestizo and Afro-descendant appearance, and the accompanying texts sometimes highlighted their looks as a sign of these musicians' national authenticity.[27] Media coverage of the tango and popular music scenes also included photographs of Afro-Argentine and Afro-Uruguayan musicians and dancers, especially from the late 1930s onward, when the fashion of *candombe* [an African-derived music of the Río de la Plata region] multiplied the opportunities for these artists not only to perform, but also to visually emphasize their African ancestry (for example, in their choice of costumes).[28] And, following the local tradition of the *lubolos* [blackface carnival groups], but due also to the international influence of American minstrel shows and of Al Jolson's films, blackface made a frequent appearance in the arts, whether it was used by white actors playing black people in films and plays, or by jazz or candombe singers impersonating Afro-descendants in their shows, as some published photos attest.[29] Comic strips also displayed nonwhite presences. The clearest example would be *Patoruzú*, introduced in 1928, one of the most successful Argentine comics of all times. Created by Dante Quinterno, an artist of nationalist sympathies, the strip narrated the adventures of a *Tehuelche* Indian who embodied the values and virtues of the criollo (and therefore genuinely Argentine) world under threat from foreign villains. Patoruzú was a rather curious synthesis of the figures of the gaucho and the Amerindian, which had traditionally been seen as inimical. Afro-Argentines were also occasionally shown in commercial advertisements and in comic strips such as Arturo Lanteri's "Las aventuras del negro Raúl" (1916) or Arístides Rechain's "La página del dólar" (1920s), although most often as objects of ridicule.[30] Finally, nonwhites also appeared in films, usually as historical characters or as representatives of barbarism, but occasionally as contemporary figures and in a more positive (or at least neutral) light.[31]

In sum, prior to the emergence of Peronism images of indigenous people and individuals of darker skin or mestizo features did appear here and there in Argentine visual productions, often presented in a positive (if sometimes folkloric) light and associated with ideas of popular and national authenticity. Afro-Argentines were more likely to appear in grotesque or exoticizing contexts, but that was not inevitably the case. Notwithstanding the relevance of these examples, we should recall that these were just a drop in a sea of visual representations of Argentines as whites.

THE RACIAL AMBIGUITIES OF PERONIST VISUAL CULTURE

As mentioned earlier, the Peronist state did not openly challenge the myth of the white-European Argentina, either through verbal and written discourse or through visual language. Indeed, the iconographic representations of common Argentines produced in these years were largely in keeping with dominant cultural canons. In marked continuity with the visual conventions of an earlier period, the vast majority of Peronist propaganda and illustrations showed Argentines of white phenotypes (in some school texts most individuals were even blond).[32] The "New Argentine 'Juan Pueblo'" depicted on the front cover of the popular humor magazine *PBT* in 1950 and in the pages of the Peronist newspaper *El Laborista* in the same year was of classically European looks – not a gaucho anymore, but a tidy industrial worker.[33] The same can be said of "José Julián, the heroic *descamisado* [the Peronist term for the "shirtless" humble-born]," the main character of the pro-Peronist comics who fought against oligarchs and communists (it should be noted, however, that he and his associates were dark-haired, while some of the villains were blond).[34] Furthermore, at least some Peronist officials were unhappy with having non-European imagery in relation to their movement. For example, when the Argentine embassy in France commissioned a sculpture of Evita from the Paris-based Argentine artist Sesostris Vitullo in 1953 and he carved a mestizo-looking Evita – envisioning her as a "liberator of the oppressed races of the Americas" – they confined the work to a basement. It remained forgotten there until its rediscovery in 1973.[35]

As I have argued elsewhere, some Peronists managed to implicitly challenge the myth of the white-European Argentina by tapping into the criollista discourse of earlier times.[36] But while Perón did much to present himself as a criollo and his government as the defender of criollo populations and national values, rarely did political authorities convey an explicitly mestizo sense to that identification, which remained to a great extent racially indeterminate. This is exemplified in a famous propaganda book's visual

FIGURE 12 The "average" family in the Peronist era. Source: *La nación argentina, justa, libre, soberana*, 3rd. ed. (Buenos Aires: Presidencia de la Nación, 1950), 799.

representation of the criollo – the "son of the country" forgotten by earlier governments and now dignified by Perón – which features a family of pinkish complexion and European looks (Figure 12). And yet, other visual renderings of Juan Pueblo, the workers, and the criollos produced by Peronists or sponsored by the state portrayed them with phenotypes that denoted miscegenation (Figure 13) or signaled African roots (Figure 14).[37] Likewise, the inclusion of illustrations of people of indigenous or mestizo features in the press often lent a racial connotation to textual stories that otherwise had no obvious or necessary racial dimension – as in the case of a story about the contribution of *provinciano* musicians to popular music, or another about the historic connection between the contemporary Peronist shirtless ones and the soldiers of the wars of Independence. Such illustrations also lent a racial dimension to abstract calls for the "ethnic unification" of the nation.[38]

FIGURE 13 "Juan Pueblo" drawn with brown skin, slanted eyes, and other "creole" features. This image received third prize in a poster contest for the Five-Year Plan sponsored by a Peronist newspaper. Source: *El Laborista*, 10 Jun. 1947, 8.

FIESTA
CRIOLLA

BUENOS AIRES
AÑO DEL LIBERTADOR GENERAL SAN MARTIN, 1950

FIGURE 14 Front cover of a Peronist propaganda pamphlet. The illustration is by the artist Gregorio López Naguil. Source: *Fiesta criolla* (Buenos Aires, 1950). Courtesy of the Instituto Juan D. Perón.

SHOWING THE (DARKER) PEOPLE

As the lower classes gained political influence and visibility during the Peronist era, they participated in all sorts of demonstrations and festivals and increasingly "occupied" public spaces. Accordingly, the lower classes acquired more prominence in photographs published in the mass-circulation press – a trend that was advanced by plebeian sectors themselves to gain greater influence and enjoy a new sense of political recognition, as well as by the state propaganda machine to display the government's popular legitimacy.

The official media reported several cases of plebeian sectors making remarkable efforts to gain visibility. The best known is arguably the "Malón de la Paz," a march that the indigenous Kolla people organized in 1946. During this political action – which involved marching on foot from Salta and Jujuy hundreds of miles to Buenos Aires, in the hopes of attracting state support to reclaim ancestral lands – the Kolla carefully chose their symbols in light of Argentina's history of race. By calling their protest a "malón" they tackled head-on the prejudice that their Indianness evoked (even if, historically, Kollas had never performed such raids), and added "of Peace" to counter it. They marched with traditional clothes and musical instruments, but also made it clear that they were proud Argentines (by participating in military parades) and good Catholics (by carrying an image of the Virgin Mary). Although the Malón ultimately failed to achieve its immediate goals, it was a success in terms of visibility; dozens of stories and photos filled the press, including the photos taken when Perón greeted the marchers in the presidential palace.[39] Lesser-known but similar episodes include marches of groups of people of largely mestizo appearance from Salta and from Santiago del Estero to demonstrate their loyalty to Perón, and the self-styled "Inca del Altiplano [Inca of the Highlands]" who arrived in Buenos Aires and knocked on the door of a newspaper's offices to manifest "the unconditional support of his racial brothers." These performances received visual coverage in high-profile Peronist media outlets like *El Laborista* or in *Mundo Peronista*. The march led by fifty *santiagueños* [residents of the Northwestern province of Santiago del Estero] – who were described by the press interchangeably as "workers" or as "criollos" and in racialized terms as "some [...] dark-skinned, others white" – was received by Perón; this made a good story about the need to "*hermanar*," or create brotherhood among, all Argentines.[40] In another case, the government itself brought from Salta to Buenos Aires a group of children of the *Diaguita* nation, also photographed and placed on the front page of a national newspaper.[41] The appointment of a *Mapuche* chief as part of the staff of the General Bureau for the Protection of Aboriginal Peoples also generated visual images and press coverage about the "autochthonous races" that formed part of the New Argentina.[42] Photographs of non-stereotypically white Argentines also appeared in diverse news reports, ranging from stories on the strength of Peronism in the Interior, to the improved social condition of the "sons of the land," to an award ceremony for the Peronist Medals.[43] But more importantly, in these years Perón and Evita were profusely photographed in the national press in the company of mestizo-looking people.[44]

People of African descent acquired a prominent place in Peronist visual culture that is particularly noteworthy, as it contrasts with their virtual absence in verbal discourse. As with representations of indigenous people and mestizos, pictures of Afro-Argentines also found their way into the press as illustrations for stories about lower-class suffering (Figure 15), as possible "faces" of Peronist supporters, or as participants in face-to-face meetings with Perón and Evita.[45] People of African descent (and, more broadly, references to Argentina's African roots) also appeared in mass culture, which, as scholars have noted, was tightly intertwined with Peronist mass politics. Indeed, Perón and Evita made use of the sentimental resonances of the melodrama genre and of *criollismo* to build a relationship with their supporters and to transmit political messages, while mobilizing movie and radio stars, artists of different musical genres, and sportsmen for political purposes.[46] Thus, a renewed interest in Argentina's African roots discernible in mass culture was present among Perón's "borrowings" from the very beginning. In the charitable event that Perón organized for the relief of the victims of the San Juan earthquake in 1944 – arguably, the event that launched his political career – Alberto Castillo and Hugo Devieri, the two best known artists behind the rebirth of candombe, were invited to perform; both artists were white, but the latter appeared in blackface, as the pictures published by the press attest.[47] Years later, the biggest Peronist tango and movie idol, Hugo del Carril, appeared in blackface as he starred in and directed a film that (despite its title) broached anti-racist themes: *The Black Man Who Had a White Soul* (1951).

Perón also went out of his way to secure the support of foreign artists and sportsmen of African descent who were popular in Argentina. Legendary African-American performer Josephine Baker, who had already visited the country twice, returned in 1947 and in 1952. She became an enthusiastic Peronist and met Perón both times (the second, while she was delivering a speech in praise of Evita at the Teatro Colón), which attracted much media photo coverage.[48] The president also photographed himself embracing African-American boxer Archie Moore and strolling with him in his residence; similarly, he had himself photographed in the company of Afro-Cuban boxing champion Kid Gavilan (who was decorated by the government with the Eva Perón Cup).[49] The Peronist press also published photos of notable Afro-Argentines, like the famous singer Gabino Ezeiza (who had died in 1916 but was routinely evoked) or the athlete Ezequiel "el Negrito" Bustamante, who was an eager Peronist.[50]

Peronism was also associated with Afro-Argentines in drawings and comic strips. In 1955, for example, *Mundo Peronista* published "Chocolate," the story of an Afro-Argentine kid who was bullied at school by his white peers. Included in the section devoted to the indoctrination of children, the tale was

El Laborista
Propulsor de Una Nueva Conciencia en Marcha

10 CENTAVOS EN TODA LA REPUBLICA

AÑO I   BUENOS AIRES, MIERCOLES 8 DE MAYO DE 1946   No. 117

UNA FAMILIA HUMILDE como tantas, una familia criolla, de trabajo, que un día tuvo que soportar las ansias de mayores ganancias en el patrón del inquilinato que comprendió lo lucrativo del negocio de "hospedajes". Le llegó el desalojo, el infortunio, la desesperación. Y así no cesa el drama de los inquilinos, víctimas propiciatorias del último gran "negocio" de Buenos Aires. (Nota ps. 8 y 9)

FIGURE 15 An elderly Afro-Argentine woman with her family being evicted from their home. The accompanying caption describes the woman as "criolla." Source: *El Laborista*, 8 May 1946, front page.

meant to explain that "in the New Argentina all children are equals." In this case, the message of equality was implicitly delivered by Perón himself, who unexpectedly visited the school and had words of appreciation for the black boy (the illustration showed the president tenderly stroking his head) (Figure 16). The section for children in the same magazine provides other good examples of Peronists' attempts to associate themselves with Afro-Argentines, with more obvious political connotations. The subsection "Our Little World" was often illustrated with the image of a bunch of children – one of whom was black – playing the bass drum or *bombo*, one of the main symbols of the Peronist movement.[51] But the most interesting example in this regard is that of "Chispita y Grillito," one of the magazine's regular comic strips. The protagonists of this strip were "Los Privilegiados [the privileged ones]," a gang of children always ready to support the government, one of whom was an Afro-Argentine boy (Figure 17).[52]

Unlike typical images of Afro-Argentines, which were belittling or stressed tropes of vanishing populations (as in depictions of elderly Afro-Argentines or their representation as part of remote historical scenes), this example is undoubtedly situated in the present – or, indeed, in the future, since the Afro-Argentine subject is a child – and it depicts Afro-Argentines as taking an active role in national politics (as they had for much of the nineteenth century). If "Los Privilegiados" represents the Peronist rank-and-file and the "authentic" people of the New Argentina, then the presence of the black boy in this collective group can be interpreted as a metonym of a racially diverse nation. It is worth noting that in this visual device the influence of mass culture may also be discerned. Gangs of children featuring a black boy or girl (a strategy for indicating that they belonged to the lower class) can be found in at least three Argentine movies of the time: the short film *Pibelandia* (1935), *Chimbela* (1939, directed by the Afro-Argentine film-maker José A. "el Negro" Ferreyra), and *Stella* (1943).[53] In turn, these inter-racial gangs of children may have been (at least visually) modeled on foreign examples and, in particular, on US children's adventure films such as Hal Roach's *Rascals*, which also included a black child and which circulated widely in mid-century Argentina.[54]

THE HIDDEN HISTORY OF THE PERONIST COAT OF ARMS

One element of Peronist visual culture that has gone surprisingly unnoticed among scholars is the use of an alternative version of the official coat of arms of the movement, in which the lower hand in the handshake symbol is painted in a darker color (Figure 18). I have thoroughly documented the circulation of this variant elsewhere.[55] It was certainly used less frequently than the official version, in which both hands were of the same tone, but it was nevertheless present as part of the official decorations of several party, union, or state gatherings, street celebrations, or

FIGURE 16 This image, titled "Chocolate," appeared in one of the most celebrated Peronist magazines of the era. Source: *Mundo peronista* 84, 15 Apr. 1955, 32. Courtesy of the Archivo Histórico de la Provincia de Buenos Aires "Dr. Ricardo Levene."

FIGURE 17 The comic strip "Chispita y Grillito." Source: *Mundo Peronista* 60, 1 Mar. 1954, 36.

FIGURE 18 President Juan D. Perón speaking at the Ministry of Labor and Welfare, with the Peronist coat of arms below. 9 Aug. 1955. Courtesy of the "Centro de Documentación e Información de la Cultura de Izquierdas en Argentina (CeDInCI)," Archivo *La Razón* [SGAL-CFV-C-8-1402] (1).

mass meetings, as well as on the banners of Perón supporters. In fact, the alternative version was part of the gigantic emblem that decorated the stage for Perón and Evita in the famous Cabildo Abierto of 1951, attended by an estimated one million people (and seen by many more in the propaganda films and photos released by the government later). While the emblems used for official stages were probably made at the same workshops as all other decorations for Perón's appearances, it is likely that the demonstrators' banners were self-made.

In the official Peronist liturgy, as Perón himself explained, the symbol represented a superior stage in the nation's development. There was an implicit narrative at play: during official events the Peronist coat of arms was usually displayed together with Argentina's national emblem – after which it was modeled – and positioned almost always to its right (from the observer's view). While the horizontal handshaking of the national emblem was a symbol of abstract equality, the vertical grasping of hands was meant to illustrate the duty of solidarity of the higher class toward the poor, a key tenet of social policy in the New Argentina. Are we then allowed to interpret the two-color variant as a racial inflection that overlapped with the class meaning? Can we read the nuance in the hands' skin color as denoting the solidarity expected between the rich/whites and the poor/darker-skinned? While contemporary texts highlighted themes of class solidarity in explaining the meaning of the unicolor coat of arms, I have been unable so far to locate similar commentary on the potential racial significance of the two-color version.

In the absence of words, interpreting images is always a risky exercise. We stand on firmer ground if we take into account the context in which they were used. First, although the main Peronist leaders did not publicly address the "racial" issue, secondary figures did speak or write about it straightforwardly. Second, as we have seen, Peronist visual culture was rich in images suggesting the racial heterogeneity of the country and even the centrality of dark-skinned people in the nation. The possible interpretation of the two-color coat of arms as denoting a racial inflexion does not rely on that image solely, but on the wider visual landscape of which it was a part. Finally, the economy of Peronist liturgy can also shed light on the matter. Take, for example, the Cabildo Abierto of 1951: that day, prior to the much-awaited entrance of Evita, the Secretary General of the CGT (General Confederation of Labor), José Espejo, delivered a speech under the giant two-color emblem. Before his appointment as chief of the labor movement, Espejo was a worker in the food industry of Buenos Aires, where he had arrived from his native San Juan looking for better opportunities. Moreover, he had black hair and brownish skin; indeed, he seemed a prototype of what the anti-Peronists used to call a *cabecita negra*. In his speech Espejo highlighted the fact that the immense crowd gathered there had arrived "from the four cardinal points" of the country, bringing with them "the voice of history." In his view, the "simple and shirtless" people of the present were directly related to those who had given their blood in the struggles for independence. Indeed, according to Espejo, Peronism meant precisely the vindication of "the old, vanquished fatherland" that had been "humiliated" for "over a century" before Perón came to reverse the situation (note that, in this chronology, humiliation had started with the process of national consolidation and extended through the era of European mass immigration).[56] The references to the criollo world, however, were not only Espejo's. As was the norm in most large Peronist public gatherings, individuals dressed up as gauchos formed part of the multitude, some of them even on horseback, a rather unusual presence in the city centers where rallies often took place. According to one newspaper report, the workers of a meatpacking factory in Greater Buenos Aires had arrived to the Cabildo Abierto "dressed in the gaucho style, while in their cart, pulled by four oxen, country men and women [*paisanos y paisanas*] sang criollo songs." Pro-government newspapers included photographs of these performances, underscoring that their participants had come from the Interior of the country and therefore were "truly criollos,"[57] while the propaganda film made by the state after the Cabildo also stressed that the multitude had arrived "from the bottom of history" after having waited for over a century to see their longings fulfilled.[58]

In such a context, it is not too hazardous to risk an interpretation that draws attention to the importance of race and class together in Peronist visual culture. The nuance in the shaking hands displayed in the giant coat of arms complemented the discourses of solidarity and inclusion uttered during and immediately after the Cabildo Abierto. In this way, visual language enabled a full elucidation of the message, pointing to something that Peronist authorities still had trouble saying verbally or setting down in writing. All people were the Peronist people, but the criollos in particular embodied them, and they in turn were particularly represented by those coming from the provinces and bearing darker skins. The brownish tone on the emblem's lower hand alluded metonymically to the mixed-race criollo, who was the heart of the nation, according to the criollista discourse in vogue in those years. The message was clear: in the New Argentina, rather than despising the cabecitas negras, those citizens and leaders positioned socially above them had the moral obligation to help improve their lives.

If this interpretation is correct, then the two-color coat of arms entered into semantic interplay with the national coat of arms, undermining the abstract ideal of the citizen in a second, arguably more unsettling way. By turning the handshake on a vertical axis, the unicolor Peronist emblem had already alluded to class differences among a nation of supposedly equal citizens. The two-color version added the recognition of a racial dimension to class inequality. True, the Peronist movement – or at least its leaders – generally referred to differences among citizens as part of a political imagination that revolved around an idea of class harmony and national unity. But despite this vision, the coat of arms, as a visual emblem, was dangerously unstable: it promised solidarity as much as it reminded viewers of persistent class (and now also color) cleavages.

METONYMS OF THE NATION

As we have seen, efforts to render nonwhite presences visible and disputes over the racial profile of the nation preceded the Peronist era. Nevertheless, these elements became more prominent in the New Argentina and, more importantly, they acquired a more overtly political tone. Examples of this orientation include "Chispita y Grillito" and the two-color coat of arms: dark skins were explicitly associated with Peronism as a political identity. In the latter case, an implicit narrative component was coupled to the image in the verbal pronouncements of leaders and in pro-Peronist press coverage. Historical allusions provided powerful ways to challenge the myth of the white-European Argentina, itself supported by potent visual and narrative devices.

In certain cases, Peronist loyalists made these connections and allusions quite explicitly. Take, for example, the following illustration by Arístides Rechain, the author of one of the comics featuring Afro-Argentines in the 1920s, printed in the Peronist magazine *Descamisada*. The image builds upon, and furthers, a common association between the May Revolution of 1810 (taken as the first step toward the birth of the nation) and October 17th 1945 (the foundational moment of Peronism), while deploying racialized imagery in powerful ways (Figure 19). In this image, the participants in the May 1810 Revolution march together with the *descamisados* or Peronist support- ers, the past and present moving forward toward a luminous future. The skin color of the men of 1810 and their Peronist counterparts is deliberately painted in a dark tone, which becomes evident by contrast with the only person of fair hair and pinkish complexion (a woman), at the bottom left of the image. The prominent cheek bones and the dark, coarse hair of the central figures are hardly accidental, nor are the slanted eyes of the man who holds the shirt as a flag and of the individual directly behind him: all these are commonly understood markers of indigenous ancestry and mixed race in Argentina. It is also worth noting that the illustrator included a very dark-skinned Afro- Argentine woman at the bottom right, almost out of the frame but still visible and at the very front. Confining nonwhite presences to Argentina's colonial past has been a common device for rendering them invisible in the present, but here the image deliberately brings the past into the present: it makes nonwhites part of the New Argentina taking shape. The eye can capture several nuances: black, brown, and white, and each of them has a presence. But the arrange- ment of the figures leaves no doubt: the Argentine people may be diverse, but they are represented above all by men of dark complexion and mestizo appearance. The classically white-European component is there, but it is notably underrepresented. This depiction of the Peronist present connects directly with Argentina such as it was before the advent of European mass immigration (one can even say that this drawing chooses to ignore its impact altogether).

Other interesting elements come into sight when we analyze this image through the lens of gender. With the exception of the Afro-Argentine figure, the only woman whose features can be clearly distinguished is the sole character repre- sented as unquestionably "white." Next to her, from behind and very closely, comes a male of darker skin and mestizo appearance. With his shirt wide open,

FIGURE 19 "May and October: Two Generations, the Same Destiny." Source: *Descamisada* 18, 20 May 1946, n.p. Courtesy of Special Collections, University of Miami Libraries, Coral Gables, Florida.

he observes her in a way that transmits a sense of erotic tension. As Sergio Caggiano has argued in his study of Argentine visual culture, in a cultural context like Argentina's, where dominant discourses have stressed the "whitening" of the population, the empirical fact of (past) miscegenation could only be visually represented through couples in which the nonwhite member was always the woman. Sexual intercourse, understood as possession, implies that it is the (white) male who is to play the active role in incorporating the native (feminine) world. As we have seen in examples of nineteenth-century paintings, Argentine visual culture did sometimes represent inter-racial unions the other way round, but primarily through the archetype of the cautiva, the woman kidnapped and taken beyond the borderline of civilization, therefore lost to the nation-building project (even if cautivas managed to return, their reputation was considered forever ruined).[59] In criollista literature we find a similar pattern: allusions were made to miscegenation, but usually by ethnically marking the indigenous woman (the so-called *china*) and not the gaucho. This Peronist image inverts the expected relation between race and gender. In the couple that marches in the vanguard of the group, leading the crowd to the future, the possibility of sexual intercourse subtly alluded to would be one in which the carrier of nonwhite ancestry is the male, while "white" purity is presented as the female attribute destined to be incorporated by plebeian male actors into the nation. Thus, this image confers upon the mestizo-looking character the power and privileges of maleness over the (feminized) sectors previously privileged by their whiteness.

CONCLUSION

This chapter has discussed several examples of images made or disseminated by Peronists that highlight the presence of nonwhites, including cases where dark-skinned bodies were clearly used as metonyms of Peronism's popular characteristics and the authentic nation. In this regard, two interrelated questions immediately come to mind: first, why would Peronist artists, journalists, photographers, and members of the rank-and-file engage in the production or dissemination of such images? Second, what impact did these images have among the general population, particularly those who felt attracted to the Peronist movement?

One way to grapple with these questions is to relate the representations of racial markers in the images directly to any actual markers that individuals may have had. In other words, the production or consumption of this kind of iconography could be analyzed in terms of how certain people, who felt discriminated against on racial grounds, tried to renegotiate the ethnic profile of the nation so as to make room for themselves, to see themselves reflected in public imagery. Indeed, some of the first Peronist figures who spoke openly about color differences in these years, like Cipriano Reyes or Buenaventura Luna, were dark-skinned and of mestizo backgrounds.[60] Additionally, it is well known that many indigenous groups expressed open support for Perón in these years,[61] and there are also some hints in this regard among Afro-Argentines.[62]

But what about those who did not identify themselves as part of these minority groups – that is, the millions of Argentines whose features did not match the European ideal phenotype but who had no references about their ethnic background, other than being criollos? It is difficult to know. To be sure, the percentage of voters who backed Perón and his party was higher in regions most inhabited by mestizos, like the Northwest, than in other areas. But as those regions were also the poorest, it is hard to tell whether there was a specifically racial/ethnic component in voters' behavior. It would not be surprising if people of mestizo phenotypes felt to some extent acknowledged and welcomed by the subtle signs emanating from Peronism, including visual ones, which could be part of the explanation for their devotion to Perón. As art historian David Freedberg has noted, the reaction that an image may produce in any given person depends, among other factors, on the possibility of establishing an empathic bond with it; we feel particularly connected to images in which we can recognize bodies like our own or our peers'.[63] Thus, in societies in which social hierarchies and ethnic differences to some extent overlap, disadvantaged people may establish an emotional connection with images that they feel reflect their own bodies – for instance metonymically, through skin color and key features – even in the absence of open, verbal discourses that deal with color differences. (The traditional cult of dark-skinned Madonnas in several Latin American countries – including Argentina – would be a good example.) It is certainly possible that Peronist visual sources, such as the mestizo Juan Pueblo (Figure 13) or the two-color coat of arms, triggered similar emotional responses among some of the people who felt attracted to the new movement.

That being said, it should be noted that the assertion of the nonwhite components of the nation was not the exclusive work of dark-skinned or mestizo Argentines. On the contrary, people who fit the white European ideal also participated in the creation and dissemination of visual products of the kind we are analyzing (painter Gregorio López Naguil, for example, author of Figure 14, who was the son of a Spanish father and a French mother). To some extent, the political and cultural logic of these images can also be understood from an alternative perspective, as a response to the views of Peronism generated by anti-Peronists. From Peronism's earliest days, critics set out to discredit this new political movement by means of racist explanations. In their eyes, the basis of Perón's support was not all workers, but only the most backward and irrational – and, in racial and ethnic terms, not those of immigrant backgrounds but criollos, particularly those who had recently arrived from the rural Interior to urban areas. The expression "cabecita negra," which became widely used in this era, synthesized the alleged features of Peronist supporters in a conspicuously racist tone; this slur was complemented by other descriptions that linked Peronist supporters to Africanness (as in insistent depictions of Peronist gatherings as candombes). This invective worked through a logic of equivalence: if the cabecitas negras were Peronists, then all Peronists were negros and Peronism itself could be considered a *"cosa de negros* [a *negro* thing]," as one conservative politician put it.[64]

In turn, there is evidence that these equivalences were soon adopted by some Peronists, albeit with the opposite appraisal. Although Peronism's identification with the cabecitas took place after Perón was overthrown in 1955, before that date some Peronists were already writing in their defense or even toying with the idea that their support was the best proof of the authentically popular and national character of the movement.[65] The visual products that we have analyzed in this article can also be interpreted in this light, as part of wider struggles over which political forces had the legitimacy to represent the Argentine people; if the authentic people were darker, then Peronism, as a *"negro* thing," was the sole force entitled to represent them. From this perspective, the subtle renegotiations of the racial profile of the nation that we have identified were driven less by the desire of nonwhites or non-stereotypically whites to be included, than by the aspiration of Peronists of whatever "race" to claim national authenticity while denying it to their opponents.

It would be a mistake, however, to consider this an either/or question. For it should be remembered that negotiations of Argentina's racial profile predated Peronism, and that in earlier examples stereotypically "white" people were also involved as producers and as consumers of racialized visual culture. The visual references to nonwhites that we have analyzed in this chapter, then, cannot be understood naïvely, as if they were part of the efforts of oppressed sections of the population (Amerindian, mestizo, or Afro-Argentine) to demand a new, multicultural definition of the nation: there was no such idea at that time. But nor can they be considered mere pieces of discursive fabrications for polemical purposes, produced "vicariously" by white people and with no relation to the social and demographic reality of the country. If certain artists, intellectuals, and eventually political actors sought to undermine the myth of the white-European Argentina, it was because they found the need or the opportunity to do so, counting on the receptivity of the population. And this cannot be understood without taking into account the disjunctures in dominant narratives of the nation regarding the physical diversity visible in its population, or the unstable meanings of "whiteness" in a country that officially extended that feature to the whole citizenry but simultaneously preserved a visual sense and a vocabulary that continually marked internal nuances within that "whiteness." Nor can it be understood without bearing in mind the serious problems that Argentine elites had previously experienced when it came to culturally "civilizing" and to politically including the lower classes – difficulties that partially derived, in turn, from the exclusionary narratives elites chose to endorse, but also from the capacity of the common people to propose alternatives, or at least to passively resist certain cultural messages and political initiatives. To borrow Nicholas Mirzoeff's words, visual production was carried out against the background of deeper struggles for "the right to look."[66]

Indeed, the transformations in visual culture that we have considered here are better understood as an episode in a long-term, painful, and probably still unfinished *ethnogenesis*: the making of a national ethnos out of Argentina's demographic heterogeneity, with all of the tensions created by overlapping class and ethnic cleavages and by the conflicting narratives by which different groups of Argentines have tried to grasp who they were. Indeed, the images we have analyzed can be interpreted through the lens of what anthropologist Guillaume Boccara has called "mestizo logics," or the capacity to redefine the ethnic Self "by means of a movement of openness to the Other." Through a metamorphosis that makes room for the Other, the ethnic Self – thus *mestizado* – overcomes potentially conflictive situations and secures its continuity over time.[67] As members of an ethnos in the making, both white and nonwhite people could be agents of such a strategy, for which, due to their fluidity and indeterminacy, visual artifacts were an ideal arena of expression and contention. Indeed, although the images we have examined illuminate a racial dimension that was still difficult to process in verbal language, there is no evidence that producing or consuming them had any racial(izing) intention. Locating a dark-skinned character as the center of the nation was not about replacing "white" with "black" or European with indigenous, but rather about making visible *metonymically* the human diversity that composed the world of the lower classes. In this case, a dark-skinned individual (whether drawn, photographed, or symbolically represented in the two-color coat of arms) functions as an encompassing signifier for the totality of the people of the lower classes, irrespective of their color. In racist discourses, metonym is used to transfer to the entire lower classes the stigma originally associated only to those of African or indigenous origin. But taken up by dissenting cultural or political strategies, the part refers to a differently valorized whole, the whole of the people with its diversity of colors recognized and accepted rather than denied. One of its parts – the dark-skinned people – takes the place of the whole to make visible the fact that that whole is not white or colorless, as the dominant discourses would have it. At the same time, the metonym also points to the subaltern condition associated with the sense of exclusion or asymmetry of power that dark skin evokes. Somehow, this metonymic operation points to a unified people, diverse but without ethnic conflicts and made of equals. In other words, a people that exists only as desire. Perhaps one of the reasons for the extraordinary vitality of Peronism is precisely that (in spite of some of its leaders) it became a political channel for that desire for equality not just in terms of class but also of race and ethnicity.

Notes

1. In this chapter I use the terms "ethnos"/"ethnic" to refer to a concrete group of people who identify with each other based on some common element, whether real or attributed (culture, ancestry, historical experience, and so forth). The terms "race"/"racial" are used here in a limited sense, to refer to physical features that some people perceive as denoting specific ancestries.

2. Adamovsky, *Clase media.*
3. Milanesio, "Peronists." See also Geler, Gordillo, this volume; Frigerio, "Negros."
4. Avena et al., "Aporte aborigen," 49; Telles and Steele, "Pigmentocracia."
5. Segato, *La nación*, 30.
6. Adamovsky, "El color."
7. Adamovsky, "El criollismo."
8. See Elena, this volume.
9. Marin, *Estudios semiológicos*, 25–61.
10. Caggiano, *El sentido*, 278–80.
11. See Poole, *Vision*, 7.
12. Caggiano, *El sentido*, 52–54.
13. Gené, *Un mundo*; Schembs, "Education"; Mestman and Varela, *Masas*; Plotkin, *Mañana*; Soria: "La propaganda"; Hollman and Lois, "Imaginarios geográficos"; Artinian, "Imaging."
14. Oscar Chamosa has called attention to these aspects in Chamosa, "Criollo."
15. Malosetti Costa, *Rapto*; Giordano, "Nación."
16. Malosetti Costa and Gené, *Atrapados.*
17. Massota, *Indios*; Andermann, *Optic*, 185–205; Chamosa, this volume.
18. Szir, *Infancia*, 46, 90.
19. Prieto, *El discurso*; Masotta, *Gauchos*; Karush, *Culture.*
20. Chamosa, *Argentine Folklore.*
21. Karush, "Blackness"; see also Karush, this volume.
22. Penhos, "Nativos"; see also Chamosa, this volume.
23. To offer but one example, "El lancero colorado" (1923), one of his paintings of mestizo-looking characters, was reproduced in *La Nación, La Prensa, Orientación,* and *Nativa,* among other periodicals; see Gutiérrez Zaldivar, *Quirós.*
24. Among others see his "¡Chismiando!" (1931); "Hijo'el país!" (1930); "Bravo Corcoveando" (1928); "Pa tizón del infierno…!" (1933); "¡Sudiadanoj!" (1936).
25. See *Nativa* (Buenos Aires) 50, 29 Feb. 1928 front cover; 30, 30 Jun. 1926, front cover; 33, 30 Sep. 1926, n.p.; 38, 28 Feb. 1927, front cover; 89, 31 May 1931, front cover; 113, 31 May 1933, 35; 116, 31 Aug. 1933 , front cover; 144, 31 Dec. 1935, front cover; 149, 31 May 1936, front cover; 172, 30 Apr. 1938, front cover; 176, 31 Aug. 1938, front cover.
26. *Caras y Caretas* (Buenos Aires) 1993, 12 Dec. 1936, front cover; 2020, 16 Jun. 1937, front cover; 2062, 9 Apr. 1938, front cover. Other representations of Juan Pueblo that seemingly make no allusion to nonwhiteness appear in the following issues: 1294, 21 Jul. 1923, front cover; 1436, 10 Apr. 1926, 51; 1974, 1 Aug. 1936, front cover; 2006, 13 Mar. 1937, front cover; 2060, 26 Mar. 1938, 67; 2061, 2 Apr. 1938, front cover; 2131, 12 Aug. 1939, front cover.
27. See for example *Sintonía* (Buenos Aires) 131, 26 Oct. 1935, 2; *Sintonía* 219, 1 Jul. 1937, n.p. (article on Andrés Chazarreta's children's ensemble).
28. "De recorrida," *Sintonía* 156, 18 Apr. 1936, n.p.; "Así es el tango," *Sintonía* 195, 14 Jan. 1937, n.p.; "¡Todo el color y la profunda sugestión del candombe rioplatense en la voz de Carlos Tajes y sus ocho tamborileros negros!," *Sintonía* 431, Jan. [n.d.] 1943, 21 and issue 433, 1 Mar. 1943, 4; *Sintonía* 12 Jan. 1944, 42–43.
29. For example *Antena* (Buenos Aires), 2 Apr. 1943, n.p. [Carlos Tajes]; and the following issues of *Sintonía*: 69, 18 Aug. 1934, n.p. [The Blackbirds]; 73, 15 Sep. 1934, n.p. ["María"]; 125, 14 Sep. 1935, n.p. [Lois Blue]; 199, 11 Feb. 1937, last page [Johnny Alvarez]; 267, 2 Jun. 1938, n.p. ["Magia negra"]; among others.

30. See for example *Sintonía* 147, 15 Feb. 1936, n.p.; 394, 30 Apr. 1941, back cover.
31. Lusnich, *El drama*, 29, 101, 105, 121, 139, 144, 149; Tranchini, "El cine"; Alvira, "Una legión"; Thompson, "From the margins."
32. Albornoz de Videla, *Evita*.
33. *El Laborista* (Buenos Aires), 30 Apr. 1950, 3.
34. See for example *Descamisada* (Buenos Aires) 57, 10 Aug. 1948, 10–11.
35. Orlando Barone, "La polémica sobre la obra Arquetipo Símbolo. Un gran escultor argentino, el necesario rescate de Sesostris Vitullo," *Crisis* 2 (1973) [n.p].
36. Adamovsky, "El criollismo."
37. For a good example of a mestizo-looking worker, see the 1948 official poster "Perón cumple, ya son nuestros," celebrating the nationalization of railways; Archivo General de la Nación [hereafter AGN], Archivo Intermedio.
38. *El Laborista*, 23 Jun. 1947, 17; 9 Jul. 1946, 9; 15 Jul. 1946, 8.
39. See Gordillo, this volume; Lenton, "The Malón."
40. *El Laborista*, 6 Jun. 1946, 5; 19 Jul. 1951, 5; 20 Aug. 1950, 6; *Mundo Peronista* (Buenos Aires) 2, 1 Aug. 1951, 9, 36–38.
41. *El Laborista*, 28 Oct. 1950, front page.
42. *Mundo Peronista* 49, 1 Sep. 1953, 9–10.
43. *Mundo Peronista* 58, 15 Jan. 1954, 12; *El Líder* (Buenos Aires), 30 Nov. 1949, 6; *El Laborista*, 18 Oct. 1950, 4.
44. For example *El Laborista*, 3 Jan. 1947, 10; 13 Feb. 1947, 10; 26 Feb. 1947, 5; 15 Jan. 1948, front page and p. 9; 3 Dec. 1948, 3; *Mundo Peronista* 50, 15 Sep. 1953, 24; 63, 15 Apr. 1954, 29.
45. An Afro-Argentine supporter of Perón interviewed and photographed in *Mundo Peronista* 16, 1 Mar. 1952, 18; an Afro-Argentine boy photographed with Perón and Evita in *El Laborista*, 15 Nov. 1948, front page.
46. See Karush, *Culture*.
47. *Sintonía* 447, 1 May 1944, 10.
48. *El Laborista*, 21 Nov. 1952, 3–4; *Mundo Peronista* 34, 1 Dec. 1952, 20.
49. *El Laborista*, 23 Aug. 1953, 9 and 24 Aug. 1953, 13; *Mundo Peronista* 72, 15 Sep. 1954, 27–29; 30, 1 Oct. 1952, 48 and 31, 15 Oct. 1952, 11.
50. *El Laborista*, 6 Oct. 1954, 6; 12 Oct. 1948, back cover; 12 Oct. 1951, 6; *Mundo Peronista* 49, 1 Sep. 1953, 49; *El Laborista*, 16 May 1954, 9.
51. *Mundo Peronista* 34, 1 Dec. 1952, 33. Repeats in issues 35, 36 and 37.
52. The Afro-Argentine boy appears in the following issues of *Mundo Peronista*: 53, 1 Nov. 1953, 41; 60, 1 Mar. 1954, 36; 64, 1 May 1954, 38; 67, 15 Jun. 1954, 40; 70, 1 Aug. 1954, 34; 73, 1 Oct. 1954, 42; 76, 15 Nov. 1954, 24; 86, 15 May 1955, 32; 86, 15 Jun. 1955, 19.
53. Photos in the following issues of *Sintonía*: 329, 9 Aug. 1939, 54 (Chimbela); 79, 27 Oct. 1934, n.p. and 389, 19 Feb. 1941, 86 (Pibelandia); 445, 1 Mar. 1944, 76 (Stella).
54. Pictured for example in *Sintonía* 107, 11 May 1935, n.p.
55. Adamovsky, "Historia del escudo."
56. *Mundo Peronista* 4, 1 Sep. 1951, n.p.
57. *El Laborista*, 23 Aug. 1951, 2–4.
58. AGN, Departamento de Cine, Audio y Video, Tambor 15 C 35 1 A.
59. Caggiano, *El sentido*, 133–38; see Alberto, this volume.

60. Reyes' mother was indigenous; in Luna's case miscegenation is not documented and was surely more distant.
61. See for example Gordillo, "Crucible."
62. See Cirio, *En la lucha*, 63–64.
63. Freedberg, *El poder*, 227.
64. Adolfo Mugica, "Merienda de negros," *Tribuna Demócrata* (Buenos Aires), no. 2, 26 Dec. 1945, 2.
65. See speech of Francisco Carnevale in Cámara de Diputados de la Provincia de Buenos Aires, *Diario de Sesiones 1952–1953*, vol. 3, La Plata, 1954, 1776. See also Eguren, "Poema;" Talamón, "Buenos Aires;" Abregú Virreira, *La cultura*, 9–14.
66. Mirzoeff, "The Right to Look."
67. Boccara and Galindo, *Lógicas mestizas*, 28.

7

Argentina in black and white

Race, Peronism, and the color of politics, 1940s to the present

Eduardo Elena

Race has long been a contentious issue in the study of Latin American politics. During the mid-twentieth century, contemporaries often viewed nationalist mass movements as testing existing racial hierarchies – challenges often welcomed by supporters and derided by opponents, which lent an added intensity to the era's political antagonisms. Typically, mid-century nationalist reforms were not framed explicitly as programs for racial uplift; their advocates preferred, instead, to emphasize ideals of modernization, social peace, and collective justice. Nevertheless, these movements promised, and in some cases delivered, improvements demanded by laboring majorities that included racially stigmatized sectors. At the same time, many of these movements embraced, to various degrees and with varying motivations, cultural nationalisms that valorized African and/or indigenous folkways and acknowledged the virtues of multiracialism and *mestizaje*. It is common in retrospect to associate this generation of nationalist movements – many of which were subsequently labeled "populist" – with paradigms of "racial democracy," a concept coined by commentators toward the end of Brazil's nationalist government under Getúlio Vargas (1930–45), and which later worked its way into the conceptual toolkit of Latin American studies.[1] The status of populist leaders as racial democrats has, however, stoked debate. If contemporary critics assailed these actors as dangerous demagogues, revisionists have focused on their limitations, arguing that ideas of racial harmony were illusory and acted as barriers to deeper change. By contrast, a more recent wave of post-revisionist scholarship is reappraising the social resonance of mid-century racial discourses.[2]

The place of Peronism – Argentina's mid-century political movement first led by Juan D. Perón and Eva Duarte de Perón – in these discussions is unclear, despite its standing as one of Latin America's most famed expressions of "populist nationalism." This isolation derives from the reasonable inclination to study Peronism within the framework of Argentine history, but also from entrenched ideas of racial exceptionalism that encourage viewing Argentina as a regional outlier. The conventional wisdom among historians has long maintained that race was of marginal importance to Peronist rule, especially compared to the centrality of class in articulating "the people" as a political subject. Researchers, however, are now subjecting these views to greater empirical scrutiny as part of a broader reconsideration of the history of race and nation in Argentina. This direction is partially inspired by recent events: under the Kirchner governments (2003–2015), Argentina adopted Peronist versions of "pluriculturalism" that celebrated racial diversity in a variety of policy areas. Gaining an understanding of the changes from and the continuities with earlier Peronist treatments of race can provide a sense of historical perspective too often missing from contemporary disputes over these measures.

This chapter advances this emerging field of inquiry in two significant directions. First, it examines how Peronist actors from the 1940s to the present have (and have not) employed racialized conceptions of citizenship, identity, and nationality commonly associated with other Latin American societies and with similar nationalist and populist movements. The goal is not to build a systematic comparison or to reduce the region's political movements to a common denominator. Instead, the chapter employs conceptual tools from other Latin American cases to more clearly illuminate the characteristics of Peronist Argentina. In pursuing this vein of research, the problem immediately arises that Peronism has a very long past. Whereas most mid-century populisms in Latin America were active but relatively fleeting, Peronism has remained the central feature of Argentina's political landscape for over seventy years and counting. During this period, Peronism has been constantly in motion: its famed ideological heterogeneity, pragmatism, and factionalism make it difficult to identify a single Peronist position on race-related questions (or, for that matter, almost any issue).

Accordingly, this chapter makes a second contribution by seeking a better appreciation of the factors behind the mutability of Peronist racial politics over the *longue durée*. My approach, by necessity, forgoes detailed treatments of individual eras, focusing instead on overall trends and key periods of transition (in particular, the 1955–76 years). It seeks a more comprehensive understanding of this movement's shifting political repertoire: that is, the various uses of race in partisan contests, intellectual efforts to define nationality, and practices of state-led mobilization and grassroots activism. In surveying these subjects, the chapter considers how race helped significantly to define Peronist/anti-Peronist oppositions over decades of intense political conflict. Yet perhaps more unexpectedly, the chapter also probes how race operated *within* Peronism itself, thereby offering new insights on the interactions among the movement's sympathizers that are too often obscured by prevailing partisan myths.

In turn, the case of Peronist Argentina allows us to view the history of race and nation in twentieth-century Latin America and elsewhere through a different set of lenses. It demonstrates how in certain contexts political contests became "colored" by racial thinking.[3] As race became decoupled from late-nineteenth-century eugenic notions of biological descent, it acquired newfound power as a mass political category – one that in places like Argentina was employed to draw fundamental distinctions between partisan allies and enemies and to define the political characteristics of social majorities and minorities. Peronist Argentina offers particularly intriguing insights into both the "politics of race" and the "race of politics" since, unlike countries such as Brazil, Mexico, and Cuba, references to race did not typically target a specific domestic racial or ethnic group like "blacks" or "Indians" long at the center of public discussion about the nation's character. Instead, political actors aimed racialized conceptions of difference more broadly at the Argentine "people," thereby exposing a complex range of cultural attitudes regarding non-European ancestry, race mixture, and whiteness that shaped prevailing ideas of nationalism in Argentina.

"NATIONALIZING WHITENESS" DURING THE FIRST PERONISM

Peronism's formative years and the first two Perón presidencies (the "First Peronism," 1943–55) established key tendencies in regard to how the movement's adherents envisioned race. Nevertheless, the scholarly consensus holds, rightly, that most Peronist authorities and followers did not make discussion of racial difference central to their project of creating a "New Argentina." If so, how then did race factor into political life? To untangle this interpretive problem, we might begin by posing a set of counterfactual questions: why did the Perón government and most of its supporters not make more overt references to race? And more generally, why the degree of obliqueness in discussing and visualizing the racial dimensions of problems such as injustice, inequality, and exclusion that were central to Peronist nationalism? To be clear, these questions do not imply that Peronists *should* have adopted a certain position on race or that somehow Argentina deviated from a supposed Latin American norm. Counterfactual suppositions of this sort are tricky, but when treated with care they can shed new light on the choices made by political actors within the constraints of their historical moment and, in this case, they offer a more nuanced understanding of Peronist formulations of nationalism.

Rather than a single Peronist line on such issues, one can identify three overlapping tendencies that help explain how race featured in the New Argentina. Depending on the circumstances and actors, these three tendencies were configured with varying emphases. First, Peronist authorities displayed little interest in challenging dominant conceptions of nationalism, which rested on the premise that massive immigration had successfully Europeanized and whitened society and that Argentina was racially different from, if not superior to, most other Latin American nations. Following largely along the path set by interwar nationalists, the regime's ideologues highlighted the nation's white, Catholic, and Hispanic character in the design of propaganda, tourism materials, and school texts.[4] Thus official Peronist representations of nation-hood made it difficult to acknowledge openly problems like discrimination against "nonwhite" citizens – after all, according to the prevailing logic these problems and populations did not really exist in Argentina.

That said, Peronist authorities muted the exclusionary features of whiteness by insisting on national unity: there was, in theory, room for all in the New Argentina. This second tendency helps explain the political reticence to walk into the potential minefield of difference. Argentina in the 1940s was a society characterized by multiple ethnic, racial, religious, and cultural traditions, some with centuries-old European, Amerindian, and African roots in the country and others associated with more recent transatlantic migrations.[5] This second tendency toward stressing inclusion had clear advantages, as it encouraged an underlying sense of partisan solidarity among supporters, regardless of their diverse ancestries, physical appearances, or other possible markers of difference. It built as well upon earlier Argentine campaigns to assimilate foreign- and native-born populations into a national mainstream. In contrast to present-day valorizations of diversity as an inherent good, the Peronists – like other mid-century nationalists – saw homogeneity in a far more positive light, and popular majorities were valued over a mosaic of distinct minorities.

Yet compared to their Latin American peers, Perón and his inner circle were even less enthusiastic about engaging categories such as "*raza*" in discussing these presumed commonalities. The third tendency – denying the very validity of race as a social category – resulted from opportunities presented to the Peronist regime in this historical moment. In the wake of World War II, notions of racial improvement came to be seen as increasingly toxic and conceptions of innate biological hierarchies fell from favor among social scientists and, in time, among political actors (as evidenced by the UNESCO statements by evolution-ary biologists in the early 1950s). Race was by no means abandoned: it was reinvented in keeping with ideas about "types" and "populations" borrowed from psychology and sociology, without fully casting off earlier notions of "bloodlines" from the biological sciences and animal husbandry.[6] In the Peron-ist case, the question of racial prejudice was a particularly live wire, thanks to accusations about the movement's fascist and anti-Semitic sympathies made by political enemies at home and abroad. Thus, timing and political opposition (and not just Argentine ideologies of whiteness) help account for the apparent reticence of Peronist authorities to explore racial dimensions of nationhood – an unease that contrasts with the attitudes of other "classic" populists such as Getúlio Vargas and Lázaro Cárdenas, who came onto the scene a decade or more earlier.[7]

Throughout the 1943–55 period, juggling these three tendencies proved a difficult task for Peronist authorities. The regime's dominant impulse was to stress the second tendency in order to "nationalize whiteness" – that is, to advance a vision of national integration premised on assimilation to a white Argentine mainstream in an immigrant-heavy, multiracial, and multiethnic society.[8] Yet ideals of inclusion clashed, at times, with the desire among some Peronists to emphasize the specifically Catholic and Hispanic character of this white nation. This tension was especially fraught in regard to Jewish Argentines and Jewish immigrants.[9] During Perón's rise to prominence, right-wing nationalists allied with the movement carried out sporadic anti-Jewish attacks, while a cohort of similarly minded intellectuals later occupied posts within the government. Peronist policymakers in the areas of education, health, and immigration espoused eugenic notions of racial improvement – although so, too, did anti-Peronist political forces, and the exact impact of eugenics on state policies during the First Peronism remains unclear.[10] The most notable case was Santiago Peralta, an anthropologist who carried out biometric measurements on Argentine convicts to test theories of white racial degeneration and who served as the director of immigration (1945–47). From this post, Peralta worked with officials abroad to bar the entry of Jewish refugees to Argentina. Regrettably, the Perón government was not alone in these efforts: in fact, many other governments in the Americas (such as Brazil's) and elsewhere in the world opposed Jewish migration at least as strongly, if not more so.[11]

Nevertheless, these actions served as ammunition for critics at home and abroad. The Peronist regime's leadership sought to counteract these attacks by emphasizing the second and third tendencies – that is, by stressing popular unity and rejecting the legitimacy of race. To this end, the government eventually removed vocal racists like Peralta from high-profile posts and took well-publicized steps to improve ties with Argentina's Jewish community. These initiatives included public statements by Perón and Evita repudiating anti-Semitism, the state-sponsored creation of a Peronist Jewish association (the *Organización Israelita Argentina*), the incorporation of anti-discrimination language into the 1949 national Constitution, the establishment of strong diplomatic and trade relations with the state of Israel, and the appointment of Argentine Jews to high-level government positions.[12] Motivations for these overtures ranged from the political desire to bring Argentina's sizable Jewish population into the Peronist fold to the imperative of altering negative public opinion abroad.

In those rare moments when the Perón government used propaganda to expound on race-related issues, its interventions revealed the extent to which authorities were driven by concerns with anti-Semitism and broader ideals of national inclusion through whiteness. One particularly telling example is the short film *Fin de semana* (The Weekend), which looks at the life of an "average citizen," José Pérez, who works as an illustrator and lives at home with his family in Buenos Aires city.[13] With its newsreel-style narration, the film highlights the high quality of life in the New Argentina: the well-dressed Pérez is shown eating abundant meals, relaxing with friends, and enjoying liberty of thought (here, the propagandists were hardly subtle, but surprising in their illustrative choices: in one scene the camera pans across the young man's bookshelf, which includes biographies of Abraham Lincoln and Jesus Christ as well as copies of *Das Kapital* and the *Qu'ran*). The themes of opportunity and freedom extend to social relations. Pérez is shown in the company of two male friends. The first, Jaime Levi, he meets on the way to work every day – and if his name did not mark him sufficiently as Jewish, the film shows Levi reading a Yiddish newspaper while the voiceover commentary adds, "Jaime Levi is of a different religion to Pérez, but race and religion have never been an obstacle to friendship in Argentina." The other friend receives much less attention and is simply referred to as "*el provinciano Funes* [Funes, the provincial]." He is not depicted as fundamentally different from the other two characters, although he appears of slightly darker complexion and has the lower-status job of gas station attendant (Pérez is employed at an advertising firm, and Levi works a cash register in a shop). In both of these examples, race is coded by the filmmakers in familiar Argentine ways: for Jews, religious and racial differences are conflated, whereas the provinciano's geographical origins provide a marker of presumed difference associated with "mixed race" populations. Nevertheless, the film closes with a vision of fraternity by showing Pérez, Levi, and Funes shooting pool together with the voiceover, "Because in Argentina equality reigns as sovereign and the only aristocracy recognized is that which is born from nobility of spirit." In this portrait of social harmony, the fact that the main characters are male is hardly coincidental; it builds on a deeper Argentine cultural tradition of imagining the nation through the actions (sociability, warfare, and so on) of male rather than female figures.

Yet this propaganda piece is just as revealing for what is not there – namely, a more forceful critique by the Peronist regime of discrimination against darker-hued individuals like Funes. It is well-known that some anti-Peronist sectors mocked the popular base of the Peronist movement with racially charged slurs such as "*cabecitas negras*" or simply "*negros*." These terms disparaged certain individuals and populations by highlighting their supposed indigenous and/or African ancestry – in other words, their nonwhiteness or "off-whiteness," in addition to their lower-class status.[14] These forms of prejudice were nothing new in Argentina. Yet by the mid-1940s, skin and hair color and other supposed markers of race quickly took on a powerful political meaning amidst the nation's growing partisan divide. In the eyes of many observers, to be a *negro* was almost by definition to be a Peronist (especially if one was a manual laborer or hailed from a province outside the Littoral region). Natalia Milanesio has skillfully shown how racist epithets were used by anti-Peronists seeking to define Peronists as tacky and barbaric, in part because of middle-class anxieties stemming from working-class consumption and social mobility.[15] By the same token, however, it is difficult to locate widespread evidence of Peronist authorities publicly repudiating these attacks. Instead, the regime's officials remained largely silent about epithets of "darkness." The inclusion of Funes in the trio of protagonists (although without so much as a last name) shows a glancing recognition of the problem. But compared to the more extended portrayal of the average Jewish young man, propagandists were clearly less interested in demarcating and defending the social type of the cabecita negra.

This film is suggestive of the profound ambivalence with which the Peronist movement approached the question of nonwhite populations as members of the New Argentina. As Ezequiel Adamovsky's chapter in this volume shows, Peronist intellectuals adapted earlier *criollista* traditions of cultural nationalism that idealized Argentina's rural past to valorize the contributions of populations with indigenous ancestry.[16] Yet the regime's propagandists did not reject prevailing norms of taste or challenge standards of beauty promoted by commercial advertising and other mass media, which privileged white skin and fair hair, among other attributes.[17] Propaganda reinforced certain racial stereotypes by depicting darker-skinned individuals engaging in folkloric celebrations, performing "archaic," manual forms of labor (such as harvesting sugar cane), and receiving the benefits of state assistance.[18] Rarely, if ever, were these *mestizo* (or *criollo* [creole], the term's closest Argentine equivalent) types shown occupying more prestigious social ranks or, for that matter, holding positions of leadership within the Peronist movement. Moreover, Peronist image-makers also employed a variety of visual tropes of Africans and Afro-descendant populations, including ones aimed at defending racial equality as well as demeaning images of black-skinned "savages" in the jungle. This imagery could be marshaled in political cartoons designed to mock the anti-Peronist tendency of equating Peronists with negros, but it did not necessarily challenge the underlying belittling of blackness and Africanness that was widespread in Argentina and the mid-century West. These contradictions help explain why a basketball fan like President Perón could be photographed in the media happily meeting the Harlem Globetrotters during their tour of Argentina, while later laughing with a group of students from the Unión de Estudiantes Secundarios (UES, a Peronist youth organization) who formed an all-star basketball team, the UES Trotters, that played in minstrel-like blackface.[19]

Perhaps no other documentary source from this period better captures the ambiguities of how Peronist authorities in this era dealt with race than the speeches of Eva Perón. These discursive acts, like those of Juan Perón, were fundamental to defining the regime's political themes and served as content for print and radio propaganda. Surveying Evita's collected speeches, it is apparent that she did not devote a great deal of attention to race, and when she did the second and third tendencies identified earlier prevailed. Contrary to what is commonly assumed, Evita made no reference to "cabecitas negras" or its variants. Of course, Evita may have used such expressions privately, but like Perón and his collaborators, she did not employ this language publicly (or, if she did, these expressions were redacted by propagandists, a move that itself would be revealing of the era's boundaries of permissible speech). That said, Evita made coded references to race in recognizing the nation's laboring majority. Her preferred synonyms for "the people" were terms like "*descamisados* [shirtless ones]" that asserted blue-collar pride. But in some settings she used the term criollo in revealing ways: she noted how social programs were uplifting *"muchachitos criollos* [criollo lads]" and how residents of Entre Rios province lived with *"entereza criolla* [criollo integrity]."[20] These expressions were usually deployed before provincial audiences, in areas of the national territory commonly associated with inhabitants of indigenous-European ancestry, suggesting perhaps an attempt to proudly acknowledge these populations as "mixed."

Nevertheless, Evita stressed themes of national inclusion over recognitions of difference. She underscored its value in speeches before various ethnic organizations as part of Peronist campaigns to attract support (for instance, appearing before the *"Comité de Residentes Japoneses"* lauding the Japanese organization's president for his "Peronist faith").[21] In other contexts Evita adopted the third tendency of explicitly rejecting race as a valid concept. In a 1951 speech, one of the longest before her death the following year, Evita cast aspersions on various theories that sought to define the people: "The *pueblo* is not Marx's proletarian class, nor the lower levels of humanity, as he affirmed. Nor can one say that the *pueblo* is the enormous human multitude. Nor is it a race, as the totalitarianisms of the last decade believed with an almost animalistic criterion."[22] After refuting the possible alternatives in her speech, Evita settled on a vaguely subalternist definition of the pueblo as "the great community of the non-privileged." This definition did not exclude concern for color discrimination in principle, but, like official Peronist formulations more generally, it left dominant myths of whiteness unchallenged and emphasized instead a vision of common struggle.

Such historical sources raise challenging questions about reception: in particular, how did Peronist sympathizers react to these moves, and did they pursue alternative visions of race and nation? Teasing out the workings of race within Peronism in this era remains a work-in-progress, but the picture so far suggests a spectrum of reactions, including the existence of racial frictions within the Peronist ranks. For instance, historian Rosa Aboy's work on the public housing project of Los Perales in Buenos Aires city reveals both the bonds of camaraderie that united the new neighborhood's residents as well as tensions among fellow Peronists – in some cases, workers of European immigrant backgrounds lambasted provincial migrants from the Northwest and populations of indigenous ancestry (dubbed *"coyitas,"* a dismissive and diminutive adaptation of "Kolla," by some of Aboy's interviewees).[23] A similarly conflicting picture has emerged from research on Peronist relations with Amerindians. Key episodes include the famed 1946 *Malón de la Paz* (Raid of Peace), a march on Buenos Aires by Kolla indigenous people from Jujuy and Salta provinces who sought to meet with Perón about land claims, an action that focused public attention on indigenous affairs, if briefly. Yet continuities remained with the colonial past: the Perón government's National Guard allegedly carried out a brutal massacre in October 1947 against the Pilagá community in Formosa province, for which the community has recently sought legal redress.[24]

Moreover, Peronist rank-and-file views were shaped not only by official discourse and images, but also by the broader social and material conditions of the day. State social policies and a booming post-war economy brought opportunities for improved living standards, and no doubt helped to cement the association between Peronism and egalitarianism among the movement's sympathizers, especially in a fractious political context where opponents lobbed racist slurs.[25] Yet as Peronist authorities increasingly centralized command of the media and ramped up propaganda-making, they constricted the spaces available to advance rival paradigms of nationhood. Visions that deviated from the tendency of nationalizing whiteness circulated largely at the margins of official Peronism.

The overall inclination was therefore to build upon rather than challenge Argentina's dominant paradigm of race and nation. Peronism remained distinct from many other contemporary mass nationalist movements in Latin America, especially regarding its views on the degrees of whiteness and nonwhiteness that were thought to constitute distinct national types. Timing mattered: the emergence of Peronism during the post-war conjuncture made "raza" a far thornier category than during the interwar period that gave rise to Varguismo, Cardenismo, and Aprismo. Yet in terms of handling potentially volatile aspects of race relations, Peronist officials adopted strategies similar to their populist peers. These mid-century nationalists rarely turned slurs into badges of honor. Populists like Colombia's Jorge Eliécer Gaitán may have been denigrated as "*el Negro Gaitán*" and his followers as a "black mob" by their enemies, but he chose to stress themes of social inclusion, improvement, and justice along similar lines as Juan and Eva Perón.[26] Even those historical actors in the Andes, Mexico, Brazil, and the Caribbean who crafted a cultural nationalism based on indigenismo and mestizaje stopped short of embracing all residents as equal members of the nation: nationalist ideologues in these and other places viewed the Chinese, Jews, and foreign-born blacks, among others, with hostility. Nevertheless, there is no denying that in Peronist Argentina as elsewhere, mid-century nationalisms resonated strongly among social majorities, even as they discouraged claims-making along explicitly anti-racist lines and would leave later activists to combat their silencing effects.

THE "BROWNING" OF PERONISM, 1955–76

The fall of the Perón regime did not, as we know, bring an end to Peronism. Although its supporters experienced waves of harassment and proscription after 1955, repression seemed only to invigorate the movement. The borders of Peronism became even fuzzier in the 1960s and 1970s, as new sectors joined the movement's ranks. Perón's return from exile for a third presidential term (1973–74) confirmed Peronism's popular appeal, but it also revealed the existence of internal factions with violently incompatible views. Compared to the 1940s and 1950s, one can detect significant shifts in the politics of race among self-professed Peronists. In particular, the 1955–76 period witnessed a far greater willingness to explicitly acknowledge – in visual, oral, and written forms – the existence of nonwhiteness in Argentina and to critique prejudice based on skin color, physical appearance, and presumed indigenous ancestry. Not all Peronists struck this new tone: intellectuals and activists on the movement's left-leaning wings took the lead, while others were ambivalent and even hostile to the emerging trend. The three earlier tendencies remained present, but a confluence of domestic and transnational influences contributed to new thinking about nationhood in Argentina. For all their limitations and contradictions, these initiatives were nevertheless significant, as they helped to establish acceptance of nonwhiteness as a far more prominent feature of Peronism's political culture. In certain respects, these historical actors brought Peronist paradigms of nationality more in line with the "mestizo nationalism" of pre-World War II Latin American political movements, while also paralleling contemporary 1960s efforts to demystify ideologies of "racial democracy" and decry racism.

The Peronists' greater political acknowledgement of race stemmed in part from broader transformations in Argentine society and intellectual life. Above all, the phenomenon of rural-urban migration served as a lightning rod of discussion for issues concerning nonwhiteness. Between 1947 and 1970, the population of the Buenos Aires metropolitan region nearly doubled; while the city remained steady at 3 million, the population of the suburbs of Greater Buenos Aires tripled from 1.8 to 5.5 million.[27] From the late 1950s onward, migration became a topic for more sustained academic inquiry and media coverage, especially in regard to a particular type of urban and suburban settlement: the *villa miseria* [shantytown].[28] The mixture of curiosity, fear, and concern about the *villeros/villeras* (as villa dwellers are called) mirrored views on rural migrants more widely: both were imagined as racial "Others" out of place in the modern city, and in the case of villeros, perceptions of foreignness were often rooted in incorrect assumptions that most were migrants from neighboring countries. These trends upended established understandings of Argentina's racial geography – in particular, the familiar contrast between a "white" Littoral (with its symbolic center in Buenos Aires city) and the "darker" Interior provinces and surrounding Latin American nations.

The fact that two of the era's most thoughtful commentators on these issues – Germán Rozenmacher and Hugo Ratier – were Peronist sympathizers is revealing of changing sensibilities within the movement. Anti-Peronist figures such as sociologist Gino Germani also researched migration and shantytown growth, but Rozenmacher and Ratier displayed arguably greater concern for specific questions of racial mixture, prejudice, and stereotyping. With Rozenmacher, his interest was conditioned by the highly polarized partisan climate of the post-1955 years, marked by state-led campaigns to "de-Peronize" society. He became involved in Peronist activism after the regime's fall, and by the early 1960s he was the director of the cultural page for the pro-Peronist weekly

Compañero. This sensitivity may have also derived from his somewhat unusual background for a Peronist activist, as he was a member of the Jewish middle class of Buenos Aires city.[29]

Whatever the exact motivation, Rozenmacher ruminated on race-related themes in his work. His best-known work of fiction, the short story "Cabecita negra," from the 1962 book of the same name, recounts a tale of misunderstanding involving a city shopkeeper, a crying woman he encounters on a foggy street late at night, and a police officer who arrives on the scene. The shopkeeper at first expects the policeman to drag the woman away ("look at these *negros*, officer, they spend their lives drunk"), but he quickly realizes, to his horror, that the policeman is himself a *"negro."*[30] Even worse, the policeman is the woman's brother and assumes that the shopkeeper has wrongly abused her; in the end, a violent conclusion is narrowly avoided. Questions of gender and honor feature centrally in this treatment of race and class conflict in Argentina, both in the story's metaphors for exploitation (the presumed sexual predation of man over woman) and the fear of violence from below (the aggrieved brother defending his sister's reputation). This portrayal is exceptional for its time in its overt consideration of possible sexual encounters across Argentina's "color lines." Its representation of a female racial Other is also unusual, as depictions of negros/negras in this era tended to center on the male masses as agents of collective liberation, national fraternity, or social danger.[31]

Rozenmacher's other writings offer reflections on his Jewish family upbringing as well as further explorations of race-related matters. These include a story titled *"Raíces* [Roots]," which probes questions of indigeneity near the Argentine-Bolivian border, and his co-authored play *El avión negro* [The Black Plane] (1970), which offers a brash satire mocking the snobbish pretensions of the middle class. In the play, one seemingly refined character exclaims *"negros de mierda* [shitty blacks]" when confronted with the Peronist masses. Another complains that blacks in Brazil are more fun-loving and have more beautiful bodies compared to Argentina's negros: "these are a bunch of trash [*una porquería*]. They're not even entirely *negro."*[32] As these examples suggest, Rozenmacher scrutinized the class dimensions of racism as well as how Argentine conceptions of white exceptionalism operated in comparison to stereotypical perceptions of neighboring Latin American societies.

By contrast, Hugo Ratier addressed racism through a more ethnographically informed account of the historical origins and struggles of racially maligned sectors. His most famous book, the similarly titled *El cabecita negra* (1972), was commissioned by the Centro Editor de América Latina, a press that specialized in cheap editions on the pressing topics of the day.[33] Ratier wrote the book while holding down a job in public education administration and working toward his doctoral degree in anthropology. His interest in race and ethnicity was informed by anthropological field work carried out in shantytowns during the 1960s (Centro Editor also published his book *Villeros y villas miseria*). Although Ratier's political loyalties were less evident in his works than Rozenmacher's, involvement in grassroots Peronist activism brought him into contact with sectors who had experienced social marginalization firsthand.[34]

Despite its brevity, *El cabecita negra* covers an impressive range of issues concerning the racial dimensions of class, gender, sex, regionalism, nationality, and Peronist/anti-Peronist politics. In particular, Ratier draws attention to what he provocatively calls "*la pluma negada* [the denied feather]" in the Argentine nation – that is, the presence of a large number of individuals with varying degrees of indigenous ancestry (by comparison, African heritage is largely unexplored).[35] Unlike most Argentine contemporaries, Ratier employs terms such as "mestizaje" to talk about nonwhiteness rather than veiled terms of mixture like "criollo"; this choice of language stems in part from his familiarity as an anthropologist with conceptions of mixture in other Latin American contexts. His book rejects the notion that the cabecita appeared out of nowhere with the rise of Perón, pointing instead to the deep indigenous roots of Argentine society: "Could it be that there weren't any here before? Why does that offending term acquire popularity in the 1940s? Why does it continue being offensive and does not become a term of pride, like *descamisado*? Yes, they existed before. They have been here always. As far back as when Mendoza and Garay made contact with the Querandíes, when the Pampas [Indians] arrived at the city to exchange their ostrich feathers for the new vices that the white man showed them."[36]

Intellectuals like Rozenmacher and Ratier were exceptional in their focus on the origins and practices of racism in Argentina, but Peronist political actors in these years also evoked the figure of the cabecita negra. Top leaders remained unwilling to broach these subjects: Perón's speeches from this period make scant references to race, still stressing the categories of class and popular-national homogeneity.[37] Nevertheless, influential second-tier leaders made occasional use of the terms cabecita negra and negro, as did scores of spokespersons and organizations within the movement. The appropriation of these terms relied on a tactic of inversion: that is, taking a derogatory slur used by political enemies and turning it into a rhetorical weapon to paint these enemies as anti-popular and anti-national. A 1962 article in a pro-Peronist paper declared that "all the *cabecitas negras* call him [Perón] 'the Old Man,' acknowledging him with all the love that one acknowledges a generous, alert, and serene father."[38] Reflecting back on the "Liberating Revolution" (1955–59), a former grassroots activist depicted the era's partisan reprisals and campaigns against suspected Peronists in racialized terms: "The white terror assassinates without pity, with perverse violence. It is a mixture of hate and fear, as can be seen in the eyes of the repressors" – an elitist hatred that, in his view, contrasted with the loyalty and sacrifice of the "*cabecitas negras*."[39] Through these "black-and-white" descriptions of political conflict, one can see how commentators came to embrace, albeit grudgingly at times, racist discourse as emblems of Peronism's identification with the people.

We have little sense, however, of the ways the intended targets of these attacks responded to the more frequent use of these terms by Peronist intellectuals and leaders. Although this remains an area in need of greater research, one can begin to discern some impressions. In the documentary film *Los resistentes* (2011), a group of elderly train workers from Tafí Viejo, Tucumán, recall their militancy during the 1950s and 1960s.[40] They belonged to a clandestine Peronist organization founded in the rail yards shortly after the 1955 coup d'état, and they engaged in acts of sabotage and protest. Anti-Peronist state authorities in Tucumán dubbed these forces the "Mau Mau" in reference to the famed anticolonial rebels in Kenya. This label reflected not only the militants' similar choice of resistance strategies, but it was also an allusion to the local usage of "negro" in reference to Tucumán's laboring populations, many of whom had some degree of indigenous and/or African ancestry. One railway worker interviewed in the film, Héctor "Toto" Romero, recounts the story of a fellow activist, "El Negro Zelaya," who complained to his comrades about his nickname: "*Qué negro, carajo, yo soy un morocho sudamericano* [I'm no Black, I'm a South American of dark complexion]." Rejection of the label "negro" in this case may have been conditioned by how partisan opponents equated local Peronists with "savage" black Africans (although some local trainworkers embraced the term Mau Mau precisely for its racial and anti-imperialist connotations). Yet Zelaya's alleged remark is open to other interpretations: was it a vague statement of Latin American solidarity, a sign of pride in being of "racially mixed" descent, or simply a joke meant to entertain his peers? The precise meaning is elusive, but elsewhere Romero himself used "negro" in gendered terms, as a way to praise the bravery of fellow male militants, one of whom he described as "a *negro* who had his balls well hung, well hung for the entire nation." Romero himself calls additional attention to the significance of racial ancestry by recognizing that his mother was a "Toba" Indian. There is little evidence, unfortunately, to reveal how these sectors reacted to Peronist intellectuals and others who increasingly appropriated and deployed this language of race, color, and masculinity.

Indeed, the early 1970s witnessed an outpouring of commentary on a wider spectrum of race-related issues by Peronist actors – above all, by activists within the loosely allied constellation of groups dubbed the "revolutionary tendency," which included mass political organizations such the *Juventud Peronista* (JP) and armed insurgents such as the *Montoneros*. Not only did these sectors enjoy greater liberty of expression in this era, but their probing social critiques were driven by a sense that revolutionary change was imminent and by a desire to distinguish their political agenda from conservatives within and outside the Peronist ranks. The weekly illustrated magazine *El Descamisado*, edited by Dardo Cabo of the Montoneros, was among the most prominent forums for presenting a range of radical concerns.[41] The magazine's focus was overwhelmingly on the ever-shifting landscape of intra-Peronist factionalism and anti-imperialist struggles across the globe. But *El Descamisado* joined contemporaries in adopting "negro" and its variants to decry the prejudice faced by popular sectors. For instance, an article on a Buenos Aires public housing project ridiculed the racial and social prejudices of those anti-Peronists who blamed the working poor for their miserable living conditions: "Of course, one understands: the *negros peronistas* have no education, they get drunk, they rape women... What burdens the Dictator left us!"[42]

Compared to the more oblique and predominately visual treatments of race during the First Peronism, activists now confronted questions of racism far more directly.[43] Publications like *El Descamisado* devoted extensive coverage to the struggles of indigenous communities in Argentina and, more vaguely, to downtrodden rural laborers in provincial zones associated with criollo and nonwhite populations. One article examined the travails endured by the "Matacos, Tobas, and Chaneses," indigenous peoples who lived in the *chaqueño* region of Salta. Replete with details about infant mortality and ruthless labor demands, the article noted the organizational efforts of the JP in the area and the selfless aid provided by a female social worker, Helena Olivier Peralta ("the white woman who lives with the Indians").[44] A report in a similar political periodical, *Posición*, lamented the poverty of populations of indigenous descent in Santiago del Estero, while striking a chord of solidarity by speaking from the place of a child and Indian Other: "*compañeros*, this night the white children are on the side of those of Indian race, despite the fact that for years we [Indians] have been considered very inferior."[45] Articles were often accompanied by extensive photography and other visual evidence. The intended messages were blunt – the caption under a photo of indigenous women and children in the *El Descamisado* article on Salta stated "our only hope is Perón," thus playing on familiar gendered understandings of populations in need of rescuing. These treatments trafficked in essentialist views of Indians and rural laborers as timeless, archaic, and passive populations who needed outside help and paternalistic tutelage to "enter the twentieth century."[46]

Yet the cumulative effect of this media coverage was a portrait of Argentine society that recognized non-European roots. These visions of a multi-shaded Argentina were notably different from the white-washed representations of earlier periods, including much of the propaganda of the First Peronism. Moreover, other left-leaning commentators (some explicitly Peronist, others less so) communicated similar textual and visual messages in magazines, books, documentary films, and artistic works: the most famous examples include the 1968 multimedia exhibit *Tucumán Arde* and the film *La hora de los hornos*, which bombarded the viewer with images of social oppression in Argentina's Interior.[47] These treatments exposed intellectuals, middle-class youth, union activists, and other audiences to representations of the pueblo that highlighted social types such as impoverished Indians, mestizo rural laborers, and dark-skinned shantytown dwellers as never before.

What explains these shifts within Peronism, especially the willingness of actors to address racial prejudice and indigeneity as politically salient concerns to a much greater degree than in the 1940s? The standard explanation marshaled by commentators is that the composition of the nation had changed in the intervening years. There is a kernel of truth to this claim, but trends like rural-urban migration and the settlement of villas miseria extended across the mid-twentieth century, and the deprivations endured by many indigenous Argentines were nothing new. Instead, what changed were not only Argentina's underlying conditions, but, more importantly, new political ideas and practices within Peronism that allowed these social features to become perceived as race-related problems.

Clearly, Peronist actors concerned by these matters were influenced by the broader intellectual currents of the day – above all, modes of revolutionary Latin Americanist and Third Worldist thinking. The Cuban Revolution was the touchstone of debate, but so, too, were de-colonization movements in Africa and Asia and the writings of revolutionaries like Franz Fanon. These currents supplied a wider variety of non-European and non-Western referents with which to think through Argentine social conditions. The translation of global trends to domestic politics was furthered by the appearance of new groups in Argentina like the *Movimiento de Sacerdotes para el Tercer Mundo* (MSTM) that espoused liberation theology, a radical form of Catholicism. Although not all members of the MSTM were allied with Peronism, the organization's leading light, Carlos Mugica, was a priest well-known for his activism among villeros and for his Peronist sympathies. In public speeches, Mugica condemned local forms of discrimination, such as the middle-class tendency to heap scorn on *"los negros"* and the impoverished Paraguayan and Bolivian immigrants who lived in shantytowns.[48] The fact that Mugica himself was the blond, blue-eyed scion of a wealthy Buenos Aires family no doubt helped to attract further attention to the racial and class implications of his activism – much as Peronist explorations of Third Worldist thinking stood out in a nation mythologized as white and European.

Less readily apparent, but no less significant, were domestic trends that contributed to the shift in the politics of Peronism and race. One influence came from *revisionismo histórico*, a school of historical thought that presented the nineteenth-century past as a dichotomous contest between Europeanizing liberal elites and the native-born pueblo. Many of the most prominent intellectuals associated with Peronism in this period – among them, Jorge Abelardo Ramos, Rodolfo Puiggrós, John William Cooke, and Juan José Hernández Arregui – espoused *revisionista* interpretations of Argentine history.[49] These thinkers did not delve into racism in depth, but they did acknowledge the role of Indians, blacks, and mixed-race types like *gauchos* (Argentina's mythic cowboys) in the nation's past. Recounting the origins of Peronism, John William Cooke wrote, "we saw the *gaucho* of flesh and bone transformed into the *cabecita negra*, the worker, who sought union leadership, guidance in their struggles, political conquests, [and] mass leaders."[50] In turn, revisionist thinking informed Peronist uses of history in ways both obvious (such as the name

Montoneros, derived from the term for gaucho insurgents) and more unexpected (such as *El Descamisado*'s cartoon series "450 Years of War Against Imperialism," which profiled the heroism of Afro-Argentine soldiers and other dark-skinned subalterns).[51]

The greater attention of some Peronist commentators to nonwhiteness was not simply a question of intellectual influences. Equally important, the political practices of this era widened opportunities for interaction among Peronists from different backgrounds. In particular, the movement's partisan networks allowed the quotidian acts of discrimination experienced by Peronists in racially stigmatized and working-class groups to catch the eye of white middle-class activists. For writers like Rozenmacher and Ratier, partisan militancy enabled them to meet and develop relationships with individuals who were workers, provincial migrants, and shantytown dwellers. This social boundary crossing was a key feature of Peronist politics. Building on the clandestine struggles of the seventeen-year-long "Peronist Resistance," those involved in organizations like Juventud Peronista tried to establish relationships with specific working-class neighborhoods or shantytowns. According to a former member, there was an almost competitive sense among JP militants that having the support of these popular communities (*"tener un barrio atrás"*) was fundamental to one's standing as a committed revolutionary.[52]

Other practices provided similar opportunities for potential consciousness-raising about racialized forms of oppression. Peronists were among a generation of young people living in Littoral cities who embarked on voyages of social discovery to Argentina's Interior; these journeys included formal trips organized by university outreach programs and Catholic groups, which allowed urban youth to witness, if briefly, the lives of the rural poor in the Northeast and Northwestern regions. Judging by testimonial accounts, the experiences of coming face-to-face with the misery endured by Argentines of indigenous descent in places like Santiago del Estero and Northern Santa Fe province were major turning points in the lives of many revolutionary militants, including for the founding leadership and rank-and-file of Montoneros.[53] For other Peronist youth and middle-class sectors, the mass rallies of the era also opened their eyes to the heterogeneity of Peronism's popular base. Seventies intellectuals like José Pablo Feinmann now recall a romantic sense of excitement that came from seeing trucks from Salta, Jujuy, and Catamarca provinces, filled with *"morochos* [darker people]" waving flags, arriving for the ill-fated 1972 Ezeiza gathering to mark Perón's return from exile, and the feeling of solidarity as he and a female companion rode alongside "villeros" on a packed train car, all chanting the same partisan songs.[54]

It is crucial, however, to keep these encounters and the wider shifts within Peronist racial politics in perspective. The growing willingness by some to critique prejudice, to acknowledge the presence of mixture and indigeneity in Argentina, and to challenge ideas of European exceptionalism did not mean that all Peronists embraced these views. Perón's own *tercermundismo*

[Third-Worldism] had a transparently tactical (if not cynical) quality, as he sought from exile in Franco's Spain to appeal to his homeland's younger, radicalized generations.[55] The manifestos issued by organizations like the Montoneros kept quiet about questions of racial oppression; so, too, did similar programmatic statements made by Peronist labor unions.[56] Even figures such as Carlos Mugica, the shantytown priest, preferred to stress categories of class when discussing social marginalization – a move facilitated by the flexibility of terms like "negro" in Argentina, which were widely considered class terms above all. In answering the question "What is the Third World?" during a 1972 event in Mar del Plata, Mugica included not just Asian and African societies in his definition but also "minority" groups such as Algerians in France and Puerto Ricans in the United States. Nevertheless, in describing conditions in Argentina he used categories of class not race, asserting that in his homeland, "the Third World is the working class but the way things are headed it will soon encompass the middle class and the entire Argentine nation."[57]

Equally important, Peronists concerned with questions of racial prejudice had to contend with opposition from many quarters, including from forces within the Peronist movement that espoused anti-Semitic and racist views. During mass gatherings in the 1970s, right-wing Peronists employed slogans such as "*Perón/Mazorca/judíos a la horca*" to characterize their leftist rivals as Jews whom they wanted to execute by hanging.[58] These were no mere threats as the cycle of bloodletting accelerated across the country. Although the role of racism in the state-orchestrated persecution of the Peronist Left remains controversial, evidence shows that the Juan Perón and Isabel Martínez de Perón governments (1973–76) harbored anti-Semitic thugs and were not above using brutal force to eradicate shantytowns and to punish activists in racially stigmatized groups.[59]

Yet even among those Peronist sectors most committed to rethinking race in Argentina, key problems remained. Conceptions of indigeneity rested on paternalistic stereotypes, and the interventions of seventies Peronists can be usefully seen within longer Latin American traditions of *indigenismo*, albeit in representations far less elaborated than in the Central Andes or Mexico. Native peoples were depicted either as hapless victims of neo-colonial exploitation or as potential agents of revolutionary change. Likewise, mestizaje as a celebration of a racially mixed society continued to receive little attention in Peronist Argentina: there were no ideologues of comparable standing to figures such as Mexico's José Vasconcelos and Brazil's Gilberto Freyre, who wrote extensively about sexual, biological, and cultural mixture among people of different races as the driving forces of nation-making.[60] Lastly, there was no real concerted effort by Peronist authorities, intellectuals, or radical organizations to pursue a cultural project in defense of Argentine "*negritud.*" Ratier's *El cabecita negra* is the closest one gets to an appraisal of a mestizo popular culture that does not simply rest on folklorist clichés of Indian authenticity. In the closing paragraph, he suggests that "*cabecitas*" have infused something new into the urban consumer landscape of Buenos Aires: "Yes, they are visible. They stroll past the colorful and cheap shop windows on Sáenz Avenue in the neighborhood of Pompeya. They are responsible for the majority of the things sold in the kiosks around the Retiro train station: Gardel dressed as a *gaucho*, Perón on horseback, the passionate life of Sandro [a popular singer]. With them arrived in the city a refreshing Latin American air that impregnates everything."[61] Only a few Peronist intellectuals followed this lead, and even fewer did so who were in positions of state leadership. Instead, the underlying motivations behind treatments of race stayed within familiar boundaries: to showcase dilemmas of collective exploitation and partisan discrimination that demanded immediate solutions via Peronist rule.

Notwithstanding these constraints, the shifts in racial politics that occurred over the 1955–76 era were significant. Activists articulated a more direct challenge to notions of European exceptionalism, while raising the visibility of nonwhiteness – in essence, they launched critiques of dominant paradigms of Argentine nationhood that had been muted during the First Peronism or treated in visual ways alone. The comparative "delay" in the Argentine case derives, ironically, from the Perón regime's command of the public sphere in this earlier period; in some cases, alternative views of the multiracial nation that circulated at the margins of the Peronist movement in the 1940s and 1950s came more into the open during the 1960s and 1970s – propelled by the racism that accompanied anti-Peronist repression and by the Peronist drift toward more revolutionary ideologies. These moves brought Peronism closer to the mestizo nationalisms of mid-century populist counterparts in Brazil, Mexico, and Cuba. But in keeping with the era's revolutionary spirit, there was far less emphasis on pacifying ideologies of racial harmony. The impact of these trends is evident in the persistent tendency of Peronist loyalists of the post-1955 era to project their overt forms of anti-racism back onto the heyday of the First Peronism. From the vantage of this later period, Evita was remembered as having lovingly addressed her cabecitas negras by that name. Despite the historical anachronism, it made perfect sense to many Peronists in the 1970s and beyond that she would have – or should have – acted in this way.

PERONIST PLURALISM AND ITS DISCONTENTS

The Proceso dictatorship (1976–83) disrupted these emerging trends. The campaign to stamp out revolutionary strains of Peronism had already begun under Perón's tenure, but the severity of military-led repression in the ensuing years reached unprecedented levels. New research suggests that the Proceso regime was not above adopting some elements of criollista nationalism in its cultural policies and that its agents cultivated relations with indigenous communities.[62] But, in general, military rulers and civilian allies styled themselves as defenders of Western Civilization and of a devoutly Catholic nation – views that informed everything from media pronouncements to the public education curriculum on the nation's history.[63] Moreover, racism and repression went hand-in-hand. The military's use of anti-Semitism as a tactic to torture detainees is well-documented, and it would appear that individuals perceived as nonwhite were treated with particular cruelty. This was very much the case for the disappeared activists who belonged to peasant leagues in Corrientes province and for the thousands of shantytown dwellers in Buenos Aires city and elsewhere, whose homes were razed by military-appointed officials.[64]

How, then, did this moment of retrenchment in the 1980s give way to the recent "Bicentennial era," during which state authorities sponsored cultural policies that accentuated multiracial and "pluricultural" diversity as essential to Argentine nationhood? Other chapters in the volume consider this transition more fully. But it is worth, if only briefly, identifying how the Peronist politics of race in the twenty-five years since the turn to democracy bear the marks of earlier dynamics. In general, earlier Peronist variations on criollismo, indigenismo, and tercermundismo survived the years of exile and military repression. These concerns acquired greater visibility as the seventies generation of left-leaning Peronists gained political prominence and access to state power in the Néstor Kirchner and Cristina Fernández de Kirchner administrations (2003–2015). These legacies are perhaps most evident in recent Peronist appropriations of historical revisionism. The Fernández de Kirchner government supported the creation of the Instituto Nacional de Revisionismo Histórico Argentino e Iberoamericano Manuel Dorrego, which offers a space for intellectuals to emphasize Argentina's membership in a wider Latin American Fatherland (*"Patria Grande"*).

But it would be wrong to view Kirchnerismo as a simple "return to the 1970s." Kirchneristas, like the members of rival factions within Peronism, have adapted earlier formulations of race and nation to fit the characteristics of a very different domestic, regional, and global political landscape. In particular, Peronists of various stripes have grappled with the emergence of multiculturalism as the dominant contemporary paradigm of imagining difference. Multiculturalism entered Argentine politics during the early 1980s, in parallel with the rising prominence of human rights discourse in the transition from military to civilian rule. Non-Peronist actors took a leading role, as witnessed in the landmark 1988 Anti-Discrimination Law passed during the Raúl Alfonsín presidency. But sectors within the Peronist ranks followed suit. The Carlos Menem presidency (1989–99) brought a return of Peronist control to national government, which saw, among other things, the creation of a new state agency, the Instituto Nacional contra la Discriminación, la Xenofobia y el Racismo (INADI) in 1995. These examples reveal the influence of multiculturalist ideologies of anti-racism backed by powerful international organizations like the United Nations, foreign governments, and a range of NGOs. Menemista officials could hardly afford to ignore these trends, and they made the requisite moves to modernize the Peronist rhetoric of national inclusion.

Yet Peronist leaders in the post-1980s years did not make a sharp break with the movement's long tradition of downplaying racial difference in favor of a language of class and popular nationalism. During the Menem presidency, the politics of nonwhiteness occupied a low profile within official Peronism, even if his presidential victory could be taken as implicit proof of Peronism's inclusive tendencies: Menem's family was of Syrian ancestry and Muslim faith; although he converted to Catholicism as a young man, these origins were unprecedented for an Argentine head of state. When issues of prejudice did surface in public discussions, the Menem government was on the defensive, as in the case of the 1994 bombing of the Asociación Mutualista Israelita Argentina (AMIA), a Jewish community center in Buenos Aires – in which state officials and others have been implicated in covering up the attack.

Peronist experiments with multiculturalism would be subsequently reworked and intensified during the Kirchnerista 2000s. Take the example of Minister of Culture Jorge Coscia's (2009–11) reflections on the significance of the Bicentennial. His views draw as much from seventies referents as from contemporary pluralism familiar the world over ("Let's celebrate variety: it's the intimate fiber of our *argentinidad*").[65] Coscia rejects the exclusionary nationalism of an earlier century: "In 1910, the ruling elite auto-celebrated its supposed standing as a white, homogeneous, Europeanized nation, relegating anything that could have a local flavor, creole or indigenous, to a second or third plane." He goes on to assert that "Argentines do not only descend from the boats [i.e., are of European immigrant ancestry]. We also come from the Indian tents, from the patrician and creole families that were here, from the Altiplano, from the other side of the Andes and the other shore of the Rio de la Plata."[66] Similarly hybrid formulations of national inclusion that showcase racial/ethnic/immigrant difference as a strength have informed cultural policies after the Bicentennial. The willingness of officials at the highest level to celebrate Argentina's nonwhite component – through state-controlled mass media and educational resources no less – is unparalleled in the history of Peronism.

There is undoubtedly much propagandistic hype in these nationalist visions of inclusion; more importantly, the feeling that Argentina has entered a new racial era is true in a different sense. The past four decades have been characterized by widening economic inequality in Argentina, manifested in various forms of income concentration, unmet basic needs, spatial segregation, and social marginalization. Although many of these trends began under military rule, problems worsened notably during the neoliberal Menemato and reached a crescendo during the 2001–2 financial crisis. The Kirchnerista era has seen some improvements, but the long-term trend has served to further racialize and politicize poverty: for many commentators, to be poor in Argentina is to be a *negro peronista*. This overlapping of class, race, and partisan politics had previously existed, but the constriction of possibilities for upward social mobility in Argentina – coupled with the pressures of downward mobility and the global turn toward multiculturalism – has made race a more publicly used category to explain both inequality and political fault lines.

Accordingly, in the eyes of some observers there are apparently more "negros" in Argentina than ever before. In the conclusion to his study on indigenismo in twentieth-century Mexico, Alan Knight remarked that forces like urbanization and industrialization were helping to shrink the number of individuals categorized as "indios" by members of Mexican society.[67] Something of the opposite may be happening in Argentina: those lumped into the category "negro" appear to be growing, thanks largely to cultural perceptions of prevailing socio-economic and political trends. This specter is apparent in dystopian visions regarding the "Andeanization" or "Indianization" of Argentina, which implicitly link anti-immigrant sentiment with a bitter sense that the nation has degenerated and lost its former superiority. The racialization of poverty is implied, if more subtly, in recent references to the dangers of the "*favelización*" of Buenos Aires city (a reference to Brazil's iconic *favelas* or shantytowns, widely associated with blackness) made by state officials, among others.[68] It is important to note that the xenophobic tendency to associate poverty and other social ills with an immigrant-driven "browning" of Argentina clashes with official census data. According to these figures, the percentage of foreign-born residents has remained unchanged in Argentina over the past fifty years and the percentage of the national population born in neighboring countries has stayed largely constant at 2–3 percent from 1869 to the mid-2000s.[69]

In turn, these racialized fears of invasion have been opposed by new cultural forms that recognize and celebrate nonwhiteness, albeit in ways quite different from official pluralism. The past two decades have seen the emergence of a new generation of indigenous and Afro-descendant movements demanding recognition.[70] Interest in questions of ancestry in Argentina has been spurred as well by advances in genetics and genomics, which have led, paradoxically, to a resurgence of older biological modes of understanding racial difference, now cloaked in the dangerously authoritative language of twenty-first-century science.[71] At the same time, however, the category "negro" has been adopted more openly by subaltern sectors and their interlocutors to express plebeian solidarity.[72] Racial binaries such as "blanco" and "negro" have become tools to demarcate lines of social contention – most famously, in the so-called D'Elía affair, in which a neighborhood activist from Greater Buenos Aires proclaimed, in the midst of a heated radio interview, his hatred of elitist "whites" and his identification with the downtrodden majority of "negros." Although Luis D'Elía's political origins lie outside the Peronist movement, his alliance with the Kirchner government during a moment of partisan clashes over state agricultural policies lent these racial comments an added political significance.[73] In the aftermath, a grassroots group of Peronists created a short-lived organization called the "*Negros de Mierda*" that presented D'Elía and other Kirchnerista officials with honorary memberships.

In short, old terms such as "negro" are now being deployed in novel ways, including as weapons to critique once-dominant paradigms of Argentine whiteness. So far, top leaders like the Kirchners have responded with caution: on rare occasions, by echoing the "black-and-white" discourse of these critics, but typically by stressing less volatile themes of pluralistic inclusion and Peronism's traditions of anti-elitism (and occasionally, making racially insensitive pronouncements of their own). From the vantage of the movement's base and intermediaries, the use of overt racial categories in politics is still being worked out. Not all Peronist supporters – nor anti-Peronists and non-Peronists, for that matter – see eye-to-eye on questions such as recent Latin American, Asian, and African immigration to Argentina or on issues related to anti-Semitism and "homegrown" indigenous and Afro-descendant populations. The future of these racial politics is uncertain, especially as Kirchnerista rule comes to a close. Nevertheless, it appears likely that challenges to existing national myths will not break down along clear Peronist/anti-Peronist lines, but will be made by actors within each bloc.

****

The association between nationalism and whiteness in Argentina is not gone – nor should one expect it to vanish entirely in a society where a majority considers itself of primarily white European ancestry. Yet older paradigms of Argentine national identity have changed over time, and those rooted in racial assertions of exceptionalism vis-à-vis the rest of Latin America have weakened. The political momentum, for now, seems to point in the direction of greater awareness and acceptance of nonwhiteness in its multiple meanings. Peronism has reflected these changing social attitudes over the past century, and in some cases, helped to spur shifts – though not necessarily in the ways that one might expect. As this chapter has shown, the Peronist movement has not been a single-minded advocate for anti-racism over its long history, and the common assertion that prejudice is only an anti-Peronist problem is flawed. Although Peronist sympathizers have played a leading role in articulating racially inclusive nationalisms, the movement's authorities were far more reactive in their approach: they adjusted strategically to forces beyond their complete control, including transnational ideologies of anti-racism, domestic socio-economic transformations, and the pressure of internal factions and political rivals. Rather than a head-on attack against racism and nationalist ideals of whiteness, this process has been one of gradual erosion across decades of intense partisan conflict.

Despite the continued tendency to view Argentina as a regional outlier and as a country where race is non-existent or irrelevant, this case has implications for how we understand the history of race and nation in the twentieth and twenty-first centuries. Expressions like "negros peronistas" strike many non-Argentines as odd, while for Argentines they are perhaps too obvious: in each case, the immediate temptation is to declare that such language is not "really" about race. Yet these reactions betray assumptions about how race should function, rather than a willingness to recognize the wide variety of ways that racial thinking operates across time and place. There are, indeed, fundamental differences in how – and, equally significant, when – Peronist actors engaged with the concepts of multiracial harmony associated with their Latin American peers. But, as we have seen, there are underlying commonalities that derived from the political dynamics of mass nationalist movements born in the mid-century moment. In contrast to places like the United States or South Africa, political controversies over race in Argentina (and most of Latin America) did not center on the creation, reform, and dismantling of formal legal systems of exclusion. Instead, questions of race informed other aspects of national politics in less obvious but still important ways. In places like Argentina, racial categories helped color national politics by defining the "friend and foe" borders of partisan identity and marking "us and them" distinctions between elite and plebeian sectors, among other applications. Race remained a question of biological ancestry and innate cultural essences, or even of class affiliation, but it was also fundamentally political – that is, shaped by the demands, contingencies, and practices of party contests and state policies. These uses have sometimes lent a powerful simplicity to partisan confrontations – depicting the nation in only black and white, so to speak – yet they belie the many shades of Argentine society and the competing modes of thinking about race both outside and inside the Peronist movement.

Notes

I would like to recognize Paulina Alberto, Victoria Ferreira, Ashli White, and the contributors to this volume for their helpful critiques of this chapter as well as the panel members and audiences at LASA conferences who commented on earlier versions. I appreciate the generous time taken by Hugo Ratier to share his reflections on the study of race in Argentina with me. Special thanks to Lila Caimari, Nicolás Quiroga, the participants of the Seminario de Historia de las ideas, los intelectuales y la cultura "Oscar Terán" of the Instituto Ravignani at the University of Buenos Aires, and the members of the History Department at the National University of Mar del Plata for the opportunity to discuss my work with them.

1. Recent works addressing the nexus of mid-century politics and race include Andrews, *Afro-Latin America*, 157–90; Dawson, *Indian*; de la Fuente, *A Nation*. On Vargas and "racial democracy," see Alberto, *Terms*; Guimarães, *Classes*.
2. Appelbaum, "Post-Revisionist," 206–17; Appelbaum et al., *Race and Nation*; de la Fuente, "Myths," 39–73.
3. For other perspectives on the political uses of racial discourses, see de la Cadena, "Are Mestizos Hybrids?" 259–84; Weinstein, "Racializing," 237–62 and *Color*.
4. On Peronist nationalism and imagery, see Plotkin, *Mañana*; Gené, *Un mundo*; Chamosa and Karush, *New Cultural*; Acha and Quiroga, *El hecho*; Elena, "New Directions."
5. According to official censuses, the ratio of foreign-born residents in the population had shrunk from a historic peak of 30 percent in 1914, but still stood at roughly

15 percent in 1947. Argentine Republic, INDEC, *Aquí se cuenta* 12 (Feb. 2004), 1–6. www.indec.gov.ar/micro_sitios/webcenso/aquisecuenta/aqui12.pdf (Accessed 9 Mar. 2015).

6. Haraway, "Universal Donors," 321–66.
7. Dawson, *Indian*; Lesser, *Welcoming* and *Negotiating*; Rénique, "Race," 211–36.
8. I have adapted the term "nationalizing whiteness" from Moore, *Nationalizing Blackness*.
9. Deutsch, *Crossing*; Lvovich, *Nacionalismo*; Newton, '*Nazi Menace*'; Rein, *Argentina, Israel*; Senkman, *Argentina*, and "Etnicidad," 5–39.
10. Vallejo and Miranda, "Los saberes," 425–44.
11. Senkman, "Etnicidad"; Vallejo and Miranda, "Los saberes," 436.
12. Rein, *Argentina, Israel*, 33–72. As this volume entered production, Rein published a new study, *Los muchachos peronistas judíos* (Buenos Aires: Sudamericana, 2015), on the subject.
13. *Fin de semana*, Actualidades Argentinas, date unknown, AGN, Departamento de Cine, Audio y Video.
14. On the complicated history of "negro" in Argentina, see Geler, Gordillo, and Alberto, this volume, and Frigerio, "Negros."
15. Milanesio, "Peronists," 53–84.
16. See Adamovsky, Gordillo, Pite, and Chamosa, this volume. See also Chamosa, *Argentine Folklore* and "Criollo," 113–42; Adamovsky, "La dimensión," 87–112 and "El criollismo."
17. On commercial advertising and state propaganda, see Ballent, *Las huellas*; Elena, *Dignifying*, 119–53; Gené, *Un mundo*.
18. Secretaría de Prensa y Difusión, *Fraternidad justicialista*, 35-mm film, date unknown, AGN, Departamento de Cine, Audio y Video.
19. See *Descamisada* (Buenos Aires) 18, 20 May 1946, 3. On the UES Trotters, see www.paginapopular.net/el-gral-peron-y-el-deporte/ (Accessed 9 Mar. 2015).
20. Perón, *Discursos*, vol. I, 86, 89, 148.
21. Ibid., 127, 340–41.
22. Ibid., 323–24.
23. Aboy, *Viviendas*, 123–36. On the further challenges of studying the internal dynamics of Peronism, see Acha and Quiroga, *El hecho*.
24. Lenton, "The *Malón*," 85–112; O' Malley, *Octubre Pilagá*; Gordillo, this volume.
25. Milanesio, "Peronists." Similar dynamics help explain why Vargas is remembered as the "father of the poor" among some working-class Afro-Brazilians and others. Wolfe, "Father of the Poor," 80–111; Levine, *Father of the Poor?*; Fischer, *Poverty*.
26. Braun, *Assassination*; Green, *Gaitanismo*.
27. Gutman and Hardoy, *Buenos Aires*, 271; Torre, "El mapa social," 164–89.
28. Key works from this era include: Verbitsky, *Villa miseria*; Germani, *Política y sociedad*. See also Auyero and Hobert, "¿Y ésto es Buenos Aires?"
29. Rozenmacher, *Cabecita negra*, 7–17; "Rozenmacher," *Clarín* (Buenos Aires) 8 Mar. 2001.
30. Rozenmacher, *Cabecita negra*, 77.
31. See Adamovsky, this volume.
32. Cossa et al., *Tres obras*, 76, 102.
33. Gociol, *Más libros*.

34. Hugo Ratier, conversation with author, Buenos Aires, Argentina, Aug. 2012. See also Hugo Ratier, interview as part of the Ciclo de Encuentro "Trayectorias," Colegio de Graduados en Antropología de la República Argentina, 2009, www.vimeo.com/7750904 (Accessed 9 Mar. 2015).
35. Ratier, *El cabecita negra*.
36. Ibid., 1.
37. For instance, in a 1967 speech about Latin American integration, Perón makes a passing reference to "*la América trigueña* [wheat-colored America]." Perón, *Latinoamérica*, 67.
38. Baschetti, *Documentos*, 188.
39. Ibid., 63.
40. *Los resistentes*; Feinmann, *Peronismo*, vol. I, 427.
41. Although determining *El Descamisado*'s circulation is impossible, memoirs written about this era suggest that it was read widely by would-be revolutionaries across Argentina. Gatica, *Tiempos*, 51; Baschetti, *Documentos*, 31.
42. *El Descamisado* (Buenos Aires) 3 Jul. 1973, 11 and 27 Nov. 1973, 12.
43. See Adamovsky, this volume.
44. *El Descamisado*, 31 Jul. 1973, 15.
45. *Posición* (Buenos Aires), 20 Dec. 1972, 11.
46. *El Descamisado*, 31 Jul. 1973, 15.
47. Longoni, *Del Di Tella*; Stites Mor, *Transition*.
48. Memorando No. 2696, 9 Oct. 1970, *Movimiento de Sacerdotes Para el Tercer Mundo*, Comisión Provincial Por la Memoria CD-ROM Collection [hereafter *Colección MSTM*], vol. IV, 173. "Entrevista Periodística al [Redacted] en el transcurso de su visita a Bahia Blanca el 03 Agosto 72," *Colección MSTM*, vol. VII, 166.
49. Goebel, *Argentina's Partisan*, 110–20, 145–80.
50. Quoted from Cooke, *Apuntes*, 98 by José Pablo Feinmann, "Cooke: Peronismo e historia," *Envido* (8 Mar. 1973), 21. A facsimile can be found in *Envido*, vol. II.
51. *El Descamisado*, 8 Jan. 1974.
52. Feinmann, *Peronismo*, vol. II, 154; "Por qué somos Peronistas de base," *Cristianismo y Revolución*, 30 (Dec. 1971), reprinted in Baschetti, *De la guerrilla*, 219; Gatica, *Tiempos*, 57.
53. Gillespie, *Soldiers*; Lanusse, *Montoneros*; Sucarrat, *El inocente*, 93; *Montoneros: una historia*.
54. Feinmann, *Peronismo*, vol. I, 272, 665–76. On the politics of youth in this era, see Manzano, *Age of Revolution*.
55. Baschetti, *De la guerrilla*, 65, 305, 330.
56. Ibid., 568–617, 630–33.
57. A full transcript of this speech can be found in the files of the police intelligence branch of Buenos Aires province. "Reuniones del Grupo de Trabajo, Cuerpo I," 17 Mar. 1972, *Colección MSTM*, vol. VI, 197.
58. These examples are taken from a recent compilation and study of the slogans chanted at public rallies in this period. Tcach, *La política*, 65, 67.
59. Feitlowitz, *Lexicon*, 110–48; Tasín, *La oculta*, 22.
60. Dynamics of sexual attraction and repulsion feature in much of the post-1955 fiction written about Peronism by authors such as Rozenmacher, Julio Cortázar,

Fogwill, Ricardo Piglia, and Néstor Perlongher, but "race mixture" as such is rarely considered. Olguín, *Perón vuelve*.

61. Ratier, *El cabecita negra*, 99.
62. See Pite, this volume, and David Sheinin (personal communication).
63. Feitlowitz, *Lexicon*; Goebel, *Argentina's Partisan*, 183–201; Novaro and Palermo, *La dictadura*.
64. Blaustein, *Prohibido vivir*; Feitlowitz, *Lexicon*, 110–48; Vernazza, *Para comprender*; Gordillo, this volume.
65. Coscia, *Encrucijada*, 20, 30, 88–93.
66. Ibid., 30.
67. Knight, "Racism," 71–113.
68. Tasín, *La oculta*, 190. See also Auyero, *Poor*; Grimson, "Nuevas xenofobias," 69–97.
69. INDEC, *Aquí se cuenta* 12 (Feb. 2004), 1–6. According to the 2010 Census, the total foreign-born population stands roughly at 4.7 percent. Of course, official figures do not take undocumented migration fully into account. Argentine Republic, INDEC, *Censo 2010*, www.censo2010.indec. gov.ar/resultadosdefinitivos_to talpais.asp (Accessed 9 Mar. 2015).
70. Briones, *Cartografías*; Gordillo and Hirsch, *Movilizaciones*.
71. Wade, et al., eds., *Mestizo Genomics*.
72. Adamovsky, "El color."
73. Frigerio, "Luis D'Elía"; Young, *Negro*; Gordillo, this volume.

PART II

RACE AND NATION IN THE NEW CENTURY

8

African descent and whiteness in Buenos Aires

Impossible mestizajes *in the white capital city*

Lea Geler

> *M. Mujica Lainez*: Were all of our black people killed off during the war with Paraguay? When did they disappear?
>
> *J.L. Borges*: I can say something based on personal experience. In 1910 or 1912 it was common to see black people [...] They were not killed off in our frontier wars nor in the Paraguayan war; but what happened to them later, I can't say [...]
>
> *M. Mujica Lainez*: It's possible that their color faded [*puede ser que se hayan desteñido*], and that many of the whites that we know are blacks.
>
> Manuel Mujica Lainez, Los porteños (1980), 27.

In 1881, José Antonio Wilde – a renowned intellectual and doctor from the capital city of Buenos Aires – published his memoirs, *Buenos Aires desde setenta años atrás*, which would become a leading primary source for the study of the early post-independence period in the Argentine capital. Wilde portrayed the "mulatto" J. Antonio Viera, a celebrated nineteenth-century actor and singer, as follows: "His courteous demeanor and his manners left nothing to be desired, and as the saying goes, *only his color was lacking* [*el color no más le faltaba*], or more accurately, he had *an excess of it.*"[1] In 2010, more than a hundred and thirty years after Wilde's book was first published, Paula, a *porteña* (or resident of Buenos Aires city) who self-identifies as an Afro-descendant, said of herself in an interview: "Only my color is lacking [*a mí me falta el color nada más*]."

The extraordinary formal similarity between these two testimonies points to the historical persistence of a troubling relationship among perceived skin color, a supposedly expected "way of being," and the (im)possibility of recognition and self-recognition within established social categories. For what does it mean for someone to *lack* or to have *an excess of color*? In regard to what standard is someone's skin color judged to be *too much* or *too little*? This verdict implies, among many other things, that there is something in that person – whether a "mulatto" or an "Afro-descendant" – that exceeds or does not fit into established social categories. In this chapter, I will explore this conceptual dislocation between appearances and ways of being, which, I argue, must be understood in relation to the absence of intermediate or mixed (*mestizo*) categories in Buenos Aires. My purpose is to illuminate the different ways in which social categories related to blackness, whiteness, and *mestizaje* – that is, racialized and racializing categories – are and have been produced and reproduced in Argentina's capital city since the late nineteenth century, with a particular focus on their present-day configurations.

It is important to note that Buenos Aires has long been represented as a white-European, modern, and "civilized" city, in opposition not only to the rest of the country, but also – since the capital city is often made to stand for the nation as a whole – to much of the rest of Latin America.[2] According to this broadly accepted representation, the city's population descends almost entirely from the European immigrants who arrived by the millions in response to the state's invitation to "populate" the country in the second half of the nineteenth century. This image of Buenos Aires and by extension of Argentina as white-European is partly supported by the widely held belief in the total extermination of the indigenous population in late-nineteenth-century wars, and by the conviction that the descendants of enslaved Africans gradually decreased in number over the course of that century until they disappeared.[3] In terms of Afro-Argentines, the focus of this chapter, several accepted hypotheses supposedly explain their "disappearance." The most frequently cited explanation is that people of African descent died *en masse* over the course of the nineteenth century due in part to the many epidemics that assailed Buenos Aires in that period (particularly the yellow fever epidemic of 1871), and in part to the overreliance on black soldiers as cannon fodder in wars, especially the Independence battles (1810–16) and the War of the Triple Alliance (1864–70, the "Paraguayan war" mentioned in the epigraph). In the same vein, the disappearance of Afro-Argentines is often attributed to disproportionately high mortality rates owing to the poor living conditions of freed people, especially following the Law of the Free Womb of 1813 or the abolition of slavery (1853 in the provinces, 1861 in Buenos Aires). Another common explanation is mestizaje – the idea that people of African descent (imagined as ever smaller in number) "mixed in" with lighter-skinned people (ever greater in number, especially during the period of mass immigration). Here, however, it is crucial to note that the idea of disappearance by mestizaje implies that the process of mixture is not imagined as having resulted in *mestizos* ["mixed" people]. Quite to the contrary: thinking about mestizaje as disappearance means imagining the dilution or absorption of one group into another, an issue I will return to shortly. All of these explanations for Afro-Argentines' "disappearance" – as well as the idea of disappearance itself – are continuously reproduced in institutions such as the school system and in a range of representational practices, such as political speeches, public policies, the media, the arts, and so forth. Consequently, even though these hypotheses have been proven wrong by several generations of researchers, they remain durable pillars of national ideologies and pervasive themes within a national "common sense."[4]

In essence, over the course of the twentieth century, *porteños* have come to accept that there are no more black Argentines, giving rise to a situation that researchers and activists call "invisibilization." The invisibilization of Afro-Argentines does not refer to an actual disappearance of people, but rather, to wide-ranging transformations in social categories and in (self) perceptions that were the desired outcome of late-nineteenth-century processes of nation-building and state consolidation.[5] As part of their attempts to achieve an "improved" and more homogeneous national population, local elites implemented policies that ranged from courting European immigrants as a way of "improving" the local population and bringing the country nearer to European ideals of progress and modernity (Law 817 of Immigration and Colonization, 1876), to passing disciplinary labor legislation (such as vagrancy laws), enacting free, obligatory and secular schooling for every child (Law 1420 of Common Education, 1884), and enforcing obligatory military service (Law 4301 of Mandatory Enlistment, 1901). As a result of these processes, around 1910, the idea that the Argentine population was a melting pot [*crisol de razas*] gained strength. That representation implied the fusion of diversity into a homogeneous "Argentine race" defined as white-European.[6] In the first decades of the twentieth century, through a range of institutions of social control and with the rise of eugenics, psychiatry, and criminology, the state set out to protect and defend the white and homogeneous national race that, it was broadly believed, had finally been achieved.[7]

The belief, in this view, that every Argentine was white brought with it the conviction that race did not play any part in Argentine social relations and that the nation was an "exception" in Latin America.[8] But in fact, the "Argentine race" contained internal hierarchies. In this supposedly racially homogeneous country, difference and diversity were channeled through the class system, the dominant paradigm that allowed citizens to be inscribed in the nation and to be recognized and included in political struggles for or against the state.[9] The class structure reproduced inequalities persisting since colonial times, when society was more visibly divided into groups that measured purity of blood, origins, colors, status, and so on.[10] For this reason, socioeconomic differences within the national population have continued broadly – but not exclusively – to correspond to recognizable phenotypical differences. Yet since the early twentieth century, with the ascendancy of the idea of a uniformly white population and the emergence of class as the only admissible paradigm of difference, race and color (other than the naturalized "white") became issues almost impossible to discuss explicitly, or even to be contemplated. As a result of these processes, during the twentieth century the invisibilization of Afro-Argentines was nearly complete.

Nevertheless, beginning in the 1990s, a deep economic crisis resulting from decades of neoliberal politics uncovered an Argentina that was much closer to Latin America than many Argentines and outsiders had previously thought. The advent of ideologies that praised diversity (such as multiculturalism), together with the efforts of several multinational organizations and financing institutions (such as the World Bank, NGOs, or private foundations) to make loans to Argentina conditional on acquiescence with these ideologies, gradually fractured the state's longstanding commitment to homogeneity and whiteness. It may be true that, as anthropologist Rita Segato points out, this process brought a "canned," flattened sort of diversity to Argentina by imposing ideas and values that originated in historical processes largely foreign to that country.[11] But this process also opened new spaces for making the Afro-Argentine population visible, promoting the activities of a growing number of their organizations and the investigations of scholars who contest the idea of Afro-Argentines' disappearance. As these activists and scholars have shown, far from being gone, Afro-Argentines have continuously negotiated their inclusion in the nation, generally from positions of great inequality and sometimes marginality.[12]

This process is locally known as "revisibilization." Revisibilization implies not only demanding public recognition of the existence of Afro-Argentines and of their historical importance, but also facing up to repressed memories, painful pasts, and discriminatory attitudes. Revisibilization also requires finding new forms of self-identification in the face of social categories still deeply rooted in a national imagination that continues to deny the very possibility of the existence of black Argentines. Indeed, it was in this spirit that a delegation of African-descended activists representing Argentina attended the preparatory encounter for the United Nations' World Conference Against Racism, Racial Discrimination, Xenophobia, and Related Forms of Intolerance in Santiago de Chile in 2000.[13] They decided to adopt the denomination of "Afro-descendants [*afro-descendientes*]" to include, first and foremost, the descendants of enslaved Africans in Argentina or Latin America more broadly, but the label was also in some cases extended to the descendants of African immigrants living and/or born in Argentina.[14] Nevertheless, in Buenos Aires there are various and sometimes competing categories of self-identification at play, as local organizations and groups champion different terms like "black [*negro*]," "Afro-Argentine of the colonial root [*afroargentino del tronco colonial*]," "African Diaspora," among others, each with its own inclusions, exclusions, and political implications.[15]

Working from the premise that every classificatory category is a historically situated and contingent social creation, this chapter analyzes how categories related to mestizaje, whiteness, and blackness work in present-day Buenos Aires.[16] To do so, it draws on the cases of three Afro-descendant porteñas: Nora, Emilia, and the previously cited Paula, all of whom I interviewed between 2008 and 2011. Focusing on these few cases allows me to perform a close reading and a historically and culturally grounded analysis of the ways in which ideas about mestizaje, "blackness [*negritud*]," and "whiteness [*blanquitud*]" take on meaning at the intersection of individual, family, and broader local or national histories. I have selected these cases to reflect some of the diversity of the Afro-porteño community. Nora, for instance, is around 80 years old and had been living in Spain for more than 20 years at the time of our interview. Emilia and Paula are approximately 40 years old and currently live in the Greater Buenos Aires area.[17] These women represent different generations of families that held great prestige and importance within the Afro-porteño community at the end of the nineteenth century and the first decades of the twentieth. Their families achieved recognition and even fame beyond the Afro-porteño community as well. These women also represent different socioeconomic backgrounds. Nora can be described as upper-middle class (having trained as a nurse in her youth), while Emilia (a school teacher and a dancer of folkloric and African music) and Paula (a government employee and visual artist) can be described as lower-middle class, both at a certain disadvantage compared to Nora.

It is important to point out, moreover, that by the standards of Buenos Aires, these three women are socially (that is, seen by society as) white.[18] As such, their cases represent a unique part of the broader "Afro field" in that city.[19] Compared to Afro-descendants who are seen as black and who experience racist attitudes every day, these women have a very different situation. Yet, as we will see, they nonetheless suffer a structural racism whose existence Argentines deny. Their words and experiences as white Afro-descendants thus shed light, from a new angle, on the workings of social categories in Buenos Aires and on the processes by which difference is marked or unmarked in everyday life. The very existence of people who self-recognize as Afro-descendants while being socially identified as white may seem strange or even contradictory in the majority of countries in Latin America, where ideologies of mestizaje played a fundamental role in the formation of local matrixes of diversity or where whiteness was not envisioned as the only possible outcome of mixture. Unpacking this strangeness through these case studies will, I hope, contribute to the discussion of racial categories in other American countries. Similarly, the dynamics described in this chapter sometimes run parallel to, and sometimes diverge from, patterns in other Argentine regions where terms like "*criollo*," "white," "black," "mestizo," and "indigenous" have often taken on different meanings.[20] This chapter also contributes, then, to furthering our understanding of the ways in which constructions of racial and ethnic difference in Argentina (as elsewhere) have been markedly region-specific.

First, in order to lay out the complexity of thinking about racial categories in present-day Buenos Aires, I will briefly introduce two different types of "negritud" or blackness that exist today, naming them "racial negritud" and "popular negritud." Second, taking into account the two main types of social paradigms that govern perceptions of race and skin color in Buenos Aires (a visual paradigm and a genetic paradigm), I will analyze how racialized and racializing categories are configured in such a way as to make the existence of mestizos impossible. Finally, I will explore the relationship between perceived colors and behaviors or "ways of being," showing how people's ways of being are continuously monitored in a society that praises whiteness and that does not allow the existence of gray zones, giving rise to lives shaped by (self) disciplining and to trajectories of concealment and oblivion. Together, these sections illuminate the ways in which the whiteness that characterizes the capital city has been, and is still, manufactured, sustained, and reproduced.

WHO IS BLACK AND WHO IS WHITE IN BUENOS AIRES? RACIAL NEGRITUD AND POPULAR NEGRITUD

In Argentina, as in most Latin American countries, "race" is very difficult to analyze as an isolated category. In fact, race is embedded within and subsumed as a dimension of other social categories, especially class and nation. This way of understanding the social world is based on longstanding processes in which the formation of an "Argentine race" became entangled with other state projects: first, in the early nineteenth century, attempts to contain and incorporate diversity through the extension of political citizenship, and later, beginning at mid-century, the quest for a homogeneous and modern-European nation.[21] If both aspects of these projects – the taming of diversity and nation-building – were initially grounded in Enlightenment and liberal ideals of equality, cosmopolitanism, and progress, by the late nineteenth and early twentieth centuries they fell under the influence of rising currents of scientific racism (though earlier ideals remained influential).

As a result of these processes, and bearing the evidence of their often contradictory political impulses, racial categories in Argentina and specifically Buenos Aires settled into a unique binomial formation that persists to this day. Argentines would come to be considered "white" by definition – for the invisible raciality of the nation is white (European)[22] – while people seen as pertaining to the "black race" would immediately be understood not only as foreigners but also as numerically insignificant.[23] As anthropologist Alejandro Frigerio has demonstrated, from the early twentieth century until the present, blackness in Buenos Aires has been reduced to a very limited and specific set of physical characteristics. This classificatory system, which rests upon the very high levels of mestizaje that took place in the city, reduces to a minimum the number of people recognizable as belonging to the "black race."[24] The cornerstone of this system of racial classification is the so-called *negro mota* ("mota" refers to tightly curled or "kinky" hair), considered the "true" black person, racially speaking. To be a proper "negro mota," a person must possess a combination of several key physical characteristics, such as very dark skin and tightly curled hair (also called *pelo viruta*), a wide nose, or thick lips. Dark skin is not enough, in this classificatory scheme, to mark someone as racially black; one or more of the other traits mentioned earlier must also be present. In this sense, what is understood locally as racial blackness is defined visually rather than by a system of descent, blood, or genetics, making it different from other classificatory systems, such as the one conventionally understood to operate in the United States.[25] Everyone who is left out of this narrow "black" category – the vast majority of the population – is seen as *not-black*, or "normal."[26] And since in Argentina what is "normal" is, by definition, white, it follows that whiteness is configured locally as a capacious category that incorporates everything that is left outside of racial blackness. This social economy of color and race – present in several parts of the country but particularly pronounced in the capital – is known as porteño dualism.[27] This dual system inscribes and reproduces locally and historically specific ways of seeing and perceiving whiteness and blackness. Meanwhile, thousands of Afro-Argentines who are seen as "racially black" according to local standards (that is, "negros mota" or "actual" black people) are treated as foreigners on a daily basis, a practice that reveals and reinforces the supposed incompatibility of blackness and Argentineness. This limited representation of what is racially black carries with it all the stereotypically racist meanings associated with blackness for centuries in the broader Atlantic world, such as innocence, stupidity, joy, strength, hypersexuality, savagery, kindness, and so forth.[28] Such racism, however, is considered "non-existent" in Argentina and is commonly denied on the grounds that there are no racially black people in the country to be racist against(!).[29] I call this particular racial construction "racial negritud."[30] The porteño version of racial negritud combines all the potentiality of the visually based classificatory system that characterizes Buenos Aires, with many elements of the genetic or biological classificatory system derived from the "scientific" ideas about race that reached their peak in Argentina in the first half of the twentieth century and have yet to be fully dislodged.

In contrast to the extreme precision of definitions of racial negritud, there exists in Argentina another kind of negritud or blackness that is much more difficult to define. These "negros" do not represent a racial alterity to the nation, for they are part of the nonblack, "normal" or white national "whole," and they are conceived – in general – as Argentines.[31] This kind of negritud does not rely, in principle, on visual markers of race, but is determined primarily by a "way of being" associated with the lower classes, the popular world, and the grotesque: a way of seeing the world (backward or outdated), (uncivilized) actions, (lack of) education, (poor, filthy) place of living, etc. Basically, the attributes of this sort of blackness reflect the pejorative way in which many members of the (generally urban) middle and upper classes conceive of the popular world and popular sectors. In a very complex field of social categorization, where phenotypes are taken into account in very confusing and entangled ways, these "negros" do not, in theory, pertain to a different race, and the use of that word as an insult is not considered (at least by those who make the insult) to be racist. However, as several scholars have noted, the people dismissively called "negros" (also "*cabecitas negras*" or "*negros cabeza* [little black heads]," "*villeros* [shantytown dwellers]," "*grasas* [tacky people]," or "*negro de alma* [black on the inside, even if visually white]") are usually of darker skin tones than the people thus naming them.[32] In this light, the use of the epithet "negro," "disguised as a social and cultural stigma, masks a clear racial discrimination toward mestizo and low-income social groups."[33] To differentiate this construction of blackness from racial negritud, I will call it "popular negritud". The emergence of this kind of classificatory system based on social class and ways of being, together with the idea that "real" black people largely "disappeared," has made possible the expulsion of the racial dimension from the realm of the explicit.

Just as both racial negritud and popular negritud derive their classifying power from mutually reinforcing cultural and biological axes, so must whiteness be thought of as possessing intertwined biological and cultural dimensions.[34] Whiteness thus consists of ideas about skin color or lines of descent *and* ideas about an expected way of being, related to European modernity and a capitalist system. Basically, whiteness is the baseline from which both forms of negritud are and have been distilled and populated. This process leaves large portions of the population – whether because of their skin color and features or because of their ways of being – on the margins or entirely outside of the (white) "normal," and thus in a space of constant vulnerability.[35]

In sum, in the porteño racial and social ideological complex, whiteness encompasses a visual shade that ranges from people "without color" (middle and upper classes) to the nonracial "black people" (the popular world). This construction of whiteness, however, is itself tacitly racialized, as the middle and upper classes see themselves as whiter and with more European (and therefore more acceptable) tastes and behaviors than the popular sectors.[36] Presenting itself as nonracial (and nonracist), this racial-social ideological complex restricts normality to whiteness while providing very strict lines of perceptibility for racial negritud. Simultaneously, it creates a structure of colors and behaviors linked to values of what is acceptable and what is not, which has very tangible consequences for the lives of people who are left outside of whiteness, or who – like Nora, Paula, and Emilia – are trapped in the classificatory system's ambiguous or intermediate zones. These women's stories can help us gain deeper insight into this ideological complex and its power to expand or limit personal possibilities and life trajectories.

HAVING TOO LITTLE OR TOO MUCH COLOR: THE IMPOSSIBILITY OF MESTIZAJE

It is important to emphasize that Nora, Paula, and Emilia recognize themselves as white people, and that they know that society classifies them as such. Paula, for instance, describes herself as "*blanca teta* [white as a breast, or literally, "tit-white"]." Similarly, Emilia says: "I am *blanca teta* and have light eyes."

The expression "blanca teta" refers to the extreme of whiteness and it means something like "the whitest that a skin can be," since it represents a zone of the (white) body at its most "natural" and supposedly never touched by sunlight. This expression works similarly to "negro mota," which (as explained earlier) defines the opposite extreme of the color spectrum and means something like "truly black." Finally, Nora says about herself: "I have green eyes and [when I was born] my hair was so blond that they cut it several times to force it to grow, they thought I had no hair ... and it was because my hair was so blond that it was almost invisible." Unlike Emilia and Paula, Nora's skin color would be defined locally as "*trigueño* [wheat-colored, brownish]." In all three cases, one of the parents of these women was of predominantly European descent.

Besides their self-recognition as white, Paula, Emilia, and Nora recognize themselves as descendants of enslaved Africans, but in slightly different ways. For example, Paula and Emilia grew up knowing that they had African ancestors, but Nora found this out as an adult by reading a history book. That book was George Reid Andrews' foundational *The Afro-Argentines of Buenos Aires*, which appeared in Spanish in 1989. Andrews' book marked a turning point in studies about Afro-Argentines, as it was the first to question their "disappearance" and simultaneously offered one of the most comprehensive historical accounts of slavery and people of African descent in Buenos Aires. Considering how deeply entrenched the idea of a white Argentina is among Argentines, it should come as no surprise that a book like this was written by a foreign scholar. Nor is it surprising that the book was only published in Argentina almost a full decade after its first edition in English (in 1980). *The Afro-Argentines of Buenos Aires* became an obligatory reference in Afro-Argentine studies, an achievement recognized even beyond the scholarly world (to the point that Andrews appears in a recent critically acclaimed novel, *Fiebre negra*, as the subject of the main character's romantic dreams and the source of her fascination with the Afro-Argentine past).[37] For Nora, then, discovering information about her family in a book that enjoyed such legitimacy and prestige marked an immediate change in the way she and her family saw themselves. For until that moment, Nora had lived her life assuming she was white-European:

NORA: I realized that my family *had been black*, but only once I was a grown-up. I was an adult. Because I had never known [...]. When I bought [...] Andrews' book, when I read it and saw that my grandfather was there, then I said: "But of course!" And then I began to *put two and two together*.

LG: You were reading and you said "This is my grandfather"?

NORA: Yes, of course [...] and there was also Tata Sosa, whose portrait we have in every one of our houses, he is family.[38]

Note that Nora stresses that her family "had been black," which means that they were not black anymore and, consequently, that she was not either. This way of constructing race is in keeping with the ideology of whitening historically at work in Buenos Aires. This ideology implies that in the event of mixing, the race that persists is the white one – because it is conceived as the strongest and most adaptable – and it is the one that is most visually "legible" according to the local system of visual racial classification. This particular ideology of whitening was crucial in the nation-building process. It made possible the promotion of European immigration in order to "improve" the population through mestizaje, both biological and cultural. But it simultan-eously created a classificatory system that did not allow for the existence of intermediate or mixed zones. In this situation, the intermingling of people considered white with those considered black would not result in mestizos or mulattos, as in other parts of Latin America; rather, as long as these newer generations did not present the full set of characteristics that would relegate them to racial negritud, they would be considered white. This explains why (to return to an earlier point), according to widely held ideas, Afro-Argentines are seen to have disappeared in part due to mestizaje (understood as dilution/ absorption): the implication is that they had "faded" or turned white. This whitening process – based on the positive appraisal of whiteness over black-ness – can be traced back to the nineteenth century or even colonial times, and even today it is discursively recreated and reinforced when, in conversations, people reveal only their European ancestors. "European" is the ancestry most commonly put forth in public settings and indeed in private ones, as occurred in Nora's case: she only spoke (and knew) about her French-Basque descent until she read Andrews' book, which allowed her to "put two and two together."

Unlike Nora, Paula and Emilia spoke of racial negritud as something that had always been present in their lives. But they framed it using terms pointedly different from those made available by the broadly accepted porteño visual system of identification. Emilia, for instance, said: "you have it in your genes [...] I am a black woman inside a white skin, but blackness doesn't show through skin. I mean, we are all equal, skin color doesn't matter. What's valuable is what is inside." Similarly, Paula explained that "it shows up everywhere ... you can't see it but it is there [...] it's genetic I guess..." In other words, unlike Nora, Emilia and Paula adhere to a racial conception of negritud linked to genetics and biology, more typical of the twentieth and twenty-first centuries, when "scientific" theories of race – even after being widely discredited in the wake of World War II – continue to insinuate them-selves into our daily lives through a range of seemingly innocuous studies in medicine, psychology, or population genetics. This "biological" way of think-ing about race and descent can be compared to the "one-drop rule" historically used in the United States to determine who is black and who is not, and it runs counter to the porteño system of classifying racial types primarily through visual means. In noting this distinction, it is important to remember that between Nora (more than 80 years old) and Emilia and Paula (both around 40), there is a gap of approximately two generations. Moreover, both Paula and Emilia are engaged in revisibilization struggles, while Nora – whether because of her age, her politics, or her location outside of the country – is not. These circumstances are relevant because they speak to the paradigm shift that took place in Argentina in the 1990s as described in the introduction to this chapter – a shift that influenced and perhaps even made possible new ways of thinking about race, even as it brought with it a new set of limitations.

One of these limitations becomes evident when Paula, who does not have any of the locally accepted visible signs of racial negritud, exposes the conceptual dislocation that prevents her from self-identifying the way she would like to: "[. . .] it's only my color that's lacking, that's how I feel, I only lack color." Indeed, in the absence of external evidence of her racial negritud – according to local visual parameters – she feels discriminated against when people dismiss her self-identification as an Afro-descendant:

PAULA: [. . .] I see a lot of "Afro" in myself. [But people] tease me, they annoy me. They offend me, I feel offended many times, and I feel more discriminated than people might think. That is, I am discriminated for the opposite [of what is usual], because they mock me, all the time. It's mockery all the time. It's "don't believe her," "Oh, as if she's really an Afro-descendant, ha ha ha." [. . .] [E]verything we feel that comes out in art [. . .] everything, dance, music [. . .], all of that comes with the genetic package, I think this is true [. . .].

Likewise, Emilia said:

EMILIA: Well, I might be dancing *malambo*[39] [and people would say] "the blond woman was seized by a convulsion" and then, well, that would drive me crazy. [. . .] But heritage [used here in a biological sense] is stronger and I would answer: "no, the blond woman wasn't seized by any sort of convulsion; the *negra* [black woman] was seized by the *Afro*."[40]

Contrary to strategies of "passing" familiar from the United States context, in which the ability to be socially recognized as white could provide a partial escape from severe anti-black discrimination, for Paula and Emilia discrimination stems from the impossibility of having their African ancestry socially recognized. This impossibility is grounded in the contradiction between their phenotype, which makes them "white" according to the visual structure used locally, and what they claim as their "black genetics," invisible to the eye but "verifiable" through their aptitude for dance and music. For these women, racial negritud emerges and becomes visible in direct relation to the stereotypical idea that black people carry music and dance in their blood or genes, an idea shared by the majority of porteños.[41] Behind this thought process lies an attempt to subvert dominant whitening ideologies by appealing to an invisible but powerful, genetically inherited knowledge. Yet Argentina's whiteness is a one-way journey – it is the nation's teleology, as anthropologist Claudia Briones has argued – and the visual system society uses to sustain it does not allow these two women to "go backward," to "stop" being white, or to (re)become nonwhite.[42]

In this regard, both the term "Afro" used by Paula and Emilia to identify themselves and the term "Afro-descendant" itself seem to introduce the possibility of mixed or mestizo categories, as they appear to be unattached to specific colors (and thus inclusive of many) and to reference instead geographical origins and cultural traditions. In fact, Afro-Argentine activists chose this terminology specifically for its ability to deemphasize color in order to leave behind any racial implications. Nevertheless, for these women, "Afro" is the materialization of a genetic profile (if not a color), of a biological "heritage" that carries specific and distinctive abilities (such as dance), of a racial negritud that should rightfully place them in one of the extremes of the racial continuum. Consequently, Paula and Emilia do not locate themselves as mestizas; instead, they use the term "Afro" as a referent for racial negritud. This same use of "Afro" is widely shared, and indeed made possible, by a society that does not permit the visibly white Paula and Emilia to self-recognize as Afro: "Oh, as if she's really an Afro-descendant, ha ha ha." "Afro," in this sense, does not allow someone to be two things at once: European-Argentine and African-Argentine, for example, or white and black, or even something entirely new or hybrid resulting from that mixture. By imposing a genetic racial matrix upon the dominant visual one, Paula and Emilia fall right back into the logic of porteño categorial dualism. Even though Paula and Emilia feel limited, on a daily basis, by their visually determined whiteness, they cannot claim a mixed category. Because their own subjectivity has developed from within dualistic categories, their attempts to fight one binomial classificatory system lead them to appeal to the other, without ever resolving their sense of dislocation.

The racial paradigm that Emilia and Paula use also becomes evident when these women speak about their ancestors. Emilia, for example, considers her grandfather "negro" while her family does not: "I knew my grandfather was black [. . .]. But afterwards [my mother and aunt] said: well, he wasn't that black, he was chocolate-colored or *morenito* [the diminutive form of *moreno*, a term denoting dark skin – here, the diminutive is intended to soften the term or diminish its presence]." According to Emilia's mother and aunt, who used a visual racial system, being "of chocolate color" or "moreno" seemed to move Emilia's grandfather away from racial negritud. Similarly, when Nora thought about her ancestors she said:

NORA: My grandfather was *moreno*. [. . .] *He was not black, he was moreno* . . . I don't
    recall that; for me he wasn't even *moreno*. I remember him as a *normal man*,
    gorgeous, handsome, very nice, but he wasn't one of these persons with *a wide nose* or
    lips . . . no, not at all. [. . .] The one who had more of those traits was my aunt. They
    called her "*negrita* [the diminutive form of negra or black woman, indicating an
    affective dimension or an intention to soften the term]," aunt Carmen, the youngest of
    all the siblings [. . .]. She wasn't *that morena*.[43]

Nora strings together her grandfather's "normality" – his unspoken whiteness untouched by any of the visible traits of racial negritud, such as a wide nose or thick lips – with a language that avoids mixed categories (mulatto or mestizo). Nevertheless, in her word choice Nora refers to a gradation of skin color, with the word "moreno" standing out, as it did in Emilia's mother's and aunt's reported speech.

The term "moreno" and others like it provide an important clue for understanding local racial ideologies. In Buenos Aires, depending on the context, "moreno" may be used to refer to a person with a dark skin tone but who is perceived as within the bounds of racial whiteness, as well as to describe (in softened terms) a person understood as racially black. This same ambiguity is also present in the term "*pardo* [brownish-colored]," and in the term "trigueño," which Andrews has signaled as key to the transfer of people from the category "black" to that of "white" in nineteenth-century official statistics.[44] Significantly, in colonial times "moreno" was not an ambiguous word; it meant "black," and "pardo" meant "mulatto." Yet as "mulatto" (like other explicitly intermediate terms) disappeared from the local vocabulary, "moreno" and "pardo" became ambiguous and interchangeable terms. In that sense, these terms can be understood as points of articulation among racial categories and enablers of movement into the category of whiteness.[45] "Trigueño" also works in this way, as it was used to describe European immigrants with darker skin colors as well as anyone whose skin color could not be placed at either extreme of the color line. These three terms ("moreno," "pardo," and "trigueño") designate people with skins that are darker than those described as "blanca teta," but the terms do not necessarily designate racial negritud or popular negritud. These terms, with their ambiguity and their ability to bridge and allow passage across racial categories, illustrate one of the ways in which the category of racial negritud is continually narrowed in favor of whiteness, a process continuously reproduced across society more broadly. Similarly, in Buenos Aires, to call someone a "negro" may connote strong feelings of affection, familiarity, and friendliness, and when used in this sense the term is not related to skin color. This is yet another way in which the racial meanings of the word "negro" are veiled or altogether voided, allowing it to move closer to whiteness. The reader will recall, for instance, Emilia's phrase "the *negra* was seized by the Afro." Since Emilia is "blanca teta," she was channeling her racial negritud through the concept of "Afro," while leaving "negra" in suspense, in an ambiguous place, signaling the term's inability or insufficiency to connote racial blackness. Or, for example, in Nora's account, her grandfather's designation as "moreno" or her aunt's as "negrita" were never clearly linked to a race that was different from the tacit "normal" (whiteness) – at least while Nora was a child and the issue of racial negritud was completely off the table (in subsequent paragraphs I will return to this question of the silencing of black ancestry in Afro-Argentine families).

The way "moreno" works as an articulating category becomes very clear when Nora describes another of her aunts, Amalia:

NORA: I always say that my aunt might have been a *cuarterona* [quadroon] or something like that, because she was very special [...]. That aunt was beautiful. I always think that she had the beauty of the quadroon, but without being black, only *morena*.[46]

Quadroon is a mixed category used in the colonial period, and in Spanish America it implied a quarter of Indian "blood" and the rest Spanish, though in some places it could also connote African ancestry in similar proportions.[47] This category of mestizaje was thus related to a biological system that tracked "blood" or descent, detached in principle from possible visual outcomes.[48] Nora, also using a biological system, assumes that a quadroon would be nearer to a racial negro than to a mestizo or a white person. That is why she hurries to remove her aunt from that definition: her aunt was a quadroon but "without being black, only *morena*." Nora is pulling her aunt back into a visual system where she would be white, though with a darker skin tone than "blanca teta"; or at least her aunt would not belong to racial negritud, understood in its biological sense. "Morena" appears again as a referent of the visual system, displacing the language of (black) "bloodlines," which mean nothing locally and which, in any case, have been understood to "disappear" through dilution in whiteness. In contrast to terms such as "Afro-descendant" or "Afro," which make it possible to remove people from the visual paradigm and situate them in the biological one (as we saw in Paula and Emilia's cases), the terms "moreno," "pardo," "trigueño," and often "negro" itself remove people from the bio-logical paradigm and situate them in the visual one. We must understand them, then, as articulators among classificatory systems.

For her part, Paula describes her family as follows:

LG: Your [great-grandfather] married [a Spanish woman]...
PAULA: Yes, she was white with light eyes.
LG: And their children?
PAULA: They all turned out black [...] All of them.
LG: And your mom?
PAULA: She is *a mulata* [...] My mom is *mulatita* ["a little bit" mulatto], and so is my aunt. Maybe my aunt has whiter features, but not my mom. My mom has the nose, the eyebrows...

It is relevant here that Paula uses the intermediate category – mulato/a – to name her mother, instead of relying on the local binomial classificatory system. However, Paula does not use the mulatto category with her grandfather, though this term would apply to him according to classifying systems that recognize mestizaje. Instead, she speaks of him as "negro." Apparently, Paula is once again combining the visual racial system with one based on descent. That is why, when returning to local visual categories to describe her mother, Paula has to search for other signs of racial negritud ("the nose, the eyebrows") while her aunt was already seen as "white." And just as with Nora and her quadroon aunt, the fact that Paula's mother could be identified as "mulata" placed her in the realm of racial negritud. Yet unlike Nora, Paula did not try to take her relative out of racial negritud. On the contrary, what Paula was seeking to emphasize was the very racial negritud that would allow her, as her mother's daughter, to be designated as an Afro-descendant as well. As a result, the terms "mulata" and "cuarterona" – which are not currently in use in the city except, as in these cases, among people looking for different ways of classifying themselves – end up adapting to the local binomial system. In that context, they work as categories denoting racial negritud, according to the system of "blood"/biology/descent, and not as the intermediate categories they were in their original contexts.

In short, "moreno," "pardo," "trigueño," and even "negro" are all categories that, in the broader local usage, signify intermediate skin tones but without a necessary association with racial negritud. They work to help bring people of darker skin tones closer to whiteness which, readers will recall, is locally determined through a visual system that comprises a broad range of phenotypes, even though it is grounded in supposedly European descent. The term "Afro" works in a parallel manner, though in the opposite direction: it helps to take people out of the visual system with its emphasis on whiteness, and to place them instead into a genetic matrix, bringing them closer to racial negritud while skipping over intermediate options. In both cases, we are dealing with articulators among classificatory systems, whose function is to mediate between visual and biological systems that are always binomial. Disguised as intermediate or mestizaje terms, these categories work by re-locating what is in the gray zones to one or another extreme ("black" or "white"), and by moving people to one or the other system of categorization (visual or genetic), depending on the context, without allowing them to occupy intermediate spaces. Both the visual and the genetic systems of classification are grounded in the positive valorization of whiteness (seen as a welcome and irreversible historical outcome), thus restricting any possibility for making visible the nonwhite/non-European. This situation illustrates how powerfully social classifications are imposed and maintained in Buenos Aires through the teleological and legitimating force of racial and cultural whiteness, as we saw (in different ways) through Nora, Paula, and Emilia's cases. At the same time, these dynamics lead us to wonder about the experiences and struggles of people on the margins of whiteness: those who, whether because of their phenotypical traits or their "ways of being," or according to what they are able to present or hide in crucial social situations, are vulnerable to being classified as nonwhite and therefore at risk of being seen as deviants from the "normal." Once again, Nora, Paula, and Emilia's family stories can help us untangle some of the past and present consequences of these experiences.

WAYS OF BEING: ON MOVING AWAY FROM (OR BEING KEPT IN) "NEGRITUD"

Racial markers are not innocuous: negritud carries with it connotations of derision and exclusion that can be traced all the way back to the origins of the slave system. And even in a supposedly "deracialized" Argentina, the power of these connotations is palpable, as can be seen in Emilia's case:

EMILIA: [My mother and aunt face] the issue of not wanting to recognize part of their roots. Because they have *pelo mota* and they straighten it with a flat-iron. It is a small detail but, well, there are other ways in which they don't accept themselves. For example, I might tell my mother or my aunt "shut up, *negrita*," and they'll answer, "I'm not black." They themselves will say this to me! And then I'll get mad and I'll reply: "And where do you think that *pelo mota* comes from?" And they'll have to shut up. [...][My sister] has really kinky hair, super kinky, but you can't tell because she straightens it. But she has *viruta* [very coarse] hair, not just the common tight curls, she has *viruta* hair, and she hates it ....

Although this reaction to tightly curled hair (known in other countries as "bad hair") is not exclusive to Argentina – it exists in the majority of Latin American countries and feminist scholar Hill Collins cites it as part of the "matrix of racial domination" in the United States – in an Argentine context that upholds whiteness as an almost totalizing normality, carrying such visible signs of racial negritud brings with it the risk of falling into abnormality or deviance.[49] In this light, the importance that Emilia's family members place on ironing and hiding their hair's original form becomes understandable. In the same way, Paula relates how her mother found, upon her body, some of the visual signs of racial negritud, and, as a perpetual inhabitant of the margins of inclusion, felt threatened and potentially defined by them at all times: "[My mom] had a lot of complexes [...] about her nose. Because she said it was broad. So my mom slept with a clothespin on her nose, during like two years of her adolescence she slept with this clothespin." As with Emilia's mother and aunt, for Paula's mother it was essential to try to modify bodily traits (in her case, a broad nose) that signaled racial negritud. In the porteño ideological-social-racial system, racial negritud is construed as a radical and negative alterity, always visible and, in principle, impossible to hide.[50] Racial negritud is also inextricably related to ugliness and strangeness. In this regard, Nora relates:

NORA: We arrived at a house. [...] What I didn't know beforehand was that the owner was a woman who was black as coal. [...] And my sister and I thought she was wearing a *virulana* [steel wool] wig. She was an old lady... and we said: "Grandfather, your friend is really ugly!" "Don't say that, girls," he responded. "She is a very elegant lady, very charming."

The ideals of beauty that have become dominant in Argentina since the end of the nineteenth century celebrate white skin, blond, straight hair, and light eyes.[51] It cannot surprise us, then, that the question of the beauty or ugliness of Nora's relatives had come up frequently in her family. For example, she added about Colonel Sosa:

NORA: Yes, our family had his portrait. [...] He was very respected by the family. Not by the kids, because we saw him as ugly, because he had ... a hairy beard with those things on the front that generals typically wear [sideburns], with his uniform and all. So we'd say, "Tata Sosa is so ugly," and aunt Carmen always replied, "You are wrong, he was a beautiful man." But in the picture we saw a dark thing, with this white hair . . . .

Beauty and ugliness were thus closely related to whiteness or negritud, with real consequences in people's lives. For instance, Emilia's sister, who has a darker skin tone than Emilia, always felt she was at a disadvantage due to this difference. Emilia recalled that her sister used to say to her: "You are the pretty one, not me; you are the white one, not me." And Emilia adds: "I know my [European] grandmother said [at my birth]: 'finally, a blond and light-eyed baby was born,' and she was in front of my sister, and my sister was thirteen. . . ." According to Nora's family account, the doctor who helped deliver Nora said something similar: "Well, the sun of the family is born." In these accounts, those who expressed joy at Emilia and Nora's appearance dramatized the widely held view that mixing with Europeans was successfully resulting in the sought-after process of whitening, gradually eliminating racial negritud from bodies (classified according to the local visual system) that then became beautiful. It is also worth noting that both Emilia and Nora's families transmitted these accounts to them, perhaps as a way of highlighting events and values that were meant to bring happiness.

In light of this, Paula explained that she thought her Spanish great-grandmother "[. . .] was exquisite, she was striking, very striking." But it is interesting to point out that this striking woman described her own husband, Paula's famous Afro-Argentine great-grandfather, as follows: "That *negrito* [the affectionate diminutive for negro], that *negrito* was charismatic, very seductive." Paula elaborates: "They say he was terribly seductive, he was not handsome, he was not handsome but he was seductive . . . charismatic and charming, a gentleman." In sum, for Paula's great-grandmother and for Paula herself, this great-grandfather was not handsome, but he had other positive qualities and manners that made it possible to "ignore" his racial negritud. Just like the "mulatto" J. Antonio Viera, described by Wilde in his famous work, Paula's great-grandfather's only defect was that he had *an excess of color*.

The charisma and gallantry that Paula attributes to her great-grandfather finds a parallel in Nora's description of her grandfather: "My grandfather [. . .] was very dapper, very well-mannered. He was such a polite man, so elegant, always so well put together [. . .]. Besides, he was a teacher in the armed forces, where he made his career. He had gorgeous handwriting. He was a cultured man, he was delicious." And about her "quadroon" aunt, Nora said: "my aunt Amalia was beautiful. How can I explain it? She was kind of strong. Not weak. She was strong but elegant, a beautiful woman." Through Nora's and Paula's testimonies, as in Wilde's before them, we can see that refined behaviors, education, and gallantry, in the case of men, or elegance in the case of women,

were conceived of as possible ways of unmarking oneself racially, of downplaying or sidestepping the pejorative meanings attached to skin color or to
perceived ugliness and strangeness. That is why for Paula's mother, hiding
one's potential racial *negritud* involved not only the modification (inasmuch
as possible) of physical traits, but also, at the urging of her family members, a
constant self-patrolling according to the standards of "polite" behavior, a
"containment" of the physical boundaries of herself:

PAULA: [My aunts] used to say to my mom: "don't wipe your nose, don't cough, don't
speak in front of people, because if a *dark one* does that it looks bad." So my mother
was all *contained* [*contenida*] all the time, all *contained*. Then when she went to [the
privacy of] the bathroom she sneezed, she did everything there. [...] All these things
built upon themselves: you were dark, or black, you came from African roots, you
couldn't [...], you had to be careful about everything because anything could
stigmatize you so much more, do you understand?[52]

It is highly disciplined people such as these – people who, at different
moments, turned themselves into models of polite conduct according to
prevailing norms of social and bodily propriety – who would be seen as
having "too much" color: their visible traits (dark color, potentially "black"
facial features) did not coincide with their ("civilized") "ways of being." This
dislocation placed them in a zone where classification standards became
blurred and porous.

The fundamental importance of measured, educated, disciplined, and "contained" behaviors in these passages speaks to one of the key ways in which
whiteness was and is constructed in Buenos Aires. The "ways of being"
explored here must be understood as learnable behaviors that enable people
to "progress" or "improve," and not as biologically determined, inherited, or
unchangeable characteristics. This definition rests upon long-term historical
processes related to nineteenth-century European modernity, Enlightenment
values, the expansion of citizenship, and capitalism, when ideas about "culture" and "race" were not completely dissociated from one another. In
nineteenth-century Buenos Aires, the nonwhite social sector previously known
(in colonial times) as *castas* – essentially blacks and mulattoes, because the
indigenous population was scarce in the city – together with everyone who did
not belong to the aristocracy, was lumped together under the category of
"popular world" or "popular sectors."[53] Porteño elites saw this urban popular
world as an amalgamation of grotesque, uneducated people, with uncouth
manners and an unrestrained sexuality, closer to barbarism than to civilization,
though politically mobilizable and, above all, potentially improvable. What is
striking here is that as the nineteenth century progressed and as the Afro-
descendant population supposedly "disappeared," black people actually held
such importance in the city's cultural and political affairs that they became the
prototypical figures of the urban popular world. As a direct reflection of this
position, during the final decades of the nineteenth century – precisely when

modern social classes were emerging and the city was changing rapidly due to immigration and economic expansion – that popular world came to be conceived of and explicitly described as "black" or "of color." In sum, "blackness" melded with and came to characterize the popular world as a whole, a popular world elites believed to be uncouth but civilizable through education and discipline.[54] In this way, blackness disappeared neither from the city's imagination nor from its lexicon; it became, rather, the concept and the term used widely to designate every form of unsuitable behavior coming from poor, "primitive," or "uncivilized" social sectors – no matter their skin color or race – thus providing the historical basis for today's popular negritud. Notably, while unacceptable behaviors by members of the popular classes were derided as "black," similar behaviors by elites would be understood, conversely, as "pranks" or "mimicry," performances that were at their most explicit during carnival. But it was exactly the possibility of "improvement," "civilization," or "regeneration" – the latter term a favorite of Afro-porteño intellectuals in the 1880s[55] – encoded in ideas about the popular world that offered the inhabitants of the margins a legitimate path to becoming part of a nation that wished to be modern and white-European, a process that simultaneously ensured their inclusion as citizens.[56] And many Afro-porteños embraced this ideology and its promise of inclusion.

According to late-nineteenth-century Afro-porteño intellectuals, achieving regeneration required education, proper manners (that is, "modern" ones patterned on European standards of behavior), shedding old ("African") traditions or reserving them only for the private sphere, working to provide stability for one's family and, of course, serving one's country.[57] Through this sort of personal effort, a person's black past (never considered a positive legacy), their non-European traditions, and the supposedly close relation between negritud and vice could be "ignored." "Civilizing" oneself in this way also brought with it the promise of social mobility, related as much to economic improvement as to social prestige. The realm of popular negritud, with its intrinsic capacity for education and improvability, allowed many Afro-descendants with "dubious" appearances, and even many socially black people, to move closer to whiteness. And in the nineteenth and early twentieth centuries, one of the paths that led Afro-descendants to gain social prestige and a more comfortable standard of living – even in the face of the obstacles that discrimination placed in their way – was undoubtedly the army. Nora's grandfather, as mentioned previously, had been a military man:

NORA: He had his military wage. His was a model family [. . .]. They helped people. He had his salary. All the children had careers. As was customary at the time, his daughters attended the Red Cross nursing courses when they were 17 years old, something only done by well-to-do families. [. . .] And in my grandparents' house there was a stairway, and upstairs there were three rooms for the help. They had only two women as help, the cook and the cleaning lady, who was a Spaniard by the way, charming. They both were named María.

This last paragraph is remarkable for the way in which Nora inverts the typical image of black people as domestic servants, reserving that place instead for the white-European immigrants who served traditional local families.[58] This image highlights Nora's family's status and upward mobility.

Aside from a military career, other kinds of government jobs allowed many Afro-Argentines to improve their economic situations, find economic stability, and even achieve social mobility. Emilia's Afro-porteño grandfather was "the first typist for the National Congress." With this grandfather, her mother and aunt "lived [...] in the city center, downtown, they even lived in [the middle-class neighborhood of] Flores. [...] My grandfather would take them on Thursdays and Fridays to the theaters, they would pick him up when he left work at the Congress." One can safely assume that this grandfather's manners and ways of being were "impeccable," surely much like those of Nora's grandfather, according to the conventions of etiquette required in spaces of great visibility, prestige, and discipline such as the Congress or the army. Historical accounts describe Paula's great-grandfather in similar terms, highlighting his elegance and gallantry as major factors in his success as a musician. One of those accounts from the nineteenth century stated: "His attire, in accordance with the importance that his art has earned in our social life, has much more of the gentleman than of the popular singer about it."[59] Accounts of Afro-porteños as refined, with excellent manners, etiquette, and education endured throughout the twentieth century, even as stereotypical, discriminatory, and demeaning ideas about racial negritud rose.[60] These circumstances made it possible – at least in the first years of the twentieth century – for color to be ignored or downplayed in favor of ways of being, bringing those who dwelled on the margins of whiteness closer to its center through performances of whiteness.[61] Performances of whiteness – that is, acting in ways that approximate the behaviors and visual standards of European-modern culture – also facilitated the move away from another way of being: popular negritud, in the development of which Afro-porteños had been so crucial. Nora, Paula, and Emilia's relatives represented different generations of Afro-descendants who, through their ways of being, sought to demonstrate – indeed, were compelled to demonstrate – that their only sin was an excess of color. In so doing, they found spaces of acceptability and some opportunities for class mobility. But in order for their color to stop being quite so visible – in order, in other words, to stop suffering from an "excess" of color – what they needed beyond manners, economic stability, and education was to hide or dilute the signs of racial negritud for themselves and their descendants. To this end, mestizaje became a fundamental resource.

Overall, moving away from racial negritud required bodily modifications, mestizaje, or concealment, and moving away from popular negritud required the imposition of a strict code of conduct or a continuous performance of whiteness. Both negritudes are dangerous, and keeping one's distance from them is an important concern in people's daily lives, even among socially white

Argentines. What makes this goal particularly difficult for Afro-descendants, however, is that these negritudes do not work apart; in fact, they feed each other. When hints of popular negritud can be detected in racial negritud (a radical alterity), or vice-versa, people go out of their way to hide them or to keep them out of sight. That is what happened to a majority of Afro-porteño families. Nora's ignorance about her family being "black" was based on specific actions taken by her family. The lengths to which they went to keep her ignorant of this fact sheds light on the suffering of those who – despite all efforts at education, "containment," or courteousness – still find themselves in danger of exclusion by the binomial system of visual classification at work in Buenos Aires:

LG: And your father did not know about [his African roots]?
NORA: He must have known, but he never breathed a word. In my house NO ONE EVER SPOKE OF THIS.
LG: You asked questions and they didn't answer?
NORA: No, no, no. I couldn't ask about what I didn't know. No, this didn't exist for us.

These kinds of actions aimed at eroding or erasing negritud – described by Alejandro Frigerio as "social micro-processes of concealment" – turned ever more urgent as Nora's family moved up the social ladder.[62] But silence and ignorance were not the only ways to conceal negritud:

NORA: One day, while looking at photographs with that aunt, the youngest of the family, I must have been about fourteen years old, I said: "Wow, aunt, look, who is this *negrita*?" because I saw in the picture a young black girl sitting in a hammock beneath the vine arbor in my grandparents' yard. She answered: "That's aunt Amalia." "That's not possible," I said, "because here she is black." "Ah, no, it's just that she came out badly here," and rip-rip-rip *she tore up the photograph and she threw it away. . .* [. . .]. *Yes, and this was never spoken of again.* This episode was stored away in my brain and later, one day, I recalled it, but at that moment it disappeared from my life, [. . .] and as a result there was no way we could discuss it.[63]

Taken together, her family's actions allowed Nora to live her life in a state that we might call "perfect whiteness": a combination of a good social position, a performance of whiteness, and light skin color. Meanwhile, the material vestiges of negritud, any traces that could have cast doubt upon this whiteness, were systematically destroyed.

In the same vein, Paula remembered: "Here is another terrible thing: it is said that there were a lot of [my great-grandfather's] writings that his own sons threw away [. . .]." And Paula's mother, in turn, took actions to edit or redact the family tree of her own daughter, in an attempt to steer her life trajectory from the moment of birth: even though she is the child of a single mother, Paula was given her stepfather's surname. According to Paula's account, her mother denied Paula her maternal surname because of the recognition it might have had in the public sphere due to her great-grandfather's fame:

PAULA: My mom took away my identity. She wouldn't give me her surname [...].
  I couldn't have my father's surname, the biological one, and I ended up having my
  stepfather's .... It's OK, he was great, to me he was my father, but he is not my
  bloodline, it's wrong, this is not my identity. [...] And I don't understand why she
  thought it was so bad to be a Larrea. That is what I don't understand [...]. Since
  I assumed the Larrea surname my life got better [...].[64]

To remove the surname was to remove a traceable mark of African ancestry.
Denying the family surname also had the effect of silencing the fact that Paula's
mother was unmarried, another shameful stigma reinforced by stereotypes of
black women's hypersexuality. Paula's mother's actions not only strengthened
the chain of concealment, discrimination, and rejection of blackness in the city,
but it also reproduced this ideology in Paula, shaping her from birth.

  In Emilia's case, her family's pointed avoidance of any discussion of blackness was strengthened by her grandfather's early death, which forced the family
to change their lives completely. "I see it as totally related to discrimination and
to a sort of abandonment from not being able to stay with [that part of the]
family, not being able to be with their roots." Episodes of discrimination
toward Emilia's mother and aunt also played a part in their silence:

EMILIA: I always knew, but they never talked to me about this issue because my mom
  has ..., she is one of the many ... let's say discriminated people, for most of her life,
  let's say her childhood, at the school, [they would call her] *negrita de mi***** [sh*tty
  little black girl]. [...] She was always discriminated, and her sister, both of them [...].
  Both used to tell me that at school they were called *negrita de mi*****, I don't want to
  finish the word because I don't like it [...]. Well, they were really discriminated ....
  But the point is that she suffered a childhood of discrimination, afterwards she
  suffered the fact that my father's family didn't accept her, that made her life
  impossible, because how was it possible that a white, blond, and blue-eyed man was
  going to marry a *negrita*!

Emilia, Nora, and Paula's accounts speak volumes about local racial ideologies.
They reveal that visual markers never cease to impact people's lives or to govern
their placement within the complex coordinates of social status and belonging.
In order to make all the discrimination and the stereotyping go away, the
answer for many Afro-porteños has been to hide any signs of negritud, constantly and indefinitely, making every trace disappear. Even now, whitening as
a national telos becomes hegemony, and it acts – and forces people to act – to
reproduce it, profoundly shaping the socio-racial ideologies and practices
of the inhabitants of Argentina's capital city. And in this sense, it is remarkable
how these families' archival vacuum, the silences surrounding their blackness,
parallel the absence of classificatory options for people like Nora, Paula, and
Emilia, for whom a non-white identification is impossible. Unable to enjoy the
stability of occupying an established intermediate category, in Buenos Aires
people who suffer dislocation among color and ways of being have to permanently take action to be classified or declassified, a constant pressure that

disempowers them, and instead empowers those who classify from their secure and stable places: in general, places of whiteness.

The success of these and other families' arduous journeys toward whitening has depended on the contingent and often random ways in which key elements in the construction of whiteness worked (or not) in their favor in different times and places: the social perception of colors and phenotypes, economic status, education, and so forth. In Nora's case, her family's trajectory permitted her to melt imperceptibly into the national "us." In Paula's and Emilia's cases, their life trajectories had the opposite result: they ended up, as adults, claiming the African roots that their families had tried so vigorously to deny. If, over the course of the twentieth century, local classifications allowed the inhabitants of the gray zones to be considered either black or white according to ways of being that were moldable and could veil racial *negritud*, today Paula and Emilia demand to be recognized according to a way of being determined by biology. They do this in the attempt to overcome their categorial dislocation, but without accomplishing it.

FINAL WORDS

The visual classificatory system on which porteño whiteness is based is certainly undergoing a process of transformation. Not only has there been a slow but steady paradigm shift away from praising homogeneity to praising diversity, but the revisibilization process led by Afro-descendant organizations and activists is yielding some of its leaders' desired results. Nevertheless, in Buenos Aires, thousands of persons must contend daily with stigmatizing experiences that vary according to the ways (largely beyond their control) in which their skin colors and ways of being are perceived in a range of contexts. The stories of Nora, Paula, and Emilia allow us to glimpse how whitening and racialized categories operate and have operated locally, suppressing any possibility of mestizaje by driving to the extremes every intermediate case, ultimately reinforcing the dualistic system in which the poles of whiteness and *negritud* (both racial and popular) are the only viable categories for self-identification. Finding it impossible to be "detected" as black women from within the porteño visual classification system – because they fall outside the local parameters for perceiving signs of racial *negritud* – and finding it even less possible to identify as *mestizas* or *mulatas* – because the system is dualistic – Paula and Emilia are continuously driven toward one or the other of the extremes of the racial continuum. Even when they seek to claim racial *negritud* according to the blood or biological system of classification, they fail to be accepted as Afro-descendants by the rest of society. For them, there are no suitable categories available for self-identification. But neither can they imagine themselves in an intermediate situation: not only is their own subjectivity dualistic, but every intermediate category with which they might experiment ends up driving them back to one or the other extreme. Through a series of articulators among systems of categorization, the inhabitants of the gray zones are continually transported from a visual system of classification toward a biological one, and vice-versa, eliminating any chance of remaining in the middle zone or of generating something new. "Pardo," "moreno," "trigueño," "negro," and "afrodescendiente" are some of the most prominent terms that work interchangeably to signal either negritud or whiteness, according to the system within which a person is being categorized and from which the term is enunciated.

The elimination of the possibility of mestizaje in Buenos Aires has real consequences. It not only configures racial negritud as a radical and negative alterity, a discrimination borne daily by black Afro-Argentines (who until not so long ago were compelled to hide and suppress any trace of their blackness). But it also denies people who wish to claim non-European roots and/or traditions the ability to situate themselves outside of whiteness. Moreover, every Afro-descendant is forced to continuously demonstrate ways of being that distance him or her from the other kind of negritud, the popular one. Even though Paula, Nora, and Emilia do not suffer the harsh racism and derision that socially black people must cope with on a daily basis, their families' trajectories starkly reveal how a less obvious, but nonetheless tenacious, structural racism works in Buenos Aires: racial and popular negritud function together to mold bodies and behaviors, containing and discouraging different forms of blackness, and thereby undercutting any potential threat to whiteness. Indeed, the very dynamics and history of the production of the (partial) distinction between racial and popular negritud is itself a fundamental cog in this machinery, reinforcing whiteness once again as the only possible means of belonging in the city and nation. Through a range of coercive and disciplinary mechanisms at work since the late nineteenth century, the life trajectories of those who dwell on the margins of whiteness are confined to a very narrow set of choices in a city that ceaselessly polices and demarcates negritud in any of its forms. Fortunately, some choices do exist, and they are becoming ever more visible.

Notes

I would like to thank Paulina Alberto, Eduardo Elena, Mariela E. Rodríguez, and Florencia Guzmán for their invaluable insights on this work; and especially Paulina Alberto for her exquisite translation of this text, which made evident how languages sustain and contribute to reproducing some of the differences between racial systems. This work is dedicated to the memory of Valentina Mauriño and Mónica Quijada. TEIAA 2014SGR532/I+D+i MEC HAR2012-34095 (Spain).

1. Wilde, *Buenos Aires*, 61 (italics in the original).
2. See Gordillo, Chamosa, this volume. See also Briones, *Cartografías*; Escolar, *Los dones*; Guzmán, *Los claroscuros*.
3. On indigenous "extermination," see Rodríguez, this volume.
4. For refutations of these hypotheses, see especially Andrews, *Los afroargentinos*.

5. The disappearing of people is, sadly, one of the things for which Argentina is known, as nearly 30,000 people were abducted by the state during the last military government (1976–83). On the transformations in social categories that produced Afro-Argentines' "disappearance," see Andrews, *Los afroargentinos*; Frigerio, "Negros"; Geler, *Andares*; and Geler, "¡Pobres negros!"

6. Adamovsky, *Clase media*, 63.

7. See Salvatore, "Criminología"; Vallejo and Miranda, "Los saberes"; Stepan, *Hour*; Rodríguez, this volume.

8. See Briones, "Mestizaje"; Frigerio, "Negros"; Elena, Adamovsky, this volume.

9. Geler and Rodríguez, "Argentina." See also Margulis and Belvedere, "La racialización."

10. Margulis and Belvedere, in "La racialización," call this structure "racialized class relations."

11. Segato, "Alteridades," 15.

12. On Afro-descendant activism since the 1980s, see Frigerio and Lamborghini, "Los afroargentinos"; Frigerio and Lamborghini, "(De)Mostrando"; Lamborghini and Frigerio, "Quebrando."

13. The conference was held in Durban, South Africa in 2001.

14. The term allows the inclusion of different national origins (Afro-Uruguayans, Afro-Ecuadorians, etc.) in a movement of collective recognition. See Frigerio and Lamborghini, "Los afroargentinos," 30. See also Maffia, "La migración," on Cape Verdean migration to Argentina.

15. See Frigerio and Lamborghini, "Los afroargentinos"; Molina, "Por qué Afroargentin@s"; Cirio, "Afroargentino."

16. On the situatedness of classificatory categories, see Wade, "Race"; de la Cadena, "Introduction."

17. In order to preserve the interviewed women's privacy, all cited names are fictitious and the ages given are approximate. The interview with Nora took place in Madrid (2008). The interviews with Paula (2010) and Emilia (2011) took place in Buenos Aires.

18. In describing a person as white or black, I follow anthropologist Luis Ferreira's idea that people are "socially" black or "socially" white. That is to say that perceptions and recognition of race and color are never simply "natural" but always respond to socially constructed, historically situated, and contingent classifications. Ferreira, "Música."

19. The term designates the discontinuous territoriality and heterogeneous temporality that includes state institutions and other public offices, groups, families and individuals of African origin, networks of Afro-descendants, students, researchers, etc. Fernández Bravo, "Qué hacemos," 243.

20. See Rodríguez, Chamosa, this volume; Guzmán, "Performatividad."

21. Quijada, "Imaginando."

22. Étienne Balibar speaks of the invisible ethnicity of the nation, which in the Argentine case would be "European." Here, I want to highlight the other facet of this nation's invisible ethnicity, which is "white" raciality. Balibar, "La forma nación."

23. The same happens with people seen as "Asian." See Ko, this volume; Balibar, "La forma nación."

24. Frigerio, "Negros."

25. Historically in the United States, even when a person did not display any visual traits assigned to the black race, he or she could be classified in the judicial system

as black due to family background. Such rules, however, could in some situations be challenged by performances of whiteness and "common sense" understandings of a person's race. See Gross, *Blood*. The "one drop rule" became less stable once the Supreme Court overturned laws banning miscegenation in 1967.

26. Frigerio, "Negros."
27. Frigerio, "Negros"; Andrews, *Los afroargentinos*.
28. Hall, "Spectacle."
29. In the last decade or so, the growing presence and visibility of migrants from Sub-Saharan Africa to Buenos Aires has unveiled the persistence of this kind of racism. See Morales, "Representaciones." On state racism, see Espiro and Zubrzycki, "Tensiones."
30. Negritud could be translated as "blackness," but I keep the Spanish word to emphasize that racialized and racializing signs are socially and historically specific, and do not result from natural or self-evident differences that can be easily transferred from region to region. On a similar use of "negridad," see Restrepo, *Intervenciones*, 195.
31. Nevertheless, this kind of *negritud* is often xenophobically used to describe immigrants, especially Latin American ones; it is often applied to indigenous peoples or their descendants as well, with the effect of expelling them from the national imaginary. See Briones, "Mestizaje," and Gordillo, Rodríguez, this volume.
32. Note the interesting phonetic recurrence in the words *grotesco* [grotesque], *grosero* [rude, uneducated], *grone* [slang for black], *groncho* [black and tacky], and *grasa* [tacky], often used to diminish lower-class people and anyone lacking in education or manners. Note too the resemblance between "groncho" and "*morocho* [a term for people with dark hair or skin]."
33. Lamborghini and Frigerio, "Quebrando," 140 (Cf. Frigerio, "Negros.") See also Frigerio, "Luis D'Elia"; Ratier, *El cabecita negra*; Margulis and Belvedere, "La racialización"; Gordillo, this volume. Scholars of other Argentine provinces are currently investigating how categorial ambiguity works in a similar fashion to designate racial/social alterities. Lina Picconi (personal communication); Fernández Bravo, "El regreso."
34. This duality is central to the emergence of whiteness as an ideological structure and to its power. Echeverría, *Modernidad*.
35. On whiteness as a civilizing system, see Echeverría, *Modernidad*.
36. On the middle classes' whiteness, see Adamovsky, *Clase media*; Garguin, "Los Argentinos."
37. See Alberto, this volume.
38. Emphasis mine. Nora is referring to Colonel Domingo Sosa, a renowned Afro-Argentine military officer of the nineteenth century, who was also appointed congressman. His portrait usually appears in books about Afro-Argentines due to his outstanding trajectory.
39. *Malambo* is an Argentine folkloric dance that involves drums and heel-and-toe tapping. Today it is believed to have African and Spanish roots.
40. Emphasis mine.
41. In fact, music and dance have become one of the main focuses of the Afro revisibilization movement in Buenos Aires, given these activities' apparent ability to capture the public's attention and to position Afro people and cultures in a favorable light. See Frigerio and Lamborghini, "(De)mostrando." Dance and music have been configured as repositories of memory for Afro-descendant families in

Argentina: because until not so long ago every non-European cultural expression was repressed or negatively valued, dance and music went deep into the private sphere of Afro-descendant communities. See Frigerio, *Cultura negra*; Geler, *Andares*. However, Afro-descendants are far from unanimous in their views of the virtues of this strategy for revindicating African culture and Afro-descendant identities.

42. Briones, "Mestizaje."
43. Emphasis mine.
44. Andrews, *Los afroargentinos.*
45. See Geler, "Un personaje"; Frigerio, "Negros."
46. Emphasis mine.
47. The dictionary of the *Real Academia Española* defines "cuarterón/a" as coming from "quarter" (having a quarter of Indian ancestry and three quarters of Spanish): "Adj. Born in America from Spanish and *mestiza/o*." I believe the use Nora makes of "cuarterona" has more to do with her living in Spain than with a specific knowledge of the term's historical meaning.
48. In colonial Spanish America, categories that referred to people's "quality" combined a range of systems for marking difference – visual, moral, sociability-based, and of so-called purity of blood – all of which worked in complex and intertwined ways and were marked by what anthropologist Anne-Marie Losonczy has dubbed "phenotypic uncertainty." Losonczy, "El criollo," 266; Guzmán, "Performatividad"; Rappaport, "¿Quién es?"
49. On the United States, see Hill Collins, *Black Feminist.*
50. Contrary, in principle, to the (assimilatable or modifiable) alterity that indigenous people supposedly represent. Briones, "Mestizaje."
51. Devoto and Madero, "Introduction."
52. Emphasis mine.
53. See Di Meglio, *¡Viva el bajo…!*
54. See Geler, "Afrodescendencia"; Geler, "Un personaje"; Geler, "¿Quién no ha sido?"
55. Geler, *Andares.*
56. This process, as it concerns Afro-porteños at the end of the nineteenth century, can be called "ethnicization," following anthropologist Claudia Briones' conception of an alterity-marking process that, being based on "cultural" differences, allows passage from one category to another. Briones, "Mestizaje." On the process of ethnicization among Afro-porteños, see Geler, "¡Pobres negros!"
57. Note the correlation between, on one hand, these lines of action as defended by Afro-porteño intellectuals committed to improving their community, and, on the other, the national laws passed in order to "improve" the population, as cited in the introduction to this chapter. This overlap reveals the reach and hegemony of state-sponsored ideas about progress among the Afro-porteño leadership. See Geler, *Andares.*
58. On images of blacks as servants, see Geler, *Andares.*
59. Di Santo, *El canto*, 9.
60. Bernardo González Arrili described the black population of 1900s Buenos Aires as follows: "Any one of them […] could give us a lesson in manners or urbanity […]. The *morenos* were usually courteous." González Arrili, *Buenos Aires*, 119. In the same vein, Alfredo Taullard recalled "In the 1890s some blacks were still visible in

the army, and the most 'refined' worked as orderlies in state offices. They were, it should also be said, more solicitous and accomplished than many of today's 'whites.'" Taullard, *Nuestro antiguo*, 357. See also Alberto's insightful analysis of the many representations of the famous porteño character "el Negro Raúl," and the way this kind of description could be used by Afro-descendants themselves to mock elite groups. Alberto, "Títere roto."

61. Geler, *Andares*; Geler, "¿Quién no ha sido?"
62. Frigerio, "Negros."
63. Emphasis mine.
64. Paula now uses her mother's surname, which links her to her famous Afro-Argentine great-grandfather.

9

The savage outside of White Argentina

Gastón Gordillo

In early December 2013, several urban centers in Argentina experienced a wave of turmoil that brought to light the sensibilities that have historically racialized the national geography – a racialization whose existence has long been denied by Argentine official discourse. In the province of Córdoba, thousands of police officers demanded a salary increase by withdrawing from the streets and remaining in their barracks, while undercover officers instigated the looting of stores in order to create a public demand for their presence. The news of the lack of police repression quickly spread, and thousands of men and women from poor neighborhoods began storming stores and supermarkets to grab anything they could, from food to television sets. The unrest spread to other provinces, most notably Tucumán, where the same pattern of a police walkout and subsequent looting unfolded.[1] With several cities shaken by riots, a significant portion of the population felt that the streets were dissolving amid a vortex formed by the expansiveness of *los negros* [the blacks] – the racialized term used in contemporary Argentina to name the poor and people of indigenous or *mestizo* [mixed] background.

On the streets as well as in social media and the online forums of Argentine newspapers, thousands of people called for the violent extermination of "*esos negros de mierda* [those fucking blacks]." Armed vigilantes promptly began shooting at "los negros" as if the latter were savage hordes determined to overrun settlers circling the wagons on a hostile frontier. When *La Nación* (Argentina's leading conservative newspaper) informed its readers that "a young man" was shot dead in Córdoba, marking the first deadly victim of the violence, most readers posting comments on the paper's online edition celebrated his death as an act of civilizing justice. Many objected to the use of the phrase "a young man" to name what was just a negro. One reader further dehumanized the victim by declaring, "Too bad it's only one. I wish there were two hundred negros dead."[2] Similar comments flooded Twitter under the hashtag #*Negros de mierda*. When the violence subsided two days later – after the federal government sent forces to Córdoba and the provincial government there and in Tucumán acquiesced to police demands – over ten people were dead and hundreds were wounded. During these incidents, many commentators compared the looters with the Indians who threatened the boundaries of civilized space in earlier centuries. Conservative writer Abel Posse wrote in *La Nación* that in Tucumán a relative of his borrowed a shotgun, formed a vigilante patrol, and locked up his wife and children. He felt as if *"un malón"* was about to attack their home, evoking the raiding parties of indigenous combatants on horseback who once controlled much of what is now national territory.[3]

It is important to think about this wave of unrest – and how it was profoundly racialized – in the context of Argentina's self-positioning as a white and racially homogeneous nation. Even in the face of these events, Argentine political and cultural elites continued to insist that "[in Argentina,] we don't have problems of racism." I personally heard center-left presidential candidate Raúl Alfonsín repeat this line with conviction at several speeches during his 1983 campaign, and almost two decades later conservative writer Marcos Aguinis began his book on the Argentine condition making exactly the same claim.[4] Yet in Argentina this self-congratulatory narrative about a racism-free society has long coexisted with the everyday use of a heavily racialized language to name, with disdain, "esos negros de mierda": the millions of Argentines who are explicitly marked as the despised nonwhite part of the nation. This racialization is part of a hierarchical class formation, for "los negros" also names the poor. Indeed, many Argentines deny that the term is a racial slur because it also names a class position, thereby subsuming race to class. However, that the poor are called "los negros" and *not* something else actually reveals how racial sensibilities inform perceptions about class in Argentina. And when "the blacks" appear as a menacing presence on the streets, as in late 2013, it is common to hear passionate calls – entangled with openly racist slurs – for their extermination, on the grounds that "los negros" are dangerous and not fully human.

Several scholars have noted this contradiction in Argentina between claims to racial homogeneity and tolerance and the everyday reality of a profoundly racialized and racist society.[5] As anthropologist Alejandro Grimson aptly put it, in Argentina the same person can claim to live in a white nation without racism and add, shortly thereafter, that half of the population is made up of "negros de mierda."[6] This tense oscillation is certainly at the core of the specific configuration of whiteness in Argentina, but its affective and spatial dimensions have been overlooked. Grimson and other authors have tackled this paradox by arguing that whiteness in Argentina is a myth or an ideology: a discourse that misrecognizes the existence of millions of Argentines of indigenous and mestizo background and seeks to make invisible, and therefore legitimize, racialized forms of hierarchy. Whiteness in Argentina does, indeed, have mythical and ideological dimensions, but I argue that it can be better understood as *an affective and geographic formation* that is in denial of its existence *because* it is not reducible to a conscious ideology and operates at a pre-discursive, emotional level.

In this chapter, I propose to name this racialized disposition toward space as *La Argentina Blanca*, White Argentina. I do not conceive of this term, it is important to note, as a bounded entity made up of Argentines of white skin. Many of the harshest critics of La Argentina Blanca are light-skinned Argentines with blue eyes (such as writer Osvaldo Bayer or musician León Gieco) and some of its staunchest defenders have dark skin and indigenous ancestry (like the former governor of Salta province, Juan Carlos Romero). I conceive of White Argentina, first and foremost, as a geographical project and an affective disposition defined by the not always conscious desire to create, define, and *feel* through the bodily navigation of space that the national geography is largely European. But this is a haunted and ever-incomplete project, a whiteness that feels under siege, for it permanently confronts the evidence that millions of Argentine citizens bear in their bodies the traces of the non-European substratum of the nation. White Argentina, in this regard, is an affect in the relational, inter-subjective, and material sense that philosopher Baruch Spinoza gives to this concept: the capacity to affect and to be affected by other bodies.[7] And few things affect White Argentina more profoundly than the appearance in prominent public spaces of expansive multitudes of "negros."

The affective nature of White Argentina is apparent in its visceral reaction to events like those of December 2013. While riots create anxiety and fear in any social setting, in Argentina these fears usually trigger widespread calls for the mass murder of "los negros," embodied in the cry *"a esos negros de mierda hay que matarlos a todos* [those fucking blacks should all be killed]." These calls for civilizing and genocidal violence (i.e., this desire to kill *all* negros) are rationalized as a condemnation of criminality; but they primarily express rage at the evidence that Argentina is *not* a white nation. The appearance of dark-skinned multitudes affects White Argentina as if these bodies could open up, from within the nation, a huge and expanding crack that reveals a terrifying vortex located "outside" Argentina: an abyss that resurrects "el malón" that the founding fathers of White Argentina thought they had exterminated in the late 1800s and that Abel Posse's relative in Tucumán *felt* had reappeared in December 2013.

El malón is one of the most extraordinary figures in Argentine history: it alludes to the indigenous cavalries that for centuries launched stealthy, high-speed attacks on frontier settlements in the Pampas (the prairies of central Argentina) and in the tropical lowlands of the Gran Chaco region (in the North), which in some cases reached the gates of Buenos Aires, Córdoba, and Santa Fe and eroded the boundaries of state territoriality. As a military configuration, el malón was destroyed by the Argentine state in the 1870s and 1880s. But el malón can also be examined as a spatial, bodily, and affective formation that outlived its original historical conditions. The old trope of el malón as a masculinized, predatory barbarism that threatened the feminized domesticity of civilized homes is still evoked in Argentina.[8] When in the twenty-first century the term "malón" is used to name looters or simply the poor taking to the streets, it suggests the bodily return of this gendered, feared barbarism from the past.

The "blackness" referenced by the colloquial uttering of the term "los negros" in Argentina, therefore, does not name African phenotypes – even if, depending on context, the word can be used in this sense as well. Ironically, White Argentina has long claimed that the country is racism-free "because we *don't* have negros," meaning *in this specific instance* black people of African ancestry.[9] This is a remarkable phrase that admits that racism would indeed exist if the country had a sizable Afro-Argentine population and, at the same time, *erases* the fact that that Argentina *does* have millions of "negros" who are subjected to racist gestures and discrimination because of their indigenous phenotypes and class background. In sum, in Argentina the nonwhiteness referenced in the phrase "esos negros de mierda" primarily evokes the legacy of the human constellations that controlled this area of South America prior to European conquest: those indigenous, mestizo conglomerates *against* which the nation's leaders defined their whitening efforts.

Philosopher Jacques Derrida argued that the ghost is something that seemed to have disappeared but always returns, reappearing again and again.[10] To speak of specters, he wrote, is to speak of their return. It is in this sense that el malón can be said to be a ghostly figure in Argentine history: a force that had allegedly been destroyed but that continues to return, haunting those who dream of a White Argentina.

THE AFFECTIVE HEGEMONY OF A BESIEGED PROJECT

A rich literature has taught us that race and whiteness are not biological objects but bio-political constructs used to divide up human beings in units allegedly different from each other. Whiteness, blackness, mestizaje, or indigeneity are shifting, conjunctural social positionings whose meanings and boundaries are arbitrary, negotiable, slippery, and policed. But more importantly perhaps, these racialized positionings are profoundly spatialized. What defines whiteness all over the world is that it is a geographical project. As theorist Sarah Ahmed has argued, whiteness "orientates bodies in specific directions, affecting how they 'take up' space."[11] But the spatial orientations defining whiteness have very diverse expressions. In the southern United States under Jim Crow, in Nazi Germany, in Apartheid South Africa, and in the Israeli-occupied territories of Palestine, this bodily orientation has demanded the creation of legally enforced forms of separation from nonwhite bodies perceived to be inferior, polluting, and threatening. In South America, racialized forms of spatial segregation have been less extreme but have existed in multiple forms. In Bolivia, for instance, parts of downtown la Paz were "whites only" places, legally off limits for indigenous people until the 1950s.[12]

In Argentina, whiteness has been a spatial and bodily orientation that in contrast to these other racialized geographies sought to *un-mark* its racial foundations by way of one of the most ambitious projects of social engineering ever devised: the attempt to *thoroughly replace* prior populations with people implanted from Europe.[13] This led to the founding myth of White Argentina, which is the story that White Argentina has long told itself about itself: that beginning in the late 1800s, European migration was so massive and the extermination of Indians so extreme that Argentina became socially homogeneous: that is, white. As historian Mónica Quijada has argued, "It is difficult to find a case in which the pressure to homogenize has been so successful in the consolidation of a collective perception of a nation allegedly uniform in cultural, ethnic, and racial terms."[14] This included the perception that this homogenization was a spatially productive force that had recoded the national geography as white.

Any hegemonic disposition implies what anthropologist Ann Stoler calls an affective condition of disregard: that is, a failure to fully notice particular features of society, which may be partly registered but are promptly relegated "to the edges of awareness."[15] In Argentina, the hegemony of the disposition to feel and desire that the national space is white implied disregarding those nonwhite places and bodies that haunted it from the edges of its own awareness. The scholarship on race has shown that in many parts of the world whiteness tends to be naturalized and made invisible as the non-racial normal, thereby projecting explicit "racial" features onto nonwhite bodies.[16] This normalization and invisibilization of whiteness became particularly deep in Argentina. The contrast to the United States or South Africa is illustrative: in those parts of the world it was always apparent, particularly at the level of policy, that dominant forms of whiteness had to confront the unavoidable presence of large nonwhite multitudes. In those countries, people of European ancestry are permanently confronted with the word that names them as "whites," and with which they identify. In notable contrast, the term *los blancos* (the whites) is hardly if ever used in Argentina to name the people who claim European ancestry, for whiteness has long been assumed to be the generalized *normal* that does *not* need to be named. But by obsessively naming "los negros" as the nonwhite part of the nation, this common sense inadvertently admits that whiteness in Argentina is an ever-incomplete spatial project that generates frustration and often rage. This is why White Argentina is a haunted, reactive project, which often acts as if the immense nonwhiteness of the nation did not exist and, then, cannot but react with contempt and calls for repressive violence at the appearance of multitudes of "negros de mierda."

This attitude reveals an affective resistance to fully accepting that people who do not look European are, or could be, full-fledged Argentine citizens. White Argentina has regarded the presence of dark-skinned bodies in the national territory as foreign intrusions, or, at most, as quaint relics from a vanishing past. In an incident in 1999, for instance, three Argentine brothers from Buenos Aires were detained at the Buenos Aires international airport and forced to miss their flight to the United States because officials thought they were too dark-skinned to be Argentines and assumed that their passports were forged. Officials mistreated, strip-searched, and insulted these men, calling them "*boliguayos*," a racist slur aimed at Bolivians and Paraguayans.[17]

The hegemonic nature of the predisposition to assume that "normal" Argentines are white is not restricted to openly right-wing, reactionary, or elite actors; rather, it is shared and accepted as natural by people in different social classes and with very different ideologies, as we shall see. The expression "esos negros de mierda," in fact, can also be heard in shantytowns and working-class districts, where people with mestizo phenotypes may use it to name neighbors viewed as undesirable or prone to criminality. Yet while the hegemony of White Argentina cuts across class boundaries, it is most apparent in the middle and upper classes. The whitening of Argentine space, after all, has historically been the project of the national elites who violently expropriated vast indigenous territories. The main actors and institutions defending the principles of White Argentina have been the landowning elites, conservative newspapers like *La Nación*, and institutions like the armed forces and La Sociedad Rural (the most powerful and elite landowning association). In this chapter I focus often on this social segment to illustrate some of the most paradigmatic expressions of White Argentina, while also revealing its affective influence among other actors and classes.

As with any hegemonic formation, the effort to create a European nation in South America has always been a contested project, opposed and challenged from very different positionings. In the pages that follow, I present a spatial and affective history of these contestations, which in the past decades have in fact gained more traction and have significantly eroded the old common sense that defined White Argentina.

THE "CONQUEST OF THE DESERT": THE FOUNDATIONAL VIOLENCE OF WHITE ARGENTINA

Argentina's early post-independence history was defined by a remarkable spatial configuration, one that was unique in South America. Between the 1810s and 1880s, over half of the territory that the new republic claimed as its own – the Pampas, Patagonia, and the Gran Chaco – was in the hands of politically autonomous indigenous societies. While these groupings also engaged with Argentine state actors through trade, wage labor, and political alliances, what best embodied their territorial autonomy was their power to generate malones that openly challenged and negated the spatial expansion of state power.

The book *Facundo: Civilization and Barbarism*, published in 1845 by journalist and future president Domingo Sarmiento, is the foundational text of White Argentina for one simple reason: Sarmiento opens his text by declaring that he feels overwhelmed by the vastness of the geography controlled by "savage hordes," a geography that he famously called "*el desierto* [the desert]." This desert did not allude to a topography devoid of water or vegetation but to a savage outside: a spatial nothingness beyond the reach of state power, civilization, and capitalism. And what voided this space were "the savages" controlling it. Sarmiento had already articulated the affective, visceral nature of White Argentina when he wrote elsewhere that he felt "an invincible repugnance" for "the savages of the Americas" and that their "extermination" would be "providential" and "sublime."[18] In *Facundo*, he added a geographical dimension to this "repugnance" when he wrote that one feels the desert "*en las entrañas* [in the guts]."[19] Nausea is a visceral, pre-discursive reflex against a feared, unwanted object that is felt as a negative pressure on the body. This is what Spinoza called the "sad passion" of bodies that react negatively to how other bodies affect them, without fully understanding what happens to them.[20] And what distinguishes nausea as a collective affect is that it calls for violence on the nauseating object in order to eliminate that feeling of disgust. The creation of a white, civilized Argentina therefore demanded an expansive violence of epic proportions, able to exterminate the Indians, dissolve their *malones*, and destroy "the desert."

While the project to create a nation free of "repugnant savages" drew from attitudes first cultivated during the period of Spanish colonialism, White Argentina forged its foundational identity through what it presented as a civilizing, nation-building enterprise: "the Conquest of the Desert."[21] General Julio A. Roca became the military hero of White Argentina for leading the 1879 campaign by the federal army to the Pampas and northern Patagonia and for presiding over the 1884 campaign to the Chaco during his first presidency (1880–86). Both campaigns destroyed the strongest military segments of indigenous political assemblages. In the 1860s, as governor of San Juan, Sarmiento had anticipated Roca by ordering the massacre of rebellious *gauchos* (rural workers of mestizo background), for whom he also felt repugnance as savages whose blood, he claimed, should be shed in abundance.[22] In a few decades, the national elites defeated subaltern and indigenous armed resistance, expropriated vast tracts of land, and encouraged massive migration from southern and eastern Europe.

The destruction of "the desert" left behind myriad mass graves, from Tierra del Fuego in the south to the Pilcomayo River in the north.[23] And this violence was followed by efforts to create a new, positive geography. The production of European-looking places was most successful in the cities of Buenos Aires and Rosario and in the region re-named "*la pampa gringa* [the Gringo Pampas]," encompassed by the provinces of Santa Fe, Entre Ríos, southern Córdoba, and northern and central Buenos Aires. This became the heart of White Argentina: the region where the majority of European migrants settled and where former indigenous territories were most dramatically erased. In the national capital of Buenos Aires, whole areas of the city, especially elite neighborhoods, were made to look and feel like a European metropolis; indeed, there are few things that White Argentina finds more gratifying than hearing Europeans or North Americans refer to Buenos Aires as "The Paris of South America," for this seems to confirm that Argentina has, indeed, become white. Similar architectonic projects were also implemented in parts of Patagonia, where towns like Bariloche were built in an effort to replicate the Swiss and German Alps.[24]

Amid this spatially expansive whiteness, the descendants of defeated indigenous groups were for decades denied citizenship rights and treated either as vanishing relics or as ongoing threats.[25] Especially in the Chaco, state agents continued massacring indigenous people over several decades, as the killing of hundreds of men and women in Napalpí in 1924 illustrates.[26] But since White Argentina was also a class project, the national elites did not hesitate to unleash similar levels of terror on European immigrants who, inspired by socialist and anarchist values, threatened the status quo. The massacre of hundreds of European workers in the streets of Buenos Aires in 1919 or on the sheep ranches of southern Patagonia in 1921 confirms that the elites who dreamed of a White Argentina had in mind, first and foremost, a hierarchical project of class domination.[27]

Throughout the twentieth century, officials and scholars repeatedly presented the whitening of the nation as a project that had been successful. In the early 1900s, for instance, it was possible to hear an elite judge proudly argue that Argentina "is the only white country of Latin America."[28] Even liberal critics of the so-called Conquest of the Desert participated in this trope of homogenization when they lamented that indigenous people had been "exterminated."[29] More notably, this image of a white nation was quantified and repeated as hard fact in textbooks and official documents that argued that Argentina was "97 percent white, 2 percent mestizo, and 1 percent indigenous." These figures are notable because they imply that Argentina had become the *whitest* nation in the world, for not even in Scandinavian countries do whites make up "97 percent" of the population. Needless to say, these percentages were performative gestures that were, literally, invented. In the late 1800s, the efforts to homogenize the nation included dropping the unwanted term *indio* (and in fact all racial categories) from the national census, which means that there was no way of knowing how many Argentines had little or no European background.[30] In school textbooks, that minuscule percentage of nonwhiteness was presented as being restricted to those areas of "the North" that had been less affected by Europeanization. This whitening also involved silencing the noticeable presence of descendants of slaves of African background in Buenos Aires and other provinces in the nineteenth century.[31]

The industrialization and urban expansion that Argentina experienced in the 1930s and 1940s, however, attracted to the city and suburbs of Buenos Aires working-class multitudes from rural areas that had not been Europeanized. These male and female migrants brought with them a nonwhiteness that had officially been declared extinct; for this reason, their presence in the national capital affected White Argentina as an unsettling force.

THE RESURRECTION OF EL MALÓN: THE INVASION OF "LOS CABECITAS NEGRAS"

Beginning in the 1940s, the growing presence of working-class bodies with little or no European ancestry in the urban fabric of Buenos Aires, their political mobilization against the privileges of the landed aristocracy, and the rise of Peronism represented traumatic trends for the actors who had dreamed of a White Argentina. On October 17, 1945, this trauma was embodied in a ghostly apparition of sorts: the unexpected materialization of huge working-class, mestizo multitudes that converged on downtown Buenos Aires to demand the release of Colonel Juan Domingo Perón, briefly jailed by the military regime (1943–46) of which he had been part. Many urban residents and commentators experienced this multitude as the return of el malón, as an invasion that "took over" the city.[32] A few months later, in February 1946, Perón was elected president in a landslide victory and his government expanded the social rights of the poor and the working class, eroded older political hierarchies, and confused prior spatial taxonomies. In this conjuncture, the terms *"los cabecitas negras* [little blackheads]" (originally the name of a bird) and "los negros" emerged to name those dark-skinned multitudes now visible in the capital city and who were instrumental in the rise of Peronism as a new and powerful political movement.[33]

Under the first Perón presidencies (1946–55), the presence of "los cabecitas" in Buenos Aires affected the traditional elites "in the guts." For conservative politician Adolfo Mugica, the country was now immersed in *"una inmensa merienda de negros* [an immense bedlam of negros]." Another observer noticed with horror that Peronist rallies were mostly made up of "mestizos and even Indians," and that Argentina was being "blackened [*se negrea*]."[34] Openly racist and classist observations of this kind were made even in formal settings. In 1947, a member of Congress declared with disgust that an *"aluvión zoológico"* [a zoological flood]" had engulfed the city of Buenos Aires.

In this period, many anti-Peronists complained explicitly that this barbarian invasion felt like the return of el malón.[35] This resurrection contradicted the assumption that Argentina's indigenous people had been exterminated. As a man cited by anthropologist Hugo Ratier put it, "We thought that many tribes were extinct, but a visit to Plaza Italia [a public space in the elegant Buenos Aires neighborhood of Palermo] made us change our minds."[36] As part of these recurring references to Peronist rallies as comprised of "Indians," the daily *La Nación* dubbed Perón "the chief of the tribe."[37] This spatial expansion of Peronist "Indians" generated vertigo and nausea. In an anti-Peronist magazine, a person was asked what he thought of "the sweating masses" that supported Perón. He replied, "They make me feel nauseous!"[38] Given that nausea calls for the suppression of its source, a journalist who wrote that "el malón" had returned to the city argued that "this evil" should be "totally extirpated."[39] Historian Ezequiel Adamovsky has shown that in Argentina the idea of a middle-class identity emerged as a reaction against the empowerment of the working class under Peronism.[40] By the same token, these emerging middle classes saw themselves as white in opposition to the expansive presence of "los cabecitas negras" and influenced by the racialized sensibilities of the elites.

Yet because White Argentina was by then a hegemonic field that operated through a common sense that was not reducible to particular ideological discourses, the Peronist governments eroded some of its most overtly racialized and hierarchical premises while reproducing many others.

EL MALÓN DE LA PAZ: THE LIMITS OF PERONIST CRIOLLISMO

As historian Oscar Chamosa has argued, the Peronism of the 1940s and 1950s defied the normalization of whiteness in Argentina by celebrating the *criollo* and thereby mestizo traditions of the Northwest.[41] Drawing from earlier criollista celebrations of the gauchos of the 1800s and of their subaltern rural world, Peronist officials made frequent references to "criollos" and supported the public dissemination of their folklore, music, and dances. In another significant break with dominant ideologies, the Peronist government officially declared that indigenous people were also Argentines by granting them, for the first time, citizenship rights and by distributing national identity documents in indigenous villages where people were undocumented.[42]

These moves partly eroded the idea of Argentina as a white and homogeneous nation, but they did not go deep enough. Peronism lacked an explicit policy toward indigenous people and reproduced a prior disregard for their plight.[43] Likewise, its celebration of criollos was a tension-free and depoliticized allusion to racial mixture that, in fact, sought to whiten the population. The word "mestizo," tellingly, was rarely if ever mentioned and references to "criollos" downplayed the indigenous legacies that had created them.[44] Chamosa as well as historian Eduardo Elena (in chapter seven of this volume) show that officials avoided mentioning or criticizing the racism to which criollos and cabecitas were subjected. Peronist ideology, in this regard, acknowledged the mestizo component of the nation yet did so only tangentially, and the movement's authorities were careful to emphasize that Argentina was a country "without racism" defined by "racial harmony."

In 1946, these contradictions became apparent during a march by indigenous people named, notably, *El Malón de la Paz* [The Malón of Peace]. Organized by indigenous people to demand land titles in the northwest of the country, this march was their first major collective attempt to assert that they were a constitutive part of Argentina. It was therefore a foundational moment of the indigenous movement in the country. Coordinated by a non-indigenous army officer sympathetic to their cause, 174 men and women walked from the highlands of Jujuy to Buenos Aires on a three-month trek. The name of the march reveals, once again, the symbolism of el malón as an expression of indigenous assertiveness, this time moving from the margins of the nation to Argentina's capital. But this malón was choreographed as a peaceful and respectful march, very different from the malones of the past. This malón stood for "peace," which implicitly accepted that the malones of combatants on horseback had been defeated. As El Malón de la Paz advanced toward Buenos Aires, its tranquil demeanor gained relative visibility and media attention in a country that had not witnessed this type of public protest by indigenous people. The presence of the army officer leading the malón further contributed to making it relatively palatable to state authorities and to generating expressions of public sympathy, at least during its slow trek to the national capital.[45]

In Buenos Aires, the march was welcomed by curious Peronist crowds, but nationalist and fascist groups protested the presence of indios in the city.[46] Perón and members of Congress briefly received the group. Yet officials promptly placed the 174 men and women in the Hotel de Inmigrantes, which was used to house recently arrived foreigners. As writer Marcelo Valko has pointed out, the symbolism was clear: El Malón de la Paz was a foreign entity that did not really belong in Argentina.[47] More importantly, a few weeks later officers forced the group out of the hotel and loaded them, using batons and tear gas, on freight trains that took them back to Jujuy. Perón subsequently declared that the Malón de la Paz did not represent "the authentic indigenous inhabitant of our North."[48] Although in the following years the government responded to the protest by expropriating some estates in Salta and Jujuy and banning labor servitude, it did not radically alter the land tenure system of the Northwest. Most notably, one of the worst massacres of indigenous people in national history took place under the first Peronist government. In October 1947, *gendarmería* (the military border police) slaughtered, over several days, close to six hundred Pilagá men and women in Formosa, amid unfounded rumors that they were about to launch "un malón."[49]

Despite their more inclusive rhetoric and policies, Peronist officials tended to view indigenous people as not fully belonging in the nation, except as exotic relics destined to dissolve into the nation's "racial crucible [*crizol de razas*]." The assumptions that defined White Argentina had become part of the common sense of different classes and sectors and were accepted as normal by people with different ideologies. Yet the disposition to feel that Argentina ought to be white continued having a class core, embodied in the elites who felt a particularly visceral contempt for "los cabecitas negras."

TERROR AS SPATIAL FORCE: THE REASSERTION
OF WHITE ARGENTINA

When the armed forces and the national elites, with substantial support from the middle classes, toppled Perón in the 1955 coup, they sought not only to negate the legacy of Peronism but also to reassert some of the racialized parameters of White Argentina as a geographic and violent project. This violence began in the failed coup attempt against Perón in June 1955, when rebel airplanes machine-gunned, bombed, and massacred hundreds of civilians who were in Plaza de Mayo demonstrating in favor of the government. When Perón was finally toppled in September 1955, the spatially expansive presence of "los cabecitas negras" in Buenos Aires was contained. "You no longer see cabecitas downtown," a supporter of the coup noted with sarcasm.[50] El malón had been repelled from Buenos Aires and the savage outside had dissipated.

With the threat of Peronist populism apparently contained, the phrase "cabecita negra" gradually disappeared from everyday language.[51] But darkskinned men and women continued moving from rural areas to the city and began concentrating in the first *villas miserias* [shantytowns] in Buenos Aires and its outskirts. These people came to be known as *villeros* and *negros*, and while they were politically contained throughout the 1960s, their poverty and nonwhiteness continued creating an unsettling presence, which lurked on the margins of the Europeanized core of the city.

By the early 1970s, however, this containment was yet again eroded, this time by the rapid rise and expansion of leftist and revolutionary movements that, drawing on mestizo and pro-Latin American imaginaries, became openly hostile to the idea of a White Argentina. Not surprisingly, the Montoneros, the most powerful guerrilla organization to emerge in those days, was named after *las montoneras*: the insurgent cavalries created by gauchos in the 1800s to fight the pro-European liberal elites who were also dreaming of a White Argentina. For radicalized youths of European background committed to overthrowing "the oligarchy," the assertiveness of these gaucho malones thus became a symbol of revolutionary struggle. The charged political climate of the early 1970s also witnessed a rise in indigenous activism. Land invasions, grassroots mobilizations, and demonstrations by indigenous people erupted from Patagonia to the Chaco, in some instances with support from revolutionary organizations.[52] It was in this politicized environment that Peronist activist and anthropologist Hugo Ratier broached the taboo topic that earlier generations of Peronists had not dared to confront: the structural racism of Argentine society. In 1972, Ratier documented this racism in gripping detail and with ironic wit in his groundbreaking book *El cabecita negra*, which examined the anti-Peronist hatred for the nonwhite poor in the 1940s.

In 1973, the left-wing Peronist government of Héctor Cámpora took office celebrating the Latin American character of the nation and attacking "the oligarchy" amid huge, resonant multitudes taking over the streets of Buenos Aires. White Argentina experienced its darkest hour. Those who desired to build a white nation felt cornered by hordes that blended subaltern savagery with the threat of impending revolution. But soon afterward, Cámpora stepped down to let a now-elderly Perón return from his exile in Franco's

Spain. An alliance among Perón, right-wing Peronists, the military, and the old national elites promptly terminated the revolutionary spring of 1973–74. The paramilitary assassinations of 1974–75 and the impact of several large-scale guerrilla operations rapidly led to the military coup of March 1976 and a full-fledged campaign of state terrorism that tortured and murdered close to 30,000 people. The state crushed the rebel multitudes through sheer terror.

The 1976–83 dictatorship was the most violent embodiment yet of the project and affective dispositions of White Argentina. In 1979, the military regime made its genealogy apparent by honoring the mythical origins of White Argentina with large celebrations and military parades that hailed General Roca and the centennial of the Conquest of the Desert. As thirteen-year-olds starting high school in 1979, my classmates and I were made to read the book *La guerra al malón* [War on the Malón] by Manuel Prado, a military officer who fought indigenous combatants in the Pampas in the late 1800s.[53] Reading *La guerra al malón* during the most repressive regime in national history, we were reminded that the project to turn Argentina into a European nation had confronted equally savage enemies in the past and in the present, from indigenous and gaucho malones to subversive urban multitudes.

During the dictatorship years, officials emphasized that the violence unleashed by the military regime was a spatially cleansing force, which hoped to rid Argentina of "*elementos ajenos al ser nacional* [elements alien to the national being]." Because this terror sought to prevent revolution and to discipline the subaltern classes in a sweeping fashion, it unleashed violence regardless of the victims' skin color. But the state violence of the late 1970s also sought to whiten space through the destruction of places of perceived barbarism. In 1977, Osvaldo Cacciatore, the air force brigadier who acted as Buenos Aires' mayor during the dictatorship, launched an ambitious project to remove and destroy the city's shantytowns, whose steady growth generated anxieties in middle- and upper-class neighborhoods. The plan also responded to the regime's goal of enhancing the global image of Argentina as a civilized (and white) nation in preparation for the 1978 World Cup. Close to 200,000 people were evicted and forced to settle in the city outskirts and by 1980 the military regime proudly claimed it had removed 76 percent of shantytown dwellers from Buenos Aires. The main target of the bulldozers was La Villa 31, a shantytown that had been a hotspot of radical activism and was located next to the upscale neighborhood of La Recoleta, the core of White Buenos Aires.[54]

Yet the dictatorship's commemoration of General Roca's victory over el malón and its removal of dark-skinned people and places from the national capital were, in retrospect, fruitless attempts to conjure away ghosts. After all, La Villa 31 and other dismantled shantytowns were reappropriated and rebuilt a few years later by spatially expansive multitudes that, despite the violence, did not fail to return to the center of the white city.

LOS NEGROS ARE COMING: THE URBAN MALONES

The neoliberal reforms applied in Argentina since the late 1970s and the resulting growth in unemployment and urban poverty have heightened middle- and upper-class anxieties about the spatial-bodily proliferation of nonwhiteness. Whereas "los cabecitas" of the 1940s had been born in rural areas and were looked down upon as clumsy peasants not used to urban habits,[55] "los negros" of today present a new kind of threat in that they are profoundly urban in nature. As a result, in moments of crisis these populations are seen as creating particularly feared, disruptive vectors of mobility.

One of the most violent and widespread of these contemporary "malones" created by the urban poor were the riots of May and June 1989, when swarms of men and women sacked thousands of stores all over the country amid the hyperinflation crisis that marked the end of the Alfonsín presidency (1983–89). During these weeks, in the well-off parts of Buenos Aires where I was living at the time, residents entered an affective state of collective hysteria. I clearly remember the paranoid, unfounded rumors circulating about "mobs of negros" from Greater Buenos Aires moving toward the city's downtown in a spree of lust, violence, and devastation, as if they were hordes of savage Indians who had breached the walled perimeter of a besieged outpost of civilization. In the upscale areas of the suburb of San Isidro, which is separated from nearby working-class areas by the Pan-American Highway, neighbors set up barricades and had firearms at the ready, waiting for the reappearance of el malón (which never arrived). During this crisis, Mariano Grondona, a conservative journalist and one of the leading voices of White Argentina, made his infamous call on television to "take the tanks out on the streets." He pleaded that the military do what the Venezuelan government had done a few months earlier during the *Caracazo* of February 1989 amid a similar explosion of subaltern unrest: to massacre the poor and, in this case, wipe out the malón. The tanks did not roll onto the streets, but the police and armed vigilantes killed twenty people during the incidents.

In the late 1990s, as an outcome of the radical neoliberal reforms implemented by President Carlos Menem (1989–99) and the resulting rise in unemployment and poverty, the growing presence of the poor on the streets created noticeable geographic transformations. The boundaries separating social classes hardened further, as evidenced by the proliferation of gated communities and malls protected by private security.[56] As in the rest of South America, this spatial segregation was racialized and expressed what political scientist George Cicciariello-Maher calls the fear of the middle classes that their everyday places will be "penetrated" by nonwhite mobs.[57]

This fear of a masculinized negro threat on the streets intensified with the appearance of *los piqueteros*: thousands of unemployed, subaltern youth who in the late 1990s began organizing politically and setting up road blockades (*piquetes*) on highways to demand jobs and state assistance. White Argentina viewed los piqueteros as negros who had mutated into particularly dangerous urban combatants. What made them look especially fearsome was that when they interrupted traffic they were prepared for self-defense against the police by covering their faces and carrying sticks. This well-organized, politically assertive trespassing of spatial boundaries triggered visceral and openly racist responses. In 2003, an editorial by *La Nación* condemned these road blockades under the memorable headline "The Savagery of the Piqueteros."[58] Demonstrating the power of Sarmiento's legacy, the newspaper editorial named the piqueteros as direct heirs to the indigenous savagery of the 1800s. This was not an innocent gesture, for in Argentina those deemed "savages" tend to become the target of state violence. In a famous incident that took place in June 2002, the police murdered two piquetero activists in the city of Avellaneda, located just outside the capital in the Greater Buenos Aires area. On a blog bluntly called "How much I hate you, negro de mierda," their death was celebrated as an "act of justice" on savage scum.[59]

Many middle-class Argentines of European background are certainly critical of these openly classist and racist celebrations of violence. But Argentines who identify as progressives or center-left are not free from inadvertently reproducing some of the racialized dispositions that have been normalized by White Argentina. In the late 1990s, two anthropologists based in the United States, Galen Joseph and Emanuela Guano, conducted fieldwork in Buenos Aires among middle-class men and women who were then staunchly opposed to President Carlos Menem's neoliberal reforms. They found out, independently of each other, that their research subjects' critiques of Menem were profoundly racialized. Many looked down on Menem for being a "darkie" (*morocho*) from a backward, mestizo province (La Rioja) and articulated a patronizing view of the dark-skinned poor who voted for him. Guano also noted that the teachers who were then mobilizing against Menem's erosion of public education celebrated Sarmiento because of his role in expanding public schooling; but when asked about Sarmiento's well-known disdain for Indians and gauchos, they casually disregarded it as politically irrelevant. And when these two ethnographers raised the topic of racism in Argentina in their interviews, people vehemently denied that racism had any salience at all in the country.[60]

A decade later, this denial of the existence of racism became harder to sustain with the dramatic rise of over thirty Facebook groups that openly and unapologetically called for the extermination of "los negros." Even *La Nación* had to acknowledge that these online expressions of hatred were racist and troubling.[61] In 2008, I saved thousands of comments posted on these pages before they were shut down for breaching Facebook anti-discriminatory rules. These postings provide rich, disturbing evidence of the sad passions that celebrate violence as a cleansing force that could whiten Argentina. Revealing the class core of White Argentina, most of the participants in these Facebook groups were teenagers attending elite private schools. The names that they chose for their groups made transparent the object of their hatred: "I hate los negros;

To kill all those bastard thieves and fucking negros; It'd be so great to have a world without negros; Say No to los negros [*Odio a los negros; Matar a todos los rastreros chorros negros de mierda; Qué bueno sería un mundo sin negros; No a los negros*]."

This "I-hate-los negros" online extravaganza articulated the affective habits of youths disgusted by the asphyxiating intrusion of "los negros" in their everyday spaces. Comments said things like, "They reproduce like rats." "They are everywhere." One admitted that it would be tough to exterminate them because of their sheer numbers: "It's going to be hard. They're many." These are the affects of a besieged White Argentina, disgusted (like Sarmiento) by the overwhelming nonwhiteness that surrounds it. As part of the fantasy of violently destroying this expansive threat, the name of one of these Facebook groups was, "If I had a bomb, I'd throw it on La Villa 31." The group's motto was the spontaneous attempt to articulate an experience of nausea: "*Negros de mierda*, you can't walk quietly in Recoleta because there's always *un negrito cabeza*, especially at the corner of Santa Fe and Callao. We should extinguish that disgusting race." These are calls for violence of a sweeping, genocidal scale, which desires to kill them *all*. That this fantasy focuses on the destruction of La Villa 31 with "bombs" reveals that this shantytown is too close for comfort: a festering source of "negros" right next to La Recoleta and "Santa Fe and Callao" (places frequented by the Buenos Aires elite). What these teenagers in the 2000s probably did not know was that the military dictatorship in the late 1970s had already sought to destroy this shantytown to no avail.

Not surprisingly, many comments on these Facebook groups denied that they were racist. Some argued that they did not refer to *negros de piel* [blacks of skin] but to *negros de alma* [blacks of soul], and that by "negro" they meant criminal, morally decadent, and dangerous creatures, independent of their skin color. This move is, in fact, a common disavowal that appears in online forums and social media. These comments make apparent how White Argentina denies its own existence as well as the phantom quality of the returning malones made up of people "with black souls," as if the savage Indians of the past had resurrected and taken over seemingly un-racialized bodies by *darkening* their souls. This emphasis on "souls" that are to be despised because they are "black" seeks to naturalize hostility toward nonwhiteness with the declaration that savagery has, indeed, a *color*.

The racism preached on these now-defunct Facebook groups may sound extreme but is in fact standard on the online forums of mass-circulation newspapers like *Clarín* and *La Nación*, as any reader can readily attest on a daily basis. And the violence that these commentators celebrate is not simply metaphorical, nor is it restricted to the elites; likewise, it is not aimed only at the Argentine poor, for it often targets immigrants from Bolivia, Paraguay, or Peru, who have added more cultural and linguistic diversity to the indigenized and mestizo nonwhiteness that increasingly threatens the spatial integrity of White Argentina.

In December 2010, yet another vortex materialized in Buenos Aires when hundreds of families living in poverty, many of them recent immigrants, occupied *en masse* El Parque Iberoamericano (a large, overgrown park on the southern, poorest area in the city) and demanded the right to build homes there. This massive occupation of public space sent intense shockwaves across the city and led to a wave of violence that lasted for several days. Neighbors from lower-middle-class families formed gangs that tried to repel "the invaders" with stones, petrol bombs, and firearms, all while articulating an anti-foreigner racism that is not rare in working class districts. The television channels, radio stations, and online discussion forums were on fire: a malón of foreigners had materialized out of nowhere and Argentine territoriality was disintegrating. *La Nación* emphasized on its front page that the land invaders spoke "Guaraní" and a journalist said live on TV that they were "immigrants of low quality."[62] "Tomorrow, it could be your home," read the title of an op-ed at *La Nación* that claimed that this urban insurgency should be crushed by the police to prevent it from taking over the city, as if private homes all over Buenos Aires were at risk of being swallowed up by swarms of foreigners.[63]

Online posts on the websites of leading newspapers blamed this conflict on the "populism" of the Peronist governments headed by Néstor Kirchner and Cristina Fernández de Kirchner and made enraged calls "to kill those negros de mierda." During these days, three people involved in the land occupation were murdered by armed gangs and the police, and dozens more were injured. The federal government eventually sent troops to stop the violence, and the park was vacated. But the massive trespassing of boundaries on the poor edges of the city of Buenos Aires had changed the nature of space to reveal, once again, a savage outside – in this case, one created by modern-day malones that came from the depths of indigenous and mestizo Latin America.

In 2000, the weekly *La Primera* published a memorable cover entitled "The Silent Invasion." With a subheading that proclaimed that "two million illegal immigrants" take jobs away from "Argentines," the cover showed a shirtless, dark-skinned male with clearly indigenous features photo-shopped to look toothless, savage, and menacing. The photo, it turns out, is that of a Toba man born on Argentine soil: a descendant of the people who have inhabited for millennia what is today national space. His Indian look, however, was used to epitomize the scary nonwhiteness of foreigners from the rest of Latin America. With the growing waves of migration from neighboring countries, the whiteness originally imported from Europe as part of the legacy of an imperial invasion is presented, through a notable reversal, as the natural condition of an Argentina "invaded" by the original inhabitants of the continent. Tellingly, the cover of *La Primera* showed that the outer limits of Buenos Aires had already been breached: the Indian-foreigner stood next to the obelisk (the symbolic core of the city) and the Argentine flag, as if he had just gotten off his horse and put his spear to rest.

THE RETURN OF THE INDIANS

In the past two decades, indigenous people from all over the country have launched myriad protests, mobilizations, land claims, and land invasions that both openly challenge the idea of Argentina as a white and homogeneous nation and reveal that indigenous people had never fully vanished. The most salient institutional impact of this activism was the inclusion in the 1994 National Constitution, after intense lobbying, of a clause that acknowledges that indigenous people are an indissoluble part of Argentina and are its original inhabitants, effectively terminating the foreign status projected onto them in the foundational 1853 Constitution.[64] This constitutional visibility was the outcome of protests by collectives that never ceased having a tangible social presence and indigenous self-identifications (such as Mapuche, Qom-Toba, or Wichí) but also by thousands of people who in previous decades had de-marked themselves as indigenous out of fear of facing discrimination or ridicule, or who simply felt ashamed of their heritage. In the 1990s, therefore, many people organized around identities that state officials and academics had deemed extinct, such as "Huarpe" or "Rankulche."[65]

Activists often articulate this expansion as the return of that old vector of indigenous, anti-hierarchical rebelliousness: el malón. This was made clear in *El Segundo Malón de la Paz* [The Second Malón of Peace] that took place in Jujuy in August 2006. This "malón" consisted of marches and road blockades organized by thousands of men and women from the Jujuy highlands seeking official land titles. As the name of the protest indicates, the participants saw themselves as heirs to the first Malón de la Paz of six decades prior. Many of the people who took to the roads were, in fact, the grandchildren of those who marched to Buenos Aires in 1946. But the six decades that had passed also revealed how different this new Malón de la Paz was. The first malón involved fewer than two hundred people, was micromanaged by an army officer, performed a non-confrontational attitude before Perón, and was eventually sent back to Jujuy by force. El Malón of 2006 could not have been more different: it was under the full control of an indigenous leadership and grassroots assemblies, and it mobilized thousands of people who peacefully but forcefully confronted state agents. The road blockades paralyzed much of the province and the governor had no option but to relent. Unlike its predecessor, el Segundo Malón de la Paz was a major political victory that forced the Jujuy government to begin distributing over a million hectares of land.[66]

The growing visibility of indigenous protests has found a receptive audience in some members of the urban middle classes who descend from European immigrants and who have begun more openly to question the violence and discrimination imposed on indigenous people throughout Argentine history. But many of those who still cling to the ideal of a White Argentina, needless to say, have followed the spatial expansiveness of indigenous demands with unease and hostility. *La Nación* columnist Rolando Hanglin is one of the proudest advocates of White Argentina; he regularly celebrates the Conquest of the Desert and unapologetically makes openly racist statements condemning indigenous activism. Not surprisingly, he frequently highlights the afterlife of el malón to make his points about the forces that are threatening White Argentina in the twenty-first century. In January 2013, Hanglin published his most detailed piece yet on the current political salience of el malón.[67] He described, first, how in the 1800s el malón was "a massive attack by an indigenous cavalry" accompanied by "the terrifying shouts of the warriors," which unleashed devastation, death, and looting on "an unarmed civilian population." These "crimes," he wrote, "have always deserved, throughout history and in all nations, the most severe forms of punishment." He thereby argued that General Roca's violence against the malones, while a bloody affair, was a civilizing and necessary measure.

Hanglin then moved on to make his main point: that el malón, actually, was not destroyed in the late nineteenth century, for it continues to return. "All this is relevant to what happened in Chile last week," he wrote. He referred to an elderly couple of landowners of German surname who died when their house was burnt down amid land conflicts with Mapuche farmers and activists. A "horde," Hanglin wrote, attacked the landowners like a malón, in an act of "terrorism" that demanded a tough response. He insisted that similar conflicts involved Mapuche people in Argentina, whom he often presents as "Chilean."[68] White Argentina can be seen here, once again, as a bodily orientation toward space that is very sensitive to the trespassing of boundaries by nonwhite multitudes and, at the same time, disregards the suffering inflicted on indigenous people and the expropriation of their land by settlers of European background. The Chilean military police had, after all, killed several Mapuche in previous years without making Hanglin blink. Yet the main point raised by Hanglin's ruminations about el malón is the admission that Roca actually *failed* to annihilate it back in the late 1800s.

Three months earlier, on October 13, 2012, a modern malón had in fact appeared on the Argentine side of Patagonia in one of the most Europeanized places of the nation: the resort town of Bariloche. A hundred activists showed up armed with ropes, tools, steel cables, and the determination to bring down the monument to General Roca in the center of the city. This monument has long been painted with graffiti with words such as "murderer" or "genocide," as part of a grassroots campaign demanding its removal.[69] But that day, the crowd tied the ropes around the monument, partly sawed off the horse's feet, and started pulling. The petrified general on horseback was beginning to tilt when the police arrived, clashing with the protesters and managing to preserve the monument.

On the online forums of *La Nación* discussing this event, most readers were enraged. Many passionately defended General Roca's civilizing legacy. One reader presented him as the pacifier of blood-thirsty, murderous hordes: "Roca didn't commit any massacres, the only massacres were committed by los malones." But the most illuminating comments were of a different nature, defending the monument but aware that this collective attack, carried out in the light of day, marked a new social reality hostile to White Argentina. One person said, "We should re-write history. There was no conquest of the desert. The Indians won. And the facts exposed in this article demonstrate it."[70] This tone of factual resignation is as notable as is its historical truth: the admission that the Conquest of the Desert failed to create a nation without Indians.

THE KIRCHNERISTA DECADE: MESTIZO RETERRITORIALIZATIONS

The cracks in the affective edifice of White Argentina have widened with the anti-neoliberal insurrection of December 2001, the economic collapse of 2002, and the center-left, openly pro-Latin American governments of Néstor Kirchner (2003–07) and Cristina Fernández de Kirchner (2007–15). Influenced by the proliferation of indigenous protests in the previous decade, this new political context has favored the dissemination of sensibilities more open to accepting that Argentina is defined by a multiplicity of legacies. In May 2010, the celebrations for the Bicentennial of national independence in downtown Buenos Aires were a major expression of this shift. Among other events, the commemorations included a huge parade attended by two million people that represented a vision of two centuries of Argentine history that did away with the old fairy tale of a homogeneous and white nation and highlighted, instead, the multiplicity, mixture, and mutual entanglement of indigenous, African, criollo, and European influences.[71] This public and massive celebration of Argentina as a nation defined by racial mixture and cultural diversity would have been unthinkable two decades earlier.

Another telling expression of these transformations is that many subaltern urban youths are embracing the term "los negros" as a marker of plebeian pride. As Ezequiel Adamovsky argues, this shift began in popular culture during the heyday of the neoliberal multiculturalism of the 1990s. In 1994, the famous performer La Mona Giménez released an album called *Raza Negra* in which he celebrated "the skin of my race, the black race [*la piel de mi raza, raza negra*]." This identification became even more salient in the growth of *cumbia villera* [slum cumbia] in the 2000s, a music genre whose lyrics focus on the reality of life in the slums and its hybrid cultural habits. Pablo Lescano, a leading figure in the genre, displays a large tattoo on his chest that reads "*100% negro cumbiero*." Soccer star Diego Maradona also said publicly he is a proud "negro."[72] These acts constitute subaltern, explicit negations of the idea of a white nation and of its associated class, cultural, and spatial hierarchies.

The public gestures against White Argentina were epitomized by the huge controversy created in early 2008 by piquetero leader and supporter of the Kirchner government Luis D'Elía. The controversy began during the "conflict with *el campo* [the countryside]," the euphemistic term used by the media in reference to the lockouts and road blockades organized by anti-Kirchner farming and landowning groups against proposed tax increases on their export earnings. In March of that year, D'Elía calmly and firmly declared on national radio, in reference to these groups, "I hate the whites [*odio a los blancos*]." He clarified he hated "the whites of the oligarchy" for their classism, racism, and violence, for "they never had any problem killing us en masse."[73] The uttering of the phrase "the whites" as the object of hatred by a person regularly called "un negro de mierda" created a national uproar. Journalists and politicians condemned D'Elía in heated terms for his "racism" and "class hatred." Most of the media coverage of this incident failed to mention that the online forums of *La Nación* or *Clarín* were in those days, more intensely than usual, full of people preaching racial and class hatred against D'Elía and "esos negros de mierda" as well as making calls for their extermination.[74]

Political scientist Ariel Armory wrote an op-ed piece in *La Nación* about this incident that made an important point: while D'Elía's remarks were obliviously blunt and crude, they also marked a breakthrough in publicly *naming* the collective that is so normalized in Argentina that it is systematically silenced: "los blancos."[75] This was disturbing to many because it ruptured the normalization of whiteness in Argentina by revealing that many Argentines do not identify as white and, therefore, that "los blancos" are just a *part* of the nation, not the whole. Yet the intervention by D'Elía had an additional affective impact because he boldly positioned himself as an uppity "negro" who spoke to White Argentina straight in the face and said that he reciprocated its hatred. His gesture resonates with a point made by psychiatrist and philosopher Frantz Fanon: that "being black" involves the awareness of being negated by the hostile white gaze.[76] D'Elía is "el negro" who spoke back, telling White Argentina that millions of citizens are *well aware* of its hostile gaze. "You think that we are disgusting, garbage, barbarism," he added. This proudly anti-elite declamation exposed what anthropologist Michael Taussig would call the public secret of White Argentina, or a secret that is well-known but is disavowed: that dreaming of a nation without Indians, mestizos, and negros is a deeply racist gesture.[77]

Subjected to reterritorializations, political forces, and bodily sensibilities that are rejecting its hegemonic power, White Argentina has responded with increasing expressions of hatred, vertigo, and nausea at this renewed resurgence of a mestizo-indigenous continent. The visceral, racialized rage that defined the anti-Peronism of the 1940s and 1950s has resurfaced in the intensely emotional contempt that the conservative core of White Argentina feels for the Kirchner governments and their supporters, whose populism and pro-Latin American rhetoric it follows with existential angst as well as transparent expressions of disgust and anger.

This is why the 2007–08 uprising by "el campo" was the genuine clamor of a besieged White Argentina, congealing in its rural core: the Pampa Gringa. Carrying their whiteness around to mark public places as rightly and naturally theirs, supporters of the protest set up blockades against the government all over the Argentine prairies by placing tractors, trucks, and pick-ups across the roads. In several cases, the largely middle-class men manning the blockades acted violently against people who sought to drive through. Only a few years earlier, the same people were calling the piqueteros "negros de mierda," "Indians," and "savages" for doing the same thing: interrupting traffic. In March 2008, Raúl Biolcatti, the president of La Sociedad Rural Argentina, was asked on national radio what he thought of this contradiction in his view of road blockades now and then. In a matter-of-fact tone, Biolcatti responded that what set their blockades apart was people's "skin color."[78] In other words, disruptions of traffic in favor of "el campo" were, to him, legitimate because the people behind them had white skin. The private media supporting the protests treated the comment as unremarkable. This disregard shocked foreign journalists who were in Argentina at the time, and who could not believe that a major political figure could get away with making openly racist statements on national radio.[79] But Biolcatti articulated what is a widespread sentiment among Argentine conservatives: that they represent the true, normal, White Argentina, threatened by millions of "negros" who blindly voted for Cristina Kirchner in exchange for "a social [welfare] plan and a pair of sneakers." In fact, the Facebook groups calling for the extermination of "los negros" peaked during the rural lockout, posted standard anti-Kirchner slogans, and were linked to other Facebook groups supporting "el campo."

Despite the partisan logic guiding political debates in Argentina in the past decade and despite having challenged the power of the old national elites through their more inclusive, progressive, and pro-Latin American agenda, the administrations of Néstor and Cristina Kirchner have not broken entirely from the White Argentina that rejects them. Many of their policies and narratives are still attached to this project's spatial and affective sensibilities. The clearest example is that the Kirchners have radicalized the racialized parameters of spatial destruction led by the landed aristocracy since the Conquest of the Desert. Exactly like a century ago, the indigenous and mestizo areas of Argentina are being devastated in the name of progress, this time by agribusinesses that are bulldozing vast tracts of forests to create soy fields. In the Argentine Chaco, the "soy boom" encouraged by the Kirchner administrations is partly undoing the indigenous expansiveness of the 1990s and pushing it back through violence and evictions.[80] In the past few years, this has included the assassination by the police and thugs of over a dozen indigenous and criollo people defending their lands in Salta, Formosa, Chaco, and Santiago del Estero.[81]

In February 2013, President Cristina Kirchner made comments that reveal how her pro-agribusiness policies reproduce White Argentina's disregard for the destruction of the nonwhite places of the nation. Reacting to the news that the conservative mayor of Buenos Aires (a major figure in the opposition) had just destroyed 150 trees in the city, she declared her passionate love for trees and said, "We won't bring down any tree! The trees are untouchable. They are sacred." She added that trees would be destroyed "only over my dead body."[82] The President's declared love for trees, however, was restricted to the trees of places dear to White Argentina, like Buenos Aires. In the previous year alone, forty million trees had been bulldozed and burnt down in northern Argentina to make space for soybean fields. Ahmed has written that places acquire the skin color of the bodies that inhabit them.[83] Drawing from the racialized disregard that has defined White Argentina, the President was clearly unmoved by the destruction of those millions of trees of dark skin. Those crowds of disposable trees are the vegetal equivalent of "esos negros de mierda," and are often destroyed – as during the military campaigns of the late 1800s – over the actual dead bodies of criollos and indigenous people.

CONCLUSION: LA ARGENTINA MESTIZA

In this chapter, I have sought to show that understanding whiteness in Argentina in its complexity requires examining it as a spatial and affective condition: as a utopian geographical project tormented (and frequently nauseated) by the impossibility of its realization. As we have seen, White Argentina is not a bounded group constituted by those citizens who are white or see themselves as such. Many Argentines of European background, in fact, have long opposed the racism that has defined much of national history. White Argentina is the not-fully conscious disposition, shared by people of multiple backgrounds, to desire a nation "without negros." For generations, millions of people simply wished that the nonwhite part of Argentina would dissolve or, at least, that it would not be too noticeable. Yet the immensity of centuries of indigenous, mestizo, African, and Spanish entanglements has recurrently overwhelmed this longing for a white nation. The violence to contain the return of el malón as well as its collective, often class-based demands has defined, with shifting levels of intensity, much of the nation's history.

While White Argentina has lost part of its past prestige and prominence, this project is still the guiding force behind the inequalities that twelve years of Kirchner administrations have not dared dismantle. Further eroding the power of this hierarchical project will entail doing much more than denouncing its constitutive racism, for the latter is not just a rational discourse reversible through the use of purely logical arguments. Political theorist Jon Beasley-Murray has proposed abandoning the notion of hegemony on the grounds that dominant forms of common sense do not operate discursively but, rather, affectively and through not-fully-conscious habits and bodily dispositions.[84] Yet the political salience of pre-discursive affects does not mean that the concept of hegemony is irrelevant to account for them. As we have seen, the dispositions that guide White Argentina have indeed been hegemonic for a long time, accepted as common sense by various groupings and classes. But this has been an unstable, ever-contested, and affective hegemony, which is now under growing pressure from an emerging yet still inchoate formation that could be called *La Argentina Mestiza*, a disposition that feels comfortable with multiplicity and does not desire to create a piece of Europe in South America. This is not the orderly diversity of neoliberal multiculturalism, in which officially sanctioned identities are placed in bounded slots.[85] This is the messy, disjointed, liberating mestizaje that confounds the very notion of an identity as a fixed, stable positioning.

Anthropologist François Laplantine and linguist Alexis Nouss have argued that mestizaje should not be considered as a process of fusion in which originally distinct elements lose their individuality to form a new, homogeneous whole.[86] In Latin America, this homogenizing mestizaje has been that of state ideologies in Brazil and Mexico, which celebrate mixture only to reproduce ongoing racial hierarchies.[87] The mestizaje hailed by Laplantine and Nouss is, on the contrary, defined by a movement of tension, vibration, and oscillation that creates an unresolved multiplicity, what philosophers Gilles Deleuze and Félix Guattari call "disjunctive synthesis," a crossing without fusion.[88] Argentina has always been a mestizo nation in this disjointed sense. The expansion of La Argentina Mestiza as an affective formation will require affirming its disjunctive multiplicity without reactive passions ("I hate the whites") and through the forceful erosion of the class hierarchies and the cult of inequality that has defined White Argentina. La Argentina Mestiza is, in short, an anti-hierarchical and therefore more egalitarian and tolerant geographical project.

The gradual expansion and territorialization of La Argentina Mestiza will also mean liberating el malón from its eternal return. Gilles Deleuze envisioned, with Friedrich Nietzsche, an eternal return that does not recreate the repetition of the same – the one that has defined the fearful and violent becoming of White Argentina – but rather the disintegration of the fantasy of stable, fixed identities and places.[89] This is the utopian, rhizomatic horizon that La Argentina Mestiza aims for: a geography peopled by a tapestry of multiplicities and lines of flight, freed from the fear of a savage outside.

Notes

1. "Nueve policías fueron detenidos en Tucumán por los saqueos," *La Nación* (Buenos Aires), 14 Dec. 2013; "Detienen a 16 policías y a una ex-agente por los saqueos en Córdoba," *La Gaceta* (Tucumán), 17 Feb. 2014.
2. "Córdoba: murió un joven de 20 años en medio de los saqueos," *La Nación*, 4 Dec. 2013.
3. Abel Posse "Hay que salir al rescate de la nación," *La Nación*, 28 Jan. 2014.
4. Aguinis, *El atroz*.
5. See, among others, Briones, "Formaciones"; Quijada, "Introduction"; Joseph, "Taking"; Segato, *La nación*.
6. Grimson, *Mitomanías*.
7. Spinoza, *Ethics*.

8. The utmost symbol of this trope is that of "*la cautiva*," a white female captured by indigenous combatants and taken to live among them in "the desert." See Alberto, Adamovsky, this volume.
9. To avoid confusion, people often use the phrases "*negro mota* [blacks with curly hair]" or "*negro negro*" to refer to people with African phenotypes. The current use of "los negros" also draws from the fact that in the 1800s Buenos Aires and provinces like Santiago del Estero or Córdoba had a sizable population of African slaves and their descendants, who gradually blended with other groups and became un-marked as Afro-Argentines. While today only a few thousand people claim an Afro-Argentine identity, DNA analysis has revealed a relatively high presence of African genetic markers in the country. But that the phrase "los negros" usually names indigenous-mestizo phenotypes reveals that the legacy of trans-Atlantic slavery has been silenced and recoded in terms of what the elites have viewed as the main obstacle to the complete whitening of Argentina: the population native to the American continent.
10. Derrida, *Specters.*
11. Ahmed, "Phenomenology."
12. Guss, "The Gran Poder."
13. Ribeiro, *Americas.*
14. Quijada, "Introduction," 10.
15. Stoler, *Archival Grain.*
16. Ahmed, "Phenomenology"; Dyer, *White*; Hill, ed., *Whiteness.*
17. "No los dejaron viajar debido a su apariencia," *La Nación*, 14 Jul. 1999.
18. *El Progreso* (Santiago de Chile), 27 Sep. 1844.
19. Sarmiento, *Facundo.*
20. Spinoza, *Ethics.*
21. Viñas, *Indios.*
22. Escolar, *Los dones.*
23. Gordillo, *Rubble.*
24. See Chamosa, this volume.
25. Gordillo, "Crucible" and *Landscapes.*
26. Cordeu and Siffredi, *De la algarroba*; Gordillo, *Rubble.*
27. Bayer, *Patagonia Rebelde.*
28. Chamosa, "Criollo."
29. Gordillo and Hirsch, "La presencia."
30. Grosso, *Indios muertos*; Lazzari, "The Autonomy."
31. Karush, this volume; Grosso, *Indios muertos*; Frigerio, "Luis D'Elía."
32. Milanesio, "Peronists."
33. Ratier, *El cabecita negra*; Milanesio, "Peronists."
34. Adamovsky, *Clase media*, 276.
35. Ibid., 277.
36. Ratier, *El cabecita negra*, 13.
37. Ibid., 38.
38. Ibid., 32.
39. Adamovsky, *Clase media*, 277.
40. Adamovsky, *Clase media.*
41. Chamosa, "Criollo."
42. Gordillo, "Crucible."

43. Lenton, "The Malón."
44. Gordillo, *Rubble*; Chamosa, "Indigenous"; Lazzari, "Indio argentino."
45. Valko, *Los indios invisibles.*
46. Ibid., 195.
47. Ibid., 206.
48. Serbín, "Las organizaciones"; Lenton, "The Malón"; Valko, *Los indios invisibles.*
49. *Octubre Pilagá.*
50. Ratier, *El cabecita negra,* 76.
51. Ratier, *El cabecita negra.*
52. Serbín, "Las organizaciones"; Gordillo and Hirsch, "La presencia."
53. Prado, *La guerra.*
54. See the *TV Pública* clip on *YouTube.* "Archivo histórico: La erradicación de villas en la gestión de Cacciatore." www.youtube.com/watch?v=XYzNIhlj8Ms.
55. Ratier, *El cabecita negra.*
56. Svampa, *Los que ganaron*; Guano, "Color."
57. Ciccariello-Maher, "Toward a Racial Geography."
58. "El salvajismo de los piqueteros," *La Nación,* 13 Jan. 2003.
59. *Cómo te odio negro de mierda* (blog). May 2008. www.odioalosnegros.blogspot.ca/2008/05/esta-nueva-entrada-es-para-recordar-los.html.
60. Joseph, "Taking"; Guano, "Color" and "Stroll."
61. "El odio, la otra cara de las redes sociales," *La Nación,* 15 Mar. 2009.
62. *La Nación,* 10 Dec. 2010.
63. Javier Miglino, "Mañana puede ser nuestra casa," *La Nación,* 12 Dec. 2010.
64. Gordillo and Hirsch, "La presencia."
65. Escolar, *Los dones*; Lazzari, "The Autonomy."
66. Gordillo, "Longing."
67. Rolando Hanglin, "Chile y Argentina, ¿Hacia una crisis mapuche?" *La Nación,* 8 Jan. 2013.
68. The claim by conservative authors that Argentine Mapuche are "Chilean" draws from the fact that centuries ago, before Argentina or Chile existed as nations, the Mapuche people lived mostly west of the Patagonian Andes and expanded across the mountains into what is today Argentina over several centuries. Briones, "Formaciones." See also Rodríguez, this volume.
69. Valko, *Desmonumentar.*
70. "En Bariloche intentaron derribar al monumento a Julio Roca," *La Nación,* 13 Oct. 2012.
71. Adamovsky, "El color."
72. Adamovsky, *Clases populares.*
73. *La Nación,* 27 Mar. 2008.
74. Frigerio, "Luis D'Elía"; Adamovsky, "El color."
75. Ariel Armory, "Lo que nos enseñó D'Elía," *La Nación,* 5 Apr. 2008.
76. Fanon, *Black Skin.*
77. Taussig, *Defacement.*
78. "Línea de conducta," *Página/12* (Buenos Aires), 31 Jul. 2009.
79. Marcelo Justo, "Cuestión de piel." *Página/12,* 8 Apr. 2008.
80. Aranda, *Argentina originaria*; Gordillo, *Rubble.*
81. Darío Aranda, "La década extractiva," in *ComAmbiental* (blog), 25 May 2013. www.comambiental.com.ar/2013/05/la-decada-extractiva.html.

82. "Cristina, contra el Metrobús: 'los árboles no se tocan,'" *Clarín* (Buenos Aires), 16 Feb. 2013.
83. Ahmed, "Phenomenology," 157.
84. Beasley-Murray, *Posthegemony*.
85. Muehlmann, "Real Indians" and *River*.
86. Laplantine and Nouss, *Mestizajes*.
87. Knight, "Racism, Revolution."
88. Deleuze and Guattari, *Anti-Oedipus*.
89. Deleuze, *Difference and Repetition*.

10

Between foreigners and heroes

Asian-Argentines in a multicultural nation

Chisu Teresa Ko

Argentina's economic crisis of 2001 triggered a crisis in national identity that cast doubt on the nation's long-held beliefs about its racial and cultural exceptionalism as a white and therefore modern nation. In the decade after the crisis, Argentina experienced a major shift in racial discourse, redefining itself as a multiracial and multicultural nation. The newly adopted multiculturalism does not entirely displace older understandings of race and nation – as Gastón Gordillo demonstrates in Chapter 9 of this volume, the increased visibility of nonwhites has heightened racial violence in contemporary Argentina – but it does mark a radical departure from previous official discourses that insisted on the nation's homogeneous whiteness. Argentina's rather abrupt multicultural turn has to do in part with the expediency of multiculturalism, which helps articulate both populist and elite reconfigurations of the national narrative. In one sense, the multicultural discourse that focuses largely on Afro-descendants and indigenous peoples disavows previous claims of Europeanness to adopt a populist Latin-Americanist position as an antidote to the globalization of neoliberal capitalism. It is within this context that a contestatory working-class coalition using the racial marker "negro" also arose.[1] Simultaneously, however, multiculturalism is often seen as a sign of neoliberal globalization – as the transnational flow of capital triggers migrations and diversifies cultural consumption – and as a marker of first world status in a global climate in which the notion of development encompasses the "preservation – or even cultivation – of ethnoracial diversity."[2] In this context, a vast network of institutional, academic, political, and cultural discourses along with popular ethnic activism dismantled notions of white homogeneity to establish Argentina as multicultural. Afro-Argentine and indigenous peoples – who had been considered "disappeared" – claimed their legitimate space within the nation; Argentines of European descent who had melted into the *crisol de razas* [melting pot] began to assert their ethnicities; and diversity became a key measure of social justice.[3]

This proliferation of ethnicities has more recently extended to Asians in Argentina, as evidenced by their changing position in cultural discourses. In the context of Argentina's incipient multiculturalism, cultural manifestations featuring Asians as protagonists, rather than as exotic or awkward peripheral characters, have gained popularity. But unlike Afro-Argentines and indigenous peoples whose existence and *argentinidad* [Argentineness] are legitimized through a multiplicity of projects on the ground and at the institutional level (ethnic activism, inclusion in the national census and history textbooks, academic research, and cultural representation), the position of Asian-Argentines within the nation remains uncertain, as their representation appears to be limited to cultural manifestations (literature and film) that intersect little with academic and political treatments of multicultural nationalism.

Asians in Argentina have alternated between hyper-visibility and invisibility. Hyper-visibility has often been negative, particularly for people of Korean and Chinese origin who have been targets of racism and xenophobia. For example, during the 1980s and 1990s, the increasing size of the Korean-Argentine community and its members' success as small-business owners attracted accusations by the media and the general public of tax evasion, taking away jobs from Argentines, and exploiting the cheap labor of other immigrant groups such as Bolivians.[4] More recently, the growing Chinese community has been accused of widespread mafia connections and of unethical business practices – it is widely rumored, for example, that Chinese grocers (the iconic niche occupation of the Chinese-Argentine community) turn off their refrigerators at night.[5] Public sentiment also reflects an assumption that people of Asian descent are physically, culturally, and linguistically too different to belong to Argentina or less prone to "become" Argentine compared to other immigrant groups. The hyper-visibility of their difference, in a sense, justifies the group's invisibility – or its irrelevance – vis-à-vis the nation, since their perceived difference disqualifies Asian-Argentines from debates of nationhood even as multiculturalism gains currency.

Scholarly and anecdotal evidence suggests that the denial of racial and cultural citizenship to people of Asian descent is not particular to Argentina but rather widespread in countries whose national identity is based primarily on Western cultures.[6] In fact, indigenous, European, and African peoples have the longest history in Argentina, but the routine exclusion of Asians is at odds with Argentina's newfound multiculturalism. While Asian-Argentines likely represent a smaller minority than other racial groups, Argentina's multiculturalism rejects the argument that numerical insignificance justifies the historical marginalization and effective erasure of indigenous and Afro-Argentine populations. Moreover, no official statistics quantify the Asian-Argentine population; the idea that they represent a tiny minority cannot hold ground if the state's policy has been not to count them. As we will see, Argentina's Asian population has been altogether excluded from sustained, institutionalized forms of counting, which renders them officially invisible.

Acknowledging that racial meanings are not formed by one single institution or ideology but rather discursively through social structures, cultural products, and individual identification, this chapter will focus on some specific discourses that produce the two main notions associated with Asians in present-day Argentina: namely, that they are essentially foreign and that they serve as symbols of multiculturality in the shifting national imaginary. On the one hand, I contend that inherited practices of exclusion based on the assumption of Asian-Argentines' foreignness (at times desirable yet fundamentally immutable) can persist even today in part because of the group's absence from state-sanctioned forms of social knowledge and academic discourses. Multicultural recognition depends a great deal on these discourses, as the cases of Afro-Argentines and indigenous peoples attest; the intersection of ethnic mobilization, academic discourses, institutional projects, and group members' own performances of "race" and culture have contributed to a general awareness that these groups exist and that they merit an important place in the Argentine nation.[7] On the other hand, by analyzing three recent films – *Un cuento chino* [*Chinese Take-Out*] (2011), *Samurai* (2012), and *Mujer conejo* [*Rabbit Woman*] (2013) – that attempt to rebuild a national identity at a time of economic and identitary crisis, I examine how non-official and non-academic cultural manifestations have appropriated the figure of the Asian as a symbolic multicultural subject that can mediate between old and new definitions of the nation.

ASIANS' INVISIBILITY IN OFFICIAL DISCOURSES

During the 2010 Bicentennial celebrations, Argentina heightened its efforts to reject previous ideas of homogeneity and redefine the nation as diverse. In this process, the state agency INADI (Instituto Nacional contra la Discriminación, la Xenofobia, y el Racismo) has become a major official promoter of diversity and tolerance, with 550 employees in 2011, up from thirty-five in 2005, and a ten-fold increase in budget in six years.[8] The agency's web channel (webINADI) reflects its understanding of diversity; the organization's video campaigns, for example, a key tool to educate the public about discrimination and to promote cultural, racial, and gender diversity, almost entirely lack Asian presence. As of 2014, only one video depicts an Asian: as part of an animated series for children, "Somos iguales y diferentes," the video asserts the equality of non-normative peoples within the nation and shows one Asian girl dressed in a kimono with chopsticks in her hair.[9] Given that the campaign's portrayal of excluded identities extends to a white woman with a British accent, the near-complete absence of Asians is striking. While no single such omission can have enormous impact, the conspicuous absence of Asians across official discourses can reproduce their invisibility and validate some common assumptions about their foreignness, numerical insignificance, inability to assimilate, and status as temporary migrants.

In another decisive example, the Bicentennial national census of 2010, which was ground-breaking for its simultaneous inclusion of two long-absent racial categories (*afrodescendiente* or "Afro-descendant" and *pueblo originario* or "indigenous peoples"), had no Asian category. In the broader context of Latin America's contemporary racial politics, Argentina's revised national census is not exceptional. Latin American nations that had previously avoided specific racial categorizations in favor of consolidating national identities under notions of "melting pots" or *mestizaje* began in recent years to reshape their nationhood through redesigned national censuses that produced statistical data about their diverse ethno-racial composition. According to sociologist Mara Loveman, by 2010 all Latin American nations except the Dominican Republic "included, or had publicly committed to include, at least one direct query to capture indigenous and/or Afro-descendant individuals."[10] But Loveman also points out that despite an overarching impulse to render visible racial diversity, "those of Asian descent remained statistically invisible in the national censuses of nearly all Latin American countries," including Argentina.[11]

Sociologists Edward Telles and René Flores note that Latin American censuses also tend to omit "white" as a category – out of seventeen national censuses carried out in the 2000s, only Brazil, Cuba, Ecuador, and El Salvador included a white category. Telles and Flores interpret this as a sign that "whites are not supposed to exist according to some national ideologies (e.g., *mestizaje* in Mexico), or perhaps [as] further evidence that whiteness is simply not problematized as it is for nonwhites."[12] Given that whiteness in Argentina has been the very founding ideal of its dominant national identity, the omission of white in Argentina's census does not render white people invisible. As much as the new census attempts to recuperate two major groups that were historically eliminated from the modern nation, it also reaffirms white as Argentina's default population. In this context, the omission of Asians, who belong neither to the deracialized normativity of whiteness nor to the newly included categories of Afro-descendant and indigenous peoples, automatically discards them from Argentina's redefined nation. Loveman rightfully asserts that official census classification can be simultaneously inclusionary and exclusionary.[13] That is, census classification does not necessarily mean inclusion, and it also risks essentialization and greater state control. However, given that Argentina has historically denied the existence of racial minorities, their inclusion or exclusion from the census can be particularly charged with political and symbolic meaning.

Asian-Argentines' statistical – and, by extension, ontological – uncertainty results not only from their omission in the census but also from a broader lack of sustained official data. Estimates cited by the government, media, and scholars come from a variety of sources – each with different measuring criteria – but no comprehensive and official information helps us understand

Argentina's Asian population. The only official statistics reflect Asians who are foreign-born, potentially excluding Asians who are born in Argentina, are naturalized, or might self-identify as Argentines.[14] This practice at once reflects and reproduces the common attitude that Asians cannot be Argentines, or that if they happen to be, their cultural difference does not merit recognition. Statistics on overseas residents compiled by foreign governments – such as South Korea's Ministry of Foreign Affairs, which counts overseas Koreans – are commonly cited, but these also represent imprecise measures at best. For example, South Korea only counts people living in Argentina who have current or previous Korean citizenship or who have been members of Korean community associations in the country.[15] Given the long and substantial history of Asian immigration to Argentina, it seems likely that available statistics greatly undercount Asian-Argentines and mixed-race people with Asian heritage in the country. From a symbolic perspective, these practices truncate the possibilities of articulating an Asian component even in Argentina's purported multicultural national identity. Without subscribing to the idea that a community's size should be a condition for inclusion, it is nonetheless possible to point out that a lack of data exacerbates the perception of Asian-Argentines as an irrelevant group and can limit their material and symbolic participation in the nation.

ASIANS AS IMMIGRANT SUBJECTS IN ACADEMIC DISCOURSE

While the study of Asians in Argentina has remained largely underdeveloped, a growing body of work, mostly from the social sciences, is filling this scholarly gap. Concentrated on three major East Asian groups – Japanese/Okinawan, Chinese/Taiwanese, and Korean – the existing scholarship is primarily concerned with the history of immigration, migration patterns, and socio-anthropological issues of discrimination, assimilation, and identity formation. More recent works have taken a new direction, placing these groups within the framework of transnational diasporas. Although the Chinese population is reportedly the largest Asian group and the fourth-largest immigrant group in Argentina (commonly estimated by government agencies, scholars, and media to be above 100,000 people), it has received the least scholarly attention, possibly because of its recent arrival, as we will see later.[16] On the other hand, the Japanese community, smaller in size, with an estimated population of 40,000, has received the most scholarly attention.[17] The prominence of Japanese-Argentines has to do with the group's relatively long history, its particularly favorable image compared to other Asian groups, and the broader development of Nikkei studies in Latin America.[18] Outside these three major groups, there are only a handful of academic and institutional publications regarding people of Southeast Asian descent, such as the Laotian refugee community.

A common thread in this multidisciplinary body of work is its approach to Asian-Argentines as immigrant subjects or as members of distinct ethnic communities or *colectividades* (e.g., *colectividad coreana*) who hold strong ties to countries of origin and are distant from the majority population, mainstream culture, and hegemonic Argentine national identity. These works attest to the reality that as non-European immigrants, Asians have shared a common experience of discrimination, stereotyping, and rejection from the nation. Through an emphasis on Asians' ethnic groupness, these works reveal a history of unequal power relations between Asians and the dominant culture, and they portray ethnic or diasporic modes of identification as a way to challenge this condition. Nonetheless, I suggest that thinking of Asians strictly as colectividades can unwittingly reproduce the boundaries that make them outsiders by overlooking spaces of hybridity and multiplicity among Asians, and, most crucially, by disregarding their role in formulations of Argentine national identity.

Among these studies of Asians in Argentina, the earliest works sketch the history of immigration of specific ethnic groups, the socio-historical circumstances that triggered migration, the complex routes of arrival and departure, and their settlement patterns. What emerges from these works is the existence of a constant flow of Asians to Argentina since the early twentieth century. Reflecting the socio-economic and historical circumstances of their countries of origin, East Asian communities settled successively in Argentina – Japanese arrived in the first half of the twentieth century, Koreans in the second half of the twentieth century, and Chinese at the start of the twenty-first century. A small but steady wave of Japanese immigration to Argentina started around 1909 and continued into the 1960s, with a break during World War II, gradually stopping as Japan emerged as a global economic power.[19] Korean immigration began substantially in the 1960s and reached a period of intense growth in the 1980s and 1990s; Mirta Bialogorski, a leading scholar of the Korean-Argentine community, estimates that the Korean-Argentine population reached 40,000 during this time.[20] This larger population stimulated the growth of Korean-Argentine associations, as well as churches, radio stations, and newspapers catering to Korean-language speakers.[21] More recently, a modest wave of Taiwanese immigration in the 1980s and a larger group of immigrants from the Chinese mainland in the 1990s and 2000s have established a significant Taiwanese/Chinese community.[22] The economic crisis of 2001 diminished the Korean and Taiwanese populations, as many re-emigrated to neighboring countries or to the United States and Canada, but a wave of immigration from mainland China reached its peak during the post-crisis years.[23]

The existing scholarship has illustrated that the majority of Asian immigrants to Argentina ended up engaging in ethnic economies – Japanese in the dry-cleaning business, Koreans in the textile industry, Chinese in the grocery business, and Taiwanese in the photo-developing business – that required few language skills and operated through family and ethnic ties. Along with the growth of Korean and Chinese ethnic neighborhoods, this concentration exacerbated the perceived distance between the dominant sector and Asian communities, supporting facile associations and stereotypes such as the "clean" Japanese dry-cleaners, "exploitative" Korean textilers, and "unethical" Chinese grocers. Anthropologist Carolina Mera argues that the Korean community's isolation and the formation of "an identity that withdraws into itself" is a reaction to mainstream "discourses of rejection" that "scorn their culture."[24] In this context, while some scholars explore how Koreans in Argentina have articulated their Koreanness through institutionalized and performative practices of Korean culture, others offer in-depth analyses of the discourses of racial prejudice and xenophobia produced in everyday language and mass media to deny Korean-Argentines access to Argentine nationhood.[25] Such works collectively show that Asians who arrived in Argentina commonly faced a dominant discourse that considered them alien on all counts, but that at the same time demanded "the adoption of 'Argentineness' as the first principle of identification." Therefore, in a context that did not even allow "a descriptive term such as 'Japanese Argentine,'" Asians were faced with the impossible task of becoming Argentine while they had already been prescribed as essentially un-Argentine.[26]

The most recent scholarship takes a new direction, building on previous works but also inquiring more emphatically about the complex ways Asians in Argentina have negotiated their identities and sense of belonging. A significant number of works analyze Argentines of Japanese, Korean, and Chinese descent from the perspective of diaspora studies, taking into consideration not only their deeply rooted connections to the country of origin but also their collective experience of "displacement."[27] These works approach Asian-Argentines as members of ethnic diasporas that maintain close ties both to their original culture and to transnational diasporic communities, increasingly connected through online communication and often institutionally supported by their countries of origin. This new framework is particularly illuminating because continuous transnational movements have characterized Asian immigration to Argentina, with many arriving from or re-emigrating to other parts of the Americas or returning to their country of origin.[28] Turning scholarly attention toward such processes of diasporization – for example, the formation of a transnational Nikkei identity – reveals a more nuanced understanding of Asian-Argentine experiences, which have formed what Mera terms "bicultural identities always marked by the experience of difference and discrimination."[29] As anthropologist Marcelo Higa points out in relation to the Nikkei, diasporic identities can be best understood as a "relative point, a simple refusal to identify with 'the Japanese of Japan'" or to completely assimilate as the "*gaijin* [foreigner] Argentine."[30] But he also indicates that the diasporic Nikkei identity can acquire "as many different meanings as the environments in which it is created" and that it is "but one possible facet or orientation, in constant transformation, and constantly connected with others."[31]

Analyzing Asian-Argentines as members of ethnic colectividades or diasporas is crucial, especially in light of previous discourses of homogeneous whiteness and continued practices of exclusion. And as these scholars have demonstrated, membership in distinct communities is central to the organization of Asian-Argentines' social, economic, and cultural lives. However, such forms of belonging should not lead us to assume that Asian-Argentines operate strictly within what Higa terms the "subsystem" of the colectividad and preclude an inquiry into Asian-Argentines' participation in the Argentine national space.[32] As long as nation is a crucial category that grants not only a sense of belonging but access to material and symbolic benefits, the place of Asians vis-à-vis the Argentine nation should not be explored only in terms of their exclusion.

Both the absence of Asian-Argentines from institutional practices of multiculturalism and the groupist assumption that informs current academic discourse can perpetuate Asians' position as outside the nation. While it could be argued that the current scholarly attention given to Asians is itself a result of multiculturalism and its desire to respect heterogeneity, the particular case of Asian-Argentines as outsiders to the historical nation highlights an impasse typical of multiculturalism: how to recognize difference without compromising the unity of the nation and, conversely, how to recognize difference without denying anyone access to the nation. In this context, recognizing people of Asian origin in discussions of Argentine nationhood is crucial in order to avoid their instrumentalization by the discourse of multiculturalism, which, as critics have pointed out, risks granting nominal cultural recognition to minorities while preserving existing racial, cultural, economic, and political hierarchies.[33]

ASIAN-ARGENTINES IN CULTURAL DISCOURSES

Considering that Asians in Argentina are often assumed to be "too few" or otherwise "too foreign" – not only because of their racial and cultural difference but also because of their imagined status as transient urban migrants – their increased visibility in contemporary cultural manifestations is remarkable. While Asians have not become principal or normative actors in Argentina's cultural imaginary, representations of Asians have notably increased in frequency and become generally more positive. An overwhelmingly negative image as laughable, inarticulate, and greedy has given way to a still stereotyped yet positive image. The global embrace of multiculturalism as an important social value has in part encouraged the visibilization of Asian cultures in the form of ethnic festivities performed for a broader public (e.g., Chinese New Year, the Korean Thanksgiving "Chuseok," parades showcasing ethnic garments and objects), some of which are institutionally sponsored by the country of origin as well as the Argentine state, which considers "the support for celebrations and festivities of foreign communities" an essential step to overcoming discrimination.[34] But they have also gained significant visibility in more spontaneous cultural manifestations including stand-up comedy, television, literature, theater, and most recently, film, suggesting that Asians have also reached the mainstream cultural imaginary.[35]

I have argued elsewhere that the new protagonism of Asians in public life and cultural products is intrinsically linked to Argentina's shift toward a new multicultural paradigm, not only because of multiculturalism's greater toler-ance toward racial others but also because Asians play a significant symbolic role in the production of contemporary multicultural discourses.[36] Historian Arif Dirlik posits that Asia's growing economic power after the Cold War has allowed it to challenge previous identifications of modernity with the West and make "alternative cultural claims on the modern."[37] In this sense, particularly regarding Japanese-Argentines, I have argued that their symbolic flexibility – which encompasses images of hyper-tradition, hyper-modernity, and global reach as well as the undesirable racial other – makes them "ideal champions of multiculturalism for their ability to articulate disparate – and at times contradictory – demands of contemporary multiculturalism."[38] In other words, because of multiculturalism's intrinsic oscillation between inclusion and exclusion – recognizing minorities on the one hand but trying to preserve racial hierarchies on the other – Asians provide symbolic unity to the simultaneous desires to be modern and traditional, multicultural and monocultural. Racially essentialized, culturally exoticized, and different not only from Argentina's dominant whiteness but also from its traditional minorities, Asians have func-tioned as a highly visible marker of the nation's incipient multiculturalism.

Three recent films with Asian protagonists – *Un cuento chino*, *Mujer conejo*, and *Samurai* – suggest, however, that Asians' role in the national narrative has come to transcend their role as tokens of multiculturalism. Given the symbolic significance of Asians in reconfigurations of modernity emblemized now by globalization and multiculturalism, coupled with the centrality of multicultural-ism in Argentina's discourses of nation (as a way to transcend the previous exclusionary version of the nation), I suggest that Asian-Argentines and their representations have become an important site of national articulation. By analyzing these three films, I will argue that in a post-crisis Argentina that aspires to be multicultural, Asians play a meaningful symbolic role: as chal-lenges to previous discourses of the modern nation and as mediators of a new national unity.

ASIAN-ARGENTINES AS MEDIATORS OF THE NATION

Sebastián Borenzstein's *Un cuento chino*, the highest-grossing Argentine film in its year of release, is a formulaic odd-couple story about Roberto (Ricardo Darín), a bitter, middle-aged Argentine recluse and Jun (Ignacio Huang), a considerate but helpless young Chinese man who comes to Argentina with no money (he was robbed by a taxi driver as soon as he landed) or language skills, and who seeks his uncle at an outdated address. Good at heart, Roberto begrudgingly gives Jun room and board, teaches him some Spanish, and helps him navigate Buenos Aires. The film follows the story of their developing bond, comically highlighting moments of cultural and linguistic miscommunication.

Gaspar Scheuer's *Samurai* presents an unsettling premise to Argentine viewers, who imagine Asians as strictly contemporary and urban migrants, through the story of a Japanese family in nineteenth-century rural Argentina. The film follows the formula of an odd-couple road movie with Poncho Negro (Alejandro Awada), a disillusioned *gaucho* or cowboy wandering the Pampas after losing both arms in the Paraguayan War, and Takeo (Nicolás Nakayama), a still-illusioned descendant of samurai who is in search of Saigo Takamori, the historical samurai leader. On his deathbed, Takeo's grandfather suggests that Saigo is hiding "in a faraway place," and Takeo interprets this to mean that he is hiding in the Argentine Pampas – where Takeo and his family live – waiting for his opportunity to return to Japan. Takeo sets out to find Saigo in order to join his fight against Japan's modernization and restore the old order in his native country.

Finally, Verónica Chen's *Mujer conejo* is a thriller about Ana Yang (Haien Qiu), a young city inspector of Chinese descent, who gets in trouble with the Chinese mafia of Buenos Aires when she refuses to authorize unlawful business permits. The conflict between the ruthless Chinese gangsters and Ana is interwoven with her personal identity conflict as an Argentine of Chinese descent who does not speak Chinese and does not identify with Chinese culture.

The three films, although apparently very different from one another, have in common not only their Asian protagonists but also a deep concern to address questions of national identity at a time of crisis. In a post-crisis Argentina that rearticulates the national as a "contestatory exercise, both denouncing the failure of the state and resisting the rhetoric of globalization," film scholar Joanna Page argues that recent Argentine cinema has played a "significant role in representing the nation to itself" and "rebuilding national identity in the absence of a functioning state."[39] All three films evidence the desire to condemn state-sponsored projects of modernity and their accompanying discourses of Argentine exceptionalism (racial, cultural, economic) while still preserving the discourses of nation. While the seminal film *Bolivia* (2001) – produced closer to the economic crisis than to the Bicentennial and concerned more with denouncing xenophobia than with a heightened rhetoric of multiculturalism – reveals "the extent to which 'nationness' as a unifying concept has broken down," these three post-Bicentennial films attempt to restore the unity of the nation that precedes or supersedes the nation in crisis.[40]

Set in the late nineteenth century, *Samurai* criticizes Argentina's modernity project at the moment of its emergence. The railway is arriving to the desolate countryside scarcely populated by hard-drinking gauchos, greedy *criollo*, or native-born, landowners, and, it turns out, an unlikely Japanese family that still wears traditional clothes, eats Japanese food, and lives in a Japanese-style house with sliding paper doors. At the same time, the state is forcing men from the countryside to join its military. None of these modernity projects, however, seems to bring progress. Poncho Negro, a war hero, has been left armless and homeless, rewarded with two medals of honor that he had to sell for food. The deception Argentina's nation-building process perpetuated on the gaucho mirrors the Japanese family's failed immigrant dream. Takeo's father, Satchiro (Jorge Takshima), seeks to improve his position through hard work and assimilation, but his family refuses to give up Japanese customs and he loses everything when he is conscripted by the military. Takeo's samurai grandfather accuses Satchiro of betraying his tradition by wearing Western clothes and speaking Spanish at home, and Takeo seeks to follow in his grandfather's tradition rather than his father's. The presentation of the railway project also appears to affirm Takeo and Poncho Negro's disillusion with modernity. When Takeo works as a hired hand to clear the land for the railway, the film resists the possibility of the railway's linear vision, insisting on short-range shots that dive deep into the density of the Pampean shrubbery. Furthermore, as he journeys with Poncho Negro in search of the famed "last samurai," they seem to go uselessly in circles, as they ride through scenic yet indistinguishable sierras and repeatedly run into the same people.

Like Poncho Negro, *Un cuento chino*'s Roberto is a war veteran disillusioned with the state. Although he was not physically disabled like Poncho Negro, his participation in the Malvinas War left him emotionally disturbed and an orphan. When British forces took the young Roberto and his fellows as war hostages, his photo ended up on the front pages of Argentine newspapers. Roberto's father, who had fled Europe to protect his family from war, suffered a heart attack upon seeing this photo and did not live to see his son's safe return. For Roberto and his first-generation Italian immigrant family, the Argentine state not only fails to deliver their immigrant dream but also fails to protect its citizens. Roberto's mistrust, however, extends beyond the Argentine state to the core of modernity itself as he has lost faith in the rational and therefore obsesses over the absurd. Outside his hardware store, Roberto fills his time collecting newspaper articles about absurd tragedies around the world, including a woman in China crushed to death by a cow that fell from the sky. He will later discover that Jun was her fiancé.

Mujer conejo interweaves its criticism of the failed state with current issues of immigration and global capitalism. The bad guys in this film are not transnational corporations sponsored by the state's neoliberal policies but the local Chinese mafia supported by easily bribed low-ranking public officials. However, Ana, the protagonist, quickly learns that the mafia's reach transcends the *barrio chino* [Chinatown] with its connections to global human-trafficking networks and access to a sophisticated genetic mutation technology that will seriously threaten the national space – both city and country. The film begins with shots of Buenos Aires' barrio chino that could be a busy Chinatown in any cosmopolitan city; Buenos Aires' iconic Europeanness is absent from the film. The Argentine characters are already at ease with their city's cosmopolitanism, delighting in Chinatown's culinary offerings, and casually accepting its impenetrability and noise ("They [Chinese people] are always fighting," a character declares as a matter of fact). While Ana has become curious about her own heritage – leaving Alonso (Luciano Cáceres), an Argentine doctor, to become close to Wang (Wu Chao Ting), a recent Chinese immigrant – she is unwilling to be bribed by the Chinese mafia. The elderly mafia leader tries to subdue her by imposing traditional Chinese hierarchies of age and gender on her, but then resorts to violence, killing her former lover, Alonso, who was involved in her anti-mafia activities. His death leaves her as the sole defender against the moral and physical degeneration of the nation. Aware of the danger she is in, she seeks refuge in her childhood home in the countryside. But the countryside turns out to be no safer than the city: carnivorous mutant rabbits have taken over the once bucolic countryside like a plague and devoured all its cattle, thus destroying the livelihood of its inhabitants. She learns eventually that the rabbits were genetically mutated by the Chinese mafia to produce cheap, self-feeding rabbits for their restaurants and to sell their fur.

All three films reflect on questions of national identity that emerge at the intersection of the 2001 economic crisis and the Bicentennial's pursuit of multiculturalism. If the crisis prompted Argentines to distrust and reexamine national narratives that constructed Argentina as a white and modern nation, multiculturalism – both as a global trend and as a strategy to reclaim its Latin Americanist position – followed naturally as a way to reject them. As Page has argued, however, the crisis ultimately heightened Argentina's desire to rearticulate the national.[41] In these films, Asian characters fill an important role in both the protest against the various projects of the state (modernization, Malvinas, neoliberalism) and the rearticulation of the national which, curiously, characters achieve by renewing an old vision of the nation that stemmed from those same projects. Bruno Latour's work on postmodernity can offer some perspective on this process; he states that "postmodernism is a way of using modernism without being sure it is right."[42] Latour proposes that postmodernity's emphasis on multiculturalism as a way of "getting out" of the discourses of modernity is deeply rooted in modernity itself as "it uses, to try to understand the former unity of modernism, the very definition of multiplicity or pluralism that modernism threw out."[43] If modernity allowed the proliferation of others, only to banish them and ensure the unity or homogeneity of the nation, multiculturalism as articulated in these new national narratives revives those very differences in order to ensure the nation's unity – to borrow theorist Sara Ahmed's words, to establish a "unity-from-diversity."[44]

The introduction of an Asian protagonist, unquestionably an outsider, validates the cultural and racial boundaries of the historical nation. When the landlord in *Samurai* asks about his new hired hand Takeo, the foreman replies, "He is a bit strange. He is not *criollo*. He is not *Pampa*. ... His name is 'Japón.'" All three films also emphasize Asians' difference through typical examples of language barriers and worn stereotypes such as the quiet and submissive Jun, the greedy and ruthless Chinese mafia that hide behind a mask of oriental

wisdom, and the honorable samurai. But most significantly, these films underscore the experience of cultural dissonance – produced by contemporary
non-European immigration and the exigencies of inclusion imposed by the
multicultural ideology – through a sort of chronological dissonance between
Asian newcomers and the preexisting "authentic" nation. That is, the Asian
characters are subjected to an odd temporality by entering a static and old
version of nation, populated by gauchos, *gringos* [the term used in the nineteenth
and early twentieth centuries to refer to immigrants, largely from Europe] and
criollos, and still insularly divided between modernity/tradition, city/
country, and civilization/barbarism, as proposed by Domingo F. Sarmiento's
foundational text *Facundo: Civilization and Barbarism*.[45] If as Latour indicates,
modernity fixes an "archaic and temporal past" from which it can break, and
which will clearly delineate the difference between the modern "victors" and the
premodern "vanquished," these films reappropriate the operation by fixing an
"archaic and temporal past" of the essentialized nation.[46] Unlike modernity's
impulse to break from a primitive past, however, these three films do not attempt
to entirely replace the nation at is foundational moment. Rather, the project of
postmodernity "extends [the nation] as it weakens it."[47]

When Ana, in *Mujer conejo*, seeks refuge in the countryside, she seems to
step into a different era as she encounters some unlikely characters: a gaucho,
two aging *polacos* [Poles] with heavy accents, and a local criollo family. The
revival of these national types, whose prominence predates multiculturalism,
highlights Ana's undeniable foreignness, and therefore makes her defense of
the nation even more heroic. The foundational trope of city and country also
frames the national space in *Un cuento chino*, where the main Argentine
characters fall neatly into a gendered national dichotomy, with the city-
dwelling Roberto as a solitary cynic and Mari as the prototype of the country
maiden – simple, good natured, and romantic. *Samurai* only alludes to the city
without showing it, but the sense that it is far too powerful and inaccessible for
these marginalized characters gives it presence. The city's absence underscores
its uneven power relation to Takeo and Poncho Negro's quixotic journey
against modernity, which we know is doomed from the beginning. While
previous discourses had held together these dichotomies through their opposition or, at times, as an antidote to one another (e.g., the countryside as a
site of national authenticity to the cosmopolitan degeneration of the city,
modernity as progress to the backwardness of tradition), the films here rather
imagine these binary spaces as a form of national unity, simultaneously
against the strangeness of the Asians and through their role as mediators. By
conjuring the nation at the moment that the discourse of modernity imposed its
splitting view and by helping to reveal a collective awakening to the failures of
this discourse, the Asian protagonists reconnect the divided nation and forge
solidarity between its peoples.

Ana's discovery of the common "plague" that has contaminated both the
city and the country in *Mujer conejo* makes this role most explicit. Before Ana's

arrival, the inhabitants of the countryside had passively and ignorantly suffered the invasion of the rabbits alone; Ana's presence inspires them to rise up and join forces. When the mafia comes looking for Ana in her country hideout, the gaucho and the two aging European immigrants, and even the local family who had looked at her with suspicion when she offered the hungry children some *alfajores* [the national sweet], take up arms in her defense. In the final fight scenes, depicted entirely through *anime*, the "national" gang defeats the Chinese gang despite the latter's superior weapons. As the Chinese men are shot, they reveal their true identities by morphing into rabbits, establishing that the Chinese not only engineered a threatening plague, but that they are the plague themselves. The film ends victoriously with the image of Ana holding a bloody dead rabbit up to the sky.

Ana helps identify both the symbolic and material threats against the Argentine nation, and uses the traditional national types – gauchos, gringos, criollos, categories that are in effect obsolete in Argentina outside the symbolic realm – to defend it. In this way, the film simultaneously ensures the unity of the nation (between the country and the city, and its different peoples) and its continuity (from the modern nation to the multicultural nation) at the moment that Argentina's hegemonic national discourses are challenged and as new identities begin to enter it. The final shot of Ana triumphantly raising a dead rabbit/Chinese establishes her clearly as the new national hero. Yet the title of the film, *Mujer conejo*, vacillates on the legitimacy of Ana's national belonging, just as she is privately torn between the Argentineness she adopted and the Chineseness she chose not to inherit. The title declares that Ana is still a *conejo* [rabbit] which, following the film's final revelation, means she is Chinese. That she is a *mujer* [woman] *conejo* sets her apart from the undesirable and masculinized Chinese immigrants but, on the other hand, this gender qualification also evokes the rabbits' dangerous fertility, rendering her a threat to Argentina and humanity itself, although the death of both of Ana's Chinese and Argentine love interests assuages this tacit reproductive threat, as does her heroic role in unifying and defending a nation in crisis. To a certain extent, Ana legitimizes her place in the nation by helping Argentines to distinguish between those desirable and undesirable immigrants – literally fleshing out their hidden identity – precisely because she is herself a *conejo* and has some inside knowledge of that invasive force.

Unlike *Mujer conejo*, which addresses social anxieties of a Chinese "invasion" and the resulting disintegration of the nation, *Un cuento chino* skirts the xenophobic discourses that accompany present-day immigration by making Jun a purely affective migrant in search of his uncle rather than an economic migrant in search of better opportunities. In a light-hearted manner, this film also entrusts Jun with the task of ensuring the unity of the nation by saving the couple and marrying the contrasting values of the city and the country that Roberto and Mari represent. Jun brings the two Argentines together, and helps Roberto in particular to learn his given role in the couple as the foundational unit of the nation, or to bring out the *eroto* in him (as Jun calls Roberto, apparently unable to pronounce his name). Jun disrupts Roberto's secluded life, organized around strict rituals that revisit his family's failed immigrant dream: he works grumpily in his father's hardware store (once a sign of having "made it" in the Americas and now just a daily drudgery), visits his parents' cemetery every weekend, and clips newspaper articles of absurd deaths like the one that befell his father. Roberto discovers a changed Buenos Aires, as when he goes to the barrio chino for clues about Jun's uncle, where he learns that all Chinese speak Spanish, and he gets scolded for not knowing the difference between Mandarin and Cantonese. Even though Roberto is good at heart, he turns out to be a terrible and at times even cruel caretaker: he places Jun in a dirty room full of junk and, at the beginning of his stay, locks the door from outside. Ever maternal, Mari shows up to make up for Roberto's shortcomings, cooking meals, organizing fun outings, and socializing Jun by introducing him to other Argentines. The presence of Jun, in essence, allows Roberto and Mari to rehearse their given gendered roles as a couple and family. The death of Jun's fiancée had truncated his own hopes of making a family and his self-imposed exile allows the couple to infantilize him as a stand-in child. After Jun leaves to reunite with his long-lost uncle in the provinces, Roberto discovers that Jun had dutifully cleared the clutter of his patio, white-washed its walls, and painted a mural of a giant cow. This cow pays homage to their common experience with life's absurd blows and also remits us to the opening scene of the film: Roberto imagines the flying cow that killed the young woman as a "marvelous tale," or even as a *cuento chino* [Chinese tale] meaning an "unbelievable story" or "lie," in which the cow interrupts the moment of betrothal between a lovely young couple dressed in traditional clothes on a peaceful lake surrounded by picturesque hills.[48] The second scene of the film takes us abruptly to China's antipode, Argentina, to a shot of a man walking down the street in front of Roberto's store, depicted not only as more modern and real, but as also physically upside down through an inverted image. The image's hundred and eighty degrees rotation then indicates that we have arrived on the other side of the world in every sense. Jun's drawing of the cow symbolically sums up this antipodal relationship: what for Jun represents loss of love and nation represents for Roberto the recuperation of those very things. The drawing of the cow – one of Argentina's most important national symbols and products – reveals the possibilities of unity and regeneration; in the final scene Roberto happily joins Mari in her *estancia* where she is milking a cow and the couple's possibility of unity and regeneration comes to stand in for the nation's possibility.

By reviving traditional tropes that symbolize the nation, these films illus-trate how "a multicultural nation takes place through the use of a monocul-tural framework" in which the cultural diversity of the stranger "must be transformed into a unifying force."[49] As we have seen earlier, these films establish such a monocultural framework by forging a temporal dissonance in which Asian characters step into an imagined nation of the past. In other words, these films propose that the newcomers and the new ideology of multiculturalism – even if produced by their own dismantling of previous national narratives – can be incorporated as long as they can return the preexisting "'us' into a static and uncontestable past."[50] *Mujer conejo* and *Un cuento chino* ultimately reveal the highly instrumental role of their Asian protagonists (in service of the nation) by providing few clues as to their ultimate fate. Jun boards a plane to the provinces to join his uncle, but the film offers no hints of what his future in Argentina will be like, and Ana emerges victorious but having lost everything.

Samurai permits a more transformative role for Takeo even as the film never loses sight of the authentic nation. The gaucho and samurai, as outlaws but also as indisputable national symbols, efficiently reiterate the critique of the modern state and the desire to preserve the nation. Poncho Negro initially takes advantage of Takeo's naiveté, encouraging the illusion that Saigo might indeed be hiding in the Pampas, to secure his care. While Takeo had been disdainful of his own father for his modern pragmatism, he becomes an exemplary son to Poncho Negro: he gently feeds the armless gaucho with his chopsticks, gives him sips of water in a cup to save him from the humiliation of drinking face down on a riverbed, and becomes the breadwinner during their journey. On the other hand, the young Takeo, who only speaks Japanese and has no experience with the countryside's hostile nature, could not survive without Poncho Negro's knowledge of Spanish and of his native land. Although the pair's attempt to restore a nostalgic old order is destined to fail against the reality and brutality of modernization, this failure does not destroy the film's construction of the nation. Rather, the gaucho and the samurai's symbolic fight against the state, however unrealistic it may be, nationalizes the foreigner and renationalizes the gaucho through a consolidating narrative of "shared experience."[51] The amputated gaucho meets his inevitable death but, gradually through the film, he passes on his gaucho qualities to Takeo, who eventually sheds his chopsticks, *katana*, traditional clothes, and pointed straw hat along with his desire to return to Japan. With his white shirt open at the chest and long hair blowing in the wind as he rides skillfully on the hills of the Pampas, the former samurai becomes a native, or as Poncho Negro describes him, a "strange *gauchito*, but like a son." This strange "gauchito" indeed signals a different future for Argentina, especially as Poncho Negro dies and Takeo's father folds his immigrant dreams and becomes a soldier. "Follow your path," says the father to Takeo, who can now renew the national character by combining the bravery and knowledge of the gaucho and the honor and hard work of the samurai. Even without Poncho Negro, Takeo finds his way out of the endless Pampas to arrive at the seashore where a couple of fishermen are about to go out to sea. Takeo proves his usefulness, and perhaps his newly acquired Argentineness, by skillfully handling a *facón*-style knife – not a katana – that the man hands him to cut the ropes of the boat.

"With will, one can learn the trade," the fisherman says to Takeo, who responds in an accentless Spanish, "*Vamos.*"

CONCLUSION

Whether united in love, honor, or against mutant rabbits, the three films here envision a multicultural nation based on a deeply rooted monocultural framework – perhaps a nation that "has" multicultural subjects instead of "being" multicultural.[52] The three Asian protagonists embody the multicultural entities that the nation can possess in order to overcome the limitations of a nation that homogenized itself by force, but they also function as mediators to reshape the national identity. The Asian characters' central role in these three examples of contemporary national narratives testifies to Argentina's growing desire to proclaim itself as tolerant and diverse. However, these films keep their distance from multicultural negotiations on the ground – such as shifting boundaries of identity and class, and ensuing cultural and racial conflicts – not only by insisting on a preexisting definition of the nation as described earlier, but also by borrowing from stereotyped notions of the traditional *oriental* and portraying the Asian heroes as caricatures, or as primarily allegorical characters that have little footing in Argentina's reality. Resorting to the figure of the samurai, both mythical and mystical, to the beautiful and morally unbendable heroine of the anime, or to notions of traditional filial piety, the films construct characters that are unmistakable allegories of values – honor, morality, hard work, patriarchy – that are thought to be lost in Western modernity but that can be rescued from an orientalized imagination of the East.

The myth of *Samurai*, the anime of *Mujer conejo*, and the fairy tale of *Un cuento chino* propose a new (but also expressly renewed) national character largely removed from the seemingly conflictive Asian-Argentine populations whose official inclusion the multicultural state still resists and whose tension with the majority population and dominant culture has been, according to the existing scholarship, central to their experience. By leaping into the mythical, the oneiric, and the fantastic, these films construct the postmodern multicultural nation through "precisely the *occlusion* of the margins and the poor," reducing Asians to values that can be appropriated into the national character but occluding their marginalized condition in today's Argentina.[53] While it is unlikely that Asian-Argentine communities would recognize themselves in the national heroes portrayed in these cinematic fables, my point is less about the lack of verisimilitude of the invoked Asians and more about the unequal power relations – of representation and recognition – that they potentially naturalize. The representations of Asians as heroic figures in the construction of the new national space are unprecedented and laudable, and certainly make great strides in changing the racial thinking of a nation that prided itself on being European from its foundation. But Asians' omission from official discourses and their reductive representations in contemporary cultural manifestations continue to limit their meaningful participation in the nation.

A cultural discourse that produces unlikely – even if idealized – images of Asian-Argentines, especially in the context of a lack of official representation and recognition, risks laying norms for national inclusion that might be impossible to meet.

If to a certain extent, the three films analyzed here can be read as instructions on how to build a multicultural nation, *La Salada* (2014), a more recent film by the Argentine-Taiwanese filmmaker Juan Martín Hsu, moves away from a prescriptive multicultural ideology to examine some on-the-ground processes of multiculturalism in today's Argentina. The title refers to the Feria La Salada in the province of Buenos Aires, reportedly the biggest informal market in South America with 30,000 stalls that sell clothing, pirated DVDs, toys, and food. The fair was first established by a few Bolivian immigrants in the 1990s but grew astronomically after the 2001 economic crisis when working-class people who could no longer afford regular prices began to pour in from all over the country. In this sense, *La Salada* represents the real margins of a nation in crisis, which the film explores through the multicultural "salad" of its occupiers.[54] Following the lives of Korean, Taiwanese, and Bolivian immigrants (some more recent than others) who work in the market, *La Salada* depicts their common experience of displacement as newcomers to the nation as well as existing power relations, not only with the dominant culture but with each other. This film is not free of common – and at times, dangerous – stereotypes and essentializations such as the subservient Bolivian who works hard despite constant abuse, and the Korean who does not know a word of Spanish after almost two decades in Argentina. However, it avoids reducing minorities to heroes, victims, or cultural ambassadors, and rather attempts to capture different aspects of Asian and Bolivian experiences (arguably the most denigrated groups in Argentina).

Asian-Americanist Lisa Lowe argues that in relation to the articulations of an Asian-American identity, acknowledging heterogeneity (of, for example, national origin, experience of immigration, and relation to the country of origin), multiplicity (as "several different axes of power" determine social relations), and hybridity (cultural practices that are produced by the "histories of unequal and unsynthentic power relations") is crucial in order to overcome the essentializing discourses of the dominant culture.[55] Although admittedly schematic, we can read the characters of *La Salada* as embodying some of the heterogeneity, multiplicity, and hybridity of multicultural Argentina: Yunjin (Yunseon Kim), the dutiful daughter of a Korean immigrant who does not feel as Korean as her father (who in her own words is a "coreano coreano") but in the end submits to an unwanted arranged marriage; Wang (Ignacio Huang), the lonely Taiwanese seller of DVDs (which he copies wearily day in and day out), whose devastatingly awkward date with a young Argentine woman he loves sends him to the arms of an equally lonely and drunk old lady who asks him to say something in Chinese; Bruno (Limbert Ticona), the recent Bolivian arrival who learns to understand his bosses' barked and abusive Korean; and Señor

Kim (Chang Sun Kim), Yunjin's patriarchal father and Bruno's fiery boss, who despairs when Yunjin talks to the *wonjumin* (literally "natives," a common term Koreans in Argentina use to refer to Argentines) men, but who eventually bonds with the hard-working and ingenious Bruno despite differences in race, language, and class.

The scene in *La Salada* in which Kim and his equally successful friend are drinking in a Korean karaoke bar, served by white hostess girls in skimpy dresses who even sing in Korean, exemplifies the threat that contemporary multiculturalism can pose to the hegemonic racial, cultural, and economic order, which the dominant discourse tries to evade by imposing notions of foreignness or by creating guided visions of a multicultural nation based on a monocultural framework. As I have tried to illustrate in this chapter, this discourse is the most predominant in present-day Argentina. However, it also appears that new insights, such as Hsu's in *La Salada*, might be emerging in a post-crisis and now post-Bicentennial Argentina to give us a different understanding of Asian-Argentines and the nation's incipient multiculturalism.

Notes

1. Adamovsky, "El color," 355.
2. Loveman, *National Colors*, 291.
3. For a detailed discussion of Argentina's paradigmatic shift to multiculturalism, see Ko, "Whiteness," 1–5.
4. Courtis, *Construcciones*, 55–61.
5. Due to the ubiquity of Chinese grocery stores, *chino* has become synonymous with "grocer" in everyday language. To disavow myths about the turned-off refrigerators, the association of Chinese grocers, CASRECH (Cámara de Autoservicios y Supermercados Propiedad de Residentes Chinos), signed an agreement with the Government of Buenos Aires to install temperature-detection chips in all Chinese-owned supermarkets. Silvia Gómez, "Controlarán con un chip las heladeras de los súper chinos," *Clarín* (Buenos Aires), 6 Mar. 2011 [online].
6. On the perceived foreignness of Asian-Americans and a denial of racial and cultural citizenship see Chang, "Eternally Foreign," and Tsuda, "I'm American."
7. See Ko, "Whiteness," 1–5.
8. *Infobae*, "En seis años, el Inadi pasó de tener 35 empleados a 550 y a manejar $50 millones," 15 Jun. 2011: www.infobae.com/2011/06/15/587738-en-seis-anos-el-inadi-paso-tener-35-empleados-550-y-manejar-50-millones (accessed 28 Aug. 2014).
9. webINADI (Instituto Nacional contra la Discriminación, la Xenophobia y el Racismo), "Somos Iguales y Diferentes 02" (YouTube video, 15 Jul. 2013): www.youtube.com/watch?v=_gs94hjBfGg&index=28&list=UUVHcPsq8G8t8Hkx WfQg85zA (accessed 29 Aug. 2014).
10. Loveman, *National Colors*, 252.
11. The exceptions were Brazil, which included the color category *amarelo* ("yellow"), Costa Rica with *chino* and Uruguay with *descendencia asiática* and *amarilla* ("Asian descent" and "yellow"). Loveman, *National Colors*, 295 n. 96.
12. Telles and Flores, "Not Just Color," 414.

13. Loveman, *National Colors*, 12.

14. INDEC (Instituto Nacional de Estadística y Censos), "Migraciones" (web publication): www.indec.mecon.ar/comunidadeducativa/migraciones.pdf (accessed 25 Aug. 2014).

15. Ministry of Foreign Affairs, Republic of Korea, "Status of Overseas Citizens," 2 (web publication): www.mofa.go.kr/travel/overseascitizen/index.jsp?mofat=001.2 (accessed 26 Aug. 2014, my translation).

16. Government of the City of Buenos Aires, "Colectividad china y taiwanesa," in *Observatorio de colectividades* (web page): www.buenosaires.gob.ar/derechoshu manos/observatorio/colectividad-china-taiwanesa (accessed 26 Aug. 2014).

17. Laumonier, "Cafés," 164. Estimates on Japanese-Argentine populations vary greatly, ranging between 30,000 and 80,000. However, there appears to be a general consensus among scholars that the current population is between 30,000 and 50,000.

18. According to Evelyn Hu-DeHart, "among the studies of non-European immigration to Latin America, those of the Nikkei may be the best developed" because of the large Nikkei populations in Peru and Brazil, the participation of highly trained scholars of Japanese descent in Latin America, and the interdisciplinary intersections created by US scholars with backgrounds in Asian-American studies and Latin American studies. Hu-DeHart, "Locating the 'Asian,'" 240.

19. Higa, "Desarrollo histórico," 471.

20. Bialogorski, "Logros," 280.

21. Mera, "La inmigración coreana," 3–4.

22. Although there is no unanimous data on Argentina's Taiwanese population, Trejos and Chiang suggest that a maximum population of 30,000 could have been reached before 2001. Trejos and Chiang, "Taiwanese," 119–20.

23. On the impact of the economic crisis on the Korean-Argentine population, see Mera, "Crisis." On recent Chinese immigration, see Pappier, "Inmigración china," 4.

24. Mera, "La inmigración coreana," 7 (my translation).

25. Courtis, *Construcciones*; Bialogorski, personal communication.

26. Higa, "Argentines," 262.

27. Mera, "Diáspora coreana," 3. For an examination of Taiwanese diasporas, see Trejos and Chiang, "Taiwanese." On Japanese diasporas see Onaha, "Diasporización y transnacionalismo," and Higa, "Argentines."

28. These patterns reflect the political and economic instability of Latin American nations, strong cultural ties to country of origin and transnational diasporas, the search for better economic opportunities, and socio-cultural issues related to education and cultural capital. Park, "Rhizomatic Diaspora," 15–26.

29. Mera, "Diáspora coreana," 12 (my translation).

30. Higa, "Argentines," 276.

31. Ibid., 277.

32. Ibid., 262.

33. Since this critique has been widely accepted, see these seminal works: Fraser, "Redistribution," and Žižek, "Multiculturalism."

34. INADI (Instituto Contra la Discriminación, la Xenofobia, y el Racismo), *Hacia un plan nacional contra la discriminación* (Web publication, 2005), 343: www.inadi .gob.ar/wp-content/uploads/2010/04/plannacional.pdf (my translation).

35. For an analysis of the representation of Asians in contemporary novels by Asian-Argentine authors, see Hagimoto, "Beyond the Hyphen." For an analysis of novels by authors of non-Asian descent, see Ko, "Argentina te incluye."

36. Ko, "Whiteness."

37. Dirlik, "Asia Pacific Studies," 158.

38. Ko, "Whiteness," 14.

39. Page, *Crisis*, 6, 113, 111.

40. Ibid., 126.

41. Ibid., 111.

42. Latour, "Recall," 16.

43. Ibid., 16.

44. Ahmed, *Strange Encounters*, 112.

45. Sarmiento, *Facundo*.

46. Latour, *Never Been Modern*, 10.

47. Latour, "Recall," 16.

48. Erausquin, "Los inmigrantes."

49. Ahmed, *Strange Encounters*, 112.

50. Ibid., 104.

51. Page, *Crisis*, 110.

52. Ghassan Hage, *White Nation: Fantasies of White Supremacy*, quoted in Ahmed, *Strange Encounters*, 117.

53. Andermann discusses these occlusions in post-crisis films, such as *Luna de Avellaneda* (2004), that attempt to represent the "nation in plight" from the comfort of middle-class interior spaces. Andermann, *New Argentine Cinema*, 42.

54. Although the name of the fair La Salada ("The Salty") derives from a nearby lake with high levels of salinity, it is possible to read the film's title as an allusion to the "salad" of diverse peoples – Bolivians, Koreans, Taiwanese – that the film portrays. "Salada" is also the Korean pronunciation of salad.

55. Lowe, "Heterogeneity," 428–29.

11

Indias blancas, negros febriles

Racial stories and history-making in contemporary Argentine fiction

Paulina L. Alberto

With the start of the new millennium, Argentine readers appear to have developed a taste for a new kind of racial storytelling. Faithful black servants pining for their white mistresses, white captive women falling for their indigenous captors, and enslaved "Hottentot" princes seducing white socialites are some of the unlikely characters populating a new crop of historical fiction, set mostly in Argentina's turbulent nineteenth century. The corpus of stories spotlighting the lives, loves, and tribulations of nonwhite Argentines is expanding rapidly, primarily through novels aimed at adult audiences but also in short story collections and youth literature.[1] Some of these works have won critical acclaim and prizes, and others – largely ignored by the literary establishment – have become mass-market bestsellers.

The popularity of these works in present-day Argentina is striking given the efforts of past generations of Argentine politicians, thinkers, and writers to set their nation apart, racially and culturally, from its neighbors. This project itself rested substantially upon a particular kind of racial storytelling – historical, political, or literary narratives that, from the mid-nineteenth century onward, idealized or asserted Argentina's homogeneous whiteness and Europeanness as part of a "civilizing" process.[2] Beginning in the late nineteenth century, proponents of this "white legend" of Argentine racial history declared indigenous people and Afro-Argentines to have disappeared through war, disease, or peaceful assimilation.[3] Throughout the twentieth century, celebrations of Argentina as a "perfectly white" country of immigrants "descended from the boats," a "melting pot" of primarily European ethnicities, came to enjoy widespread acceptance among Argentina's urban educated sectors.[4] The notion of Argentine whiteness and exceptionalism has also been indirectly reinforced by what we might call a "black legend" of Argentine racial history.[5] This critical counter-narrative, embraced at different times by historians, politicians, ethnic activists, and other public figures, provides a dark (rather than rosy) vision of Argentine whiteness: it sympathizes with the indigenous and Afro-Argentine victims of

nineteenth-century "civilizing" campaigns and denounces the violence and discrimination that led to their "extermination" or "genocide."[6]

Yet this newer crop of tales offers a different kind of racial storytelling,
paralleling the recent rise in Argentine public life of what I call "brown
legends" of Argentine racial identity. Since the devastating economic crisis
of 2001 and especially in the years surrounding the 2010 Bicentennial, groups
of ethnic activists, politicians, historians, and other producers and consumers
of high and popular culture have sought to force into the national spotlight an
alternative vision of a diverse or even *mestizo* Argentina. Although Argentines
do not use the term "brown" or its Spanish equivalents in relation to these
projects, I find the term analytically useful to describe emerging narratives
of Argentine racial identity that occupy a symbolic third space between
white and black legends, and to reflect ideas of the mixed nation that, unlike
the term "mestizo," can encompass not only indigenous people but Afro-
descendants as well. As we will see, the project to "brown" Argentina has
many contemporary manifestations, ranging from the creation of anti-racist
government agencies to the recent inclusion of indigenous people and Afro-
Argentines in the national census. But it is also deeply historical and historiographic in nature. In Argentine public life, the nation's past and how it
should be told in the present have become lively grounds for political debate
as vocal historians and other public figures attempt to discredit both "white"
and "black" legends of Argentine exceptionalism. Drawing Argentina closer
to its neighbors, and questioning or nuancing Argentine whiteness, many
public commentators increasingly highlight the country's Indo-Afro-*criollo*
populations, past and sometimes present, and the significance of mestizaje
(as a social process, if not as an explicit ideology of state) in the creation of
modern Argentina.[7]

In a similarly revisionist vein, the new crop of historical fiction spotlights
the protagonism, rather than the erasure or subsidiary role, of indigenous
people, mestizos, blacks, or mulattos in Argentina's past, implicating readers
personally and politically in their fates. As stories of interracial love, moreover,
these tales retroactively provide Argentina with a mixed-race genealogy. Above
all, these authors make the process of historical revision central to their story-
lines. Heroes and heroines become historian-detectives whose personal quests
compel them to uncover the role of indigenous people or Afro-Argentines in the
nation's past, exposing Argentine whiteness itself as the result of fictional
storytelling. Historians, histories, documents, and bibliographies appear
throughout, arming readers with the knowledge needed to revise their racial-
historical imaginaries.

Literary scholars and cultural historians have long noted the role that racial
stories played in the foundation of new American nations – in particular, their
cultures and political constituencies – in the nineteenth century.[8] There is little
chance that any of these contemporary racial fictions will become canonical in
the way that Argentina's *Facundo* (1845), Brazil's *Iracema* (1865), or Cuba's

Sab (1841) did in their time. Yet like the tales of mixture that served as symbolic "foundational fictions" in many other parts of Latin America over a century earlier, these new Argentine fictions are rich sources for understanding shifting ideas about race and national identity in their own time and place. These novels, with their powerful counter-narratives of national history,[9] are part of the noteworthy, if uneven and incomplete, attempts by a broader range of public figures to symbolically "re-found" the nation upon a more inclusive matrix two hundred years after independence. As part of their didactic mission, they crystallize for readers the main strains of racial storytelling circulating in public life – from "mainstream" discussions of race (in the media, political pronouncements, popular culture, or schools) to "specialist" views (scholarship or activist discourse). In the process, these works draft a valuable blueprint of the components, mechanisms, and functions of these racial stories and of their potential sites of intersection with readers' private passions.

This chapter focuses on three novels: the two-book saga *Indias blancas* and *Indias blancas II: La vuelta del ranquel*, by Florencia Bonelli (2005), and *Fiebre negra*, by Miguel Rosenzvit (2008). Bonelli is the leading figure in the popular historical romance subgenre in Argentina and *Indias blancas* [White Indian Women] is her best-selling work, as well as the one that deals most centrally with race.[10] Rosenzvit's *Fiebre negra* [Black Fever] is both less popular and more self-consciously literary, but it received attention in notable media outlets and was a finalist for the Premio Planeta.[11] In *Indias blancas* the main racial "others" are indigenous people, whereas in *Fiebre negra* they are Afro-Argentines. The books are also quite different in style and structure. Yet both authors make inter-racial relations central to their plot lines, and both use their historical imaginations and contemporary debates over history to reframe national identity in more inclusive terms. They also both intentionally reject the entrenched white legend of Argentine racial history, drawing instead on some variant of historical revision: from black legend denouncements of the evils and effectiveness of genocide, to brown legend accounts of the persistence of histories of mixture and diversity, to the more subtle revisionism of academic historiography or (less frequently) racial activists' own demands for visibility and reparation. All three works, finally, reveal the power of these competing racial stories to shape the public's historical imaginary in ways that are trans-formative, but also limiting.

Indias blancas: PROMISES AND PERILS OF THE BROWN LEGEND

Set in the nineteenth century, *Indias blancas* and its sequel imagine a love affair between a young white woman of the Buenos Aires elite (the daughter of a general of the independence wars) and an indigenous man. The story begins in 1873 when the heroine, Laura Escalante, receives unsettling news: her beloved half-brother Agustín, a Franciscan priest who ministers to the indigenous Ranquel people in the frontier town of Río Cuarto, Córdoba, has been stricken with a deadly case of anthrax. Against the prohibitions of her family and fiancé, Laura flees her elegant home in Buenos Aires for Río Cuarto. Yet in the process of caring for her brother, Laura meets and falls in love with Nahueltruz Guor, one of her half-brother's closest companions and the fictional son of the historical Ranquel chief Mariano Rosas.

Though the story opens at a moment of relative peace between the state and the Ranqueles, Bonelli repeatedly foreshadows the approach of the "Conquest of the Desert" (1879–85), the state's massive military campaigns to subdue Argentina's autonomous indigenous groups in the Pampas and Patagonian regions and occupy their territories.[12] Bonelli thus relies on the prevalence in Argentine society of both white and black legend narratives of indigenous extermination to shroud the love affair with a sense of doom. At the same time, drawing on reinvigorated brown legend narratives in present-day Argentina, her novels push against the sense that conflict and destruction are inevitable to find the plausible spaces – geographic, cultural, ideological – in which such a romance could have taken place. In *Indias blancas*, Bonelli provides Argentina with a new mestizo history and genealogy, made possible by the interracial love affairs of intrepid female heroines.

Bonelli pursues this historiographic goal not just by telling us a new story about Argentina's multiracial past, but by making the process of historical discovery and the revision of Argentine racial stories central to the plot itself. Early on in the novel, Laura intercepts a manuscript addressed to her ailing half-brother Agustín, which she keeps and reads avidly in secret. It turns out to be the memoirs of a woman named Blanca Montes: Laura's aunt, as well as the first wife of Laura's father (and mother of Agustín). This "primary source" is rendered in italics and interspersed throughout the main storyline at the moments when Laura reads from it. The memoir, written toward the end of Blanca's life, reveals to Laura the fate of this mysterious aunt, never publicly discussed in her family. Blanca (the name is the female adjective for "white" in Spanish) relates how, on a trip across the countryside with her husband in the 1840s, she was taken captive by a group of Ranqueles and made into the unwilling concubine of chief Mariano Rosas. Blanca's memoirs narrate her initial repulsion toward Mariano and her eventual amorous and cultural conversion, resulting in the realization – following a climactic sexual encounter – that "Mariano Rosas was my destiny and that I had become an *india blanca*."[13] In the course of her time as a captive, Blanca gave birth to a young boy with the gray eyes of her ancestors – none other than Laura's lover, Nahueltruz.

Blanca's memoirs, with their romantic captivity story, provide a seemingly unique precedent for Laura's own intrepid and unconventional love affair. Reading long passages from the *Memorias* just before or after her trysts with Nahueltruz helps strengthen Laura's resolve to brave social conventions and set aside her doubts, to vow to become another "india blanca," even before she is assured of a happy ending for her aunt.[14] Yet Blanca's memoir soon reveals her story of interracial love to be far from exceptional. Blanca, too, is a historian, gathering oral histories of her family's deep past from a beloved (and ancient) family servant. These stories, retold in the *Memorias*, gradually disclose to Laura a host of love affairs in the history of her family and household in which respectable men and women became entangled with people of the "wrong" race, class, region, or political party. These transgressive romantic matches begin with the first members of the Montes family to reach Argentina in the late eighteenth century (a blonde Spanish beauty and a part-Moorish man) and continue down the generations to Blanca's own mother Lara (whose last name, Pardo, a term denoting partial African descent, is but one of many suggestions of her ambiguous whiteness). The memoirs invent a new family tree even for the famous non-fictional Ranquel chief Mariano Rosas – in the story, Mariano was the product of a night of passion between Governor Juan Manuel de Rosas (the famous nineteenth-century Argentine head of state) and a beautiful mestiza. Gradually, the process of historical discovery turns nearly every character in the novel into a product of mestizaje – conceived either as a kind of amorous transculturation (like Blanca or Laura, white women "colored" by their love affair with a nonwhite man) or, more traditionally, as the offspring of these relationships.

What do we make of Bonelli's hyperbolic attempts to re-center mestizaje in Argentine history? In an article exploring the uses of fiction for history, historian and novelist Richard Slotkin asks why, given the historiographic shifts that have helped demolish master narratives and national mythologies in the last few decades, there should not be "a type of historical fiction that is responsive to the new, critical historiography, and uses its insights?" Historical novels written in this mode, Slotkin explains, can explore "alternative possibilities for belief, action and political change, unrealized by history, which existed in the past. In so doing, the novelist may restore, as *imaginable possibilities*, the ideas, movements and values defeated or discarded in the struggles that produced the modern state – may produce a *counter-myth*, to play into and against the prevailing myths of the nation."[15] Bonelli, it would seem, is trying to use her copious inter-generational stories of mixture to create a "counter-myth" – a brown legend, to be precise – to "play into and against" the traditional representations of a white Argentina.

This, Bonelli demonstrates through Laura's discoveries, is a revisionist project – one in which historians will recognize broader trends transforming Argentine academia and public life in the last few decades. Since at least the 1980s, historical writing on indigenous people and Afro-Argentines has begun to move beyond the black legend denunciations of "extermination" that had largely characterized earlier scholarship. These newer, revisionist works lay bare the mechanisms – concrete and discursive – by which non-whites were excluded from the nation: how they were *made invisible*, rather than (or in addition to) how they physically disappeared. This has included paying greater attention, among other things, to processes of mestizaje and cultural hybridity, complicating earlier interpretations that stressed unidirectional whitening or assimilation. In their concern with dismantling the "myth" of a "white Argentina," newer academic works have echoed a broader tendency among Latin American historians in the past few decades to debunk "myths" of racial harmony or peaceful amalgamation, to demonstrate the consequences of these ideological constructs, and to lay the groundwork for narratives centered on the participation, resistance, and persistence of black and indigenous populations despite the violence, marginalization, and enforced invisibility to which they were subjected.[16]

Bonelli's attempts to draw from this newer scholarship on Argentina's non-white past are most evident in her treatment of one facet of the mestizaje story: Blanca's captivity. Aside from being a personal and family history, Blanca's memoirs are a first-person captivity narrative written by a white woman who was rescued – a document that does not actually exist for Argentina. In contrast to the United States, where captivity narratives written by "redeemed" white women became the first best-sellers, in Argentina no such narratives were published in the nineteenth century, nor have any yet been discovered.[17] This relative absence likely reflects a broader historical reticence in Argentine society toward rescuing captive women (for reasons partly involving the shame and dishonor of presumed interracial sex); the reluctance of many of those captives to leave behind their mestizo children as a condition for their return home; and the fact that most historical captives were lower-class, and probably illiterate, frontier women (unlike Laura or Blanca).[18] Even without such first-person narratives, however, the theme of the white female captive is a recurring one in Argentine literature from the seventeenth century onward. But in most of these narratives, the captive woman ultimately dies to avoid, or to expiate, the shame and dishonor of capture and rape at the hands of Indians.[19] Literary scholars have read this treatment of white female captivity as a reflection of anxieties, particularly in the nineteenth century, about the possibility of establishing a white lineage for Argentina, and as a way of exorcising the dreaded specter of mestizaje, of kinship with the racial "other," raised by female captivity.[20]

Bonelli's novel, by contrast, gleefully steps into the spaces left by these silences, imagining a document that captures the excitement, romance, and eroticism of captivity in the voice of an educated white woman. Indeed, it revels in inverting what historian John Demos, in his classic study of captivity in early North America, calls the "nightmare prospect" (for European settlers) of "civilized people willingly turned savage."[21] Blanca, following her cultural conversion, does not wish to be rescued. Like several historical captives, she prefers her new life to a return to a society where she and her mestizo child would be disdained. She becomes an "india blanca" – in the novel, a person transformed in culture and ethnicity by her love for an Indian man and her motherhood to their child. This aspect of Blanca's *Memorias* reprises an alternative and lesser-known tradition of narrating female captivity in Argentina, from travelers' accounts of white women who wished to remain "unredeemed" to novels like Eduarda Mansilla's *Lucía Miranda* (1860), which explores the possibility of mutual attraction between indigenous captor and white captive.[22] Moreover, through the device of the rediscovered diary and through scenes of Blanca's tortured return to "civilization," Bonelli allows Laura and her readers to witness the ways that family (and by extension national) histories were reconstructed to hide or forget episodes of captivity, interracial sex, and mestizaje (echoing themes in recent histories of indigenous people and Afro-Argentines), as well as to downplay the protagonism of strong women.

Yet as we can already begin to see, Bonelli's exaggerated use of mestizaje in the novel is more than just a revision of racial narratives per se. Her project to establish a mestizo or brown genealogy for Argentina is part of a broader set of revisions – common to the works of other writers in this genre, and drawing explicitly or implicitly on several decades of work among academic historians – that introduce nuances, hidden stories, or silenced voices into dominant historical narratives. Bonelli dramatizes one of these historiographic revisions in her choice to situate part I of *Indias blancas* on the frontier. In this setting, she recreates the complex contact zone described by nineteenth-century explorer Lucio V. Mansilla, whose account of his embassy to the group of Ranqueles under Mariano Rosas (*Una excursión a los indios ranqueles*, 1870) reveals "the whole motley frontier society of outlaws, captives, criminals, political dissidents, fugitives from military service, honest men, and rogues that has gathered around Mariano Rosas's tents."[23] By lingering in this space just beyond the reach of the Argentine state, Bonelli seems to be reminding us (as historians have done) both of the fiction of stark national frontiers and of the historical existence of complex, interethnic contact spaces.[24]

As she does with Laura's historical discoveries, Bonelli dramatizes this revision through emplotment. Toward the end of Part I, Laura's lover Nahueltruz takes up residence in an abandoned shack along the frontier, reportedly haunted by the ghost of its former inhabitant (a female healer of both African and indigenous background). Nahueltruz resolves to transform this site into a temporary home for himself and Laura, where they might take refuge from both of their families and the world at large. Yet this plan fails when Laura's chaperone and would-be suitor Julián Riglos discovers the affair and drives the lovers apart by relaying false information to both sides. Riglos's jealousy is the proximate motive, but Bonelli makes a deeper historiographic point. Riglos is a historian, engaged in compiling one of the first histories of independent Argentina (from the perspective of wealthy, prominent Liberal males). The "official" historian, with his biases, lies, and stark nineteenth-century antinomies of "civilization" and "barbarism," thus destroys the possibility of a contented life in the intermediate, mixed, almost otherworldly space of the frontier, forcing Laura and Nahuel back to her or his side of a divided Argentina. Another

prominent – though much more literary and academic – writer of racial fictions,
María Rosa Lojo, captured this historiographic project best in her interview
with the national daily *La Nación* just before the May 2010 Bicentennial
(interviews with Bonelli, by contrast, are relentlessly superficial and tell us
nothing of her views on race).[25] Lojo eloquently describes the ways in which
reading the works of Lucio Mansilla and his sister and fellow writer Eduarda
allowed her to enter "a distant and not-so-distant *pampa,* inhabited by
gauchos, indigenous people and blacks: ethnic and cultural currents that com-
mingled in an *Argentina criolla.*" These readings introduced her to "an Argentina [...] far beyond the usual dichotomies and simplifications," "more
profound and complex than the one described in textbooks."[26] Before Bonelli,
Lojo reimagined this alternative Argentina in novels about Lucio and Eduarda
Mansilla or Manuelita Rosas – people unusual in their attitudes toward race,
gender, and authority.[27]

Another broader historiographic revision that Bonelli strives to popularize is
the use of gender as a category of historical analysis, which (in Argentina as
elsewhere) has resulted, in the last decades, in new kinds of histories focused on
women, gender roles and expectations, or private life.[28] Indeed, Bonelli states
this goal in the preface to the novel's 2005 edition, and throughout the early
chapters of the novel, she introduces Laura to her twenty-first-century female
readers as a kindred spirit: independent, possessed of "a powerful will," and an
articulate feminist *avant la lettre* (a message underscored by Laura's willingness
to pursue a sexual affair with an indigenous man). Blanca's memoirs, moreover,
are Bonelli's version of a history written in this gendered tradition. They present
a bottom-up history of private lives and intimate details, centered on women
and written in a female voice, revealing a history that intersects with and
transforms official ones. It is in contrast to Riglos's official history – androcen-
tric, dichotomous, and authoritarian – that Blanca's fine-grained account of the
multiple gender, class, and racial transgressions of the Montes family takes on
particular meaning.

In her search for precedents for a more inclusive Argentina, Bonelli also
rebuilds the pantheon of Argentine heroes. She does this in part by creating
new heroes: giving voice to alternative, eccentric, or counter-hegemonic individuals from Argentine history, like Eduarda and Lucio Mansilla (upon whose
Excursión Bonelli seems to base most of her descriptions of Ranquel life and
characters, and which, in the novel, serves as Laura's other literary obsession
alongside her aunt's memoirs) and assorted other boundary-crossing figures. At
the same time, like authors of other Latin American "new historical novels,"[29]
Bonelli uses her plot lines to de-mythify official national heroes linked to the
Conquest of the Desert, like Presidents Domingo Sarmiento and Julio A. Roca
or explorer Estanislao Zeballos (all rendered as unappealing characters in
Indias blancas). In *La vuelta del ranquel,* Laura returns to Buenos Aires as
Riglos's wife, soon widows, and becomes influential as the owner of a printing
press that leads the opposition to the Conquest of the Desert. At the same time,

Laura begins an affair with General Roca himself – the main architect and executor of those military campaigns. Though absurd, this relationship allows Bonelli to write scenes in which Laura directly confronts and condemns Roca's plans, ideologies, and morals, teaching readers to revise their views of the illustrious general.

In their use of racial mixing to highlight other dimensions of diversity, rebelliousness, or resistance in Argentine history, Bonelli's novels reflect (and likely reinforce) a key facet of broader debates about race, history, and identity in contemporary Argentina. In the period when these novels were published, discussions of the nation's ethnic and racial diversity – including allusions to a mestizo Argentine people – became increasingly salient in public history, popular culture, and political life. As we might expect, the 2001 economic crisis exacerbated feelings of xenophobia against foreigners and discriminatory sentiments against poor and dark-skinned Argentines that had been on the rise among sectors of Argentina's urban middle and upper classes since at least the 1990s.[30] But the crisis also, perhaps unexpectedly, intensified a renegotiation of Argentina's racial and ethnic character that had begun more gradually in the 1980s and 1990s, following Argentina's return to democracy. The 2001 economic catastrophe deepened the crisis of legitimacy faced by the state since the dictatorship, and definitively destabilized official visions of national identity that, for most of the twentieth century, had stressed Argentina's exceptional status in Latin America as a homogeneously white, largely middle-class nation. These processes widened the space for alternate definitions of national identity to emerge at various levels of society, accelerating the processes of ethnic and racial re-visibilization already underway.[31]

Yet the particular history of "race" in modern Argentina – the circumstances that produced its invisibility for so long – has conditioned the forms through which race has reemerged as an issue of national debate. Official ideologies have long denied the significance of racial differences within the homogeneously "white" national community. Since the late nineteenth century, a centralized state helped to produce and sustain this image through powerful institutions of social control that incorporated diverse residents as (theoretically) unmarked citizens, while class-based identifications increasingly subsumed (nonetheless persistent) racial and ethnic tensions.[32] If "race," as a discourse and practice of demarcation of difference, became invisible for most of the century by being silently absorbed into more explicitly articulated ideas about power, space, gender, class, and culture, it stands to reason that today, as race resurfaces a problem or an identity, it comes characteristically entangled with the multiple modalities of power it helped to produce. Especially given the historical absence, in Argentine public life, of legitimized ways of articulating experiences of racism, the imbrication of race with a range of other dimensions of social struggle and inequality also reflects attempts by those who would denounce racist attitudes and acts to draw on and adapt denunciatory frameworks (such as human rights discourse) that already had strong resonance in

Argentina.[33] In many of these post-crisis histories and historical fictions, then, the recuperation of race as an issue and the defense of racial diversity as a moral good are not primarily – and perhaps not even – about race itself. Instead, taking advantage of the shape-shifting history of race in Argentina and its power to stand for many things, emerging counter-narratives use the browned nation (whether conceived as multiracial or simply as a darker shade of white-ness) as a metaphor for an Argentine identity that might newly be conceived as anti-authoritarian, anti-hegemonic, nationalist, populist, gender-inclusive, and plebeian.

For instance, following the 2001 crisis, many working-class and poor Argen-tines increasingly spoke of themselves as "*negros*" (reclaiming a common insult) and celebrated "lo negro" as authentically Argentine in a range of public contexts. As historian Ezequiel Adamovsky explains, although these recent redeployments of "lo negro" have some racial and anti-racist undertones, they are in no way claims to belonging to a particular ethnic or racial group (though the use of the term can recognize some amount of mestizaje among popular sectors). The term, rather, relies on the mark and stigma of "*negritud*" or blackness to "make visible, metonymically, the human diversity that makes up the popular."[34] This metonymic operation rests upon an even earlier one (beginning in the late nineteenth century) by which, as historian and anthro-pologist Lea Geler has shown, the term "negro" and the supposed attributes of African blackness were symbolically transferred onto popular sectors as a whole, linking "negritud" primarily to class and behavior and de-linking it from Africanness.[35] As deployed by members of popular sectors today, "negro" operates as a strategic marker of difference, a reminder of power asymmetries, a rejection of dominant definitions of Argentine identity as purely white and European, and an assertion of affinity with the Afro-Latin-Indigen-ous cultures of Argentina's neighbors.

Similar "metonymic" uses of race are visible across many public efforts to rewrite Argentine history and identity in a counter-hegemonic register in the wake of the crisis. Historian Felipe Pigna, with his vast array of books, TV documentaries, historical exhibits, and journalistic production, best exemplifies the growing taste among educated audiences for revisionist histories in a "popular" mode. His best-selling *Los mitos de la historia argentina* (2004) begins with a denunciation of the erasure of indigenous people from Argentine history. Yet the attention to indigenous groups is but the opening salvo in a broader battle to "reconquer" Argentina's history from the memory of "offi-cial" historians and the military dictatorship.[36] In a similar vein, public histor-ian Osvaldo Bayer has undertaken a campaign to "de-monumentalize" General Roca, removing his name and image from public spaces (the famous portrait of his army on the 100-peso bill has been replaced by a profile of Eva Perón). In place of a statue to Roca in a prominent Buenos Aires plaza, Bayer and his supporters proposed plans in 2004 to erect a double statue to native and immigrant women, highlighting mestizaje (and the role of mothers) in the creation of a "criollo" population. Here, as in Bonelli's fictionalized equivalent of these "de-monumentalization" campaigns, the racial violence practiced by Roca extends metonymically into broader recurrent injustices in Argentine history, such as military authoritarianism, fascism, patriarchy, and the writing of repressive or exclusionary histories.[37]

Yet insofar as these emerging visions of Argentine identity either stress racial mixture or use race indirectly to allude to other kinds of power asymmetries, they stand in tension with the narratives put forth by indigenous and Afro-Argentine activists and allied academics. Despite sharing with brown legend narratives the goals of debunking histories of whiteness and effective extermination, indigenous and Afro-Argentine activists deviate from emerging conceptions of a "mestizo" Argentina by stressing their historical and contemporary presence as ethnically or racially distinct groups (and in the case of indigenous people, politically autonomous ones). These groups tend, moreover, to center issues of racial violence and discrimination in their analyses of the Argentine past and present, rather than use them as a manifestation or metonym of something else. Above all, they demand visibility, official state recognition, and (to different degrees) reparations as historically aggrieved communities.[38] Academic historians, for their part, have looked to the past not simply to celebrate a new, more inclusive vision of a multiracial or mestizo nation – indeed, several have critiqued the reductionism of revisionist glorifications of mestizaje which, in their celebration of a purportedly peaceful form of racial integration, hide the usually violent conditions under which racial mixing historically took place.[39] Instead of creating new Manichean narratives with heroes and villains, most recent works on indigenous people and Afro-Argentines (in step with the scholarship on race in Latin America more broadly) have examined critically how ideas about race are produced and circulated from above and below, and how race conditions citizenship. Scholars have focused on indigenous people and Afro-Argentines as actors central to major historical processes, seeking to document the presence of these groups into and through the twentieth century and to place racialized subjects at the center of their accounts.[40]

Bonelli's novels, with their extremely literal insistence on interracial love and sex as the basis of a mestizo (and matrilineal) national genealogy, bring into particularly clear focus the limitations of these brown legends as they circulate in fiction and in public life. The existence of several popular Facebook pages for *Indias blancas*, where adoring and almost exclusively female fans discuss the novels in highly personal terms, affords some insight into how present-day readers receive, act upon, or revise such celebrations of a mestizo past.[41] First, by configuring inclusion as mestizaje or interracial romance, Bonelli's brown legend reduces the spaces for indigenous or black characters to assert and maintain their ethnic or cultural difference. Bonelli's insistence on mestizaje, for instance, means that she does not actually go so far as to describe the beauty of "purely" indigenous or black characters. The attractive Mariano Rosas and

Nahuel are both light-eyed mestizos in the fictional rendering, and the dignified and appealing "negra" María Pancha, Laura's black maidservant, turns out to be a *mulata*. We can begin to glimpse the contradictory effects of this kind of message through readers' Facebook posts. On one hand, the page is full of images (found or created by fans) depicting sensual embraces between strong, bare-torsoed, bronzed men and scantily clad blonde women. In these pictures, the idealized Nahueltruz balances exotic good looks (dark skin, high cheek-bones, sleek black hair) with a few Europeanized features (light eyes, aquiline nose) for a mestizo aesthetic that departs from traditional Argentine ideals of white male beauty. His indianness is lightly acknowledged by clothing or adornments: a feather, a headband, a lance. On the other hand, there is clear evidence of the limits of the mestizo's appeal. In response to a set of posts containing images of the real Mariano Rosas – a man with dark skin, brown eyes, and a deeply creased, mustachioed face – some fans expressed (comical) disappointment and others questioned the authenticity of this "supposed por-trait" because the image did not fit their vision of the handsome light-eyed man Bonelli described.[42] That fans can write the actual indigenous cacique out of their historical imaginaries for failing to live up to fictional standards of mestizo beauty exposes the limits of the transformational power of Bonelli's counter-myth of mestizaje.

Bonelli's romance story also pushes toward the negation or fusion of cultural differences through the devices of love, sex, and reproduction. Thus, the novel fails (or chooses not) to imagine a counter-myth in which indigenous people might have fought for their right to cultural difference and political autonomy. Instead, it consistently imagines the resolution of inter-ethnic tensions through indigenous people's adaptation to the cultural norms of Euro-Argentine soci-ety – whether in Nahueltruz's conversion (in Part II) into the polished and educated "Lorenzo Rosas," or in Bonelli's imaginative re-writing of passages of Mansilla's *Excursión* to highlight Mariano Rosas's eagerness and ability to adopt "civilized" habits like sedentary agriculture. Bonelli thus replaces black legends of extermination with a history of gradual vanishing through cultural assimilation – indeed, she often describes both Mariano Rosas and Nahueltruz as shadowy, ghostly presences, presaging their eventual evanescence. The image of the "vanishing Indian" is a recognizable trope in Argentine (and other American) creolization narratives, and it clashes frontally with contemporary scholars' and activists' attempts to assert indigenous people's presence and to make them visible.[43]

At the same time, throughout the novel, difference (cultural, racial, social) fulfills a primarily erotic purpose – it is seductive and fetishized. When Blanca Montes tells her future husband why her personal history makes her an unsuit-able match for a man of his status, Escalante answers passionately, "your past seduces me" – he is attracted to Blanca because of her unconventional history, not in spite of it.[44] Similarly, María Pancha's father (the Khoikhoi prince Mugabe) woos her mother (the wealthy white Sebastiana Balbastro) with "stories of his land and of his strange customs" and by speaking to her in Khoisan, just as Nahueltruz's command of the history and mores of the Ranqueles leaves Laura and other listeners "seduced."[45] As critics of mestizaje, racial democracy, and other brown legends have noted, these ideologies often reify and claim an indigenous, African, or creole past for whites in problematic ways, while sugar-coating the histories of ethnic and gender violence that often underlay racial mixture. This fetishizing of difference not only titillates; it also proposes a simplistic way of fulfilling a fantasy of racial progressivism without requiring much social change. Bonelli offers her readers, faced with new messages about the virtues of multiculturalism, the possibility of becoming "indias blancas" themselves by reading this romantic fantasy of transgression with an exotic lover. (Bonelli is part "india blanca" herself; she dedicates the novels to an aunt who told her of a distant relative of theirs who had been a captive). Indeed, this seems to be one of the most appealing messages of these two novels, judging from the responses of female readers on Facebook. The inaugural post of the *Indias Blancas* Facebook page asks the rhetorical question that becomes a recurring theme throughout subsequent posts: "who would not want to be an india blanca after meeting nahueltruz….[?]"[46] In subsequent posts, many women affirm this desire for captivity, expressing their longing to be "indias" or to be Laura in the arms of Nahueltruz. A few more realistic ones simply begin calling their existing lovers "mi Nahueltruz" or "mi indio," suggesting just how little accommodation in one's actual life is required by the seductive fantasy of difference.[47]

Wanting to be an "india blanca" and to embrace an Indian prince, however, is different from wanting to be (or to embrace) a contemporary "negro" (though the suggestive parallel between the two might give some readers a thrill). Despite implying, through Blanca and Laura's processes of historical discovery, that the recovery of a mestizo past can influence choices and a sense of identity in the reader's own present, the novels offer few clues that similar romances are possible across contemporary racial and class divides. Indeed, most of the characters who enjoy the privilege of mestizaje in *Indias blancas* are elites – Indian chiefs, African princes and their offspring, and the cream of white society. This results in an emphasis on class distinctions even as racial barriers are crossed – it allows for romance between privileged whites and "exotic" others of similar class backgrounds, but immediately writes off the possibility of romance with Argentina's socio-economically marginalized, non-Afrodiasporic "negros" (who are in any case not legible as a racial or ethnic "minority" in contemporary multicultural discourses). It might be possible to read Laura and Nahuel's mestizo son as the precursor to the "negros" of the twentieth century's popular movements, whose claims and popular culture have become more salient since the 2001 crisis. But because the novel ends before the twentieth century, any connections between its fictional, aristocratic, by-gone world and the present are completely opaque. This is most likely an intentional choice: the lavishly reconstructed past is in part a mechanism for escapist pleasure. And it is clear from the responses on Facebook that this aristocratic fantasy is a major part of the novels' appeal: for example, almost all the posts and comments relating to the faithful black nursemaid María Pancha refer to her as "*mi negra* María Pancha," ventriloquizing Laura and Blanca's affective/possessive relationship, while one fan goes so far as to declare that she wants "a María Pancha for myself."[48]

Bonelli's complex historiographic interventions and revisions, then, ultimately diverge from the more race-centered discourses of ethnic activists and scholars to reprise the key elements – and limitations – of contemporary brown legends. Specifically, they echo the strain of brown legend thinking enunciated or embraced by educated, white Argentines and focused principally on the events of the past (in contrast to the strain voiced by self-identified "negros" who stress plebeian pride in the present). Bonelli's novelized brown legend offers her readers – primarily white middle-class women – a triple fantasy: illicit romance with an exotic other (and the ability to appropriate or tame the other through mestizaje); female empowerment; and a gesture toward progressive ideals in the face of a historically racist society – carefully channeled and contained through temporal distance.

Fiebre negra: POWER AND PERSISTENCE OF THE BLACK LEGEND

In *Fiebre negra*, the story of a young, white, middle-class anthropologist living in post-crisis Buenos Aires (2008) frames a second story, set in the nineteenth century (1820s–70s), focused on Afro-Argentines. In the present-day story, the young anthropologist, Diana, inherits the keys to an old family house in the historic neighborhood of San Telmo. The house lay abandoned and locked up since 1871, when Diana's ancestors, like other well-to-do San Telmo families, fled their homes in the midst of the yellow fever epidemic that devastated the south side of the city. For over a century, the house was considered cursed or haunted (not even the neighborhood's ubiquitous squatters dared break in). When Diana enters, we begin to discover why. In the back of the building, off the kitchen, she finds a boarded-up room, which she pries open in one of the novel's more suspenseful scenes. Inside, underneath a thick layer of dust, she finds, among other objects, writing implements, a long manuscript, and two skeletons. At the urging of a geneticist friend, Diana takes DNA samples from the human remains and finds out that they belonged to two black men. The novel then tacks back and forth between chapters dedicated to Diana's attempts to uncover the mystery of these men's fate, and chapters on those men's lives (based, it is implied, on the contents of the manuscript itself).

This is not an innocent tale of sleuthing. As in *Indias blancas*, the author's historiographic intent – revealing the work of uncovering a hidden past – is written directly into the novel through the investigations of a main character (in this case, a historically minded anthropologist) and her discovery of primary sources (here, both a manuscript and a set of physical remains). As the author makes clear in a range of interviews and promotional materials, *Fiebre negra* is intended to highlight present-day Argentines' ignorance of the foundational role played by Afro-Argentines in the nation's past, and to correct a history plagued by "half-truths" and outright "nonsense."[49] Rosenzvit renders the intentionally buried black presence as a haunting: the "horror," "mystery," "malevolent forces," and "phantasmagorias that surround this house's history."[50] This haunting, however, is less about the supernatural than it is about history: it marks (as scholars have noted for other cases) a bad conscience, the site of a social and moral crime that cries out for scholarly investigation.[51] Thus, when Diana first pries open the boards that seal off the mysterious room, she is struck by a change in the very quality of the air, which she at first mistakenly attributes to "putrefaction": "Reconsidering, I laughed at my mistake: not even putrefaction can persist for so many years."[52] Argentina's black past was boarded in for over a century, but even racism's evil emanations cannot persist in the face of efforts by historically minded scholars like Diana to bring that past to light.

Yet though Diana is a scholar, she is also, at first, no more educated about Argentina's black past than the average middle-class *porteño* or resident of Buenos Aires (though she is a particularly open-minded one). When Diana finds out that the human remains in her family's house belonged to black people, she thinks to herself: "If they were slaves, what were those papers doing there? Maybe it was more common than I imagined for slaves to know how to read and write. In all honesty, I realized that I knew nothing about black Argentines."[53] After spending a night reading the entire manuscript, Diana is both enlightened and embarrassed to have needed such enlightenment. This discovery holds up a mirror to the reader's own experience as a well-educated yet – on this matter – probably ignorant citizen.

Even more explicitly than Bonelli, Rosenzvit relies on historical scholarship to set the story straight. Here, too, that process of historical discovery becomes part of the plot. When Diana realizes her ignorance about Afro-Argentines, she runs to the Biblioteca Nacional to do some research. There, she comes across issues of Buenos Aires's late-nineteenth-century black press and discovers a range of classic works on Afro-Argentine history. In itemizing these works through the voice of Diana, Rosenzvit gives his readers a history lesson and a reading list: "I gorged myself on Ortíz Oderigo, Goldberg, Rodríguez Molas, Lanuza, and I lingered over Andrews."[54] This embedded bibliography, like Bonelli's repeated references to Mansilla's *Excursión*, reveals the author's own scholarly reference points and gives us insight into his interpretive framework. Most of the authors Rosenzvit lists belong to an early or "classic" period of Afro-Argentine historiography – a body of work that revealed the importance of Afro-Argentines in the national past, but which was still heavily shaped by the presumption of their eventual disappearance – in other words, a black legend view.[55] George Reid Andrews's work, *The Afro-Argentines of Buenos*

Aires, is the exception to this trend, inaugurating a wave of revisionist historiography on Afro-Argentines that moved beyond assumptions about extermination (and for this reason, perhaps, Rosenzvit sets it apart). By examining the
power of whitening ideologies in the nineteenth century and tracing how racial
categories were transformed to efface blackness (especially in official censuses),
Andrews famously demonstrated that Afro-Argentines did not so much "disappear" as become statistically and ideologically invisible.[56]

By drawing on this scholarship, Rosenzvit attempts first to debunk a central
element of white legend ideas of Argentine exceptionalism: the "nonsensical"
notion that blacks were never a significantly important part of Argentina's
population to begin with. In one scene, toward the end of a dinner party, Diana
shares her historical discoveries with her friends and informs them that,
according to census records, 30 percent of the population of Buenos Aires in
the early nineteenth century was Afro-Argentine. Yet her friends dismiss this
(historically accurate) information, leading Diana to realize that the negation of
Argentina's black presence was "as authentic an element of historical truth as
the census itself."[57] To convince any such potential skeptics among his readers
(or to provide readers with ammunition for their own future dinner parties),
Rosenzvit bolsters his heroine's discovery of the historical manuscript with
"harder" scientific evidence. By having Diana's geneticist friend use a DNA
sample to determine the skeletons' partial African ancestry (rendered somewhat
simplistically in the novel as proof of "black skin"), Rosenzvit references the
extent to which scientific evidence of nonwhite ancestry in recent DNA samples
from the populations of several Argentine cities has helped provide definitive
"proof" of Argentina's racially mixed background, transforming discussions of
national identity in some quarters.[58] The other material remains Diana finds –
the pens, pieces of furniture, or shattered pottery – echo the increasing involvement of archeologists in unearthing Buenos Aires's black past.[59]

In this vein, Rosenzvit uses the nineteenth-century narrative to flesh out a
strong and dignified, culturally vibrant community persisting in the face of
adversity. Indeed, in order to do so, Rosenzvit appears to have packed all of
the knowledge gleaned from his academic reading list (especially Andrews) into
his small cast of black characters. The nineteenth-century story, documented in
the found manuscript, narrates the story of Joaquín, an Afro-Argentine man
born in 1820 to a domestic slave belonging to a well-to-do white family
(Diana's ancestors) in San Telmo. Joaquín bears the burden of representing
the "black experience" in nineteenth-century Argentina, gathering into his
person the key events and circumstances shaping the Afro-porteño community.
Joaquín is born conditionally free, a *liberto,* following the passage of the Free
Womb Law of 1813 (though like other libertos, he is obliged to work for his
mother's owners until his legal majority, and is subjected to vicious private
regimes of punishment, illustrating the limits of this "freedom"); he fights as a
soldier in a succession of wars (including the Paraguayan War, where he loses a
leg); he is an active member of a *nación* or Afro-Argentine mutual aid society;

he revels in *candombe* dances and in black carnival parades; and he writes for the nascent black press, eventually becoming the director and editor of his own newspaper.

But Rosenzvit is not interested in simply illustrating the historical Afro-Argentine presence. In the frame story (as in several interviews), Rosenzvit makes it clear that he is also conversant with revisionist arguments about "invisibilization," and that he sees these – with their rejection of black legend themes of "disappearance" – as progressive and anti-racist positions. He introduces this interpretation through Diana, who in the same dinner party conversation cited earlier laments that each of her friends "had well-formed opinions about the *supposed* extinction and its causes."[60] Readers' education in revisionist hypotheses continues as Diana meets Eva Sevilla, a contemporary Afro-Argentine activist whom Diana first encounters through a newspaper article about Buenos Aires's hidden but re-emerging black presence (a fictional nod to the media's increased coverage of Afro-Argentine issues in the last decade). Eva directly voices Andrews's famous thesis about the role of census manipulation in erasing Argentina's significant black population, as well as other scholarly arguments about the ways this population was made invisible through the everyday denial of African ancestry within Argentine families.[61] Contradicting the usual black legend explanations for disappearance, Eva explains: "A presence that large cannot be annihilated just like that [...] Not even with wars. Nor with diseases."[62] Here, Rosenzvit clearly aligns himself with the position of contemporary Afro-Argentine activists and allied academics, dramatizing the claim that Afro-Argentines – far from being "annihilated" – were still very much among us, though suffering from a lack of recognition.

Despite these very intentional revisions in favor of a continued Afro-Argentine presence, Rosenzvit's commitment to undercutting the white legend often leads him, perhaps unwittingly, to reprise powerful black legend accounts of Afro-Argentine victimization and disappearance. In the interest of debunking the myth of Argentina's benevolent slavery and post-abolition colorblindness, for instance, Rosenzvit hems in the lives of his fictional black community, and of Joaquín in particular, with racism and a range of structural disadvantages and limitations. The tale takes on a patina of pathos and unremitting suffering as it ends up fleshing out, one by one, the key explanations for the classic "extermination" narrative: Afro-Argentines' disproportionately heavy and dangerous service in national armies (almost all black male characters in the book are maimed or killed by military service); their intermixture with and marginalization by waves of white immigrants (who, in the story, displace Afro-Argentines violently in both physical and symbolic terms); and their succumbing to disease (in the yellow fever epidemic of 1871, the book's climactic episode).[63] Rosenzvit's rendition of Joaquín's love life illustrates this tendency as well. Joaquín's birth coincides with that of Valeria Beltrán, the daughter of his mother's masters. Valeria and Joaquín's destinies are thenceforth intertwined, and their young adulthood is marked by romantic tension.

But unlike in Bonelli's novels, here the interracial romance is never consummated – perhaps more realistically than in *Indias blancas*, contemporary prejudices make an explicit love story between Valeria and Joaquín impossible, despite the fact that Valeria (like Laura) is an intrepid, liberated young woman. Yet if Bonelli is downright outlandish in her willingness to imagine pervasive interracial desire, there is something prudish and even politically timid in Rosenzvit's reluctance to develop that relationship (despite a vivid sexual scene between Joaquín and a *trigueña* or light-brown-complexioned woman).

Above all, Rosenzvit rehearses black legend themes in his account of Joaquín's demise, one of the novel's opening scenes. Black legend narratives of Afro-Argentine "extermination" usually emphasize the role of the 1871 yellow fever epidemic in decimating the Afro-Argentine population. Historians have found no positive evidence that Afro-Argentines died disproportionately from the disease.[64] Still, Rosenzvit chooses to make Joaquín die during that devastating outbreak. Whether or not Joaquín contracts the disease is unclear, but death comes because he agrees to let Valeria barricade him and his nephew Lucas into the servants' quarters of the house that she and her family have abandoned (where Diana eventually finds them over a century later). This desperate measure was meant to save the men from the certain death they would have faced by vigilante mobs who wrongly identified blacks as the source of the disease. Valeria promises to return, but given Diana's discovery of these two bodies, we know that this does not happen. This plot twist allows Rosenzvit to drive home an important historical lesson: regardless of the actual means of death, what ultimately killed Joaquín and his nephew was racism. Yet especially given the symbolic weight the author invests in Joaquín as a representative of the nineteenth-century Afro-Argentine community, the choice to kill him off in such a stereotypically black-legend episode leads Rosenzvit's novel to read, ultimately, as a mystery gradually unlocking the story of Afro-Argentines' effective disappearance and death.

As in Bonelli's case, the politics of Rosenzvit's historical imagination are difficult to parse, particularly in relation to the present. Despite choosing to set his story partly in post-crisis Buenos Aires, with its visible ethnic resurgences and the fever for all things Afro-cultural among a subset of young porteños, the contemporary presence of Afro-Argentines is remarkably underdeveloped. The character of Eva Sevilla lightly voices black activists' main contention – the idea that they are *still here* despite racism and invisibilization – but her presence is fleeting and isolated. Also as in Bonelli's novels, the twentieth century is missing from Rosenzvit's tale, reinforcing the idea of late-nineteenth-century black "disappearance" and making it even harder to trace Afro-Argentines' existence into Diana's (and our) present.[65] The victory of black legend narratives in a novel otherwise intent on emphasizing Afro-Argentine agency and survival points to the power and persistence of these narratives in Argentine public life more broadly (as we will see), seemingly for their ability to voice a righteous denunciation of racism and of discredited white legends without fully overturning widely held notions of Afro-Argentine "disappearance" and of the nation's overall whiteness. Yet the powerful undertow of the black legend in *Fiebre negra* also points to a tension inherent in revisionist scholarly and activist interpretations of "invisibilization" themselves, which, in their emphasis on denunciation, sometimes risk re-enacting Afro-Argentine absences and reinforcing narratives of victimization.[66]

The conventions of the romance novel are also partly to blame for the apparently irresistible pull toward the narrative of extermination. The present-day story is about Diana's search for her own romantic self-fulfillment, specifically, her choice between two white men: her controlling, unappreciative, sexually unfulfilling boyfriend, and Marco, a more loving young man, quirkily obsessed with robotics and supportive of Diana's own unusual intellectual interests. Even at his most explicitly historiographic, Rosenzvit chooses to subsume the search for Argentina's African past to contemporary romance between white people. The scene in which Diana visits the Biblioteca Nacional to educate herself about Afro-Argentine history ends with the heroine – exhausted and elated from her research – laying her head on the desk and beginning to daydream. She day-dreams not about Argentina's black past but, romantically, about George Reid Andrews, the white historian, whose moving words to his wife in his book's dedication page prompt her to put herself in the other woman's place: "I imagined that I was Andrews's wife, that I was the light of his life."[67] And it is just then, upon awakening from her daydream, that Diana meets Marco, the man she ends up choosing over her boyfriend, in large part because (as Diana says to him), "I find it very seductive when you're interested in my things. And when you share your things with me, too."[68] As in Bonelli's novels, difference is seductive, and so is a lover's ability to appreciate it. Yet here, the seductive difference is at an even further remove: it is not Diana's own racial or cultural difference that makes her attractive, but her quirky interest in exhuming the Afro-Argentine past, rendered as a "hobby" on par with Marco's bizarre obsession with robot soccer.[69] In that modern world of circuitry, Afro-Argentines have no place, except as traces of the past. Despite this novel's attempts at historio-graphic nuance, then, Rosenzvit, too, ultimately offers his readers a fantasy of political progressivism: rejecting racism and myths of benevolence (mostly in the past) and deploying race metonymically (or indeed only metaphorically) to support the cause of female self-actualization in the present.[70]

FINAL THOUGHTS

These novels, with their clear and at times compelling historiographic intents, are intimately intertwined with shifting ideas about race, history, and identity in contemporary Argentina. If their historiographic revisions have a patchwork quality, it is partly because novelists have multiple projects, having to do with gender, race, romance, and myth-making; multiple potential audiences; and multiple resources to draw on, including recent historiography, as well as longstanding legends, "white," "black" and "brown," with their various political implications. Yet the romance genre is only partly to blame for this historiographic cacophony, which more broadly characterizes racial storytelling in contemporary Argentine public life. As more and more voices search for alternatives to white legends of the nation's racial history, they often cling to the appealing denunciatory strength and moral outrage of black legends, or to the fashionable, yet often exoticizing or reductionist, messages of mixture or diversity of contemporary brown legends. Neither of these counter-myths seems able fully to escape the terms or the homogenizing logic of the dominant story: the former places nonwhiteness squarely in the past, while the latter imagines a "brownness" that only ambiguously contests or modifies racial whiteness in the present. Nonetheless, both counter-myths point to the noticeably widening spaces available for claims about race or ethnicity in public discourse, and to the ability of race and ethnicity to channel and amalgamate a range of political projects largely imagined as progressive.

It is impossible to gauge how much influence any of these particular novels, or others like them, may have exercised upon Argentine debates about race in the years since their publication. Yet it is striking how closely the racial stories told in these fictions – from *Indias blancas'* romantic version of the brown legend to *Fiebre negra*'s capitulation (in spite of its historiographic erudition) to black legend narratives – prefigured key themes in the discussions of Argentine identity surrounding the 2010 Bicentennial.

The opportunity for historical reflection occasioned by the Bicentennial, along with the particular politics of President Cristina Fernández de Kirchner's administration, opened space for emerging counter-narratives of social and ethnic inclusion to gain visible official backing. As Ezequiel Adamovsky has argued, the Bicentennial celebrations offered an opportunity for an "attempted suture" between the people and the state, in which the state could publicly address multiple constituencies and incorporate their various challenges to dominant discourses of racial, ethnic, and cultural identity.[71] The presidential decree of 2008 that created a government body to oversee the Bicentennial celebrations alluded to this historiographic intent and its hoped-for effects: "the Bicentennial of the May Revolution of 1810 constitutes a unique opportunity to reflect upon and debate the history and identity of the Argentine Republic, as well as to project toward the future a collectively constructed national project marked by social and federal inclusion and by integration into the Latin American region."[72] In this formulation, "integration into the Latin American region" is meant not just as a proclamation of political solidarity with other Latin American states, but also as an embrace of an "inclusive" vision of Argentina that rejects exceptionalist narratives of whiteness and Europeanness (thus echoing broader visions of national identity put forth by the Kirchner administrations of 2003–2015).[73] Whether intentionally downplaying the period of mass European immigration in historical parades or explicitly featuring indigenous, mestizo, and Afro-descendant faces in historical re-enactments, the state-produced histories on display during the Bicentennial manifestly rejected Liberal narratives of Argentine history and identity that portrayed Argentines as "descending from the boats," focusing instead on transmitting images of a popular, nationalist, browner Argentina, with roots in the deep colonial past and in the less Europeanized Interior.[74] In the Bicentennial celebrations, what was once a politically marginal or geographically peripheral reading of Argentine history moved center stage, resulting in what some observers called the triumph of a "mestizo" Argentina.[75] In the historical imaginary of the Bicentennial celebrations, then, we have a version of Bonelli's counter-myth writ large and backed by the state – a brown legend using racial mixture as one powerful tool (together with gender, class, geography, and politics) to revise Argentine history away from nineteenth-century Liberal narratives.

The themes central to *Fiebre negra* have been somewhat slower to appear at the highest levels of political discourse, but appear they have. In 2010, the Senate and Chamber of Deputies of the Province of Buenos Aires passed a law proclaiming October 11 as the "Día de la Cultura Africano-Argentina." The law honors an Afro-Argentine woman, María Remedios del Valle, whose distinction as a fighter and healer in Argentina's independence wars earned her the informal title of "Madre de la Patria" among contemporaries, yet who was reduced to begging for years before she received recognition and a pension from the fledgling national government. Using del Valle's case as an emblem and citing the occasion of the Bicentennial, the law seeks to repay a broader outstanding debt: "to recognize and recover the role of African culture [. . .] since it constitutes an undeniable cornerstone of our nationality."[76] Similarly, in her presidential address of May 25, 2012 (two years after the Bicentennial), President Cristina Fernández de Kirchner spoke fondly of her recent trip to Angola (itself an index of shifting ideas about Argentina's geopolitical identity),[77] and used this connection to give a rather remarkable public history lesson about Argentina's African past. "Our sister republic of Angola," she declared, is "a place that may seem very distant from us, but which in fact [. . .] has had more importance and presence [here] than you might imagine. In the city of Buenos Aires and throughout the countryside, half of the population according to the census of 1778 [. . .] was black and the majority of those blacks came from Angola. [. . .] I would like to inform anyone out there who might be lacking a history lesson or two, that for the most part, the armies that liberated the Argentine Republic were comprised of *negros*, *mestizos*, *mulatos*, and *indios*, and these were the soldiers who fought at the front lines." Fernández de Kirchner also highlighted important soldiers of African ancestry, noting that their Africanness was often zealously hidden by "official histories."[78] In both the provincial law and the presidential speech, the desire to give a corrective history lesson about the presence and protagonism of Afro-Argentines (especially as soldiers) runs parallel to the historiographic intent of the nineteenth-century story in *Fiebre negra*.

These more inclusive conceptions of Argentine identity expressed in the years surrounding the Bicentennial have allowed for the increased visibility of Afro-Argentines and indigenous people in public life. Yet these state-backed formulations of a revised Argentine identity reveal some of the limitations of brown and black legend narratives exhibited so clearly in the novels. As with the emphasis on mestizaje in *Indias blancas,* state-sponsored versions of the brown legend provide limited spaces for Afro-Argentines and indigenous people to assert their rights to racial and cultural difference. In these narratives, the "authentic" national subjects are members of the "popular sectors" (poor or working-class, marginalized Argentines of mixed ethnic origin) – a social majority subjected to racist attitudes, but whose members by and large do not explicitly identify with indigenous or African descent. To the extent that these national narratives make race or color more visible in order metonymically to highlight broader structures of inequality, they also contribute to eliding difference when it concerns members of racially or ethnically distinct minorities. We can see this lumping of various ethnic or racial groups into an undifferentiated Argentine "people" in another segment of the earlier-cited speech by Fernández de Kirchner. Having highlighted the role of nonwhites in Argentina's independence wars, the President goes on to explain: "And this is how all liberation struggles would be throughout different stages of Argentina['s history]: in the civil wars that followed [independence], *criollos, el mestizaje,* the poorest, those who had the least were the ones sent to the front lines – even in the Malvinas [War] this was the case." Note the trajectory of the soldiering "people" in the President's historical imaginary as she moves through time: from *"negros, mestizos, mulatos, indios"* through *criollos* and *mestizaje* to "the poorest, those who had the least" – in effect, from ethnic/racial categories in the 1800s to social or class ones by the late 1900s. It is a national-populist narrative, however broadly inclusive, that continues to impose a homogeneous, hegemonic idea of Argentine citizenship and of an authentic national subject marked primarily by class or subalternity. This narrative undercuts the claims of indigenous communities, who demand a plurinational state and political autonomy.[79] And it is a narrative that (as in Bonelli's novels) underscores the success of assimilation – despite the existence, in the present, of politically organized, active, and increasingly visible indigenous communities (such as those who, during the Bicentennial celebrations, staged massive marches from the Interior to the capital city, and mounted parallel or counter-commemorations of their own).

Black legends of outright (if lamented) extermination, for their part, also continue to weigh heavily upon even the most progressive contemporary official initiatives to highlight diversity. As in *Fiebre negra,* state-sponsored historical narratives about Afro-Argentines during and after the Bicentennial rehearse the tenacious idea of their disappearance. This occurs, for instance, in the emphasis on blacks' soldiering visible across these initiatives, which often highlights self-sacrifice or even immolation for the sake of the motherland.[80]

It also occurs through discussions of a primarily historical and cultural, rather than contemporary and politicized, Afro-Argentine element. For instance, although the legislation decreeing a "Día de la Cultura Africano-Argentina" boasts an extensive and up-to-date academic bibliography, the law's rationale nonetheless overwhelmingly emphasizes the historical character of Afro-Argentines and their contributions, with no mention of the community's present existence and demands. As in *Fiebre negra*, historiographic erudition and the best intentions of denouncing injustice ultimately give way to black legend lamentations of disappearance. In this sense, the spirit of the law honoring María Remedios del Valle closely parallels a prize-winning novel about that historical character (Ana Gloria Moya's *Cielo de tambores*) from 2002. Though the author celebrates María and places her (as a first-person narrator) at the center of the novel, she chooses to end with María's mestizo lover (who outlives her) lamenting that "they [blacks] were shamelessly exterminated."[81]

To return to literary scholar Doris Sommer's classic formulation, these novels can be understood as "foundational fictions" for a post-crisis, leftist-nationalist-populist, Bicentennial Argentina. They disseminate comforting messages, for progressively minded middle-class white Argentines, of female empowerment and multiculturalism. Through appealing stories of mestizaje and disappearing blackness, they allow white Argentine readers to feel ethnically inflected without having to fully face contemporary issues of race and racism or the continued privileging of whiteness. Indeed, in a world in which modern, industrialized societies all have their immigrants and internal others, these plotlines seem to reflect what some critics have identified as a recent attempt to use Argentina's racial diversity as evidence of its rightful (if not actual) belonging in the "first world."[82]

Yet even when they make us wince, these novels reveal important transformations in Argentine racial ideologies. Like much of the recent historical scholarship on race, they suggest that the classic contrast between a white Argentina and its mixed-race neighbors has been overdrawn, and that this distinction was itself a product of the political victory of stories of white nationhood and the suppression of alternative ones. Like other contemporary Argentine historians and commentators, these novelists appear to want to plot new paths through the Argentine past, trajectories that can better explain and connect to the nation's present-day diversity. These are important counter-narratives to the white legend, and they seem to be well received – even, on occasion, by racial activists who appreciate their corrective historiographic intentions.[83] Who would have thought that Argentine readers would seek out romances in which the didactic anti-racism of the heroes is part of the story? They are fantasies, no doubt – but imagined stories are, after all, what racial identities are made of. Perhaps these stories, with their as-yet rhetorical use of race, can help fuel the imaginary of a future politics more fully attentive to leveraging the intersections among various forms of exclusion.[84]

Notes

For their insightful comments, I would like to thank Eduardo Elena, Jesse Hoffnung-Garskof, Graciela Montaldo, Fernando Coronil, George Reid Andrews, Alex Stern, Tiya Miles, John Mack Faragher, Florencia Guzmán, Teresa Ko, Lea Geler, Marc Hertzman, Amy Chazkel, Rebekah Pite, Keila Grinberg, Gastón Gordillo, and Carrie Rosenzweig. I am indebted to Julieta Pereira for first putting *Indias blancas* in my hands; thanks too to Alejandro Frigerio for pointing me to other important novels in this genre.

1. In addition to the three novels examined in this chapter, see (among others): Florencia Bonelli, *El cuarto arcano* and *El cuarto arcano II: El puerto de las tormentas* (Suma, 2007 and 2008); Ana Gloria Moya, *Cielo de tambores* (Emecé, 2003 [2002]); Daila Prado, *José Francisco, esclavo* (Córdoba: Raíz de dos, 2012); Mirta Fachini, *Susurros negros* (Córdoba: Ediciones del Boulevard, 2010) and *Herencia Negada* (Córdoba: El Emporio, 2013); Ernesto Mallo, *El relicario* (Planeta, 2010); Javier Aguirre, Eduardo Blanco, and Fernando Sánchez, *Ucronías argentinas: Diez historias que pudieron haber cambiado la Historia* (Sudamericana, 2008); Washington Cucurto, *1810. La revolución de mayo vivida por los negros* (Emecé, 2008); Silvia Grau, *Curumbamba y Curumbé* (Cántaro, 2008); and María Rosa Lojo, *Historias ocultas en la Recoleta* (Alfaguara, 2000), *Amores insólitos de nuestra historia* (Alfaguara, 2001), and *Finisterre* (Sudamericana, 2005) [all published in Buenos Aires except as noted]. These works expand upon an incipient attention to non-white characters in late twentieth-century historical fiction by authors like María Rosa Lojo, Cristina Bajo, César Aira, and others. See Giuffré, *En busca*. For an inventory of historical fiction featuring Afro-Argentines, see Cirio and Cámara, "Black Letters."

2. For an overview, see Shumway, *The Invention*; Nouzeilles, *Ficciones*.

3. On these discourses, see Rodríguez, Geler, this volume; Andrews, *Afro-Argentines*; Geler, "¡Pobres negros!"; Quijada, "Indígenas"; Briones, "Formaciones."

4. Garguin, "Los argentinos"; Segato, "Una vocación"; Adamovsky, *Clase media*; Joseph, "Taking"; Guano, "Color."

5. I use "black legend" to evoke the famous discourse (dating back to the sixteenth century) about Spain's excessive cruelty in and decimation of its American colonies. This "black" mark on Spain's reputation has been contested over the centuries, leading to (among other positions) a countervailing "white legend" (in Spanish, "rosy legend") defending Spanish conquest and allied projects over the centuries. Powell, *Tree of Hate*; Greer and Mignolo, *Rereading*. Cf. Adelman, *Colonial Legacies*. For a critique of the "black legend's" effacement of native presences, see Silver Moon and Ennis, "The View."

6. On these narratives in academia and public life, see Gordillo and Hirsch, "Indigenous Struggles"; Delrio et al., "Discussing"; Frigerio, "De la 'desaparición'"; Cirio, "La desaparición"; Frigerio, "Luis D'Elía."

7. See Elena, Gordillo, and Geler, this volume.

8. Sommer, *Foundational Fictions*; Rosenthal, *Race Mixture*; Earle, *Return*.

9. On this trend in regional context, see Pizarro Cortés, "Decentring."

10. "Una radiografía del lector argentino: Los 100 libros más vendidos del 2009," *Diario Perfil* (Buenos Aires), 27 Dec. 2009; Alejandra Rey, "El amor nunca muere y cada vez vende más," *La Nación* (Buenos Aires), 5 Jul. 2008. In 2010 and again in 2012, the prominent daily *La Nación* issued inexpensive editions of Bonelli

novels; *Indias blancas* was the first installment. The novels are even available in the United States as Amazon Kindle e-books.

11. Ángel Berlanga, "Tras los pasos perdidos," *Página/12* (Buenos Aires), 28 Sep. 2008; Lucila Rolón, "La historia negra postergada," *Newsweek Argentina* (Buenos Aires), 27 Aug. 2008: www.infonews.com/nota.php?id=3995&bienve nido=1, accessed 29 Jul. 2013.

12. Viñas, *Indios*; Mases, *Estado.*

13. Bonelli, *Indias blancas*, 315.

14. Ibid., 227.

15. Slotkin, "Fiction," 230–31. (Emphasis in original). I also draw here from Linda Hutcheon's concept of historiographic metafiction; see Hutchins, *Poetics.*

16. For recent historiographic overviews of these fields, see Vela, "Historia y actualidad"; Frigerio, "De la 'desaparición'"; Gordillo and Hirsch, "Indigenous Struggles"; Geler and Guzmán, "Sobre esclavizados/as"; Briones and Lanata, *Contemporary Perspectives*. Historical scholarship rarely considers indigenous people and Afro-Argentines together; as exceptions, see Quijada, Bernand, and Schneider, *Homogeneidad*; Adamovsky, *Clases populares*; Grosso, *Indios muertos*; and Geler and Rodríguez, "Argentina."

17. Rotker, *Captive Women*, 8.

18. Socolow, "Spanish Captives"; Altube, "Mujeres"; Malosetti Costa, *Rapto de cautivas.*

19. Classic accounts include the legend of Lucía Miranda in Ruy Díaz de Guzmán's "La Argentina Manuscrita" (1612) and Esteban Echeverría's poem "La cautiva" (1837).

20. See especially Rotker, *Captive Women*. Cf. Masiello, *Between*; Gruesz, "Facing"; Frederick, "Reading"; Hanway, "Property"; Pratt, *Imperial Eyes.*

21. Demos, *Unredeemed Captive*, 4.

22. See the introduction to Mansilla de García, *Lucía Miranda*; Rotker, *Captive Women*, chapter 5. Another important predecessor in this vein is Rosa Guerra's *Lucía Miranda* (1860).

23. Eva Gillies, "Introduction," in Mansilla, *A Visit*, xxxvi.

24. See, for instance, Mandrini, *Vivir*; Boccara, "Fronteras."

25. See, e.g., Leonardo Blanco, "Florencia Bonelli: La nueva reina de la novela rosa," *La Nación*, 7 Feb. 2010; Fabiana Scherer, "Florencia Bonelli: La vida en rosa," *La Nación*, 24 Jun. 2012 ("she loves the color pink, she considers herself romantic by nature, and she collects teapots").

26. Analía Testa, "La literatura, camino para pensar y recrear la idea de Nación," *La Nación*, 22 May 2010.

27. María Rosa Lojo, *La pasión de los nómades* (Buenos Aires: Atlántida, 1994), *Una mujer de fin de siglo* (Buenos Aires: Planeta, 1999), and *La princesa federal* (Buenos Aires: Planeta, 1998).

28. See Pite, "Engendering."

29. Menton, *Latin America's*; Pizarro Cortés, "Decentring."

30. Grimson, "Nuevas xenofobias." On processes underway in earlier decades, see Margulis and Urresti, *La segregación.*

31. Adamovsky, "El color"; Ko, "Whiteness"; Escolar, "El 'estado.'" Cf. Grimson, "Nuevas xenofobias," for a different interpretation of the crisis' short-term effects.

32. Geler and Rodríguez, "Argentina"; Briones, "Mestizaje." See also the introduction to this volume.

33. See Sutton, "Contesting."

34. Adamovsky, "El color," 355. On "metonymy" as the process by which "negro" comes to denote the popular more broadly, see Geler, "Afrodescendencia."

35. Geler, *Andares* and this volume.

36. Pigna, *Mitos*, vol. 1, 13, 17–18.

37. Lenton et al., "Argentina's," 68–75. Cf. Bayer, *Historia*; Viñas, *Indios*.

38. On indigenous social movements, see Lenton, "The Malón"; Gordillo and Hirsch, *Movilizaciones*; Briones, *Cartografías*. On Afro-Argentine social movements, see Frigerio and Lamborghini, "(De)mostrando cultura"; Frigerio and Lamborghini, "Los afroargentinos," 26–37. Notably, these activists often face the accusation that their identities are inauthentic or spurious; that they too use race metonymically as a strategy to advance other, purportedly unrelated, political or material goals (access to land, political positions, and so forth).

39. The proposed monument to indigenous and immigrant women as mothers of a mixed-race nation, for instance, has come up for debate on these grounds. Lenton et al., "Argentina's"; Lenton, "Próceres genocidas."

40. It would be impossible to highlight all of the important works and trends here. In addition to the historiographic overviews cited in n. 16, see for a discussion of recent trends in these fields: Lenton et al., "Argentina's," 75–79; Geler and Guzmán, *Dossier sobre esclavizados/as*.

41. I conducted research for this chapter using the "Indias blancas" Facebook fan page, which was available from early 2010-ca. Sep. 2013. Similar pages, still available as this volume goes to press, include several named after the novels' main characters, like "Nahueltruz Guor" (www.facebook.com/pages/NAHUELTRUZ-GUOR/ 175303102540016), or a page dedicated to advocating for the movie version of the books (www.facebook.com/pages/Juntemos-firmas-para-que-Indias-Blancas-se-haga-pelicula/232254083464177).

42. Indias Blancas [page owner]. "Don Mariano Rosas [...] fotografiado en Santa Rosa junto a una de sus esposas," www.facebook.com/photo.php?fbid=13429400 9955130&set=a.132468053471059.31627.1324608268051115&type=1, 19 Oct. 2010 [Facebook post], accessed 7 Mar. 2013; Flavia Zalazar: "me kdo [quedo] con el mariano d[e] mi imaginación," www.facebook.com/photo.php?fbid=13429 4009955130&set=a.132468053471059.31627.1324608268051115&type=1& 09955130&set=a.132468053471059.31627.1324608268051115&type=1&com 955130&set=a.132468053471059.31627.1324608268051115&type=1&commen t_id=121243&offset=0&total_comments=3, 20 Oct. 2010 [Facebook comment], accessed 7 Mar. 2013. Two subsequent comments heartily agreed: Indias Blancas (20 Oct. 2010) and Alicia Martínez Escalante (13 Nov. 2010). On the "supuesto retrato," see Elida Guzmán, "Retrato de Mariano Rosas," www.facebook.com/ permalink.php?story_fbid=366782583385621&id=1324608268051115&commen t_id=3854283&offset=0&total_comments=3, 23 May 2012 [Facebook comment], accessed 7 Mar. 2013. See also two subsequent comments by Marcela Binnier (23 May 2012) and Elida Guzmán (24 May 2012).

43. Lazzari, "Aboriginal."

44. Bonelli, *Indias blancas*, 207.

45. Ibid., 151; 140.
46. Indias Blancas [page owner], www.facebook.com/permalink.php?story_fbi
    d=161304957231584&id=13246082680511 5, 12 Oct. 2010 [Facebook post],
    accessed 7 Mar. 2013. See also e.g. by Indias Blancas: "hola a todas las mujeres
    blancas q quisieran ser indias solo por nahueltruz, o ser cautivas de mariano!!"
    (www.facebook.com/permalink.php?story_fbid=159316940758354&id=132460
    826805115, 14 Oct. 2010 [Facebook comment]) and "quien no quisiera estar en el
    lugar de laura para calmar la furia del indio ♥" (www.facebook.com/permalink
    .php?story_fbid=180967648621099&id=13246082680511 5, 28 Apr. 2011 [Face-
    book comment], both accessed 7 Mar. 2013.
47. See comments to Indias Blancas [page owner], www.facebook.com/permalink.php?
    story_fbid=191093534275177&id=13246082680511 5, 9 Jun. 2011 [Facebook
    post], accessed 7 Mar. 2013.
48. Vero Guell, www.facebook.com/permalink.php?story_fbid=309460285771834&
    id=13246082680511 5, 26 Jan. 2012 [Facebook post], accessed 7 Mar. 2013.
    Three commenters agreed.
49. Miguel Rosenzvit, interview with "Voces," Radio Nederland, Sep. 2008 (www.you
    tube.com/watch?v=4Ud1BhraMX0).
50. Rosenzvit, *Fiebre negra*, 17.
51. Miles, *Tales*; Hay, *History*; Gordon, *Ghostly Matters*.
52. Rosenzvit, *Fiebre negra*, 23.
53. Ibid., 78.
54. Ibid., 79. Almost all works in this genre include similar embedded or indirect
    bibliographies; a few, like Mallo's *El relicario*, Lojo's *Historias ocultas*, and Pra-
    do's *José Francisco* include formal ones. Cirio and Cámara also comment on the
    importance of this "paratext" in what they call "neo-slave narratives": "Black
    Letters," 14–16.
55. Cf. Frigerio, "De la 'desaparición'"; Cirio, "La desaparición."
56. Andrews, *Afro-Argentines*.
57. Rosenzvit, *Fiebre negra*, 117–18.
58. Since the late 1990s, DNA studies on samples of the population of Buenos Aires
    and other major cities have provided new evidence of Argentina's "genetic admix-
    ture." Depending upon the methods used, these studies have revealed up to 54% of
    their sampled populations to have significant indigenous ancestry, and up to 10%
    of their sampled populations to have significant African ancestry. (Corach et al.,
    "Inferring"; Fejerman et al., "African Ancestry.") Popular discussions of these
    studies (as in Rosenzvit's novel) have drawn on genetic science to buttress a
    "brown" view of Argentina, but they often simplistically equate continental genetic
    markers with "race," "color," or "blood," or they conflate very high percentages
    of indigenous genetic ancestry within *individuals* with the population as a whole.
    See Briones, "La nación," 46; Seldin et al., "Argentine Population." Historian
    Hugo Chumbita has been leading a public campaign to conduct DNA analysis
    on the remains of Argentine independence hero José de San Martín, to test for
    maternal indigenous heritage in order to prove that the national hero was "*mestizo
    y plebeyo*." This episode, too, resulted in a convergence of history, race, and fiction,
    in José Ignacio García Hamilton's controversial novelized biography of the leader,
    Don José (Buenos Aires: Sudamericana, 2000). In this way, DNA studies are being

used to revise official histories of race, just as they have been used to discredit the "official story" of the military dictatorship.

59. Schávelzon, *Buenos Aires negra*.
60. Rosenzvit, *Fiebre negra*, 117–18. Emphasis mine.
61. Frigerio, "Negros." See also Geler, this volume.
62. Rosenzvit, *Fiebre negra*, 179.
63. For a fuller account of these traditional explanations, see Andrews, *Afro-Argentines*, chapter 1.
64. Andrews, *Afro-Argentines*, 91–92.
65. There are, however, a couple of tantalizing suggestions about the possible historical continuities between the "negritud" ascribed to Afro-Argentines and to today's marginalized popular sectors: through a character's use of the contemporary insult "negro" (118) and through the character of Umbelina, Diana's maid, whose life history as a migrant from the Interior is unveiled as she acts as Diana's guide through the working-class neighborhood where the Afro-Argentine Eva Sevilla lives (174–76).
66. What we might call "post-revisionist" accounts, by contrast, pay closer attention to the role of Afro-Argentines in shaping and contesting the circumstances of their "disappearance." See especially Geler, *Andares*. Cf. Appelbaum, "Post-Revisionist."
67. Rosenzvit, *Fiebre negra*, 79.
68. Ibid., 180.
69. This parallel is underscored by a reference to a mess of Marco's electronics as "robot bones." Rosenzvit, *Fiebre negra*, 152.
70. This reading echoes scholars' critiques of the use, in US popular culture, of stereotyped African-American characters (the "magical Negro," the "Mammy") to support the self-realization of white characters. For a critique of the controversial film *The Help* on these grounds by the Association of Black Women Historians, see www.abwh.org/images/pdf/TheHelp-Statement.pdf.
71. Adamovsky, "El color," 361–64. See also Elena, this volume.
72. Decreto no. 278 (18 Feb. 2008).
73. Biglieri, "El retorno."
74. Adamovsky, "El color," 362; Tamagno and Maffia, "Lo afro y lo indígena."
75. "El triunfo de la patria mestiza," *Miradas al Sur*, 30 May 2010, 14–15 (cited in Adamovsky, "El color," 364). As Adamovsky notes, the extent to which this was a true transformation or just a politically expedient one was hotly debated.
76. Senado y Cámara de Diputados de la Provincia de Buenos Aires, Ley 14276.
77. On the implications of Argentina's relatively underdeveloped bilateral relations with sub-Saharan Africa and its privileging of South Africa in earlier decades, see Lechini, "Evolución."
78. Full text of the speech is available at www.lanoticia1.com/noticia/revolucion-de-mayo-cristina-y-el-acto-en-bariloche-recordando-a-nestor-kirchner-30232.html. Overly celebratory attempts to equate the Law of the Free Womb (1813) with full "abolition" and references to the mythical soldier Falucho (an emblem of blacks' "disappearance" in wars), however, make the President's history lesson problematic.
79. For this critique, see Briones, "La nación"; Delrio et al., "Discussing."

80. On this theme and its role in narratives of black "disappearance," see Geler, "¡Pobres negros!"
81. The novel's title is a fragment from Jorge Luis Borges' hyperbolically elegiac verse on Afro-Argentines: "¿A qué cielo de tambores/ y siestas largas se han ido?/ Se los ha llevado el tiempo,/ el tiempo, que es el olvido." J.L. Borges, "Milonga de los morenos," in *Para las seis cuerdas* (Buenos Aires: Emecé, 1996 [1965]).
82. Grimson, "Nuevas xenofobias," 69.
83. See the enthusiastic review of *Fiebre negra* ("Cuando la historia adolece de fiebre negra") in *Raíz Afro* [online], 22 Aug. 2008.
84. For a thoughtful discussion of politics that have begun to move in this direction, see Sutton, "Contesting."

Epilogue

Whiteness and its discontents

George Reid Andrews

In July 1975, I arrived in Buenos Aires to begin a year of dissertation research on the city's black population. My plan was to use municipal censuses to document the disappearance of that population over the course of the 1800s. Settling in to the Archivo General de la Nación, I was welcomed by the community of historians – mostly Argentine, some foreign – carrying out research there. They were friendly and helpful but somewhat nonplussed by my project. My colleagues were well aware that Africans and Afro-Argentines had formed a significant part of the city's population in the late colonial period and early 1800s. But they also knew that by the end of the 1800s black people were no longer a significant component of the city's society (the 1887 municipal census set their numbers at less than 2 percent of the total population). The big story of the 1800s, and even more of the 1900s, was the arrival of the immigrants and the resulting transformation of Argentine society, culture, and politics. Why, then, spend my time investigating a topic of purely antiquarian interest, and a people who had left no visible traces in the nation of which they had once formed part?

What a difference forty years make! As this volume makes clear, the terms of that scholarly conversation have decidedly shifted, as the notion of White Argentina (to use the term proposed in the chapter by Gastón Gordillo), hegemonic during most of the 1900s, has now been challenged by visions of a multiracial, multicultural Argentina.[1] As the volume's introduction suggests, one of the effects of this rather seismic shift has been to undermine claims of Argentina's national exceptionalism and to bring the country into much closer dialogue not just with its Latin American neighbors but with multiracial societies across the globe. Argentina is hardly alone, after all, in having its longstanding claims to whiteness called into question. In recent decades intensifying migration from Latin America, Asia, and Africa has transformed the ethnic and racial composition of the United States, Canada, and much of

Europe. Argentina's transition from hegemonic whiteness to highly contested multiculturalism is an experience that cries out for comparison with those North Atlantic cases (not to mention Australia, where similar demographic shifts are currently under way).

These concluding reflections, however, focus mainly on Latin America and take up the volume's challenge to reconsider Argentina's supposed "racial exceptionalism." It was mainly in relation to other Latin American societies, after all, that Argentine elites initially constructed their claims of national whiteness and, therefore, uniqueness. Nor were they entirely wrong. Their national history was indeed unique, as is every country's national history. But if all countries share that quality, then uniqueness becomes, by definition, unexceptional. And while Argentina's racial history is certainly distinctive, it also has many points in common with other nations in the region, beginning with its supposedly most distinctive feature, its success in attracting European immigrants. Between 1880 and 1935 Argentina had net European immigration of 3.4 million people, a figure far exceeding its 1869 population of 1.9 million. By 1914 the national population was one-third foreign-born, with another 25 percent the children or grandchildren of immigrants.[2]

Within a continental Latin American context – in comparison, for example, with Mexico or Colombia – the Argentine experience does indeed stand out; but within a narrower Atlantic South American context, somewhat less so. As demographer Nicolás Sánchez-Albornoz noted some years ago, Europeans entered South America all "along the two thousand kilometers of coastline between Rio de Janeiro and Buenos Aires."[3] Between 1880 and 1940, Brazil received net migration of 3.3 million Europeans, almost the same number as Argentina. Since Brazil's population (9.9 million in 1872, 30.6 million in 1920) was so much larger than Argentina's, those immigrants formed a much smaller proportion of the national population (6 percent in 1900, 5 percent in 1920). However, the majority of those immigrants settled in the single state of São Paulo, where by 1920 18 percent of the population was foreign-born.[4] In Uruguay, Europeans accounted for about the same proportion of the national population as in São Paulo (17 percent in 1900), and fully 50 percent of the population in the capital city of Montevideo.[5]

Jumping ahead a century to 2010, we find that three other Latin American nations, plus the four southernmost states of Brazil, have racial and demographic profiles fairly similar to Argentina's. Argentina, Chile, Costa Rica, and Uruguay all have populations that are majority (52–73 percent) white, with large (18–32 percent) *mestizo* minorities.[6] The southern states of Brazil – Paraná, Rio Grande do Sul, Santa Catarina, and São Paulo – also have white populations that account for 70 percent of the regional total, and populations of racially mixed *pardos* that account for one-quarter of the total.

As those figures (which we will revisit later in this epilogue) suggest, Argentina was not alone in its avid pursuit of whiteness. Residents of early-twentieth-century São Paulo cast their state as the most modern, "civilized,"

TABLE I *Whites and* Mestizos *in Selected Latin American Countries, as a Percentage of Total Population, 2010*

	Whites	Mestizos	Total population (in 000,000s)
Argentina	73	24	40.1
Southern Brazil[a]	70	24[b]	68.9
Chile	66	30	17.1
Costa Rica	52	32	4.3
Uruguay	73	18	3.3

[a] Paraná, Rio Grande do Sul, Santa Catarina, São Paulo
[b] Pardos
Sources: Argentina, Chile, Costa Rica, Uruguay: LAPOP (Latin American Public Opinion Project) 2010 national surveys, available at http://lapop.ccp.ucr.ac.cr/Lapop_English.html. Brazil: Brasil, *Síntese*, table 8.1.

and progressive region in Brazil, qualities directly tied, they argued, to its "unimpeachably white" population. Not to be left behind, successive federal and municipal administrations in Rio de Janeiro sought to rebuild their city in the image of Belle Époque Paris. Perhaps most enthusiastic of all were the Uruguayans, who announced their country's success at creating "a new ethnic type [. . .] All the countries of the white race have contributed to our formation and perfection, working in common." "No other country of the Americas can display a population like ours," noted another local observer, writing in 1929, "in which the Caucasian race so clearly prevails."[7]

Where Argentina *was* unique, the chapters in this volume suggest, was in the distinctive racial imaginary to which whitening in that country gave rise. Rather than embracing race mixture and the mestizo identities celebrated by most Latin American nations (including Brazil, Chile, and Costa Rica), Argentines created a broad, all-embracing whiteness as the national norm. The racial category of mestizo (along with all other racial categories) was removed from national recordkeeping and from daily social practice and consciousness as well.[8]

But as Alberto and Elena suggest in the volume's introduction, might a broadly inclusionary conception of whiteness in Argentina function in ways similar to conceptions of mestizaje in other countries? "Whiteness prevailed in Argentina because of a system of racial classification and perception that broadened North Atlantic definitions of the category 'white' to include an array of racial origins, phenotypical variations, and shades of color [. . .] This broad definition of whiteness and its conferral, at least in theory, on most of the nation's inhabitants is thus markedly similar to the tropes of racial and cultural inclusion that came to characterize other Latin American nations in the twentieth century" (p. 11).

Whiteness as the Argentine version of Brazilian or Venezuelan racial democracy: could it be? Absolutely, and not least because, as virtually all of the
chapters demonstrate, all-embracing whiteness, like racial democracy, could
simultaneously be inclusionary in theory and hierarchical and exclusionary in
practice. While "all Argentines were formally considered 'white' [...] in terms
of physical appearance there was a substantial grey area between those who
clearly displayed the right ('European') skin tones and facial features, and those
who obviously did not."[9] Neither Jews nor Asians fit neatly into Argentine
conceptions of whiteness; nor did the country's indigenous and mestizo inhabitants, many of whom were re-labeled as *criollos* and assigned a deeply ambivalent role in the country's racial imaginary. "White Argentina recognized in the
criollos [...] the purveyors of the ancient spirit of the Argentine nation and
linked them to both the epics of early national history and to the romanticized
landscape of the vast Interior. Thus, while in symbolic terms indigenous and
criollo Argentines moved to the center as archetypes of the nation, they
remained in the geographical and temporal periphery. In the meantime, the
dynamic center of modern Argentina continued to be occupied by the business
and political elite, the European immigrants that arrived after 1870 and
their Argentine-born children."[10]

The parallels with Brazilian racial democracy are striking. Jews and Asians
were just as ambiguously situated in the Brazilian racial hierarchy as they
were in Argentina.[11] And while racially mixed mulattoes were symbolically
proclaimed as the essence of the Brazilian nation, census data from
1940 to the present make clear their enormous economic and social disadvantage in comparison to the nation's white population.[12] In the face of those
inequalities, observers of racial democracy in Brazil and other countries
have noted the same "seeming paradox" raised by Adamovsky: that "despite
skin-color discrimination and the pervasive presence of racist aggression,
during most of the twentieth century there seems to have been no collective
or sustained public reaction by members of the lower classes to these problems" (p. 156).

During the 1980s and 1990s, some scholars sought to ascribe the alleged
absence (in Colombia, Venezuela, and other countries) or the limited appeal
(in Brazil and Cuba) of such movements to the "mystifying" effects of racial
democracy ideology, which disguised the realities of racial discrimination and
persuaded nonwhites that their problems were rooted in inequalities of class
rather than race.[13] More recent scholarship has sought to address the paradox
in two different but related ways. One is to note that racially-defined black and
indigenous movements have in fact been more widespread, and more conse-
quential in regional and national politics, than had previously been thought.[14]
The other is to show how class-based populist movements, even when they
espoused no explicitly racial program or message, proved to be an important
means for racially excluded nonwhites to take part in national politics and
receive the benefits, even if limited, of such participation.[15]

Here, of course, we come to the central drama of twentieth-century Argentine history: the decades-long struggle between the populist movement(s) led by Juan Domingo Perón and his successors, and opposition forces based in rightist and centrist political parties and in the armed forces. The volume's two chapters on Peronism agree that "the Peronist state did not openly challenge the myth of the white-European Argentina, either through verbal and written discourse or through visual language."[16] This was so, Elena suggests, in part because of the global disinclination to talk about race that followed World War II, and in part because, as in other Latin American countries, populist movements were reluctant to openly discuss race for fear that it might aggravate potential racial and ethnic divisions within those movements. Peronism's reticence on questions of race and discrimination was thus fairly typical of mid-century populist movements throughout the Americas (including in the United States).

Yet popular movements in multiracial societies inevitably drew on constituencies that spanned the color and racial spectrum. Indeed, it was the very openness of such movements to previously excluded nonwhite groups that helped give them their "popular" character. And here again, Peronism was no exception. Adamovsky and Elena bring us fascinating information on the movement's use in its visual propaganda of black and indigenous themes and faces (or, in the case of its coat of arms, hands). Those images both provoked and responded to conservative denunciations of Peronist meetings and demonstrations as *candombes* and of the Peronist masses as *negros*.[17] As a result, during its first nine years in power (1946–55), Peronism acquired a subtle but definitive racial coloration that echoed (or prefigured) the multiracial character of Acción Democrática and Hugo Chávez's Bolivarian movement in Venezuela, of left Liberalism and Gaitanismo in Colombia, and of *trabalhismo* in Brazil.[18]

Peronism thus challenged not just traditional conservative and liberal hegemony in Argentina but longstanding notions of whiteness as well. Those challenges in turn helped pave the way for two intriguing developments that bring us up to the present: the adoption of "negro" social and political identities by people who are not phenotypically black; and recent (since the early 2000s) acknowledgements, both official and unofficial, of Argentina as a multiracial, multicultural society and nation.

The use of "negro" as a non-racial term has a long history in Argentina, dating from at least the early 1900s. At that time the racial term "'negro' was unmoored from biological references to African descent and extended more broadly onto working-class sectors and certain provincial populations [...] mark[ing] these populations off as less deserving of full citizenship due to their perceived poverty, uncouth behavior, lack of education, or place of residence."[19] Geler explores in depth the distinction between "racial blackness" and "popular blackness," and Gordillo and Elena examine the upsurge of "popular blackness" in the 1990s and early 2000s as members of the urban poor and working class "embrac[ed] the term 'los negros' as a marker of plebeian pride." Especially in the context of the political and economic turmoil of those years, this discursive racialization of class divisions aggravated already intense feelings on both sides of that divide, with *piquetero* leader Luis D'Elía publicly announcing his hatred of "the whites," and some middle- and upper-class Argentines calling for the violent purging of "blacks" and "blackness" from Argentine society.[20]

The adoption of "black" identities by people who are not racially black does strike me as a fairly distinctive aspect of Argentina's racial history, with no obvious parallels (at least that I know about) in other Latin American countries. Less distinctive, though equally unexpected, is the official acknowledgement in recent years of Argentina as a multiracial society. As Alberto and Ko both demonstrate, that acknowledgement has taken place in the cultural realm as well, in films and novels. But almost all the chapters point to the Bicentennial celebrations of 2010 as a watershed moment in Argentine racial history, and one that "would have been unthinkable two decades earlier." For the first time in Argentine history, the national government officially recognized the country's multiracial character with events, parades, and commemorations that openly acknowledged Argentina's indigenous, African, and mestizo past and, to a certain degree, present.[21]

The importance of such a redefinition of state policy can hardly be over-stated. Brazil experienced a similar moment in 1988, the centennial of the abolition of slavery, when government officials formally acknowledged, for the first time in Brazilian history, the yawning gap between the ideals of racial democracy and the realities of racial inequality and discrimination in that country. That acknowledgement, combined with continuing pressure from black organizations, opened the way for on-going debate in the 1990s about how best to reduce racial disparities in education, health, employment, and earnings. By the first decades of the 2000s that debate had led to the adoption of affirmative action policies and other government programs aimed at redu-cing racial and social inequalities.[22]

The centennial celebrations of 1988 coincided with the writing of the new constitution of that year, which further contributed to state recognition of the racial dimension of Brazil's extreme social inequalities. In other countries as well – Colombia in 1991, Venezuela in 2000, Bolivia and Ecuador in 2009 – the drafting of new constitutions led to formal acknowledgment of the plural, multi-ethnic character of each nation's society. The same was true of Argentina, where the constitutional revisions of 1994 recognized the "ethnic and cultural pre-existence" of the nation's indigenous peoples and their rights to commu-nally controlled land and bilingual education.[23]

Shortly thereafter, Argentina agreed to gather data on indigenous peoples in the census of 2001.[24] Throughout Latin America, the gathering of such data was a principal demand of black and indigenous movements in the 1990s and early 2000s. Most countries in the region had dropped racial information from their censuses after World War II, as part of the global disenchantment at that time with concepts of race. Others, such as Argentina and Venezuela, had never gathered information on race at the national level. Yet without such data, black and indigenous groups argued, it was impossible to know the conditions under which nonwhites lived and worked, or even how many of them there were.

Black and indigenous demands for census data were further supported by international agencies, including the United Nations (UN), the International Labor Organization (ILO), the World Bank, the Inter-American Development Bank (IDB), and international foundations and NGOs. The UN demanded census data as part of its institutional mission to combat racial and gender inequality around the globe and the ILO to monitor national compliance with its Convention 169 on the Rights of Indigenous and Tribal Peoples. Meanwhile, the World Bank and IDB had come to see racial and gender inequality as a principal obstacle to economic growth and development. They concurred with the UN on the need for national and local-level census data to investigate and measure such inequality and lobbied national governments to gather that information.[25]

By 2010 every Latin American nation except the Dominican Republic had agreed to include racial and ethnic data in the national census, though the questions used to elicit that data varied greatly from country to country.[26] Argentina (2010) and Colombia (2005) both opted to count their black and indigenous populations but not their white, mestizo, or Asian-origin populations. Census forms in those countries asked respondents whether they self-identified as blacks/Afro-descendants or as indigenous peoples. Those who did not – 86 percent of the population in Colombia, 97 percent in Argentina – were grouped into a single residual category that in Colombia was labeled as having "no ethnic identity."[27]

The results of Argentina's census could easily be interpreted as confirming longstanding assertions of the country's whiteness. Fewer than 3 percent of Argentines identified themselves as indigenous or Afro-descendant.[28] However, the 2010 LAPOP survey data reported earlier in this epilogue tell a somewhat different story. While tending to confirm the census' count of indigenous people (2.4 percent in the census, 1.6 percent in the survey) and Afro-Argentines (0.4 percent in the census, 0.7 percent in the survey), the LAPOP questionnaires also gave respondents the opportunity to self-identify as white or mestizo. While most (73 percent) did identify as white, nearly one-quarter (24 percent) identified as mestizo, a term that supposedly has little currency in Argentina. Could it be that mestizo consciousness is in fact more broadly diffused in that country than we thought? Or might this large mestizo minority reflect relatively recent changes in racial thought and practice?

In addition to gathering data on racial identity, LAPOP interviewers also measured respondents' skin color, using a calibrated "color palette." Researchers using those data for Brazil, Colombia, Mexico, and Peru have demonstrated that inequalities in earnings, education, and other social goods correlate more closely with skin color than with self-identified racial categories (i.e., an individual's skin color is a better predictor of social and economic disadvantage than is his or her self-selected racial identity).[29] The consistency of those findings suggest that the same correlation will hold true in other Latin American countries as well; if so, this would be yet another point of convergence between Argentina and the rest of the region. Here's hoping that we will see the results of such research in the not-too-distant future.

To conclude, the White Argentina project that enjoyed unquestioned social and cultural hegemony in the 1900s is now in serious crisis, opening the way for new visions of an Argentina Mestiza.[30] As in other Latin American countries, that transition will not be a smooth or easy one.[31] If anything, the depth and intensity of Argentina's historical commitment to whiteness may well make the process of reconsidering and abandoning that goal even more painful and difficult than it has been for other countries. But the experience of Argentina's neighbors suggests that once societies openly acknowledge the racial (and gender) dimensions of social and economic inequality, and the contradictions between those inequities and national ideals of fairness and equality, there is no turning back. Like the rest of the region, Argentina is now irrevocably embarked on the path of re-interpreting its racial past and re-imagining its racial future. Those wishing to contribute to those tasks will be well served by the chapters in this provoking and illuminating volume.

Notes

1. In addition to the chapters in this volume, see Rosal, "Bibliografía afroargentina"; Briones, *Cartografías*; and "There Are No Blacks."
2. Sánchez-Albornoz, *Population*, 155; Rock, "Argentina in 1914," 113.
3. Sánchez-Albornoz, *Population*, 159.
4. Nugent, *Crossings*, 125; Brazil, *Recenseamento 1920*, vol. 4, part 5, book 1, 84–85; Lesser, *Immigration*, 82.
5. Nahum, *Manual*, vol. 2, 107; Sánchez-Albornoz, *Population*, 159.
6. On the commonalities in racial composition among those four countries, see Telles and Flores, "Not Just Color."
7. Weinstein, "Racializing," 247; Fischer, *Poverty*, 34–49; Andrews, *Blackness*, 3.
8. See chapters in this volume by Geler, Pite, and Rodríguez.
9. Adamovsky, this volume, 155.
10. Chamosa, this volume, 69; see also Pite, this volume, and Chamosa, "Indigenous."
11. Lesser, *Welcoming*; *Negotiating*; and *Discontented Diaspora*.
12. Telles, *Race*; Andrews, "Racial Inequality."
13. For Brazil, see Hanchard, *Orpheus and Power*; Twine, *Racism*. For Venezuela, see Wright, *Café con leche*; Montañez, *El racismo oculto*.
14. See for example Andrews, *Afro-Latin America*; Alberto, *Terms*; Pisano, *Liderazgo*; Gotkowitz, *Revolution*.
15. De la Fuente, *Nation for All*; Fischer, *Poverty*; Green, *Gaitanismo*.
16. Adamovsky, this volume, 163.

17. *Candombes* were nineteenth-century Afro-Argentine community events, focusing on drumming and dance.
18. In addition to the chapters by Adamovsky and Elena, this volume, see Karush and Chamosa, *New Cultural History*, and Adamovsky, "La dimensión."
19. Alberto and Elena, this volume, 9.
20. In addition to chapters by Gordillo and Elena, this volume, see Frigerio, "Luis D'Elía."
21. Quotation from Gordillo, this volume, 260. In addition to Adamovsky, Alberto, Elena, Gordillo, and Ko in this volume, see Adamovsky, "El color."
22. Htun, "Racial Democracy"; Andrews, "Racial Inequality."
23. Rodríguez, this volume, 149.
24. Barrientos, "Are There Still 'Indians'?"
25. Loveman, *National Colors*, 250–300.
26. For those questions, see Loveman, *National Colors*, 256–63.
27. Colombia, *Colombia*, 34.
28. Argentina, *Censo Nacional 2010*, vol. 1, 277, 298.
29. Telles and PERLA, *Pigmentocracies*.
30. Adamovsky, Gordillo, this volume.
31. On recent debates on racial hierarchy in the region, see Cottrol, *Long, Lingering Shadow*, 238–91; Hernández, *Racial Subordination*.

Collective bibliography

Abregú Virreira, Carlos. *La cultura tradicional en el Segundo Plan Quinquenal.* Buenos Aires: Subsecretaría de Informaciones, 1953.

Acha, Omar. "Dos estrategias de domesticación de la mujer joven trabajadora: La Casa y el Hogar de la Empleada." In *La fundación Eva Perón y las mujeres: entre la provocación y la inclusión*, edited by Carolina Barry, Katrina Ramacciotti, and Adriana Valobra. Buenos Aires: Editorial Biblios, 2008.

Acha, Omar and Nicolás Quiroga. *El hecho maldito. Conversaciones para otra historia del peronismo.* Rosario: Prohistoria, 2012.

Adamovsky, Ezequiel. *Historia de la clase media argentina: apogeo y decadencia de una ilusión 1919–2003.* Buenos Aires: Planeta, 2009.

"El color de la nación argentina: conflictos y negociaciones por la definición de un ethnos nacional, de la crisis al Bicentenario." *Jahrbuch für Geschichte Lateinamerikas* 49 (2012): 343–64.

Historia de las clases populares en la Argentina: desde 1880 hasta 2003. Buenos Aires: Sudamericana, 2012.

"La dimensión étnico-racial de las identidades de clase en la Argentina: el caso de Cipriano Reyes y una hipótesis sobre la 'negritud' no diaspórica." In *Cartografías afrolatinoamericanas. Perspectivas situadas para análisis transfronterizos*, edited by Florencia Guzmán and Lea Geler, 87–112. Buenos Aires: Biblos, 2013.

"La cuarta función del criollismo y las luchas por la definición del origen y el color del ethnos argentino: desde las primeras novelas gauchescas hasta 1940." *Boletín del Instituto Ravignani* 41 (2014): 50–92.

"El criollismo en las luchas por la definición del origen y el color del ethnos argentino, 1945–1955," *Estudios Interdisciplinarios de América Latina y el Caribe* 26:1 (2015): 31–63.

"Historia del escudo peronista: sus inflexiones de clase y de 'raza' (1945–1955)." *Iberoamericana* 15:59 (Sept. 2015): 65–86.

Adelman, Jeremy, ed. *Colonial Legacies: The Problem of Persistence in Latin American History.* New York: Routledge, 1999.

Aguinis, Marcos. *El atroz encanto de ser argentinos.* Buenos Aires: Planeta, 2001.

Ahmed, Sara. "A Phenomenology of Whiteness." *Feminist Theory* 8 (2007): 149–68.
  Strange Encounters: Embodied Others in Post-Coloniality. London: Routledge,
  2013.
Aizenberg, Edna. *Parricide on the Pampa? A New Study and Translation of Alberto
  Gerchunoff's Los gauchos judíos.* Madrid and Frankfurt am Main: Iberoameri-
  cana-Vervuert, 2000.
Alberdi, Juan Bautista. *Bases y puntos de partida para la organización política de la
  República Argentina.* Buenos Aires: Eudeba, 1966 [1852].
Alberto, Paulina L. *Terms of Inclusion: Black Intellectuals in Twentieth-Century Brazil.*
  Chapel Hill: University of North Carolina Press, 2011.
  "Títere roto: vidas (posibles) y vidas póstumas del 'Negro Raúl.'" In *Cartografías
  afrolatinoamericanas 2. Perspectivas situadas desde Argentina,* edited by Florencia
  Guzmán, Lea Geler and Alejandro Frigerio. Buenos Aires: Biblos, in press.
Albornoz de Videla, Graciela. *Evita: libro de lectura para Primer Grado Inferior.* Buenos
  Aires: Luis Lasserre, 1952.
Alpersohn, Marcos. *Colonia Mauricio: memorias de un colono judío.* Translated
  by Eliahu Toker. Carlos Casares, Argentina: Archivo Central Cultural José Inge-
  nieros, n.d.
Alsogaray, Julio L. *Trilogía de la trata de blancas (Rufianes, Policía, Municipalidad).*
  Buenos Aires: L. J. Rosso, 1933.
Altube, María Inés. "Mujeres en 'tierra adentro'. Las cautivas en las sociedades indí-
  genas de la región pampeana y norpatagónica (siglos XVIII y XIX)." In *Historia y
  género: seis estudios sobre la condición femenina,* edited by Daniel Villar, María
  Herminia Beatriz di Liscia, and María Jorgelina Caviglia de Villar, 89–120. Buenos
  Aires: Biblos, 1999.
Álvarez, Marcelo and Luisa Pinotti. *A la mesa: ritos y retos de la alimentación argentina.*
  Buenos Aires: Grijalbo, 2000.
Alvira, Pablo. "'Una legión de espectros': La cuestión indígena en *El último malón.*"
  Anuario de la Escuela de Historia 24 (2012): 169–86.
Amadeo, Tomás. *El falso dilema. Fascismo o Bolcheviquismo.* Buenos Aires: Librería del
  Colegio, 1939.
Aboy, Rosa. *Viviendas para el pueblo: espacio urbano y sociabilidad en el barrio Los
  Perales, 1946–1955.* Buenos Aires: Universidad de San Andrés/Fondo de Cultura
  Económica de Argentina, 2005.
Ambrosetti, Juan B. *Viaje a la Puna de Atacama.* Buenos Aires: Imp. La Buenos Aires,
  1904.
American Jewish Yearbook 56. Philadelphia: Jewish Publication Society of America, 1955.
Andrews, George Reid. *The Afro-Argentines of Buenos Aires, 1800–1900.* Madison:
  University of Wisconsin Press, 1980.
  Los afroargentinos de Buenos Aires. Buenos Aires: de la Flor, 1989.
  Blacks and Whites in São Paulo, Brazil, 1888–1988. Madison: University of Wiscon-
  sin Press, 1991.
  Afro-Latin America, 1800–2000. New York: Oxford University Press, 2004.
  Blackness in the White Nation: A History of Afro-Uruguay. Chapel Hill: University of
  North Carolina Press, 2010.
  "Racial Inequality in Brazil and the United States, 1990–2010." *Journal of Social
  History* 47: 4 (2014): 829–54.

Andermann, Jens. *The Optic of the State: Visuality and Power in Argentina and Brazil.* Pittsburgh: University of Pittsburgh Press, 2007.

New Argentine Cinema. London: I.B. Tauris, 2012.

Anreus, Alejandro, Diana L. Linden, and Jonathan Weinberg, eds. *The Social and the Real: Political Art of the 1930s in the Western Hemisphere.* University Park: Penn State University Press, 2006.

Anreus, Alejandro. "Siqueiros' Travels and 'Alternative Muralisms' in Argentina and Cuba." In *Mexican Muralism: A Critical History,* edited by Alejandro Anreus, Leonard Folgarait, and Robin Adele Greeley, 177–95. Berkeley: University of California Press, 2012.

Appelbaum, Nancy P. *Muddied Waters: Race, Region, and Local History in Colombia, 1846–1948.* Durham: Duke University Press, 2003.

"Post-Revisionist Scholarship on Race." *Latin American Research Review* 40:3 (2005): 206–17.

Appelbaum, Nancy P., Anne S. Macpherson, and Karin Alejandra Rosemblatt, eds. *Race and Nation in Modern Latin America.* Chapel Hill: University of North Carolina Press, 2003.

Appelbaum, Nancy P., Anne S. Macpherson, and Karin Alejandra Rosemblatt. "Racial Nations." In *Race and Nation in Modern Latin America,* edited by Nancy P. Appelbaum, Anne S. Macpherson, and Karin Alejandra Rosemblatt, 1–31. Chapel Hill: University of North Carolina Press, 2003.

Aranda, Darío. *Argentina originaria: genocidios, saqueos y resistencia.* Buenos Aires: La Vaca, 2011.

Archer-Straw, Petrine. *Negrophilia: Avant-Garde Paris and Black Culture in the 1920s.* New York and London: Thames & Hudson, 2000.

Archetti, Eduardo. "Hibridación, pertenencia y localidad en la construcción de una cocina nacional." In *La Argentina en el siglo XX,* edited by Carlos Altamirano, 217–37. Quilmes: Universidad Nacional de Quilmes, 1999.

Arcondo, Aníbal. *Historia de la alimentación en Argentina: desde los orígenes hasta 1920.* Córdoba: Ferreyra Editor, 2002.

Ardiles Gray, Julio. *Historias de artistas contadas por ellos mismos.* Buenos Aires: Belgrano, 1981.

Argentina. Instituto Nacional de Estadística y Censos (INDEC). *Censo Nacional de Población, Hogares y Viviendas 2010: Censo del Bicentenario. Resultados definitivos, Serie B N° 2.* 2 vols. Buenos Aires: INDEC, 2012.

Arrom, José Juan. "Criollo: definición y matices de un concepto." *Hispania* 34:2 (1951): 172–76.

Artinian, Juan Pablo. "Imaging Argentina: Politics, Protest and the Cultural Politics of Representation 1950–1966." Ph.D. diss., Stony Brook University, 2013.

Auyero, Javier. *Poor People's Politics: Peronist Survival Networks and the Legacy of Evita.* Durham: Duke University Press, 2000.

Auyero, Javier and Rodrigo Hobert. "¿Y ésto es Buenos Aires? Los contrastes del proceso de urbanización." In *Nueva Historia Argentina,* vol. IX, edited by Daniel James, 213–44. Buenos Aires: Sudamericana, 2003.

Avena, Sergio et al. "Aporte aborigen y africano de diferentes regiones de la Argentina en Buenos Aires." *Revista Argentina de Antropología Biológica* 5:1 (2003) [online, n.p.]

Avni, Haim. *Argentina & the Jews: A History of Jewish Immigration*. Translated by Gila Brand. Tuscaloosa: University of Alabama, 1991.

Babb, Florence. *The Tourism Encounter: Fashioning Latin American Nations and Histories*. Stanford: Stanford University Press, 2011.

Baily, Samuel L. "Sarmiento and Immigration: Changing Views on the Role of Immigration in the Development of Argentina." In *Sarmiento and his Argentina*, edited by Joseph T. Criscenti, 131–42. Boulder: Lynne Reinner, 1993.

   Immigrants in the Lands of Promise: Italians in Buenos Aires and New York City, 1870–1914. Ithaca: Cornell University Press, 1999.

Balibar, Etienne. *"La forma nación. Historia e ideología."* In *Raza, nación y clase, Etienne Balibar and Immanuel Wallerstein*, 133–63. Madrid: IEPALA, 1991.

Ballent, Anahí. *Las huellas de la política: vivienda, ciudad, peronismo en Buenos Aires, 1943–1955*. Buenos Aires: Universidad Nacional de Quilmes, Prometeo, 2005.

Ballent, Anahí and Adrián Gorelik. "País urbano, país rural." In *Crisis económica, avance del estado e incertidumbre política, 1930–1943*, edited by Alejandro Cattaruzza, 143–200. Buenos Aires: Sudamericana, 1998.

Barbería, Elsa. *Los dueños de la tierra en la Patagonia Austral, 1880–1920*. Río Gallegos: Universidad Nacional de la Patagonia Austral, 1995.

Barrientos, Pilar. "Are There Still 'Indians' in Argentina? Indigenous Peoples and the 2001 and 2010 Population Censuses." In *Everlasting Countdowns: Race, Ethnicity and National Censuses in Latin American States*, edited by Luis Fernando Angosto Ferrández and Sabine Kradolfer, 41–68. Newcastle upon Tyne: Cambridge Scholars Publishing, 2012.

Baschetti, Roberto, ed. *De la guerrilla peronista al gobierno popular: documentos, 1970–1973*. Buenos Aires: de la Campana, 1995.

   ed. *Documentos de la Resistencia Peronista, 1955–1970*. Buenos Aires: de la Campana, 1997.

Bauer, Arnold. *Goods, Power, History: Latin America's Material Culture*. New York: Cambridge University Press, 2001.

Bayer, Osvaldo, ed. *La Patagonia Rebelde*. Buenos Aires: Planeta, 1995.

   Historia de la crueldad argentina. Julio Roca y el genocidio de los Pueblos Originarios. Buenos Aires: El Tugurio, 2010.

Beasley-Murray, Jon. *Posthegemony: Political Theory and Latin America*. Minneapolis: University of Minnesota Press, 2010.

Beckett, Jeremy. *Past and Present. The Construction of Aboriginality*. Canberra: Aboriginal Studies Press, 1988.

Bederman, Gail. *Manliness & Civilization: A Cultural History of Gender and Race in the United States, 1880–1917*. Chicago: University of Chicago Press, 1995.

Beerbohm, Julius. *Wanderings in Patagonia or Life Among the Ostrich-Hunters*. New York: Henry Holt and Company, 1879.

Bejarano, Margalit. "From Turkey to the United States: The Trajectory of Cuban Sephardim in Miami." In *Contemporary Sephardic Identity in the Americas: An Interdisciplinary Approach*, edited by Margalit Bejarano and Edna Aizenberg, 141–58. Syracuse: Syracuse University Press, 2012.

Benton-Cohen, Katherine. *Borderline Americans: Racial Division and Labor War in the Arizona Borderlands*. Cambridge: Harvard University Press, 2009.

Bergmeier, Horst P. J. and Rainer E. Lotz. "James Arthur Briggs." *Black Music Research Journal* 30:1 (2010): 93–181.

Bialogorski, Mirta. "Logros de una inmigración reciente." In *Cuando Oriente llegó a América: contribuciones de inmigrantes chinos, japoneses y coreanos*, 178–94. Washington D.C.: Banco Interamericano de Desarrollo, 2004.

Bialogorski, Mirta and Daniel Bargman. "The Gaze of the Other: Koreans and Bolivians in Buenos Aires." *Patterns of Prejudice* 30 (1996): 17–26.

Biglieri, Paula. "El retorno del pueblo argentino: entre la autorización y la asamblea. Argentina en la era K." In Paula Biglieri and Gloria Perelló, *En el nombre del pueblo: la emergencia del populismo kirchnerista*, 61–84. Buenos Aires: UNSAM, 2007.

Billarou, María José. "El ama de casa 'moderna': los mensajes de la política sanitaria en los primeros gobiernos peronistas." *La aliaba: Revista de Estudios de la Mujer* 5 (2000): 145–63.

Blaustein, Eduardo. *Prohibido vivir aquí: una historia de los planes de erradicación de villas de la última dictadura*. Buenos Aires: Gobierno de la Ciudad de Buenos Aires, 2001.

Boccara, Guillaume. "Antropología diacrónica. Dinámicas culturales, procesos históricos y poder político." In *Lógicas mestizas en América*, edited by Guillaume Boccara and Silvia Galindo, 21–59. Temuco: Universidad de La Frontera, 1999.

"Fronteras, mestizaje y etnogénesis en las Américas." In *Las fronteras hispanocriollas del mundo indígena latinoamericano en los siglos XVIII-XIX: un análisis comparativo*, edited by Raúl Mandrini and Carlos Paz, 63–93. Tandil: Universidad Nacional del Comahue, 2003.

Boccara, Guillaume and Sylvia Galindo, eds. *Lógicas mestizas en América*. Temuco: Universidad de La Frontera, 1999.

Bockelman, Brian. "Between the Gaucho and the Tango: Popular Songs and the Shifting Landscape of Modern Argentine History, 1895–1915." *American Historical Review* 116:3 (2011): 577–601.

Bolivia. Directed by Adrián Caetano. Cinema Tropical, 2001.

Bonelli, Florencia. *Indias blancas*. Buenos Aires: Debolsillo/Sudamericana, 2008 [2005]. *Indias blancas II: la vuelta del Renquel*. Buenos Aires: Debolsillo/Sudamericana, 2009 [2005].

Bontempo, Paula. "Para Ti: una revista moderna para una mujer moderna, 1922–1935." *Estudios Sociales* 41:1 (2011): 127–56.

Borge, Jason. "Dark Pursuits: Race and Early Argentine Jazz Criticism." *Afro-Hispanic Review* 30:1 (2011): 63–80.

Bra, Gerardo. *La organización negra: la increíble historia de la Zwi Migdal*. Buenos Aires: Corregidor, 1999.

Brasil. Directoria Geral de Estatística. *Recenseamento do Brasil realizado em 1 de setembro de 1920*. 5 vols. Rio de Janeiro: Typ. da Estatística, 1922–30.

Instituto Brasileiro de Geografia e Estatística (IBGE). *Síntese de indicadores sociais: uma análise das condições de vida da população brasileira, 2010*. Rio de Janeiro: IBGE, 2010.

Braun, Herbert. *The Assassination of Gaitán: Public Life and Urban Violence in Colombia*. Madison: University of Wisconsin Press, 1985.

Briones, Claudia, ed. "Mestizaje y blanqueamiento como coordenadas de aboriginalidad y nación en Argentina." *Runa* 23 (2002): 61–88.

"Formaciones de alteridad, contextos globales, procesos nacionales y provinciales."
In *Cartografías argentinas: políticas indígenas y formaciones provinciales de alteridad*, edited by Claudia Briones, 9–40. Buenos Aires: Antropofagia, 2005.

"La nación argentina de cien en cien: de criollos a blancos y de blancos a mestizos." In *Nación y diversidad: territorios, identidades y federalismo*, edited by José Nun and Alejandro Grimson, 35–62. Buenos Aires: Edhasa, 2008.

Cartografías argentinas: políticas indigenistas y formaciones provinciales de alteridad. Buenos Aires: Antropofagia, 2005.

Briones, Claudia and José Luis Lanata, eds. *Contemporary Perspectives on the Native Peoples of Pampa, Patagonia, and Tierra del Fuego: Living on the Edge*. Westport: Bergin & Garvey, 2002.

Briones, Claudia and Morita Carrasco. *Pacta Sunt Servanda. Capitulaciones, convenios y tratados con indígenas en Pampa y Patagonia (Argentina 1742–1878)*. Buenos Aires: IWGIA, 2000.

Brodkin, Karen. *How the Jews Became White Folks and What That Says about Race in America*. New Brunswick: Rutgers University Press, 1998.

Brodsky, Adriana. "The Contours of Identity: Sephardic Jews and the Construction of Jewish Communities in Argentina, 1880 to the Present." Ph.D. diss., Duke University, 2004.

"Re-configurando comunidades. Judíos sefardíes/árabes en Argentina (1900–1950)." In *Árabes y judíos en Iberoamérica: similitudes, diferencias y tensiones*, edited by Raanan Rein, 117–34. Sevilla: Tres Culturas del Mediterráneo, 2008.

Bronfman, Alejandra. *Measures of Equality: Social Science, Citizenship, and Race in Cuba, 1902–1940*. Chapel Hill: University of North Carolina Press, 2004.

Brown, Jonathan C. *A Brief History of Argentina*. New York: Checkmark Books, 2004.

Bunge, Alejandro. *Una nueva Argentina*. Buenos Aires: Guillermo Kraft, 1940.

Caggiano, Sergio. *El sentido común visual: disputas en torno a género, 'raza' y clase en imágenes de circulación pública*. Buenos Aires: Miño y Dávila, 2012.

Caldo, Paula. *Mujeres cocineras: hacia una historia sociocultural de la cocina argentina a fines del siglo XIX y primera mitad del XX*. Rosario: Prohistoria, 2009.

Canals Frau, Salvador. "La Araucanización de la Pampa." *Anales de la Sociedad Científica Argentina* 120 (1935): 221–32.

"Expansions of the Araucanians in Argentina." In *Handbook of South American Indians*, edited by Julian Steward, 143:2 (1946): 761–66.

Las poblaciones indígenas de la Argentina. Buenos Aires: Sudamericana, 1986 [1953].

Cara, Ana C. "The Poetics of Creole Talk: Toward an Aesthetic of Argentine Verbal Art." *The Journal of American Folklore* 116:459 (2003): 36–56.

Cariou, André. *L'Aventure de Pont-Aven et Gauguin*. Milan: Skira Editore, 2003.

Casamiquela, Rodolfo. *Rectificaciones y ratificaciones, hacia una interpretación definitiva del panorama etnológico de la Patagonia y área septentrional adyacente*. Bahía Blanca: Instituto de Humanidades, Universidad Nacional del Sur, 1965.

Casamiquela, Rodolfo, Osvaldo Mondelo, Enrique Perea and Mateo Martinic Beros. *Del mito a la realidad. Evolución iconográfica del pueblo tehuelche meridional*. Buenos Aires: Fundación Ameghino, 1991.

Castro, Donald S. *The Afro-Argentine in Argentine Culture: El Negro del Acordeón*. Lewiston: Edwin Mellen, 2001.

"The Sainete Porteño, 1890–1935: The Image of Jews in the Argentine Popular Theater." *Studies in Latin American Popular Culture* 21 (2002): 29–57.

Castro, Hortensia. "Otras miradas, otros sujetos: los relatos de viajeros en la construcción de la Puna argentina." In *Viajes y geografía: exploraciones, turismo y migraciones en la construcción de lugares*, edited by Perla Zusman, Carla Lois, and Hortensia Castro, 93–114. Buenos Aires: Prometeo, 2007.

Caterina, Luis María. *La Liga Patriótica Argentina: un grupo de presión frente a las convulsiones sociales de la década del '20.* Buenos Aires: Corregidor, 1995.

Censo Indígena Nacional, *Vol. 3, Resultados definitivos 1966–1968.* Buenos Aires: Ministerio del Interior. Secretaría de Estado de Gobierno, 1968.

Chamosa, Oscar. "Indigenous or Criollo: The Myth of White Argentina in Tucumán's Calchaquí Valley." *Hispanic American Historical Review* 88 (2008): 71–106.

"Criollo and Peronist: The Argentine Folklore Movement during the First Peronism (1943–1955)." In *The New Cultural History of Peronism: Power and Identity in Mid-Twentieth-Century Argentina*, edited by Matthew B. Karush and Oscar Chamosa, 113–42. Durham: Duke U. Press, 2010.

The Argentine Folklore Movement: Criollo Workers, Sugar Elites and the Politics of Cultural Nationalism. Tucson: University of Arizona Press, 2010.

Chang, Gordon H. "Eternally Foreign: Asian Americans, History, and Race." In *Doing Race: 21 Essays for the 21st Century*, edited by Paula M. L. Moya and Hazel Rose Markus, 216–33. New York: Norton, 2010.

Chasteen, John Charles. *National Rhythms, African Roots: The Deep History of Latin American Popular Dance.* Albuquerque: University of New Mexico Press, 2004.

Ciccariello-Maher, George. "Toward a Racial Geography of Caracas: Neoliberal Urbanism and the Fear of Penetration." *Qui Parle* 16 (2007): 1–33.

Cirio, Norberto Pablo. "La desaparición del candombe argentino. Los muertos que vos matáis gozan de buena salud." *Música e Investigación*, 12–13 (2003): 181–82.

En la lucha curtida del camino. Buenos Aires: INADI, c. 2008.

"Afroargentino del tronco colonial. Una categoría autogestada." *Novamérica/Nuevamérica* 127 (2010): 28–32.

Cirio, Norberto Pablo, and Dulcinea Tomás Cámara. "'Black Letters': Problems and Issues in the Research, Dissemination and Reception of Literature by Afro-Argentines and on Afro-Argentines." *African and Black Diaspora: An International Journal* 7:2 (2014): 129–51.

Civantos, Christina. *Between Argentines and Arabs: Argentine Orientalism, Arab Immigrants, and the Writing of Identity.* Albany: State University of New York Press, 2006.

Coffey, Mary. *How a Revolutionary Art Became Official Culture: Murals, Museums, and the Mexican State.* Durham: Duke University Press, 2012.

Cohen, Judith R. "The Role of Music in the Quebec Sephardic Community." In *Contemporary Sephardic Identity in the Americas: An Interdisciplinary Approach*, edited by Margalit Bejarano and Edna Aizenberg, 202–20. Syracuse: Syracuse University Press, 2012.

Coleman, Bill. *Trumpet Story.* Boston: Northeastern University Press, 1991.

Colombia. Departamento Administrativo Nacional de Estadísticas [DANE]. *Colombia una nación multicultural: su diversidad étnica.* Bogotá: DANE, 2007.

Cooke, John William. *Apuntes para la militancia*. Buenos Aires: Schapire, 1972.

Corach, Daniel, Oscar Lao, Cecilia Bobillo, Kristiaan Van Der Gaag, Sofia Zuniga, Mark Vermeulen, Kate Van Duijn, et al. "Inferring Continental Ancestry of Argentineans from Autosomal, Y-Chromosomal and Mitochondrial DNA." *Annals of Human Genetics* 74:1 (2010): 65–76.

Corbin, Alain. *Women for Hire: Prostitution and Sexuality in France after 1850*. Translated by Alan Sheridan. Cambridge: Harvard University Press, 1990.

Cordeu, Edgardo, and Alejandra Siffredi. *De la algarroba al algodón: movimientos milenaristas del Chaco argentino*. Buenos Aires: Juárez Editora, 1971.

Coscia, Jorge. *Encrucijada del bicentenario*. Buenos Aires: Peña Lillo, Continente, 2011.

Cossa, Roberto, Germán Rozenmacher, Carlos Somigliana, and Ricardo Talesnik. *Tres obras de teatro*. Havana: Casa de las Américas, 1970.

Cottrol, Robert J. *The Long, Lingering Shadow: Slavery, Race, and Law in the American Hemisphere*. Athens: University of Georgia Press, 2013.

Courtis, Corina. *Construcciones de alteridad: discursos cotidianos sobre la inmigración coreana en Buenos Aires*. Buenos Aires: Eudeba, 2000.

Courtis, Corina, María Inés Pacecca, Diana Lenton, Carlos Belvedere, Sergio Caggiano, Diego Casaravilla, and Gerardo Halpern. "Racism and Discourse: A Portrait of the Argentine Situation." In *Racism and Discourse in Latin America*, edited by Teun A. van Dijk, translated by Elisa Barquin and Alexandra Hibbett, 13–55. Lanham: Lexington Books, 2009.

Crosby, Alfred W. Jr. *The Columbian Exchange: Biological and Cultural Consequences of 1492*. Westport: Praeger, 2003.

Dalton, Karen C. C. and Henry Louis Gates, Jr. "Josephine Baker and Paul Colin: African American Dance Seen through Parisian Eyes." *Critical Inquiry* 24:4 (1998): 903–34.

Dann, Graham. "The People of Tourist Brochures." In *The Tourist Image: Myths and Myth Making in Tourism*, edited by Tom Selwyn, 61–81. New York: John Wiley & Sons, 1996.

Dávila, Jerry. "Ethnicity, Identity, and Nationality in Latin America." *Jewish History* 18 (2004): 95–113.

Davis, Darién J. *White Face, Black Mask: Africaneity and the Early Social History of Popular Music in Brazil*. East Lansing: Michigan State University Press, 2009.

Dawson, Alexander S. *Indian and Nation in Revolutionary Mexico*. Tucson: University of Arizona Press, 2004.

De Agostini, Alberto María. *Andes patagónicos: viajes de exploración a la Cordillera Patagónica Austral*. Buenos Aires: Guillermo Kraft, 1945.

De Castro Esteves, Ramón. "En pro de las danzas nativas." In *Memoria general del Primer Congreso Nacional de Turismo y Comunicaciones*, organized by the Touring Club Argentino Buenos Aires, Sept. 1938. Buenos Aires: Talleres Gráficos Argentinos, 1939.

De la Cadena, Marisol. *Indigenous Mestizos: The Politics of Race and Culture in Cuzco, Peru, 1919–1991*. Durham: Duke University Press, 2000.

"Are Mestizos Hybrids? The Conceptual Politics of Andean Identities." *Journal of Latin American Studies* 37 (2005): 259–84.

"Introduction" to *Formaciones de indianidad: Articulaciones raciales, mestizaje y nación en América Latina*, edited by Marisol de la Cadena, 7–34. Popayán: Envión, 2008.

De la Fuente, Alejandro. "Myths of Racial Democracy: Cuba, 1900–1912." *Latin American Research Review* 34:3 (1999): 39–73.

A Nation for All: Race, Inequality, and Politics in Twentieth-Century Cuba. Chapel Hill: University of North Carolina Press, 2000.

De Pigafetta, Antonio. *Primer viaje en torno al globo.* Madrid: Calpe, 1922 [1524–25].

Degreff, Walter. *Judiadas, judiones, judíos y judihuelos. Acción usurpadora de los judíos en el mundo moderno.* Buenos Aires: Francisco A. Colombo, 1936.

Delaney, Jeane H. "Imagining 'El Ser Argentino': Cultural Nationalism and Romantic Concepts of Nationhood in Early Twentieth-Century Argentina." *Journal of Latin American Studies* 34:3 (2002): 625–58.

Deleuze, Gilles. *Difference and Repetition.* New York: Columbia University Press, 1994.

Deleuze, Gilles and Félix Guattari. *Anti-Oedipus: Capitalism and Schizophrenia.* Minneapolis: University of Minnesota Press, 1983.

Delrio, Walter. *Memorias de expropiación. Sometimiento e incorporación indígena en la Patagonia (1872–1943).* Bernal: Universidad Nacional de Quilmes, 2005.

Delrio, Walter, Diana Lenton, Marcelo Musante, Mariano Nagy, Alexis Papazian, and Pilar Pérez. "Discussing Indigenous Genocide in Argentina: Past, Present, and Consequences of Argentinean State Policies toward Native Peoples." *Genocide Studies and Prevention* 5:2 (2010): 138–59.

Demos, John. *The Unredeemed Captive: A Family Story from Early America.* New York: Vintage, 1995.

Derrida, Jacques. *Specters of Marx: The State of the Debt, the Work of Mourning, and the New International.* New York: Routledge, 1994.

Deutsch, Sandra McGee. *Counterrevolution in Argentina, 1900–1932: The Argentine Patriotic League.* Lincoln: University of Nebraska Press, 1986.

Las derechas: The Extreme Right in Argentina, Brazil, and Chile, 1890–1939. Stanford: Stanford University Press, 1999.

"Contra 'el gran desorden social': los nacionalistas y la sexualidad, 1919–1940." *Sociohistórica (Cuadernos del CISH)* 17–18 (2006): 127–50.

Crossing Borders, Claiming a Nation: A History of Argentine Jewish Women, 1880–1955. Durham: Duke University Press, 2010.

Devoto, Fernando J. *Nacionalismo, fascismo, tradicionalismo en la Argentina moderna: una historia.* Buenos Aires: Siglo XXI, 2002.

Historia de la inmigración en la Argentina. Buenos Aires: Sudamericana, 2003.

Historia de los italianos en la Argentina. Buenos Aires: Biblos, 2006.

Devoto, Fernando and Marta Madero. "Introduction" to *Historia de la vida privada en la Argentina. La Argentina plural: 1870–1930* (Tomo II), directed by Fernando Devoto and Marta Madero, 7–15. Buenos Aires: Taurus, 2000.

Di Meglio, Gabriel. *¡Viva el bajo pueblo!: la plebe urbana de Buenos Aires y la política entre la Revolución de Mayo y el rosismo (1810–1829).* Buenos Aires: Prometeo, 2006.

Di Santo, Víctor. *El canto del payador en el circo criollo.* Buenos Aires: Tall. Gráf. Offset 25, 1987.

Díaz-Mas, Paloma. *Sephardim: The Jews from Spain.* Translated by George K. Zucker. Chicago: University of Chicago Press, 1992.

Dirección Nacional de Artes Visuales (Argentina). *Primera muestra de obras premiadas en los salones nacionales: 30 pintores premiados.* Buenos Aires: AmigArte, 1990.

Dirlik, Arif. "Asia Pacific Studies in an Age of Global Modernity." *Inter-Asia Cultural Studies* 6:2 (2005): 158–70.

Dixie, Florence. *Across Patagonia.* London: Richard Bentley and Son, 1880.

Dregni, Michael. *Django: The Life and Music of a Gypsy Legend*. New York: Oxford University Press, 2004.

Dyer, Richard. *White*. London: Routledge, 1997.

Earle, Rebecca. *The Return of the Native: Indians and Myth-Making in Spanish America, 1810–1930*. Durham: Duke University Press, 2007.

    The Body of the Conquistador: Food, Race, and the Colonial Experience in Spanish America, 1492–1700. Cambridge: Cambridge University Press, 2012.

    "The Columbian Exchange." In *The Oxford Handbook of Food History*, edited by Jeffrey M. Pilcher. New York: Oxford University Press, 2013.

Echeverría, Bolívar. *Modernidad y blanquitud*. Mexico: Era, 2011.

Edison, Paul. "Conquest Unrequited: French Expeditionary Science in Mexico, 1864–1867." *French Historical Studies* 26 (2003): 459–95.

Edwards, Elizabeth. "Postcards: Greetings from Another World." *The Tourist Image: Myths and Myth Making in Tourism*, edited by Tom Selwyn, 197–221. New York: John Wiley & Sons, 1996.

Eguren, Alicia. "Poema a los cabecitas negras." In *El talud descuajado*, 57–60. Buenos Aires: Sexto Continente, 1951.

Eichelbaum, Samuel. "Aaron the Jew." In *Argentine Jewish Theatre: A Critical Anthology*, edited and translated by Nora Glickman and Gloria F. Waldman, 19–54. Lewisburg: Bucknell University Press, 1996.

Elena, Eduardo. "What the People Want: State Planning and Political Planning in Peronist Argentina, 1946–1955." *Journal of Latin American Studies* 37:1 (2005): 81–108.

    Dignifying Argentina: Peronism, Citizenship, and Mass Consumption. Pittsburgh: University of Pittsburgh Press, 2011.

    "New Directions in the History of Peronism." *Estudios Interdisciplinarios de América Latina y el Caribe*. 25:1 (2014): 17–40.

Elkin, Judith Laikin. *The Jews of Latin America*. New York: Holmes & Meier, 1998.

Endere, María. *Management of Archeological Sites and the Public of Argentina*. Oxford: Archeopress, 2007.

Envido: Revista de política y ciencias sociales, vols. I and II. Buenos Aires: Colección Reediciones y Antologías, Biblioteca Nacional, 2011.

Erausquin, Estela. "Los inmigrantes en el cine argentino. Panorama general y estudio de un caso actual: *Un cuento chino*, 2011." *Amérique Latine Histoire et Mémoire. Les cahiers ALHIM*, 23 (2012) [online] http://alhim.revues.org/4264?lang=en.

Escalada, Federico. *El complejo Tehuelche: estudios de etnografía patagónica*. Buenos Aires: Coni, 1949.

Escobar, Arturo. "Culture Sits in Places: Reflections on Globalism and Subaltern Strategies of Localization." *Political Geography* 20 (2001): 139–74.

Escolar, Diego. "El 'estado del malestar.' Movimientos indígenas y procesos de desincorporación en la Argentina : el caso Huarpe." In *Cartografías argentinas: políticas indigenistas y formaciones provinciales de alteridad*, 41–72. Buenos Aires: Antropofagia, 2005.

    Los dones étnicos de la nación. Identidades huarpe y modos de producción de soberanía estatal en Argentina. Buenos Aires: Prometeo, 2007.

Espiro, María L. and Bernarda Zubrzycki. "Tensiones y disputas entre migrantes africanos recientes y organismos de control estatal. El caso de los senegaleses en la ciudad de La Plata." *Questión* 1:39 (2013): 109–21.

Fanon, Franz. *Black Skin, White Masks*. London: Pluto, 1986.

Farberman, Judith and Raquel Gil Montero, eds. *Los pueblos de indios del Tucumán colonial: pervivencia y desestructuración*. Quilmes: Universidad Nacional de Quilmes, 2002.

Farberman, Judith and Silvia Ratto, eds. *Historias mestizas en el Tucumán colonial y las pampas*. Buenos Aires: Biblos, 2009.

Fazio, Lorenzo. *Memoria descriptiva de la Provincia de Santiago del Estero*. Buenos Aires: Compañía General de Billetes de Banco, 1989.

Feinmann, José Pablo. *Peronismo: filosofía política de una persistencia argentina*, vols. I and II. Buenos Aires: Planeta, 2010–11.

Feitlowitz, Marguerite. *A Lexicon of Terror: Argentina and the Legacies of Torture*. New York: Oxford University Press, 1998.

Fejerman, Laura, Francisco R. Carnese, Alicia S. Goicoechea, Sergio A. Avena, Cristina B. Dejean, and Ryk H. Ward. "African Ancestry of the Population of Buenos Aires." *American Journal of Physical Anthropology* 128:1 (2005): 164–70.

Fernández Balzano, Oscar. *El turismo en la República Argentina desde la Fundación Eva Perón hasta la creación de una secretaría específica*. Buenos Aires, [n.e.]: 1973.

Fernández Bravo, Nicolás. "'¿Qué hacemos con los afrodescendientes?' Aportes para una crítica de las políticas de la identidad." In *Cartografías afrolatinoamericanas. Perspectivas situadas para análisis transfronterizos*, edited by Florencia Guzmán and Lea Geler, 241–60. Buenos Aires: Biblos, 2013.

"El regreso del cabecita negra. Ruralidad, desplazamiento y reemergencia identitaria entre los santiagueños 'afro'." In *Cartografías afrolatinoamericanas 2. Perspectivas situadas desde Argentina*, edited by Florencia Guzmán, Lea Geler, and Alejandro Frigerio. Buenos Aires: Biblos, in press.

Ferreira, Luis. "Música, artes performáticas y el campo de las relaciones raciales. Área de estudios de la presencia africana en América Latina." In *Los estudios afroamericanos y africanos en América Latina*, edited by Gladys Lechini, 225–50. Córdoba: CEA-CLACSO, 2008.

Filc, Judith. *Entre el parentesco y la política: familia y dictadura, 1976–1983*. Buenos Aires: Biblos, 1997.

Finchelstein, Federico. "The Anti-Freudian Politics of Argentine Fascism: Anti-Semitism, Catholicism, and the Internal Enemy, 1932–1945." *Hispanic American Historical Review* 87 (2007): 77–110.

Fischer, Brodwyn. *A Poverty of Rights: Citizenship and Inequality in Twentieth-Century Brazil*. Stanford: Stanford University Press, 2010.

Flier, Patricia Graciela. "Historia y memoria de la colonización judía agraria en Entre Ríos: la experiencia de Colonia Clara, 1890–1950." Ph.D. diss., Universidad Nacional de La Plata, 2011.

Forn, Juan. "La construcción de la memoria." In *Pintura argentina: panorama del período 1810–2000*, vol. 7, 9–17. Buenos Aires: Proyecto Arte Para Todos–Banco Velox, 2001.

Foucault, Michel. *La arqueología del saber*. Mexico: Siglo XXI, 2003 [1969].

Fraser, Nancy. "From Redistribution to Recognition? Dilemmas of Justice in a 'Post-Socialist' Age." *Theorizing Multiculturalism: A Guide to the Current Debate*, edited by Cynthia Willet, 19–49. Oxford: Blackwell, 1998.

Frederick, Bonnie. "Reading the Warning: The Reader and the Image of the Captive Woman." *Chasqui* 18:2 (1989): 3–11.

Freedberg, David. *El poder de las imágenes: estudios sobre la historia y la teoría de la respuesta*. Madrid: Cátedra, 1992.

Freidenberg, Judith. *The Invention of the Jewish Gaucho: Villa Clara and the Construction of Argentine Identity*. Austin: University of Texas Press, 2009.

Frigerio, Alejandro. *Cultura negra en el Cono Sur: representaciones en conflicto*. Buenos Aires: Ediciones UCA, 2000.

"'Negros' y 'blancos' en Buenos Aires: repensando nuestras categorías raciales." In *Buenos Aires negra: identidad y cultura*, edited by Leticia Maronese, 77–98. Buenos Aires: CPPHC, 2006.

"De la 'desaparición' de los negros a la 'reaparición' de los afrodescendientes: comprendiendo la política de las identidades negras, de las clasificaciones raciales y de su estudio en la Argentina." In *Los estudios afroamericanos y africanos en América Latina: herencia, presencia y visiones del otro*, edited by Gladys Lechini, 117–44. Buenos Aires: CLACSO, 2008.

"Luis D'Elía y los negros: identificaciones raciales y de clase en sectores populares." *Claroscuro: Revista del Centro de Estudios sobre la Diversidad Cultural* 8 (2009): 13–43.

Frigerio, Alejandro and Eva Lamborghini. "(De)mostrando cultura: estrategias políticas y culturales de visibilización y reivindicación en el movimiento afroargentino." *Boletín americanista*, 63 (2011): 101–20.

"Los afroargentinos: formas de comunalización, creación de identidades colectivas y resistencia cultural y política." In *Aportes para el desarrollo humano en Argentina/ 2011: afrodescendientes y africanos en Argentina*, coordinated by Rubén Mercado and Gabriela Catterberg, 2–45. Buenos Aires: PNUD, 2011.

Gaffet, Hernán. *Oscar Alemán: vida con swing*. DVD. Buenos Aires: La pintada, 2002.

Gálvez, Manuel. *Recuerdos de la vida literaria*, vol. 1. Buenos Aires: Taurus, 2002 [1944].

García, Amelia and Brenda Miralles, eds. "Tierra de promisión: la Patagonia en los manuales Estrada durante el primer peronismo." *Quinto Sol: Revista de Historia Regional* 12 (2008): 203–25.

Garfunkel, Boris. *Narro mi vida*. Buenos Aires: Optimus, 1960.

Garguin, Enrique. "'Los Argentinos Descendemos de los Barcos': The Racial Articulation of Middle Class Identity in Argentina (1920–1960)." *Latin American and Caribbean Ethnic Studies* 2:2 (2007): 161–84.

Garrett, Charles Hiroshi. *Struggling to Define a Nation: American Music and the Twentieth Century*. Berkeley: University of California Press, 2008.

Gatica, Oscar. *Tiempos de liberación: memorias de un militante de la JP, 1973–1976*. Santa Rosa, Argentina: Pitanguá, 2007.

Geler, Lea. "'¡Pobres negros!' Algunos apuntes sobre la desaparición de los negros argentinos." In *Estado, región y poder local en América Latina, siglos XIX-XX*, edited by Pilar García Jordán, 115–53. Barcelona: PiEUB, 2007.

Andares negros, caminos blancos. Afroporteños, estado y nación argentina a fines del siglo XIX. Rosario: Prohistoria, 2010.

"'¿Quién no ha sido negro en su vida?' Performances de negritud en el carnaval porteño de fines del siglo XIX e inicios del XX." In *El estado en América Latina: control de los recursos, organización sociopolítica e imaginarios, siglos XIX-XXI*, edited by Pilar García Jordán, 183–211. Barcelona: PiEUB, 2011.

"Un personaje para la (blanca) nación argentina. El negro Benito, teatro y mundo urbano popular porteño a fines del siglo XIX." *Boletín Americanista* 63 (2011): 77–99.

"Afrodescendencia y mundo popular en Buenos Aires (1895–1916): el caso de Zenón Rolón y Chin Yonk." In *La articulación del Estado en América Latina*, edited by Pilar García Jordán, 207–26. Barcelona: PiEUB, 2013.

"Afro-Porteños at the End of the 19th Century: Discussing the Nation." *African and Black Diaspora: an International Journal* 7, 2 (2014): 105–18.

Geler, Lea and Florencia Guzmán. "Sobre esclavizados/as y afrodescendientes en Argentina: nuevas perspectivas de análisis." *Boletín americanista* 63 (2011): 1–12.

eds. *Boletín americanista. Dossier sobre esclavizados/as y afrodescendientes en Argentina: nuevas perspectivas de análisis*, vol. 63 (2011).

Geler, Lea and Mariela Rodríguez. "Argentina." In *Encyclopedia of Race, Ethnicity and Nationalism*, edited by John Stone, Rutledge Dennis, Polly Rizova, Anthony Smith, and Xiaoshuo Hou. Chicester: Wiley-Blackwell, in press.

Gendron, Bernard. *Between Montmartre and the Mudd Club: Popular Music and the Avant-Garde*. Chicago: University of Chicago Press, 2002.

Gené, Marcela. *Un mundo feliz: imágenes de los trabajadores en el primer peronismo, 1946–1955*. Buenos Aires: Universidad de San Andrés, 2005.

Gerber, Jane S. *The Jews of Spain: A History of the Sephardic Experience*. New York: Free Press, 1992.

"Sephardic and Syrian Immigration to America: Acculturation and Communal Preservation." In *Contemporary Sephardic Identity in the Americas: An Interdisciplinary Approach*, edited by Margalit Bejarano and Edna Aizenberg, 38–65. Syracuse: Syracuse University Press, 2012.

Gerchunoff, Alberto. *Los gauchos judíos*. La Plata: Joaquín Sesé, 1910.

Germani, Gino. *Política y sociedad en una época de transición: de la sociedad tradicional a la sociedad de masas*. Buenos Aires: Paidós, 1962.

Getino, Octavio. *Turismo entre el ocio y el negocio: identidad cultural y desarrollo económico para América Latina y el Mercosur*. Buenos Aires: CICCUS, 2002.

Gillespie, Richard. *Soldiers of Perón: Argentina's Montoneros*. New York: Oxford University Press, 1982.

Gilman, Sander L. *The Jew's Body*. New York: Routledge, 1991.

Smart Jews: The Construction of the Image of Jewish Superior Intelligence. Lincoln: University of Nebraska Press, 1996.

Gilroy, Paul. *Against Race: Imagining Political Culture Beyond the Color Line*. Cambridge: Belknap Press of Harvard University Press, 2000.

Ginio, Alisa Meyuhas. "The Sephardic Diaspora Revisited: Dr. Ángel Pulido Fernández (1852–1932) and his Campaign." In *Identities in an Era of Globalization and Multiculturalism: Latin America in the Jewish World*, edited by Judith Bokser Liwerant, Eliezer Ben-Rafael, Yossi Gorny, and Raanan Rein, 287–96. Leiden: Brill, 2008.

Giordano, Mariana. "Nación e identidad en los imaginarios visuales de la Argentina. Siglos XIX y XX." *ARBOR Ciencia, Pensamiento y Cultura* 185:740 (2009): 1283–98.

Giuffré, Mercedes, ed. *En busca de una identidad: la novela histórica en Argentina*. Buenos Aires: Ediciones del Signo, 2004.

Gociol, Judith. *Más libros para más: colecciones del Centro Editor de América Latina*. Buenos Aires: Biblioteca Nacional, 2007.

Goebel, Michael. *Argentina's Partisan Past: Nationalism and the Politics of History*. Liverpool: Liverpool University Press, 2011.

Overlapping Geographies of Belonging: Migrations, Regions, and Nations in the Western South Atlantic. Washington, DC: American Historical Association, 2013.

Goldberg, Florinda F. "La telenovela El clon (Brasil, 2001): diálogos interculturales y sorpresas de la historia." In *Árabes y judíos en Iberoamérica: similitudes, diferencias y tensiones*, edited by Raanan Rein, 439–60. Sevilla: Tres Culturas del Mediterráneo, 2008.

Goldstein, Eric L. *The Price of Whiteness: Jews, Race, and American Identity*. Princeton: Princeton University Press, 2006.

González Arrili, Bernardo. *Buenos Aires 1900*. Buenos Aires: CEAL, 1967.

Gordillo, Gastón. *Landscapes of Devils: Tensions of Place and Memory in the Argentinean Chaco*. Durham: Duke University Press, 2004.

"The Crucible of Citizenship: ID-Paper Fetishism in the Argentinean Chaco." *American Ethnologist* 33:2 (2006): 162–76.

"Longing for Elsewhere: Guaraní Reterritorializations." *Comparative Studies in Society and History* 53 (2011): 855–81.

Rubble: The Afterlife of Destruction. Durham: Duke University Press, 2014.

Gordillo, Gastón and Silvia Hirsch. "Indigenous Struggles and Contested Identities in Argentina: Histories of Invisibilization and Reemergence." *Journal of Latin American Anthropology* 8:3 (2003): 4–30.

"La presencia ausente: políticas estatales, invisibilizaciones y emergencias indígenas en la Argentina." In *Movilizaciones indígenas e identidades en disputa en la Argentina*, edited by Gastón Gordillo and Silvia Hirsch, 15–38. Buenos Aires: FLACSO-La Crujía, 2010.

eds. *Movilizaciones indígenas e identidades en disputa en la Argentina*. Buenos Aires: FLACSO-La Crujía, 2010.

Gordon, Avery. *Ghostly Matters: Haunting and the Sociological Imagination*. Minneapolis: University of Minnesota Press, 1997.

Gotkowitz, Laura. *A Revolution for Our Rights: Indigenous Struggles for Land and Justice in Bolivia, 1880–1952*. Durham: Duke University Press, 2007.

Gould, Jeffrey. *To Die in This Way: Nicaraguan Indians and the Myth of Mestizaje, 1880–1965*. Durham: Duke University Press, 1998.

Green, W. John. *Gaitanismo, Left Liberalism, and Popular Mobilization in Colombia*. Gainesville: University Press of Florida, 2003.

Greer, Margaret Rich Quilligan and Walter Mignolo, eds. *Rereading the Black Legend: The Discourses of Religious and Racial Difference in the Renaissance Empires*. Chicago: University of Chicago Press, 2007.

Grimson, Alejandro. "Nuevas xenofobias, nuevas políticas étnicas en la Argentina." In *Migraciones regionales hacia la Argentina: diferencia, desigualdad, y derechos*, edited by Alejandro Grimson and Elizabeth Jelin, 69–97. Buenos Aires: Prometeo, 2006.

Mitomanías argentinas: cómo hablamos de nosotros mismos. Buenos Aires: Siglo XXI, 2012.

Gross, Ariella. *What Blood Won't Tell: A History of Race on Trial in America*. Cambridge: Harvard University Press, 2008.

Grosso, José Luis. *Indios muertos, negros invisibles: hegemonía, identidad, y añoranza*. Córdoba: Encuentro, 2008.

Gruesz, Kirsten Silva. "Facing the Nation: The Organic Life of 'La Cautiva.'" *Revista de Estudios Hispánicos* 30:1 (1996): 3–22.

Guano, Emanuela. "A Color for the Modern Nation: The Discourse of Class, Race and Education in the Porteño Middle Class." *Journal of Latin American Anthropology* 8:1 (2003): 148–71.

"A Stroll Through La Boca: The Politics and Poetics of Spatial Experience in a Buenos Aires Neighborhood." *Space and Culture* 6 (2003): 356–76.

"The Denial of Citizenship: 'Barbaric' Buenos Aires and the Middle-Class Imaginary," *City & Society* 16 (2004): 69–97.

Guber, Rosana. "Linajes ocultos en los orígenes de la antropología social de Buenos Aires." *Revista Avá* 8 (2006): 1–35.

Guimarães, Antonio Sérgio Alfredo. *Classes, raças e democracia*. São Paulo: Editora 34, Fundação de Apoio à Universidade de São Paulo, 2002.

Guss, David. "The Gran Poder and the Reconquest of La Paz." *Journal for Latin American Anthropology* 11 (2006): 294–328.

Gutiérrez Zaldivar, Ignacio. *Quirós*. Buenos Aires: Zurbarán, 1991.

Gutkowski, Hélène. *Érase una vez ... Sefarad. Los sefaradíes del mediterráneo. Su historia – su cultura. 1880–1950 – testimonios*. Buenos Aires: Lumen, 1999.

Gutman, Margarita and Jorge Enrique Hardoy. *Buenos Aires: historia urbana del área metropolitana*. Madrid: Editorial Mapfre, 1992.

Guy, Donna J. *Sex and Danger in Buenos Aires: Prostitution, Family, and Nation in Argentina*. Lincoln: University of Nebraska Press, 1991.

Guzmán, Florencia. *Los claroscuros del mestizaje: negros, indios, y castas en la Catamarca colonial*. Córdoba: Encuentro, 2010.

"Performatividad social de las (sub)categorías coloniales. Mulatos, pardos, mestizos y criollos en tiempos de cambios, guerra y política, en el interior de la Argentina." In *Cartografías afrolatinoamericanas. Perspectivas situadas para análisis transfronterizos*, edited by Florencia Guzmán and Lea Geler, 57–83. Buenos Aires: Biblos, 2013.

Hagimoto, Koichi. "Beyond the Hyphen: Representation of Multicultural Japanese Identity in Maximiliano Matayoshi's *Gaijin* and Anna Kazumi Stahl's *Flores de un solo día*." *Transmodernity* 3:2 (2014) [online] http://escholarship.org/uc/item/0sj2j5gx.

Hale, Dana. *Races on Display: French Representations of Colonized Peoples, 1886–1940*. Bloomington: Indiana University Press, 2008.

Hall, Stuart. "The Spectacle of the 'Other'." In *Representation. Cultural Representations and Signifying Practices*, edited by Stuart Hall, 223–90. London: Sage, 1997.

Halperín Donghi, Tulio. *Proyecto y construcción de una nación: Argentina, 1846–1880*. Caracas: Biblioteca Ayacucho, 1980.

Hanchard, Michael George. *Orpheus and Power: The Movimento Negro of Rio de Janeiro and São Paulo, Brazil, 1945–1988*. Princeton: Princeton University Press, 1994.

Hanway, Nancy. "Valuable White Property: Lucía Miranda and National Space." *Chasqui* 30:1 (2001): 115–30.

Haraway, Donna J. "Universal Donors in a Vampire Culture: It's All in the Family: Biological Kinship Categories in the Twentieth-Century United States." In *Uncommon Ground: Rethinking the Human Place in Nature*, edited by William Cronon, 321–66. New York: Norton, 1996.

Hay, Simon John. *A History of the Modern British Ghost Story*. New York: Palgrave Macmillan, 2011.

Hazan, Luiza. "Historia de la Sociedad Latina de Corrientes (1a. parte)." www.comu nidadjudiadecorrientes.com. Accessed Feb. 27, 2012.

Helg, Aline. "Race in Argentina and Cuba, 1880–1930: Theory, Policies, and Popular Reaction." In *The Idea of Race in Latin America, 1870–1940*, edited by Richard Graham, 37–69. Austin: University of Texas Press, 1990.

Hernández, Tanya Katerí. *Racial Subordination in Latin America: The Role of the State, Customary Law, and the New Civil Rights Response*. New York: Cambridge University Press, 2013.

Hertzman, Marc A. *Making Samba: A New History of Race and Music in Brazil*. Durham: Duke University Press, 2013.

Higa, Marcelo. "Desarrollo histórico de la inmigración japonesa en la Argentina hasta la segunda guerra mundial." *Estudios Migratorios Latinoamericanos* 10:30 (1995): 471–512.

"The Emigration of Argentines of Japanese Descent to Japan." In *New Worlds, New Lives: Globalization and People of Japanese Descent in the Americas and from Latin America in Japan*, edited by Lane Ryo Hirabashi, Akemi Kikumura-Yano, and James A. Hirabayashi, 261–78. Stanford: Stanford University Press, 2002.

Hilarión Lenzi, Juan. *Historia de Santa Cruz*. Buenos Aires: Alberto Segovia, 1980.

Hill Collins, Patricia. *Black Feminist Thought: Knowledge, Consciousness, and the Politics of Empowerment*. New York: Routledge, 2000.

Hill, Mike, ed. *Whiteness: A Critical Reader*. New York: New York University Press, 1997.

Hollman, Verónica and Carla Lois. "Imaginarios geográficos y cultura visual peronista: las imágenes geográficas en la revista *Billiken* (1945–55)." *Geografia em Questão* 4:2 (2011): 239–69.

Holmberg, Eduardo A. *Viaje por la gobernación de los Andes*. Buenos Aires: Imp. La Nación, 1900.

"Investigación agrícola en la Provincia de Jujuy." *Anales del Ministerio de Agricultura Argentina* 6 (1904): 6–7.

Htun, Mala. "From Racial Democracy to Affirmative Action: Changing State Policy on Race in Brazil." *Latin American Research Review* 39:1 (2004), 60–89.

Hu-DeHart, Evelyn. "Multiculturalism in Latin American Studies: Locating the 'Asian' Immigrant; Or, Where Are the Chinos and Turcos?" *Latin American Research Review* 44:2 (2009): 235–42.

Hutcheon, Linda. *A Poetics of Postmodernism: History, Theory, Fiction*. New York: Routledge, 1988.

Imbelloni, José. *Informe preliminar sobre la expedición a la Patagonia*. Buenos Aires: Ministerio de Obras Públicas de la Nación, Administración General de Parques Nacionales y Turismo, 1949.

"Los Patagones. Características corporales y psicológicas de una población que agoniza." *Runa*, 2 (1949): 5–58.

Itzigsohn, Sara, Isidoro Niborski, Ricardo Feierstein, and Leonardo Senkman. *Integración y marginalidad: historias de vidas de inmigrantes judíos en la Argentina*. Buenos Aires: Pardes, 1965.

Jackson, Jeffrey H. *Making Jazz French: Music and Modern Life in Interwar Paris*. Durham: Duke University Press, 2003.

Jacobson, Matthew Frye. *Whiteness of a Different Color: European Immigrants and the Alchemy of Race*. Cambridge: Harvard University Press, 1999.

James, Daniel. *Resistance and Integration: Peronism and the Argentine Working Class, 1946–1976*. Cambridge: Cambridge University Press, 1994.

Johnson, Dexter. Liner notes to *Oscar Alemán: Swing Guitar Masterpieces, 1938–1957*. Acoustic Disc, 1998.

Joseph, Galen. "Taking Race Seriously: Whiteness in Argentina's National and Transnational Imaginary." *Identities* 7:3 (2000): 333–71.

Jules-Rosette, Bennetta. *Josephine Baker in Art and Life: The Icon and the Image*. Champaign: University of Illinois Press, 2007.

Karush, Matthew B. "Blackness in Argentina: Jazz, Tango, and Race Before Perón." *Past and Present* 216:1 (2012): 215–45.

  Culture of Class: Radio and Cinema in the Making of a Divided Argentina, 1920–1946. Durham: Duke University Press, 2012.

Karush, Matthew B. and Oscar Chamosa, eds. *The New Cultural History of Peronism: Power and Identity in Mid-Twentieth-Century Argentina*. Durham: Duke University Press, 2010.

Kirshenblatt-Gimblett, Barbara. *Destination Culture: Tourism, Museums, and Heritage*. Berkeley: University of California Press, 1998.

Klich, Ignacio. "Arab-Jewish Coexistence in the First Half of 1900's Argentina: Overcoming Self-Imposed Amnesia." In *Arab and Jewish Immigrants in Latin America: Images and Realities*, edited by Ignacio Klich and Jeffrey Lesser, 1–37. London: Frank Cass, 1998.

Klich, Ignacio and Jeffrey Lesser, eds. *Arab and Jewish Immigrants in Latin America: Images and Realities*. London: Frank Cass, 1998.

Knight, Alan. "Racism, Revolution, and Indigenismo: Mexico, 1910–1940." In *The Idea of Race in Latin America, 1870–1940*, edited by Richard Graham, 71–113. Austin: University of Texas Press, 1990.

Ko, Chisu Teresa. "From Whiteness to Diversity: Crossing the Racial Threshold in Bicentennial Argentina." *Ethnic and Racial Studies* 37:14 (2014): 2529–46.

  "'Argentina te incluye': Asians in Argentina's Multicultural Novels." *Symposium: A Quarterly Journal in Modern Literatures* (forthcoming).

Koert, Hans. "Online Oscar Alemán Discography." http://oscar-aleman.opweb.nl/tuneo.htm.

  "Oscar Alemán 1930–1931." http://oscar-aleman.blogspot.com/2009/10/oscar-aleman-1930–1931.html.

  "Oscar Alemán: star of the 7de Jazzwereldfeest in Scheveningen (1939)." http://oscar-aleman.blogspot.com/2011/03/oscar-aleman-star-of-7de.html.

Kropff, Laura. "Debates sobre lo político entre jóvenes mapuche en Argentina." *Revista Latinoamericana de Ciencias Sociales, Niñez y Juventud* 9:1 (2011): 83–99.

"La inmigración después de la guerra." Special issue of *Boletín Mensual del Museo Social Argentino* nos. 85–90 (1919).

La Salada. Directed by Juan Martín Hsu. Sudestada Cine, 2014.

Lake, Marilyn and Henry Reynolds. *Drawing the Global Colour Line: White Men's Countries and the International Challenge of Racial Equality*. Cambridge: Cambridge University Press, 2008.

Lamborghini, Eva and Alejandro Frigerio. "Quebrando la invisibilidad: una evaluación de los avances y las limitaciones del activismo negro en Argentina." *El Otro Derecho* 41 (2010): 139–66.

Lanusse, Lucas. *Montoneros: el mito de sus 12 fundadores*. Buenos Aires: Vergara, 2005.

Laplantine, François and Alexis Nouss. *Mestizajes: de Arcimboldo a zombi*. Buenos Aires: Fondo de Cultura Económica, 2007.

Laskier, Michael M. *The Alliance Israélite Universelle and the Jewish Communities of Morocco, 1862–1962*. Albany: SUNY Press, 1983.

Lasso, Marixa. *Myths of Harmony: Race and Republicanism during the Age of Revolution, Colombia, 1795–1831*. Pittsburgh: University of Pittsburgh Press, 2007.

Latour, Bruno. *We Have Never Been Modern*. Cambridge: Harvard University Press, 1993.

"The Recall of Modernity: Anthropological Approaches." *Cultural Studies Review* 13:1 (2007): 11–30.

Laumonier, Isabel Jacqueline. "Cafés, tintorerías y tango." In *Cuando Oriente llegó a América: contribuciones de inmigrantes chinos, japoneses y coreanos*, 161–78. Washington D.C.: Banco Interamericano de Desarrollo, 2004.

Lazzari, Axel. "Indio argentino, cultura (nacional): del Instituto de la Tradición al Instituto Nacional de Antropología." In *Historias y estilos de trabajo de campo en Argentina*, edited by Sergio Visacovsky and Rosana Guber, 154–201. Buenos Aires: Antropofagia, 2002.

"Aboriginal Recognition, Freedom, and Phantoms: The Vanishing of the Ranquel and the Return of the Rankülche in La Pampa." *Journal of Latin American Anthropology* 8:3 (2003): 59–83.

"Antropología en el Estado: el Instituto Étnico Nacional (1946–1955)." In *Intelectuales y expertos. La constitución del conocimiento social en la Argentina*, edited by Federico Neiburg and Mariano Plotkin, 203–29. Buenos Aires: Paidós, 2004.

"The Autonomy of the Appeared: Phantom Indian, Selves, and Freedom (on the Rankulche in Argentina)." Ph.D. diss., Columbia University, 2010.

Lazzari, Axel and Diana Lenton. "Araucanization and Nation: A Century Inscribing Foreign Indians over the Pampas." In *Living on the Edge: Native Peoples of Pampa, Patagonia, and Tierra del Fuego*, edited by Claudia Briones and José Luis Lanata, 33–46. Westport: Greenwood Publishing Group, 2002.

Lechini, Gladys. "Evolución de las vinculaciones entre África y Argentina desde la perspectiva de las relaciones internacionales: aspectos políticos, económicos y culturales." In *El negro en la Argentina: presencia y negación*, edited by Dina V. Picotti, 479–510. Buenos Aires: Editores de América Latina, 2001.

Leguizamón, Martiniano. "Prólogo" to *Los gauchos judíos*, by Alberto Gerchunoff, x–xii. La Plata: Joaquín Sesé, 1910.

Lehmann, David. "Gilberto Freyre: The Assessment Continues." *Latin American Research Review* 43:1 (2008): 208–17.

Lenton, Diana. "Los araucanos en la Argentina: un caso de interdiscursividad nacionalista." In *Actas del III Congreso Chileno de Antropología* (Temuco, 1998). www.ceppas.org/gajat/index.php?option=com_docman&task=doc_view&gid=90

"De centauros a protegidos. La construcción del sujeto de la política indigenista argentina desde los debates parlamentarios (1880–1970)." Ph.D. diss., Universidad de Buenos Aires, 2005.

"The Malón de la Paz of 1946: Indigenous Descamisados at the Dawn of Peronism." In *The New Cultural History of Peronism: Power and Identity in Mid-Twentieth-Century Argentina*, edited by Matthew B. Karush and Oscar Chamosa, 85–111. Durham: Duke University Press, 2010.

"Próceres genocidas: una indagación en el debate público sobre la figura de Julio A. Roca y la Campaña del Desierto." In *Topografías conflictivas: memorias, espacios y ciudades en disputa*, edited by Anne Huffschmid and Valeria Durán, 243–63. Buenos Aires: Nueva Trilce, 2012.

Lenton, Diana, Walter Delrio, Pilar Perez, Alexis Papazian, Mariano Nagy, and Marcelo Musante. "Argentina's Constituent Genocide: Challenging the Hegemonic National Narrative and Laying the Foundation for Reparations to Indigenous Peoples." *Armenian Review* 53:1–4 (2012): 63–84.

Lesser, Jeffrey. *Welcoming the Undesirables: Brazil and the Jewish Question*. Berkeley: University of California Press, 1995.

"'Jews are Turks Who Sell on Credit': Elite Images of Arabs and Jews in Brazil." In *Arab and Jewish Immigrants in Latin America: Images and Realities*, edited by Ignacio Klich and Jeffrey Lesser, 38–56. London: Frank Cass, 1998.

Negotiating National Identity: Immigrants, Minorities, and the Struggle for Ethnicity in Brazil. Durham: Duke University Press, 1999.

A Discontented Diaspora: Japanese-Brazilians and the Meanings of Ethnic Militancy, 1960–1980. Durham: Duke University Press, 2007.

"How the Jews Became Japanese and Other Stories of Nation and Ethnicity." In *Rethinking Jewish Latin Americans*, edited by Jeffrey Lesser and Raanan Rein, 41–54. Albuquerque: University of New Mexico Press, 2008.

Immigration, Ethnicity, and National Identity in Brazil, 1808 to the Present. New York: Cambridge University Press, 2013.

Lesser, Jeffrey and Raanan Rein, eds. *Rethinking Jewish Latin Americans*. Albuquerque: University of New Mexico Press, 2008.

"Together yet Apart: Arabs and Jews in Latin America." Special issue of *Latin American and Caribbean Ethnic Studies* 6 (2011).

Levine, Robert M. *Father of the Poor? Vargas and His Era*. Cambridge: Cambridge University Press, 1998.

Lewin, Boleslao. *Cómo fue la inmigración judía a la Argentina*. Buenos Aires: Plus Ultra, 1971.

Lewontin, Richard. *La diversidad humana*. Barcelona: Labor, 1984.

Lista, Ramón. *Mis exploraciones en la Patagonia, 1877–1880*. Buenos Aires: Marymar, 1975 [1879].

Los indios tehuelches. Una raza que desaparece. Buenos Aires: Colección del Bicentenario Editores, 2006 [1894].

Viaje al país de los tehuelches. Buenos Aires: Colección del Bicentenario, 2006 [1879].

Löfgren, Orvar. *On Holiday: A History of Vacationing*. Berkeley: University of California Press, 1999.

"Know your Country: A Comparative Perspective on Tourism and Nation Building in Sweden." In *Being Elsewhere: Tourism, Consumer Culture and Identity in Modern Europe and North America*, edited by Shelley Baranowski and Ellen Furlough, 137–54. Ann Arbor: University of Michigan Press, 2001.

Logan, Joy. "Constructing Indigeneity in Argentina: At the Crossroads of Mountaineering, Tourism, and Re-Ethnification." *Journal of Latin American and Caribbean Anthropology* 14:2 (2009): 405–31.

Lois, Carla. "La Patagonia en el mapa de la Argentina moderna. Política y 'deseo territorial' en la cartografía oficial argentina en la segunda mitad del siglo XIX." In *Paisajes del progreso. La resignificación de la Patagonia Norte, 1880–1916*, edited by Pedro Navarro Floria, n.p. Neuquén: Educo, 2007.

Lomnitz-Adler, Claudio. *Exits from the Labyrinth: Culture and Ideology in the Mexican National Space*. Berkeley: University of California Press, 1992.

Longoni, Ana. *Del Di Tella a "Tucumán Arde": vanguardia artística y política en el 68 argentino*. Buenos Aires: Eudeba, 2008.

Lorandi, Ana M. "Ni tradición ni modernidad, el mestizaje en contextos sociales desestructurados." *Relaciones de la Sociedad Argentina de Antropología* 18 (1992): 108–29.

Los resistentes: relatos de la lucha clandestina entre 1955 y 1966. Directed by Alejandro Fernández Mouján. Buenos Aires: INCAA, 2009.

Losada, Leandro. *La alta sociedad en la Buenos Aires de la Belle Epoque: sociabilidad, estilos de vida e identidades*. Buenos Aires: Siglo Veintiuno Iberoamericana, 2008.

Losonczy, Anne-Marie. "El criollo y el mestizo. Del sustantivo al adjetivo: categorías de apariencia y de pertenencia en la Colombia de ayer y de hoy." In *Formaciones de indianidad. Articulaciones raciales, mestizaje y nación en América Latina*, edited by Marisol de la Cadena, 261–77. Popayán: Envión, 2008.

Loveman, Mara. *National Colors: Racial Classification and the State in Latin America*. New York: Oxford University Press, 2014.

Lovera, José Rafael. *Food Culture in South America*. Westport: Greenwood Press, 2005.

Lowe, Lisa. "Heterogeneity, Hybridity, Multiplicity: Marking Asian American Differences." In *Asian American Studies: A Reader*, edited by Jean Yu-wen Shen Wu and Min Song, 423–42. New Brunswick: Rutgers University Press, 2000.

Ludmer, Josefina. *The Gaucho Genre: A Treatise on the Motherland*. Durham: Duke University Press, 2002.

Lusnich, Ana Laura. *El drama social-folclórico: el universo rural en el cine argentino*. Buenos Aires: Biblos, 2007.

Lvovich, Daniel. *Nacionalismo y antisemitismo en la Argentina*. Buenos Aires: Javier Vergara, 2003.

"Argentina: entre las puertas abiertas y el rechazo a los indeseables." In *Nación y extranjería. La exclusión racial en las políticas migratorias de Argentina, Brasil, Cuba y México*, edited by Pablo Yankelevich, 23–58. Mexico: UNAM, 2009.

Maffia, Marta. "La migración subsahariana hacia Argentina: desde los caboverdianos hasta los nuevos migrantes del siglo XXI." In *Aportes para el desarrollo humano en Argentina/2011: Afrodescendientes y africanos en Argentina*, coordinated by Rubén Mercado and Gabriela Catterberg, 53–89. Buenos Aires: PNUD, 2011.

Mallon, Florencia. "Constructing Mestizaje in Latin America: Authenticity, Marginality, and Gender in the Claiming of Ethnic Identities." *Journal of Latin American Anthropology* 2:1 (1996): 170–81.

Malosetti Costa, Laura. *Rapto de cautivas blancas: un aspecto erótico de la barbarie en la plástica rioplatense del siglo XIX*. Buenos Aires: Facultad de Filosofía y Letras/ UBA, 1998.

Malosetti Costa, Laura and Marcela Gené, eds. *Atrapados por la imagen: artes y política en la cultura impresa argentina*. Buenos Aires: Edhasa, 2013.

Mandrini, Raúl. *Vivir entre dos mundos: conflicto y convivencia en las fronteras del sur de la Argentina, siglos XVIII y XIX*. Buenos Aires: Taurus, 2006.

Mandrini, Raúl and Sara Ortelli. "Los 'araucanos' en las Pampas (1700–1850)." In *Colonización, resistencia y mestizaje en las Américas*, edited by Guillaume Boccara, 237–57. Quito/Lima: Abya-Yala/IFEA, 2002.

Mansilla, Lucio V. *A Visit to the Ranquel Indians*. Translated by Eva Gillies. Lincoln: University of Nebraska Press, 1997.

Mansilla de García, Eduarda. *Lucía Miranda.* Edited by Martina Guidotti. Madrid and Frankfurt am Main: Iberoamericana-Vervuert, 2007.

Manzano, Valeria. "The Making of Youth in Argentina: Culture, Politics, and Sexuality, 1956–1976." Ph.D. diss., Indiana University at Bloomington, 2009.

The Age of Youth: Culture, Politics, and Sexuality in Argentina, 1950–1970s. Chapel Hill: University of North Carolina Press, 2013.

Margulis, Mario and Carlos Belvedere. "La racialización de las relaciones de clase en Buenos Aires: genealogía de la discriminación." In *La segregación negada: cultura y discriminación social,* edited by Mario Margulis and Marcelo Urresti, 79–122. Buenos Aires: Biblos, 1999.

Margulis, Mario and Marcelo Urresti. *La segregación negada: cultura y discriminación social.* Buenos Aires: Editorial Biblos, 1998.

Marin, Louis. *Estudios semiológicos (La lectura de la imagen).* Madrid: Comunicación, 1978.

Martel, Julián. *La bolsa.* Excerpted in *La cuestión judía en la Argentina,* edited by Juan José Sebreli, 61–71. Buenos Aires: Tiempo Contemporáneo, 1968. Originally published in *La bolsa.* Buenos Aires: La Nación, 1891.

Martínez Sarasola, Carlos. *Nuestros paisanos los indios: vida, historia y destino de las comunidades indígenas en la Argentina.* Buenos Aires: Emecé, 2005.

Martínez, María Elena. *Genealogical Fictions: Limpieza de Sangre, Religion, and Gender in Colonial Mexico.* Stanford: Stanford University Press, 2008.

Mases, Enrique Hugo. *Estado y cuestión indígena. El destino final de los indios sometidos en el sur del territorio (1878–1910).* Buenos Aires: Prometeo, 2002.

Masiello, Francine. *Between Civilization and Barbarism: Women, Nation, and Literary Culture in Modern Argentina.* Nebraska: University of Nebraska Press, 1992.

Masotta, Carlos. *Gauchos en las primeras postales fotográficas argentinas del siglo XX.* Buenos Aires: La Marca, 2007.

Indios en las primeras postales fotográficas argentinas del siglo XX. Buenos Aires: La Marca, 2007.

Matallana, Andrea. *"Locos por la radio": Una historia social de la radiofonía en la Argentina, 1923–1947.* Buenos Aires: Prometeo, 2006.

Mello, Jorge. "Gastão Bueno Lobo: The man who introduced the banjo to Brazil," *Musica Brasiliensis,* Jul. 18, 2007, http://daniellathompson.com/Texts/Investigations/Gastao_Bueno_Lobo.htm.

Menton, Seymour. *Latin America's New Historical Novel.* Austin: University of Texas Press, 1993.

Mera, Carolina. "La diáspora coreana en América Latina." Web publication. Instituto de Investigaciones Gino Germani, Facultad de Ciencias Sociales, Universidad de Buenos Aires, 2006. http://www.uba.ar/ceca/download/mera.pdf.

"La inmigración coreana en Buenos Aires: historia y actualidad." In *Memoria electrónica del XI congreso internacional de ALADAA.* México: Secretaría General de ALADAA, 2007. http://ceaa.colmex.mx/aladaa/imagesmemoria/carolinamera.pdf.

"Crisis and Social Change: The Impact of the 2001 Crisis on the Life of the 1.5 Generation in Argentina." Web publication. UCLA Center for Korean Studies, 2009. http://web.international.ucla.edu/korea/article/112641.

Mestman, Mariano and Mirta Varela, eds. *Masas, pueblo, multitud en cine y televisión.* Buenos Aires: EUDEBA, 2013.

Milanesio, Natalia. "'The Guardian Angels of the Domestic Economy': Housewives' Responsible Consumption in Peronist Argentina." *Journal of Women's History* 18:3 (2006): 91–117.

"Food Politics and Consumption in Peronist Argentina." *Hispanic American Historical Review* 90:1 (2010): 75–108.

"Peronists and Cabecitas: Stereotypes and Anxieties at the Peak of Social Change." In *The New Cultural History of Peronism: Power and Identity in Mid-Twentieth-Century Argentina*, edited by Matthew B. Karush and Oscar Chamosa, 53–83. Durham: Duke University Press, 2010.

Miles, Tiya. *Tales from the Haunted South: Dark Tourism and Memories of Slavery from the Civil War Era*. Chapel Hill: University of North Carolina Press, 2015.

Miller, Marilyn. *Rise and Fall of the Cosmic Race: The Cult of Mestizaje in Latin America*. Austin: University of Texas Press, 2004.

Mintz, Sidney. *Sweetness and Power: The Place of Sugar in Modern History*. New York: Viking, 1985.

Mirelman, Victor A. "La comunidad judía contra el delito: el caso de la trata de blancas en Buenos Aires." *Megamot* 2 (1987): 5–32.

Mirzoeff, Nicholas. "The Right to Look." *Critical Inquiry* 37:3 (2011): 473–96.

Molina, Lucía D. "Por qué afroargentin@s del tronco colonial y por qué nuestra bandera." *Carta Informativa de la Junta de Estudios Históricos de La Matanza*, 34 (2013): 64–71.

Montañez, Ligia. *El racismo oculto de una sociedad no racista*. Caracas: Editorial Tropykos, 1993.

Montoneros: una historia. Directed by Andrés Di Tella. 1995. Argentina: SBP Worldwide, 2006.

Moore, Robin. *Nationalizing Blackness: Afrocubanismo and Artistic Revolution in Havana, 1920–1940*. Pittsburgh: University of Pittsburgh Press, 1997.

Morales, Orlando G. "Representaciones de alteridades 'negras,' africanas y afrodescendientes en la sociedad nacional argentina. Primera década del siglo XXI." Ph.D. diss., Universidad Nacional de La Plata, 2014.

Moreno, Francisco P. *Viaje a la Patagonia austral*. Buenos Aires: El elefante blanco, 1997 [1879].

Moya, José C. *Cousins and Strangers: Spanish Immigrants in Buenos Aires, 1850–1930*. Berkeley: University of California Press, 1998.

"A Continent of Immigrants: Postcolonial Shifts in the Western Hemisphere." *Hispanic American Historical Review* 86:1 (2006): 1–28.

"What's in a Stereotype? The Case of Jewish Anarchists in Argentina." In *Rethinking Jewish-Latin Americans*, edited by Jeffrey Lesser and Raanan Rein, 55–88. Albuquerque: University of New Mexico Press, 2008.

Moyano, Carlos María. *A través de la Patagonia. Informe del viaje y exploración* [sic], *desde Santa Cruz al Chubut*. Buenos Aires: Imprenta de la Tribuna Nacional, 1881.

Muehlmann, Shaylih. "How Do Real Indians Fish?: Neoliberal Multiculturalism and Contested Indigeneity in the Colorado Delta." *American Anthropologist* 111 (2009): 468–79.

Where the River Ends: Contested Indigeneity in the Mexican Colorado Delta. Durham: Duke University Press, 2013.

Mujer Conejo. Directed by Verónica Chen. Aura Films, 2013.

Mujica Lainez, Manuel. *Los porteños*. Buenos Aires: Librería La Ciudad, 1980.

Museo Social Argentino. *Primer congreso de la población*. Buenos Aires: Gerónimo J. Pesce, 1941.

Musters, Charles. *At Home with the Patagonians. A Year's Wandering Over Untrodden Ground from the Straits of Magellan to the Rio Negro*. London: John Murray, 1873.

Napal, Dionisio R. *El imperio soviético*. Buenos Aires: Imprenta López, 1933.

Newton, Ronald. *The 'Nazi Menace' in Argentina, 1931–1947*. Stanford: Stanford University Press, 1992.

Nicoletti, María Andrea. "Los Salesianos y la conquista de la Patagonia: desde Don Bosco hasta sus primeros textos escolares e historias oficiales." *Revista Tefros* 5:2 (2007): 1–24.

Nouzeilles, Gabriela. *Ficciones somáticas: naturalismo, nacionalismo y políticas médicas del cuerpo (Argentina 1880–1910)*. Rosario: Beatriz Viterbo, 2000.

Novaro, Marcos and Vicente Palermo. *La dictadura militar, 1976–1983*. Buenos Aires: Paidós, 2003.

Nugent, Walter. *Crossings: The Great Transatlantic Migrations, 1870–1914*. Bloomington: Indiana University Press, 1992.

O'Malley, Mike. "Blind Imitation," *The Aporetic* http://theaporetic.com/?p=683.

Octubre Pilagá: relatos sobre el silencio. Directed by Valeria Mapelman. Buenos Aires: Zona Audiovisual, 2010.

Ohnuki-Tierney, Emiko. *Rice as Self: Japanese Identities through Time*. Princeton: Princeton University Press, 1993.

Olguín, Sergio S., ed. *Perón vuelve: cuentos sobre peronismo*. Buenos Aires: Norma, 2000.

Onaha, Cecilia. "Historia de la migración japonesa en Argentina. Diasporización y transnacionalismo." *Revista de Historia*, 12 (2011): 82–96.

Onega, Gladys. *La inmigración en la literatura argentina, 1880–1910*. Buenos Aires: Galerna, 1969.

Osés, María Antonia. *Léxico de la carne*. Buenos Aires: Academia Argentina de Letras, 2007.

Ospital, Silvia. "Turismo y territorio nacional en Argentina. Actores sociales y políticas públicas, 1920–1940." *Estudios Interdisciplinarios de América Latina y el Caribe* 16:2 (2005): 63–84.

Otero, Hernán. "Estadística censal y construcción de la nación. El caso argentino, 1869–1914." *Boletín del Instituto de Historia Argentina y Americana "Dr. Emilio Ravignani"* 3:16–17 (1997): 123–49.

Page, Joanna. *Crisis and Capitalism in Contemporary Argentine Cinema*. Durham: Duke University Press, 2009.

Pagés Larraya, Fernando, Jorge Filippo, and Carla Sacchi. *Tehuelches: antropología psiquiátrica de la extinción*. Río Gallegos: Ediciones Culturales Santa Cruz, Hotel Santa Cruz, 1988.

Pappier, Andrea. "Inmigración china en Argentina: el barrio chino de Bs. As. como caso de estudio cultural." In *Memoria electrónica del XIII congreso internacional de ALADAA*. Bogotá: Secretaría General de ALADAA, 2011.

Park, Kyeyoung. "A Rhizomatic Diaspora: Transnational Passage and the Sense of Place among Koreans in Latin America." Web publication. UCLA Center for Korean Studies, 2009. www1.international.ucla.edu/article.asp?parentid=112643.

Parsonage, Catherine. *The Evolution of Jazz in Britain 1880–1935*. Aldershot: Ashgate, 2005.

Paschel, Tianna. "'The Beautiful Faces of My Black People': Race, Ethnicity and the Politics of Colombia's 2005 Census." *Ethnic and Racial Studies* 36:10 (2013): 1544–63.

Pastoriza, Elisa. *La conquista de las vacaciones: breve historia del turismo en Argentina.* Buenos Aires: Edhasa, 2010.

Payró, Julio E. "La Pintura." In *Historia general del arte en Argentina*, vol. 6, edited by Academia Nacional de Bellas Artes (ANBA), 131–98. Buenos Aires: ANBA, 1988.

Payró, Roberto J. *Por tierras del Inti.* Buenos Aires: Ed. Rodríguez Giles, 1909.

Paz, Gustavo. "Campesinos, terratenientes y estado: control de tierras y conflicto en la Puna de Jujuy a fines del siglo XIX." In *Sociedad y articulación en las tierras altas jujeñas*, edited by Alejandro Isla, 219–35. Buenos Aires: Proyecto ECIRA, MLAL, 1992.

Penhos, Marta N. "Nativos en el Salón: artes plásticas e identidad en la primera mitad del siglo XX." In *Tras los pasos de la norma: Salones Nacionales de Arte (1911–1989)*, edited by Marta Penhos and Diana Wechsler, 111–46. Buenos Aires: del Jilguero, 1999.

Pérez Montfort, Ricardo. "Indigenismo, hispanismo y panamericanismo en la cultura popular mexicana de 1920 a 1940." In *Cultura e identidad nacional*, edited by Roberto Blancarte, 343–83. Mexico: Fondo de Cultura Económica, 1994.

Perón, Eva. *Discursos completos*, vols. I and II. Buenos Aires: Editorial Megafón, 1985.

Perón, Juan D. *Latinoamérica: ahora o nunca.* Montevideo: Editorial Diálogo, 1967.

Picotti, Dina V. *La presencia africana en nuestra identidad.* Buenos Aires: del Sol, 1998.

Pigna, Felipe. *Mitos de la historia argentina*, vol. I. Buenos Aires: Planeta, 2009.

Pilcher, Jeffrey. *¡Que Vivan Los Tamales! Food and the Making of Mexican Identity.* Albuquerque: University of New Mexico Press, 1998.

"Eating a la Criolla : Global and Local Foods in Argentina, Cuba, and Mexico." *IdeAs* 3 (2012): 2–16.

Pisano, Pietro. *Liderazgo político "negro" en Colombia, 1943–1964.* Bogotá: Universidad Nacional de Colombia, 2012.

Pite, Rebekah E. "Entertaining Inequalities: Doña Petrona, Juanita Bordoy, and Domestic Work in Argentina, 1952–1969." *Hispanic American Historical Review* 91:1 (2011): 97–128.

Creating a Common Table in Twentieth-Century Argentina: Doña Petrona, Women, and Food. Chapel Hill: University of North Carolina Press, 2013.

"Engendering Argentine History: A Historiographical Review of Recent Gender-Based Histories of Women during the National Period." *Estudios Interdisciplinarios de América Latina y el Caribe* (forthcoming).

Pizarro Cortés, Carolina. "The Decentring of the Historical Subject in the Contemporary Imaginary of the Independence Process." *Journal of Latin American Cultural Studies* 20:4 (2011): 323–42.

Plotkin, Mariano. *Mañana es San Perón: propaganda, rituales políticos y educación en el régimen peronista (1946–1955).* Buenos Aires: Ariel, 1994.

Poole, Deborah. *Vision, Race, and Modernity: A Visual Economy of the Andean Image World.* Princeton: Princeton University Press, 1997.

Powell, Philip Wayne. *Tree of Hate: Propaganda and Prejudices Affecting United States Relations with the Hispanic World.* New York: Basic Books, 1971.

Prado, Manuel. *La guerra al malón.* Buenos Aires: Eudeba, 1960.

Pratt, Mary Louise. *Imperial Eyes: Travel Writing and Transculturation.* New York and London: Routledge, 1992.

Prieto, Adolfo. *El discurso criollista en la formación de la Argentina moderna.* Buenos Aires: Sudamericana, 1988.

Pujol, Sergio. *Jazz al sur: historia de la música negra en la Argentina.* Buenos Aires: Emecé, 2004.

Pulido Fernández, Ángel. *Españoles sin patria y la raza sefaradí.* Madrid: E. Teodoro, 1905.

Quijada, Mónica. "De Perón a Alberdi: selectividad étnica y construcción nacional en la política inmigratoria argentina." *Revista de Indias* 52 (1992): 867–88.

"Imaginando la homogeneidad: la alquimia de la tierra." In *Homogeneidad y nación: con un estudio de caso: Argentina, siglos XIX y XX,* edited by Mónica Quijada, Carmen Bernand, and Arnd Schneider, 179–217. Madrid: CSIC, 2000.

"Indígenas: violencia, tierras y ciudadanía." In *Homogeneidad y nación: con un estudio de caso : Argentina, siglos XIX y XX,* edited by Mónica Quijada, Carmen Bernand, and Arnd Schneider, 57–92. Madrid: CSIC, 2000.

"Introduction" to *Homogeneidad y nación: con un estudio de caso: Argentina, siglos XIX y XX,* edited by Mónica Quijada, Carmen Bernand, and Arnd Schneider, 7–14. Madrid: CSIC, 2000.

"'Hijos de los barcos' o diversidad invisibilizada: la articulación de la población indígena en la construcción nacional argentina." *Historia Mexicana* 53:2 (2003): 469–510.

Quijada, Mónica, Carmen Bernand, and Arnd Schneider. *Homogeneidad y nación: con un estudio de caso: Argentina, siglos XIX y XX.* Madrid: CSIC, 2000.

Quiroga, Adán. *Calchaquí.* Buenos Aires: La Cultura Argentina, 1923.

Raíces que dieron alas. Buenos Aires: A. Weiss, 1993.

Rama, Ángel. "Hispanismo, mesticismo, indigenismo." *Cuadernos Americanos* 33:6 (1974): 136–73.

Rappaport, Joanne. "Mischievous Lovers, Hidden Moors, and Cross-Dressers: Passing in Colonial Bogotá." *Journal of Spanish Cultural Studies* 10:1 (2009): 7–25.

"¿Quién es mestizo? Descifrando la mezcla racial en El Nuevo Reino de Granada, siglos XVI y XVII." *Varia Historia* 25:41 (2009): 43–60.

Ratier, Hugo. *El cabecita negra.* Buenos Aires: CEAL, 1972.

"La antropología social argentina: su desarrollo." *Publicar* 8:9 (2010): 17–46.

Reboratti, Carlos. "Una visión de la Quebrada." In *La Quebrada: geografía, historia, y ecología de la Quebrada de Humahuaca,* edited by Carlos Reboratti, 17–46. Buenos Aires: La Colmena, 2003.

Rein, Raanan. ed. *Argentina, Israel, and the Jews: Perón, the Eichmann Capture and After.* Bethesda: University Press of Maryland, 2002.

"Diplomacy, Propaganda, and Humanitarian Gestures: Francoist Spain and Egyptian Jews, 1956–1968." *Iberoamericana* 6 (2006): 21–33.

Árabes y judíos en Iberoamérica: similitudes, diferencias y tensiones. Sevilla: Tres Culturas del Mediterráneo, 2008.

"Introduction" to *Árabes y judíos en Iberoamérica: Similitudes, diferencias y tensiones,* edited by Raanan Rein, 11–26. Sevilla: Tres Culturas del Mediterráneo, 2008.

Remedi, Fernando J. *Entre el gusto y la necesidad: la alimentación en la Córdoba de los principios del siglo XX.* Córdoba: Centro de Estudios Históricos, 1998.

Rénique, Gerardo. "Race, Region, and Nation: Sonora's Anti-Chinese Racism and Mexico's Revolutionary Nationalism, 1920s-1930s." In *Race and Nation in Modern Latin America*, edited by Nancy P. Appelbaum, Anne S. MacPherson, and Karin Alejandra Rosemblatt, 211–36. Chapel Hill: University of North Carolina Press, 2004.

Report of the Jewish Association for the Protection of Girls and Women (1906, 1911, 1915). London: Women's Printing Society, n.d., 1912, 1916.

República Argentina, Ministerio de Educación y Justicia, Departamento de Documentación e Información Educativa. *Constitución de la Nación Argentina.* Buenos Aires: n.p., 1961.

Restrepo, Eduardo. *Intervenciones en teoría cultural.* Popayán: Editorial Universidad del Cauca, 2012.

Etnicización de la negridad: la invención de las "comunidades negras" como grupo étnico en Colombia. Popayán: Editorial Universidad del Cauca, 2013.

Ribeiro, Darcy. *The Americas and Civilization.* New York: Dutton & Co, 1972.

Rock, David. "Lucha civil en la Argentina. La Semana Trágica de enero de 1919." *Desarrollo Económico* 11 (1972): 165–215.

"Antecedents of the Argentine Right." In *The Argentine Right: Its History and Intellectual Origins*, edited by Sandra McGee Deutsch and Ronald H. Dolkart. Wilmington: SR Books, 1993.

"Argentina in 1914: The Pampas, the Interior, Buenos Aires." In *Argentina since Independence*, ed. Leslie Bethell, 113–38. New York: Cambridge University Press, 1993.

Rodríguez, Julia. *Civilizing Argentina: Science, Medicine, and the Modern State.* Chapel Hill: University of North Carolina Press, 2006.

Rodríguez, Mariela Eva. "¿Indígenas, obreros rurales o extranjeros? Migraciones chilotas en la literatura de viaje de los años treinta." *Nuevo Mundo-Mundos Nuevos* 4 (2004) [online] http://nuevomundo.revues.org/document451.html

"'Empezaron sacándoles las tierras, después las familias, después la identidad': Trayectorias de una recuperación en suspenso (lote 119, provincia de Santa Cruz)." *Revista Avá* 14 (2009): 85–102.

"De la 'extinción' a la autoafirmación: procesos de visibilización de la Comunidad Tehuelche Camusu Aike (Provincia de Santa Cruz, Argentina)." Ph.D. diss., Georgetown University, 2010.

Roediger, David R. *Working toward Whiteness: How America's Immigrants Became White – The Strange Journey from Ellis Island to the Suburbs.* New York: Basic Books, 2005.

Rojas, Ricardo. *La restauración nacionalista. Crítica de la educación argentina y bases para una reforma en el estudio de las humanidades modernas.* Buenos Aires: A. Peña Lillo, 1971 [1909].

Rollansky, Samuel. *Sarmiento y los judíos.* Buenos Aires: IWO, 1993.

Romero, Luis Alberto. "Los sectores populares en las ciudades latinoamericanas del siglo XIX: la cuestión de la identidad." *Desarrollo Económico* 27:106 (1987): 201–22.

Rosal, Miguel Ángel. "Bibliografía afroargentina," *Quilombo: Revista digital de arte y cultura afro* (2012), http://www.revistaquilombo.com.ar/documentos/bibliografiaafroargentina.pdf.

Rosenthal, Debra J. *Race Mixture in Nineteenth-Century U.S. and Spanish American Fictions: Gender, Culture, and Nation Building*. Chapel Hill: University of North Carolina Press, 2004.

Rosenzvit, Miguel. *Fiebre Negra*. Buenos Aires, Argentina: Planeta, 2008.

Rotker, Susana. *Captive Women: Oblivion and Memory in Argentina*. Translated by Jennifer French. Minneapolis: University of Minnesota Press, 2002.

Rozenmacher, Germán. *Cabecita negra*. Buenos Aires: de la Flor, 1997.

Rubinzal, Mariela. "El nacionalismo frente a la cuestión social en Argentina (1930–1943): discursos, representaciones y prácticas de las derechas sobre el mundo del trabajo." Ph.D. diss., Universidad Nacional de La Plata, 2011.

"Women's Work in Argentina's Nationalist Lexicon, 1930–1943." In *Women of the Right: Comparisons and Interplay across Borders*, edited by Kathleen M. Blee and Sandra McGee Deutsch, 226–41. University Park: Pennsylvania State University Press, 2012.

Rye, Howard. "Southern Syncopated Orchestra: The Roster." *Black Music Research Journal* 30:1 (2010): 19–70.

Sábato, Hilda and Luis A. Romero. *Los trabajadores de Buenos Aires. La experiencia del mercado: 1850–1880*. Buenos Aires: Sudamericana, 1992.

Salvatore, Ricardo. "Criminología positivista, reforma de prisiones y la cuestión social/ obrera en Argentina." In *La cuestión social en Argentina. 1870–1943*, edited by Juan Suriano, 127–58. Buenos Aires: La Colmena, 2004.

Samurai. Directed by Gaspar Scheuer. Aura Films, 2012.

San Martín, Celina. "Memorias que dearqueologizan." In *Tramas de la diversidad. Patrimonio y Pueblos Originarios*, edited by Carolina Crespo, 101–36. Buenos Aires: Antropofagia, 2013.

Sánchez de Bustamante, Teodoro. "Ponencia." In *Memoria general del Primer Congreso Nacional de Turismo y Comunicaciones*, organized by the Touring Club Argentino, Buenos Aires, Sept. 1938, 649–53. Buenos Aires: Talleres Gráficos Argentinos, 1939.

Sánchez-Albornoz, Nicolás. *The Population of Latin America: A History*. Translated by W.A.R. Richardson. Berkeley: University of California Press, 1974.

Sanjinés, Javier. *Mestizaje Upside-Down. Aesthetic Politics in Modern Bolivia*. Pittsburgh: University of Pittsburgh Press, 2004.

Saragoza, Alex. "The Selling of Mexico: Tourism and the State." In *Fragments of a Golden Age: The Politics of Culture in Mexico Since 1940*, edited by Gilbert M. Joseph, Anne Rubenstein, Eric Zolov, and Emily S. Rosenberg, 91–115. Durham: Duke University Press, 2001.

Sarmiento, Domingo F. *Facundo*. Buenos Aires: Emecé, 1999 [1845].

"Somos extranjeros." In *La cuestión judía en la Argentina*, edited by Juan José Sebreli, 58. Buenos Aires: Tiempo Contemporáneo, 1968. Originally published in *El Censor*, 1886.

"Prevenciones e insinuaciones de Peuser y Crespo." In *La cuestión judía en la Argentina*, edited by Juan José Sebreli, 59–60. Buenos Aires: Tiempo Contemporáneo, 1968. Originally published in *El Diario*, 1888.

Schávelzon, Daniel. *Historias del comer y del beber en Buenos Aires: arqueología histórica de la vajilla de mesa*. Buenos Aires: Aguilar, 2000.

Buenos Aires negra: arqueología histórica de una ciudad silenciada. Buenos Aires: Emecé, 2003.

Schembs, Katharina. "Education through Images: Peronist Visual Propaganda between Innovation and Tradition (Argentina 1946–1955)." *Paedagogica Historica* 49:1 (2013): 90–110.

Schlüter, Regina, ed. *Áreas protegidas y turismo en Argentina*. Buenos Aires: Centro de Investigaciones y Estudios Turísticos, 1997.

El turismo en Argentina: del balneario al campo. Buenos Aires: Centro de Investigaciones y Estudios Turísticos, 2001.

Schoijet, Ezequiel. *Páginas para la historia de la colonia Narcis Levén (En adhesión a su cincuentenario)*. Buenos Aires: n.p., 1961.

Schwarzstein, Dora. "Entre la tierra perdida y la tierra prestada: Refugiados judíos y españoles en la Argentina." *Historia de la vida privada en la Argentina*, vol. 3, edited by Fernando Devoto and Marta Madero, 111–40. Buenos Aires: Taurus, 1999.

Scott, Rebecca. *Degrees of Freedom: Louisiana and Cuba after Slavery*. Cambridge, MA: Belknap Press of Harvard University Press, 2005.

Segato, Rita L. "Alteridades históricas/identidades políticas: una crítica a las certezas del pluralismo global." *Série Antropologia* 234 (1998): 2–28.

"The Color-Blind Subject of Myth; Or, Where to Find Africa in the Nation." *Annual Review of Anthropology* 27 (1998): 129–51.

La nación y sus otros: raza, etnicidad y diversidad religiosa en tiempos de políticas de la identidad. Buenos Aires: Prometeo, 2007.

"Una vocación de minoría: la expansión de los cultos afro-brasileños en la Argentina como proceso de re-etnización." In *La nación y sus otros: raza, etnicidad y diversidad religiosa en tiempos de políticas de la identidad*, by Rita L. Segato, 243–71. Buenos Aires: Prometeo, 2007.

Seibel, Beatriz. "La presencia afroargentina en el espectáculo." In *El negro en la Argentina: presencia y negación*, edited by Dina V. Picotti, 199–208. Buenos Aires: Editores de América Latina, 2001.

Seigel, Micol. *Uneven Encounters: Making Race and Nation in Brazil and the United States*. Durham: Duke University Press, 2009.

Seldin, Michael F., Chao Tian, Russell Shigeta, Hugo R. Scherbarth, Gabriel Silva, John W. Belmont, Rick Kittles, et al. "Argentine Population Genetic Structure: Large Variance in Amerindian Contribution." *American Journal of Physical Anthropology* 132:3 (2007): 455–62.

Semmens, Kristin. *Seeing Hitler's Germany: Tourism in the Third Reich*. Hampshire: Palgrave Macmillan, 2005.

Senkman, Leonardo. *La identidad judía en la literatura argentina*. Buenos Aires: Pardes, 1983.

"Nacionalismo e inmigración: la cuestión étnica en las elites liberales e intelectuales argentinas: 1919–1940." *Estudios Interdisciplinarios de América Latina y el Caribe* 1 (1990): 83–105.

Argentina, la segunda guerra mundial y los refugiados indeseables, 1933–1945. Buenos Aires: GEL, 1991.

"Etnicidad e inmigración durante el primer peronismo." *Estudios Interdisciplinarios de América Latina y el Caribe* 3:2 (1992): 5–39.

"Identidad y asociacionismo de sirios, libaneses y 'jálabes' en Argentina." In *Árabes y judíos en Iberoamérica: similitudes, diferencias y tensiones*, edited by Raanan Rein, 181–221. Sevilla: Tres Culturas del Mediterráneo, 2008.

Serbín, Andrés. "Las organizaciones indígenas en Argentina." *América Indígena* 41 (1981): 407–33.

Sharfstein, Daniel J. *The Invisible Line: Three American Families and the Secret Journey From Black to White.* New York: Penguin, 2011.

Shumway, Nicolás. *The Invention of Argentina.* Berkeley: University of California Press, 1991.

Silver Moon and Michael Ennis. "The View of the Empire from the Altepetl: Nahua Historical and Global Imagination." In *Rereading the Black Legend: The Discourses of Religious and Racial Difference in the Renaissance Empires,* 150–66. Chicago: University of Chicago Press, 2007.

Silverstein, Michael. "Shifters, Linguistic Categories, and Cultural Description." In *Meaning in Anthropology,* edited by Keith Basso and Henry Selby, 11–56. New York: Harper and Row, 1976.

Skidmore, Thomas. *Black into White: Race and Nationality in Brazilian Thought.* Durham: Duke University Press, 1992.

Slidin' on the Frets: The Hawaiian Steel Guitar Phenomenon. CD. Yahoo 2056, 2000.

Slotkin, Richard. "Fiction for the Purposes of History." *Rethinking History* 9:2–3 (2005): 221–36.

Snipes, Marjorie M. "Creating Identity out of Place: An Indigenous Community in Argentina." In *Negotiating Identities in Modern Latin America,* edited by Hendrik Kraay. Calgary: University of Calgary Press, 2007.

Socolow, Susan Migden. "Spanish Captives in Indian Societies: Cultural Contact along the Argentine Frontier, 1600–1835." *Hispanic American Historical Review* 72:1 (1992): 73–99.

Sofer, Eugene. *From Pale to Pampa: A Social History of Jews in Buenos Aires.* New York: Holmes and Meier, 1982.

Solberg, Carl. *Immigration and Nationalism: Argentina and Chile, 1890–1914.* Austin: University of Texas Press, 1970.

Solomianski, Alejandro. *Identidades secretas: la negritud argentina.* Rosario: Beatriz Viterbo, 2003.

Sommer, Doris. *Foundational Fictions: The National Romances of Latin America.* Berkeley: University of California Press, 1991.

Sopeña, Gerardo. *"Oscar Alemán 'abrazado a mi cavaquinho'."* *Crisis,* January 1975, 29–35.

Soria, Claudia. "La propaganda peronista: hacia una renovación estética del Estado nacional." In *Políticas del sentimiento: el peronismo y la construcción de la Argentina moderna,* edited by Claudia Soria, Paola Cortés Rocca, and Edgardo Dieleke, 31–48. Buenos Aires: Prometeo, 2010.

Spektorowski, Alberto. "The Ideological Origins of Right and Left Nationalism in Argentina, 1930–43." *Journal of Contemporary History* 29:1 (1994): 166–69.

Spinoza, Baruch. *The Ethics and Selected Letters.* Indianapolis: Hackett, 1982.

Spitzer, Leo. *Hotel Bolivia: The Culture of Memory in a Refuge from Nazism.* New York: Hill & Wang, 1998.

Stepan, Nancy. *"The Hour of Eugenics": Race, Gender, and Nation in Latin America.* Ithaca: Cornell University Press, 1991.

Stern, Alexandra. "From Mestizophilia to Biotypology: Racialization and Science in Mexico, 1920–1960." In *Race and Nation in Modern Latin America,* edited by

Nancy P. Appelbaum, Anne S. Macpherson, and Karin Alejandra Rosemblatt, 187–210. Chapel Hill: University of North Carolina Press, 2003.

Stites Mor, Jessica. *Transition Cinema: Political Filmmaking and the Argentine Left since 1968*. Pittsburgh: University of Pittsburgh Press, 2012.

Stoler, Ann Laura. *Along the Archival Grain: Epistemic Anxieties and Colonial Common Sense*. Princeton: Princeton University Press, 2009.

Stovall Tyler. *Paris Noir: African Americans in the City of Light*. New York: Houghton Mifflin, 1996.

Stowe, David W. *Swing Changes: Big-Band Jazz in New Deal America*. Cambridge: Harvard University Press, 1994.

Sucarrat, María. *El inocente: vida, pasión y muerte de Carlos Mugica*. Buenos Aires: Grupo Editorial Norma, 2010.

Sutton, Barbara. "Contesting Racism: Democratic Citizenship, Human Rights, and Antiracist Politics in Argentina." *Latin American Perspectives* 35:6 (2008): 106–21.

Svampa, Maristela. *El dilema argentino: civilización o barbarie. De Sarmiento al revisionismo peronista*. Buenos Aires: El Cielo por Asalto, 1994.

Los que ganaron: la vida en los countries y barrios privados. Buenos Aires: Biblos, 2001.

Szir, Sandra. *Infancia y cultura visual. Los periódicos ilustrados para niños (1880–1910)*. Buenos Aires: Miño y Dávila, 2007.

Tabanera, Juan Antonio. "Organización de los establecimientos termales." *Memoria del Primer Congreso Nacional de Turismo y Comunicaciones*, organized by the Touring Club Argentino, Buenos Aires, Sept. 1938, 480–82. Buenos Aires: L. J. Rosso, 1939.

Talamón, Gastón. "Buenos Aires se provincializa." *Continente* (1947): 154.

Tamagno, Liliana and Marta Maffia. "Lo afro y lo indígena en Argentina. Aportes desde la antropología social al análisis de las formas de la visibilidad en el nuevo milenio." *Boletín americanista* 63 (2011): 121–41.

Tasín, Jorge. *La oculta: vivir y morir en una villa miseria argentina*. Buenos Aires: Ediciones B, 2008.

Tasso, Alberto. *Historia testimonial argentina: documentos vivos de nuestro pasado*. Buenos Aires: CEAL, 1984.

Ferrocarril, quebracho y alfalfa: un ciclo de agricultura capitalista en Santiago del Estero. Santiago del Estero: Alción, 2007.

Taub, Emmanuel. "La conformación estereotípica de un otro-incivilizado a través de la revista Caras y Caretas (1898–1918)." In *Árabes y judíos en Iberoamérica: similitudes, diferencias y tensiones*, edited by Raanan Rein, 59–82. Sevilla: Tres Culturas del Mediterráneo, 2008.

Taullard, Alfredo. *Nuestro antiguo Buenos Aires*. Buenos Aires: Talleres Peuser, 1927.

Taussig, Michael. *Defacement: Public Secrecy and the Labor of the Negative*. Stanford: Stanford University Press, 1999.

Tcach, César, ed. *La política en consignas. Memoria de los setenta*. Rosario: Homo Sapiens, 2003.

Telles, Edward E. *Race in Another America: The Significance of Skin Color in Brazil*. Princeton: Princeton University Press, 2004.

Telles, Edward E. and Liza Steele. "Pigmentocracia en las Américas: ¿cómo se relaciona el logro educativo con el color de piel?" *Perspectivas desde el Barómetro de las Américas*, 73 (2012). [online] www.vanderbilt.edu/lapop/insights/IO873es.pdf

Telles, Edward E. and René Flores. "Not Just Color: Whiteness, Nation, and Status in Latin America," *Hispanic American Historical Review* 93:3 (2013), 411–49.
Telles, Edward E. and the Project on Ethnicity and Race in Latin America (PERLA). *Pigmentocracies: Ethnicity, Race, and Color in Latin America*. Chapel Hill: University of North Carolina Press, 2014.
"'There Are No Blacks in Argentina': Policing the Racial Border." Special issue of *African and Black Diaspora* 7:2 (2014).
Thompson, Currie. "From the Margins to the Margins: The Representation of Blacks in Classic Argentine Cinema." *Post Script* 29:1 (2009): 2–13.
Thompson, Daniella. "The globetrotting Romeu Silva," *Música Brasiliensis,* November 17, 2003. http://daniellathompson.com/Texts/Investigations/Romeu_Silva.htm.
Thompson, Era Bell. "Argentina: Land of Vanishing Blacks." *Ebony*, October 1973, 74–85.
Thompson, Robert Farris. *Tango: The Art History of Love*. New York: Pantheon, 2005.
Tierra de promesas: 100 años de colonización judía en Entre Ríos. Colonia Clara, San Antonio y Lucienville. N.p.: Nuestra Memoria, 1995.
Tobin, Jeffrey P. "Manly Acts: Buenos Aires, 24 March 1996." Ph.D. diss., Rice University, 1998.
Torre, Horacio A. "El mapa social de Buenos Aires en 1943, 1947 y 1960: Buenos Aires y los modelos urbanos." *Desarrollo Económico* 18:70 (1978): 164–89.
Tranchini, Elina. "El cine argentino y la construcción de un imaginario criollista." In *El cine argentino y su aporte a la identidad nacional*, 103–70. Buenos Aires: FAIGA, 1999.
Trejos, Bernardo and Lan-Hung Nora Chiang. "Young Taiwanese Immigration to Argentina: The Challenges of Adaptation, Self Identity and Returning." *International Journal of Asia Pacific Studies* 8:2 (2012): 113–43.
Tsuda, Takeyuki. "'I'm American, not Japanese!': The Struggle for Racial Citizenship among Later-Generation Japanese Americans." *Ethnic and Racial Studies* 37:3 (2014): 405–24.
Twine, France Winddance. *Racism in a Racial Democracy: The Maintenance of White Supremacy in Brazil*. New Brunswick: Rutgers University Press, 1998.
Un cuento chino. Directed by Sebastián Borensztein. Pampa Films, 2011.
Ursini, Sonia. *La supervivencia de un artista en el tiempo*. Buenos Aires: Corregidor, 1993.
Valko, Marcelo. *Los indios invisibles del malón de la paz*. Buenos Aires: Madres de Plaza de Mayo, 2010.
Desmonumentar a Roca: estatuaria oficial y dialéctica disciplinadora. Buenos Aires: Sudestada, 2013.
Vallejo, Gustavo and Marisa Miranda. "Los saberes del poder: eugenesia y biotipología en la Argentina del siglo XX." *Revista de Indias* 64:231 (2004): 425–44.
Vasconcelos, José. *La raza cósmica. Misión de la raza iberoamericana: Notas de viaje a la América del Sur*. Barcelona: Agencia Mundial de Librería, 1926.
Vela, María Elena. "Historia y actualidad de los estudios afroargentinos y africanos en la Argentina." In *El negro en la Argentina: presencia y negación*, edited by Dina V. Picotti, 49–62. Buenos Aires: Editores de América Latina, 2001.
Verbitsky, Bernardo. *Villa miseria también es América*. Buenos Aires: Kraft 1958.
Verdesio, Gustavo. "Invisible at a Glance: Indigenous Cultures of the Past, Ruins, Archeological Sites and Our Regimes of Visibility." In *Ruins of Modernity*, edited by Julia Hell and Andreas Schönle, 339–56. Durham: Duke University Press, 2010.

Vernazza, Jorge. *Para comprender: una vida con los pobres: los curas villeros.* Buenos Aires: Editorial Guadalupe, 1989.

Vignoli, Marcela. "Formación de un campo intelectual en torno a la Sociedad Sarmiento." In *Ese ardiente jardín de la República: formación y desarrollo de un campo cultural en Tucumán 1880–1975,* edited by Fabiola Orquera, 41–72. Córdoba: Alción, 2010.

Vilar, Juan Bautista. "La emigración judeo-marroquí a la América Latina en la fase preestadística (1850–1880)." *Sefárdica* 11 (1996): 11–54.

Villagrán, Andrea. *Un héroe múltiple: Güemes y la apropiación del pasado en Salta.* Salta: UNSA, 2012.

Viñas, David. *Indios, ejército y frontera.* Mexico: Siglo XXI, 1982.

Voloshinov, Valentin. *Marxism and the Philosophy of Language.* Cambridge: Harvard University Press, 1973.

Wade, Peter. *Blackness and Race Mixture: The Dynamics of Racial Identity in Colombia.* Baltimore: Johns Hopkins University Press, 1993.

"'Race', Nature and Culture." *Man* 28 (1993): 17–34.

"Race and Nation in Latin America: An Anthropological View." In *Race and Nation in Modern Latin America,* edited by Nancy P. Appelbaum, Anne S. Macpherson, and Karin Alejandra Rosemblatt, 263–82. Chapel Hill: University of North Carolina Press, 2003.

Wade, Peter, Carlos López Beltrán, Eduardo Restrepo, and Ricardo Ventura Santos, eds. *Mestizo Genomics: Race Mixture, Nation, and Science in Latin America.* Durham: Duke University Press, 2014.

Weinstein, Barbara. "Racializing Regional Difference: São Paulo versus Brazil, 1932." In *Race and Nation in Modern Latin America,* edited by Nancy P. Appelbaum, Anne S. Macpherson, and Karin Alejandra Rosemblatt, 237–62. Chapel Hill: University of North Carolina Press, 2003.

The Color of Modernity: São Paulo and the Making of Race and Nation in Brazil. Durham: Duke University Press, 2015.

Wells, Allen. *Tropical Zion: General Trujillo, FDR, and the Jews of Sosua.* Durham: Duke University Press, 2009.

Wigmore, Deedee. *American Scene Painting: Dominant Style of the 1930s and 1940s.* New York: D. Wigmore Fine Art Editors, 1985.

Wilde, José A. *Buenos Aires desde 70 años atrás.* Buenos Aires: Fondo Nacional de las Artes, 1998 [1881].

Winston, Colin M. "Between Rosas and Sarmiento: Notes on Nationalism in Peronist Thought." *The Americas* 39:3 (1983): 305–32.

Wolfe, Joel. "Father of the Poor or Mother of the Rich? Getúlio Vargas, Industrial Workers, and Constructions of Class, Gender, and Populism in São Paulo, 1930–1954." *Radical History Review* 58 (1994): 80–111.

Wood, Ean. *The Josephine Baker Story.* London: Sanctuary, 2000.

Wright, Winthrop. *Café con leche: Race, Class, and National Image in Venezuela.* Austin: University of Texas Press, 1990.

Young, Gerardo. *Negro contra blanco: Luis D'Elía y el recurso del odio.* Buenos Aires: Planeta, 2008.

Zanatta, Loris. *Dallo stato liberale alla nazione cattolica: chiesa ed esercito nelle origini del peronismo, 1930–1943.* Milano: Angeli, 1996.

Zeballos, Estanislao. *La conquista de quince mil leguas: estudio sobre la traslación de la Frontera Sud de la República al Río Negro.* Buenos Aires: "La Prensa," 1878.

Viaje al país de los araucanos. Buenos Aires: Anaconda, 1923.

Zimerman de Faingold, Raquel. *Memorias.* Buenos Aires: n.p., 1987.

Zimmermann, Eduardo A. "Racial Ideas and Social Reform: Argentina, 1890–1916." *Hispanic American Historical Review* 72:1 (1992): 23–46.

Ziperovich, Rosa W. de. "Memoria de una educadora: experiencias alternativas en la provincia de Santa Fe durante los últimos años de la década del 10, la del 20 y primeros años de 1930." In *Historia de la educación argentina,* vol. 3, edited by Adriana Puiggrós, 161–256. Buenos Aires: Galerna, 1992.

Žižek, Slavoj. "Multiculturalism, Or, the Cultural Logic of Multinational Capitalism." *New Left Review* 1:225 (October 1997): 28–51.

Zolov, Eric. "Discovering a Land Mysterious and Obvious: The Renarrativizing of Postrevolutionary Mexico." In *Fragments of a Golden Age: The Politics of Culture in Mexico Since 1940,* edited by Gilbert M. Joseph, Anne Rubenstein, Eric Zolov, and Emily S. Rosenberg, 234–72. Durham: Duke University Press, 2001.

Index